The Behavioral Sciences and Health Care

The Behavioral Sciences and Health Care

4th Edition

Editors

Olle Jane Z. Sahler, MD

Professor of Pediatrics, Psychiatry, Medical Humanities and Bioethics, and Oncology at the University of Rochester School of Medicine and Dentistry, Rochester, NY

John E. Carr, PhD

Professor Emeritus of Psychiatry & Behavioral Sciences and Psychology at the University of Washington School of Medicine, Seattle, WA

Julia B. Frank, MD

Clinical Professor of Psychiatry at the George Washington School of Medicine and Health Sciences, Washington, DC

João V. Nunes, MD

Associate Medical Professor at the City University of New York (CUNY) School of Medicine, New York, NY

Library of Congress Cataloging in Publication information for the print version of this book is available via the Library of Congress Marc Database under the Library of Congress Control Number 2017941758

Library and Archives Canada Cataloguing in Publication

The behavioral sciences and health care / editors, Olle Jane Z. Sahler, MD (Professor of Pediatrics, Psychiatry, Medical Humanities, and Oncology at the University of Rochester School of Medicine and Dentistry, Rochester, NY), John E. Carr, PhD (Professor Emeritus of Psychiatry & Behavioral Sciences and Psychology at the University of Washington School of Medicine, Seattle, WA), Julia B. Frank, MD (Clinical Professor of Psychiatry at the George Washington School of Medicine and Health Sciences, Washington, DC), João V. Nunes, MD (Associate Medical Professor at the City University of New York (CUNY) School of Medicine, New York, NY). -- 4th edition.

Includes bibliographical references and index.
Issued in print and electronic formats.
ISBN 978-0-88937-486-7 (softcover).--ISBN 978-1-61676-486-9 (PDF).--ISBN 978-1-61334-486-6 (EPUB)

1. Medicine and psychology--Textbooks. 2. Social medicine--Textbooks. 3. Psychology, Pathological--Textbooks. 4. Textbooks. I. Carr, John E., editor II. Frank, Julia (Julia B.), editor III. Sahler, Olle Jane Z., 1944-, editor IV. Nunes, João Vieira, editor

R726.5.B452 2017	616.001'9	C2017-903355-7
		C2017-903356-5

The authors and publisher have made every effort to ensure that the information contained in this text is in accord with the current state of scientific knowledge, recommendations, and practice at the time of publication. In spite of this diligence, errors cannot be completely excluded. Also, due to changing regulations and continuing research, information may become outdated at any point. The authors and publisher disclaim any responsibility for any consequences which may follow from the use of information presented in this book.

Registered trademarks are not noted specifically in this publication. The omission of any such notice by no means implies that any trade names mentioned are free and unregistered.

Cover image: © RapidEye – istockphoto.com

The pentagram on the cover formed by human arms depicts the five domains of determinants of health and health care: behavioral, biological, environmental, sociocultural, and cognitive.

© 2018 by Hogrefe Publishing
http://www.hogrefe.com

PUBLISHING OFFICES

USA:	Hogrefe Publishing Corporation, 7 Bulfinch Place, Suite 202, Boston, MA 02114 Phone (866) 823-4726, Fax (617) 354-6875; E-mail customerservice@hogrefe.com
EUROPE:	Hogrefe Publishing GmbH, Merkelstr. 3, 37085 Göttingen, Germany Phone +49 551 99950-0, Fax +49 551 99950-111; E-mail publishing@hogrefe.com

SALES & DISTRIBUTION

USA:	Hogrefe Publishing, Customer Services Department, 30 Amberwood Parkway, Ashland, OH 44805 Phone (800) 228-3749, Fax (419) 281-6883; E-mail customerservice@hogrefe.com
UK:	Hogrefe Publishing, c/o Marston Book Services Ltd., 160 Eastern Ave., Milton Park, Abingdon, OX14 4SB, UK Phone +44 1235 465577, Fax +44 1235 465556; E-mail direct.orders@marston.co.uk
EUROPE:	Hogrefe Publishing, Merkelstr. 3, 37085 Göttingen, Germany Phone +49 551 99950-0, Fax +49 551 99950-111; E-mail publishing@hogrefe.com

OTHER OFFICES

CANADA:	Hogrefe Publishing, 660 Eglinton Ave. East, Suite 119-514, Toronto, Ontario, M4G 2K2
SWITZERLAND:	Hogrefe Publishing, Länggass-Strasse 76, CH-3000 Bern 9

Hogrefe Publishing

Incorporated and registered in the Commonwealth of Massachusetts, USA, and in Göttingen, Lower Saxony, Germany

Printed and bound in Canada

ISBN 978-0-88937-486-7 (print) • ISBN 978-1-61676-486-9 (PDF) • ISBN 978-1-61334-486-6 (EPUB)
http://doi.org/10.1027/00486-000

About the Editors

Olle Jane Z. Sahler, MD, is the George Washington Goler Professor in Pediatrics, and Professor of Psychiatry, Medical Humanities and Bioethics, and Oncology at the University of Rochester School of Medicine and Dentistry, Rochester, New York. She is a behavioral pediatrician with a special interest in the care of chronically and terminally ill children and their families, and in the treatment of children and adolescents with chronic pain syndromes, using an integrative medicine approach. She has written widely on medical student, resident, and practitioner education in the areas of child development, management of behavioral problems at home and in school, and on palliative care, end-of-life care, and bereavement counseling. The W. T Grant Foundation and the National Cancer Institute have funded her multi-institutional research focused on siblings and mothers of children with cancer for over 30 years. She has also been funded by the National Center for Complementary and Alternative Medicine (now the National Center for Complementary and Integrative Health) of the National Institutes of Health to study the effects of using music therapy on symptom control and immune reconstitution in patients undergoing stem cell transplantation. Lastly, she has been the principal investigator and project manager of the Rochester Area Collaborative Center of Excellence in Pain Education since 2012. The goal of this project, which is funded by the Pain Consortium of the National Institutes of Health, is to develop online educational materials appropriate for interprofessional education about responsible pharmacological as well as nonpharmacological management of both acute pain and chronic pain syndromes.

As an educator, she was Director of the Pediatric Clerkship at the University of Rochester School of Medicine for 17 years and Director of the Department of Education of the American Academy of Pediatrics in 1995–1996. She was the founding chairperson of the Medical Student Education Special Interest Group of the Academic Pediatric Association, in McLean, Virginia (formerly the Ambulatory Pediatric Association), the founding president of the Council on Medical Student Education in Pediatrics (COMSEP), also in McLean, Virginia, and the founding chairperson of the Alliance for Clinical Education (ACE) of the Association of American Medical Colleges, in Washington, DC.

As President of the Association for the Behavioral Sciences and Medical Education (ABSAME) in 1992–1993, she began a project to develop a comprehensive curriculum guide for medical student and resident education in the behavioral sciences, which was published in 1995. An updated version of this curriculum guide, reflecting the many advances in our understanding of the importance of the integration of the behavioral and social sciences into medical education that occurred around the turn of the 21st century, forms the foundation for this present book, now in its fourth edition. The authors and editors who contributed to this text represent the diverse experience and expertise of ABSAME's former membership, working in conjunction with other expert professionals dedicated to excellence in education.

A graduate of Radcliffe College/Harvard University, Dr. Sahler received her MD degree with Distinction in Research at the University of Rochester, was a resident in pediatrics at the Duke University Medical Center, and completed a fellowship in Behavioral and Developmental Pediatrics and Child and Adolescent Psychiatry at the University of Rochester. She served as a Captain in the US Army Medical Corps and received a Special Commendation Award for her work in identifying and managing cases of child abuse in the military.

John E. Carr, PhD, is Professor Emeritus of Psychiatry and Behavioral Sciences and Psychology at the University of Washington where he served a 4-year term as the acting chair of the Department of Psychiatry and Behavioral Sciences, was Director of Undergraduate Medical Education, and played a principal role in developing behavioral science curricula for the School of Medicine. He has written extensively about the need for an *integrated sciences model* for the behavioral and biological sciences in medical education and clinical psychology graduate training. He has served as a consultant to the World Health Organization (WHO) on behavioral sciences in health care training, and co-coordinated a cooperative venture between ABSAME, the Association of Medical School Psychologists, and the International Union of Psychological Societies in developing behavioral science training modules for WHO.

Dr. Carr received an MA in industrial psychology and a PhD in clinical psychology from Syracuse University. He is a diplomate in health psychology of the American Board of Professional Psychology. He is a fellow of the American Psychological Association, Association of Psychological Science, Society of Behavioral Medicine, and the Academy of Behavioral Medicine Research. He has served on the National Board of Medical Examiners Behavioral Sciences Test Committee, and is a founding member and was twice elected to the presidency of the Association of Psychologists in Academic Health Centers. His promotion of an integrated sciences model in medical education and graduate psychology training reflects his bio-behavioral orientation and a research career focused on identifying the mechanisms of bio-behavioral interaction in stress, anxiety, and depression.

Dr. Carr is the recipient of a Distinguished Educator Award from the Association of Psychologists in Academic Health Centers, the Gary Tucker Award for Lifetime Achievement in Teaching and Dedication to Education from the Department of Psychiatry of the University of Washington, and Distinguished Psychologist Awards for Contributions in Scholarship and for Contributions to the Field of Psychology from the Washington State Psychological Association. He is the 2016 recipient of the American Psychological Association Award for Distinguished Professional Contributions to Institutional Practice.

Julia B. Frank, MD, LDFAPA, is a member of the voluntary faculty of the Department of Psychiatry at the George Washington University School of Medicine and Health Sciences (GWU). While serving at GWU as Director of Medical Student Education in Psychiatry (2003–2015), she organized the preclinical behavioral sciences curriculum and integrated it with the psychiatry clerk-

ship. A graduate of the Master Teachers program of the GWU School of Education and Human Development, she has cultivated an interest in multiple modes of learning, including team-based learning, problem-based learning, medical readers theater, medical humanities, and self-directed learning. She became a coeditor of the third edition specifically to help align it with current thinking about the principles of psychopathology.

Dr. Frank is a member of the Society of Distinguished Teachers, a former board member of ABSAME, a diplomate of the American Board of Psychiatry and Neurology, and a Lifetime Distinguished Fellow of the American Psychiatric Association. She was named Psychiatrist of the Year by the Washington Psychiatric Society in 2005, based on organizing colleagues to work with survivors of Hurricane Katrina. Her other scholarly writing includes coauthorship with her father, Jerome D. Frank, MD, PhD, of *Persuasion and Healing: A Comparative Study of Psychotherapy* (1991), a classic work explaining the universal processes and effects of psychotherapy, written especially for medical students and trainees in other mental health disciplines. More recently, she coedited, with Renato D. Alarcón, *The Psychotherapy of Hope: The Legacy of Persuasion and Healing* (Baltimore, MD: Johns Hopkins University Press; 2012). Other scholarly interests include research into the pharmacological treatment of posttraumatic stress disorder and writing about women's mental health, victims of violence, and various topics in the history of medicine. She has also published medical comic poetry in the *New England Journal of Medicine*.

A graduate of Harvard University and the Yale University School of Medicine, Dr. Frank completed an internal medicine internship at Michael Reese Hospital in Chicago. She pursued psychiatry residency at the Yale Department of Psychiatry. Dr. Frank has provided clinical psychiatric care to chronically mentally ill veterans, medically ill patients, university students, and refugees seeking asylum. Her current practice serves outpatients with anxiety, mood disorders, perinatal psychiatric syndromes, and a wide range of other adaptive disorders.

João V. Nunes, MD, is Associate Medical Professor at the City University of New York (CUNY) School of Medicine in New York City.

Through the years, he has been instrumental in developing behavioral science, neuropsychiatry, and doctoring curricula at the school. A Harvard-Macy Scholar in the Harvard-Macy Institute for Physician Educators (a joint Harvard Medical/Education Schools/Joaiah Macy Foundation program), he developed his interest in the principles and methods of active, self-directed learning, especially problem-based learning, team-based learning, and service learning. He is a diplomate of the American Board of Psychiatry and Neurology, a psychiatrist, and child and adolescent psychiatrist with a special interest in brain and behavior, clinical neuroscience, childhood development, psychopathology, psychotherapy, health disparities related to sleep disorders and chronobiology, and exploring personal narratives to understand behavior, including food-related behavior. He has written and presented on medical student education, on sleep and chronobiology, and on health disparities. He has dedicated much of his career to providing leadership, directorship of ambulatory services, and direct clinical psychiatry care in underserved areas of Harlem and The Bronx in New York City (where he still practices), to undergraduate and graduate medical education, and to the cause of facilitating access of underrepresented minorities to medical education. He currently helps develop the undergraduate medical education curriculum, which he teaches extensively. He has founded and directed required courses, and has directed a psychiatry clerkship and a psychiatry residency training program.

Dr. Nunes played an important role in the development of the *Behavioral Science Curriculum Guide,* published in 1995 by ABSAME, one of the first ever efforts to provide an educational template in the behavioral sciences for medical students and residents, allied health students, and teachers. These efforts were followed by participating extensively in all editions of the present book.

Beyond the medical field, he composes and performs music and writes poetry, having published a bilingual (English/Portuguese) anthology titled *True Word*, with two other poets.

A graduate of the Faculty of Medicine of Espírito Santo Federal University, Brazil, he completed residencies in pediatrics, psychiatry, and child psychiatry at the Rio de Janeiro Federal University. After moving to New York, he completed residency and fellowship training in psychiatry and child and adolescent psychiatry at the Albert Einstein College of Medicine. He holds a certificate in psychotherapy and psychoanalysis from the Post Graduate Center for Mental Health (University of the State of New York). He is a full fellow of the American Academy of Psychoanalysis and Dynamic Psychiatry.

Preface to the Fourth Edition

In prior editions, we stressed the critical importance of combining the principles of the behavioral and social sciences with those of the biological sciences to develop a comprehensive understanding of health and illness. This concept of an integrated sciences model of research, clinical training, and health care delivery anticipated the explosion of interdisciplinary studies focused on the mechanisms by which biological and behavioral and social factors interact to influence health outcomes, which has occurred since the beginning of the 21st century. Simultaneously, there has been increasing recognition that interprofessional education leading to interdisciplinary collaboration among health care professionals is essential if we are to create unified, efficacious, and cost-effective delivery systems.

Our objectives in this new edition are twofold: (1) to amplify our understanding of the mechanisms and processes contributing to bio-behavioral interactions, by reviewing recent research advances from behavioral genomics, the cognitive and social neurosciences, psychoneuroendocrinology, and other interdisciplinary research fields relevant to health care and (2) to examine how interdisciplinary practice can promote the broader application of knowledge gained from integrating the biological and behavioral and social sciences in the training of all health care professionals.

The Association for the Behavioral Sciences and Medical Education (ABSAME) gave rise to this textbook through the development of a set of educational guidelines for the behavioral sciences, and has supported its evolution over the past decade. In 2013–2014, ABSAME changed its focus and broadened its membership to reflect a growing understanding that it is only through interdisciplinary efforts that we can keep the world's population as free of disease as possible and maximize the sense of self-efficacy and well-being that is essential to living a full and productive life. Regrettably, ABSAME is no longer active as an organization, but members have joined with other organizations (e.g., Association of Psychologists in Academic Health Centers) that foster behavioral and social sciences education within the traditions of the disciplines of medicine, psychology, nursing, and social work, among others.

There are limits to the resources that professionals can rely on to improve and maintain the health of society. It is clear that the expertise of many different disciplines and the accountability of all members of the team are crucial elements of an efficient, effective health care system. Thus, it is incumbent on all of us to integrate scientific knowledge and apply our respective skills cooperatively toward achieving our mutual goals.

In keeping with these objectives, this work is designed to provide an understanding of how the behavioral, social, and biological sciences interact to influence health care. It is also designed to provide information and insight from the behavioral and social sciences that can be applied to the clinical practice of any health care provider regardless of discipline. In Section IX, we use the provider–patient relationship as an example of the broader clinician–client relationship that is the backbone of health care. Clearly, the professional responsibility to provide information, teach, advise, guide decision making, and advocate for the best interest of the person seeking our counsel – all with the utmost integrity – is inherent in the standards of all provider groups. We trust that the universal role the behavioral and social sciences play in optimizing well-being will be self-evident and that you will find these principles applicable in every health care encounter you have, in what we hope will be a rich and fulfilling career.

Resources for teachers, including an instructor's manual, are available via the publisher's website at https://www.hogrefe.com

The Editors

Contents

Introduction and How to Use This Book

In the course of human experience, people are born, mature, feel emotion, develop relationships, produce and reproduce, and struggle to cope with a myriad of challenges to their survival and well-being. This book is about the diverse ways in which health can be compromised; the many factors that contribute to an individual's predisposition, vulnerability, and resilience; the wide range of precipitating events that can trigger a disease, injury, or malfunction; and the complex array of individual differences that determine each patient's unique response to a disease as well as its treatment.

When health and well-being are challenged, humans have, for millennia, sought the aid of healers, individuals who are purported to possess special knowledge about the etiology and treatment of various disorders. History has witnessed the evolution of health care from a spiritually based healing art to a scientifically based technical profession, reflecting advances in our knowledge of the biological functioning of the human body. After World War II, there was a gradual shift away from medicine's exclusive focus on linear causal relationships between a disease and its biological etiology. Physicians began to refer to a "biopsychosocial model," which proposed that psychosocial variables were as important as biological variables in determining health status.

Although a major step forward in understanding that complex interactions exist, the biopsychosocial model failed to explain *how* psychosocial variables actually interact with biological variables. That is, what are the specific connections that exist among the biological (e.g., neurotransmitter systems), psychological (e.g., emotional reactions to stress or memory), and social (cultural prescriptions and proscriptions about appropriate physical and interpersonal responses) factors that define health and illness, and by what mechanisms are they established and maintained? In the final decades of the 20th century, medical researchers began to explore the knowledge and methodology of psychology, sociology, anthropology, and other behavioral and social sciences as they apply specifically to medicine. Focusing on bio-behavioral connections, their studies have given rise to new fields such as behavioral genetics, behavioral neuroscience, psychoneuroendocrinology, behavioral pharmacology, social biology, and behavioral medicine.

The growing integration among the behavioral and biomedical sciences, coupled with the development of interprofessional education, has revolutionized training, so that behavioral and social science concepts are typically taught within other curricular domains (e.g., organ systems-based courses in medical schools, provider–patient relations in many different professions) without being connected to a particular academic tradition or research domain. We expect that educators responsible for different courses and curricular themes will use different sections of this book separately. The more clinical chapters include case vignettes to facilitate integration with current educational strategies that emphasize case-based or problem-based rather than discipline-based approaches.

The model presented in this book calls attention to the clinical significance of the *interaction* among biopsychosocial variables, and focuses on identifying the mechanisms that interconnect these variables. We call this extension of the biopsychosocial model the *integrated sciences model* (ISM) because it emphasizes the interdependence of the contributions made by *all of the sciences* basic to medicine.

In Section I, we briefly trace the evolution of health care practices and models, the development of contemporary health care provider practice, and the integrated sciences model. In Section II, we present a brief review of the human nervous system and how its evolution has contributed to the unique survival capabilities of *homo sapiens*. In

Section III, we discuss the basic homeostatic systems and the critically important role that the stress response plays in human adaptation. In Section IV, we review basic psychological principles and the higher order bio-behavioral mechanisms involved in sensation, learning, cognition, emotion, and social interaction and cooperation. In Section V, we review human development through the life cycle and important aspects of major developmental theories as they apply to the individual and to the family. In Section VI, we examine social behavior and groups, and the influence of culture, ethnicity, and other social factors on health and health care. In Section VII, we explore several contemporary social issues that contribute to, complicate, or are major problems in health care.

In Section VIII, we examine the organization and functioning of the health care system, in particular the US health care system, the role that certain areas of special focus such as palliative care play, the rise of integrative medicine (the inclusion of complementary therapies in conventional health care plans), and some of the ethical and legal issues faced by health care providers. In Section IX, we discuss the clinical encounter and examine the relevance of basic, clinical, and social science to understanding the patient's complaints, eliciting and interpreting findings, making a diagnosis, negotiating a treatment plan, and motivating patient behavior. We also explore the importance of patients' health literacy and provider impairment in effecting health outcomes. In Section X, we summarize the field of psychopathology, present brief descriptions of the more common psychiatric disorders, and show how basic behavioral science principles help us to understand this complex area of health care.

Each chapter in this volume begins with a set of bulleted questions designed to focus attention on key learning points. Each chapter also concludes with a short set of review questions based on information in the text. We have chosen to emphasize ideas, principles, and established research findings, and to minimize references in favor of providing selected recommended readings. Finally, significant scientific observations from the behavioral and social sciences as well as clinical applications and examples have been included to make the theoretical practical.

In the Appendix, we have presented several of the psychological tests commonly used in the assessment of cognition, emotion, and behavior in both normal and clinical populations. Lastly, we have included 335 multiple-choice questions with explanations of the correct answer and why the incorrect choices are, in fact, incorrect. Some of the questions in this section provide additional review of material in the text. However, many questions are focused on new material to make the contents of the book even more comprehensive through the use of brief, directed discussions. The construction of these questions is designed to give you a sense of the kind of material and question format you may encounter later in training.

Good medicine is science artfully applied. The laws of probability should be interpreted in the light of experience and intuition, and common sense appreciated as a useful guide to decision making. Respect for the autonomy and self-efficacy of the patient will usually lead to the best outcome – although not everyone may agree with what the patient wants as the outcome.

We have tried to be explicit in defining the mechanisms of bio-behavioral interaction where they are known and to incorporate typical patient experiences where relevant. Some of the material will seem self-evident, some will seem counterintuitive, but all derives from the amalgam of research findings from the biological, behavioral, cognitive, sociocultural, and environmental sciences that contribute to our knowledge of the determinants of health and illness important for you as well as your patients.

Olle Jane Z. Sahler, MD
John E. Carr, PhD
Julia B. Frank, MD
João V. Nunes, MD

Section I
The Behavioral Sciences and Health

1 Evolving Models of Health Care

John E. Carr, PhD, Olle Jane Z. Sahler, MD, Julia B. Frank, MD, and João V. Nunes, MD

- How does the World Health Organization define health?
- How do disease, sickness, and illness differ?
- What is the difference between direct and indirect health risks?
- What shared concepts underlie traditional and modern health care systems?
- Why is the biomedical model discipline specific?
- What is the biopsychosocial model?
- What is an integrated sciences model?

Health, Disease, Sickness, and Illness

How does the World Health Organization define health?

The **World Health Organization** (WHO) defines **health** as a *state of physical, social, and mental well-being*, measured by the patient's ability to cope with everyday activities, and fully function physically, socially, and emotionally. At its optimal level, good health provides for a life marked by spiritual serenity, zestful activity, a sense of competence, and psychological well-being.

How do disease, sickness, and illness differ?

Disease is the manifestation of impaired bodily functions. Disease is recognized and classified by the type of organ damage (e.g., cirrhosis of the liver, myocardial infarction), by functional impairment (e.g., diabetes), or by homeostatic system failures (e.g., infectious disease, autoimmune disorder). **Sickness** refers to those behaviors manifested by an individual who believes that they are suffering from a disease or functional impairment. An individual can feel sick, yet have no identifi-

able disease. Conversely, someone may have a disease but not feel or act sick. Being perceived as sick or feeling sick leads to adopting the **sick role** relative to the rest of the community. This frees a person from the obligation to perform the tasks of everyday living without blame (i.e., to take sick leave). However, the sick person has obligations to (1) pursue and accept help and (2) adhere to culturally or professionally prescribed regimens that facilitate a return to health.

Illness represents the totality of a patient's experience: how a patient feels, how a patient behaves and perceives their condition, and how others respond. Responses vary according to the person's place within the family or community, as shaped by cultural beliefs and expectations. Beliefs about how or why the illness occurred (**explanatory models**) and the course the illness takes determine how the patient behaves and how the larger community responds.

Risk and Prevention

What is the difference between direct and indirect health risks?

Direct risks to health include dangerous practices (e.g., reckless driving, smoking) and various environmental pathogenic conditions (e.g., environmental toxins, contaminated water). *Indirect risks* to health are lower risk practices or prevention failures (e.g., high fat diet, not exercising). While some risk factors (e.g., age, race, genetic makeup) are not modifiable, many risk factors are related to a person's **lifestyle** (e.g., diet) and are, therefore, modifiable. Other risk factors, such as occupation, social class, religious practices, and cultural traditions, affect health status in complex ways that may or may not be modifiable.

The concept of health care extends from the *treatment* of disease; to the *prevention* of disease, injury, sickness, and illness; to the *promotion* of health. To achieve these goals, health care professionals not only apply medical treatments, but also seek to change patient behaviors, beliefs, social and cultural practices, and environmental conditions. *Such work requires knowledge of the ways these factors interact, how they affect patient health, and the methods by which they can be effectively modified.*

Primary prevention involves practices to protect, promote, and maintain health. These include the concerns of specialized public health professionals, whose role is to promote sanitation and occupational safety and to monitor environmental conditions. Primary prevention in medical settings involves advising patients about personal habits such as exercising regularly, maintaining normal weight, eating nutritional foods, and avoiding smoking, substance use, or other activities that jeopardize health. **Secondary prevention**, for which many types of health professionals may assume responsibility, involves practices such as immunization, medical surveillance, **harm reduction**, and health screening to enhance resistance to, or buffer the impact of, risk factors.

Evolving Approaches to Health Care

Archeological evidence suggests that humans have practiced some form of health care for at least the past 30,000 years. Early human beliefs about sickness encompassed observable *natural causes* such as climatic events, personal behaviors, and unobservable, incomprehensible, or *supernatural causes* such as sorcery. Naturalistic treatments presumably involved simply accept-

ing fate, or using herbs, tonics, and oils whose healing or curative properties would have been discerned empirically over time. Since healing and religion have been so intertwined in human history, treatment of supernaturally caused conditions involved rituals that were interpreted and administered by priests or Shamans knowledgeable about the relations between the mystical and natural realms.

Recorded information about the human body and theories of health care appeared roughly 6,000 years ago in the time of the Babylonians. The **Code of Hammurabi** defined the different surgical operations to be performed, a scale of fees, and penalties for malpractice. Five thousand-year-old Egyptian records describe symptoms of abdominal, eye, and heart disorders; treatment of wounds, fractures, and dislocations; and an understanding that brain lesions may be associated with paralysis of the opposite side of the body.

> **What shared concepts underlie traditional and modern health care systems?**

Major systems of traditional Chinese, Ayurvedic, and Greek medicine began to evolve between 1,500 and 500 BC and constitute the basis for many current health care practices. Despite cultural and geographic differences, knowledge moved freely throughout the ancient world, likely through trade and conquest, resulting in common doctrines fundamental to all of these systems:

1. The universe is an integrated whole that is subject to laws governing all phenomena including human behavior and health.
2. The individual is an integrated system of physical, mental, cultural, and spiritual qualities.
3. Health is a state of balance (homeostasis) between the individual and the outside world, and among the elements, humors, and forces within the individual.
4. All living things are endowed with a life force composed of vital energies that must be kept in balance (e.g., male/female, yin/yang) to maintain optimal health.
5. Disease results from disruption or imbalance within the life force, an imbalance between the life force and external events (stress), or an imbalance among humors and bodily functions.

6. Symptoms represent the body's efforts to restore balance and health.
7. Healers supplement or strengthen the body's efforts to restore balance by applying treatments based on universal principles.

These conceptualizations of disease and health, rooted in indigenous cultural beliefs, constitute the subject matter of **ethnomedicine** (see Chapter 17: Culture and Cultural Competence in Health Care) and reflect an awareness of certain concepts found in both traditional and modern health care systems. Common or universal principles include the interaction and interdependence of *etiological factors*, the principle of "balance" or **homeostasis**, the influence of **stress**, and an appreciation of the *role of the healer*.

Modern concepts of health care have their roots in the writings of **Hippocrates** (b. 460 BC), who is credited with establishing the first school dedicated to the scientific study of medicine. Hippocratic medicine was the definitive standard for medical knowledge and professional ethics until the work of **Galen**, a Roman practitioner in the 2nd century AD who compiled the medical knowledge of his time and began anatomical and physiological investigations. Because of religious constraints, Galen could carry out dissections only on animals. As a result, many of his anatomical findings proved to be in error, although he made significant contributions to understanding the functioning of the respiratory, circulatory, digestive, and neural systems.

Galen laid the scientific foundations for **allopathic medicine** by asserting that lesions in specific body organs led to dysfunctions, establishing the principle that persons schooled in the study of pathology (physicians) should be the definitive healers in society. Galenic *treatments*, only loosely grounded in his scientific work, were based on the **law of opposites** – that is, diseases were treated with medicines or interventions that created an effect opposite to the symptom.

Despite its limitations, Galenic medicine dominated medical dogma for 1,400 years. Galen's work was rediscovered in Europe through the preservation and translation of Roman, Greek, and Arabic texts, and its worldwide dispersal influenced most major medical systems but, paradoxically, stifled scientific advancement. While the applied law of opposites presumably benefited

some cases (e.g., applying cooling remedies in cases of fever), it often justified inappropriate and dangerous "treatments" such as the indiscriminate use of enemas, bloodletting, purging, and other toxic and invasive procedures.

The resurgence of rationality, critical discourse, and experimental investigation that marked the **Renaissance** and the later **Age of Enlightenment** led to important advances in the development of medicine. Seventeenth-century developments in the natural sciences led to important discoveries of the physical, mechanical, and chemical functions of the human body, but these scientific advances had limited impact on the development of health care practices for some time. Subsequent challenges to Galenism reaffirmed the **physician's role** in mobilizing and assisting the body's own healing efforts. This led to the development of **homeopathic**, **osteopathic**, **naturopathic**, and **chiropractic** approaches to medicine (see Chapter 32: Complementary and Integrative Medicine).

Biomedical Model – Discipline Specific

Why is the biomedical model discipline specific?

By the end of the 19th century, the scientific foundation of medicine included **systematic observation**, **objective measurement**, and **experimental tests of theories**. These activities were developed and taught within specific disciplines such as pathology, microbiology, physiology, and pharmacology. Corresponding clinical techniques gradually became more sophisticated and disease specific. Advances in *microbiology*, for example, showed that microorganisms contributed to disease and could be controlled by sterilization, antiseptics, and immunization.

Despite these advances, medicine and medical training were still primitive, reflecting vestiges of Galenism and a lack of scrutiny into the efficacy of various practices. However, at the beginning of the 20th century, medicine's increased scientific sophistication finally led to intense examination of the quality of North American medical training. The *Flexner Report*, issued by the Carnegie Foundation in 1910, critically evaluated the scientific curricula of all the medical schools in the US and Canada. The report called for the establishment of higher standards for medical education, grounded in the *biological sciences* and *scientific methodology*. These recommendations became the defining criteria for the **biomedical model**, making medicine **discipline specific**. Flexner downplayed, even discounted, the contributions of the behavioral and social sciences to medicine. As a consequence, post-Flexnerian medical education and practice became heavily biomedical and partly lost sight of the broader behavioral and social context of disease and health care.

Although the domain of biomedicine expanded rapidly in the beginning of the 20th century, critical academic disciplines, especially public health, and the behavioral sciences of anthropology, psychology, and sociology fostered continued awareness of the limitations of a strictly biological approach. Experience with the effects of severe stress on the health of soldiers in two world wars underscored the influence of psychosocial factors on illness and treatment outcome (see Chapter 47: Stress Disorders, Bereavement, and Dissociative Disorders). Despite their value, rigorous social science studies of the contextual determinants of health and processes of health care were too often constrained by their unique methodologies. Researchers lacked the tools to explore how psychosocial variables *interact* with biological processes in the etiology or causality of both illness and disease. Beginning in the mid-1970s, the intellectual pendulum had swung back to a midpoint that seeks to *integrate* a wide variety of methods and insights into the multidisciplinary study of health and disease.

Biopsychosocial Model – Multidisciplinary

> What is the biopsychosocial model?

In 1977, **George Engel** published an article in *Science* titled "The Need for a New Medical Model: A Challenge for Biomedicine." He further explored the model in a 1980 article entitled "The Clinical Application of the Biopsychosocial Model" in the *American Journal of Psychiatry* (pp. 535–544). Engel asserted that, in contrast to the biomedical model, the **biopsychosocial model** recognized (1) *multiple determinants* of

disease and the resultant illness process and (2) a *hierarchical organization* of biological and social systems that contribute to the disease and illness experience. The systems hierarchy and levels of organization were as follows:

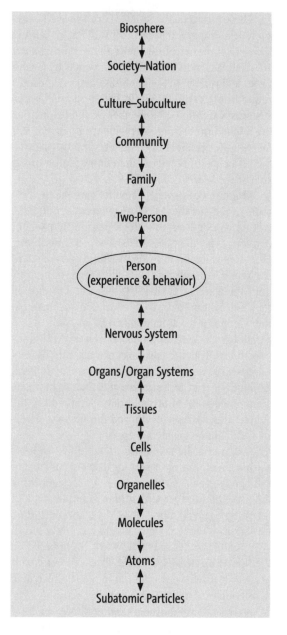

Each system was seen as a component of a higher, more abstract system. Therefore, change in one system would effect change in other systems, especially those most closely linked to it. In the biopsychosocial model, the behavioral and social sciences were as important as the biological sciences in understanding the determinants of illness, and researchers began to focus on identifying specific psychosocial factors associated with specific diseases or illnesses.

Clinical Application of the Biopsychosocial Model

Since people can function normally physiologically with only one kidney, a kidney donor will continue to have normal renal functioning. In the biomedical model, once recovered from surgery, a donor returns to full health. By contrast, the biopsychosocial model directs attention to the psychosocial parameters of the donor's and recipient's conditions. For example, this model recognizes that a donor's recovery and sense of self-worth may be facilitated, even enhanced, if they know the recipient was helped by the donation, the community applauds the donor for the gift, and the donor believes the recipient will make a full recovery. However, the model also recognizes that the knowledge of having only one kidney may leave the donor feeling damaged or otherwise impaired; the donor also may feel diminished if insufficient gratitude was expressed. These latter perceptions may impair full functional recovery.

While no *biomedical* intervention beyond appropriate postoperative care for a donor is required, care provided according to the principles of the *biopsychosocial* model posits that education is essential to reassure a donor of their biological integrity, that information about the benefits to the recipient will reinforce a donor's sense of self-worth, and that the support of family and community are essential to recovery and return to a state of full health.

Integrated Sciences Model – Interdisciplinary

What is an integrated sciences model?

Determinants of health are not simply a collection of individual psychosocial and biologic variables, each linearly related to some specific health outcome, nor are they discipline-specific systems only hierarchically related to one another. Rather, health is determined by *multiple etiological variables*, continuously interacting via complex mechanisms and interdependent processes (see Figure 1.1). Identifying the determinants of disease and

illness requires identifying not only the biological processes involved in the etiology of the condition and the psychosocial factors that influence these processes, but also the mechanisms by which psychosocial and biological factors *interact* to determine health outcomes. Efforts to identify these mechanisms of bio-behavioral interaction have prompted the growth of a number of interdisciplinary fields (see Box 1.1), in which behavioral and biological scientists collaborate by combining theoretical and methodological efforts.

These research collaborations reflect the evolution of the biopsychosocial model from a multidisciplinary view of behavioral and biological sciences as distinct from, although equal in importance to, a more complex **interdisciplinary** view that focuses on (1) the interdependence of biological and behavioral processes; (2) the mechanisms of their interaction; and (3) the integration of biological and behavioral scientific principles, concepts, and theories into a more integrated sciences model.

The survival of the human species is largely attributable to the evolution of the human brain. Over many eons, in response to genetic anomalies and epigenetic events, the brain and the associated neuroendocrine subsystem developed an array of remarkable abilities that enable *Homo sapiens* to survive in an inhospitable environment. These abilities allowed the organism to respond to threat reflexively and through experience by adapting, avoiding, anticipating, and planning as it coped with challenges from multiple domains. Eventually, humans became able to relate to, cooperate with, care for, and communicate with other humans. Such functions provide our species with extraordinary tools for mastering the environment and insuring survival.

In an **integrated sciences model** (ISM), all psychosocial and biological phenomena are viewed as *interdependent* and functionally *interactive*. The principles of interaction involve common universal scientific principles and processes, such as homeostasis, stress, adaptation, learning, development, and genetic modification. The individual can be viewed as a complex adaptive organism with homeostatic capabilities that enable adaptation not only to biological challenges, but also to environmental, cognitive, sociocultural, and behavioral challenges (see Figure 1.1). Homeostatic challenges from within each domain contribute to the individual's condition, trigger-

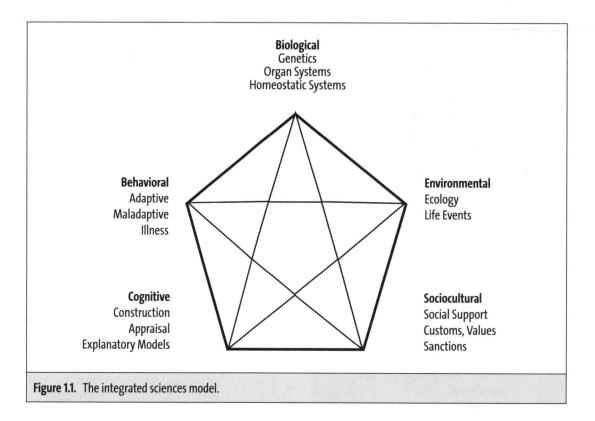

Figure 1.1. The integrated sciences model.

ing adaptive responses in all other domains. As in the original biopsychosocial model, change in any domain effects a change in all others, as the organism constantly strives to maintain *optimal balance* or homeostasis within and among domains.

Box 1.1. Interdisciplinary research fields in health care	
Genomic sciences	Seek to identify the genetic processes associated with normal and abnormal development and functioning, and the mechanisms by which these processes influence, and are influenced by, human behaviors, social and biological functioning, and environmental interaction.
Cognitive neurosciences	Seek to determine the brain structures and neuroendocrine mechanisms that contribute to, and are influenced by, specific cognitive processes (perception, learning, memory, problem solving).
Social neurosciences	Seek to determine the specific biological systems and mechanisms that implement social processes and behaviors, and the mechanisms by which those social processes modify and influence organ-based, neural, neuroendocrine, and immunological functions.
Psychoneuroimmunology	Seeks to define the mechanisms by which stressful events and emotional responses influence neurological and immune system functioning.

Integrated Sciences Model

1. The human organism possesses an integrated network of homeostatic systems enabling it to adapt to any challenge to homeostasis from biological, behavioral, cognitive, sociocultural, and environmental domains. This homeostatic network is regulated by the brain and associated neuroendocrine systems.
2. Any challenge to homeostasis constitutes "stress" and initiates a multivariate stress response.
3. Variables within each domain interact with those in other domains via diverse bio-behavioral mechanisms. Hence, stress in one domain initiates responses in all domains.
4. Challenges to the organism are ongoing, and this interactive system is constantly evolving as it is continuously adapting.
5. Diseases and disorders are byproducts of the failure of the homeostatic stress response system. Therefore, accurately addressing the differential role of stress conditions and other risk factors in each domain is essential to determining the best intervention strategy.
6. Treatment of the disease may alleviate or, in turn, initiate new stress responses within any of the domains of variables.

Stress – The Engine of Adaptation

Any challenge to homeostasis is defined as **stress**. This term is derived from physics and refers to the interdisciplinary principle of a **system under strain** (i.e., the systemic effects of any challenge within any domain). Stress or biological, developmental, environmental, behavioral, cognitive, or sociocultural challenges to homeostasis initiate *adaptive responses* in other domains, whereby the organism attempts to resolve, cope with, and learn from the stressful condition. Thus, stress is the engine that drives adaptation, the raison d'être for the evolution of the brain's remarkable capabilities and, therefore, is not necessarily destructive. Instead, the nature, intensity, and outcome (adaptive or maladaptive) of the stress response are determined, in part, by the **degree of stress**. Every college student is familiar with the *inverted U*-shaped curve describing the relationship between stress and productivity. Too little

challenge (stress) undermines motivation and may result in poor performance. Too much challenge (stress) may discourage effort and impair performance. Optimal challenge (stress) motivates and inspires, but does not overwhelm.

The adaptive success of the **stress response** in this highly complex network of homeostatic systems defines individual health; its maladaptive breakdown or dysfunction contributes to disease or disorder. Ironically, an overfunctioning stress response may also contribute to disease and disorder, as in *autoimmune diseases* where the immune system that normally protects against external pathogens attacks the host body. The bio-behavioral mechanisms of the stress response involved in adaptation and illness are discussed in greater detail in Chapter 7: Stress, Adaptation, and Stress Disorders.

Integrated Assessment

Assessment should involve a detailed exploration of the differential and *interactive* contributions of biological, behavioral, cognitive, sociocultural, and environmental risk factors. This information informs the health care professional about the bio-behavioral mechanisms and processes that contribute to a particular disorder and which, therefore, may be appropriate targets for treatment.

Clinical Application of an Integrated Sciences Model

Frank Howard has been diagnosed with chronic obstructive pulmonary disease (COPD) and advised by his physician, Dr. Elizabeth Knight, to give up smoking. Working collaboratively, Dr. Knight and Mr. Howard carefully review Mr. Howard's lifestyle to identify variables or situations that influence his smoking. Reviewing each of the domains shown in Figure 1.1, they come up with the following information:

- **Biological:** While he recognizes the implication of a diagnosis of COPD, Mr. Howard's nicotine dependence is making it difficult for him to quit smoking.
- **Behavioral:** The stress relief he experiences is a strong incentive for smoking.
- **Cognitive:** He previously believed he could quit anytime he chose. The knowledge that smoking contributes to his COPD is powerful, but not enough

by itself to deter his behavior, although he is now willing to consider a change in smoking behavior.

- Sociocultural: Previous role models and cultural sanctions had strong reinforcing value, but Mr. Howard is now getting increasing social and familial support for not smoking.
- Environmental: Tobacco had been readily accessible and smoking opportunities available and reinforcing. However, as the cost of tobacco has increased and places and opportunities for smoking have decreased, Mr. Howard is becoming more open to change.

An integrated sciences model illustrates the complexity and interdependence of factors contributing to smoking addiction and why treatments that focus only on one domain (e.g., changing a smoker's cognitions) or one variable (e.g., stopping cigarette advertisements) are likely to fail. The probability of changing complexly determined health behaviors is maximized only if treatments address as many of the contributing factors as possible. Mr. Howard and Dr. Knight, as described in the example, decided on a multimodal approach and agreed to implement the following strategies:

Biological: nicotine patches to counter nicotine dependence;

Behavioral: alternative work break and stress relief activities such as taking a walk, social gatherings in nonsmoking venues, stress management training, and meditation;

Cognitive: explaining to others (e.g., young people) how smoking is harmful; exposure to high-profile, high-status nonsmokers;

Sociocultural: encouraging family to praise, reward, reinforce nonsmoking; encouraging membership in a "smoke-enders" group; pursuing cultural and sports activities that preclude smoking behavior;

Environmental: make smoking materials and opportunities less accessible (e.g., restrict access to tobacco and limit smoking to inconvenient and uncomfortable places).

As can be seen, a multimodal treatment plan is likely to have a better outcome than a treatment plan that focuses on only a single domain. Since certain interventions may not always be practical or worthwhile, multimodal perspectives allow for greater flexibility in treatment strategizing. Also,

even though a specific factor may be important in the etiology of a condition, it may not be an effective target in treatment (e.g., while new drugs improve survival rates in HIV/AIDS patients, behavioral management of the social and psychological aspects of the disease is still a major focus of disease management).

In the chapters that follow, we explore the biological, behavioral, cognitive, sociocultural, and environmental domains that influence human adaptive functioning, and the bio-behavioral mechanisms and processes by which factors in these domains interact and, thereby, contribute to human health and illness.

Recommended Readings

Berntson, G. G., & Cacioppo, J. T. (2009). *Handbook of neurosciences for the behavioral sciences*. Hoboken, NJ: Wiley. http://doi.org/10.1002/9780470478509

Carr, J. E. (1999). Proposal for an integrated sciences curriculum in medical education. *Teaching and Learning in Medicine, 10*, 3–7. http://doi.org/10.1207/S15328015TLM1001_1

Cuff, P. A., & Vanselow, N. A. (Eds.). (2004). *Improving medical education: Enhancing the behavioral and social science content of medical school curricula*. Washington, DC: National Academies Press.

Engel, G. L. (1977). The need for a new medical model: A challenge for biomedicine. *Science, 196*, 129–136. http://doi.org/10.1126/science.847460

Gazzaniga, M. S. (Ed.). (2010). *The cognitive neurosciences* (4th ed.). Cambridge, MA: MIT Press.

Review Questions

1. A manifestation of impaired bodily functions that is caused by environmental trauma, biologic malfunction, or an identifiable agent or substance is defined by which of the following concepts?
   A. Disease
   B. Illness
   C. Injury
   D. Sick Role
   E. Sickness

2. The *Flexner Report* promoted scientific and educational standards consistent with which of the following models?
   A. Biomedical
   B. Biopsychosocial
   C. Explanatory
   D. Integrated sciences
   E. Interdisciplinary

3. Defining all the variables and processes that contribute to health, disease, sickness, and illness and the complexity of bio-behavioral mechanisms by which they interact and are interdependent, defines which of the following models?
   A. Behavioral
   B. Biomedical
   C. Biopsychosocial
   D. Integrated sciences
   E. Sociocultural

Answer Key on p. 465

Section II
Regulatory Systems

2 Predisposition

João V. Nunes, MD, Ian M. Kodish, MD, PhD, and John E. Carr, PhD

- What distinguishes genotype from phenotype?
- What do genes do, and how does the environment influence genetic functioning?
- What information is provided by a pedigree study?
- How does gene–environment interaction differ from gene–environment correlation?
- What does diathesis–stress interaction mean?
- How does personality contribute to illness vulnerability?

Genetic Predisposition

What distinguishes genotype from phenotype?

Eons of evolutionary development have provided the central nervous system (CNS) with the mechanisms that enable humans to interact with the environment, learn from experience, and adapt to ever-changing environmental demands. Because the CNS of the newborn has not yet accumulated experience, it must rely on preprogrammed expressions shaped by the collective evolutionary experience through genetic adaptations. Each cell's genetic code (genotype) functions to help scaffold the anatomical, biochemical, physiological, behavioral, and personal characteristics (phenotype) of the individual.

The **genotype** is the genetic constitution (genome) of a cell. The **phenotype** is the developmental result of the interaction of the genotype with the environment, and refers to the composite of biological and behavioral characteristics manifested by the individual under certain environmental circumstances. Each personal characteristic is called a **trait**, and virtually all traits are expressions of gene–environment interaction. Indeed, the activation of an individual's genes (**gene expression**) is dependent upon the influence of environmental events, occurring even before birth, that prompt selective activation of genes, thus shaping expression across development and setting the stage for subsequent behaviors, traits, resiliencies, and vulnerabilities.

What do genes do, and how does the environment influence genetic functioning?

Each gene carries the **DNA code** for the production of a protein. Genes are expressed through an initial copy of **messenger RNA** (mRNA), which serves as a template for the subsequent assembling of amino acids to match the coded string and form a protein (translation). To transcribe the genetic code to a particular protein, DNA uses RNA as an intermediary molecule: A nocleotide sequence in the DNA molecule is initially copied into an RNA sequence in a process called transcription. The modified RNA molecules become templates to assemble amino acids into the synthesis of a protein. That is, each RNA molecule is translating an amino acid into a protein. These molecules are essential modulators of cellular functions, and some even serve to further regulate gene expression by stimulating **promoter regions** to initiate more copies.

The expression of our genetic code is also regulated by **epigenetic processes** that modify the ability of genetic material to be transcribed without changing the DNA sequence. DNA is stored as heterochromatin, a form of chromatin

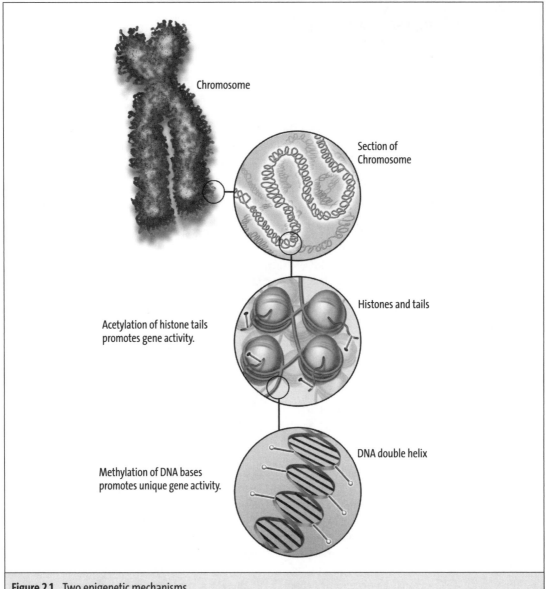

Chromosome

Section of Chromosome

Histones and tails

Acetylation of histone tails promotes gene activity.

DNA double helix

Methylation of DNA bases promotes unique gene activity.

Figure 2.1. Two epigenetic mechanisms.

that, being tightly wound, limits transcriptional activity. By modifying the supporting histone proteins to relax the folds in the DNA molecule (through acetylation), cells can regulate the physical access required for RNA polymerase to "read" the DNA code to produce mRNA. The relaxed state, called **euchromatin**, promotes gene transcription while enzymatically mediated deacetylation reverses chromatin to a recondensed state (see Figure 2.1).

The addition or removal of methyl groups from DNA sequences is another epigenetic mech-

anism used to regulate gene expression. Through DNA methylation, the addition of a methyl group to DNA sequences within the promoter region, the gene is silenced by preventing enzymes from accessing and transcribing the gene. The patterns of methylation are heritable and influence cell differentiation during development by enabling the cell to produce unique patterns of gene activity, which can be modulated across development, creating different cell types. Such gene modulation determines the chemical organizers that mediate cell migration in embryonic brain cortex formation as well as the enzymatic synthesis of neurotransmitters and neurotrophins. Fascinatingly, patterns of gene methylation determining stress responses in adult rats can be influenced by early experiences and maternal nurturing, emphasizing the lasting environmental imprints on future gene expression. More dynamically, neuronal signaling can further prompt shuttling of mRNA sequences to distant connections so they are primed to translate proteins in response to rapidly changing signals at the synapse.

Since environmental and epigenetic factors influence the structure and functioning of the nervous system, even minor variations and alterations can have significant behavioral and biological consequences on individual functioning. These may be adaptive or maladaptive. That is, mutations may contribute to resilience or vulnerability. For example, individuals often inherit susceptibilities to certain environmental factors that can then precipitate disease or play a role in its etiology. In fact, several diseases are thought to result from excess methylation caused by abnormal numbers of trinucleotide repeats in the genetic code that attach to a methyl group (Huntington's disease, fragile X syndrome), and disease severity is highly correlated with the number of repeats.

Research Approaches to Defining Heritable Diseases

Family Risk Studies

Family risk studies determine the rate of occurrence of a condition or trait in **first-degree relatives** (e.g., parents, siblings, children) who share 50% of their genetic material, as well as more distant relatives of an affected person (the **proband**). These rates are then compared with rates for the general population. A genetic component is suggested if probands have higher *concordance rates* with their first-degree relatives than with more distant relatives; the lowest concordance rates would be with the general population.

Twin Studies

The concept of **heritability** is derived from comparisons of concordance rates between monozygotic twins (who share essentially 100% of their genetic code) and dizygotic twins (who share 50%). Higher concordance rates between monozygotic twins have been interpreted as evidence of the primacy of genetic factors in determining the condition. Environmental experiences are thought to be shared across development within a sibling cohort.

Adoption Studies

Adoption studies are used in determining the risk of adopted children having a trait or disorder by comparing the risk in biological and adoptive relatives. If the risk is higher among biological relatives, a genetic factor is likely. If the risk is higher among adoptive relatives, environmental factors are suspected.

In **cross-fostering analyses**, the risk of having the trait or disorder can also be determined by comparing the risk in genetically susceptible adoptees whose adoptive parents are normal, with the risk in adoptees whose biological parents are normal, but who are raised by an affected adoptive parent. Such comparisons help identify both genetic and environmental influences.

Pedigree Studies

> What information is provided by a pedigree study?

Pedigree (ancestral lineage) **studies** rely on the construction of a **family tree**, beginning with an individual who manifests the trait or disorder (the proband), and then tracing evidence of the trait or disorder in relatives spanning many generations. **Linkage mapping** in pedigree studies involves identifying markers along the human genome (single nucleotide polymorphisms) as points of reference to determine what alterations in strands of DNA are linked to a certain trait or disease. These studies further seek to associate the trait or disease with another gene (the *marker*), which has a *Mendelian* mode of inheritance and whose chromosomal position (locus) is known. If the trait under study and the marker are neighbors on the same chromosome, they are likely to be inherited together, or linked. Traditional markers include human leukocyte antigens (HLAs), blood groups, and color blindness. To be conclusive, linkage studies depend on a large pedigree (a large number of relatives) whose condition is known or who are willing to be studied, usually through blood or tissue testing. Linkage studies are less successful with low heritability traits or small family trees, or when the condition is highly influenced by environmental factors.

The study of genetic traits and disease often relies on plant and animal models. For example, Gregor Mendel (1822–1884) established the laws of monogenic inheritance using pea plants. More sophisticated methods have enabled researchers to modify genetic expression by knocking out the function of a gene in a mouse strain. Researchers may also insert a viral DNA vector into DNA strands, thus controlling the expression of specific genes at a specific time. Although helpful in aiding our understanding of human disease, use of animal models is more limited in developing therapy since the reciprocity between animal models and humans is not perfect.

DNA Markers

DNA markers can be used to identify the chromosomal locations of genes responsible for several disorders, such as

- Early-onset forms of Alzheimer's disease, which have been linked to genetic polymorphisms on chromosomes 14 and 21 that contribute to abnormal amyloid precursor protein accumulation;
- Huntington's disease, which is linked to excessive methylation of DNA repeats (CAG) on an encoding region of a gene on chromosome 4.

With recent advances in sequencing and analytic technology, it has become possible to compare the entire genome sequences of a proband with those of unaffected individuals. Any differences become potential foci for identifying candidate trait-specifying genes. This advanced methodology has enabled researchers to discover complex arrays of genes associated with **multigenic disorders**, such as asthma and diabetes, thought to result from accumulation of many different susceptibility genes. Other illnesses, particularly those associated with advanced parental age, are thought to result from nonlethal spontaneous mutations that do not arise from a heightened genetic predisposition from parents. As the complexities of genetic predisposition in disease and illness are unraveled, the impact of environmental factors on genetic processes has become an important focus of research.

Gene–Environment Interactions

> How does gene–environment interaction differ from gene–environment correlation?

Genetic characteristics predispose the individual to react to, or be influenced by, certain environmental conditions. In the early stages of development, some genetic expression is activated by interactions with specific environmental conditions only during specific **critical periods**, when the organism is primed to respond. **Imprinting**, **bonding**, and **language development** are examples of time-specific gene–environment–development interactions. As the organism develops, these reciprocal interactions become more complex:

1. *Gene–environment interaction:* Individuals react differently to the same environmental conditions. This differential reactivity may be genetically influenced or modified by the environment and the effects of experience.
2. *Gene–environment correlation:* How individuals tend to interact with the environment is correlated with their genetic predisposition.
   a. *Passive* – refers to the correlation between the genotype a child inherits from parents and the environment in which the child is raised, which is also influenced by the parents' heritable characteristics.
   b. *Evocative* – refers to the correlation between an individual's heritable behavior and the environmental response such behavior evokes (e.g., hostile, aggressive behavior elicits hostile, aggressive responses).
   c. *Active* – refers to the correlation between an individual's heritable characteristics and the environmental conditions the individual

seeks out (e.g., extroverted individuals seek out highly social situations).

3. *Gene–environment–developmental interactions:* Developmental changes in the nature of learning reflect a temporal transactional process. At birth, in response to a survival imperative, genetic influences are manifested in reflexive responses to environmental stimuli. As development progresses, genetic predisposition requires specific environmental stimuli during critical periods to activate certain survival responses (e.g., imprinting, bonding). With further development, the organism begins to respond to experience in more nuanced and refined ways, supporting emotional learning and executive functioning during cognitive tasks (see Chapter 9: Emotion and Learning). Interestingly, traits understood to be due to both genetic and experiential determinants often show a greater heritability during later stages of development.

Temperament

The human newborn has observable genetically determined patterns of personal attributes and behavioral tendencies that are stable and develop into distinctive personality and behavioral characteristics. Differences in these tendencies contribute to differences in infant reaction patterns. **Temperament** is perceived as the pattern of these tendencies that leads to parental perceptions that a child may be "easy," "slow-to-warm-up," or "difficult." Such perceptions are based on how the child responds to various environmental stimuli, and the ease with which the child achieves contentment.

Elements of Temperament

1. Activity level
2. Rhythmicity
3. Approach
4. Adaptability
5. Intensity of reaction
6. Threshold of responsiveness
7. Mood
8. Distractibility
9. Attention span and persistence

Contemporary concepts of temperament emphasize neurophysiological reactivity and self-regulation of emotion. Beyond parent-reported increases in anxiety symptoms, inhibited children have higher sustained heart rates and more widely dilated pupils than uninhibited children. Heritability of temperament is considered to be high, accounting for 0.2–0.6 of the phenotypic variance. Yet differences in temperament may be modified by environmental experiences that foster or inhibit certain behaviors, such as parental intervention (acclimating the inhibited child to peer interactions by inviting a friend to a sleepover) or age-related expectation ("I'm too old to be afraid of the dark"). Furthermore, physiological responses that guide temperament can be moderated through use of biofeedback and mindfulness techniques, or manipulated by pharmacological intervention.

Diathesis–Stress Interactions

> How do disease, sickness, and illness differ?

With increasing recognition of the importance of gene–environment interaction, researchers have broadened the concept of predisposition. For example, behavioral genetics focuses on the role that genes and postconception biological, developmental, social, and environmental events play in determining individual differences in predispositions. These, in turn, determine an individual's **diathesis** or vulnerability to particular stressors, and subsequently define temperament, personality, and coping.

Diathesis–Stress Interaction and Depression

Individuals who possess a certain form of the familial serotonin transporter gene and are exposed to high levels of stressful life events are at heightened risk for depression. They are especially vulnerable to loss (e.g., of a valued person, role, self-esteem), to perceive events negatively, and to persistently engage in maladaptive behavior that further increases their vulnerability to stressors. This combination of diatheses increases the risk of behaviors and cognitions (e.g., reduced initiative, avoidant behavior, learned helplessness, self-criticism, anticipated bad outcomes) that contribute to depression.

Personality

Personality is the distinctive and consistent set of characteristics that predict how an adult individual will respond in various situations (response patterns). It is the developmentally advanced version of temperament, but unlike childhood temperament, personality reflects a more developmentally refined and more dynamic correlation between the response style (personality trait) and a specific situation.

Personality traits show a pattern of normative change across the lifespan. There is an increase in *social dominance, conscientiousness*, and *emotional stability* in early adulthood that is matched by broader societal rights and responsibilities. *Social vitality* and *openness* tend to increase during adolescence, but decrease during old age.

Personality assessment is, in part, a function of the observer's implicit biases and perspectives. That is, while a personality characteristic may be observable, how it gets labeled is in the eye of the beholder. A personality characteristic is typically labeled a *trait* if it is unique, distinctive, and enduring, in contrast to a *state*, which is a more situation-specific response.

Personality and Illness Vulnerability

> How does personality contribute to illness vulnerability?

Resilience

As a result of genetic predisposition, early socialization, and life experiences, some people are more resistant to stress, disease, and illness (**resilience**), while others are more vulnerable. The development of resilience has predictable aspects and often requires structure from stable value systems and communities that foster emotional support. Resilient children often demonstrate the ability to be autonomous, to cope effectively, and also to ask for needed help. Across gender and ethnic lines and at major life transition points (e.g., adolescence, early adulthood), resilient individuals are able to adapt to, and rebound from, obstacles, negative experiences, and setbacks.

In adults, resilience, or **hardiness,** is characterized by commitment, challenge, and control. *Commitment* refers to the tendency to see the world as meaningful. *Challenge* involves seeing stresses or new experiences as opportunities to learn. *Control* refers to confidence in one's ability to influence life events, sometimes referred to as **self-efficacy**.

Locus of Control

Control has been further studied with regard to the **locus of control**, which is the individual's perception of whether life events are under their personal control (*internal* locus of control) or under the control of others (*external* locus of control). **Learned helplessness** is a process whereby individuals gain the sense they have no control over a situation (external locus of control) even when presented with a choice to change it, and is thought to correlate with hopelessness and depression.

Positive Reappraisal

Resilience requires the ability to reevaluate a situation, adapt, and find new solutions, and thus cope more effectively by changing the emotional impact of the situation. This process, referred to as *positive reappraisal,* is linked to the functioning of the limbic system, the prefrontal cortex, and the reward system (see Chapter 3: The Nervous System, and Chapter 7: Stress, Adaptation, and Stress Disorders); it is an essential component of cognitive therapy. Conversely, the inability to utilize positive reappraisal is thought to contribute to lack of resiliency, creating vulnerability to both psychopathology and medical illness. These vulnerabilities are comparable to other health risks such as hypertension or hypercholesterolemia, and exacerbate the impact of chronic conditions such as diabetes. For example, Type A individuals respond to stress with hard-driving, time-urgent, and hostile behaviors with deficits in positive reappraisal. This lack of resilience may mediate heightened susceptibility to the neurophysiological and cardiovascular consequences of excess stress responses.

Personality and Brain Functioning

There is considerable evidence to suggest that the personality traits researchers have identified can be subsumed under five general personality factors (the *Big Five*): extraversion, neuroticism, agreeableness, conscientiousness, and openness or intellect. Efforts have been made to associate these personality factors with the functioning of specific brain regions, and significant correlations between trait functioning and volumetric increases in specific brain regions have been reported (see Chapter 3: The Nervous System).

Bio-behavioral predisposition is thought to have a strong genetic basis, yet is clearly influenced by a tremendously complex interplay between genetic expression and the environment. These processes also feed into each other, as experiences can have a substantial impact on how an organism progresses on a developmental trajectory, including how genes are subsequently expressed. Genetic predisposition guides the unfolding of developmental processes, but an organism still requires a dynamic interaction with the environment to maintain the learning and plasticity processes that sustain and refine adaptive functions.

Recommended Readings

Briley, D. A., & Tucker-Drob, E. M. (2014). Genetic and environmental continuity in personality development: A meta-analysis. *Psychological Bulletin, 140*, 1303–1331. http://doi.org/10.1037/a0037091

Champagne, F. A. (2011). Early adversity and developmental outcomes: Interaction between genetics, epigenetics, and social experience across the life span. *Perspectives on Psychological Science, 5*, 564–574.

DeYoung, C. G., Hirsh, J. B., Shane, M. S., Papademetris, X., Rajeevan, N., & Gray, J. R. (2010). Testing predictions from personality. Neuroscience: Brain structure and the big five. *Psychological Science, 21*, 820–828. http://doi.org/10.1177/0956797610370159

Ennis, C. (2014, April 25). Epigenetics 101: A beginners guide to explaining everything. *The Guardian (US)*.

Weaver, I. C. G. (2014). Epigenetics: Integrating genetic programs, brain development and emergent phenotypes. *Cellular and Developmental Biology, 3*, 132. http://doi.org/10.4172/2168-9296.1000132

Review Questions

1. The entire genetic information that codes for the phenotype of a cell or an individual, most likely corresponds to which of these concepts?
   A. Epigenetic effect
   B. Genotype
   C. Phenotype
   D. Genome
   E. Trait

2. The association between the genotype a child inherits from their parents and the environment provided by the parents for the child's development is an example of
   A. active gene–environment correlation
   B. diathesis–stress interaction
   C. epigenetic–environment interaction
   D. evocative gene–environment correlation
   E. passive gene–environment correlation

3. During clinical assessment of a person, the provider detects her ability to evaluate new situations, to take into account new contextual information, to adapt, and to derive new solutions to problems. This ability most likely refers to which of the following personality concepts?
   A. Hardiness
   B. Locus of control
   C. Positive reappraisal
   D. Resilience
   E. Type A personality

Directions: The items below consist of lettered headings followed by numbered descriptions. For each numbered description, choose the one lettered heading to which it is *most* closely associated. Each lettered heading may be used *once, more than once,* or *not at all.*

Match the study design with the numbered description.
   A. Adoption
   B. Family risk
   C. Linkage
   D. Pedigree
   E. Twin

4. Look for trait and disease within families by connecting trait and marker.

5. Use a family tree as a major tool.
6. Investigate how often a disease occurs in family members of a proband compared with the general population.

Answer Key on p. 465

3 The Nervous System

João V. Nunes, MD, Ian M. Kodish, MD, PhD, and Julia B. Frank, MD

- What is neuronal plasticity?
- What role does synaptic pruning play in the development of executive functions?
- How does experience-dependent plasticity differ from experience-expectant plasticity?
- How do neurotransmitters work?
- How does the limbic system contribute to learning, memory, and emotional responsivity?
- What are mirror neurons and what do they do?

The Nervous System and Environmental Adaptation

In all animals, the nervous system promotes survival by maintaining homeostasis and organizing adaptive responses to diverse, ever-changing environmental challenges. Species differ in the size, shape, and organization of their brain. While basic elements – like the structure of neurons and the processes of neuronal transmission – appear in both simple and complex organisms, neuroanatomical differences are determined by the complexity of demands placed upon a nervous system and the functions that have evolved to meet those demands.

> The human brain is complex, comprising many specialized areas utilizing multiple parallel networks that integrate to convey the unique qualities of perception, thought, and social behavior that have allowed our species to adapt to an extraordinary range of existential demands.

Evolutionary–Experiential Interaction

What is neuronal plasticity?

Species also differ in the degree to which **evolution** influenced the development of one brain structure over another. Rats have elaborate olfactory systems that encompass a large portion of their brain, contributing to exquisite olfactory sensitivity. Humans have evolved to possess an elaborate cortex that encompasses a large portion of the brain that overlies more primitive brain structures. It folds in upon itself, maximizing the number of neurons and synaptic connections, enabling humans to engage in highly sophisticated abstract cognitive functions, such as understanding the context of behavioral demands and appreciating the impact of one's behavior on another person.

All mammalian nervous systems have specialized cells and discreet areas for registering touch, vision, odors, tastes, and sounds, but the sensitivity of these functions varies across species. The sensitivity of a particular area often correlates with the local density or **arborization** of neurons. In humans, for example, the volume of the brain area devoted to processing sensation from the fingertips or lips is far larger than that devoted to processing sensation from the lower back. Similarly, the elaborate neuronal arborizations within the human prefrontal cortex, which extend into multiple integrative circuits, permit greater cognitive processing than the simpler networks that encode basic sensory information.

Nervous system structures are shaped by experience, as well as evolving genetic programs, as they continually adapt to meet environmental demands. This process, termed **neuronal plasticity**, is continuous throughout the lifespan, although it is more robust in certain species and during certain developmental periods than others.

While human brains have regions that resemble the brains of lower animals, human neuronal networks have become more specialized and elaborate to suit human needs. The autonomic nervous system, which controls visceral functions, is often viewed as a "lower" aspect of the nervous system, regulated by "primitive" brain regions. Yet the autonomic nervous system also has evolved to respond to the demands of the environment, exhibiting neuronal arrangements similar to those in higher cortical regions.

In early (embryonic and early postnatal) development, neurons have limited synaptic connections and exhibit spontaneous activity. In response to experience, neurons begin to form more specialized connections (**synapses**) with other neuronal elements. Neurons not stimulated atrophy or die, while others proliferate in response to neurotropic expression patterns. In rats, for example, if one eye is kept closed at birth, the cortical regions that process visual information from that eye atrophy, while regions that process visual information from the other eye proliferate to accommodate for the heightened processing demands placed on them. While brain plasticity drives anatomic specialization across development, refinements are also made in response to experiences meeting specific environmental demands. Synaptic density also increases in response to the complexity of the demands it has evolved to meet. For example, rats challenged by treadmill activity show increased density of cortical blood vessels, but those exposed to more complex acrobatic training develop increased synaptic connectivity in motor areas.

Evolutionary Refinement

Over time, evolution has equipped the nervous system to respond more effectively to environmental demands, building refinement and complexity on adaptive successes achieved over broad time periods. Humans and sea slugs share similar reflex arcs. The neuronal interpretation of a signal (in humans, tapping on the patellar tendon) rapidly results in a behavioral effect (extension of the leg). Reflexes are simple (peripheral, without synapsing in the brain) and typically unconscious. Thus, much of the nervous system's responsiveness in humans occurs outside the individual's awareness (e.g., breathing more rapidly in higher altitudes).

The human brain processes, integrates, and interprets information relayed by the five common senses, but has other conscious and unconscious means of obtaining information as well. For instance, the brain is able to perceive balance, orientation, temperature, hunger, and pain, and impairments in these areas can have profound effects on a person's ability to function.

The brain structures and functions required to process complex information have become increasingly specialized through evolution. When someone looks at something, the retinas perceive the object and, through the optic nerve, convey signals to thalamic centers, which send the signals to various parts of the brain specialized to respond to the information. While the bulk of the information goes to occipital regions that code information (e.g., shape and color) from each eye into visual streams, some information is directed to emotionally attuned regions of the brain, which rapidly appraise the salient features of an object (threat? harmless? novel?).

The information that generates visual details from the occipital regions undergoes further processing in integrative parallel networks, creating various streams of additional information. These streams independently enhance the meaning of the visual input (e.g., form, depth, and motion) and then converge to form an integrated perception of a coherent object. Eventually, meaning and context are assigned to the information, which can now guide behavioral responses. This use of **parallel processing** and **regional specialization** within the brain enables humans to adapt to the environment in increasingly complex and detailed ways.

Developmental Fine Tuning

> What role does synaptic pruning play in the development of executive functions?

With development, there is "fine tuning" of neuronal networks on many levels. The volume of the human brain at age 3 years is close to that of an adult, yet a 3-year-old is not as capable of responding to environmental cues as an adult is. As development unfolds, synaptic connections undergo a cycle of increased density because of vast overproduction, followed by a reduction in synaptic connectivity. The process, called **synaptic pruning**, results in the formation of more stable and functional networks. Pruning is most pronounced in prefrontal regions during adolescence. Primary sensory regions undergo *developmental tuning* earlier than more integrative regions. Network refinements build on one another over the normal course of development, as networks become more elaborate in response to environmental stimuli. This reorganization results in the development of refined networks that facilitate the acquisition of complex behaviors and abstract thinking, collectively named **executive functions**. This permits adolescents to develop strategies to handle tasks requiring an appreciation of goals and contexts, and to shift behaviors in response to changing demands and circumstances.

> Following extensive pruning in adolescence, overall synaptic density diminishes gradually throughout adulthood. Conversely, myelin (the insulating lipid that comprises white matter and supports neuronal function) continually increases across development, resulting in gradually less dense but increasingly efficient neuronal networks.

Experiential–Developmental Interaction and Brain Development

> How does experience-dependent plasticity differ from experience-expectant plasticity?

Brain networks vary in their sensitivity and readiness to respond to stimulus cues over the lifespan. This pattern of variability in readiness to respond reflects developmental changes in experiential learning. There are two recognized processes by which brain network development can be influenced by experience: unanticipated experiences that are not affected by developmental sensitivity (experience-*dependent* plasticity), and common, early experiences, such as visual and sound (especially voices) stimulation and bodily movement that the brain has developed through evolution to "expect." These experiences activate particular synoptic systems involved in the senses, in a programmed developmental sensitivity timed to that specific experience (experience-*expectant* plasticity).

In **experience-dependent plasticity**, behavior is altered as a result of learning from experience and occurs throughout the lifespan. **Experience-expectant plasticity**, however, involves specific experiences occurring during time-limited sensitive periods of development (**critical periods**). For example, the coordinated use of two eyes leads to the experience of a single three-dimensional image rather than the two-dimensional images created by light in each eye. This effect depends on visual experiences during the second half of the first year of life that occur during a critical period when the neural system is ready to respond to these inputs. Experience-expectant plasticity works to fine-tune aspects of development that could not proceed to optimum outcomes as a result of environmental or genetic factors working alone.

Neuronal Structures and Functions

Neurons are the defining cellular units of the central and peripheral nervous systems. They gather and transmit information from the environment and from other neurons via *synapses* to specific neural networks which, in turn, process, appraise, plan, and elicit appropriate responses for survival.

Glial cells, derived from neuronal progenitor cells, are uniquely specialized to physically and chemically support neuronal functioning. They are the building blocks of the *myelin sheaths* that insulate neuronal projections thus protecting the quality and strength of neuronal signals. They also participate in synaptic transmission by inactivating certain neurotransmitters and maintaining chemical homeostasis, form scar tissue after central nervous system injury, line the fluid-filled brain ventricles, and function as immune defenses by removing cellular debris and monitoring the synaptic milieu to defend against infection.

Neuronal Development

Gene expression and experience-dependent plasticity are the primary guides to neuronal development and the modification of brain functioning throughout postnatal life. Initially, neuronal development is guided by morphogenic processes such as differential cell proliferation; migration; cell growth (*neurogenesis*); neural connectivity balanced among synaptogenesis, dendritic branching, and pruning; myelination; and programmed cell death (*apoptosis*).

Brain structures and circuitry are grossly established by birth, guided by physical cell-to-cell communication and chemical signals. This is followed by maturation, which is, at first, very rapid, then slower, then of variable speed at different points during the life cycle. Throughout this developmental process, dendritic branching and pruning and refinement of synaptic connections and neurotransmitter systems lead to the establishment and maturation of increasingly interconnected and parallel neuronal networks.

Action Potentials and Neurotransmission

The impetus for the propagation of information in the nervous system is an electrical current that travels along the neuronal membrane. This semipermeable membrane permits and sustains different concentrations and gradients of positively and negatively charged ions in the internal environment of the cell (cytosol side of the membrane) compared with the surrounding extracellular fluid. The net electrical charge of the cytosol is negative relative to the charge of the extracellular fluid, with a *resultant resting potential* of –65 mV.

Activation of **membrane ion channels**, such as (a) *ligand-gated channels*, responsive to chemical signals; (b) *voltage-gated channels*, responsive to changes in the membrane potential; and

(c) *channels sensitive to heat or mechanical distortion of the membrane,* cause changes to the resting potential of the membrane. Excitation elicits the opening of membrane sodium ion (Na+) channels to allow an influx of Na+ into the cell, turning the cytosol side of the membrane progressively less negative (less polarized). If this depolarization proceeds beyond a certain threshold, an **action potential** is generated – that is, an "all-or-nothing" electrical event that propagates along the neuronal membrane of the axon toward the synaptic junction.

Neurotransmission

How do neurotransmitters work?

In the axon terminal, action potentials promote the release of **neurotransmitters** from synaptic vesicles into the synaptic cleft and onto postsynaptic receptors, permitting neurons and their projections to transmit to networks in distant brain regions that are interconnected via multiple circuits. These circuits can be examined anatomically (histology and imaging), chemically (radioactive labeling), functionally (blood flow changes during cognitive tasks), and electrically (electroencephalography) to promote understanding of specific brain functions and malfunctions.

Neurotransmitters bind to specific receptors in the postsynaptic cell membrane, which triggers opening or closing of ion channels in the postsynaptic neuronal membrane; this binding leads to depolarization (excitation) or hyperpolarization (inhibition) of postsynaptic cells. Neuronal activity owes its complexity in part to mechanisms that control electrical activation of cellular regions.

Receptors can be classified into transmitter-gated ion channels (ionotropic) and G-protein-coupled (metabotropic) receptors. *Ionotropic receptors* have an ion channel core that responds directly to neurotransmitter action, opening or closing ion channels; responses are very fast and brief. *Metabotropic receptors* are indirectly connected to ion channel activity by activating intracellular mechanisms such as *second messenger* enzymatic cascades. Prominent second messengers include cyclic nucleotides, Ca++, and inositol triphosphate (IP$_3$). Activation of **second messen-**

ger systems typically leads to *phosphorylation of ion channels*, which changes their functional state and induces slower but longer-lasting postsynaptic responses.

> The major neurotransmitters in the brain include glutamate, gamma-amino-butyric acid (GABA), acetylcholine (ACh), norepinephrine (NE), dopamine (DA), serotonin (5-HT), and histamine. Molecules such as neuropeptides and hormones play modulatory roles that modify neurotransmission over longer time periods.

Neurotransmitter activity is terminated through (1) **diffusion** away from the synaptic cleft; (2) **enzymatic degradation**; and (3) **reuptake** (active transport) back into the presynaptic terminal. After reuptake, neurotransmitters may be reloaded into synaptic vesicles for future use or degraded enzymatically. Both neuronal and glial cell membranes possess active transport mechanisms that assist in neurotransmitter removal from the synaptic cleft. For specific examples relating neurotransmitter activity to clinical syndromes, see Section X: Psychopathology.

Brain Structures and Functions

The **central nervous system** (CNS) comprises the brain and spinal cord. The brain consists of three major parts – **hindbrain**, **midbrain**, and **forebrain** (cerebrum) – each with anatomical and functional subdivisions. The midbrain and hindbrain constitute the brainstem; the hindbrain includes the cerebellum. The forebrain consists of the two cerebral hemispheres and the diencephalon (to visualize these and other neuronal structures, see http://www.radnet.ucla.edu/sections/DINR/index.htm).

Brainstem

The **brainstem** integrates and regulates vital bodily functions such as respiration, cardiovascular activity, and consciousness. Sensory information from the spinal cord ascends through brainstem tracts to specific cerebral and cerebellar sites. After incoming information is processed, a motor response is elicited via the brainstem back to the spinal cord, and then onto motor systems for bodily action.

Forebrain

The **diencephalon** includes the thalamus and hypothalamus. The **thalamus** is the gateway to the cerebral cortex for all sensory information except olfaction, which synapses directly into the cerebrum (entorhinal cortex) and the amygdala. Thalamic nuclei reciprocally connect with most of the cerebral cortex through thalamic radiations, which are fiber bundles that constitute a large portion of the **internal capsule**. The thalamus relays information from the basal ganglia and cerebellum to the cerebral cortex, which then formulates plans for the execution of smooth and coordinated motor responses. The thalamus also plays a role in regulating emotional expression, memory, and cognition by relaying information to the limbic system and integrative cortical regions. These reciprocal thalamocortical radiations are thought to be involved in the abnormalities of emotion processing and regulation found in disorders such as schizophrenia and obsessive-compulsive disorder (see Chapter 42: Schizophrenia and Other Psychotic Disorders, and Chapter 48: Obsessive-Compulsive and Related Disorders).

The **hypothalamus** is central to the functioning of the **autonomic nervous system**. Anterior and medial hypothalamic areas control *parasympathetic* activity while the lateral and posterior hypothalamic areas control *sympathetic* activity. The hypothalamus integrates input for appropriate autonomic and somatic responses that maintain homeostatic balance. It mediates neuroendocrine-induced physiological changes related to feeding, drinking, pleasure, displeasure, aversion, emotional functioning, and behavioral inhibition (see Chapter 5: Energy Homeostasis).

Anatomically, hypothalamic nuclei project neuroendocrine fibers to the anterior pituitary gland to regulate systemic stress responses in the adrenal cortex. This circuit is termed the **hypothalamic-pituitary-adrenocortical** (HPA) axis or the hypothalamic-pituitary-endocrine axis, and utilizes the neuroendocrine system to up- or down-regulate other hormonal responses in a coordinated effort to respond to environmental demands.

In response to stress, the hypothalamus releases cortico-tropin-releasing hormone (CRH), which stimulates the anterior pituitary to release adrenocorticotropic hormone (ACTH) into the bloodstream, where it prompts the adrenal cortices to release cortisol (glucocorticoid), the stress hormone. Cortisol, in turn, triggers epinephrine and norepinephrine release from the adrenal medulla, and then feeds back to the HPA axis to down-regulate further secretions. This neuroendocrine feedback loop is common to all mammals and most vertebrates, and there is evidence that dysregulation contributes to clinical impairments in mood, anxiety, and posttraumatic stress disorders.

The Limbic System

How does the limbic system contribute to learning, memory, and emotional responsivity?

The **limbic system** is considered to be part of the telencephalon like the rest of the cerebral cortex and consists of structures that initiate evaluative responses to incoming affective information, thereby contributing to learning, memory, and emotional responses to experience. Which structures are considered components of the limbic circuits has varied over time, but generally these include the amygdala, the septal nucleus, and the hippocampus, and their pathways with the anterior thalamic nuclei, cingulate gyrus, parahippocampal gyrus, and several regions of the prefrontal cortex. Emotional responsivity is coordinated in parallel by the limbic system and neocortical regions, and modulated via reciprocal connections to and from subcortical regions.

The **amygdala** receives information from every sensory modality. This information is rapidly integrated via its internal interconnections, and is then passed on to the hypothalamus and brainstem centers, which regulate autonomic function. The amygdala also connects with areas associated with interpretation of the meaning of stimuli (frontal and cingulate cortices) and with episodic memory (hippocampus). Thus, the amygdala shapes the interpretation of a sensory stimulus, drawing on cortical processes and memories to initiate an adaptive emotional response.

The **hippocampus** is located in the lower medial wall of the temporal lobe, behind the amygdala, and interacts with the hypothalamus, the amygdala, and the neocortex to promote learning and memory.

Hippocampal input provides temporal and spatial context to incoming information and, together with the amygdala, refines the interpretation of sensory stimuli. It is thought to contribute images, words, and ideas to dreaming, and is generally considered a gatekeeper for consolidation of working memory.

The **septal nucleus**, located anterior to the third ventricle near the hypothalamus, generally inhibits extreme arousal in order to preserve quiescence and readiness for action. Connections with the hippocampus and hypothalamus modulate the autonomic and neuroendocrine reactivity of the amygdala and hypothalamus, primarily through inhibition.

Cerebro-Spinal-Cerebellar-Peripheral Connections

Ascending and descending tracts relay information between the cerebrum, peripheral nervous system, and other bodily systems via the brainstem and the spinal cord. The dorsal column-medial lemniscal pathway and the anterior-lateral pathway are long ascending tracts that start from the spinal cord and carry sensory information originating in the body. The **dorsal column-medial lemniscal pathway** transmits tactile and vibratory senses, whereas the **anterior-lateral pathway** conveys pain and temperature.

At the brainstem, pathways for hearing, taste, and general sensory modalities from the face merge with the spinal sensory pathways to form the **lemniscal system**. The lemniscal system carries information to the cerebral cortex via the thalamus for the perception of pain, temperature, touch, taste, hearing, discriminative touch, and the appreciation of form, weight, and texture. The conscious experience of these sensations is mediated by the **reticular system**, which originates in the spinal cord, courses through the brain stem, hypothalamus, and thalamus, and terminates in the frontal lobes. The reticular system is essential for consciousness, arousal, sleep, and attention, and also organizes patterns of visceromotor activity (e.g., gastric motility and respiratory and cardio-vascular activities).

Incoming sensory information that demands motor action triggers commands from the motor cortex. These commands travel through the corticospinal tract to reach the cranial nerve nuclei, pons, and medulla, and continue on to lateral and ventromedial pathways (descending tracts within the spinal cord that synapse to form peripheral connections to the skeletal muscles). The lateral pathways control voluntary movement of the distal musculatures, while the ventromedial pathways control the trunk musculature for posture and locomotion.

The **cerebellum** receives information from the cerebral cortex, spinal cord, and vestibular system. It transforms the information into cerebellum-modulated motor commands and directs them back to the motor cortex and brainstem motor centers. The cerebellum-modulated motor commands are then sent to the lower motor neurons, which turn them into precise, smooth, and coordinated motor activity.

The Cerebral Hemispheres

Each **cerebral hemisphere** contains basal ganglia and cerebral cortex. The **cerebral cortex** on either side is divided into four lobes: frontal, parietal, temporal, and occipital. Each lobe has a primary sensory or motor region surrounded by larger association cortices. Though serving some specific functions, cortical regions are highly interconnected anatomically and functionally by association and commissure fibers, within and between hemispheres. The **corpus callosum** is a large midline structure underlying the cortex, comprising white matter fibers, which transmits information between cortical hemispheres. The **limbic lobe**, a cortical strip encircling the corpus callosum and part of the medial surface of the temporal lobe, is occasionally considered the fifth lobe as its anatomical organization resembles other cortical regions.

The **basal ganglia** include four nuclei deeply situated within each cerebral hemisphere: *caudate*, *putamen*, *globus pallidus*, and *subthalamic nucleus*, and one midbrain structure, the *substantia nigra*. The basal ganglia connect to the cerebral cortex via the thalamus and also receive direct cor-

tical projections. The structures of the basal ganglia are organized in three functional loops. The **motor loop**, which facilitates the initiation of willed movement, is formed as the putamen receives projections from the sensorimotor cortex and sends projections to the motor and premotor cortices. The **executive loop**, which facilitates cognitive functions, involves the caudate, which receives projections from cortical association areas and sends projections to the prefrontal cortex. The **limbic loop**, which regulates emotional behaviors, involves reciprocal projections between limbic structures and the *nucleus accumbens*. Activation of this region is associated with the experience of reward. The nucleus accumbens is located in a portion of the basal forebrain known as the *ventral striatum*.

Frontal Lobe

The **frontal lobe** makes up about half the area and volume of the cerebral cortex and has three functional regions: (1) the primary motor cortex, (2) the premotor cortex, and (3) the prefrontal cortex.

The **primary motor cortex** is located in the precentral gyrus. Its neuronal projections comprise about 40% of the volume of the corticospinal tract and make monosynaptic and polysynaptic connections with motor neurons in the spinal cord. The monosynaptic connections primarily move individual fingers during skillful tasks, while the polysynaptic connections move the limbs during complex behaviors such as walking and reaching for objects.

The **premotor cortex**, which lies anterior to the primary motor cortex and contributes about 30% to the volume of the corticospinal tract, selects movements and initiates motor planning.

The **prefrontal cortex** comprises the rest of the frontal cortex and has three main regions: (1) the dorsal prefrontal association area, (2) the ventral orbitofrontal cortex, and (3) the medial prefrontal cortex.

The **dorsal prefrontal association area** integrates motor information with multimodal sensory information coming from the parietal and temporal lobes. After processing, the information contributes to cognitive judgments and more complex motor planning. Connections to the premotor and motor cortices allow for subsequent implementation via other bodily systems – for example, the voluntary muscles. Broca's speech area and the frontal eye field exemplify this sensory–motor integration. **Broca's speech area** receives and integrates information from sensorimotor and visual cortices and from **Wernicke's area** (verbal understanding) before initiating the motor responses that produce speech. Through its connections with cortical and brainstem structures, the **frontal eye field** integrates information to initiate saccades, moving the eyes toward objects of interest, and coordinating eye-head movements.

The **ventromedial prefrontal cortex** (VMPFC) plays a role in emotional appraisal during decision making, preference judgment, and risk taking to influence reward responses, including those related to social appraisal, and is thought to be involved in the development of empathy. The **orbitofrontal cortex**, which is also associated with social functions, is often included as part of the VMPFC since the areas work in unison. They have direct connections with the limbic system, and studies of patients with *posttraumatic stress disorder* (PTSD) indicate that these are the important connections that link events with their emotional associations. The influence of the VMPFC may be unconscious (mediated by the brainstem and ventral striatum) or conscious (through cortical involvement).

> According to the somatic marker hypothesis, the VMPFC enables individuals to use emotional reactions (somatic markers) to decide between positive or negative alternatives in social situations. Damage or dysfunction of the VMPFC impairs this ability, resulting in maladaptive social behavior.

Mirror Neurons

> What are mirror neurons and what do they do?

Some neurons have been found to fire not only when a person performs an action, but also when that person observes another person performing a similar action. These neurons "mirror" the actions of another person's neurons as though they were engaged in the action being observed. This suggests that **mirror neurons** are important for *social learning* (e.g., affiliation, imitation, empathy, social cognition, and language acquisition) and

may play a role in the etiology of *autism*. Mirror neurons have been found in the premotor cortex, supplementary motor area, primary somatosensory cortex, and inferior parietal cortex. In the human brain, these areas overlap with Broca's area, highlighting the important social function of language.

Parietal Lobe

The **parietal lobe** processes and integrates somatosensory and visuospatial information for localizing the body and surrounding objects, and for learning tasks requiring coordination of the body in space. The parietal lobe has three functional regions: (1) the primary somatosensory cortex, (2) the somatosensory unimodal association area, and (3) the multimodal sensory association area.

The **primary somatosensory cortex** (PSC) is located in the postcentral gyrus and receives and interprets somesthetic (concerned with or relating to bodily sensations) information from the contralateral part of the body.

The **somatosensory unimodal association area** (SUAA), located immediately posterior to the PSC, further processes somesthetic information to facilitate improved recognition (e.g., identify an object based solely on tactile information such as size, shape, texture, and weight).

The **multimodal sensory association area** (MSAA) receives and integrates somesthetic, visual, auditory, and movement-related information from several association cortices. It enables a person to discern (a) the three-dimensional position of objects in space; (b) body image and the space in which the body moves; (c) direction of movement; and (d) location of sound. The *left inferior parietal lobule* is thought to integrate sensorimotor information for performance of skilled, temporally sequential motor acts; perception and production of written language; and arithmetic calculations.

Temporal Lobe

The **temporal lobe** processes auditory, gustatory, visceral, and olfactory stimuli, while the inferior temporal cortex allows facial recognition. The temporal lobe has several functional regions: (1) the primary auditory cortex, (2) the auditory unimodal association cortex, (3) the visual uni-modal association cortex, (4) the multimodal sensory association area, and several limbic system structures, such as (5) the limbic association area, (6) the amygdala, and (7) the hippocampus.

Lateralization, although more pronounced in the neocortex, is also observed in limbic structures. The right amygdala-hippocampus complex processes nonverbal, emotional memory, while the left amygdala-hippocampus complex processes verbal memory.

Occipital Lobe

The **occipital lobe** has two functional regions: (1) the *primary visual cortex*, located along the calcarine fissure, processes visual information relayed by the thalamus, and (2) the *visual unimodal association area* further processes the visual information coming from the primary visual cortex. These regions extend beyond the anatomical boundaries of the occipital lobe to occupy the inferior-lateral surfaces of the occipital and temporal lobes, and contribute to parallel processing of visual information that later converges into an integrated perception.

Hemispheric Dominance

At birth, the left and right cerebral hemispheres are functionally disconnected because the **corpus callosum** and anterior and posterior **commissures** are not yet myelinated. Therefore, until the age of 5–8 months, when myelination becomes complete, each brain hemisphere primarily develops independently. **Hemispheric dominance** is defined in terms of the *laterality of functions* or functional specialization of one hemisphere over the other. The left hemisphere is dominant for language in up to 99% of right-handed people, and in up to 70% of left-handed people. The right hemisphere is dominant for spatial location and orientation, but not to the same degree that the left hemisphere is dominant for language.

Left hemisphere functions include verbal comprehension and differentiation, identification, and linguistic labeling of visual, auditory, and somesthetic information. *Right hemisphere functions* include visuospatial perception, facial recognition, body image, voice tone, melody and rhythm perception, and various aspects of emotionality.

Recommended Readings

Bavelier, D., Levi, D. M., Li, R. W., Dan, Y., & Hensch, T. K. (2010). Removing brakes on adult brain plasticity: From molecular to behavioral interventions. *Journal of Neuroscience, 30*, 14964–14971. http://doi.org/10.1523/JNEUROSCI.4812-10.2010

Eroglu, C., & Barres, B. A. (2010). Regulation of synaptic connectivity by glia. *Nature, 468*, 223–231. http://doi.org/10.1038/nature09612

Gogtay, N., & Thompson, P. M. (2010). Mapping gray matter development: Implications for typical development and vulnerability to psychopathology. *Brain and Cognition, 72*, 6–15. http://doi.org/10.1016/j.bandc.2009.08.009

Holtmaat, A., & Svoboda, K. (2009). Experience-dependent structural synaptic plasticity in the mammalian brain. *Nature Reviews Neuroscience, 10*, 647–658. http://doi.org/10.1038/nrn2699

Striedter, G. F. (2016). *Neurobiology: A functional approach.* London, UK: Oxford University Press.

Additional Resources

Salamon's Neuroanatomy and Neurovascular Web-Atlas Resource. Available at http://www.radnet.ucla.edu/sections/DINR/index.htm

Review Questions

1. A 7-year-old boy is diagnosed with attention-deficit/hyperactivity disorder (ADHD) based on his restlessness, difficulty focusing attention, and tendency to blurt out things without thinking. Failure to regulate impulsive behavior suggests dysfunction at which of the following areas of the brain as a site affected by his disorder?

    A. Brainstem
    B. Hypothalamus
    C. Limbic system
    D. Occipital lobe
    E. Prefrontal cortex

2. Strategies for developing drugs that would increase and stabilize the activity of a particular neurotransmitter in the synapses of the brain might usefully include
    A. adding compounds that block ligand-gated receptors
    B. altering cell DNA to increase production of neurotransmitters
    C. blocking enzymes that degrade the transmitters after they are released
    D. changing the pH of cerebrospinal fluid to inhibit diffusion
    E. enhancing reuptake into the releasing neuron

3. Closing one eye of a rat pup for 3 weeks after birth, then opening it, will result in an adult rat with
    A. exaggerated stress responses
    B. neural atrophy in the area receiving input from the closed eye
    C. no perception of the side of the body of the closed eye
    D. normal vision
    E. reduced total brain volume

4. During adolescence, sex steroids change the architecture of the brain, leading to acceleration in cell death and increase in the density of the cell connections that remain. This process results in
    A. increased ability to acquire and process language
    B. increased brain size and head circumference
    C. increased experience-expected learning
    D. more appreciation of the context of perceived information
    E. new critical periods for skill acquisition

Answer Key on p. 465

4 Brain Networks in Health and Illness

Michael I. Posner, PhD, and Mary K. Rothbart, PhD

- What is a functional brain network?
- What is the significance of connectivity in defining a functional brain network?
- How is brain network efficiency measured?
- How do genes influence brain network development?
- How do brain networks contribute to health and illness?

Functional Brain Networks

The ability to image the human brain at rest and during task performance has transformed our understanding of normal and atypical brain function. When cells in a particular region of the brain become more active, blood flow to the region increases. Changes in blood flow can be examined using radionuclides that emit particles that can be sensed by detectors outside the head, while changes in hemoglobin can be examined using *functional magnetic resonance imaging* (fMRI). These methods provide (1) structural images of the brain, (2) maps of brain activity, and (3) measures of connectivity between brain areas.

In the late 1980s, *positron emission tomography* (PET) was used to examine blood flow in people as they heard or read individual words. One set of brain areas was active when words were read aloud, and additional areas were active when word associations were required. A major development in the 1990s was the use of *magnetic resonance imaging* (MRI) to measure localized changes in blood oxygen as a means of mapping brain activity noninvasively. MRI was not only able to show well-defined localized activity, but, because it did not rely on radioactivity, a given person could safely be scanned repeatedly. This made it possible to present different types of trials in random order and then average the outcomes of the trials, preventing participants from developing special strategies for each trial type.

What is a functional brain network?

In the 1970s and 1980s, extensive work in cognitive science and artificial intelligence in areas of cognition, such as attention, memory, and language, led to the development of computerized laboratory tasks and experimental methods that could be associated with specific mental operations. Mental operations can compute different forms of internal representation (e.g., the name of a visual word). Imaging methods often involved subtracting reaction times found in simpler conditions from those in more complex conditions, to isolate the added time required for mental operations of the more complex tasks. Using this subtractive method, it was possible to isolate the **mental operations** involved in the task and, via the scanner, to map the areas of the brain found to be active during the performance of the tasks. For example, the reading of individual words could be divided into visual, phonological, and semantic operations that could then be isolated by tasks such as visual matching, reading aloud, and classifying word meanings. Use of these tasks indicated that one posterior brain area (left fusiform gyrus) seems to be involved in grouping the letters of a word into a single unit, while another area (left temporal parietal cortex) is involved in assigning a sound for the word. These two areas are connected to brain areas involved in temporary storage (left ventral frontal), word meaning

(Wernicke's area), and attention (anterior cingulate). Thus, what seems like a simple act of reading a word is actually a complex set of functions made possible by a network of widely separated brain areas working together. Imaging with MRI has been applied widely to many areas associated with cognition and emotion such as arithmetic, autobiographical memory, fear, object perception, self-reference, and spatial navigation. In all of these studies, a set of widely scattered neural areas was activated by a specific task. Taken together, these brain areas are called **functional brain networks,** and the component mental operations performed by each individual area are gradually being identified as research progresses. Moreover, new methods of analysis of MRI data are allowing us to discover complex patterns of activity within the brain related to representations of the outside world.

Network Connectivity and Efficiency

> What is the significance of connectivity in defining a functional brain network?

Correlations in the fMRI signal between remote neural areas have been used to study their **connectivity** within a specific functional brain network. These correlations indicate which areas are working together during the performance of a task. Connectivity can also be determined by use of *diffusion tensor imaging* (DTI), a noninvasive method that shows the location, orientation, and directionality of white matter connections between the brain areas of a functional network, by measuring the diffusion of water molecules. These white matter bundles of axons connect large groups of neurons over varying distances to form connected networks. This extensive connectivity makes communication possible between anatomically separate areas both within and between functional brain networks. Currently there is a large national effort in the US to examine the full set of connections in the human brain.

Brain Network Efficiency

> How is brain network efficiency measured?

Since vascular changes measured by MRI are slow, recordings from electroencephalography (EEG) scalp electrodes or magnetic detectors (magnetoencephalography; MEG) can be used to follow the flow of information over time between brain areas. The speed of information processing along a pathway provides a measure of the efficiency of the connection. Measuring the speed of performing laboratory tasks provides a behavioral method for measuring the efficiency of brain networks. For example, an important brain network is involved in monitoring and resolving conflict induced by presenting stimuli that lead to conflicting responses. In the laboratory, a participant is instructed to respond to a central arrow by pressing one key when it points to the right and another key when it points to the left. Conflict is induced by presenting flanking arrows that point in the same or opposite direction to the central arrow. Reaction times for responding when the flanking arrows point in the same direction (congruent condition) are subtracted from reaction times when the flanking arrows point in the opposite direction (conflict condition). The difference in reaction times provides a measure of the efficiency of a high-level attention network involved in monitoring conflict among response tendencies. Brain images taken during the performance of this conflict task show increased activity in the *dorsal anterior cingulate*. In addition, the efficiency of transmission along white matter pathways leading from the cingulate to *frontal* and *parietal* areas is correlated with the speed of resolving the conflict, further indicating that these three areas are important components of an attention network involved in dealing with conflict among response tendencies.

> Both behavioral and imaging methods show that it is possible to measure not only the **connectivity**, but also the **efficiency** of brain networks involved in carrying out high-level tasks. These measurements show that connectivity and efficiency differ among normal individuals, change with experience and development, and can be influenced by training.

Gene–Environment Interaction in Network Development

The degree of **genetic influence** in the development of brain networks can be studied by comparing differences between identical twins, who share the same genes, and fraternal twins, whose genes are only as similar as those of non-twin siblings. Comparing the two types of twins provides an **index of heritability**, which indicates the relative importance of genes. Results from twin studies indicate that the efficiency of brain networks, as measured by processing speed, is about 50% heritable.

> There are no specific genes that determine functional brain networks. Rather, an array of genes code for different proteins that provide the instructions for neuronal development. These instructions specify the various neuromodulators that contribute to the connectivity and efficiency of brain networks.

Although, in general, all humans have the same genes, many of the genes are *polymorphic*; that is, they may be expressed in different forms. Among genes having a great deal of variability are those associated with *dopamine D4 receptor* (DRD4), *dopamine transporter* (DAT1), *monoamine oxidase A* (MAO-A), *catechol-o-methyl transferase* (COMT), and *serotonin neurotransmitter* systems. This variability helps to explain individual differences in behavior. For example, the dopamine D4 receptor (DRD4) gene has a 48-base pair sequence that may be repeated a different number of times, and these differences change the sensitivity of the receptor to dopamine. One version of this gene, the *seven-repeat allele* (in which the 48 base pairs are repeated 7 times) has been associated with **attention-deficit/hyperactivity disorder** (ADHD) and with the tendency to take risks, among individuals in the normal population.

There is evidence that the prevalence of the seven-repeat allele is increasing in human evolution. A possible explanation is suggested by studies of child behavior, in which children with the seven-repeat allele are found to be more susceptible to social and cultural influences provided by, for example, caregivers and peers. This greater susceptibility to social and environmental influence could increase reproductive success and, thus, influence natural selection. This explanation would be consistent with the view that individual differences in efficiency of brain networks are dependent upon *genetic* variation, *epigenetic* or environmental influences, and *development*. One particular epigenetic mechanism that is receiving considerable attention is *DNA methylation*. Gene expression can be changed when a methyl chemical group attaches to the promoter region of the cell and essentially silences the gene.

> Methylation and demethylation and other similar transcription processes (e.g., acetylation) can be rapidly altered by environmental stimuli, and are used, for example, by the hippocampus in the consolidation of memory, turning "off" memory suppressor genes, and turning "on" memory promoter genes.

In addition to network connections that are activated during the performance of tasks (e.g., attention, alerting, object perception), there are network connections that are in evidence even when the person is at rest. For example, a **default mode network** (DMN) links the posterior cingulate cortex with the medial prefrontal, medial temporal, and bilateral inferior parietal regions. Two large **attention networks** have also been shown to be connected and active at rest: a set of frontoparietal brain areas related to orienting to sensory stimuli regardless of modality, and a cingulo-opercular network related to the resolution of conflict. The frontoparietal network in adults is involved in short-term control operations common when orienting to sensory signals. The cinguloparietal network is involved in longer, more strategic control, which is an important property of executive system functions like conflict resolution.

Because the analysis of resting connectivity does not require performance of a task, it can readily be studied in infants. During the first year of life, the anterior cingulate shows little or no connectivity to other areas; but after the first year, infants begin the slow process of developing the long-range connectivity typical of adults. The functional organization of the brain also becomes increasingly differentiated. Thus, children show evidence of many shorter local connections, while adults have longer network connections. In addition, adults have separate networks related to orienting and executive attention, but this separation between networks is less well defined in children.

New Learning and Network Development

Since, as mentioned above, fMRI is noninvasive, it is possible to use multiple scans to examine the network changes that occur with learning and development. The connectivity of brain networks can be enhanced by practicing the tasks with which they are associated. In addition, goal-directed learning experiences, or training, contribute to a progressive change from the primarily local network connections, dominant in children, to the longer network connections prominent in adults. These changes reflect how learning from adaptive life experiences interacts with maturation and genetic predisposition (**gene–environment–developmental interaction**) to enhance development of brain network organization, connectivity, and efficiency.

Two types of **training** influence brain network functioning. The first type of training involves practice on a task specific to a particular network that may generalize to other tasks using that network. For example, training in working memory has been shown to affect other tasks that involve working memory (near generalization). Whether it generalizes to more remote tasks such as general intelligence is still in dispute. The second type of training involves training a brain state that influences performance of many networks. For example, not only does aerobic exercise affect aspects of an individual's physical condition, such as respiration and muscle tone, but also affects cognitive functions related to memory and attention. Training with forms of *mindfulness meditation* also has been shown to improve attention and mood, reduce stress, and enhance immune function.

Network Disorders and Health

How do brain networks contribute to health and illness?

There is evidence that impaired brain network activity contributes to several specific disorders such as *multiple sclerosis* and *callosal agenesis*, due to degradation of the myelination of axonal tracts, and decreased structural integrity of the fibers at the corpus callosum. Disruption of brain organization is also believed to be involved in conditions like **autism spectrum disorders** and ADHD. Decreased levels of cognitive performance in aging also have been related to reduced resting state activity, decreased functional connectivity, and degeneration of the microstructural organization of white matter tracts, as well as to altered microstructural organization of the cingulum tract.

Imaging studies have also provided a perspective on brain network functioning associated with other disorders. Patients with **schizophrenia** have been found to have alterations in both resting state activity and organization of white matter tracts. A brain network that includes cortical and subcortical areas has been found to reduce activation in persons suffering from depression. Treatment with antidepressant medications, shown to be effective in some patients, influences primarily subcortical areas, while equally effective behavioral therapy influences primarily cortical areas.

The structure and organization of brain systems, like all human organ systems, have evolved in the service of the survival of the species, and determine the ability of individuals to adapt to and cope with conditions that challenge homeostasis and normal functioning. As the executive coordinator and regulator of multiple organ and life support systems, the brain is critically important in managing the survival of an individual. The brain's success in that endeavor appears to be directly related to the structural integrity, interconnectedness, and efficiency of functional brain networks.

Recommended Readings

Fair, D. A., Cohen, A. L., Power, J. D., Dosenbach, N. U. F., Church, J. A., Miezin, F. M., ... Petersen, S. E. (2009). Functional brain networks developed from a "local to distributed" organization. *PLoS Computational Biology*, 5, e1000381. http://doi.org/10.1371/journal.pcbi.1000381

Poldrack, R. A., & Farah, M. J. (2015). Progress and challenges in probing the human brain. *Nature, 526,* 371–379. http://doi.org/10.1038/nature15692

Raichle, M. E. (2009). A paradigm shift in functional imaging. *Journal of Neuroscience, 29,* 12729–12734. http://doi.org/10.1523/JNEUROSCI.4366-09.2009

Rothbart, M. K. (2011). *Becoming who we are: Temperament and personality in development.* New York, NY: Guilford Press.

Tang, Y.-Y., & Posner, M. I. (2014). Training brain networks and states. *Trends in Cognitive Science, 18*(7), 345–350. http://doi.org/10.1016/j.tics.2014.04.002

Review Questions

1. Positron emission tomography (PET) and magnetic resonance imaging (MRI) produce brain images that researchers and clinicians rely on. Among the following, which is most likely the purpose of these imaging techniques?
   A. Determine the efficiency of brain matter
   B. Identify active brain waves
   C. Identify connections between brain areas
   D. Identify the role of the brain in survival
   E. Map brain activity invasively

2. The set of widely scattered brain areas that may be activated by a specific task is called a
   A. bilateral insular region
   B. cortical hub
   C. functional brain network
   D. goal-directed learning experience
   E. grouping of DNA methylation and other similar transcription processes

3. There is evidence that impaired functional brain network activity is involved in some fashion in brain disorders. Among the following, which disorders are most likely included?
   A. Autism spectrum and attention-deficit disorders
   B. Multiple sclerosis and callosal agenesis
   C. Schizophrenia and depression
   D. All of the above
   E. None of the above

Answer Key on p. 465

Section III
Basic Homeostatic Systems

5 Energy Homeostasis

Eric D. LaMotte, MD, and Ellen A. Schur, MD, MS

- How does the body orchestrate energy homeostasis to maintain a stable weight?
- Which physiological variables affect the balance of energy intake and energy expenditure within an organism?
- How can the maintenance of energy homeostasis actually work against an individual's goals for weight change?

Defining Energy Homeostasis

The body must maintain a relatively constant internal state, or **homeostasis**, over time in order to survive. If, for example, weight is to remain stable over time, caloric intake must closely match energy expenditure. An excess of just 10 kilocalories per day, less than 1% of caloric intake, is enough to cause an individual to gain a pound (0.45 kg) of body weight per year. Numerous neurological and endocrine processes coordinate this matching of intake and expenditure, which is experienced as a series of decisions about what to eat, when to eat, when to stop eating, and when to increase physical activity. The process whereby energy intake and expenditure is balanced is called **energy homeostasis**.

Coordination of Energy Intake (Eating)

How does the body orchestrate energy homeostasis to maintain a stable weight?

The brain integrates many types of information to control eating behaviors, including sensory information and physiological signals about short- and long-term nutritional status. Sensory information

sent by neurological and endocrine pathways is integrated within the **hypothalamus**, especially the **arcuate nucleus**, to create alternating states of hunger and satiety. As the primary brain structure involved in regulating body weight, the hypothalamus receives input from cortical areas, the **basal ganglia**, and the brainstem, and is sensitive to the concentrations of nutrients and hormones in the blood. Hypothalamic outputs project to the **pituitary gland**, other brain areas (especially the basal ganglia), and, via the **autonomic nervous system**, the rest of the body.

Neural Signaling

Several senses inform decisions about eating. Visual presentation, aroma, and memories and social cues can initiate a sense of hunger or cause a person to ignore satiety ("fullness") signals from the gut (e.g., during Thanksgiving dinner).

These phenomena occur because visual, olfactory, and somatosensory cortical areas project to the hypothalamus where signals promoting hunger and satiety are integrated. The hypothalamus then projects to other brain areas responsible for behavioral motivation and reward processing, such as the **amygdala** and **nucleus accumbens**. These ultimately project onto the basal ganglia and motor cortex to initiate or suppress food consumption and maintain the body's energy supply.

Gut Hormones

> Which physiological variables affect the balance of energy intake and energy expenditure within an organism?

Several hormones carry information about nutritional state from the gut to the brain, contributing to hunger or satiety. Consumption of a meal increases the blood concentration of *satiety signals* such as **cholecystokinin** (CCK), **glucagon-like peptide-1** (GLP-1)**, and peptide YY** (PYY). Duodenal cells are stimulated to secrete these hormones by the presence of fatty acids and amino acids in the small intestine after ingestion of a meal. In addition to acting within the gastrointestinal (GI) tract to slow gastric emptying and stimulate the pancreas to release digestive enzymes, these hormones also signal back to the brainstem, via the vagus nerve, to stimulate a sense of satiation that terminates a meal. In contrast, **ghrelin** is a neuropeptide hormone secreted by the empty stomach that stimulates appetite and food intake. These hormones, and others such as **insulin**, circulate in the bloodstream and act directly via receptors in the hypothalamus and other brain regions to signal whether adequate nutrients are being delivered to the gut.

Nutrient signals

The hypothalamus is sensitive to bloodstream concentrations of glucose and fatty acids that have been absorbed from the gut. Dietary **long-chain fatty acids** enter the bloodstream, bind to albumin, and then unbind and diffuse across the blood–brain barrier to be absorbed by hypothalamic cells, inducing downstream signaling and contributing to the termination of a meal. An individual's **gut microbiome** (the unique ecology of bacterial organisms living within the intestines) may affect the absorption of these nutrients and, thereby, influence energy homeostasis. As a result, stool transplantation is currently being investigated as an experimental therapy to promote weight loss by changing the patient's gut microbiome.

Myokines and Adipokines

If weight loss is the goal, exercise is usually paired with restricted intake. **Myokines** are hormones released by myocytes (muscle cells). Exercise stimulates the production of the myokine, **irisin**, which acts on metabolically inactive *white* adipose tissue to uncouple mitochondrial phosphorylation. This process increases thermogenesis and energy expenditure, so that the metabolic profile of white adipose tissue more closely resembles that of *brown* adipose tissue. This *browning* effect has been shown in mice to lead to a higher basal metabolic rate (BMR). Determining whether these are the processes involved in exercise-induced weight loss in humans is an active area of investigation. Irisin is an example of a hormone relevant to energy homeostasis that does not achieve its effect by acting on the hypothalamus.

Whereas the effects of gut hormones cycle several times per day as meals alternate with fasting, hormones from the body's muscle and fat cells convey information about longer-term nutritional status. Adipokine hormones are released by adipocytes (fat cells). The most important adipokine in energy homeostasis is **leptin**. Leptin can directly suppress food intake and raise metabolism via its action in the arcuate nucleus of the hypothalamus. Leptin also enhances satiety signaling by cholecystokinin and other gut hormones. Although a greater volume of adipose tissue in obese individuals creates higher blood levels of leptin, the hypothalamus becomes resistant to the signaling effects of leptin, at least in part by down-regulating leptin receptors. Just as individuals with type 2 diabetes have high levels of insulin yet are insulin-resistant, individuals with obesity have high levels of leptin yet are leptin-resistant. Unlike with diabetes and insulin, supplemental administration of exogenous leptin has not been shown to be beneficial in treating obesity.

Other Hormones and Cytokines

While the mechanisms described above are the core signaling pathways by which the body achieves energy homeostasis, variations in other hormones can affect the regulation of body weight as well. For example, thyroid hormone stimulates metabolic activity and, therefore, excess thyroid hormone (as seen in conditions such as Graves' disease) causes weight loss.

> Chronic stress arising from threats to well-being such as homelessness, food insecurity, and violence can also affect energy homeostasis.

Individuals who are chronically exposed to excess **cortisol** levels, either from chronic stress or steroid medications such as prednisone, are at increased risk for weight gain, insulin resistance leading to type 2 diabetes, and other aspects of the **metabolic syndrome**, including hypertension, high triglyceride levels, and low serum high-density lipoprotein (HDL) levels. Elevations in **inflammatory cytokines** (e.g., TNF-α) due to diseases such as cancer or AIDS can cause **cachexia**, which is the wasting of lean body mass due to an increased metabolic rate. Unlike malnutrition, cachexia is not readily reversible with increased caloric intake.

Energy Expenditure: The Other Half of Homeostasis

Similar to regulation of energy *intake,* energy *expenditure* is also subject to regulation.

Describing Energy Expenditure

> How can the maintenance of energy homeostasis actually work against an individual's goals for weight change?

Basal metabolic rate (BMR) describes the calories consumed within a day by an organism at complete rest, powering only essential biological processes such as breathing and circulation. Daily **total energy expenditure** is the sum of the BMR plus **activity-induced energy expenditure** plus **diet-induced thermogenesis**, since the physiological processes of digestion require energy. A sedentary individual's total energy expenditure may be 1.1 to 1.4 times their BMR, while an active individual's total energy expenditure may be upwards of twice their BMR. Energy expenditure can be estimated by analyzing O_2/CO_2 exchange, using **indirect calorimetry**. Free online calculators are available to help estimate BMR and total energy expenditure based on weight, activity level, and other variables (see Additional Resources).

Adjustment of Energy Expenditure to Maintain Homeostasis

The body's homeostatic control mechanisms manipulate energy expenditure to balance it with energy intake. A person who is fasting might feel lethargic, and thereby decrease their activity-induced energy expenditure. However, a calorie-restricted diet can also lead to a decrease in BMR, which is not subject to an individual's conscious control and is not readily observable without calorimetry.

> The maintenance of energy homeostasis poses a challenge to an overweight or obese individual trying to lose weight. The system tries to preserve body weight, working against the individual's efforts to lose it. This phenomenon has been called **maladaptive homeostasis**, because the body works to maintain an unhealthy level of body fat.

Because of this phenomenon, patients seeking to lose weight are typically advised to cut their caloric intake by about 500 kcal per day from their pre-diet intake. If it were not for homeostatic regulation, this change in energy intake would cause a sustained weight loss of 1 pound (lb) per week. This amount of weight loss might be seen in the early phase of a diet, but usually maladaptive homeostasis becomes operative and prevents further weight loss.

Changes in behavior that patients might notice when physiological adaptation has occurred include hunger, increased thoughts about food, increased appeal of energy-dense food, difficulty sustaining behavior changes, cravings, or even weight regain despite persistent weight loss efforts. These experiences can be highly frustrating. As health care providers, understanding how processes of energy homeostasis are engaged by weight loss can help support patients. One option is to change the treatment plan to work toward fitness goals rather than weight loss goals. Another option is to address issues ranging from weight discrimination to self-image that may prevent patients from feeling comfortable at their current size.

Energy Homeostasis in Obesity

An initial abundance of energy intake relative to energy expenditure contributes to weight gain. In genetically susceptible individuals, obesity can result if this energy is stored as fat rather than as lean body mass (e.g., skeletal muscle; see Chapter 22: Obesity, for a discussion of obesity's epidemiology and health consequences). In this chapter, we will focus on the implications of the homeostatic regulation of body weight on obesity.

The **regulatory set point** for weight (the weight that an individual's homeostatic apparatus tries to defend) will tend to reflect the person's historical maximum stable weight. If a person loses body weight below the regulatory set point, the body decreases its BMR, via signaling mechanisms that are not fully understood but appear to involve decreases in circulating leptin levels. For example, a man who reached 250 lb (113 kg) by dieting and losing 25 lb (11 kg) will have a lower metabolic rate than a man who is the same age, weighs 250 lb, and has never dieted or lost weight before. A lower metabolic rate will make further weight loss more difficult and accelerate weight regain.

Some obese individuals chronically restrict calories in an effort to lose weight, and develop a very low BMR as a result. They could be described as having a slow metabolism, or a very effective homeostatic regulatory mechanism that is preventing further weight loss. In such individuals, further caloric restriction risks depriving them of needed nutrients. Achieving a patient's goal for weight loss may first paradoxically require increasing caloric intake to reset a higher BMR, before caloric intake can again be restricted to achieve weight loss.

Therapies Targeting Energy Homeostasis in Obesity

As discussed above, the body's mechanisms to preserve energy homeostasis can oppose weight loss, which is a primary clinical goal in the care of obese patients to reduce risk of cardiovascular disease and other associated health problems. Current first-line recommendations for assisting weight loss include behavioral modifications such as increasing physical activity and eliminating distractions while eating to better attune to satiety signals. However, in most studies, few people are able to sustain a weight loss of more than 5% to 10% of their maximum bodyweight, perhaps because of the resetting of their homeostatic apparatus. Fortunately, this amount of weight loss is sufficient to achieve measurable health benefits such as lowering blood pressure or blood sugar level, but often falls short of a patient's wishes.

Medications can also be used to treat patients with obesity or overweight with medical complications. The safety profile of such medications is more favorable than those of prior generations of weight loss drugs, and they seem to effectively lower the homeostatic set point for weight. However, these medications can be expensive, and when patients stop taking them, the homeostatic set point for weight tends to return to what it was prior to initiating therapy.

Surgical therapies for obesity, such as **gastric bypass** and **sleeve gastrectomy**, have had dramatic success in helping patients lose a much higher percentage of excess weight, although such surgeries have inherent risks, require significant lifestyle changes, and can lead to nutrient deficiencies due to malabsorption. Although the original rationale for their efficacy included restriction of meal size and induction of macronutrient malabsorption, these surgeries have been shown to have a beneficial effect on metabolism that seems too rapid to be explained by either of these mechanisms. Whereas metabolic rate decreases after weight loss from diet and exercise alone, weight loss due to bariatric surgery does not reduce energy expenditure to the same extent. Also, the production of gut hormones is likely altered by bariatric surgery in a way that promotes reduction in energy intake and frequently cures type 2 diabetes mellitus. Therefore, bariatric surgery reduces energy intake, while preventing the reduction in energy expenditure that usually occurs in weight loss.

> Maintaining a stable body weight is an important component of overall homeostasis. The nervous system and a variety of hormones released by the gastrointestinal tract, fat cells, and muscle can be conceptualized as a coordinated system that regulates the maintenance of a stable body weight, or regulatory set point. The body's defense of this set point makes weight change difficult.

Recommended Readings

Morton, G. J., Cummings, D. E., Baskin, D. G., Barsh, G. S., & Schwartz, M. W. (2006). Central nervous system control of food intake and body weight. *Nature, 443,* 289–295. http://doi.org/10.1038/nature05026

Cummings, D. E., & Overduin, J. (2007). Gastrointestinal regulation of food intake. *Journal of Clinical Investigation, 117*(1), 13–23. http://doi.org/10.1172/JCI30227

Additional Resources

Body Weight Planner. https://www.supertracker.usda.gov/bwp/index.html. Based on Hall, K. D., Sacks, G., Chandramohan, D., Chow, C. C., Wang, Y. C., Gortmaker, S. L., & Swinburn, B. A. (2011). Quantification of the effect of energy imbalance on bodyweight. *Lancet, 378*(9793), 826–837.

Review Questions

1. Which of the following individuals has the highest basal metabolic rate? Assume they are all 45 years old.
   A. A 5'9" man whose body weight is stable at 135 lb
   B. A 5'8" man whose body weight is stable at 145 lb
   C. A 5'6" woman whose body weight is stable at 200 lb
   D. A 5'6" woman who recently lost 40 lb by dieting, but whose weight has now stabilized at 200 lb
   E. A 5'1" woman who recently lost 20 lb by dieting, but whose weight has now stabilized at 95 lb

2. Which of the following hormones reaches peak concentrations before a meal?
   A. Cholecystokinin
   B. Ghrelin
   C. Insulin
   D. Leptin
   E. Thyroid

3. A patient recently switched from a low-fat diet to an Atkins diet. If he eats fewer calories, it may be due to increased
   A. absorption of long-chain fatty acids
   B. cholecystokinin signaling
   C. ghrelin signaling
   D. absorption of long-chain fatty acids and cholecystokinin signaling
   E. all of the above

Answer Key on p. 465

6 Chronobiology and Sleep Disorders

João V. Nunes, MD, Girardin Jean-Louis, PhD, Ferdinand Zizi, MBA, and Azizi Seixas, PhD

- What is circadian rhythm?
- How does circadian rhythm affect organ system functioning?
- What is the difference between REM and non-REM sleep?
- How do the sleep patterns of infants, middle-age adults, and older persons differ?
- Why is it easier to accommodate to a flight from London to New York than from New York to London?
- What are the potential outcomes of severe obstructive sleep apnea?
- What are the differences between nightmares and night terrors?

Biological Rhythms

Homeostatic control and coordination of basic life support functions are achieved through hypothalamic regulation of rhythms of hormonal secretion and autonomic nervous system activity. These biological rhythms provide the individual with a unique adaptive capability – to vary the timing and duration of biological and behavioral activity in each system – in response to environmental change. **Chronobiology** is the discipline that studies the effect of these biological rhythms on essential processes such as physical activity, eating, and sleeping, and how these biological rhythms are adaptive to solar and lunar cycles.

Circadian Rhythm

What is circadian rhythm?

The most important biological rhythm is the **circadian rhythm**. It affects fluctuations in the release of critical hormones that affect core body functions, such as temperature regulation, metabolic activity, and serum cortisol level, in 24-hr cycles. Temporal fluctuations observed in physi-ological and behavioral processes are sensitive to environmental factors and are classified according to the time of day they routinely occur (such as diurnal, nocturnal, and crepuscular [twilight] cycles).

Other rhythms important to human functioning are **ultradian rhythms** (< 24 hr) such as the 180-min growth hormone production cycle and the 90-min REM sleep cycle, **infradian rhythms** (> 24 hr) such as menstrual and reproduction cycles, and **gene oscillation**, which describes a pattern of differential gene expression at different times during the day.

The timing of biological rhythms is governed by endogenous biological mechanisms in concert with exogenous cues, or *zeitgebers* (German for *time givers* or *synchronizers*). The strongest zeitgeber for animals is daylight. The earth's approximate 24-hr light/dark cycle synchronizes the endogenous time-keeping system, or clock, in a process called *entrainment*. Zeitgebers promote changes in the molecular components of the biological clock to match the specific phase of the 24-hr period. Humans, like other organisms, have been entrained to synchronize activity and rest to specific times of the earth's light/dark cycles. For example, changes in ambient light may induce or inhibit sleep.

Control of the Sleep/Wake Cycle

The endogenous biological clock that controls the sleep/wake cycle is composed of cells located in the suprachiasmatic nucleus (SCN) of the hypothalamus. The SCN induces pineal gland secretion of melatonin when environmental light decreases (sunset) and inhibits secretion when environmental light increases (sunrise).

The earth's light/dark cycle also cues other environmental rhythms responsive to nonphotic zeitgebers, such as ambient temperature, eating/drinking patterns, pharmacological responsivity, and exercise. For example, eating late at night has the ability to shift the phase of circadian rhythms and interfere with sleep. Eating, for its periodicity, is a nonphotic zeitgeber and may blunt melantonin secretion.

The complex *neuroendocrine network*, which connects the hypothalamic-pituitary-adrenocortical (HPA) axis to all homeostatic systems, enables the organism to selectively activate or deactivate functions, depending on conditions affecting the organism. However, because of this interlinking, hormonal fluctuations can affect multiple systems. For example, *orexin* or *hypocretin*, a hypothalamic neuropeptide, plays a role in maintaining sleep/wakefulness states. Orexin neurons, which are regulated by monoamines and acetylcholine, respond to metabolic cues such as leptin, glucose, and ghrelin (regulators of feeding and energy metabolism), and are linked to the dopaminergic reward system. Thus, fluctuations in any of these hormones can influence sleep, eating behavior, reward processes, emotional regulation, and vigilance to potential stressors. As a result, dysfunction in one system can ripple throughout the entire homeostatic system. For example, disorders in eating can trigger disorders in sleep, sexual behavior, immune system functioning, and, subsequently, every organ system.

Circadian Rhythm and Organ System Functioning

How does circadian rhythm affect organ system functioning?

Circadian rhythm in animals affects several biological systems, including the cardiac, respiratory, gastrointestinal, musculoskeletal, and immune systems.

Cardiac contractility (CC), which refers to the ability of heart muscle to shorten and contract when activated by a stimulus, is influenced by circadian rhythm. The circadian timing of CC follows a gradient over a 24-hr period, with activity peaks during daytime and activity troughs during nighttime. Specifically, there is a trough in the early morning before typical wake-up time, a rising phase just prior to wake-up time, a peak in the early afternoon or evening, a fall before bedtime, and a steep decline at sleep onset continuing into the sleep period. The incidence of cerebral vascular accident, myocardial infarction, and sudden death increases between 6 a.m. and noon. The association of typical chronophysiological patterns of cardiac contractility with adverse cardiac events suggests that imbalance between cardiac demand and myocardial oxygen supply is most likely to occur in the morning, along with other physiological changes (e.g., increased arterial blood pressure, increased platelet agreeability, and decreased fibrinolytic activity) that may contribute to adverse vascular events.

Respiratory changes occur during sleep. Changes in the carbon dioxide (CO_2) chemoreceptor increase the CO_2 threshold (the concentration of CO_2 that triggers breathing), which decreases the ventilatory drive. This decreases respiratory accessory muscle tone and the volume of air breathed per minute during sleep and increases bronchoconstriction.

Chemical and mechanical challenges to breathing during sleep contribute to low nocturnal oxygen levels (hypoxemia) and high carbon dioxide levels (hypercapnia).

Gastrointestinal motor activity, such as the gastric emptying rate, slows during the evening and overnight. Many drugs taken by mouth in the evening are absorbed more slowly, possibly delaying their onset of action. Fasting gastric acid secretion is markedly elevated between 9 p.m. and midnight, consistent with the observation that gastrointestinal symptoms often worsen around midnight. Evening administration of antacids provides protection during the period of greatest vulnerability of the gastrointestinal system.

Musculoskeletal system activity also changes with the time of day. Morning joint swelling and stiffness, diagnostic hallmarks of rheumatoid arthritis, appear to be associated with the rhythmic nocturnal fall in circulating endogenous corticosteroids.

In the *immune system*, allergen skin testing shows a greater response if done in late evening compared with in the morning. Results from tests done in the morning should be viewed cautiously to avoid false-negatives. In contrast to skin reactivity, hay fever symptoms are more pronounced upon awakening. Total T lymphocyte and CD4 T lymphocyte concentrations peak around 4 a.m., about the same time that kidney transplant rejection is most likely to occur. The efficacy and rate of adverse effects of platinum and other agents used to treat ovarian cancer are influenced by time of day. Similarly, maintenance chemotherapy for acute lymphoblastic leukemia administered in the evening appears to be more effective.

> Immunosuppressant treatment to avoid tissue rejection is most beneficial when administered at night.

Sleep

> What is the difference between REM and non-REM sleep?

Sleep is divided into **rapid eye movement (REM) sleep** and three levels of **non-REM sleep** (Stage 1, or light sleep, to Stage 3, or deep sleep). During REM sleep, the brain is highly active and is driven by spontaneous neural discharges originating primarily in the *pontine reticular formation*. However, the neural pathways associated with sensory input and motor output are inhibited. Thus, vivid dreaming and decreased perception of, and reaction to, the environment are characteristic of REM sleep.

In contrast, during non-REM sleep, the brain is less activated, and there is less cognitive activity. Stage 3, the deep sleep stage, is called **slow-wave sleep** (SWS). Throughout the night, non-REM sleep and REM sleep alternate in approximately 90-min cycles. SWS typically occurs during the earlier portion of the night, and REM sleep predominates in the last third of the night.

During REM sleep, the brain activates cortical areas normally involved in visual perception and motor activity, leading the individual to perceive seeing objects and making movements, but actually doing neither.

Sleep Patterns and Architecture

> How do the sleep patterns of infants, middle-age adults, and older persons differ?

Sleep patterns vary across age groups. Average daily total sleep time decreases from up to 18 hr during infancy, to about 10 hr in early childhood, to about 8 hr in adulthood. Among older persons, nighttime sleep diminishes, but daytime napping increases; as a result, total sleep time is similar to that of middle-age adults.

Sleep architecture, the pattern and structure of phases of sleep (REM and non-REM), changes with age. Newborn infants spend about 50% of their sleep time in REM sleep and 50% in non-REM sleep with predominantly slow-wave activity. Infant sleep is polyphasic and occurs in 3- to 4-hr cycles. During the second year of life, children develop a diurnal pattern of sleep that includes a long episode of nocturnal sleep and a brief nap during the afternoon. As children mature, the percentages of REM sleep and SWS decrease. For example, the time spent in REM sleep decreases to about 20% to 25% by late adolescence and remains stable until older age. The percentage of SWS, however, diminishes gradually throughout life. Complaints of difficulty maintaining sleep are more common among older people. These sleep difficulties may be due to an underlying health condition, medication, or types of sleep disorder that are more prevalent among older persons (e.g., breathing disturbances, periodic limb movements).

Sleep Phase Disorders

Assessment

The assessment of sleep disorders requires a thorough clinical history including the sleep-related history, a mental status exam, a review of systems, and a physical examination and indicated laboratory studies. Thorough assessment is warranted since sleep disorders may be primary or secondary to other medical disorders, including psychiatric conditions. Additionally, subjective and objective behavioral aspects of sleep must be carefully assessed and accurately recorded. Patients should be referred to a sleep disorders center for polysomnography if the diagnosis is not clear or they need special help (e.g., specific diagnosis, sleep staging, determination of severity of the disorder, precise determination of daytime sleepiness, or fitting a mask for continuous positive airway pressure [CPAP] therapy).

Sleep Hygiene

A set of simple measures, collectively called **sleep hygiene**, can help persons who have sleep difficulties regain consistent sleep.

Sleep Hygiene Measures

1. Use the bed for sleep and sex only (e.g., not for eating, reading, or using electronic devices)
2. Go to bed only when sleepy
3. If not asleep after 20 min, do some boring activity in another room; return to bed when sleepy
4. Sleep only the amount of time to feel refreshed, and sleep the same length of time every night (no sleeping in)
5. Maintain sleep conditions close to ideal and avoid excessive ambient warmth or coldness
6. Go to bed and wake up around the same time each day
7. Exercise regularly but not close to bedtime
8. Avoid napping
9. Avoid substances such as alcohol, tobacco, and caffeine near bedtime
10. Limit use of sedatives
11. If eating near bedtime, eat lightly
12. Practice relaxation
13. A body-temperature-raising 20-min hot bath near bedtime may be helpful

---

Sleep/Wake Schedule Disorders

Sleep disorders can arise either from a defect in the **circadian oscillator** (the *suprachiasmatic nucleus*, which serves as the endogenous timing system) or from the limited capacity of the internal timing system to adjust to changes in external clock time. The shifting capacity of the human circadian rhythm is 2 hr per day or less. Therefore, sleep difficulties can occur whenever the sleep/wake schedule is shifted outside an individual's range of entrainment.

Disorders of the sleep/wake schedule, also known as **circadian rhythm disorders**, result from disturbances in the timing of actual sleep/wake behavior relative to the person's circadian sleep/wake rhythm. Such disturbances can be transient (e.g., jet lag or work shift changes) or more persistent (e.g., delayed sleep phase syndrome, advanced sleep phase syndrome, permanent rotating shift work). Affected individuals cannot stay awake or stay asleep when it is necessary or desired to do so.

Why is it easier to accommodate to a flight from London to New York than from New York to London?

Jet lag results from rapid changes in time zone due to transmeridian travel. Symptoms include insomnia, fatigue, and gastrointestinal complaints. Westbound travel is generally less disruptive than eastbound travel because delaying the sleep/wake cycle (to adjust to the prevailing clock time after westbound travel) is easier to accomplish than advancing the sleep/wake cycle. Sleep disruptions can persist for up to 8 days after travel, but jet lag usually requires no treatment. Jet lag during brief trips is minimized by adhering to the clock time of the original time zone.

Shift work, or any acute change in work schedule, can desynchronize sleep within the circadian cycle. The problem is transient if the worker remains on the new work schedule; however, it can become a persistent disorder if the worker is required to rotate shifts continually. Insomnia, mood changes, and gastrointestinal symptoms are common side effects. The shift worker who is required to work at night and sleep during the day must also contend with lower levels of arousal at night, which can cause performance deficits, as well as with higher levels of arousal during the day, which can impair the ability to sleep. Unacceptable error rates associated with erratic and prolonged shift work have led to efforts to attune work patterns to normal.

Advanced sleep phase syndrome (ASPS) is characterized by the inability to stay awake in the evening and stay asleep in the early morning. Persons with ASPS typically have the irresistible urge to fall asleep at 8–9 p.m. and wake up at 4–5 a.m. Because their circadian rhythm cycle occurs earlier than that of the average person, affected individuals have normal sleep, if it occurs early evening to the early morning. Most people with the syndrome do not come to the attention of health care providers, unless they feel isolated and are unable to participate in family, social, or occupational activities. At that point, they may report *sleep-maintenance insomnia*. They become sleep deprived from postponing their bedtime, since they remain unable to sleep later in the morning. Under such circumstances of interference with functioning, the name of the condition changes to **advanced sleep phase disorder** (ASPD), which occurs in about 1% of the population and affects mostly older persons of either sex. Although the exact etiology remains elusive, ASPD has a strong genetic link: Persons with the syndrome have a 50% chance of passing it to their offspring. Early evening exposure to bright light that can emulate sunshine, and chronotherapy (see the section "Treatment of Sleep Phase Disorders," below) may reset the circadian clock, leading to later bedtimes. Such treatments require informed consent and should be undergone under the supervision of an experienced provider.

Delayed sleep phase syndrome (DSPS) is a habitual sleep pattern that typically develops during childhood, adolescence, or early adulthood, in which the individual's timing of sleep, peak alertness, hormonal and core temperature fluctuations, and other circadian rhythms are delayed relative to societal norms. Affected individuals have essentially normal sleep if conditions permit them to go to sleep late and wake up late, typically from 1–4 a.m. to 8–11 a.m. However, they often suffer from *sleep-onset insomnia* if they attempt to fall asleep earlier to obtain an adequate amount of sleep before arising at the time required for school or work. Symptoms include grogginess

and irritability in the morning. Allowing themselves to sleep in on weekends or vacations does not completely relieve symptoms and reinforces DSPS. When DSPS interferes with life functioning, it is referred to as delayed sleep phase disorder (DSPD), which is the most prevalent of all circadian rhythm sleep disorders. DSPD and ASPD are opposites. DSPD may affect 15% of teens and adults, and it accounts for as many as 10% of all chronic insomnia cases. Although the exact etiology remains to be elucidated, DSPD is genetically linked: Persons with a family history of DSPD are 3 times more likely to have or develop it than those without a family history. Environmental conditions, such as underexposure to morning sunlight and overexposure to late afternoon and evening sunlight, can lead to the development of DSPD.

Although difficult to treat, DSPD may respond to chronotherapy (see the section "Treatment of Sleep Phase Disorders," below), exposure to early morning sunlight, avoidance of late afternoon and evening sunlight, and exposure to bright artificial light in the early morning upon awakening.

Treatment of Sleep Phase Disorders

Transient sleep disorders (e.g., jet lag) usually require no treatment if the dyssynchrony is isolated. However, short-acting hypnotics and melatonin can be used to promote sleep and improve alertness during wakefulness, following abrupt changes in the sleep/wake schedule.

ASPS and DSPS have been treated successfully using **chronotherapy**, a technique intended to reset the internal clock by manipulating bedtime. The process is not without unintended consequences. Informed consent and management by experienced professionals are essential. A useful step before starting chronotherapy is for the person to be rested, so they are allowed to keep their habitual sleep pattern for at least 1 week. The individual is instructed to delay bedtime by a stipulated amount of time daily until the desired bedtime is attained. The new schedule is then maintained rigidly. The maneuver is designed to shift the sleep phase while preserving sleep duration. Since the natural tendency is for the schedule to revert back to the habitual schedule, especially in DSPD, the process should be repeated at stipulated intervals.

Narcolepsy

Narcolepsy has been conceptualized as an abnormal intrusion of components of REM sleep into wakefulness. It is a chronic neurological disorder characterized by four major symptoms:

1. *Excessive daytime sleepiness* may be relatively continuous or episodic. Severity varies from a mild desire to sleep to an irresistible "sleep attack." Daytime sleep bouts vary from seconds of nodding to short naps of 20 min. Patients with narcolepsy usually awaken feeling refreshed.
2. *Cataplexy* is a sudden loss of muscle tone triggered by strong emotions. The patient is awake during the weakness, which typically lasts seconds to minutes. The muscle weakness may be localized or affect all postural muscles. The loss of muscle tone during cataplexy is the result of the same neural mechanisms that produce the active inhibition of the musculature typical of REM sleep.
3. *Sleep paralysis* is the inability to move at sleep onset or upon awakening. It is a manifestation of REM sleep muscle inhibition.
4. *Hypnagogic hallucination*, or dreaming while still awake, is the result of a normal component of REM sleep occurring during wakefulness.

The diagnosis of narcolepsy is confirmed using the *multiple sleep latency test* (MSLT), which consists of four or five naps spaced 2 hr apart. The patient is placed in a quiet, dark bedroom and monitored by polysomnography. The time from lights out to sleep onset (sleep latency) is measured for each nap, and the appearance of REM sleep within 15 min, called a sleep-onset REM period, is noted. Findings consistent with narcolepsy include an average sleep latency of 6 min or less, which documents pathological sleepiness, and the appearance of at least two sleep-onset REM periods. Treatment consists of stimulant medications, good nocturnal sleep, and prophylactic naps. Cataplexy, sleep paralysis, and hypnagogic hallucinations are responsive to tricyclic and some selective serotonin reuptake inhibitor antidepressants.

Mechanical and Structural Sleep Disorders

Sleep-disordered breathing results when respiratory control is adversely affected by chemical information (chemoreceptor changes in PaO_2, $PaCO_2$, and pH), behavioral information derived from cortical activity, and mechanical feedback via stretch receptors in the chest wall, upper airway, and lung. Arousal from sleep is produced by low oxygen levels (hypoxemic response), high levels of carbon dioxide (hypercapnia response), or occlusion or obstruction to airflow. The arousal threshold to these stimuli is state related; awakening is more difficult from REM sleep than from non-REM sleep.

> Benzodiazepines, barbiturates, sedating antidepressants, antihistamines, antipsychotics, narcotics, and alcohol can all suppress ventilation. A careful drug history is essential when screening for sleep-disordered breathing.

Obstructive Sleep Apnea

> What are the potential outcomes of severe obstructive sleep apnea?

According to the American Academy of Sleep Medicine, **obstructive sleep apnea syndrome** (OSA) affects 26% of adults in the US between the ages of 30 and 70 years. Historically, OSA affected primarily middle-aged men and postmenopausal women. The recent rise in obesity might be contributing to the higher levels of OSA, even outside these demographics. The condition consists of temporary but recurrent obstruction of the upper airway during sleep that produces apneic episodes (cessation of airflow for ≥ 10 s). The most common sites of occlusion are the soft palate and the base of the tongue.

During an episode of obstructive apnea, chest and abdominal movements are ineffective in moving air. A brief period of electrocortical arousal follows the episode and is accompanied by deep gasping resuscitative breathing and loud snoring. In severe cases, up to 500 episodes of apnea can occur each night producing abnormal hemodynamics, blood gas changes, cognitive deficits, disrupted sleep, and daytime sleepiness. Some cases are fatal.

> In addition to age and gender, risk factors for sleep apnea include obesity, diastolic hypertension, large neck circumference, and structural abnormalities of the upper airway.

Treatment options include mechanical devices, behavioral interventions, and surgery. The most common treatment for moderate and severe cases is *continuous positive airway pressure* (CPAP) via the nose and mouth. In milder cases, an oral appliance that advances the mandible and frees up space in the oropharynx is worn during sleep. Behavioral therapy strategies include promoting weight loss and avoiding the supine sleeping position, alcohol, and sedating medications. Surgical options include uvulopalatopharyngoplasty, removal of enlarged tonsils or adenoids (tonsillectomy-adenoidectomy), and a variety of mandible advancement procedures. Tracheostomy may be necessary in extreme cases associated with life-threatening cardiopulmonary complications.

Central sleep apnea syndrome is an uncommon sleep disorder manifested by insomnia, gasping for air, arousals from sleep, and either mild or absent snoring. In this form of apnea, the absence of ventilatory effort results in the cessation of airflow. Cardiac, neurological, and cerebrovascular disease play a role in the pathophysiology of this disorder.

Cheyne-Stokes respiration with central sleep apnea is a form of periodic breathing characterized by recurrent cessation of breathing alternating with increased airflow (hyperpnea) in a crescendo–decrescendo pattern. The condition is seen most commonly in patients with congestive heart failure and central nervous system (CNS) disease. The reduced circulatory time from alveolar unit to chemoreceptor and the length of the crescendo–decrescendo cycle have been implicated in the etiology of this breathing pattern. Treatment can be difficult. Nasal CPAP, oxygen, respiratory stimulants such as acetazolamide or theophylline, and mechanical ventilation all have specific risks and benefits.

Insomnia

Insomnia is a sleep disorder that happens in the presence of unrestricted opportunity to sleep, manifested by difficult falling or staying asleep, or early morning awakening, which leads to problems with daytime functioning. It has a significant negative effect on quality of life, mood, cognitive functioning, performance capacity, and alertness. According to the American Academy of Sleep Medicine, insomnia is the most common sleep disorder. Although more common in adults, women being more likely to report it, insomnia may affect people of all ages. It has been estimated that one-third to one-half of the US population will experience insomnia at least once. Ten percent report chronic insomnia. In addition to psychiatric disorders that interfere with adequate sleep, the etiology of insomnia includes conditions such as sleep-related breathing dysfunction, periodic limb movements, conditioning, circadian rhythm dysregulation, worry about sleeplessness, late night exercise, caffeine ingestion, daytime napping, and medical conditions. General treatment includes following sleep hygiene guidelines, such as setting a regular wake-up time; eliminating napping, alcohol, and caffeine; and relaxing before bedtime with a ritual to reduce physiological hyperarousal. In addition, patients should be instructed to get out of bed if they do not fall asleep in 20 min. Cognitive approaches target arousing, worrisome, and self-defeating thoughts that can sustain insomnia. Used for a short period, a variety of rapid-acting hypnotic drugs are safe when taken alone and can help induce and maintain sleep.

Nightmares and Night Terrors

> What are the differences between nightmares and night terrors?

A **nightmare** is a terrifying dream that awakens the dreamer from REM sleep. Nightmares tend to occur during the early morning when REM periods are naturally more intense. They are common in children and decrease with age. Nightmares may be induced by stressful conditions or events. Nightmares can be caused by certain medications such as L-dopa and beta blockers. Alcohol and other drugs have a REM-suppressing effect. When these drugs are discontinued, an increase in the amount and intensity of REM sleep (rebound) can cause emotional and frightening dreams.

Night terrors, unlike nightmares, occur during SWS, in the first half of the night. They are characterized by a confused arousal in which the person appears to be terrified, often crying out. Attempts to rouse or calm the person are futile. Unlike the person who has nightmares, the person who has night terrors cannot recall details about what was going through their mind. In fact, in the morning, the person usually does not remember the event at all. Night terrors are common in children younger than 10 years, and uncommon in adults.

Recommended Readings

Espana, R. A., & Scammell, T. E. (2011). *Sleep neurobiology from a clinical perspective, SLEEP, 34*(7), 845–858.

Olaithe, M., & Bucks, R. S. (2013). Executive dysfunction in OSA before and after treatment: A meta-analysis. *SLEEP, 36*(9), 1297–1305. http://doi.org/10.5665/sleep.2950

Palmer, J. D. (2002). *The living clock.* Oxford, UK: Oxford University Press.

Sadock, B. J., Sadock, V. A., & Ruiz, P. (2015). *Kaplan and Sadock's synopsis of psychiatry: Behavioral sciences/clinical psychiatry* (11th ed.). Philadelphia, PA: Wolters Kluwer.

Additional Resources

Division of Sleep Medicine at Harvard Medical School and WGBH Educational Foundation. Available at http://HealthySleep.med.harvard.edu

Iliff, J. (2014). *One more reason to get a good night's sleep* [TED talk]. Available at https://www.ted.com/talks/jeff_iliff_one_more_reason_to_get_a_good_night_s_sleep

Online Videos

Sleep Research Society. (Producer). (2015). *Normal human sleep: Sleep in the older adult* [Video]. Available at http://www.sleepresearchsociety.org/store/product.aspx?pid=1312

Sleep Research Society. (Producer). (2015). *Normal human sleep: Infancy to adolescence* [Video]. Available at http://www.sleepresearchsociety.org/store/product.aspx?pid=1305

Sleep Research Society. (Producer). (2015). *Neurobiology of sleep* [Video]. Available at http://www.sleepresearchsociety.org/store/product.aspx?pid=1373

Review Questions

Directions: The items below consist of lettered headings followed by numbered descriptions. For each numbered description, choose the one lettered heading with which it is most closely associated. Each lettered heading may be used *once*, *more than once*, or *not at all*.

Match the sleep stage with the numbered descriptions.

- A. REM sleep
- B. Stage 1 non-REM
- C. Stage 2 non-REM
- D. Stage 3 non-REM

1. Peter dreams a lot. He keeps a pad and pencil by his bed because he often wakes up in the morning from a dream and wants to record it. He aspires to become a best-selling author and believes that his dreams give him good ideas for plots and imagery. Which is Peter's favorite sleep stage?
2. During this sleep stage, Isabel is oblivious to all but the greatest disruptions. If awakened from this stage, she will not be able to report vivid dream imagery.
3. During this sleep stage, a patient is most quickly and easily aroused.
4. During this sleep stage, information transmitted from the sensory organs to the cortex is attenuated and the motor neurons of most skeletal muscles are inhibited.

Answer Key on p. 465

7 Stress, Adaptation, and Stress Disorders

John E. Carr, PhD, Ian M. Kodish, MD, PhD, and Peter P. Vitaliano, PhD

- What are the bio-behavioral mechanisms of the stress response?
- How does the acute stress response differ from the chronic stress response?
- What role do glucocorticoids play in regulating the stress response?
- Most illnesses seen in primary care are by-products of what evolutionary objective?
- By what bio-behavioral mechanisms does stress contribute to cardiovascular disorders?
- By what bio-behavioral mechanisms does stress contribute to immune system disorders?

Stress, Adaptation, and Evolution

The human organism is the unique product of eons of evolutionary change enabling *Homo sapiens* to survive by adapting to hostile, ever-changing conditions. Essential to this capacity for adaptation was the development of a series of homeostatic life support systems (e.g., respiration, circulation, digestion, metabolism, and elimination) which made it possible for the organism to survive independently. An *executive system* was required to communicate with, coordinate, and control these homeostatic systems. To fulfill this function, the brain and neuroendocrine systems evolved to regulate coordination among the homeostatic systems, and enable the organism to interact adaptively with the environment, learn from experience, and innovate.

Derived from physics, the concept of *stress* originally referred to forces causing structural or *systemic strain.* Applied to medicine, **stress** refers to any challenge to the integrity or survival of the organism, be it *biological, behavioral, cognitive, sociocultural,* or *environmental changes* that can disrupt homeostatic balance. Any such challenge will trigger "strains" within the body's systems and activate a **stress response**, designed to utilize adaptive mechanisms to restore **homeostasis** within each of these systems. This process of restoring stable functioning is referred to as **allostasis**. Disease and dysfunction typically occur in

response to the failure of allostasis, but can also occur as the result of **allostasis overload** (i.e., sustained responses that wear down the body's ability to appropriately adapt, as can occur in chronic disorders). Thus, many of the illnesses that physicians treat can best be understood as by-products of the body's stress response, the mechanisms involved in its function, and the consequences of their actions.

The Stress Response

What are the bio-behavioral mechanisms of the stress response?

The **stress response** involves a complex *gene–environment interaction* in which the individual is sensitive to certain precipitating stressor conditions that, over time, effect changes in gene expression through a variety of epigenetic alterations. Thus, a gene–environment–stress interaction results in a medley of physiological, cognitive, emotional, and behavioral reactions that vary with the intensity and duration of the stressor. In his **general adaptation syndrome (GAS)** model, Selye defined the initial stage of the stress response as the *alarm stage* in which the body's adaptive defenses are mobilized. This is followed by a *resistance stage*, during which the organism attempts to adapt using available resources. During this stage, the individual is susceptible to *diseases of adaptation* that are by-products of the stress response. The final *exhaustion stage* occurs when demand overwhelms resources, defenses fail, and the individual is increasingly vulnerable.

Chronic Versus Acute Stress

> How does the acute stress response differ from the chronic stress response?

Whereas the **acute stress response** evolved to protect and "heal" the body, under conditions of sustained or chronic stress (allostasis overload), the body's adaptive mechanisms can be overwhelmed, resulting in disease and dysfunction. Adaptation to chronic as well as acute stress requires two types of stress response. First, there is an *immediate nervous system response* that focuses on *emergency functions* in keeping with the organism's survival imperative. Energy is mobilized from storage sites while further storage is temporarily halted; muscles are fueled with glucose, simple fats, proteins, and oxygen for **fight or flight**. Sympathetic

nervous system (SNS) activation increases heart rate, blood pressure, and respiration providing rapid delivery of oxygen and fuel to muscle cells. Simultaneously, noncritical functions such as digestion, growth, and reproduction are put on hold. The SNS also stimulates the immune system, which activates T cells, B cells, and proinflammatory cytokines to fight infection.

Stress, Performance, and Learning

Selye distinguished between *eustress*, or healthy stress, and *distress,* or unhealthy stress. **Eustress**, typically evoked in response to moderate challenges, represents the optimal degree of arousal required to perform well or learn effectively. **Distress,** typically evoked in response to high stress, occurs when arousal impedes performance. The **Yerkes-Dodson law** (see Figure 7.1) states that performance and adaptive learning are optimal under moderate rather than either high or low stress (arousal) conditions. High stress may interfere with performance, as evidenced by overly anxious students who cannot concentrate on an exam. Low stress (arousal) may lead to low motivation and impaired performance. Two corollaries to the Yerkes-Dodson law apply to specific

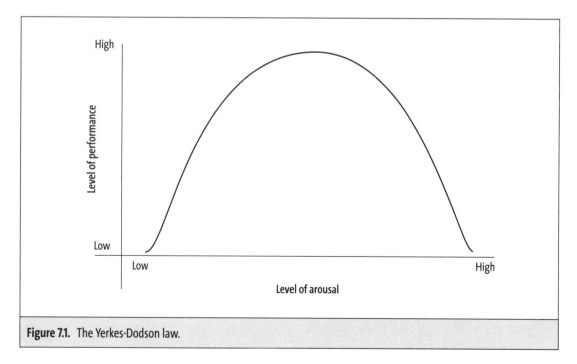

Figure 7.1. The Yerkes-Dodson law.

learning situations: (1) *Learning new or difficult tasks* is optimal under low or moderate stress conditions (recall how difficult it is to learn new material when anxious); and (2) *performance of well-learned tasks* is optimized by high stress conditions (e.g., the sprinter runs fastest when "pumped").

While *little or no stress* may be insufficient to stimulate a response, *moderate stress* conditions activate the limbic system, facilitating the coordinated ability of the amygdala, hippocampus, and prefrontal cortex to analyze, respond to, and learn from the challenge. *Chronic stress,* however, can result in persistently increased activation of the amygdala, excessive release of glucocorticoids and other stress hormones, and decreased modu-

lation of the hippocampus, resulting in impaired learning and performance (see Chapter 9: Emotion and Learning).

Bio-Behavioral Mechanisms of the Stress Response

Emotional, cognitive, and physiological reactions mutually influence each other. For example, in response to a stressor condition, sensory information is collected by the thalamus and forwarded simultaneously to the amygdala, hippocampus, and cortical association areas (see Figure 7.2).

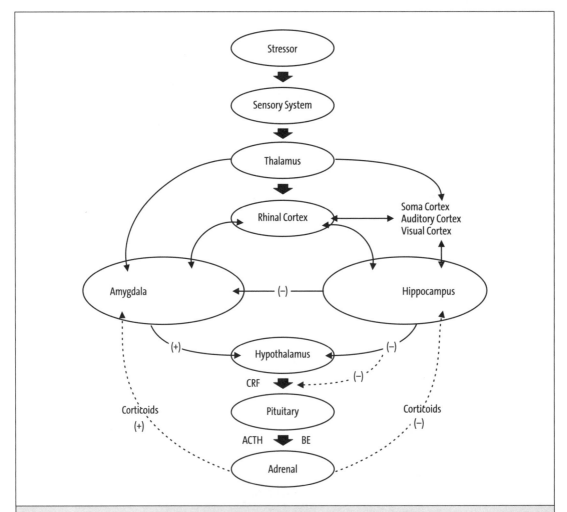

Figure 7.2. Schematic showing initial nervous system response to incoming stress information. ACTH = adrenocorticotropic hormone; BE = beta endorphine; CRF = corticotropin releasing factor.

Analogous to a "first responder," the **amygdala** coordinates an emergent reaction (fight or flight), arousing and mobilizing the organism via the **sympatho-adreno-medullary** (SAM) **system**, which triggers the release of catecholamines and glucocorticoids through activation of the **hypothalamic-pituitary-adrenocortical** (HPA) **axis**. The amygdala's response is modulated by the **hippocampus** and **prefrontal cortex**, analogous to a "command and coordinating center" that references learned experiences relevant to the incoming information to determine its importance, meaning, and an appropriate response. If the incoming information is judged to be important, the emergent response continues. If it is judged to be of limited or no importance, the response may be altered or terminated.

With activation of the HPA axis, sympathetic neural pathways originating in the hypothalamus trigger release of *epinephrine* from these synapses and the adrenal medulla. Concurrently, *norepinephrine* is released at all other sympathetic synapses in the body to act on the postsynaptic receptors of end organs. These two catecholamines promote generalized sympathetic arousal. Once the acute stress ceases, parasympathetic pathways originating in the hypothalamus activate glucocorticoid, cholinergic, and other inhibitory system receptor neurons that feedback this information to the hypothalamus, which then "turns off" the arousal. Thus, the body's initial reaction to stress is an immediate but relatively brief **autonomic nervous system**–initiated response.

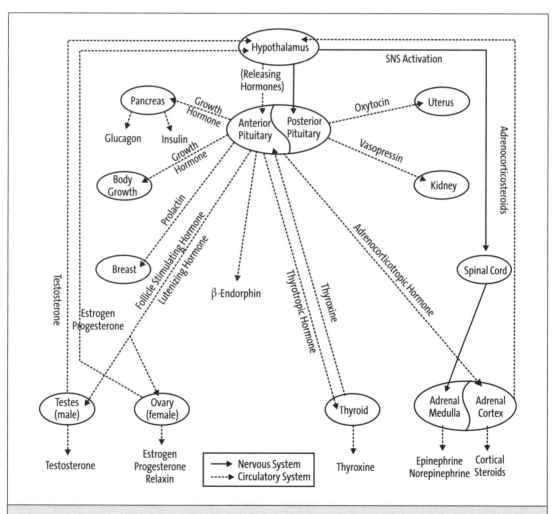

Figure 7.3. Schematic showing neuro-endocrine system response to incoming stress information. SNS = sympathetic nervous system.

What role do glucocorticoids play in regulating the stress response?

Glucocorticoids are steroid hormones that regulate and influence biological functions including growth, development, and homeostatic adaptation. In response to stress, the hypothalamus secretes *corticotropin-releasing hormone* (CRH), which is transported to the pituitary via hypothalamic-pituitary-portal circulation (Figure 7.3). The anterior pituitary secretes several hormones into the bloodstream when stimulated, including *adrenocorticotropic hormone* (ACTH), which then stimulates *glucocorticoid* secretion from the adrenal cortex. Eventually glucocorticoid receptors in various brain structures (e.g., hippocampus) signal the coordinated down-regulation of the bio-behavioral stress response. In some individuals, despite the persistence of stress, HPA axis activity may be modulated, and glucocorticoid secretion returns to normal. However, often, as severe stress becomes chronic, *glucocorticoid overstimulation* contributes to detrimental changes in receptor profiles and cellular metabolism, inhibiting protein synthesis and contributing to neuronal atrophy. This further compromises the ability of limbic networks to modulate the amygdala and the HPA-activated stress response.

When Homeostatic Systems Fail

Most illnesses seen in primary care are by-products of what evolutionary objective?

Homeostatic systems evolved to optimally serve two primary objectives: the survival of the organism and the survival of the species. The diverse homeostatic systems that carry out these objectives are coordinated via interlinked pathways and a common neuroendocrine system. The failure of any of these adaptive homeostatic functions increases the risk of disorder or disease, not only in the failed systems but in all systems, due to the highly integrated network that connects them. Since the survival of the organism depends on the organism's coordinated efforts to maintain homeostasis, it follows that the majority of illnesses seen by primary care physicians are by-products of the body's failed or incomplete efforts to adapt to these environmental challenges and restore homeostasis.

Stress and Metabolic Processes

Acute stress triggers an emergency physiological response that includes shunting of stored nutrients to muscle and organ sites while reducing digestion and other nonemergency functions. Chronic stress causes this process to turn on and off repeatedly. As a result, nutrient stores are depleted faster than they are replaced, and the body begins to catabolize muscle tissue to make up for the loss. The stressors driving this process can be serendipitous or purposeful (e.g., exercise or weight management programs) and, if not well managed, can contribute to eating disorders (see Chapter 23: Eating Disorders).

In some individuals, excess glucocorticoids resulting from chronic stress can impair the cells' ability to respond to insulin, resulting in increased glucose and fat in the blood stream and impeding oxygen flow and organ efficiency. In fact, hyperinsulinemia in response to chronic stress and poor health habits (e.g., poor diet, sedentary lifestyle) increases the risk for type 2 diabetes and coronary artery disease, and is a major process in the development of the metabolic syndrome, a collection of cardiometabolic risk factors that includes obesity, insulin resistance, hypertension, and dyslipidemia. With insulin resistance, the body does not respond to insulin, so blood sugar (glucose) cannot be appropriately utilized by cells. As a result, the insulin and blood sugar levels rise excessively, which impairs kidney function and raises the level of blood lipids. Studies of older adults have shown that chronic stress is more highly associated with elevated insulin levels than with any other physiological measure (see Chapter 22: Obesity, and Chapter 21: Geriatric Health and Successful Aging).

Stress and Growth Processes

Like other aspects of human functioning, growth is determined by the interaction of genetic predisposition and environmental events. Moderate stress has a facilitative effect on growth processes optimizing pituitary secretion of *growth hormone*, bone growth, cell division, and distribution of nutrients for tissue growth. However, chronic stress also impairs normal growth and development via (1) SNS arousal (where growth functions are put on hold, and digestion and metabolism are disrupted), (2) inhibited growth hormone release (due in part to excess levels of glucocorticoids that reduce target cell sensitivity and impair synthesis of new proteins and DNA in cell division), and (3) the shortening of *telomeres* (the DNA sequences that program the number of cell divisions).

Stress and Reproductive Processes

Because of the interconnectedness of homeostatic systems, biological and behavioral processes combine to contribute to obesity, resulting in the release of *adipose-derived hormones* (e.g., leptin, adiponectin, kisspeptin, and ghrelin), which, in turn, influence reproductive functions such as puberty and fertility. High levels of **chronic stress** can result in glucocorticoid inhibition of hypothalamic release of *luteinizing hormone* (LH) and *follicle stimulating hormone* (FSH). The effect is to limit *estrogen* secretion and *egg production* in females and *testosterone* secretion and *sperm production* in males. **Stress** can also impede the parasympathetic activation required for male penile erections resulting in *impotence* or *premature ejaculation*. **Stress-induced fat cell consumption** in females can impede *estrogen* production, resulting in a relative buildup of male hormone that contributes to *amenorrhea*. The lowering of *progesterone* levels combined with glucocorticoid blockade of bone recalcification can lead to *osteoporosis*. Other consequences may include *atherosclerosis* and impaired uterine wall nutrition increasing the risk of miscarriage and preterm labor.

Stress and Cardiovascular Disorders

By what bio-behavioral mechanisms does stress contribute to cardiovascular disorders?

Cardiovascular disorders are the product of a complex **gene–environment interaction** where individuals who are genetically predisposed (positive family history) and behaviorally vulnerable (poor diet, little exercise) to cardiovascular disease are especially susceptible to precipitating stressor conditions (sudden shock or major loss).

Individuals who regularly smoke, consume excessive alcohol, are overweight, and have a sedentary life style and unhealthy diet are at risk for diabetes, hypertension, hypercholesterolemia, and hyperlipidemia, each of which increases their vulnerability, when stressed, to cardiovascular disease.

Acute stress alters the normal cardiovascular system by diminishing arterial flow; increasing blood pressure and heart rate; diverting blood flow from the digestive tract, kidneys, and skin to brain and muscles; decreasing urine production to conserve water and blood volume; and emptying the bladder to reduce weight. Conditions of high or **chronic stress** amplify the severity of these same responses, raising the risk of organ system dysfunction and damage. Otherwise unexplained, or *essential hypertension* (BP > 140/90 mmHg), is the cardiovascular sign in 90% of cases. **Stress-induced chronic arterial constriction** combined with high cholesterol levels can result in clogging (*atherosclerosis*) and impeded blood oxygen flow (*myocardial ischemia*). This, in turn, can lead to chest pain (*angina*), or in more severe cases, to cardiac cell death (*infarct*). **Chronic stress** can also result in the heart muscle fibers lapsing into an asynchronous or disorganized rhythm (*arrhythmia* or *fibrillation*). In addition, persons with coronary artery disease who are exposed to chronic stress, have significantly higher insulin levels than those without chronic stress exposure.

Raynaud's phenomenon, another vasospastic disorder, involves excessive vasoconstriction of the fingers and toes in response to cold temperature. *Migraine headaches* may also result from spasms of the arterial vasculature in response to stressor-induced SNS activity, and may be precipitated by an array of biological, environmental, cognitive, or sociocultural stressors. Box 7.1 lists other common stress disorders that are consequences of chronic stress-induced system breakdowns.

Box 7.1. Examples of other disorders associated with chronic stress-induced system failures	
Gastrointestinal	Irritable bowel syndrome, esophageal reflux
Respiratory	Hyperventilation, asthma
Dermatological	Eczema, acne, alopecia universalis
Musculoskeletal	Muscle strain, low back pain

Stress and the Immune System

By what bio-behavioral mechanisms does stress contribute to immune system disorders?

Defense against infection and injury is essential for survival and involves a complex network of coordinated nervous system and immune system interactions throughout the body. Emerging research into the nature of these complex interactions has given rise to a new interdisciplinary field, **psychoneuroimmunology**. The immune system is an extremely elaborate "sense organ." It alerts and informs the brain of threats to the organism's integrity, identifying the location and nature of the invasion, and triggers an immediate *innate immune system response,* by releasing macrophages into the blood stream to attack the intruders. The release of targeted immunomodulators (e.g., cytokines) initiates an inflammatory response that (a) delivers reinforcement killer cells, (b) produces a barrier against further infection, and (c) stimulates tissue repair. The cytokines released also trigger additional more complex changes throughout the body (the acute phase response) by signaling the central nervous system. In response, the brain initiates an array of system changes designed to further aid in the body's defense against infection. These include fever, reductions in activity, altered sleep patterns, decreased social and sexual activity, increased pain sensitivity, reduced nourishment or food intake, and altered cognitive functions. This constellation of changes can be readily recognized in the common symptoms of a cold or flu, initiated for the purpose of conserving energy that can be redirected toward combating the infection. The HPA axis and SNS are activated (the classic

physiological stress response) which, among other things, serves to release energy from bodily stores (e.g., converting glycogen to glucose). Note that the initiation of the stress response is consistent with the principle that any challenge to the body's homeostatic integrity constitutes a stressor condition.

Immune system disorders illustrate gene–environment interactions in the etiology of disease.

Although acute or moderate stress generally activates the immune response, chronic stress and the resultant excess levels of glucocorticoids in the blood may impair the production of B cells and T cells, and induce premature migration of T cells from the thymus, leading to immunodeficiencies. Ironically, chronic stress may also heighten the immune system's response, leading it to attack organs or tissues in the host body. Such autoimmune disorders include multiple sclerosis, pernicious anemia, rheumatoid arthritis, juvenile diabetes, and various allergies. Autoimmune diseases can be organ specific, where the antigenic response focuses on a specific tissue or organ, like Hashimoto's thyroiditis (thyroid) or multiple sclerosis (nerve cell myelin sheaths). Autoimmune diseases can also be non-organ specific, where the antigen is universal, attacking parts of every cell.

Stress and Cancer

Because chronic stress can impair normal cell processes, including **apoptosis** (programmed cell death and recycling), cells can exhibit altered growth and differentiation. In addition, *regulatory genes* can be mutated by carcinogens, such as UV rays or toxic chemicals, further impairing cell growth processes. Chronic stress can also impair the ability of the immune system to mobilize defenses against invading tumor cells, inadvertently enhance tumor cell growth, and facilitate *angiogenesis* (increased capillary growth), which nurtures tumor cells. Thus, especially with tumors that are viral in origin, stress may not only enhance the growth of the tumor, but also indirectly contribute to its origin by impairing the immune response.

Stress and Emotional Consequences

Chronic stress that induces continued emotional arousal can have serious psychological consequences. Conditions leading to an excessive fight-or-flight response can result in chronic **anticipatory anxiety**, a dread that pending situations will trigger a fear response, especially the physiological components (see Chapter 9: Emotion and Learning, and Chapter 44: Anxiety Disorders). Similarly, exposure to repeated loss, failure, or interpersonal disappointment can lead to **depression** and a sense of **learned helplessness** (see Chapter 43: Depressive and Bipolar Disorders).

> Emotional responses and physical symptoms can become conditioned to specific thoughts, memories, self-statements, or acts, so that whenever these cognitions or events occur, they activate these same emotional states and physical symptoms (e.g., "Every time I fail, I get depressed").

Sudden, life-threatening, *traumatic events* can generate intense feelings of *helplessness* and *powerlessness* leading to the development of **post-traumatic stress disorder** (PTSD). The precipitating event, although necessary, is not responsible for PTSD; rather PTSD is the result of a stress response so severe that the emergency function of the amygdala overwhelms the ability of the hippocampus to act as modulator (to analyze past relevant contextual experience, learn, and offer an appropriate adaptive response). The emotional consequences of the stressor event cannot be anchored by any identifiable contextual memory (cognition), contributing to nightmares and *flashbacks* (re-experiencing the emotional memory as if the original event is actually happening), as well as insomnia, heightened physiological arousal, and emotional hypervigilance.

Moderating the Stress Response

As stated earlier, a stress or a stressor condition is any agent (including pathogens), event, or condition that challenges the homeostatic integrity of the human organism or any of its component systems and can originate under an array of genetic,

biological, behavioral, cognitive, sociocultural, or environmental conditions. However, the term *stress* is commonly used to describe daily life events (i.e., changes in health, finances, or social interactions). The relationship between life events and physical or psychological well-being was the object of research by Holmes and Rahe, who attempted to quantify the relative importance of life changes in terms of distress or *morbidity load* on the individual. They investigated the relationship between stress and illness and developed a life stress scale composed of 43 **life events**, each weighted for the severity of the stressor (see Box 7.2). By correlating life events with illnesses that occurred in the following 6 to 12 months, they found that the total number of *life change units* accumulated in a year's time provided an estimate of the impact of life stress on the individual's health. While negative events such as the death of a family member or economic hardship were obviously stressful, positive events, such as a wedding or holiday, could also be stressful.

The predictive validity of a life events scale is improved by taking into account the degree to which an event or condition is stressful "in the eye of the beholder." One person's severe "stressor" may be only another person's moderate challenge. Thus, the impact of a stressor is determined in part by the individual's **appraisal** of its significance and meaning. The impact is also influenced by an individual's **vulnerabilities** – for example, genetically (Down syndrome), cognitively (defeatist beliefs), behaviorally (a smoker), or socioculturally (denied health care or economic opportunities). Among the individual's resources are **coping skills**, adaptive abilities in the form of behavioral skills; cognitive strategies, sense of self-efficacy or confidence; and motivation. Another resource, **social support**, refers to support and assistance that the individual receives from others. Additional resources may include financial, educational, intellectual, creative and social skills, and benefits such as access to health care the individual can call upon.

While individuals may seek to limit exposure, learning to effectively manage stress is a more realistic and appropriate goal than trying to eliminate stress. Thus, a person's stress response can best be moderated and regulated by interventions that reduce predisposing vulnerabilities, enhance appraisal abilities and coping skills, and increase

Box 7.2. Life events and their respective life stress units

Death of spouse 100	Divorce 73	Marital separation 65
Jail term 63	Death of close family member 63	Personal injury or illness 53
Marriage 50	Being fired 47	Marital reconciliation 45
Retirement 45	Health change of family member 39	Change in finances 38
Death of a close friend 37	New line of work 36	Increased fighting with spouse 35
Large mortgage 31	Foreclosure 31	Son or daughter leaving home 30
In-law troubles 29	Spouse starts or stops work 26	Begin or end school 26
Trouble with boss 23	Moving into new home 20	Change in sleeping habits 16
Change in eating habits 16	Vacation 13	Total: _____

Note. The number of *life change units* accumulated in the past year of an individual's life provides an estimate of the impact of stress on health. If the total score is 300+, there is an 80% risk of illness. If the score is 150–299+, there is a 50% risk of illness. If the score is ≤ 150, there is a slight risk of illness. Adapted from "The Social Readjustment Rating Scale," by T. Holmes and R. Rahe, 1967, *Journal of Psychosomatic Research, 2,* pp. 213–218. © Elsevier.

skills for recruiting social support and identifying and utilizing other resources (see Chapter 9: Emotion and Learning).

Recommended Readings

Baum, A., & Contrada, R. (Eds). (2011). *The handbook of stress sciences: Biology, psychology, and health.* New York, NY: Springer.

Erickson, K. I., Creswell, J. D., Verstynen, T. D., & Gianaros, P. J. (2014). Health neuroscience: Defining a new field. *Current Directions in Psychological Science, 23*(6), 446–453. http://doi.org/10.1177/0963721414549350

Holmes, T., & Rahe, R. (1967). The Social Readjustment Rating Scale. *Journal of Psychosomatic Research, 11*(2), 213–218. http://doi.org/10.1016/0022-3999(67)90010-4

McEwen, B. S. (2009). Stress and coping. In G. B. Berntson & J. T. Cacioppo (Eds.), *Handbook of neurosciences for the behavioral sciences.* Hoboken, NJ: Wiley.

Selye, H. (1955). Stress and disease. *Science, 122,* 625–631. http://doi.org/10.1126/science.122.3171.625

Sharma, S., Powers, A., Bradley, R., & Kerry, J. (2016). Gene × environment determinants of stress- and anxiety-related disorders. *Annual Review of Psychology, 67,* 239–261. Retrieved from http://papers.ssrn.com/sol3/papers.cfm?abstract_id=2711696 (abstract) or http://www.pubpdf.com/pub/26442668/Gene-Environment-Determinants-of-Stress-and-Anxiety-Related-Disorders http://doi.org/10.1146/annurev-psych-122414-033408

Review Questions

1. The concept of stress refers to any challenge to the homeostasis or integrity of the organism. Stress disorders originate from stressors in which of the following domains?

A. Biological
B. Cognitive-behavioral
C. Environmental
D. Sociocultural
E. All of the above

2. Among the following, which brain structure plays a key role in modulating the stress response, based on memories of past experience relevant to incoming sensory information?
A. Amygdala
B. Hippocampus
C. Hypothalamus
D. Pituitary
E. Thalamus

3. Which of the following is a true statement about the effect of chronic stress on the immune system?
A. Chronic stress can suppress but not heighten immune system responses.
B. Chronic stress contributes to non-organ specific but not organ-specific autoimmune disorders.
C. Chronic stress induces migration of T cells into the thymus resulting in thymus swelling.
D. Excess levels of circulating glucocorticoids damage T cells.
E. Immune system stress responses occur primarily in the setting of genetic vulnerability.

4. Intense chronic stress can overwhelm the body's adaptive efforts, resulting in a variety of medical disorders. This debilitating effect is mediated primarily by the
A. cardiovascular system
B. hematopoietic system
C. immune system
D. neuroendocrine system
E. sensory system

Answer Key on p. 465

8 Pain

Jayanth Dasika, MD, Nguyen Mai, PhD, and Joel L. Kent, MD

- What is pain?
- How is pain classified?
- What are the bio-behavioral mechanisms involved in the experience of pain?
- What are the main treatments for chronic pain?

What is pain?

The International Association for the Study of Pain (IASP) defines pain as "the unpleasant sensory and emotional experience associated with actual or potential tissue damage." The scope of this definition goes beyond a sensory response to tissue damage to include the affective dimension of past experience, anxiety, and expectations. Pain is a complex phenomenon involving cognitive, emotional, behavioral, and environmental feedback. As a consequence, treatment often requires a multidisciplinary approach.

Pain as a Homeostatic Function

How is pain classified?

Pain can be divided into two broad categories: adaptive and maladaptive. **Adaptive** or **acute pain** relates to survival by protecting the organism from injury or promoting healing when injury has occurred. The body attempts to deal with the associated stress by achieving homeostasis through neural, hormonal, and behavioral activities. Healing can occur without intervention. However, medical interventions may be useful to reduce or prevent pain and speed up the healing process.

Maladaptive or **chronic pain** represents pathological functioning of the nervous system that lasts beyond the ordinary duration of time an injury to the body needs to heal. IASP defines normal healing time as less than 3 months. Pain duration shorter than 6 months, but present beyond the expected healing period, has been termed **subacute pain**. It has been proposed that it is not the duration of pain that distinguishes acute from chronic pain but, more importantly, the inability of the body to restore its physiological functions to normal homeostatic levels.

Pain can further be divided into nociceptive and neuropathic pain. **Nociception** is the detection and perception of tissue damage by nerve fibers. It is further subdivided into somatic and visceral pain. *Somatic pain* is well localized and arises from injury to body tissues. *Visceral pain* arises from activation of visceral pain receptors such as stretch receptors. It is poorly localized and often described as deep, dull, and cramping in quality.

Neuropathic pain arises from abnormal neural activity (central or peripheral) secondary to disease, injury, or dysfunction of the nervous system. It usually persists without ongoing tissue injury. Neuropathic pain can be subdivided into peripheral and central pain. *Peripheral neuropathic pain* arises from damage to a peripheral nerve (e.g., postherpetic neuralgia, neuroma formation). *Central neuropathic pain* arises from an abnormality in the central nervous system (e.g., phantom limb pain, pain from spinal cord injuries, poststroke pain).

An alternative classification described by Loeser and Melzack (1999) considers the emotional and behavioral responses to pain under four broad categories: nociception (described above), perception of pain, suffering, and pain behaviors. The *perception of pain* can exist without nociception, and, as a result, the intensity of chronic pain frequently bears little or no relation to the extent of tissue injury. *Suffering* is a negative response induced by pain and also by fear, anxiety, stress, loss of loved objects, and other psychological states. *Pain behaviors* result from pain and suffering. They are things a person does in response to actual or expected environmental consequences. Examples of pain behaviors are saying "ouch," grimacing, limping, lying down, and refusing to work.

Bio-Behavioral Mechanisms of Pain

What are the bio-behavioral mechanisms involved in the experience of pain?

The sensation of pain begins through the activation of specialized nociceptors in the peripheral nervous system, which transmit pain signals to the dorsal horn of the spinal cord. As noted above, nociception is the physiological process of activation of neural pathways by stimuli that are potentially or currently damaging to tissue. The signal is then relayed through the central nervous system to be processed and eventually interpreted in the somatosensory cerebral cortex. Multiple ascending and descending pathways along with a vast number of neurotransmitter systems are involved in modulating the incoming messages and relaying the information to the brain. There are four bio-behavioral processes associated with these pathways:

- **Transduction** is the conversion of a noxious stimulus into electrical activity in the peripheral terminals of nociceptor sensory fibers.
- **Transmission** refers to the passage of action potentials from the peripheral to the central nervous system.
- **Modulation** is alteration either by enhancement or suppression of sensory input. A major

site of modulation is within the dorsal horn of the spinal cord.
- **Perception** is the interpretation of afferent input in the somatosensory cerebral cortex resulting in a subjective sensation of pain.

Of these four processes, modulation and perception largely account for individual variability in the experience of pain. That is, individuals differ in the degree to which pain signals are modulated, and these modulated signals are in turn variously perceived due to differences in past learning and experience.

Modulation: Segmental Inhibition

A-δ and C nerve fibers transmit sensory information from the periphery to cells in the dorsal horn. In the substantia gelatinosa (lamina II) of the dorsal horn gray matter, pain sensation is filtered by modulation of the sensory nociceptive input prior to ascending up to the brain via the neurons in the spinothalamic tract. One source of this modulation of afferent nociceptive signals is in response to input from sensory touch fibers. This is referred to as *segmental inhibition*, when sensory touch fibers modulate nociceptive input from the same vertebral segment (vertebral level). This modulation can alter or completely block the nociceptive signal.

This form of modulation is better known as the **gate control theory,** of Melzack and Wall (see Figure 8.1). This theory describes how input along low-threshold A-β fibers (carrying touch sensation impulses) inhibits the signals emanating from small diameter fibers (carrying pain impulses). Hence, the perception of pain can be diminished or not felt at all when touch is applied at the same level. Gate theory can be explained through the example of rubbing a body part after it has been injured. Rubbing the painful area activates touch A-β fibers, which modulate (in this case, decrease) the nociceptive impulses to higher brain centers, providing a decrease in the sensation of pain. This is also the analgesic mechanism behind *transcutaneous electrical nerve stimulation* (TENS), which is a widely used therapy for pain management.

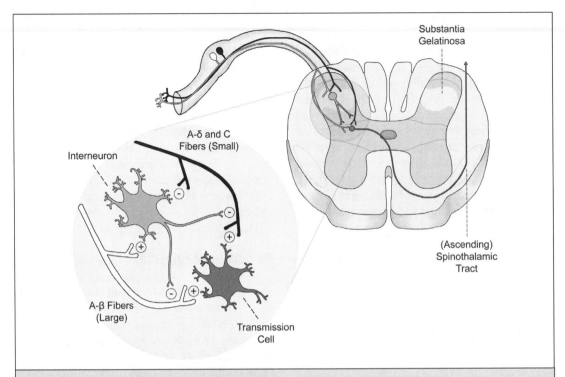

Figure 8.1. Gate control theory of pain modulation: Large and small afferent fibers synapse on interneurons in the substantia gelatinosa and transmission cells that give rise to the ascending spinothalamic tract. Input from large touch fibers excites the inhibitory interneuron, which then dampens input from pain fibers, mitigating pain perception.

Modulation: Descending Inhibitory Nerve System

Descending modulation of pain sensation is a well-known phenomenon that affects nociceptive processing in the dorsal horn. Activity in these descending pathways tends to inhibit nociceptive neurons in the dorsal horn of the spinal cord. The most recognized pathway is the periaqueductal gray (PAG) and rostral ventromedial medulla (RVM) pathway (see Figure 8.2). The PAG and RVM receive descending projections from a range of cortical and limbic structures, including the amygdala, anterior cingulate cortex, and prefrontal cortex. While the PAG has a few direct projections to the spinal cord, it mainly projects to the RVM, which, in turn, modulates nociceptive neurons in the dorsal horn of the spinal cord. Interestingly, stimulating electrodes implanted in the PAG can cause a state of analgesia. Investigations have corroborated that the effect of electrical stimulation in the PAG results in the inhibition of nociceptive neurons of laminae I, II, and V of the dorsal horn. Enhanced activity in the descending inhibitory system is also the putative mechanism of action for a range of behavioral modalities commonly used in pain management such as relaxation techniques, guided imagery, meditation, and other behavioral pain management modalities.

Modulation: Central Sensitization

Nociceptive neurons in the central nervous system can also become increasingly sensitive to nociceptive input over time. This phenomenon is known as *central sensitization* and will tend to promote and exaggerate the perception of pain. Central sensitization is a condition associated with the development and maintenance of chronic pain. As a response to physiological activity and neural injury, central sensitization causes an enhancement in the function of nociceptive pathways through activation of N-methyl-D-aspartate

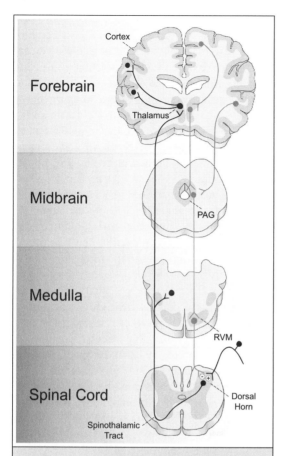

Figure 8.2. Pain perception and modulation pathways. Afferent pain fibers (black) synapse in the dorsal horn of the spinal cord. Fibers from second order neurons decussate and ascend via the spinothalamic tract, synapsing in the medulla and thalamus, which relays the stimuli to somatosensory and insular cortex. Descending inhibitory fibers from the forebrain (gray) synapse in the periaqueductal gray (PAG), which projects to the rostral ventromedial medulla (RVM). Projections from the RVM synapse on the ascending afferent fibers in the dorsal horn and modulate their input.

(NMDA) receptors and changes in the dorsal horn. This results in increases in membrane excitability and plasticity of the somatosensory system. This central facilitation can, therefore, manifest as a reduction in pain threshold (allodynia), and an increase in pain responsiveness (hyperalgesia). There are several mechanisms that appear to contribute to central sensitization. One is the con-

version of nociceptive-specific neurons to wide-dynamic neurons that then respond to both innocuous and noxious stimuli. Another is the concept of temporal windup, where there is a progressive increase in the responses elicited by a series of repeated innocuous stimuli. Finally, there are physiological changes that endure past the initiating trigger. All of these phenomena can contribute to the development and maintenance of chronic pain states.

Perception

Perception is the final stage of the pain-signaling process. This is the subjective sensation of pain as a result of the transmission of noxious stimuli. The threshold for the perception of pain can be changed by a process of sensitization as well.

The thalamus recognizes a noxious stimulus, and the parietal cortex further appreciates the stimulus intensity, localization, and other discriminatory aspects. The cerebral cortex governs the patient's emotional reaction to pain, and is thought to be responsible for attention and emotional variance of the overall pain experience. Psychological factors, such as anxiety and depression, can alter the subjective perception of pain, which is why it is no surprise that pain and affective disorders are often linked.

Managing Chronic Pain

What are the main treatments for chronic pain?

Pain is an enormous health care challenge in the US. It is the most common cause of long-term disability with over one third of the population suffering from chronic pain. Roughly 80% of affected patients report that pain disrupts activities of daily living, while 65% report that pain has negatively altered their personal relationships. Lost economic production is estimated at 50 million work days per year. Pain complaints account for 20% of all outpatient visits and 12% of all prescriptions. Despite recent advances in knowledge and treatment, pain remains an undertreated medical problem and a difficult social challenge.

Pharmacological Interventions

Opioids

Opioids can play an important role in the management of chronic pain. However, their euphoric and addictive qualities have made their use controversial and highly regulated, particularly when prescribed for nonmalignant pain. The name itself is derived from opium, one of the oldest known drugs in the world dating back to roughly 3,000 BC. Opium was widely used by ancient civilizations for medicinal and recreational purposes. However, it was not until the early1800s that the German pharmacist Friedrich Sertürner isolated morphine from opium sap. Morphine is 10 times more potent than opium and became widely used for the treatment of severe pain, particularly on the battlefield. After the structure of morphine was determined in the 1920s, various synthetic and **semisynthetic** opioids were developed with a wide range in pharmacokinetic and pharmacodynamic effects.

The **endogenous opioid system** consists of various peptides and a receptor family involved in several regulatory functions including nociceptive, stress, emotional and hedonic responses and modulation of thermoregulation, breathing, neuroendocrine function, GI motility and immune responses. The receptor family classically includes the µ-, κ- and δ-opioid receptors. Exogenous opioids act with varying affinities at these receptor sites modifying both nociception and the perception of a noxious stimulus. Activation of µ-opioid receptors within the central nervous system stimulates analgesia by activating descending inhibitory pathways that inhibit nociceptive dorsal horn firing in the spinal cord. Opioids are also effective peripherally by acting directly on A-δ and C-fibers. One of the main concerns with prescribing opioids is opioid-induced respiratory depression for which the µ-receptor has also been implicated.

Examples of **short-acting opioids** commonly prescribed in an outpatient setting include oxycodone, hydrocodone, tramadol, and tapentadol. They are commonly prescribed for a short course postoperatively and in select patients in an outpatient setting. Due to their potential for addiction and abuse, these opioids are highly regulated on the federal and state level in the US and many other countries. Oxycodone, in particular, was largely overprescribed in the 1990s and early 2000s leading to a sharp increase in overdose mortality. As recently as 2012, health care providers wrote 259 million prescriptions for opioid pain medication in 1 year. In 1998, the House of Delegates of the US Federation of State Medical Boards (FSMB) established the Model Guidelines for the Use of

Box 8.1. Definitions of addiction, pseudoaddiction, tolerance, physical dependence, and substance abuse	
Addiction	Primary, chronic, neurobiological disease, with genetic, psychosocial, and environmental factors influencing its development and manifestations. It is characterized by behaviors that include impaired control over drug use, craving, compulsive use, and continued use despite harm.
Pseudoaddiction	Iatrogenic syndrome resulting from the misinterpretation of relief-seeking behaviors as though they are drug-seeking behaviors indicative of addiction. The relief-seeking behaviors resolve upon institution of effective analgesic therapy.
Tolerance	Physiological adaptation in which exposure to a drug induces changes that result in diminution of one or more of the drug's effects over time. Tolerance is common in opioid treatment, has been demonstrated following a single dose of opioids, and is not the same as addiction.
Physical dependence	State of biological adaptation that is evidenced by a class-specific withdrawal syndrome when the drug is abruptly discontinued or the dose rapidly reduced and/or by the administration of an antagonist. Physical dependence does not equate with addiction.
Substance abuse	Use of any substance(s) for nontherapeutic purposes or use of medication for purposes other than those for which it is prescribed.

Based on Federation of State Medical Boards model policy on the use of opioid analgesics in the treatment of chronic pain, July 2013. Retrieved from http://www.fsmb.org/Media/Default/PDF/FSMB/Advocacy/pain_policy_july2013.pdf

Controlled Substances for the Treatment of Pain. This model offered clear practice standards for opioid prescribers and includes recommendations for monitoring and periodic drug testing. These guidelines were updated in 2004 and converted to a model policy. The policy included the definitions of addiction, pseudoaddiction, tolerance, physical dependence, and substance abuse (see Box 8.1). In March 2016, the Centers for Disease Control and Prevention released guidelines aimed directed at primary care providers, with an emphasis on conservative use of opioids. Various risk assessment tools have been made available by the American Pain Society (APS) and the American Academy of Pain Medicine (AAPM) in published guidelines for approaches to prescribing opioids:

- Screener and Opioid Assessment for Patients with Pain,
- Opioid Risk Tool,
- Diagnosis, Intractability, Risk, Efficacy (DIRE) score: Patient Selection for Chronic Opioid Analgesia.

In summary, chronic opioid therapy (COT) can be integral to a multimodal approach to acute and chronic pain management. However, it is usually best considered after more conservative treatments have been tried and found unsuccessful. Outpatient treatment with opioids should generally be avoided in patients with a history of personal or family substance abuse, drug-seeking behavior, or severe mental illness. Opioids should always be initiated at the lowest dose possible in the opioid-naïve patient and titrated to effect.

Nonsteroidal Anti-Inflammatory Drugs

Nonsteroidal anti-inflammatory drugs (NSAIDs) are among the most prescribed drugs in the world, with most being available over the counter (OTC). They are primarily used to reduce pain, fever, and inflammation. NSAIDs act by inhibiting production of prostaglandins from **cyclooxygenase (COX)**, an enzyme produced from arachidonic acid. Prostaglandins are produced at sites of inflammation leading to the sensation of pain through sensitization of nerve fiber endings. Two isoforms, COX-1 and COX-2, are important from a pharmacological standpoint. COX-1 is constitutive, meaning that it is active at all times. It is expressed primarily in the GI tract, kidneys, and platelets. COX-2 is an inducible isoform primarily activated in macrophages, fibroblasts, and other

cells leading to inflammation. COX-1 is thought to be primarily responsible for the side effects attributed to NSAIDs such as GI bleeding. Nonselective NSAIDs such as aspirin, ibuprofen, ketorolac, and naproxen inhibit both enzymes. Selective COX-2 inhibitors such as celecoxib (Celebrex) and etoricoxib (Arcoxia) target inflammation with reduced risk of bleeding. Only celecoxib is available in the US at this time. Aspirin is unique in that is a nonselective, irreversible inhibitor of COX, favoring inhibition of COX-1. Thus, it has excellent antiplatelet properties and is widely prescribed by cardiologists for that reason. It is not commonly prescribed for pain management due to its side effects. While not technically classified as an NSAID, acetaminophen is frequently prescribed for its analgesic and antipyretic properties. Its analgesic effect is mediated through inhibition of central prostaglandin synthesis. It has weak anti-inflammatory effects compared with NSAIDs due to weak inhibition of COX in the presence of peroxides, which are found at sites of inflammation. However, it has been used in the management of postoperative pain to decrease the need for higher doses of opioids without the risk of bleeding associated with NSAIDs. Liver toxicity is the most important consideration when prescribing acetaminophen.

Antidepressants

Research suggests that at least 40% to 50% of chronic pain patients suffer from depressive disorders. Patients with psychiatric illness report greater pain intensity, more pain-related disability, and a larger affective component to their pain. *Chronic pain can cause depression and vice versa,* in what becomes a mutually reinforcing relationship. An important study by Jarvik and colleagues in 2005 demonstrated that levels of depression predicted the development of low back pain 3 years following the initial assessment. Patients with depression were 2.3 times more likely to report back pain compared with those who did not report depression. In fact, depression was a stronger predictor of chronic back pain than any other clinical or anatomic risk factor.

Prior to publication of the Melzack-Wall gate control theory in 1965, the amount of pain experienced by an individual was generally considered to be directly proportional to tissue pathology. The article was the first to provide a physiological explanation for psychological effects on pain. Pain signals can either be altered or blocked from traveling in the CNS. In gate control theory, painful signals are blocked in the dorsal horn of the spinal cord, which diminishes the pain intensity perceived by the patient. In a similar manner, activity along descending inhibiting tracks, which lead from the brain to the spinal cord, also serve to inhibit pain transmission. Activity of these tracks can be promoted with a range of behavioral therapy modalities such as deep relaxation techniques and mindfulness to help diminish pain perception in patients experiencing chronic pain. In a similar manner, treatment of comorbid psychiatric disorders such as depression and anxiety will help normalize activity along the descending inhibitory tracks, which can assist in decreasing pain intensity.

Based on these mechanisms, it is not surprising that many antidepressant medications have been found to have analgesic effects even in patients who are not depressed. **Tricyclic antidepressants** (TCAs) and **serotonin and norepinephrine reuptake inhibitors** (SNRIs) are classes of antidepressants that have significant analgesic efficacy (Box 8.2). TCAs act by inhibiting both serotonergic and noradrenergic reuptake. They are inexpensive and have analgesic properties that are particularly effective for treating neuropathic pain independent of their antidepressant effect. However, they are potentially proarrhythmic and can prolong the QTc interval. Thus, any patient over 40 years old or with a history of cardiac disease should undergo a baseline EKG. Additionally, sedation and weight gain are important anticholinergic side effects of TCAs. SNRIs are a newer class of antidepressants, which, similar to TCAs, work by inhibiting serotonin and

norepinephrine reuptake. They have a safer risk profile with fewer cardiac and anticholinergic side effects compared with TCAs. Other antidepressants such as traditional selective serotonin reuptake inhibitors (SSRIs) as well as bupropion, mirtazapine, and trazodone may be effective in treating chronic pain, although less evidence is available regarding their analgesic efficacy.

Behavioral Interventions

Social and environmental factors can have a profound impact on the way an individual experiences and expresses pain. Pioneering work by Fordyce and colleagues in the early 1970s emphasized the importance of viewing clinical pain in a **biopsychosocial context**. His study on operant conditioning published in 1973 demonstrated positive outcomes by reducing medication and increasing activity levels in patients with chronic pain. An important distinction, explored in later work, was that suffering and pain behaviors can exist irrespective of a nociceptive stimulus. Additional work by Turk and colleagues in the 1980s detailed the application of cognitive behavior interventions in chronic pain management. Psychological treatment has had the clearest benefit for patients suffering from major depression and anxiety.

Operant interventions are designed to reduce maladaptive responses to a pain behavior and replace them with more adaptive behaviors. For example, an individual's pain complaints will largely be ignored, while more adaptive behaviors such as attending physical therapy, exercise, and increasing overall activity levels are reinforced. To avoid the negative pattern of individuals pushing themselves to the point of pain exacerbation and giving up, it is important to utilize "shaping" in operant programs. *Shaping* is the process of gradually increasing the nature, frequency, or duration of a behavior while managing the consequences, which include removing any punishment (e.g., pain) and introducing reinforcement (e.g., experience of success, social attention). Family members and significant others can play a vital role in this process.

Relaxation techniques have been particularly useful for the management of anxiety and stress management. For example, progressive muscle relaxation techniques involve reducing stress by

Box 8.2. Examples for drug classes	
SSRIs	Citalopram, fluoxetine, fluvoxamine, paroxetine, sertraline
TCAs	Amitriptyline, nortriptyline
SNRIs	Duloxetine, venlafaxine

Note. SNRIs = serotonin and norepinephrine reuptake inhibitors; SSRIs = selective serotonin reuptake inhibitors; TCAs = tricyclic antidepressants.

systematically tensing and relaxing specific muscle groups while focusing on breathing and using guided imagery. Biofeedback involves providing a patient with physiologic information about muscle tension, typically through electromyographic (EMG) feedback, in order to learn voluntary control over what is usually an involuntary process.

Cognitive behavioral therapy (CBT) studies have provided excellent evidence supporting its use in the treatment of chronic pain (particularly lower back pain), rheumatoid arthritis, and osteoarthritis. CBT focuses on cognitions, such as attitudes and beliefs, that underlie maladaptive pain behaviors and emotions. Components of relaxation and operant conditioning may also be practiced in CBT. Individuals with chronic pain treated with CBT have been shown to have improvements in pain intensity, pain-related interference, health-related quality of life, and depression. Other methods such as learning constructive coping skills, cognitive restructuring, and hypnosis have also been shown to be effective in treating chronic pain.

A multidisciplinary approach that includes a combination of behavioral interventions, medications, injections, and physical therapy is generally necessary to provide lasting benefits. Behavioral interventions may provide the most benefit to those at high risk of responding poorly to treatment. These include individuals who are highly distressed, see their pain as uncontrollable, experience highly negative life events, perceive themselves to be disabled, or have low readiness to engage in self-management.

Acupuncture

Acupuncture is an important component of traditional Chinese medicine for treating illness or providing local anesthesia through the insertion of needles at specific sites on the body. The English translation derives from the Greek *acus* (needle) and *punctura* (puncture). It is based on the Chinese concept of *qi* or the "vital energy" that flows through meridians or channels in the body connecting it to the outside world. Pain and illness can arise from obstruction in the flow of *qi*. External stimulation of acupuncture points (acupoints) can modulate *qi* where the meridians emerge at the surface of the body.

Acupuncture is now more widely prescribed by Western pain physicians as an alternative treatment for certain patients, particularly those with lower back pain, neck pain, tension headache, migraine, and osteoarthritis of the knee. Although there is no clear scientific explanation for acupuncture, there is evidence that acupuncture triggers the release of endogenous opioid-like substances and monoamine neurotransmitters, resulting in analgesia. Unfortunately, most studies to date have been too poorly designed to properly assess efficacy.

As the rates of adverse effects and complications are generally low, acupuncture can serve as a useful adjunct to a pain treatment plan. In the future, more randomized controlled trials will be necessary to better assess the efficacy of this treatment for various pain conditions.

Recommended Readings

Dowell, D., Haegerich, T. M., & Chou, R. (2016). *CDC guideline for prescribing opioids for chronic pain – United States*, 2016. *JAMA, 315*(15), 1624–1645.

Ehde, D. M., Dillworth, T. M., & Turner, J. A. (2014). Cognitive-behavioral therapy for individuals with chronic pain: Efficacy, innovations, and directions for research. *American Psychologist, 69*(2), 153–166. http://doi.org/10.1037/a0035747

Fordyce, W. E. (1995). On pain illness and disability. *Journal of Back and Musculoskeletal Rehabilitation, 5,* 259–264. http://doi.org/10.3233/BMR-1995-5310

Jarvik, J. G, Hollingworth, W., Heagarty P. J., Haynor, D. R., Boyko, E. J., & Deyo, R. A. (2005). Three-year incidence of low back pain in an initially asymptomatic cohort: clinical and imaging risk factors. *Spine, 30*(13), 1541–1548. http://doi.org/10.1097/01.brs.0000167536.60002.87

Loeser, J.D., & Melzack, R. (1999). Pain: An overview. *Lancet, 353,* 1607–1609. http://doi.org/10.1016/S0140-6736(99)01311-2

Melzack, R., & Wall, P. (1965). Pain mechanisms: A new theory. *Science, 150,* 971–979. http://doi.org/10.1126/science.150.3699.971

Wegener, S., Wolfman, J., & Haythornthwaite, J.A. (2011). Psychological interventions for chronic pain. In H. Benzon (Ed.), *Essentials of pain medicine* (3rd ed., pp. 180–183). Philadelphia, PA: Elsevier.

Review Questions

1. Saying "ouch" is an example of
   A. nociception
   B. pain behavior
   C. physical dependence
   D. suffering
   E. tolerance

2. A patient with severe lower back pain and long-standing major depression comes to clinic for an evaluation. What would be the most appropriate medication to prescribe?
   A. Duloxetine
   B. Hydrocodone
   C. Naproxen
   D. Sertraline
   E. Trazodone

3. A trial of low-dose opioid therapy in an out-patient setting would be most appropriate in which of the following situations?
   A. A 22-year-old woman taking oxycodone for the past 3 years after a skiing accident because "nothing else works"
   B. A 54-year-old man with a remote history of alcoholism with long-standing severe degenerative hip pain, who has abstained from alcohol use for over 15 years
   C. A 58-year-old woman with fibromyalgia currently on vacation in your area, who is requesting a one-time prescription for 2 weeks until she gets a refill from her regular physician
   D. A 65-year-old otherwise healthy man with symptomatic L4-L5 disc herniation refractory to treatment with several NSAIDs, injections, and physical therapy
   E. A 75-year-old man with a history of bipolar disorder and severe arthritic pain of the left knee

4. Acupuncture
   A. can lead to hyperalgesia
   B. has no scientific evidence to support its use
   C. may release endogenous opioid-like substances
   D. often leads to nerve damage
   E. works primarily through distraction

Answer Key on p. 465

Section IV
Higher Order Homeostatic Systems

9 Emotion and Learning

John E. Carr, PhD, and Ian M. Kodish, MD, PhD

- What role does emotion play in homeostatic adaptation?
- What role does learning play in evolution?
- What bio-behavioral mechanisms are involved in implicit vs. explicit learning?
- What is the developmental significance of different kinds of learning?
- What bio-behavioral mechanism makes reinforcement possible?

Emotion

What role does emotion play in homeostatic adaptation?

As noted earlier (Chapter 7: Stress, Adaptation, and Stress Disorders), any challenge to homeostasis initiates a **stress response**, a complex neuroendocrine-mediated state of arousal. Such states of physiological arousal are affectively experienced as an emotion that alerts the organism to the heightened significance of incoming sensory information. How the information and the *physiological arousal* are interpreted depends on the *situational context* in which it occurs, and the *cognitive interpretation*, or meaning, assigned to that context, based on the individual's past experience. Emotions orchestrate diverse neurophysiological systems to flexibly signal the importance of various thoughts and experiences, serving to enhance memory consolidation and adaptive functioning.

The earliest emotions in the newborn are reflexive expressions of distress, designed to generate caregiving behaviors in parents. The *most basic emotion* is pleasure–displeasure, which differentiates into more refined *primary emotions* (e.g., joy, sadness, fear, anger, interest, surprise, disgust) as the infant develops. These early emotional expressions are universal, suggesting they are genetically determined for their survival value. As the individual develops, emotional expression becomes increasingly complex and nuanced, influenced by physiological, cognitive, sociocultural, and environmental stimuli. As emotion is increasingly influenced by culture (see Chapter 17: Culture and Cultural Competence in Health Care), expression is governed by *social norms* that define when, where, and how specific emotions are expressed. While primary emotions are predominately individual and reflexive, *social emotions* (e.g., guilt, shame, embarrassment, empathy, compassion, admiration, respect) develop in response to interactions with others (e.g., family, community).

Emotional expressions and associated social roles are common to many cultures, suggesting an evolutionary interaction between heredity and sociocultural sanctions.

Bio-Behavioral Mechanisms of Emotion

The amount of *glucocorticoids* released from the adrenal cortex and *catecholamines* released from the adrenal medulla and other sympathetic nerve endings defines the physiological *intensity* of a stress response and, therefore, contributes to the perceived importance of the event. These actions, and the associated emotional state, induce associative learning, and become *conditioned* to the contextual stimulus. This input converges in the basolateral *amygdala* and is forwarded to the *hippocampus, caudate nucleus,* and *cortex,* where it is consolidated, stored, and readily accessed in similar future situations. The *strength* of a memory is proportional to the *intensity* of the emotional response and emotional learning serves to alert the individual in the future to potentially threatening, benign, or pleasurable situations.

Bio-Behavioral Mechanisms of Emotion Regulation

Any emotional response that can be conditioned can be "unconditioned" or *extinguished.* However, this does not mean that the response is eliminated. Rather, the response becomes less relevant in light of new information or a change in circumstances. The ability to alter a response as circumstances change is essential to successful adaptation and survival. The *situation* to which fear (or any emotion) is conditioned defines the context of the fear. Thus, situations previously perceived as threatening may be reappraised in a new context and found to be benign.

Fear can be replaced with more adaptive emotional responses through emotion regulation strategies involving specific bio-behavioral mechanisms. When the circumstances of an emotional response are altered, the prefrontal cortex and hippocampus exercise greater inhibitory control over the amygdala and thereby introduce new contextual information. The new coping response is gradually learned, takes priority over the old response, and establishes a new context. All of these strategies are especially effective immediately following the activation of the emotional response, before memory has been reconsolidated and while it is, therefore, still malleable. These mechanisms underlie and explain the effectiveness of behavioral interventions in emotion regulation.

Learning and Adaptation

What role does learning play in evolution?

Human adaptation is possible because the brain can associate and store sequences and patterns of events in time and space. This capability contributes to the development of the behaviors, traits, and characteristics that are most successful in overcoming environmental challenges. These successful adaptations are then genetically passed on to offspring through **natural selection**. Thus, the current human genome is the result of an accumulation of *gene–environment–developmental interactions* that promote survival. However, the genetic contribution to this evolutionary process is not *what was learned* but rather the development of the brain systems that facilitate the *ability to learn.* As a result, learning enables the organism to adapt and modify behavior, incentives, and future goals. **Behavior modification** involves altering behavior associated with events contiguous in time and space. **Incentive modification** involves anticipating outcomes and altering the value of future goals based on lessons learned from past experience. Incentive modification may also involve learning how to *delay gratification* or inhibit certain responses in order to achieve, at a later date, desired outcomes that cannot be fully achieved immediately.

Principle of Association

The **principle of association** refers to the ability of organisms to "record" relationships between environmental events, biological responses, cognitions, or behaviors and their consequences. Associations range from *simple sequential connections* (*if* I press the button, *then* the horn will sound) to more *complex associations* incorporating temporal, spatial, and causal relationships, contextual cues, and consequences (if I sound the horn late at night in a residential area, I may get an angry response). Thus, *contextual cues* play an important role in guiding attention, emotional response, learning, and memory retrieval, thereby influencing subsequent behavior.

Time is an especially important contextual cue because the passage of time constantly changes the context.

Bio-Behavioral Mechanisms of Learning

Stimulus characteristics are stored or consolidated in memory in the form of patterned neuronal responses and activity-dependent synaptic alterations in distributed networks. The extensive dendritic tree of a single vertebrate neuron can form 100,000–200,000 receptive synaptic contacts with other neurons, thus providing an extraordinary array of potential associative networks. There are two types of learning based on the level and complexity of the neuronal mechanisms involved:

1. **Implicit learning** is the association of immediately sequential sensory and motor system responses via lower levels of cortical mediation. The information stored is limited to predictive relationships between events. Implicit learning can be immediate (reflexive) or cumulative over time, but tends to be *automatic*, often *without conscious participation* of the individual.

2. **Explicit learning** involves more abstract associations between diverse stimuli and events that vary across time and space. Explicit learning tends to be *intentional*, and typically requires more active *conscious participation* by the individual. Explicit learning outcomes may be immediate (e.g., instantaneous *insight*) or delayed (e.g., extended *reflection*).

Implicit Learning

> What bio-behavioral mechanisms are involved in implicit vs. explicit learning?

Implicit learning involves the acquisition of skills or knowledge without awareness of what is learned, such as in riding a bicycle. Implicit learning is known to involve diverse brain systems utilizing neurochemical changes common in other forms of learning. This process requires a convergence of neuronal activity. The first signal sensitizes the synapse, which potentiates or amplifies the effect of the second signal and enhances the associative link between the two neurons. Through this mechanism, the organism records information in the form of **sensory memories** derived from environmental interactions. These sensory memories are short lived due to the limited time span of synaptic firing. However, the process can be enhanced and made more durable by repeated associations with other sensory or motor signals occurring in connection with the same stimulus event. **Procedural memory** involves the acquisition and retrieval of motor sequences (tying shoelaces) and cognitive sequences (organizing a schedule). Information of low interest or infrequent utility may be retained for a few minutes in **short-term memory** areas such as the prefrontal cortex, but these if not consolidated, will erode. Unlike explicit learning which requires hippocampal and cortical processing, amnesia or hippocampal damage do not affect implicit learning skills.

Explicit Learning

Explicit learning requires activation and coordination of structures in the cortex, especially the temporal lobe, and other mediating brain networks, for the longer-term processing, coding, and storing of complex information. The **limbic system** (hippocampus, amygdala, basal forebrain, and thalamus) receives and integrates diverse sensory information. These are collated by the thalamus, and then referred on to the amygdala, which records its *emotional* significance, and the hippocampus, which assigns it a temporal and spatial context. These contextual cues facilitate learning by enabling the limbic system to reference the new incoming information to related memories already in the cortex.

The hippocampus and its associated structures in the limbic system serve as a central switchboard, connecting the various storage sites distributed throughout the cortex to form combined memories. When new learning occurs, these connections constitute temporary or short-term memory and are easily lost or reorganized as additional information is received. However, over time, as some memories are repeatedly activated and continue to have predictive value, they are eventually forwarded by the hippocampus to the prefrontal cortex to become part of long-term memory.

Major neural pathways of the hippocampus use the excitatory amino acid, **glutamate**, as a neurotransmitter. After neuronal excitation, glutamate binds with two types of protein receptors on the cell membrane of the postsynaptic neuron: (1) N-methyl D-aspartate receptors **(NMDA receptors)** and (2) all other or **non-NMDA receptors.** The NMDA receptor response is blocked by magnesium ions until the cell is unblocked by depolarization due to the stimulation of non-NMDA receptors. The *intensity* of the stimulus determines the *magnitude of the depolarization* and, therefore, the *intensity* of the cell response. The convergence of NMDA and non-NMDA receptor activation produces a slow, long-lasting synaptic response. In complex learning situations requiring multiple stimulus associations, the repeated convergence of these excitatory changes on two or more neurons serves to potentiate and prolong the sensitivity of the synaptic link. This **long-term potentiation** effect, however, requires that the two signals – glutamate binding to the receptor and depolarization of the postsynaptic cell – take place simultaneously, resulting in cell-mediated alterations in synaptic components that preserve the associative linkage.

Neurogenesis

The human capacity for learning is facilitated by **neurogenesis**, the ability of the nervous system to generate new neurons and neuronal connections. The process involves the proliferation, survival, migration, differentiation, and integration of neuronal cells essential to learning. The new cells are generated from stem cells and, although there is evidence of neurogenesis in several areas of the brain, its occurrence in the dentate gyrus of the hippocampus is especially important, as it explains the significant role the hippocampus plays in the mediation and processing of new information.

Learning and Developmental Demands

What is the developmental significance of different kinds of learning?

From birth to maturity, humans must adapt to increasingly demanding interactions especially with the environment, requiring progressively more complex and sophisticated learning processes.

Reflexive behavior represents the cumulative result of ancestral learning genetically programmed into the organism. Reflexes (e.g., distress cries, nursing reflexes) require minimal interaction with the environment and promote survival during early life, before the individual can learn from experience.

Critical period learning is also the result of genetic programming but requires a developmentally tuned interaction with the environment. **Imprinting** and **bonding** occur in response to specific stimulus cues in the environment (e.g., nurturing or "maternal" figures) essential to continued survival. Critical period learning, however, is time limited (i.e., the organism is responsive to the stimulus for only a brief time before the plasticity underlying that learning is lost).

One-trial learning behaviors are reflexive in their survival value, but involve even more interaction with the environment. The *strength* or *durability* of learning depends on the intensity of the stimulus, the intensity of the subsequent biological and/or emotional response, and the relevance to the organism's survival. Examples include touching a hot stove or ingesting an intensely noxious substance.

Classical conditioning reflects the ability of the organism to learn from increasingly complex interactions with the environment. It involves the association of two sequential events (A and B) such that one event (B) acquires the ability to elicit responses (R) formerly associated with the other event (A).

After repeated trips to the hospital for chemotherapy (unconditioned stimulus [US]), the side effects of which include nausea (unconditioned response [UR]), a patient may begin to experience nausea (conditioned response [CR]) as soon as the hospital (conditioned stimulus [CS]) comes into view. Thus, through associative learning, the hospital acquires the ability to induce nausea.

Operant conditioning is an advanced form of learning that makes it possible for the individual to learn from the positive or negative *consequences* of interactions with the environment, thus becoming more effective in assessing and adapting to stressful challenges. **Social learning**, an advanced form of operant conditioning, is a further adaptation of human learning to environmental demands, especially the complexities of interpersonal relationships (see Chapter 10: Cognition, Communication, and Social Interaction).

Reinforcement

A fundamental principle of operant conditioning, the law of effect states that if a behavior is followed by positive consequences (reinforcement) that behavior will increase in frequency over time. Conversely, if a certain behavior is followed by negative consequences (punishment), that behavior will decrease over time.

A **reinforcer** is any biological, behavioral, cognitive, sociocultural, or environmental event that reduces stress and restores homeostasis. Since stress reduction and the restoration of homeostasis are positive consequences, any behavior that contributes to them will be rewarded and, thereby, increase in frequency over time.

The Premack Principle

If an individual engages repeatedly in an activity, it implies that the activity is rewarding. Based on this observation, psychologist David Premack proposed that a frequently performed behavior can be used as a reinforcer for a preferred target of behavior. A mother invokes this principle when she tells her 6-year-old, "If you pick up your toys, you can watch your favorite TV show."

Having a rewarding experience is *positively reinforcing*, while avoiding an unpleasant or punishing experience is *negatively reinforcing*. In both cases, the behavior is reinforced and, therefore, will continue or increase over time. **Negative reinforcement** underlies several aspects of human behavior, such as studying to *avoid* failing or obeying the speed limit to *avoid* getting a traffic ticket. It also explains why many patients *avoid* going to the doctor to *avoid* experiencing pain (e.g., injec-

tions, blood draws), unpleasant examinations (e.g., prostate or pelvic examinations), bad news (e.g., diagnosis of cancer), or unpleasant treatments (e.g., dietary changes, abstinence from alcohol).

Stimulus generalization is a process by which a response can be elicited by other stimuli in a common context. Stimulus generalization explains why a long-time smoker finds it difficult to stop smoking behavior that has been conditioned to an array of contextual cues, all of which can trigger the smoking response (e.g., coffee breaks, social events, specific times or locations).

Bio-Behavioral Interaction in Reinforcement

What bio-behavioral mechanism makes reinforcement possible?

The **endogenous reward system** is the mechanism that drives adaptive learning in enabling the individual to identify and reinforce those cognitions and behaviors that have adaptive and survival value. The core of this endogenous system is a neuronal conduit, the **median forebrain bundle**, which includes the *nucleus accumbens* (NAcc), the *ventral tegmental area* (VTA), the *ventromedial* and *lateral nuclei of the hypothalamus*, and the *amygdala*. This conduit connects to all the structures within the limbic system, including the hippocampus, septal nuclei, and anterior cingulate gyrus, as well as the hypothalamus and amygdala. Recall that the limbic system regulates homeostasis, emotion, learning, and memory, and coordinates the neuroendocrine response to stress. Since it *regulates* almost every endocrine, visceral, and autonomic function, it is in a position to *assess* all incoming information, determine what functions, behaviors, substances, or strategies constitute an *optimal response*, and provide a *rewarding inducement* for the retention of that response. The inducement comes primarily in the form of increased release of the neurotransmitter dopamine at the neuronal synapses within the endogenous reward system, which continues to mature into adulthood.

As incoming sensory information is processed by the brain (new learning), the amygdala assesses the emotional impact of the information, and the hippocampus and prefrontal cortex assess the adaptive value of the information, contrasting it with already stored memories. If the new experience is judged less adaptive than comparable past experiences, then the new information or behavior is not rewarded and unlikely to be retained. If the new information is more valued, the association is strengthened by the rewarding impact of the dopaminergic neurotransmitter system, and the memory and behaviors are more likely to be reinforced and retained.

A patient receives pain medication PRN (as needed) and attentive care, but, over time, complains more frequently of increased pain. The pain reduction associated with receiving medication and attention from nursing staff reinforces the pain complaints, they become more frequent, and the perceived intensity of the pain increases. The attending physician orders pain medication administered every 4 hr and limited attention to pain complaints. The patient's pain complaints and pain intensity decrease. Why?

The HPA axis also plays a role in the endogenous reward system. Recall that stress-induced activation of the HPA axis releases a cascade of hormones that includes *endogenous opioids (*e.g., endorphins, enkephalins), whose antipain, antianxiety properties can also have significant reinforcing effects.

Clinical Applications

Since many illness behaviors, symptoms, emotional responses, and health-related beliefs are learned, clinical strategies using learning principles have been developed to assist patients to modify maladaptive responses and learn more adaptive and healthy behaviors.

Conditioning therapy is based on classical conditioning principles. This technique has been applied in the treatment of cancer where chemotherapies to suppress immune functioning may have severely noxious side effects. By repeatedly pairing the treatment with a pleasant odor, the odor acquires the ability to elicit the treatment effect (immunosuppression) but with fewer of the noxious side effects of the chemotherapy (see Chapter 7: Stress, Adaptation, and Stress Disorders).

Aversive conditioning involves conditioning a noxious stimulus to an undesired response, leading to the extinction of the undesired response. This approach has been used in alcohol treatment programs by conditioning noxious substances (e.g., disulfiram) to drinking behavior.

Contingency management involves selectively manipulating the consequences of a behavior to (1) increase desired behaviors via positive reinforcement, (2) extinguish undesirable behaviors, and (3) avoid undesirable consequences via negative reinforcement. Contingency management is effective in the treatment of chronic pain, as shown in the patient example on this page. Reinforcers of pain-related complaining behavior (e.g., attention) are identified, eliminated, or gradually reduced *(fading),* leading to the extinction of this undesirable behavior. The approach is also used to develop desirable health behaviors through *shaping* (i.e., reinforcing progressive steps in a diet program such as cutting intake of carbonated beverages by 25% each week for a month to attain abstinence).

Stimulus control involves the use of anticipatory cues to guide behavior toward more rewarding consequences. If a child sees reminders to brush their teeth when entering the bathroom, brushing is more likely to occur and can be reinforced by the parent ("What sparkling teeth you have!"). In addition to rewarding desirable behavior, undesirable behavior can be extinguished by removing the opportunity for reinforcement (timeout), or forfeiture of positive reinforcers (response cost). Positive reinforcement is the basis of **token economy** programs where patients accumulate "tokens" or points for successful completion of treatment sequences (e.g., rehab) which they can use to obtain rewards or privileges.

Feedback, based on the principle that information is reinforcing, involves reflecting relevant information that promotes self-monitoring and adaptive change. **Biofeedback**, utilizing displays of physiological monitors, provides the patient with information about otherwise unperceived autonomic and neuroendocrine responses to stress. Feedback on progress can reinforce regulation skills, and thus increase the likelihood that these skills will be utilized in the future. Maintaining behavioral records of stimulus events, symptom frequency, associated cognitions and behaviors, and outcomes is the most useful and fundamental feedback technique.

Cognitive restructuring refers to modifying the patient's assumptions and cognitive appraisals of various stimuli. This can apply to the perceived significance of bodily sensations, self-esteem, self-efficacy, approach to illness, effectiveness of treatments, competence of health professionals, and other perceptions that influence health outcomes.

A 35-year-old man with no history of cardiac risk factors visits the emergency room several times with complaints of "pain in my chest." He presents with elevated heart rate, sweating, dizziness, and shortness of breath, yet cardiac function tests are normal, and the symptoms disappear within an hour. A careful history reveals that the patient interpreted a twinge in his chest as a sign of an impending heart attack. This "catastrophic" belief apparently initiated the stress response, which, in turn, produced even more sympathetic nervous system activation. A cognitive restructuring intervention would involve (a) teaching the patient to challenge his "catastrophic" belief by considering the evidence (e.g., cardiac testing normal; no personal or familial risk factors), (b) explaining the nature of the stress response, and (c) considering alternative explanations (e.g., current life stress, heartburn, muscle strain).

Relaxation and breathing training teaches patients how to modulate physical symptoms of the stress response (e.g., muscle tension, hyperventilation) that contribute to or complicate illnesses. Relaxation training is often used in conjunction with biofeedback techniques. Through self-monitoring, the patient in the example above might learn that once he notices atypical chest sensations and interprets them as dangerous, he immediately starts hyperventilating. The patient could then learn to regulate his breathing under these circumstances and abort the cycle of sympathetic nervous system arousal.

Exposure therapy invokes a number of *relearning* and context-changing strategies to reduce fear reactions and the associated maladaptive behavioral responses. Instead of avoiding triggers, the patient is exposed to stimuli that elicit undesirable symptoms (e.g., anxiety), but under conditions that minimize reinforcement (e.g., by not showing sympathy) or maladaptive responses (e.g., avoidance, dissociation). To control the intensity of the response, exposure therapies can be applied via imagery (i.e., imagining a stressful situation), virtual reality situations (e.g., computer generated), or in vivo (i.e., real life and real time). The patient can be exposed gradually from minimal to more intense stimuli (*systematic desensitization*), which has a more positive and longer-lasting treatment outcome than a single "flooded" exposure *(immersion)*.

Interoceptive exposure refers to exercises in which patients allow themselves to experience and then observe the bodily sensations of the stress response, but under controlled conditions. The primary goal is to familiarize the patient with the normal unfolding of the stress response, to better understand, and thereby tolerate, and control their reaction to it. The patient may be instructed to hyperventilate, climb stairs, or spin on a chair to induce the feared sensations, and then notice how they dissipate homeostatically.

Imaginal exposure refers to exercises that encourage the patient to recall stressful events or conditions, thereby cognitively inducing conditioned stress response symptoms. The goal, as in all exposure exercises, is to enable the patient to better understand the stress response mechanisms that produce their symptoms and thereby increase their tolerance and control of them. Gradual and repeated exposures to these memories will eventually lead to associated reductions in the fear response when thinking about or actually participating in a stressful behavior (e.g., flying in a plane, riding a horse, speaking in public.)

In vivo exposure refers to exercises carried out in real time and real life with the same goals of assisting the patient to experience and better understand the stress response mechanism so they can increase tolerance and control. For example, a patient avoids driving their car on busy streets for fear of losing control of the vehicle. In vivo exposure exercises involve having them drive in progressively denser traffic and busier roadways. Teaching individuals to gradually approach previously avoided situations is a learning experience that provides new contextual information (i.e., the event is not as frightening as anticipated).

Bio-Behavioral Mechanisms of Exposure

There is evidence to suggest that exposure, imaginal or real, triggers the stress response, which includes the simultaneous release of **adrenocorticotropic hormone** (ACTH), which has excitatory effects, and **beta endorphin** (BE), which has analgesic and anxiolytic effects. The ACTH contributes to the *fight-or-flight* response, and, because it is antagonistic to BE, temporarily blocks BE receptors. Within minutes, however, the ACTH decays biochemically; the BE, which has a longer half-life, moves into the receptors, producing an anxiolytic effect. This mechanism appears to coincide with the patient's report of initial heightened arousal (due to the release of stress hormones including ACTH), followed, in minutes, by a reduction in anxiety (due to the continued presence of BE). Confronting the stress situation, tolerating the stress, and being rewarded by biologically mediated stress reduction (new context), reinforces coping behavior and increases a sense of self control (see Carr, 1996, in Recommended Readings).

Problem-solving therapy (PST) involves developing skills for resolving stressful situations and enhancing self-esteem. The five major steps of problem solving include (1) identifying the problem, (2) generating possible solutions, (3) choosing the most plausible solution, (4) implementing the solution, and (5) evaluating the outcome.

Using **cognitive behavioral therapy** (CBT), stress response symptoms can be conditioned to the patient's cognitions, as well as their behavior. These can be maladaptive, contributing to the disease–illness process. CBT strategies modify the patient's maladaptive beliefs by restructuring negative cognitions, teaching more effective coping skills, and educating about the nature of the stress response. This increases the patient's ability to effectively problem solve and adapt to subsequent stressors. Evidence of the effectiveness of CBT for medical and psychiatric disorders is well established. The application of *these* treatments has given rise to the fields of *health psychology* and *behavioral medicine*, and recognition of the value of combined biomedical and behavioral treatments to ensure effective intervention, follow-up, and prevention.

Mindfulness training involves teaching the individual to experience, observe, and be more attentive to their own inner processes (thoughts, feelings, and sensations). Without passing judgment, patients practice ways to accept and observe their life objectively in the moment. Such exercises have evolved out of various forms of meditative training (note the similarity in outcomes to interoceptive exposure exercises).

Motivational interviewing (MI) is a guided intervention designed to help patients resolve ambivalence about behavior change. Developed as a strategy for motivating behavioral change in problem drinkers, it is based on five psychotherapeutic principles: (1) *accurate empathy* (understanding the patient's viewpoint and communicating that to the patient); (2) *expressing respect* for and affirmation of the patient; (3) *eliciting and selectively reinforcing* the patient's problem recognition, desire to change, and self-efficacy; (4) *monitoring* the patient's resistance to change until ready to change; and (5) *affirming the patient's control* over their decisions and behavior.

Recommended Readings

Cahill, L. F. (2009). Emotional modulation of learning and memory. In G. G. Berntson & J. T. Cacioppo (Eds.), *Handbook of neurosciences for the behavioral sciences* (pp. 606–613). Hoboken, NJ: Wiley.

Carr, J. E. (1996). Neuroendocrine and behavioral interaction in exposure treatment of phobic avoidance. *Clinical Psychology Review, 16*, 1–15. http://doi.org/10.1016/0272-7358(95)00047-X

Hartley, C. A., & Phelps, E.A. (2010). Changing fear: The neurocircuitry of emotion regulation. *Neuropsychopharmacology, 35,* 136–146. http://doi.org/10.1038/npp.2009.121

Nelson, E. E., Lau, J. Y., & Jarcho, J. M. (2014). Growing pains and pleasures: How emotional learning guides development. *Trends in Cognitive Science, 18*(2), 99–108. http://doi.org/10.1016/j.tics.2013.11.003

Premack, D. (1959). Toward empirical behavior laws: I. Positive reinforcement. *Psychological Review, 66*, 219–233. http://doi.org/10.1037/h0040891

Steinmetz, J. E., & Lindquist, D. H. (2009). Neuronal basis of learning. In G. G. Bertson & J. T. Cacioppo (Eds.), *Handbook of neurosciences for the behavioral sciences*. Hoboken, NJ: Wiley.

Review Questions

1. Among the following, which brain structure assigns temporal and spatial context to incoming sensory information?
   A. Amygdala
   B. Hippocampus
   C. Limbic system
   D. Prefrontal cortex
   E. Thalamus

2. The acquisition of associations between diverse stimuli and events that vary in time and space requires conscious participation and is called
   A. critical period learning
   B. explicit learning
   C. implicit learning
   D. passive learning
   E. reflexive learning

3. The labeling of an emotion requires which of the following combinations?
   A. Cognitive interpretation, social sanction, emotional regulation
   B. Physiological arousal, situational context, cognitive interpretation
   C. Physiological arousal, situational context, emotional regulation
   D. Situational context, reinforcement, social sanction
   E. Stimulus, response, reinforcement

4. The neurotransmitter system that appears to be most involved in the reinforcement of new experiences is
   A. dopamine
   B. epinephrine
   C. glutamate
   D. norepinephrine
   E. serotonin

5. A CBT technique that includes encouraging the patient to focus upon and become familiar with the bodily sensations of the stress response under controlled conditions is
   A. imaginal exposure
   B. *in vivo* exposure
   C. interoceptive exposure
   D. virtual reality exposure
   E. all of the above

Answer Key on p. 465

10 Cognition, Communication, and Social Interaction

John E. Carr, PhD, and Ian M. Kodish, MD, PhD

- What are the components of long-term memory?
- What is cognitive style?
- What purpose does attachment serve?
- What is empathy?
- What neuronal development most likely made human speech possible?
- How do culture and cognition influence one another?

Cognition

Cognition refers to those bio-behavioral processes by which the information acquired through sensation, emotion, and learning is analyzed, distributed, and organized to engage in problem solving and social communication.

Cognitive Processes

Consciousness: State of cognitive arousal that enables awareness of self and the environment.

Alertness: Level of responsivity to the environment. Maximal alertness occurs at times of stress or challenge.

Attention: Ability to focus. Characterized by intensity, selectivity, voluntary control, and concentration.

Memory: Ability to process, retain, store, and retrieve information.

Concept formation: Ability to identify, record, and label commonalities and distinctions among stimuli.

Perception: Analyzing and interpreting incoming information.

Thinking: Applying stored concepts, schemas, and strategies to appraise something, and effectively utilize them in problem solving.

Intelligence: Ability to use information to learn and adapt to new experiences.

Language: Ability to communicate one's own meaning and comprehend the thoughts and intentions of others.

Memory

What are the components of long-term memory?

Memory refers to the ability of the brain to acquire, store, retain, and retrieve information. The brain is especially "tuned" to retain information that has adaptive value or is critical to the survival of the individual (see Chapter 3: The Nervous System, and Chapter 4: Brain Networks in Health and Illness). Research delineates three types of memory functions:

1. **Sensory memory**, the acquisition of incoming information from each of the sensory systems: This includes *evaluative memory*, which records the emotional significance of stimuli, and *procedural memory*, which includes the encoding of basic motor sequences (tying shoelaces) and, later, through maturation, the encoding of cognitive sequences (organizing a schedule). Sensory memory is prioritized to encode in short-term memory over less salient information.

2. *Short-term*, or **working memory,** serves as a temporary "inbox" for the constant influx of perceptual information necessary for day-to-day tasks such as language comprehension, learning, and problem solving. Short-term memory has three subcomponents: an attention controlling system, a visual imagery "sketch

pad" system, and a phonological system for speech-based information. As the term implies, short-term memory is continually turning over, and decays rapidly. Information in working memory is temporarily retrievable by activation in the prefrontal cortex, and then, if indicated, it is consolidated and transmitted via the amygdala, hippocampus, and prefrontal cortex to cortical areas for storage as long-term memory. *Consolidation* of long-term memory is the process required for memory to become sufficiently permanent that it cannot be erased or altered by pharmacological or electrical interventions. In humans, consolidation that is resistant to pharmacological erasure may take only a few hours. Seizures including those induced by electroconvulsive therapy (ECT) may produce temporary loss of both *anterograde* (immediately before an event) and *retrograde* (immediately after an event) memory, but memory loss is usually restricted to hours or days.

3. *Long-term memory* comprises **declarative memory**, which includes **semantic memory**, the retention and retrieval of structured information (e.g., facts, events, dates, concepts), more complex **procedural memory** (e.g., tying a shoelace, riding a bike), and contextual or **episodic memory** (the retention of sequential events and contextual details around meaningful experiences that become the basis for the concept of self).

In general, episodic memory does not develop until around age 2 years due to the delayed maturation of the hippocampus, which is essential to the processing of contextual information like personal experiences.

The bio-behavioral mechanisms of memory retrieval involve information from cortical association areas being transmitted to **prefrontal cortical areas** surrounding the hippocampus. The perirhinal cortex receives input from prefrontal cortical areas that process information about specific objects ("what" and "who"), while the parahippocampal cortex receives input from areas that process contextual or temporal and spatial information ("where" and "when"). The *perirhinal* and *parahippocampal cortices* project to the *entorhinal cortex*, which feeds the information to the hippocampus where object and context are inte-

grated. Through its circuitry and neuroplasticity properties, the hippocampus is able to represent complex sequences of events and links between them in relational networks that make inferential problem solving possible under moderately challenging conditions. However, under conditions of severe or chronic stress, the ability of the hippocampus to encode or retrieve declarative information is impaired. This impairment is largely due to the impact of excessive *glucocorticoid* release, reduced glucocorticoid receptor response, and the resulting reduction in neuronal plasticity that jeopardizes the individual's adaptive capability (see Chapter 44: Anxiety Disorders, and Chapter 46: Neurocognitive Disorders: Dementia).

Memory, Stress, and Coping

Neurogenesis, learning, and memory acquisition are promoted by moderate levels of stress but are impaired by chronic or severe stress that increases glucocorticoid and other stress hormone levels, which

- stimulate amygdala functions and
- impair hippocampus functions, which
- impair explicit learning and memory and, thereby,
- impair adaptive response to stress, which
- can result in chronic anxiety, learned helplessness, and depression.

Concept Formation

In **concept formation**, the brain identifies and records commonalties among classes of stimuli (e.g., objects, places, events), sorts them into relevant categories (*concepts*) that share the same features, and stores this information in *semantic memory*. Conceptualizations of operations (e.g., how to bake a cake, repair a motor, plan a trip) are called *schemas,* and are stored in *procedural memory*. Concepts and schemas are learned and refined as the individual attempts to continually adapt to life challenges. As new challenges are experienced, these new events are compared with the memories of past experiences through *hypothesis testing*. If the hypothesis is confirmed, it is rewarded and retained. If disconfirmed, it is not rewarded but may heighten attentional vigilance to either refine the hypothesis or extinguish it.

Intelligence

Intelligence refers to the quality and power of the individual's ability to learn from, and adapt to, new situations and is determined by both heredity and experience. It is operationally defined in terms of *verbal ability* and *spatial problem-solving skills*, but cultural definitions vary. In Western cultures, speed of processing information is valued. In other cultures, cautious introspection may be more highly valued. All cultures regard social judgment as a measure of intelligence but differ widely with regard to specific behaviors.

> It is generally agreed that there are no significant differences in intelligence across populations distinguished by race, ethnicity, or culture. Studies that claim to identify such differences have been faulted on the basis of linguistic, ethnic, and cultural bias of the measuring instruments.

Intelligence usually reflects *convergent thinking* (the individual responds with familiar solutions to a problem) and *divergent thinking* (the individual responds with alternative solutions to a problem). Divergent thinking is more creative (events are perceived in unusual ways that generate novel solutions) and reflects unique associative links in the brain applied to particular learning experiences. Sleep is also thought to facilitate this cognitive process.

Perceptual Development

Perception refers to the process of interpreting and assigning meaning to new experience based on concepts and schemas learned from past experience. As experiences accumulate, perceptions develop throughout childhood. Early learning prompts **neurogenesis** in the hippocampus and synaptogenesis in the prefrontal cortex, contributing to increases in gray matter in the frontal lobes, up to adolescence. With continuing experience and refinement, the brain begins to "prune" incorrect or maladaptive neuronal connections. Adaptive information is reinforced and supportive neuronal networks are progressively insulated within a myelin sheath. Thus, a complex integrated cognitive structure, capable of mature perception and judgment, becomes available only in late adolescence or early adulthood.

Cognitive Style

> What is cognitive style?

Cognitive style refers to the individual's unique manner in which a new experience is perceived, interpreted, and organized, ultimately producing a predictable *coping response*. One cognitive style is *locus of control* (generalized expectations that rewards are understood as being brought about through one's own efforts – internal locus of control – or instead due to factors outside one's control – external locus of control). Other cognitive styles include *learned helplessness* (self-defeating passivity), *hardiness* or *resiliency* (a sense of resolve in which stress is viewed as challenge rather than threat), *self-efficacy* (level of confidence in coping with a challenge), and *Type A personality*, characterized by excessive competitiveness, impatience, time urgency, and hostility (see Chapter 2: Predisposition).

> High levels of *external locus of control* and learned *helplessness* are characteristic of patients with chronic depression. Individuals with a *Type A personality* are at heightened risk for coronary artery disease. Low levels of *hardiness* or *resiliency* are associated with poor immune system response.

Defense Mechanisms

The concept of **defense mechanisms** is derived from *psychoanalytic theory* and refers to cognitive processes that influence the ways individuals perceive, interpret, and respond to situations that challenge cognitive, emotional, or biological homeostasis. The following is a list of the more common defense mechanisms, redefined in terms of the cognitive processes involved:

Common Defense Mechanisms

Denial: Incoming information that is threatening to one's sense of self or contradictory to stored memory is refuted.

Repression: Perceptions of events that are threatening or contradictory to past experiences may be consciously avoided or irretrievable from memory.

Intellectualization: An event or memory is reconceptualized in sufficiently abstract terms to distance it from its original meaning and associated uncomfortable emotional responses.

Projection: An idea, feeling, or behavior inconsistent with one's ideal self-concept is attributed to another person.

Regression: Using cognitive processes and coping behaviors from earlier developmental stages associated with periods of less stressful demands.

Other cognitive processes that may buffer or exacerbate stress include *cognitive distortions*. These include *catastrophizing* (magnifying consequences to disastrous proportions), *overgeneralizing* (sweeping conclusions based on a single example), *personalization* (applying general information to oneself), *mind reading* (making assumptions about others' motives without evidence), and *unsubstantiated expectations* (of others' behaviors and motives based on one's own). These are also commonly employed by patients suffering from depressive and anxiety disorders and are often identified as treatment targets using cognitive behavior therapy.

Social Processes

An especially important contribution to the successful evolution of *Homo sapiens* has been the brain's facilitation of **social processes** that make collaborative efforts for adaptation and survival possible. While many species developed social processes to facilitate reproduction, care of offspring, and limited collaboration among immediate clan or pack members, humans are capable of contributing to significantly more complex social perceptions, functions, and organizations to facilitate mutual benefits.

Attachment and Separation

> **What purpose does attachment serve?**

The earliest social relationship is the **attachment** that develops between parent and offspring. Designed to provide safety and nurturance during the offspring's most vulnerable maturational phase, the bond facilitates the development of social processes necessary for survival. Early attachment is manifested by smiling and the infant's preference for sensations associated with the primary caregiver (e.g., the mother's odor).

> The attachment bond is an adaptive social process that has evolved to provide human offspring with the degree of nurturance, safety, and social guidance required to survive, appropriate to their developmental needs.

Gradually, the child develops into an increasingly self-sufficient social being. However, during the early childhood years, any disruption in the attachment bond (separation, abandonment, abuse) can have serious *developmental* as well as *epigenetic* consequences (see Chapter 43: Depressive and Bipolar Disorders, and Chapter 44: Anxiety Disorders). Separation from familiar caregivers (usually the mother) results in the withdrawal of the infant's primary source of nutrition, body heat, sensorimotor contact, and general comfort. As a consequence, the infant experiences a traumatic emotional reaction, the *biphasic protest-despair response*, in which the child first cries out to and seeks to locate the parent (protest), followed by a period of decreased responsiveness (despair). Thus, important regulatory processes, critical to the infant's physical as well as social development, are dependent upon stable relationships with primary caregivers (see Chapter 47: Stress Disorders, Bereavement, and Dissociative Disorders).

As the child develops, caregivers form a safe base from which to explore the world. Through the attachment bond, the caregiver provides training in more complex social interactions such as *affiliation, empathy*, and *communication and language,* as well as *imitation, reciprocity*, and *play*, progressively developing the social perception and relational skills required for successful survival and social adaptation in adulthood.

Affiliation

The attachment bond is the evolutionary foundation for the development of the **affiliation** response, the tendency to share resources and receive joint protection in response to threat or other stressors. The caring for offspring and affiliating with others has been called the *tend and befriend response*, and this describes basic relational survival skills that are universal to all cultures and ethnic groups. There is evidence that the release of *oxytocin* from the hypothalamus during autonomic nervous system activation in response to social stressors is a key component of the biobehavioral mechanism of the affiliation response. The release of oxytocin appears to be facilitated by estrogens and, together with dopaminergic and opioid systems, prompts affiliative behavior in females. Androgens, such as testosterone, inhibit oxytocin release, and may contribute to reduced affiliative behaviors in males.

Social learning in childhood is largely *vicarious* or *observational*. Through *imitation* of parents, and through *reciprocity* and *play* with peers, the child acquires social and coping skills that may, or may not, be appropriate and adaptive. Social learning can be positively reinforced through attention, praise, and affection, or negatively reinforced through efforts to avoid punishment or abandonment. Since *information is reinforcing*, an important element of social learning is *evaluative feedback*, provided by parents, significant others, and the community, or by the consequences of the social activity itself. The degree of success the individual experiences not only reinforces the social behavior, but also helps to define a sense of self-efficacy and confidence in one's ability to function well in social contexts.

Empathy

What is empathy?

An evolutionary development in affiliation is **empathy**, or the ability to intuitively comprehend and share another's cognitive perceptions and emotional experiences. Empathy is a complex phenomenon that involves both cognitive and emotional components, and is not to be con-

fused with **sympathy**, which reflects an emotional response to the situation of others, without necessarily appreciating how the other perceives the situation.

> Accurate empathy requires the ability to (1) *comprehend* the perceptions and emotions of another person; (2) *communicate* that understanding to the other person, in their conceptual terms; and (3) have that understanding *confirmed* by the other person.

Helping and comforting behavior has been observed in children as young as 1 year, although it more commonly appears between the ages of 2 and 3 as children become more prosocial. The biobehavioral mechanisms contributing to empathy appear to include (1) a bottom-up processing of affective arousal involving the amygdala, hypothalamus, and orbitofrontal cortex; (2) emotional understanding and self and other awareness that involve the superior temporal and ventromedial cortices; and (3) a top-down process of emotion regulation involving the executive functions served by the network of connections within the prefrontal areas linked to the limbic system.

Recent research indicates that **mirror neurons** may play a central role in the development of empathic responses. That is, mirror neurons appear to be able to respond to the intention of the behavior observed, a defining characteristic of empathy (see Chapter 3: The Nervous System).

> Individuals with lower socioeconomic status (SES) are, on average, more empathic than individuals with higher SES. It may be that, because lower SES individuals have less influence or control over the social and economic environment in which they must function, they must constantly be sensitive to and able to read the actions and intentions of others who do have influence.

Communication and Language

Given the evolutionary trajectory of *attachment*, *affiliation*, and *empathy*, the ability *to communicate* interpersonally was a logical next step in the unfolding of social processes that facilitate mutual support, social collaboration, and survival of the species. The ability to comprehend others' cognitions and intentions, and communicate that comprehension in social interactions is critical to achieving mutually beneficial social goals. Early in the evolutionary process, prior to the development of language, communication was based largely upon *interactive behavior* – that is, gestures, or imitative and demonstrative actions and sounds that convey semantic information. Thus, from the beginning, the *ability to communicate* behaviorally preceded and was separate from the process of coding and decoding *linguistic information*. In fact, the ability to conceive and design a communicative message requires cortical systems different from those required for activating and carrying out linguistic tasks. The *intention to communicate* with another activates the medial prefrontal cortex (MPFC), left temporal-parietal junction, and portions of the temporal lobes, which together constitute the *mentalizing network*. In contrast, linguistic coding and decoding activates the left inferior frontal cortex and the left inferior parietal cortex.

> The ability of humans to communicate was advanced by an important evolutionary change in brain structure that appeared over 100,000 years ago. A mutation of the **FOXP2 gene** enabled the brain to learn, remember, and conceptualize auditory representations of experience – that is, transfer the meaning of a gesture into the meaning of an abstract sound. Since the genetic change leading to the development of spoken language is presumed to have occurred at about the same time as the "out of Africa" migration of *Homo erectus*, this suggests that the increased ability to communicate enabled proto humans to plan and coordinate group actions like migrations.

> **What neuronal development most likely made human speech possible?**

While the first human communications were behavioral responses to visual events, in time these behaviors and events became associated with unique sounds that acquired specific situational or object meanings. These associations among observed events, behaviors, and vocal expression suggest that the biological basis for language occurred with the development of complex neural networks involving connections among visual association areas, auditory association areas,

hand and arm and facial motor areas, and speech production areas. The key to this transition from gesture to speech appears to have been the advent of the **mirror neuron** system, which provided a direct visual and auditory link between sender and receiver (i.e., a neuronal "Wi-Fi system"). The gestural behavior of the sender involves motor acts or action sounds that, via the premotor cortex, initiate similar motor responses in the receiver, allowing the receiver to "understand" the sender's message. Thus, neural networks linking cognitive components of human language – for example, phonology and syntax – to the motor system, provide the foundation for linguistic communication.

Gene–Environment Interaction in Language Development

> All human languages are composed of the same basic structural elements:
>
> | | |
> |---|---|
> | Phonemes: | Basic *sound units* |
> | Morphemes: | Basic *meaning units* (the smallest number of sounds that will produce a meaning) |
> | Syntax: | Rules for combining words into phrases and sentences (*grammar*) |
> | Semantics: | *Meaning* associated with words and sentences |
> | Prosody: | *Vocal intonation* that modifies the meaning of words and sentences |

The universality of language structure suggests that language is *genetically primed* by the structure and function of the brain. Indeed, by 3 to 6 months of age, there is evidence of a biological readiness to develop language that includes an inherent mechanism for imposing structure on whatever language the child learns. Language structure is also influenced by the *ecology* in which a specific language develops, which in turn influences the speaker's perception of the environment. For example, the multiple specific words used by Alaska Natives to describe ice and snow would be incomprehensible to Bedouins in the desert. In contrast, because trade languages evolve to facilitate communication and understanding among peoples from widely varying cultures, they tend to be more general and have less ecological specificity.

While language structure has universal components, the semantic meaning inherent in language is more a function of learning, experience, culture, and interaction with the environment. As a result, the concepts, memories, and perceptions that underlie language are highly idiosyncratic in meaning, with the result that the same words or phrases may have significantly different meanings to different individuals (even those that use the same language). Thus, communication requires ongoing clarification and accommodation as each person strives to assure that what is being communicated is accurately being comprehended.

> A physician cannot assume that because a patient uses a term familiar to the physician to describe a symptom, that the patient's meaning is the same as the physician's. Failure to clarify that meaning can result in the misdiagnosis and improper treatment of the patient's disorder.

Culture–Cognition Interaction

> How do culture and cognition influence one another?

The continued evolution of social collaboration in the service of human survival inevitably led to social groupings based upon similarities in beliefs and behavioral practices. Research on **cultural mapping**, which seeks to identify the ways that cognitions and behaviors converge within groups, suggests that there are three bio-behavioral mechanisms that contribute to culturally specific cognitions and behaviors.

The first mechanism is **gene–culture interaction**. European and Japanese populations differ with regard to the nature of the 5-HTT (serotonin transporter) gene. Japanese tend to carry more short vs. long alleles of the 5-HTT gene, while Europeans tend to carry more long vs. short alleles. The difference has significant cultural implications, since individuals carrying the short allele are thought to be prone to higher levels of depression in the context of stressful life experiences as compared with carriers of the long allele.

The second mechanism is a **neuroplasticity–culture interaction**. Cultural learning in the form of bilingual education and culturally specific display rules for emotional expression show unique patterns of activation in the left inferior frontal cortex and the amygdala, respectively. Both reflect the important role of neuroplasticity in new cultural learning.

The third bio-behavioral mechanism is a **brain function–environmental structure interaction**. There is evidence of culture- and language-specific patterns of activation in response to environmental stimuli and patterns. For example, Chinese and Japanese writing require greater activation of visual areas in the brain than does Western writing.

Recommended Readings

Haas, B. W., Filkowski, M. M., Cochran, R. N., Denison, L., Ishak, A. Nishitani, S., & Smith, A. K. (2016). Epigenetic modification of OXT and human sociability. *Proceedings of the National Academy of Sciences of the United States of America U S A, 113*(27), E3816–E3823. http://doi.org/10.1073/pnas.1602809113

Kuhl, P. K. (2014). Early language learning and the social brain. *Cold Spring Harbor on Quantitative Biology, 79*, 211–220. http://doi.org/10.1101/sqb.2014.79.024802

Rizzolatti, G., & Fogassi, L. (2014). The mirror mechanism: Recent findings and perspectives. *Philosophical Transactions of the Royal Society of London, Series B, Biological Sciences, 369*(1644), 20130420. http://doi.org/10.1098/rstb.2013.0420

Tousignant, B., Eugène, F., & Jackson, P. L. (2016). A developmental perspective on the neural bases of human empathy. *Infant Behavior & Development*. Advance online publication. http://doi.org/10.1016/j.infbeh.2015.11.006

Willems, R. M., & Varley, R. (2010). Neural insights into the relation between language and communication. *Frontiers in Human Neuroscience, 4*, 1–8. http://doi.org/10.3389/fnhum.2010.00203

Review Questions

1. The retention and retrieval of abstract information involves what kind of memory?
   A. Declarative
   B. Episodic
   C. Procedural
   D. Semantic
   E. Sensory

2. People with amnesia acquire and retrieve information regarding motor and cognitive sequences but do not know they have such information, because of impaired
   A. consolidated memory
   B. declarative memory
   C. procedural memory
   D. sensory memory
   E. short-term memory

3. An idea, feeling, or behavior inconsistent with one's self-concept is attributed to another person. This defines which of the following defense mechanisms?
   A. Denial
   B. Intellectualization
   C. Projection
   D. Regression
   E. Repression

4. The earliest social relationship that develops between a parent and offspring is called
   A. affiliation
   B. attachment
   C. empathy
   D. sympathy
   E. tend and befriend response

Answer Key on p. 465

Section V
Development Through the Life Cycle

11 Selected Theories of Development

Lisa D. Herzig, MD, Emily F. Myers, MD, and Forrest C. Bennett, MD

- How does conservation relate to compensation in cognitive development?
- What are the basic concepts of psychoanalytic theory?
- How is libidinal energy expressed during psychosexual development?
- How do Erikson's "ages" compare with Freud's developmental stages?
- How do Kohlberg's moral stages relate to Piaget's cognitive stages?
- According to social learning theory, how does a person "unlearn" maladaptive behaviors?

Many theories have been proposed to explain the cognitive, social, and emotional developmental processes that transform the simple reflexive behaviors of the infant into the complex informed behaviors of the adult. In this chapter, we discuss different theorists' views of developmental processes. The list below organizes each theorist by his domain of developmental theory:

Jean Piaget:	Cognitive development
Sigmund Freud:	Psychosexual development
Erik Erikson:	Psychosocial development
Lawrence Kohlberg:	Moral and ethical development
Arnold Gesell:	Neuromotor development

Each theory uniquely contributes to our understanding of separate developmental processes. Piaget's theory of cognitive development asserts that children go through four discreet stages and play an active role in their own cognitive growth and development. Freud's theory discusses the five stages of psychosexual development, which are based on biological drives expressed within the family setting. Erikson's theory, on the other hand, proposes that biological drives are expressed and developed through society. Both Freud and Erikson postulate that impaired resolution at any stage can lead to specific maladaptive adult behaviors. Kohlberg hypothesizes that the sense of right and wrong follows an orderly and predictable sequence and can be broken down into three basic levels, each with two stages of development. Lastly, Gesell's theory of maturational development postulates that genetics primarily dictates development of the neuromotor system and that this development will occur regardless of environmental influences.

Social learning theory, as outlined by Bandura, asserts that learning and development occur through observation and imitation of social models within the environment. Lastly, we will explore the field of behavioral epigenetics and examine how nurture shapes nature.

Piaget's Theory of Cognitive Development

According to **Jean Piaget**, children are born with two cognitive functions: *organizational ability* and *adaptive ability*. Children construct their understanding of the world by organizing their experiences into *concepts*, and concepts into more complex structures called *schemas*. In effect, children are theory builders who use concepts and schemas to make sense of the environment, employing two strategies: *assimilation* and *accommodation*.

In **assimilation**, experiences are interpreted and acted upon within the framework of an existing cognitive schema: "all objects that can be fitted into the mouth provide nutrition." In **accommodation**, schemas are altered to fit disconfirming experiences that cause disequilibrium between cognitive understanding and external reality: "a thumb [put] into the mouth does not, in fact, provide food." As development progresses, schemas are modified further to fit ongoing experiences with reality. An integral part of Piaget's theory is that children play an active role in their own growth and development.

Four Major Stages of Cognitive Development

In Piaget's theory there are four major stages of cognitive development (see Table 11.1).

Sensorimotor Stage (Birth to 2 Years)
During the first year of life, cognitive schemas progress from performing inborn reflexive activity, to repeating interesting acts, and finally to combining acts to solve simple problems. The concept of *object permanence* is established during this stage. That is, the infant learns that objects that

have moved out of sight or been concealed continue to exist and can be searched for and found.

> How does conservation relate to compensation in cognitive development?

Preoperational Stage (2 to 7 Years)
During this stage, children learn to use language and other symbols. Problem solving is intuitive rather than logical or rational, and analytic thinking is poorly developed. For example, intuitive reasoning, common in children this age, is illustrated by a child's failure to appreciate the law of **conservation** (recognition that a given property of a substance remains the same despite irrelevant changes such as physical rearrangement). This is illustrated in Piaget's classical conservation experiment in which children in the preoperational stage were not able to appreciate that two identical portions of liquid, transferred from identical containers to two differently shaped containers (one taller and thinner than the other), are still equal in volume although unequal in height.

Piaget suggests that the inability to conserve is due to the preoperational child's inability to carry out a cognitive function called **compensation** (considering multiple dimensions of a problem simulta-

Table 11.1. Piaget: stages of cognitive development		
Age (approx. years)	**Stage**	**Distinguishing Characteristics**
0–2	Sensorimotor	*Preverbal* Development of object permanence and rudimentary thought Reflexive activity leading to purposeful activity
2–7	Preoperational	*Prelogical* Development of semiotic functioning (use of symbols, representational language) Inability to deal with several aspects of a problem simultaneously
7–12	Concrete operational	*Logical* Problem solving initially restricted to physically present objects/imagery Development of logical operations (e.g., classification, conservation)
12+	Formal operational	*Abstract* Comprehension of purely abstract or symbolic content Development of advanced logical operations (e.g., complex analogy, deduction)

neously and appreciating the interaction between them). In the case presented, the child is unable to consider both height and width simultaneously.

Concrete Operational Stage (7 to 12 Years)

In this stage, the child is able to conceptualize the world from an external point of view; thinking becomes dynamic, decentralized, reversible, and relational. Relational thinking is characterized by **transitivity** (mental arrangement of dimensions of objects) and **seriation** (appreciation of relationships among objects in a serial order). During the early concrete operational stage, children can only solve a problem if the elements of the problem are physically present (*concrete*); often they must actually manipulate the elements for full understanding. Later in this stage, they can solve problems of time and space; *conserve* substance, quantity, weight, and volume; and *classify* objects into hierarchical systems based on past experiences with similar issues or objects, often without any actual experience with the specific issues or objects being considered.

Formal Operational Stage (12 Years through Adulthood)

Formal operational thinking is characterized by the ability to use *abstraction*. Both tangible and intangible problems can be solved through flexible, complex reasoning and **hypothesis formation**. Being able to conceive an ideal situation forms a backdrop for evaluating specific life circumstances and participating in social action and civil disobedience.

Piagetian Stages and Health-Related Behaviors

Piaget's cognitive developmental stages clarify how children and adolescents view illness causation and death. *Stress* can impair an individual's ability to use higher order cognitive skills and regressed cognition is common. *Magical thinking* (my wish equals action) or *egocentrism* (my action caused some externally determined and unrelated event), which are common among preschoolers, can occur even in adults who are in crisis. The inability to think futuristically, characteristic of children's thinking prior to late adolescence, hinders their ability to understand the long-term consequences of current actions (e.g., lung cancer as a result of smoking; becoming a parent as a result of sexual intercourse without contraception).

Freud's Theory of Psychosexual Development

What are the basic concepts of psychoanalytic theory?

The major concepts of psychoanalytic theory are:
1. Behavior is motivated by unconscious biological urges, instincts, or drives.
2. Behavior is influenced by unconscious memories that are kept from awareness by defense mechanisms.
3. Psychic energy is channeled through three parts of the personality: id, ego, and superego.

The **id** is the original reservoir for all psychic energy. It expresses drives and impulses based on biological needs, such as food, sleep, and procreation. The **ego** serves as the id's intermediary with the external world. It operates on the reality principle and energizes learning and logical thinking. The **superego**, or conscience, assures that the ego's actions are socially and morally correct.

Five Stages of Psychosexual Development

How is libidinal energy expressed during psychosexual development?

Sigmund Freud proposed five stages of psychosexual development. These stages reflect the developmental sequence of body areas invested with *libidinal energy* (sexual or life force). *Fixation*, or impaired resolution of certain psychological conflicts that arise at the oral, anal, and phallic stages, is presumed to result in specific adult behaviors.

Oral Stage (Birth to 1 Year)

Libidinal energy is concentrated in the mouth, lips, and tongue. It serves the basic need of the infant to take nutrition. Fixation in the oral stage may manifest itself in adults as excessive smoking, eating, or craving for social contact.

Anal Stage (1 to 3 Years)

Libidinal energy is invested in the anal sphincter and bladder. Toilet training demands that urges be inhibited or delayed. Fixation in the anal stage may show itself as excessive orderliness or obstinate, retentive behaviors.

Phallic Stage (3 to 6 Years)

Children become aware of male–female differences and derive pleasure from self-stimulation or masturbation. They develop sexual longing for the parent of the opposite gender and jealousy toward the parent of the same gender (*Oedipal conflict*). Fixation in the phallic stage may manifest as difficulties with sexual relationships.

Latency Stage (6 Years to Puberty)

During this period, sexual strivings are largely suppressed by the superego. Libidinal energy is channeled into socially acceptable behaviors, such as study or sports.

Genital Stage (Puberty to Adulthood)

The onset of this stage coincides with physiological maturation and reinvestment of libidinal energy in the sex organs. The underlying goal is reproduction through a sexual relationship.

Erikson's Theory of Psychosocial Development

Erik Erikson agreed with Freud that people are born with biological drives, but he focused on *society* rather than the family as the setting in which these drives are expressed. Erikson is considered an *ego psychologist* because he emphasized visible, rational, and adaptive aspects of personality.

Erikson's emphasis on relevant, adaptive behavior and the integration of social and cultural factors into classical psychoanalytic theory highlights the interplay between internal and external reality. Psychotherapy based on Erikson's theory is directed at working through unresolved conflicts, starting at the stage where the person is *developmentally arrested*. Erikson's psychosocial theory was among the first to formulate personality development as a lifelong, sequential process.

Eight "Ages" of Psychosocial Development

> How do Erikson's "ages" compare with Freud's developmental stages?

For each of his eight developmental stages or *ages of man*, Erikson defined the major psychosocial conflict and its possible resolutions in active, behavioral terms.

Basic Trust Versus Basic Mistrust (Birth to 1 Year)

This age corresponds to the Freudian oral stage. The task is to learn to trust a caregiver. If care is not given or only inconsistently given, infants come to see human relationships as too disappointing or dangerous to rely on.

Autonomy Versus Shame and Doubt (1 to 3 Years)

This age corresponds to the Freudian anal stage. The challenge is to become independent in rudimentary aspects of living: feeding, making choices, keeping, and letting go. Failure to pass through this stage successfully will lead to self-doubt.

Initiative Versus Guilt (3 to 6 Years)

This age corresponds to the Freudian phallic stage. The need to have mastery over the environment can lead to conflicts with others (e.g., parents) producing guilt. The child must learn to set internal limits and to achieve balance between their own and another's desires.

Industry Versus Inferiority (6 to 12 Years)

This age corresponds to the Freudian latency stage. Primary challenges are learning to meet school and social demands and acquiring academic and athletic skills. Output is measured and graded, and competition with peers increases. Failure leads to feelings of inequality, inferiority, and worthlessness.

Identity Versus Role Confusion (12 to 20 Years)

This age corresponds to the beginning of the Freudian genital stage and marks the transition from childhood to young adulthood. Experiences with role models outside the family (e.g., teachers) broaden the individual's value system. The primary challenge is to establish a sense of self as a physical, sexual, and vocational being. Failure leads to indecision, vacillation, and a sense of purposelessness.

Intimacy Versus Isolation (20 to 40 Years)

In this age, the individual moves from a self-centered focus to affiliation and partnership with others. Love and companionship transcend interpersonal boundaries and permit commitment to another. Lack of friendships and intimate relationships lead to loneliness, emptiness, and isolation.

Generativity Versus Stagnation (40 to 65 Years)

During this age, individuals become teachers of the next generation. They repay society for having nurtured them by sharing their work and creativity and assisting younger people. They develop a sense of responsibility for society. Failure leads to stagnation and boredom.

Ego Integrity Versus Despair (65 Years to Death)

This age involves the acceptance of one's life, with its successes and failures. Reflection leads to an integration of experiences and sense of order and meaning. Without self-acceptance, a person experiences cynicism and hopelessness.

Kohlberg's Theory of Moral Development

> How do Kohlberg's moral stages relate to Piaget's cognitive stages?

Stages of moral development: The development of *morality* (i.e., the sense of right and wrong) has been postulated to follow an orderly sequence. **Lawrence Kohlberg** proposed three basic levels of morality encompassing six stages of development (see Table 11.2).

Preconventional morality

This stage is characteristic of children in Piaget's sensorimotor and preoperational stages of cognitive development. Judgments about right and wrong are based on external consequences (rewards and punishments) and external higher authority (parent). Personal benefit is a highly motivating factor.

Conventional Morality

Conventional morality is characteristic of children in Piaget's concrete operational stage of cognitive functioning. Moral judgments are based on fulfilling the expectations of others and following the rules. Thus, an action is morally good if others say it is, and maintaining law and order is essential. In decision making, intent is emerging as a more important factor than outcome.

Postconventional Morality

This stage is characteristic of individuals who are in Piaget's formal operational stage of cognitive functioning. Judgments are based on personal adherence to principles that are perceived as valid by the individual, apart from any external author-

Table 11.2. Kolberg: development of moral judgment

Age (years)	Level	Basis of Moral Judgment	Developmental Stage	Characteristics
0–6	I. Preconventional (premoral)	Consequences (reward or punishment)	1. Punishment-obedience	Egocentric, no moral concepts
			2. Instrumental-relativistic	Satisfaction of own needs
6–12	II. Conventional (moral)	Good and right roles	3. "Good Boy" – "Nice Girl"	Desire to please others
		Principles, rights, values	4. "Law and Order"	Obligation to duty Respect of authority
12+	III. Postconventional (principled)	Individual beliefs	5. Social contract-legalistic	Relativism of personal values and opinions
			6. Universal-ethical-principled	Conscience dictates action in accord with self-chosen principles

ity or convention. Laws are judged with regard to their conformity with obligations and contracts, and their congruence with basic standards of human rights. Under certain circumstances it may be morally right to disobey a law in the service of broader social principles (*civil disobedience*). Self-chosen *ethical principles* of justice, reciprocity, respect, and equality inform morality. The moral person who has attained this stage of development can transcend his own person and see issues and dilemmas from the perspective of all others involved. This blend of regard for universal justice and compassion and respect for all individuals is considered to lead to optimal moral decision making. Other research in moral development has focused less on rules and punishment and more on children's increasingly complex awareness of their own and other's emotional needs and responses (see Chapter 14: The School Years).

Gesell's Maturational Theory of Development

Contrasting with both Freud's and Erikson's interactional theories of human development, the *maturational theory* of **Arnold Gesell** postulates that human development progresses in a regimented and mostly predetermined biological manner. Gesell's biological theory states that cognitive development and motor development occur in parallel and in regular sequence according to a *genetic blueprint* through a process called *maturation.* According to Gesell, teaching or outside environmental influences cannot override the natural biological progression of human development; children develop when they are ready. Innate neurophysiological differences underlie human diversity and brain-based neurological processes control the sequence and timing.

As a result of his research, Gesell identified many of the developmental milestones seen in the early years of life, and described their progression throughout childhood. These milestones are still used regularly today to assess development.

Social Learning Theory

> According to social learning theory, how does a person "unlearn" maladaptive behaviors?

In contrast to Gesell's maturational theory, social learning theory postulates that the broad constellation of behaviors that constitute "personality" is the result of the individual's social learning history. Learning occurs through *observation* and *imitation* of the behavior of others (see Chapter 10: Cognition, Communication, and Social Interaction). Learning is a cognitive activity during which internal representations of modeled behavior are constructed. Subsequently, these representations are used to *imitate* (reproduce behaviorally what was observed). Behaviors that are *reinforced* (praised, rewarded, gain attention) are repeated. Both adaptive and maladaptive behaviors are acquired or extinguished through social learning.

Extinction of maladaptive behaviors requires the elimination of the reinforcers of those behaviors by pairing those behaviors with noxious consequences; then, by imitating others, the person learns more adaptive responses. Thus, observing adaptive role models can modify nonfunctional behavior patterns.

In social learning theory, development is the result of an ongoing *interaction between the individual and the environment.* Although genetic and biological factors influence individual predispositions early in life, developmental changes are increasingly influenced by social factors as the individual matures. Critics of social learning theory argue that this view of development is too simplistic and that it deemphasizes biological influences on behavior. Proponents counter that this view of behavior reflects the increasing influence of social factors with age and provides a theoretical framework for society-based clinical interventions.

Current Considerations: Behavioral Epigenetics

Behavioral epigenetics is the study of alteration in gene activity not caused by changes in the

DNA sequence, but rather the environmental and other nongenetic events that can influence genetic expression of behavioral, cognitive, mental health, and personality traits. The first documented example of this occurred in 2004 when scientists discovered that the type and amount of nurturing provided by a mother rat will change how the baby rat responds to stress later in life. Stress sensitivity in rat pups was eventually linked to down-regulation in the expression of the glucocorticoid receptor in the brain, meaning that rats who received less nurturing were more prone to stress throughout their lifespan. Interestingly, it is thought that these changes in gene expression can be passed down to subsequent generations (see Chapter 2: Predisposition).

Further research is needed to connect early human life experience to behavior or health problems later in life. Obtaining such scientific evidence has proved to be difficult given the ethical and moral dilemmas that would arise, as well as the complexity involved in objectively characterizing adverse events. Despite these challenges, behavioral epigenetics is contributing to our understanding of the mechanisms linking human genetics to environmental and other nongenetic events. In fact, in 2011, the Board of Directors of the American Academy of Pediatrics (AAP) added epigenetics as a priority initiative to the AAP's Agenda for Children.

Recommended Readings

Bandura, A. (1977). *Social learning theory*. Englewood Cliffs, NJ: Prentice-Hall.

Crain, W. (2000). *Theories of development: Concepts and applications* (4th ed.). Upper Saddle River, NJ: Prentice Hall.

Erikson, E. (1963). *Childhood and society* (2nd ed.). New York, NY: Norton.

Freud, S. (1937). *New introductory lectures in psychoanalysis* (2nd ed.). London, UK: Hogarth Press.

Kohlberg, L. (1980). *The meaning and measurement of moral development*. Worcester, MA: Clark University Press.

Piaget, J., & Inhelder, B. (1969). *The psychology of the child*. New York, NY: Basic Books.

Sahler, O. J. Z., & Wood, B. L. (2001). Theories and concepts of development as they relate to pediatric practice.
In R. A. Hoekelman, H. M. Adam, N. M. Nelson, M. L. Weitzman, & N. H. Wilson (Eds.), *Primary pediatric care* (4th ed., pp. 637–654). St. Louis, MO: Mosby.

Wright, R., & Saul, R. A. (2013). Epigenetics and primary care. *Pediatrics, 132*(Suppl. 3), S216–S223. http://doi.org/10.1542/peds.2013-1032F

Review Questions

Directions: The items below consist of lettered headings followed by numbered descriptions. For each numbered description choose the one lettered heading to which it is *most* closely associated. Each lettered heading may be used *once, more than once,* or *not at all.*

Match the Piagetian concept with its definition.
   A. Accommodation
   B. Assimilation
   C. Concrete operational thinking
   D. Conservation
   E. Magical thinking

1. Understanding that a given property of a substance remains the same despite irrelevant changes.
2. An object must be physically present for understanding or problem solving.
3. Schemas are altered based on experience
4. My wish equals action.

Match the Eriksonian age with the descriptor that fits it best.
   A. Ego integrity vs. despair
   B. Generativity vs. stagnation
   C. Industry vs. inferiority
   D. Initiative vs. guilt
   E. Trust vs. mistrust

5. The age of learning that others are consistent and reliable.
6. The age of reflection about one's successes and failures in life.
7. The age most closely aligned with Freud's oral stage.
8. The age of the elementary school child.

Match the Kohlberg stage of moral development
with the moral action.
  A. Good boy – nice girl
  B. Instrumental – relativistic
  C. Law and order
  D. Punishment – obedience
  E. Universal – ethical – principled

 9. A 5-year-old puts the cookie back in the jar
    when he hears his mother coming
10. A 3rd grader does homework to comply with
    household rules
11. A college student marches against ethnic dis-
    crimination

Answer Key on p. 465

12 The Fetus, Newborn, and Infant

Emily F. Myers, MD, Lisa D. Herzig, MD, and Forrest C. Bennett, MD

- What effects do maternal health and environment have on the developing fetus?
- What does the Apgar score assess?
- How do growth parameters change during infancy?
- What changes in motor skill and response to stimuli occur during infancy?
- What is object permanence?
- What is attachment?

Throughout the entire life cycle, there are both critical (biologically dependent) and sensitive (environmentally dependent) periods of development; most of these occur during childhood and adolescence. Careful attention to these periods is necessary to promote healthy development. Biological (genetic and health) and environmental (family and culture) dependent processes influence not only when but also which behaviors and skills are learned. Further, disruption of these periods in development can have influences across generations, constituting a transgenerational as well as biopsychosocial model of health.

The Fetus

Prenatal Growth and Development

Fetal growth is strongly influenced by biological (maternal health, family history, and ethnicity), and environmental health factors. Generally, the mature human fetus is delivered at 38 to 42 weeks after conception, and is called a **full-term infant**. Full-term infants have a mean birthweight of 7 lb 11 oz (3,500 g). Other growth parameters that are measured at birth include head circumference and total body length, with means of 14 in. (35 cm) and 19.5 in. (50 cm), respectively.

Alterations in growth during fetal life can have significant effects on an infant's future developmental capacity. Weight is one such growth factor. **Low birthweight** refers to infants weighing less than 5 lb 8 oz (< 2,500 g); **very low birthweight** refers to weight less than 3 lb 5 oz (< 1,500 g); and **extremely low birthweight** is defined as being born weighing less than 2 lb 3 oz (< 1,000 g).

Adequate weight gain during the fetal period is vital for long-term neurodevelopment. Infants who are growing too little or too much for their gestational age are at increased risk of having negative developmental and medical consequences.

Head size can be too large (**macrocephaly**) or too small (**microcephaly**). Macrocephaly is head size greater than two standard deviations above the mean, or greater than 14.5 in. (> 37 cm) for a term newborn. Microcephaly is less than 13 in. (< 33 cm) for a term newborn. Head size greater than two standard deviations above or below is associated with increased risk of negative developmental consequences.

Genetic/Chromosomal Influences

Genetic influences in brain development are considered critical periods of development in the neonate and young child. Genetic or chromosomal differences result in alterations in the central nervous system (CNS) and other organ development, and account for more chronic childhood disability than all of the acquired brain insults combined. While Down syndrome (trisomy 21) is the best known and most common chromosomal syndrome, trisomy 13 and trisomy 18 are also well known, and are associated with more severe disability. New and evolving techniques for examining the human genome, including microarray and exome sequencing, are revealing novel chromosomal rearrangements and genetic mutations that affect growth and development in a multitude of ways. Maternal infection, such as that caused by the Zika virus, which has been associated with microcephaly, can disrupt genetic processes governing the formation of the nervous system.

Maternal-Fetal Health

Maternal Health Problems

What effects do maternal health and environment have on the developing fetus?

Certain maternal medical conditions may have significant effects on neonatal development and beyond. For example, *maternal diabetes mellitus* (particularly insulin-dependent disease) increases the likelihood of major congenital malformations (e.g., spina bifida, congenital heart disease, cleft lip and/or palate), and impaired neurodevelopmental performance (e.g., poorer physiological control and interactive capacities, immature motor processes, reduced cognition). This is of particular concern because of the increasing incidence of obesity in the US, leading to rising rates of gestational diabetes. *Persistent maternal hypertension* can produce uteroplacental insufficiency, leading to intrauterine growth retardation and asphyxia, often resulting in premature birth or neurodevelopmental impairment.

Intrauterine Exposures

Maternal use of *prescribed medications*, such as anticonvulsants used to treat seizures (e.g., val-

proic acid, carbamazepine, hydantoins) have been linked to physical birth defects, malformation syndromes, and long-term neurodevelopmental abnormalities. Other commonly used medications for a variety of different medical problems can cause birth defects as well. Examples include retinoic acid, methotrexate, and lithium, used to treat acne, cancer, and bipolar disorder, respectively.

Several *recreational drugs* can have a variety of both physical and developmental effects on the fetus. Fetal alcohol spectrum disorder (FASD) is the most common preventable nongenetic cause of intellectual disability. Approximately 4 million infants born each year were exposed to alcohol during gestation. The diagnosis is made through the identification of facial features, growth retardation, and CNS anomalies. FASD is one diagnosis among a range of disorders associated with fetal alcohol exposure, which affect all aspects of development and behavior, causing language delays, attention-deficit disorder, and learning disabilities.

Maternal *tobacco consumption* can result in fetal growth retardation from decreased uterine blood flow during pregnancy; birthweight decreases in a dose-response manner to tobacco exposure. Fetal brain growth has been shown to be adversely affected by heavy maternal smoking with suboptimal language, social, and cognitive outcomes.

Certain *recreational substances* including cocaine, methamphetamines, and marijuana produce varying combinations of neonatal symptomatology and long-term developmental-behavioral dysfunction. Opiates such as *heroin* can cause neonatal addiction as well as withdrawal (*neonatal abstinence syndrome*) after the infant is born. Maternal use of cocaine may affect placental blood flow but usually does not produce an acute withdrawal syndrome in the newborn. However, the children of cocaine-abusing mothers do frequently suffer from neurobehavioral problems as well as academic and social difficulties that have been linked to low birthweight, interruptions in maternal care, and low socioeconomic status.

Maternal-Fetal Infections

Maternal-fetal infections during pregnancy can have significant effects on the neurodevelopmental outcome of an infant. Although there are many infections that significantly affect the fetus, cytomegalovirus, herpes simplex virus, and human immunodeficiency virus (HIV) are among the most common and best studied. *Cytomegalovirus* (CMV) affects approximately 30,000 to 40,000 infants in the US each year. Up to 20% of congenitally infected neonates are left with adverse outcomes including severe sensorineural hearing loss, visual deficits, hydrocephalus, cerebral palsy, and cognitive disabilities.

Neonatal herpes simplex virus is an infection that can be passed to the neonate traveling through the birth canal at delivery. Its incidence is 1 in 3,500 births. Organ systems commonly involved in infected neonates include the CNS, skin, liver, and lung. Infants can have seizures, microcephaly, brain atrophy, and visual deficits.

Maternal human immunodeficiency virus infection can be transmitted to the fetus either through the placenta, during birth, or through breastfeeding, especially if the mother is not being treated with antiretrovirals. However, advice to infected mothers about breastfeeding is a matter of debate, and the risk must be weighed against the benefits of breastfeeding. If the mother is untreated during pregnancy, 25% of infants develop an infectious or neurological complication within the first year of life. The virus itself can enter the nervous system causing progressive motor impairment, loss of developmental milestones, and poor brain growth. Congenital HIV can lead to early infant death. Fortunately, in the US and increasingly elsewhere, vigorous drug treatment during pregnancy has reduced the congenital infection rate to approximately 1%.

Congenital Birth Defects

There are several known developmental defects which occur prenatally that significantly affect long term childhood outcomes. These include CNS malformations (e.g., neural tube defects and neuronal migration abnormalities), and congenital heart disease (e.g., single ventricle physiology and endocardial cushion defects).

The Newborn

Prematurity

Preterm birth, or birth at < 37 weeks of gestation, is a major cause of neurodevelopmental complications. About 12% of births in the US are preterm, and account for 64% to 75% of infant deaths. The incidence of preterm births is rising, as is the survival rate. Survival at 23- to 25-week gestational age is becoming more common (approximately 50% at 24 weeks).

The complications associated with preterm birth are caused by the immaturity of fetal organ systems, delivery complications, and medical interventions that are required to sustain life. *Fetal hypoxia, ischemia, intracranial hemorrhage, hydrocephalus, hypoglycemia,* and *infection* are all risks for neurodevelopmental and behavioral disorders, and are common in infants born prematurely.

Major adverse outcomes associated with prematurity include cerebral palsy, intellectual disability, and hearing and visual impairments. *Minor adverse outcomes* include mild gross motor impairments and coordination problems, difficulties with fine motor tasks, attention-deficit/hyperactivity disorder, executive dysfunction, language delays, learning disabilities, and behavior problems.

Birth Complications

Fetal distress from intrapartum asphyxia can result from uteroplacental insufficiency, umbilical cord compression, or placental abruption. The *asphyxia syndrome* includes components of hypoxia, ischemia, hypotension, and impaired perfusion of multiple organs, particularly the brain. If brain damage occurs before the infant is delivered and adequately resuscitated, any of a wide range of neurodevelopmental disabilities such as cerebral palsy, intellectual disability, seizures, and learning and behavior problems can occur.

Birth trauma can adversely affect the development of the infant. Malpresentation (e.g., breech, transverse lie), an exceptionally large fetus, or a delivery requiring instrumentation with forceps or vacuum extraction can lead to intracranial contusions or hemorrhages, fractures, spinal cord injuries, and other nerve damage.

Jaundice, or *hyperbilirubinemia*, is a common newborn condition, and if severe, it can lead to significant adverse developmental outcomes. Jaundice, the yellow discoloration in the skin of neonates, is caused by a buildup of bilirubin, which can be deposited not only in the skin but also in other organs, including the brain. It can be treated effectively in most cases with phototherapy. However, if inadequately treated and the bilirubin reaches critical levels, a neurological condition known as kernicterus can occur. *Kernicterus* (bilirubin encephalopathy) affects areas of the brain responsible for balance, motor coordination, and hearing (basal ganglia and brainstem). This damage is permanent and can lead to severe motor and sensory disabilities.

Developmental Assessment of the Newborn

What does the Apgar score assess?

The **Apgar score** is a numerical rating of the adequacy of the neurophysiological transition to extrauterine life in the newborn infant and is the standard method of postdelivery assessment. Its principal utility is assessment of current status, and it serves as an indicator of the potential need for neonatal resuscitation. The score is assigned and recorded at 1 and 5 min of life, but can be extended to 10, 15 and 20 min. Scores of 7 to 10 indicate no CNS depression; 4 to 6 indicate some depression; and 0 to 3 indicate severe depression that requires resuscitation. These early scores, particularly if very low, may presage long-term neurodevelopmental abnormalities.

Another neonatal assessment tool is the **Ballard neonatal examination,** which is used to estimate gestational age and determine the adequacy of intrauterine growth. This examination is particularly useful when the length of the pregnancy is uncertain and can be used in conjunction with birthweight in anticipating potential problems.

The **Brazelton Neonatal Behavioral Assessment Scale** provides a neurobehavioral assessment of such characteristics as visual attention, alertness, auditory responsivity, and habituation. The scale can be administered serially to provide an objective measure of change over time. Although these scores do not necessarily have predictive value for future developmental capabilities, they can be used to promote more sensitive interactions between at-risk newborns and mothers.

The Infant (Birth to 12 Months)

How do growth parameters change during infancy?

Infancy is marked by rapid growth and development. Whereas the average newborn infant weighs 7 lb 11 oz (3.5 kg) and spends virtually the entire day sleeping, crying, eating, and eliminating waste, the average 12-month-old infant weighs approximately 22 lb (10 kg), has a distinct personality, can crawl or walk, feeds themselves, and communicates with gestures and a few words. As with the fetus, infant development is punctuated by both critical and sensitive developmental processes. Biological factors that directly affect infant development include genetic makeup, temperament, and state of health. The most significant environmental factors affecting infants are parents, extended family, and the skills, attitudes, culture, and socioeconomic status of the family.

Infant Physical Growth

Birthweight is doubled by 4 to 5 months of age and tripled by 12 months. Length increases by 50% in the first year of life. Head growth is very rapid early on, increasing by approximately 2.4 in. (6 cm) during the first 3 months and an additional 2.4 in. (6 cm) over the next 9 months. The volume of the infant's brain at birth is about 25% of adult volume; by 12 months, it is more than 50% of adult volume. Physiological changes that occur during infancy include improvement in respiratory pattern, coordination of sucking and swallowing, and temperature control. Changes in respiratory pattern include a gradual decline in respiratory rate from 30 to 50 breaths per minute at birth to 25 to 35 breaths per minute at 12 months. By 12 months of age, the infant has progressed from taking only liquid food to being able to personally put solid food into their mouth and then chew and swallow without difficulty. Temperature regulation is established during the first few days of life, making the infant capable of maintaining a core temperature of 37 °C under normal ambient conditions.

Motor Development

> **What changes in motor skill and response to stimuli occur during infancy?**

Development of the infant's motor capabilities facilitates learning about the social and inanimate world. During the first year, infant movement progresses in an orderly cephalocaudal sequence from a mainly supine or prone position to sitting, crawling, and even walking independently. To create volitional movement, primitive reflexes gradually recede during the first few months of life and are replaced by planned *gross motor movements* such as rolling over (4 to 5 months), sitting independently (8 to 9 months), and walking (10 to 15 months). Wide variation exists in the exact timing of gross motor milestones; however, the sequence of the developing motor milestones remains predictable.

Fine motor movements progress in a stepwise proximal-distal fashion, as the sensory system becomes more refined. Grasping and reaching for objects emerges and solidifies between 3 to 6 months of age. By 9 months of age, infants can orient their hands to pick up an object. A pincer grasp (securing an object between thumb and forefinger) is mastered by approximately 10 to 11 months. Less variability is seen in the normal acquisition of fine motor milestones than of gross motor milestones.

Language Development

At birth, although infants do not have the motor control to form words, they *communicate* through other sensory modalities (e.g., gestures, cry, gaze). Infants acquire **language** through reciprocal interactions with caregivers and others. With early vocalizations and nonverbal cues, caregivers and infants learn to respond to one another or to take turns communicating. By 1 month of age,

an infant has developed a range of cries to signify different needs that parents can recognize. At 4 to 6 months of age, infants can produce consonant sounds; by 10 to 12 months of age, they can speak their first words.

Cognitive Development

> **What is object permanence?**

An infant's developing sensory systems (tactile, visual, and auditory) have vital roles that allow observation and interaction with the social and inanimate environment. By 1 month of age, infants are able to visually track an object to midline, and by 2 months, can track an object past midline. At 3 to 6 months of age, an infant is able to coordinate extraocular muscles, permitting binocular vision; at 6 to 8 months, there is evidence of depth perception. Infants just after birth will be alert to sounds, and by 3 months, can turn to a sound. At 4 months of age, an infant not only turns to sound but can look toward the origin of the sound as well. The ability to localize sound approaches that of an adult by 12 months.

Early cognitive development is characterized by sensory-motor exploratory behaviors and interactions with the environment. During the first several months, major change occurs as the infant's behaviors develop from reflexive responses to learned intentional activities such as reaching.

One of the core milestones of infant cognition is **object permanence**, which is the concept of knowing that an object exists even if it is not in the field of vision. During the first month of life, images cease to exist when they are no longer perceived. By 7 to 9 months of age, the infant learns that objects exist even when they are not visible, and will search for objects that are not in view.

Social-Emotional Development

> **What is attachment?**

Bonding and **attachment** describe the affectional relationships that develop between primary caregivers (usually parents) and infants. Bonding begins before and immediately after birth and reflects the feeling of the parents toward the newborn. Attachment refers to the reciprocal feelings between parent and infant that gradually develops over the first years. Thus, the infant is an active participant in the development of attachment (see Chapter 10: Cognition, Communication, and Social Interaction).

By 10 days of age, infants can distinguish the smell of their own mother's breast milk from that of other women. At about 5 to 6 weeks of life, the infant becomes able to recognize individuals and smiles responsively. By 3 to 5 months of life, the infant will show preference for a primary caregiver by smiling and vocalizing. Parents respond to the infant's "social smile" with mutual gaze, friendly facial expressions, "parentese" (high-pitched, vowel-rich verbal messages), and touching. The infant follows the parents intently, first with the eyes and later by crawling after them. Although the mother is usually the primary attachment figure if she is the person most constantly present, infants will form an attachment to whoever is consistently responsive to them. Most infants form multiple attachments, which helps protect them in the event of an absence or loss of their primary caregiver.

Separation anxiety becomes apparent at 6 to 9 months. The infant begins to understand simple cause-and-effect relationships and anticipates separations (e.g., seeing mother putting on her coat). When the mother actually leaves the infant's presence, the infant will cry and actively look for her. This behavior persists to about 2.5 to 3 years of age, when, through experience, the child learns the mother will return and no longer fears her going. However, if the primary caregiver(s) never leave the infant with others (to "practice" going and then returning), the child may have difficulty passing through this stage, particularly if they have a shy, fearful, or anxious temperament.

Stranger anxiety develops at about 8 to 9 months of life when the infant becomes fretful at the sight of a stranger and seeks parental comfort and reassurance. Such behaviors reinforce the parent's protectiveness in response to the infant's signaling of potential danger. Stranger anxiety often peaks again at 12 to 15 months, and then diminishes.

Temperament refers to the patterns of personal attributes and behavioral tendencies of a person. It has a distinct role in social-emotional development and has been classically categorized as "difficult," "slow-to-warm-up," and "easy." *Difficult infants* are described as having traits such as largely negative mood, high intensity, and poor adaptability. The *slow-to-warm-up infant* can have a negative mood initially, but gradually becomes more positive as the encounter evolves. An *easy infant* has a positive mood and adapts well to change. The behavioral makeup of a given individual can include traits from all temperament categories. Temperament can have a significant effect on bonding, attachment, and, in fact, all interactions between infants and caregivers. As a precursor to personality, temperament persists, in modified form, into adulthood.

Bonding, attachment, stranger anxiety, and separation anxiety are tasks that are typically mastered by the end of infancy. Mastery is dependent on an infant's recognition that its caregivers are responsive to their physical and emotional needs. Further, a knowledge that individuals who are not caregivers do exist and should be regarded with caution is vital not only for an infant's social-emotional development but also for survival.

Developmental Surveillance and Screening

Early assessment for atypical or delayed development is a critical component of health care for all fetuses and infants. Growth and development of the fetus is measured through prenatal ultrasound and maternal growth during pregnancy, and growth and development of the infant is measured at regular intervals after birth. Well child checks with developmental surveillance are performed at 2, 4, 6, 9, and 12 months of age, and the American Academy of Pediatrics recommends a formal developmental screen for every infant at 9 months of age. Identification and treatment of developmental concerns is critical to optimize health outcomes in the pediatric population.

Recommended Readings

Bennett, F. C. (2005). Developmental Outcome. In M. G. MacDonald, M. D. Mullett, & M. M. K. Seisha (Eds.), *Avery's neonatology: Pathology and management of the newborn* (6th ed.). Philadelphia, PA: Lippincott, Williams & Wilkins.

Committee on Practice and Ambulatory Medicine. (2016). 2016 Recommendations for preventive pediatric health-care. *Pediatrics, 137*(1), 25–27. http://doi.org/10.1542/peds.2015-3908

Lu, M. C., & Halfon, N. (2003). Racial and ethnic disparities in birth outcomes: A life-course perspective. *Maternal and Child Health Journal, 7*(1), 13–30. http://doi.org/10.1023/A:1022537516969

Shelov, S. P. (Ed.). (2015). *Your baby's first year* (4th. ed.). Elk Grove Village, IL: American Academy of Pediatrics.

Additional Resources

American Academy of Pediatrics. *Healthy children website.* Available at https://www.healthychildren.org/English/Pages/default.aspx

Centers for Disease Control and Prevention. *Learn the signs. Act early: Milestones.* Available at http://www.cdc.gov/ncbddd/actearly/milestones/index.html

Review Questions

1. Which of the following factors are considered to influence infant development?
   A. Ethnicity
   B. Birthweight
   C. Maternal mental health
   D. Socioeconomic status
   E. All of the above

2. In the US, a pregnant woman's use of which of the following substances is responsible for the greatest number of cases of neurodevelopmental dysfunction in childhood?
   A. Alcohol
   B. Cocaine
   C. Heroin
   D. LSD
   E. Tobacco

3. By which of the following ages has a child learned object permanence, or that objects still exist even when they are not visible?
   A. 3 months
   B. 6 months
   C. 9 months
   D. 12 months
   E. 15 months

Answer Key on p. 465

13 Toddlerhood and the Preschool Years

Emily F. Myers, MD, Lisa D. Herzig, MD, and Forrest C. Bennett, MD

- When is a child ready for toilet training?
- How does language evolve between 12 and 36 months?
- How does a child's play change between 12 and 36 months?
- Why do preschool children obey rules?

Toddlerhood (Ages 1 to 3 Years)

As children move through infancy and enter the toddler and preschool years, their activities mature and become more nuanced. A child's mobility dramatically changes, moving from crawling to walking, running, and jumping. Increasing receptive and expressive language capacity allows children to use words and gestures to communicate. Social-emotional relationships become more rich and complex as they begin to include greater interaction and experience with people outside the family. With this rapid period of complex development, there remains a dependence on both biological and environmentally driven processes, which strongly influence the development of the young child (see Chapter 11: Selected Theories of Development).

Physical Development

Early in the second year of life, children complete the transition from crawling to walking. Multiple factors are involved in this process, including the development of an upright posture and the ability to shift weight, alternate leg movements, and process sensory information while moving. Most 1-year-old children initially walk with a wide-based gait and short, waddling steps that have given rise to the term *toddler*.

The average age of taking first independent steps is 12 months, although some children will not begin walking until 16 to 18 months. By 24 months, toddlers are beginning to jump, and some can walk up and down stairs by themselves. By age 36 months, most toddlers have an adult-like *heel-to-toe* gait; they are able to run and change direction with agility; they like to try new types of movements such as galloping; and they are fully able to jump with both feet. Many toddlers can pedal a tricycle at 36 months of age. However, because there is such a wide range of normal variation in the development of most gross motor milestones, no single motor skill can or should be used to describe overall neuromotor development (see Table 13.1).

Two-year-old children can toss or roll a ball. They progress from finger feeding to self-feeding with a spoon and fork, and can build a tower of 4 to 6 blocks. This progression parallels the toddler's ability to recognize objects and associate them with their functions. Thus, the toddler begins to use objects appropriately rather than just mouthing and banging them. Three-year-old children can dress with help and can hold a glass with one hand. These fine motor milestones are necessary for mastering activities that occur in preschool settings, and are important precursors to the development of handwriting skills.

Toilet Training

When is a child ready for toilet training?

Table 13.1. Selected developmental milestones from 12 months to 36 months

Age (months)	Gross Motor	Fine Motor	Language	Cognitive
12	Wide-based independent walking	Pincer grasp	"mama" "dada" + 2–3 other words	Object permanence
15	Runs	Imitates scribbling	3–6 words	Turns pages in a book
18	Walks upstairs while holding on	Brushes teeth with help	10–20 words	Matches pair of objects
24	Jumps with two feet	Builds tower of 4–6 blocks	50–100 words Combines two words 25–50% intelligibility	Shows use of familiar objects
36	Heel-to-toe gait Pedals tricycle	Copies a circle	3–4 word sentences 50–75% intelligibility	Knows age and gender

Toilet training is one of the most important examples of the physiological neuromotor maturation process of toddlerhood. Before voluntary bladder and bowel control can occur, the sensory pathways from the bladder and bowel must be mature enough to transmit signals to the cortex indicating bladder and bowel fullness. Toddlers must also demonstrate an interest in control of elimination, as well as an ability to follow adult instruction. These abilities together demonstrate a *developmental readiness* for toilet training. Toddlers must then learn to associate these signals with the need to (1) eliminate, followed by the need to (2) tighten the sphincter to prevent immediate elimination, and finally, after tightening, the need to (3) loosen the sphincter to permit elimination at the proper moment. The child must have the fine motor skill to remove clothing quickly and reliably before urinating and defecating. Toddlers are not able to voluntarily postpone elimination until they are at least 15 to 18 months of age. By 2 years of age, some toddlers are able to remain dry during the day, although many children wear diapers until age 3. Most children are not fully bowel trained until they are 4 years old. Environmental and cultural expectations and demands influence the exact timing of these events.

Language Development

> How does language evolve between 12 and 36 months?

At 12 months, toddlers' use of specific words is often limited to "mama" and "dada" for their parents, and two or three other words. *Jargoning,* utterances that sound like statements but contain no real words, is common. During the second year, their repertoire of words accumulates slowly and then increases dramatically. By 18 months, they will express 10 to 20 words, and by 2 years, 50 to 100 words. At 2 years, toddlers begin to combine words. The earliest word pairings before true noun–verb combinations are actually phrases ("go bye-bye") or labels ("baby baby") that the child perceives and uses as a single entity.

Because **receptive language** ability (what a child is able to understand) generally precedes the development of **expressive language** (what a child is able to produce), toddlers can point to pictures and understand body parts before they can name them. Similarly, they can follow one- or two-part commands before they are able to express such commands themselves.

By the end of the third year, utterances are typically three to four words long. Grammar becomes more correct, and plural nouns are used occasionally. The speech of most 3-year-old children is 50% to 75% intelligible to a stranger, although imperfect diction is still common. Problems with the rhythm and pacing of speech (*developmental dysfluencies*) frequently occur. These dysfluencies usually resolve without specific intervention. Factors associated with slower acquisition of language milestones include, but are not limited to, male gender, prematurity, multiple gestation (twins, triplets), bilingualism, and disadvantaged socioeconomic status.

Cognitive Development

> **How does a child's play change between 12 and 36 months?**

Beginning at about 7 to 9 months and extending into the second year of life, the toddler learns that an object exists even when it is not present, by developing a mental image of it (**object permanence**). During the second year, toddlers will quickly look for an object that they observed being moved through a series of displacements. By 18 to 24 months, toddlers begin to search for a hidden object even if it was moved while they were not watching; furthermore, they will check several possible locations in an attempt to find it.

In the second year of life, toddlers begin to understand that their actions can cause novel reactions and they become experimenters within their environment. They learn that seemingly unrelated behaviors can have certain consequences. For example, by age 2, a toddler will know to wind a toy to make it move.

Long-term memory develops in the second year of life, allowing toddlers to make associations such as matching a place at the table with one person. In fact, they may get upset if someone else sits in that place. They also "memorize" stories, making it close to impossible to skip a few pages of bedtime reading.

Play is an important aspect of development that reflects increasing mental abilities. At 12 months, toddlers begin to use objects in play (e.g., banging a spoon). After this stage, they begin to use the object functionally (e.g., pretending to eat with the spoon). In the next stage, typically at about 18 to 24 months, the toddler uses a toy to represent a real action (e.g., using a toy telephone to "call Daddy"). These activities are known as *symbolic play* (one object [toy] stands for another object [telephone]). Toddlers at this stage also engage in *parallel play* (despite being situated near one another, they play independently with little interaction or joint play).

Toddlers in the third year of life continue to develop the ability to represent reality to themselves through the use of words and symbols, including gestures. Their thinking is **preoperational** (they can solve simple problems, understand ordination [one book, two books] and classification [a dog is an animal], and sort by color and shape).

Egocentrism, the belief that they are the center and initiator of all activity and the inability to put themselves in the place of others, are prominent features of children's thinking at 2 to 3 years of age. As toddlers enter their fourth year, egocentrism begins to recede, and they start to understand that others may have a different perspective from their own.

Social-Emotional Development

Toddlers become increasingly adept at reading the primary caregiver's cues regarding the safety of novel social interactions. For example, a toddler is more easily calmed if the caregiver smiles and is reassuring while in a new situation like a doctor's office. This behavior is called **social referencing** and is typically mastered during this time and continues to be a useful skill throughout life.

By 18 months of age, toddlers can guide the attention of one person to share in their experiences of other objects. This is called **joint attention**, and shows the emergence of understanding that other people have their own interests and behaviors. This allows toddlers to be able to respond to others' distress. For example, when confronted with the distress of someone else, they are capable of understanding that the distress is affecting another person and not themselves. They may even try to comfort the other person.

Walking and using language promote new forms of social relations as toddlers learn that they can share experiences and compare reactions. The process of developing a *sense of self* leads to a new awareness of their own ability to create plans or do things independently. This increasing competence is the basis for the emerging autonomy characteristic of this time.

A toddler's sense of **autonomy** is also accompanied by a strong desire to see personal wishes fulfilled. Given that they lack the ability to think rationally and logically, they cannot understand their parents' rational and logical arguments for or against specific behaviors. They are also unable to understand postponement of their immediate desires and so are in frequent conflict with others. Because they lack sufficient language skills to express their disappointment or frustration, they demonstrate these feelings behaviorally through *tantrums*, the hallmark of the "terrible two's." Other hallmark features of toddlerhood include *negativism* (this is the age of the mandatory "no"), rigidity, and emotional lability. All of these make calm, controlled parenting a challenge.

Between 12 and 24 months of age, toddlers begin to experience such learned *secondary emotions* as embarrassment, jealousy, pride, shame, guilt, and envy. These secondary emotions do not appear until toddlers are able to think about and evaluate themselves in terms of some social standard, rule, or desired goal. Thus, secondary emotions can be considered social emotions because they involve either challenge to, or enhancement of, the toddler's sense of self.

Increasing autonomy and sense of self enhance the development of **gender identity**. By 2 years of age, toddlers are able to discriminate whether a playmate is male or female. Identification of gender is based on anatomical inspection as well as an understanding of core gender identity. By 3 years of age, toddlers know their own identity as male or female. Although in their fantasy life, there may be mixtures of male and female elements in how they see themselves, toddlers will nonetheless be protective of their gender identity.

Health Risks

Although toddlers eat a variety of foods, it is common for them to go through periods when they will eat only certain foods (e.g., peanut butter and jelly sandwiches every day). Despite their idiosyncrasies, toddlers virtually always take in what they need to grow appropriately. In fact, research has shown that children are responsive to the energy content of their diets. Routine monitoring of growth is mandatory, however, and each year children should have growth parameters entered onto an appropriate height and weight growth chart to verify adequate progress over time. In addition to the standard curves developed for the average child in the US, the World Health Organization has developed dozens of charts representing average growth in height and weight for children in a number of countries. Using the chart most appropriate for a newly immigrated child can be very useful in assessing the adequacy of the child's growth.

The significant risk of injury during toddlerhood is a function of the child's increasing motor ability and desire to explore. During this period, accidental injury, poisoning, and drowning are major concerns because an energetic 2-year-old child can get into trouble quickly. The strong sense of autonomy that is characteristic of toddlers puts them at high risk of child maltreatment from excessive physical and emotional punishment in response to their negative and egocentric behaviors. Health care at this age should include parental guidance in accident prevention and management of temper tantrums.

Preschool Years (Ages 3 to 5 Years)

Physical Development

Between the ages of 3 and 5 years, preschool children begin to master more complex gross and fine motor tasks. By 4 years of age, children are learning to skip, climb stairs independently, catch bouncing balls, and swing. By 5 years of age, most children are able to ride a bicycle with training wheels. Children at this age also draw circles, crosses and squares, and faces with bodies; cut with scissors; and use the toilet independently. At 4 to 5 years, the typical child will be able to print their first name.

Preschool Language Development

Preschool children can carry on a conversation reflecting their ability to describe several activities that occurred during the day. Three-year-old children are also full of "why" questions. Their grammar and syntax is becoming increasingly correct. Mean length of utterance should equal chronological age in the first 5 years of life; thus, the typical 5-year-old child speaks in sentences that average five words. Articulation continues to mature with the speech of most 5-year-old children being at least 90% intelligible. The rhythm and pacing of speech is also improving rapidly and developmental dysfluencies are disappearing.

Preschool Cognitive Development

As children progress beyond 3 years of age, their play matures from *symbolic* to *imaginary*. For example, the child may have a "mother" doll feed a "baby" doll. *Joint* or *associative play* emerges where groups of children cooperate and take turns with one another, laying the foundation for group activities. *Learning to share* is a major milestone that requires understanding ownership and delaying gratification.

At this age, the preschool setting facilitates learning through *imitation*. Sociocultural rules are integrated into learning at this time, and children are assessed for their readiness to attend school based, in part, on many of these preacademic skills. In fact, most experts agree that school readiness decisions should consider all developmental and behavioral domains as well as factors such as gender, birth date, and physical size.

Preschool Social-Emotional Development

Gender role identification is solidified in the preschool years. As children's concept of gender identity forms, they become adept at labeling themselves as boys or girls. Soon, they develop a gender role schema for "boy" and "girl" and are able to identify objects and behaviors that are associated with each gender role. Social reinforcement of gender-specific behaviors leads children to place value on those behaviors associated with their gender role and they imitate them.

Sexual play among preschool children is a natural consequence of their cognitive, social, and emotional development. Children are interested in "private parts" and what distinguishes "boys" from "girls." They are fascinated with toileting activities. Preschool children may participate in games of "mommy and daddy" or "doctor" to further explore gender differences. Sexual play is common and does not predict fixation on these behaviors as an adult. However, preschool children should be educated about the differences between "good touching" and "bad touching."

Why do preschool children obey rules?

An important part of social-emotional development at this time is the development of a **social conscience** or **morality**. Preschool children apply the concepts of morality independently of what is right or wrong, and their primary motivation for good behavior is to avoid punishment. Preschool children obey adult rules even though they do not understand why the rules exist. They have little understanding of intent or motive behind a particular behavior because (1) they still have difficulty understanding another person's perspective, and (2) they cannot focus on more than one characteristic of an object or event at a time (amount of damage done vs. intent). As a result, the degree of guilt or blame a child typically ascribes to a behavior is associated with the degree of damage. As children move through the later preschool years, they are better able to understand reasons for rules, particularly in group settings.

In combination with the development of a moral sense of self, preschool children develop greater **autonomy** and are interested in trying new tasks and experiences on their own. At the same time, they are becoming more aware of others' emotions and agendas, and they want to share their experiences with others. "Terrific three's" describes an age of relative emotional calm and equilibrium. However, this respite is often followed by the "out of bounds four's," characterized by high energy, boisterousness, and general disequilibrium.

Preschool Health Risks

Trauma is the greatest health risk during the preschool years, most likely because of children's increasingly facile complex motor abilities. In addition, however, caregivers often have difficulty containing the child's willfulness and limit testing. Because children of this age often attend childcare or preschool, exposure to *communicable diseases* is another common health concern.

Developmental Considerations

As with fetal and infant development, toddlerhood and the preschool years are considered both critical and sensitive periods of child development. Identifying and treating early developmental delay are essential to optimizing health and development. Significant social or emotional delays and conditions such as autism spectrum disorder are often first identified in children this age. The American Academy of Pediatrics recommends developmental screening at 18 months and 30 months of age, including administration of a formal autism spectrum disorder screen.

Recommended Readings

Augustyn, M., Frank, D.A., & Zuckerman, B.S. (2009). Infancy and toddler years. In W. B. Carey, A. C. Crocker, W. L. Coleman, E. R. Elias, & H. M. Feldman (Eds.), *Developmental-behavioral pediatrics* (4th ed.). New York, NY: Saunders Elsevier.

Gerber, R. J., Wilks, T., & Erdie-Lalena, C. (2010). Developmental milestones: motor development. *Pediatrics in Review, 31*(7), 267–277

Goswami, U. (Ed.). (2010). *The Wiley-Blackwell handbook of childhood cognitive development* (2nd ed.). Oxford, UK: Wiley-Blackwell. http://doi.org/10.1002/9781444325485

Hamel, S. C., & Pelphrey, A. (2009). Preschool years. In W. B. Carey, A. C. Crocker, W. L. Coleman, E. R. Elias, & H. M. Feldman (Eds.), *Developmental-behavioral pediatrics* (4th ed.). New York, NY: Saunders Elsevier.

Siegel, D. J. (2012). *The developing mind* (2nd ed.). New York, NY: Guilford Press.

Smith, P., & Hart, C. (Eds.). (2010). *The Wiley-Blackwell handbook of childhood social development* (2nd ed.). Oxford, UK: Wiley-Blackwell. http://doi.org/10.1002/9781444390933

Review Questions

1. The most common age for children to become bowel and bladder trained is
   A. 18 months
   B. 24 months
   C. 3 years
   D. 4 years
   E. 6 years

2. The manner in which toddlers play with one another is often described as
   A. imaginary
   B. magical
   C. obstinate
   D. parallel
   E. reciprocal

3. Which of the abilities below is a gross motor milestone typically associated with a 3-year-old child?
   A. Has a pincer grasp
   B. Jumps with two feet
   C. Pedals a tricycle
   D. Pushes a toy while walking
   E. Snips with scissors

4. The stable conceptualization of being either male or female despite superficial features such as dress or mannerism is
   A. gender identity
   B. sex role schema
   C. sex role stereotype
   D. sexual orientation
   E. sexual preference

Answer Key on p. 465

14 The School Years

Elizabeth A. McCauley, PhD, ABPP

- Why is thinking during middle childhood called "concrete operational"?
- What are the characteristics of peer groups during middle childhood?
- What motivates a 10-year-old child to "do the right thing"?
- What are the major health concerns during middle childhood?
- How does timing of pubertal development influence self-concept?
- How do different "developmental trajectories" manifest themselves during adolescence?

Middle Childhood (6 to 12 Years)

Although **middle childhood** is a period of significant physical, cognitive, social, and emotional development, changes are more gradual and subtle than the dramatic growth surges found during the infancy and preschool, and adolescent years.

Physical Development

From the age of 6 years until the adolescent growth spurt, children grow about 2.5 in. (6.35 cm) and gain approximately 6.6 lb (3 kg) each year. As early as age 7, **hormonal changes** begin including the increased production of *adrenal steroids* in both boys and girls, followed by increases in *estrogen* and then *androgen* production. As a result, fat is deposited in subcutaneous tissues beginning at approximately age 8 in girls and age 10 in boys. In many girls, the first pubertal changes of breast budding, followed by pubic and axillary hair growth, occur during middle childhood. *Menarche* (onset of menses) occurs after the growth spurt. In girls, the growth rate begins to accelerate as early as 10 years of age, with most girls experiencing their major growth spurt between 11 and 13 years. Boys typically develop later than girls but can have signs of puberty, such as testicular enlargement, as young as 10 years of age. Most of the major growth spurt in boys occurs during

adolescence (13 to 15 years of age). The timing of pubertal development has shifted downward for girls in the US over the last 30 years. While many factors may contribute to this trend, the rise in obesity in US children has been a central focus, given that increased body fat or a rapid increase in weight are associated with earlier onset of puberty for girls. The relation between obesity and timing of puberty is less clear for boys. Early puberty is associated with less positive body image and greater risk for depression in girls but response to early puberty may differ across ethnic and social subgroups.

Bone and muscle growth during middle childhood results in enhanced physical coordination and more complex motor skills. Whereas 5-year-olds can run, ride a tricycle, print their name, and throw a ball, most 10-year-olds have mastered a two-wheel bike, can run and dribble a ball simultaneously, and write in cursive.

Permanent teeth begin erupting during the early elementary school period. Loss of the primary or deciduous (baby) teeth occurs at a rate of about four teeth per year, from age 6 to 14.

Neurological changes promote important cognitive developments. Continued *myelinization of the cortex* is accompanied by increased numbers and density of dendrites and synaptic connections. Brain cell genesis, nerve myelinization, and dendritic pruning, particularly in the frontal cortex, increase during late childhood and early adolescence and continue into young adult life. During childhood, the thickness of the cerebral cortex varies with periods of thickening and thinning, and cortical fissures become more prominent. Electroencephalographic (EEG) activity transitions from primarily delta wave (frequency: 3 to 5/s) to predominantly alpha wave (frequency: 8 to 13/s) activity after age 6. EEG activity also becomes increasingly stable, localized, and function specific, depending on the task the child is doing.

Cognitive Development

> **Why is thinking during middle childhood called "concrete operational"?**

By the age of 7, most children can consider more than one characteristic of an object or issue simultaneously, and understand that an object does not change merely because its appearance varies. For example, the child recognizes that the amount of liquid remains the same even if poured from a tall container into a shorter but wider container. Piaget termed this phenomenon **conservation**.

Other important skills learned at this time include **seriation**, the ability to conceptualize quantifiable differences (e.g., Jane is taller than Sue), and **transitivity**, the ability to infer relations among elements in a serial order (e.g., if I am taller than Jane, and Jane is taller than Sue, then I am taller than Sue). These new mental skills allow children to perform simple mathematical functions, and enhance the child's conception of time, so that waiting for a turn, anticipating a holiday, and planning for a future event become possible.

Memory improves as children learn to use rehearsal or categorizing to help organize daily tasks. However, these skills are still connected to the physical world (things the child can see, feel, or manipulate). Thus, this stage is termed the **concrete operational stage** of thinking. It is not until adolescence that the cognitive ability to manipulate ideas, possibilities, and abstract concepts emerges.

Cognitive structures and early problem-solving skills evolve during middle childhood through complex *fantasy play* and following *rules*. The elementary school–aged child typically enjoys board games and team sports. A major developmental step is the transition from the need to interpret rules strictly, to the ability to negotiate changes in rules, and the ability to apply rules from one situation to another similar situation (generalization). These skills are typically learned by trial-and-error and repetition.

Social Cognition

Social cognition refers to skills that reflect a person's sense of self and relations to others. At age 6 to 7, children compare their personal qualities with those of others, but are bound to observable physical attributes, such as who runs the fastest or counts the highest. At age 8 to 10, children begin to recognize *psychological attributes* such as fairness or generosity. Late middle childhood children can evaluate traits like shyness or reliability. Despite this progress, they remain tied to concrete (observable) representations of behaviors, and cannot yet understand that different social or emotional situations may elicit different behaviors without changing the basic characteristics of a person.

As children develop a more complex sense of self and others, they demonstrate increased ability to *take another person's perspective*. Most 10-year-old children are able to consider another person's point of view but cannot easily consider two points of view (theirs and the other person's) simultaneously. By age 12, however, almost all children can consider multiple perspectives simultaneously as long as the issue is tied to the concrete world (e.g., discussion of how a parent, teacher, and child might react differently to a rule-breaking situation). As children move into early adolescence, they begin to understand that ability is a stable trait and to infer that repeated failures may represent a lack of ability rather than a chance occurrence.

> **What are the characteristics of peer groups during middle childhood?**

During elementary school, children belong primarily to same-sex **peer groups**. These groups are more formalized than previously, and selection of friends is based on common interests or personality traits rather than merely living close by or being in the same classroom. Members of a peer group interact on a regular basis, have a shared set of *norms*, and a sense of belonging to the group. Gradually, roles emerge with particular members becoming leaders or followers. As the child matures, peers become less interchangeable, and lasting friendships are established. The importance of peers and the time spent with them increases steadily throughout middle childhood.

Personal and Social Competence

According to **Erikson**, the major task of middle childhood is developing a sense of *personal competence* by mastering new physical, cognitive, and social skills introduced by school and community activities. School work, athletics, and hobby groups all focus on practice, motivation, and *accomplishment.* Children who do not find areas of success and accomplishment, even in doing such activities as chores around the house or self-care, develop a sense of inferiority and failure that can lead to decreased self-esteem and reluctance to take on new challenges and responsibilities.

Children who have poor *social skills* (e.g., inaccurate sense of personal space, inadequate hygiene, clinging, demanding, or aggressive behavior) have difficulty maintaining social relationships despite a strong desire for companionship. They are usually bewildered by their lack of acceptance because their behaviors result from not perceiving the subtle intricacies of relationship rather than from any conscious rudeness or disrespect. "She just doesn't get it" is a perfect description. Children with *learning and attention problems* are vulnerable to social rejection as they may, because of their leaning difficulties or impulsivity, have problems reading and responding to social cues. For some children, intentional buffoonery or antisocial behavior becomes the only means of peer "acceptance."

Moral Development

> What motivates a 10-year-old child to "do the right thing"?

Early research on **moral development** suggested that children move through a predictable sequence

of stages of moral judgment, transitioning from an early childhood focus on rules, expectations of authority figures, and avoiding punishment to, in middle childhood, a more internalized set of rules that culminates, in late adolescence, with an individualized set of moral values based on personal principles. Using this early paradigm, for the 6- to 7-year-old child, goodness or badness is determined by the *consequences* of an act. By age 9, children become fascinated with *rules.* Most children of this age have a strong sense of right and wrong with difficulty appreciating and accommodating to changing circumstances. By about age 10, children begin to consider *intent* in understanding their own and others' behavior, and the cognitive process underlying moral judgments shifts to a desire to behave in ways that gain *social approval.*

More recent developmental research has provided a richer understanding of the process and suggests that moral judgments are influenced by the child's social interactions. This newer research revealed that moral decisions are shaped by emotional responses and social judgments. Moral emotions such as sympathy increase significantly during middle childhood and help children develop moral action and values setting the stage for the developmental of moral identity in adolescence. Moreover, this research suggests that moral development does not follow an invariant sequence of developmental stages, noting that even toddlers are capable of sympathetic and empathetic reactions to others. Further, children in early and middle childhood appear to be able to make distinctions between moral, social, and personal judgments, allowing them to decide whether or not something is right or fair, based on the circumstances of the situation rather than merely following a rule or doing what is most socially acceptable.

Sex Role Development

By age 6 or 7, *gender-related behavioral patterns* are well-established, and children are clear about "boy" vs. "girl" behaviors. Open curiosity about other children's bodies and bodily functions is less common during middle childhood than it was at earlier ages. Many children are modest about their body and want privacy while bathing or toileting. Bedwetting may still occur among 6- to

8-year-old children and may interfere with social activities that involve an overnight stay away from home. Jokes about embarrassing bodily functions are common, but given the strong taboos against sexual play in Western culture, most sexual interactions become covert during middle childhood. Many children engage in some same-sex sexual play, consisting primarily of comparing genitalia and some touching.

> Practicing boy–girl social relationship roles is common during middle childhood. In the primary grades, boys and girls engage in chasing and teasing games; later, many children experience their first real crush. Many gay and lesbian adults report knowing they had "different" romantic interests as early as middle childhood, even before having a clear cognitive understanding of sexual orientation.

Gender Identity Development

During the preschool years, a small group of children experience gender dysphoria and express a strong desire to be the sex opposite to their birth sex. While this appears to be a developmental phase for many, this identification persists into middle childhood for a number of children. Some go through a "social" transition into living in the desired gender gradually over the elementary to middle school years, and some seek hormonal intervention to suppress pubertal development. There is also a trend in the US for a growing number of young adolescents to question their gender, with many identifying as *transsexual* or transgender while some prefer to adopt a gender neutral status. It is not clear if this reflects a change in the number of youths who question their gender or changes in society that have allowed for more open expression of gender variance. Many of these youths pursue hormonal treatments to either suppress pubertal development if younger or to masculinize or feminize their bodies. These youths frequently describe having gone through a period of questioning of their sexual orientation, thinking first they were bisexual, then lesbian or gay, and then coming to identify as *trans*. Surgical interventions are typically not available for youths until they are 18 or older.

Health Risks

> What are the major health concerns during middle childhood?

The major health concerns arising during middle childhood fall into three categories: (1) *chronic medical conditions* such as diabetes or asthma; (2) *injuries* associated with increasing involvement in physical activities including "I dare you" games; and (3) *learning, attention, or emotional health disorders*. Approximately 20% of children struggle with a learning or behavioral problem. Problems with attention and anxiety are most common. Attention difficulties can affect school and social success and may contribute to the various anxiety-related problems that commonly present during middle childhood. If attentional problems are severe enough to meet criteria for a diagnosis of attention-deficit/hyperactivity disorder, they are typically managed with a combination of behavioral and parenting strategies and use of a stimulant medication if indicated. Anxiety-related problems including social anxiety and tics are common during the middle childhood years. In general, the anxieties of middle childhood are responsive to brief behavioral interventions, and most resolve as children mature.

It is critical that children who have a chronic medical condition be treated within the context of their developmental needs. This means encouraging the child and family to normalize the child's life as much as possible by encouraging appropriate school and peer activities. Because children of this age are forming their sense of self, it is essential that they, and their families, not define themselves in terms of the child's medical or behavioral condition. The physician can assess and reinforce this sense of balance by including questions about participation in school, athletic, and social activities as part of every health care visit.

Adolescence (12 to 19 Years)

Adolescence is defined as extending from the appearance of secondary sex characteristics to the cessation of somatic growth. After the neonatal period, it is the time of dramatic physical, cognitive, social, and emotional change.

Physical Development

How does timing of pubertal development influence self-concept?

Physical changes associated with **pubertal development** are a primary concern for most adolescents. The onset and course of pubertal events are organized around a feedback mechanism that involves the integration of protein peptide hormones released by the hypothalamus and pituitary with steroid hormones secreted by the gonads. **Gonadotropin releasing hormone** (GnRH) is synthesized and stored in the hypothalamus. When released, this small peptide regulates the production and release of two anterior pituitary hormones, or gonadotropins, **luteinizing hormone** (LH) and **follicle stimulating hormone** (FSH). The two primary sex steroids produced by the gonads, **estradiol** and **testosterone,** act on peripheral target organs and tissues and within a negative feedback loop to suppress hypothalamic release of GnRH. The notable exception to this negative feedback loop is the regulation of **ovulation,** where positive feedback of ovarian steroid ultimately produces an LH surge and ovulation.

The *hypothalamus* acts as a central common pathway for impulses from the cortex, limbic system, and pineal gland and is sensitive to *catecholamine* and *indolamine* stimulation. Neuroendocrine response to stress and nutritional status influence pubertal manifestations like linear growth and menstruation.

As these feedback systems are activated, the individual moves through a series of physical changes that have a dramatic effect on appearance. These changes begin gradually during middle childhood and culminate with completed pubertal development and linear growth during adolescence when the final 25% of adult height and 50% of adult weight are attained. Significant visible changes focus the teenager's attention on the *self* and heighten concern about **body image**.

The pubertal **growth spurt** occurs earlier in females than in males. On average, 12-year-old girls are taller than 12-year-old boys although there is marked variability. When boys begin to grow, their spurt is longer and of greater magnitude than that of girls. Given the considerable variation in the timing of pubertal change, most young people need reassurance that they are normal. Concerns related to body changes should be taken seriously and explained to allay unnecessary anxiety. Youths who experience their development as "out of synch" with their peers are at increased risk for behavioral and emotional problems. Early maturation was long considered to have positive effects on boys' self-confidence and social status, but more recent research suggests that both early and late maturation confer increased risk for depression and anxiety in boys (see Table 14.1).

Table 14.1. Phases of adolescence

	Age	Sexual Maturity Rating
Early	12–13	1–2
Middle	14–16	3–5
Late	17+	5

Early-maturing girls, especially those with obvious physical changes such as early breast development, are the group at most risk for increased behavioral problems. Early-developing girls may seek out peers who are like them physically (although a year or more older) and find themselves in demanding social and emotional situations without the necessary coping skills. Early development is most problematic when friendships with more deviant peers develop in the context of lax parental supervision. Parents should be encouraged to help their child cope with the physical changes of puberty by promoting healthy activities that are in keeping with the youth's skills and developmental status.

Recent research has shown that adolescence involves a period of marked *brain development* with increased cell genesis, myelinization, and dendritic pruning, particularly in the frontal and prefrontal cortex. Adolescence, however, marks a period of differential development of the subcortical and cortical systems. Whereas these systems are equally immature in children and equally mature in adults, during adolescence, the prefrontal cortex matures less quickly than the subcortical region. The prefrontal cortex as it develops controls self-regulation skills such as inhibitory control and the perception and evaluation of risks and rewards. Brain development in early and middle adolescence lays the foundation for the development of more sophisticated problem-solving skills in late adolescence and early adulthood.

Some neurodevelopmental changes occurring in adolescence are triggered by pubertal hormones. These hormones are thought to stimulate the brain systems that regulate arousal and appetite, contributing to the moodiness, changes in the sleep/wake cycle, increases in romantic interests, risk taking, and novelty-seeking behavior observed in many adolescents. The increased intensity of reactions in these systems reflects the greater influence of the subcortical or approach system and the weaker influence of the prefrontal cortex or regulatory system.

Early adolescence is also marked by a physiological alternation in melatonin production that leads to a shift in circadian rhythm affecting adolescent **sleep patterns** and later bedtimes. Changes in adolescent sleep architecture result in less deep, slow wave sleep. Adolescents need 8 to 10 hrs of sleep per night; insufficient sleep negatively affects mood and ability to perform in school. To address the negative effects of sleep deprivation on students, many middle and high schools have moved to delayed school start times. Later school start time leads to improvements in academic and test performance and reduced tardiness.

Therefore, it is important to educate adolescents and their parents about normative shifts in sleep patterns, while stressing the importance of getting adequate sleep, including increasing opportunities for sleep by turning off computers and cell phones.

> In a recent survey, about 65% of adolescents reported not getting enough sleep; lack of sleep was associated with daytime sleepiness, negative mood, poor school performance, and increased risk taking. About 25% of youths reported falling asleep in class on a weekly basis.

Cognitive Development

The ability to use abstract thought, consider theoretical notions, devise hypotheses, examine cause-and-effect relationships, and make judgments based on future considerations emerges during adolescence. This stage of **formal opera-**

tions typically does not begin to develop until late adolescence with only 35% of 16- to 17-year-old adolescents exhibiting this skill. Many adolescents can think more abstractly when considering topics such as political issues, but are less flexible in their thinking about personal, social, or emotional issues. Further, not all individuals ever fully develop these abilities, and many reach adulthood with only a limited ability to deal with abstract concepts like religion, morality, philosophy, and ethics. During adolescence, **regression** in cognitive processing to a more concrete stage of thinking is common in the face of physical or emotional stress.

Moral Development

Past research suggested that children in middle childhood and early adolescence made moral judgments based on *conventional moral reasoning* – that is, internalization of societal rules and decision making that reflects what is best for the community, not just what is best for the individual. Recent research finds that delayed or immature moral reasoning is strongly associated with juvenile delinquency regardless of socioeconomic status, gender, age, and intelligence, and that mature moral development acts as a barrier to engaging in antisocial acts. Research further suggests that adolescents' moral motivation is positively associated with the quality of the parent–child relationship and the adolescent's own rating of the importance of social justice (see Chapter 11: Selected Theories of Development).

Emotional Development

Emotional regulation, the ability to identify, process, and express feelings appropriately, is an important milestone in adolescent development. Both brain maturation and experience help youths to gradually master the skills needed to make sound decisions, even in the face of intense emotions. As cognitive coping skills mature, adolescents become better able to resist emotional impulses and make decisions based on longer-term goals. Problem solving and planning are intellectual functions still under active reorganization during the adolescent years.

> **How do different "developmental trajectories" manifest themselves during adolescence?**

Studies of both normal healthy adolescents and those with a variety of chronic illnesses describe three **developmental trajectories**: continuous, surgent, and tumultuous. Long-term follow-up of youths in each of these categories has shown that no group experiences significantly more psychopathology than any other group, and overall adjustment in young adulthood is comparable across groups. It is normal for teenagers to experience transient disturbances in self-esteem, anxiety and depression, and oversensitivity to shame and humiliation in response to stressful situations. Less than a third of all teenagers experience severe turmoil.

Types of Developmental Trajectories	
Continuous:	No major crises, high self-esteem, stable environment
Surgent:	Prone to depression, less socially active
Tumultuous:	Anxious, dependent on peers, less secure self-concept, family problems

Social Development

Learning the responsibilities and nuances of **peer friendships** is a prerequisite to healthy adult friendships. Being "popular" is not as important as having at least a small group of accepting friends. Social isolation during adolescence increases risks for academic difficulty, delinquency, and feelings of inadequacy. Purely social, rather than athletic or task-oriented activities, become increasingly common during this period. This is also a time when adolescents experiment with more **intimate relationships**, and social learning becomes based less on peer group influences and more on the influence of a boyfriend or girlfriend. Social development also plays an important role in the process of **identity formation** as youths try out different roles and interests.

Establishing a sense of identity is an ongoing process that extends into early adulthood. The pro-

cess takes shape in adolescence as youths search for **personal identity** or that sense of self that combines the person's diverse and often conflicting social roles (e.g., child, friend, student, athlete), talents (artistic, musical, analytic), values, and attitudes.

Early adolescents are preoccupied with the *physical changes* associated with puberty. Although early adolescents engage in role experimentation and seek independence via close relationships with peers, family relationships and parental approval remain important. Younger adolescents focus on "being like" their friends in terms of dress, hairstyles, and interests.

Middle adolescents are preoccupied with their *social role* and are intensely aware of how they appear to, and are judged by, their peers. They begin experimenting with risk-taking behaviors and asserting their independence from family. By the end of middle adolescence, many teens feel more confident and begin to express more nonconformity.

Older adolescents are preoccupied with decisions about *work and career*. Family influences become less important as *intimate relationships* are established. Some older adolescents postpone physical and financial independence from the family because of their need for resources to complete their education or training. This period of continued family reliance, termed the **psychosocial moratorium**, extends into the mid-20s and even early 30s for some.

Gender Identity and Sexual Development

During puberty, **sexual functioning** matures and takes on new meaning. **Menarche** represents the culmination of puberty in the adolescent female and the beginning of the reproductive years for the mature female. Although relative infertility without regular ovulatory cycles is common during the first 3 to 24 months following menarche, **contraception** is indicated for any sexually active adolescent female. Most hormonal forms of contraception can be used safely beginning immediately after menarche.

Virtually all adolescent boys and many adolescent girls engage in **masturbation**. Recent trends suggest declining rates of adolescent sexual activity, pregnancy, and childbirth; however, many youths engage in risky sexual behavior. In a recent survey of high school students, 48% of male and 46% of female students reported having had **sexual intercourse**: 34% of these students had sexual intercourse during the previous 3 months, and, of these, 41% did not use a condom the last time they had sex. **Sexually transmitted diseases**, especially chlamydial and human papillomavirus infections, are common, and infection rates remain higher among US teens than those among teens in other developed nations. This finding is particularly true among ethnic minority youths in the US. Nearly 10,000 young people (aged 13 to 24) were diagnosed with HIV infection in the US in 2013. Use of alcohol or drugs during sexual encounters was common, and 10% of dating high school students report dating violence including sexual violence. Social media has also influenced communications about sex. *Sexting* is the exchange of explicit sexual messages or images by mobile phone. More than 10% of 14- to 24-year-olds describe sexting, which involved sharing a naked photo or video via the Internet or text messaging.

Homosexual fantasies occur among both male and female heterosexual teenagers. Some young adolescents have exploratory homosexual experiences. These experiences do not necessarily predict future **sexual orientation**. The percentage of the overall population who identify themselves as exclusively homosexual is difficult to determine, but appears to be between 4% and 10%. Although many gay and lesbian adults report having had feelings of marginality or of being different during childhood, homosexual identity formation (personally acknowledging, exploring, and accepting) generally occurs during midadolescence. Youths are now "coming out" more commonly during the adolescent years, and, as noted above, there is greater diversity in sexual and gender identification among today's youths than was recognized in the past. Recent statistics suggest that twice as many young adults (aged 18 to 29) identify as lesbian, gay, bisexual, or transgender than adults in the 30- to 49-year-old age range.

Health Issues

Approximately 20% of presumably healthy teens (aged 12 to 19) have previously unrecognized health problems, mostly related to the rapid growth and maturation of puberty. These problems include structural (e.g., idiopathic scoliosis) and functional (e.g., "shin splints") disorders of the skeletal system, and failure to achieve puberty at the appropriate time (e.g., pituitary insufficiency).

> A sense of self-competence is the most important predictor of adherence to a medical regimen. The teenager who has a positive self-image is likely to follow a health care provider's advice. Other factors that promote adherence include a treatment schedule tailored to the teenager's personal lifestyle (few side effects; simple, easy-to-follow; requires minimal time and effort) and satisfaction (feels fully informed; feels privacy and confidentiality will be respected).

However, most common adolescent health concerns, such as **sexually transmitted disease, pregnancy, injury due to violence,** and **substance abuse**, are closely related to risk-taking behaviors that are common during this period. Mental health concerns, particularly **depression**, also become more prevalent during adolescence.

The three leading causes of death among adolescents are **accidents**, **homicide**, and **suicide**. Many accidental deaths are preventable, including motor vehicle collisions and drowning. In deaths due to homicide, the perpetrator is often an acquaintance or family member.

The first use of **illicit drugs** can occur in elementary school children but is most common among adolescents. Youths who are rebellious, place a low value on achievement, are alienated from their parents and community, and live in a chaotic environment are most likely to be substance abusers.

Tobacco use remains a major public health problem among adolescents. Approximately 30% of teenage females in the US smoke on a regular basis; the percentage is somewhat lower among males.

The prevalence of **violence** increased dramatically over the last two decades of the 20th century. Active school and community antiviolence programs led to small but promising declines just before the turn of the century. However, the percentage of high school students who have carried a gun, knife, or other weapon at least once during the preceding month still exceeds 75% in some urban areas.

Longitudinal studies suggest that, by age 18, 20% of adolescents have experienced a significant episode of **depression,** and 65% of adolescents report some depressive symptoms. Vulnerability to depression during adolescence may be heightened given the neurodevelopmental changes that are thought to alter perception and evaluation of risks and rewards and intensify emotional reactivity. Sensitivity to social stress and peer rejection is enhanced particularly during early adolescence, which can, in turn, trigger depression. Health care providers must be alert to signs of depression, as many adolescents have difficulty verbalizing their feelings, allowing depression and suicidal thoughts to go unrecognized.

Suicide is the third most common cause of death among adolescents, so providers need to ask directly about self-harming behaviors and thoughts of suicide. Suicidal behaviors are frequently impulsive responses to a personal disappointment, and suicide attempts are sometimes masked or missed as accidents. When the risk of suicide is present, precautions must be taken to ensure the adolescent's safety, including informing guardians or other responsible adults.

Recommended Readings

Carskadon, M. (2011). Sleep in adolescents: The perfect storm. *Pediatric Clinics of North America, 58*(3), 637–647. http://doi.org/10.1016/j.pcl.2011.03.003

Craig, W. (2000). *Childhood social development.* Oxford, UK: Blackwell.

Dahl, R. E., & Spear, L. P. (Eds.). (2004). *Adolescent brain development: Vulnerabilities and opportunities.* New York, NY: New York Academy of Sciences.

Davies, D. (2011). *Child development* (3rd ed.). New York, NY: Guilford Press.

Fisher, M. M., Alderman, E., Kreipe, R. E., & Rosenfeld, W. D. (Eds.). (2011). *Textbook of adolescent health care.* Elk Grove Village, IL: American Academy of Pediatrics.

Killen, M., & Smetana, J. G. (2006). *Handbook of moral development.* Mahwah, NJ: Erlbaum.

Steinberg, L. (2005). Cognitive and affective development in adolescence. *Trends in Cognitive Sciences, 9*(2), 69–74. http://doi.org/10.1016/j.tics.2004.12.005

Review Questions

1. Hormonal changes that lead to puberty are
   A. evident as early as age 7 with increases in adrenal steroids
   B. marked by estrogen increases in girls only
   C. seldom observed during the middle childhood years
   D. undetectable until after pubic hair develops
   E. unrelated to increases in subcutaneous fat during middle childhood

2. Neurological development during middle childhood is characterized by a significant increase in
   A. delta wave EEG activity
   B. glial cell proliferation
   C. head circumference
   D. number of neurons
   E. synaptic connections

3. During middle childhood, most children prefer
   A. being with older adults
   B. peer groups with common interests
   C. playing with mixed groups of boys and girls
   D. simple fantasy games
   E. structured games and sports

4. Which of the following statements concerning adolescence is true?
   A. Adolescents are quite flexible in thinking about personal, social, and emotional issues.
   B. Adolescents' moral motivation is associated with the quality of parent–child relationships.
   C. Boys' growth spurt is shorter and of lesser magnitude than girls'.
   D. Contraception is unnecessary until regular ovulation is established.
   E. The growth spurt occurs earlier in males than females.

Answer Key on p. 465

15 The Adult Years

James A. H. Farrow, MD

- How do relationships with parents change during young adulthood?
- What are some of the risks and benefits of becoming a parent?
- How does sexual functioning differ between men and women of middle age?
- Why do some people have a "mid-life crisis"?
- Why do some "empty" nests become "elastic" nests?
- What organ system changes occur with increasing age?

Young Adulthood (20 to 40 Years)

The human body reaches peak strength, flexibility, functioning, and efficiency between the ages of 20 and 30. The combination of strong musculature, exceptional stamina, high resistance to disease, and rapid repair of tissue damage allows the young adult to develop specialized motor skills and maximal athletic and physical prowess. Poor health during this time is usually related to lifestyle choices and behaviors such as alcohol and substance abuse, poor exercise and nutritional habits, obesity, and mental health problems such as depression and stress-related conditions.

Cognitive Development

Brain cell development peaks during the 20s. However, new **synaptic pathways** are formed throughout adulthood, permitting the individual to learn new information and skills at any age. Young adults are informed, knowledgeable, and able to make complex decisions using cognitive abilities termed **formal operations**. They can organize, plan, and consider the short- and long-term consequences of actions.

Intellectual functioning continues to evolve throughout adulthood into an advanced phase of problem solving. This level of cognitive functioning is influenced by education, tolerance of diverse viewpoints, and **dialectical thinking** (i.e., ability to reexamine ideas as a result of critique). Cognitive and learning impairments identified during childhood and adolescence (e.g., attention-deficit/hyperactivity disorder [ADHD]) may continue well into adulthood. These disorders may be manifested by difficulty with the more challenging academic work in college or graduate studies or in organizing activities of daily living (**executive functioning**).

Moral Development

By adulthood, most individuals have developed a personal standard of behavior and adhere to **universal ethical principles**, including abiding by a *social contract* and respecting individual rights. When an individual's principles do not conform to existing law, conscience directs behavior. Accepting responsibility for one's actions and empathizing with others are part of that development. Key features of sociocultural development during this time are increasing prosocial behavior, civic engagement, and sense of purpose within society's standards of morality.

Gender and Sexuality

The **reproductive system** of both males and females is fully mature by the age of 20. The maximum capacity for reaching orgasm peaks in the late teens for males and in the 30s for females. Sex hormone production is highest in the 20s, but sex drive remains active in most persons for several decades, often into their 70s and 80s.

Observable behaviors and roles are easy for the young adult to evaluate and either incorporate or reject. However, intimate behavior is less observable and so less readily modeled. Discussion about comfort with **intimacy** is virtually unavailable to the young adult, and rarely addressed in clinical settings. Thus, many young adults abandon an otherwise promising relationship because of feeling unsure about how to achieve true psychosocial intimacy rather than merely perform intimate acts (e.g., fondling, intercourse). The impersonal nature of social media may contribute to the lack of human to human interpersonal skills.

Consolidation of **gender identity** and **sexual orientation** occurs during late adolescence and early adulthood. For lesbians and gay males, defining oneself as homosexual internally and then to others with same-sex attractions, is the first stage of disclosure, called "coming out." Retrospective studies of adult homosexuals have found that gay males typically define themselves as homosexual between 16 and 21 years of age. Adult lesbians reach self-definition somewhat later, between 21 and 23 years of age. These milestones have been occurring earlier in some populations as a result of improved social acceptance of sexual minorities including transgender persons.

Sexual Relationships

Between 2000 and 2009, the share of young adults aged 25 to 34 who are married dropped from 55% to 45%, according to data from the US Census Bureau. During the same period, the percentage that has never been married increased sharply, from 34% to 46%. In a dramatic reversal, the proportion of young adults in the US who have never been married now exceeds those who are married.

Delay in marriage is due, in part, to more women choosing to take advantage of educational and career opportunities. Living together and sharing sexual activities without being married is common among both heterosexuals and homosexuals. In 2005, unmarried households, including same-sex couples that are now being counted, became

the majority of all US households. Most of these relationships are short-term and average about 2 years.

Most individuals will marry eventually, but many choose long-term singlehood. **Singlehood** has the advantage of freedom to spend time, money, and other resources according to individual choice, more career opportunities, greater geographic mobility, enhanced sense of self-sufficiency, and more psychological autonomy. About 80% of both male and female singles report some kind of coital activity between the ages of 25 and 50.

Most women prefer to bear their children before age 45 when the complication rate begins to increase dramatically. With higher average life expectancy, bearing children before age 45 also allows women to parent their children into middle adulthood.

Social Development

Erikson described the major task of young adulthood as intimacy vs. isolation. **Intimacy**, as defined by Erikson, includes the ability to form an interpersonal relationship characterized by commitment, reciprocity, attachment, and interdependency. Because intimacy entails self-disclosure, achieving a truly intimate relationship requires a strong sense of self (identity). Intimacy is not limited to sexual or spousal relationships. Close and lasting friendships are formed during this period.

Isolation, in contrast to intimacy, includes feeling victimized or exploited by others, experiencing difficulty cooperating with others, and having such a fragile sense of identity that the self-disclosure and analysis required in an intimate relationship are too threatening. Traditionally, women have been able to establish intimate relationships earlier than men, who usually find it easier to engage in intimacy after they develop a secure occupational identity. The increased number of occupational options for women has made this gender difference in timing less pronounced than in the past.

Collegiality With Parents

How do relationships with parents change during young adulthood?

Once a stable and satisfying sense of **self** has developed, young adults begin to discover their parents as complex people. The change to exploring the interests, feelings, and values of parents is the beginning of a **period of mutuality** that extends until the individual assumes a caretaking role for an ill or elderly parent. In this initial stage, the young adult tentatively gives support and direction as well as receives it. The response of the parents can range from a reluctance to give up their parental authority, to an appreciation for the contemporary perspective their children can provide. Members of the **millennial generation** (young adults reaching age 18 around the turn of the century) have been brought up by parents who generally have been more protective than parents of past generations. This protective relationship often continues during the college and postcollege years, as young adults continue to depend on parents for support and advice and, more recently, access to health care insurance.

Generation Z (Gen Z) is the most common name given to the cohort born between 1995 and 2015. Characteristics from this generation include comfort with technology, interacting through social networking media, and having feelings of insecurity as a result of growing up through the Great Recession of December 2007 to June 2009.

Intergenerational Relationships

- Young adults are most likely to form stable intergenerational relationships within their family of origin when they adopt a lifestyle similar to, but independent of, their parents, if that choice is an authentic reflection of what the young adult wants to do.
- Conflicted relationships occur when young adults reject parental values and adopt an antagonistic or antithetical lifestyle, or they adopt the lifestyle desired by the family of origin but wish they had chosen differently.

Gender and Career Choices

Today, many women have **occupational goals** that have traditionally been reserved for men. Many men prefer a partner with job aspirations for economic reasons and for the prospect of shared interests. Both men and women who are career oriented are more likely to postpone marriage, delay parenthood, and have fewer children. However, for women, commitment to a career remains problematic. Women are still vulnerable to an employer's concerns about the potential work-related effects of pregnancy, maternity leave, or relocation to accommodate the husband's career, and are occasionally asked many potentially discriminatory questions about marital status and family situation, even though such questions are unlawful. In recent years, there has been a dramatic increase in domestic partner protections and benefits in the workplace, although equal pay for equal work among men and women still remains problematic.

Women who assume the multiple roles of wife–mother, homemaker, and career may find the combination too stressful for their physical and emotional health. On the other hand, the physical and emotional health of women who have no career other than wife and mother also may be in jeopardy. Women who work solely in the home have more depression, acute illnesses, chronic conditions, and health care visits than women who work both inside and outside the home.

Marriage and Parenthood

Having a satisfying marriage and family life is the goal of 80% of college students. Marriage partners typically share race, religion, age, social class, level of education, and mutual physical attraction. This includes same-sex couplings. Although the durability of marriage is influenced by many factors, marrying later appears to lead to more stable and satisfying relationships. Over the past 20 years, the average age of first marriage for men has increased from 27 to 29 years and for women from 25 to 27 years.

Men who marry in their teens have twice the risk of divorce as those who marry in their late 20s.

Women who marry between 14 and 17 have 4 times the risk of divorce as women who marry in their late 20s.

What are some of the risks and benefits of becoming a parent?

Life changes that challenge those who become parents include reduction in personal freedom, increased financial pressure, and concerns about being a good parent. The joys of parenthood stem from the pleasure derived from the child's development, the companionship, bonding, and awareness that the child is an extension of the parent's own self even when a child is adopted, and the sense that children are the individual's link with immortality. Parenthood often promotes a sense of true adulthood.

With age, the gradual lowering of *basal metabolic rate* results in reduced energy expenditure and caloric requirements. Although it may be typical to be overweight and less physically fit as a result of aging, research has shown that these body changes can be delayed by increased activity and better conditioning. Regular exercise slows both calcium loss from bones and the loss of muscle, helps maintain pulmonary functioning, and reduces kyphotic changes in the spine. Maintaining normal weight mitigates against the development of adult-onset type 2 diabetes.

Middle Age (40 to 65 Years)

After growth and development peaks in the 20s and 30s, middle age declines in physical, cognitive, affective, and social functioning begin. Many declines are subtle, slowly progressive, and so universally anticipated that the changes are virtually imperceptible until the latter half of middle age. **Loss of neurons** and **degeneration of neuronal pathways** result in slower nerve conduction, which lengthens reaction times. Unless skills are practiced, they are lost because of active **dendritic pruning**. Relearning is possible, however, and may require less time and effort if remnants of the neuronal pathways are still functional. **Alzheimer's disease, Parkinson's disease,** and **Huntington's disease** are specific neurodegenerative disorders. Genetic forms of these conditions typically appear in late middle and early old age. Outside of genetics, the onset of neurodegenerative disorders, especially **vascular dementia** (was *multi-infarct dementia*), is affected by the lifestyle choices (smoking, drinking) and stresses of early and middle adulthood (see Chapter 46: Neurocognitive Disorders: Dementia).

Although certain immunological responses (T cell function, wound healing) and physiological functions (bladder reflex, hair growth) are diminished, the most significant change with age is the diminished ability of the body to maintain homeostasis, particularly during periods of stress. When confronted with temperature extremes, emotional strain, or physical injury, middle-aged adults recover less rapidly than younger adults. Many self-regulatory processes are under neuroendocrine control suggesting that either neurostimulation, end organ response, or both may be diminished.

Cognitive Development

Cross-sectional studies of traditional IQ test scores show that overall **intelligence** begins to decline at about age 30. However, while *fluid intelligence* (response speed, memory span), which depends on smooth functioning of the central nervous system (CNS), clearly declines beginning in the middle adult years, *crystallized intelligence* (reading comprehension, vocabulary), which depends on education and experience, may continue to increase throughout the adult years.

Affective Development

The middle adult years are characterized by **reflection about life goals**, assessment of personal and professional accomplishments, and critical thinking about the future. Some midlife adults experience short-term distress over transitions but ultimately handle and learn from these crises. Other adults find that change cripples their decision-making skills, undermines their marriage or partner relationships, or interferes with their ability to be a parent. Good support systems enhance coping ability. Other positive factors include higher intelligence, flexible temperament, past successes in other areas of life, and absence of a significant mood disturbance.

Gender and Sexuality

The menstrual cycle becomes less regular in the late 30s and 40s and ceases for most women during their 50s. Factors associated with later menopause include childbearing, early puberty, maternal history, thin physique, higher socioeconomic status, northern European ancestry, and White race. The onset of menopause is associated with a decrease in the size of the reproductive organs and vaginal dryness and atrophy due to decreased estrogen production. This process is called the climacteric. Despite these changes, assistive reproductive technology enables some postmenopausal women to bear children, suggesting that the pace of the aging process varies among different organs even within a single system.

Men experience no single event to mark a **male climacteric**. The circulating level of testosterone does, however, decline with age. Although men remain fertile until late in life, developing an erection requires more time and stimulation, and both the volume of seminal fluid and the force of ejaculation diminish with age. Men with low testosterone in middle age report lower energy and libido. The metabolic changes accompanying low testosterone explain a constellation of clinical symptoms and signs that mimic menopause, and may produce the metabolic syndrome (see Chapter 5: Energy Homeostasis). Many symptoms may be partially corrected with testosterone supplementation.

Sexual Functioning

How does sexual functioning differ between men and women of middle age?

After the peak in male potency during the late teens and early adulthood, a decrease in interest and desire may occur at about age 50; a more significant drop in sexual activity occurs after age 70. Women, who reach peak sexual potency in their mid-30s, experience relatively little loss in capacity thereafter. However, the number of women who remain sexually active and the frequency of these activities decline with age and are correlated with the health of the spouse or partner. In contrast, partner health and marital status are poor predictors of sexual activity among older men.

The frequency of sexual intercourse drops to a level of 3–4 times/month among couples married 30 years. Older adults who have access to a regular partner report having intercourse about

2–3 times/month even at the age of 70. There are limited data about the relationship between aging and homosexual activity. Older gay men report continued sexual activity and satisfactory relationships. Less is known about the sexual activity of older lesbian women.

Social Development

Why do some people have a "mid-life crisis"?

Erikson proposed that the nuclear conflict of the adult years is generativity vs. stagnation. **Generativity** is concerned with guiding and contributing to the next generation. **Stagnation** refers to lack of productivity or creativity, self-centered behavior, and exploitation of others. Midlife is typically the time for attaining maximal job and career satisfaction and achievement, especially among men. Prestige and power are at their peak, and many middle-aged adults mentor younger colleagues to achieve a sense of generativity. Jobs requiring heightened sensory capabilities may be subject to age-related performance decrements and provoke early retirement. Job retraining in middle-age especially in technical fields may be more challenging. In contrast, artists and musicians may continue to be creative into very old age.

Many factors, such as health, personality, social environment, income, and educational level, affect the feelings and behaviors of the midlife adult. Marriage, parenthood, career, physical health, and general quality of life may be different from what was expected. Thus, many of the expectations of young adulthood must be reevaluated as time and energy become limited. Feelings of helplessness and a sense of being "trapped" can lead to a **midlife crisis**, during which individuals reexamine themselves and the meaning of life. As reevaluation of life goals occurs, many people experience an "identity crisis" similar to that typically associated with adolescence. Extramarital affairs are not uncommon during this period, reflecting uncertainty and disappointment about the value of previous commitments, or the need to be reassured about physical attractiveness. If the original marriage or relationship survives, reorganization of roles, redirection of energy, and rejuvenation of sexual activity may result.

Typical midlife issues include increasing assertiveness and independence among women and increasing emotionality and sensuousness among men.

Parent–Child Relationships

> Why do some "empty" nests become "elastic" nests?

The period a couple spends together from the time the last child leaves home to the time one partner dies is known as the **empty nest** period. This can be a challenging time for both, but particularly for the woman who loses the role of mother. Although there is a sense of loss, there is also relief from the responsibility of daily childrearing, more opportunities to pursue other interests, and increased personal freedom and privacy.

The **elastic nest** describes the phenomenon of children leaving the family of origin and then returning *(boomerang effect)* in response to job changes, divorce, or other life changes. This intermittent dependency can be fulfilling to the parents who still feel needed; reassuring to the child who still feels protected; and frustrating to all as they struggle with the challenge of trying to move forward developmentally.

Even before the financial crisis of the early 21st century, with its uncertain resolution worldwide, the phenomenon of **household consolidations**, where parents and children with loss of job and benefits, depletion of life savings, and foreclosure make mutual decisions to pool resources to avoid poverty and homelessness, began to take hold. Although the elastic nest was usually seen as a temporary arrangement, the duration of household consolidation remains unknown, but in many instances is likely to be permanent.

The middle-aged population of the late 20th century has been called the **sandwich generation**, caught between the continuing needs of their children and the new needs of their now-aging parents. Assuming responsibility for social, financial, emotional, or physical aid to their parents can be stressful for adult children. Such role reversal requires giving up reliance and dependency on the aging parent and assuming significant new responsibilities. How aging parents and their adult children negotiate these changes depends on competing obligations (e.g., to other family members, work, social networks) and the previous parent–child relationship.

Later Life (65+ Years)

From a health standpoint, 65 is not old. For example, any man who reached the age of 65 by the turn of the century could expect to live into his early 80s; any woman could expect to live into her mid-80s. Factors that affect longevity include health, access to regular health care, and socioeconomic status, with higher levels of income and economic security being associated with longer lifespan. Older persons, especially those ≥ 80, are the fastest growing age group. In 2000, the number of Americans ≥ 65 years of age exceeded the number ≤ 25. This trend has continued over the past decade with increasing numbers of *baby boomers* reaching retirement age.

Is There a Limit to Human Life Expectancy?
Certain molecular processes appear to regulate the lifespan of individual cells and the more complex tissues they make up. These processes include:

1. the number of individual cell replications;
2. the production of free radical by-products of energy metabolism, which creates an intracellular electrical imbalance that can damage other molecules (including DNA); and
3. glycosylation (glucose bonding to proteins to form sticky, web-like networks or cross-linkages producing changes such as cataracts and arteriosclerosis).

> What organ system changes occur with increasing age?

Changes in biological functioning due to aging are highly variable. Some older persons exhibit marked declines, while others exhibit little or no diminution in organ system functioning. Although most people aged 65–80 are not significantly limited by a chronic physical condition, they do have *diminished reserve*, reduced ability to adjust to physical or psychological challenges, and prolonged recovery following injury or disease. Some problems create more widespread dysfunction. *Neurosensory system losses*, such as decreased hearing and vision, are common in the elderly and may cause significant difficulty with eating, following instructions, and ambulation. Gerontologists refer to this as impairments in the **activities of daily living** (ADLs). Impaired regulation of core body temperature may lead to reduced fever response to severe infection, increased risk for heat stroke during the summer, and increased risk for hypothermia during the winter.

> While older individuals have an essentially intact immune system, there is some impairment in T cell function, and antibody responses are reduced. These and other changes in host defenses account for increased rates of infection of the skin and the urinary, gastrointestinal, and respiratory tracts in older adults, the last resulting in increased mortality from pneumonia and influenza.

Reduced cardiac and pulmonary reserve, along with frequent coexisting medical conditions such as arthritis and decreased exercise tolerance, contribute to the more sedentary lifestyle typical of many older adults. Many older individuals show evidence of *coronary arteriosclerosis*, although this finding is not predictive of any particular functional limitations. Diminished lung elasticity and total lung capacity decrease respiratory reserve and increase vulnerability to the effects of otherwise minor pulmonary diseases or insults such as smoking.

Kidney function gradually diminishes with age, usually at a rate of about 0.6% per year. This loss of renal function is attributable to both a reduced number of nephrons and a decrease in tubular functioning. Structural and functional changes in the **gastrointestinal system** include reduced peristalsis and gastric acid secretion and slower emptying times, which contribute to indigestion. Because of slowed metabolic rate and more sedentary lifestyle, obesity is common. Decreased hepatic drug oxidation rates and renal function lead to slower drug metabolism and excretion and, thus, higher blood levels of medications and their active metabolites. Age-related changes in drug pharmacokinetics also include increasing tissue sensitivity, especially in the CNS, resulting in more drug side effects. Given

that the standards for the use of most therapeutic agents were determined in younger adults, loading and maintenance doses of medication should usually be reduced when treating older patients.

Cognitive Development

Deterioration of mental functioning, or **dementia** (in DSM-5, dementia is principally referred to as *major neurocognitive disorder*, although the term *dementia* is retained "for continuity"), is an acquired, chronic impairment in global cognitive functioning that affects comprehension, memory, communication, and daily activities. Fewer than 10% of individuals ≥ 65 years of age have any form of measurable impairment in cognitive functioning. When dementia does occur, the patient's level of consciousness is usually normal, and the onset of cognitive impairment is so gradual that it may not be noticeable until some consistent threshold of impairment is reached. The typical course is chronic and progressive.

The dementia associated with **Alzheimer's disease**, which is diagnosable by classic symptoms, signs, course, and autopsy findings, accounts for about half to two thirds of all cases of dementia. A variety of other specific conditions, such as vascular dementia, account for the remaining cases. Approximately 10% to 15% of patients with dementia have treatable, potentially reversible disorders such as CNS tumor, subdural hematoma, hydrocephalus, drug toxicity, hypothyroidism or hyperthyroidism, alcoholism, cerebrovascular insult, or depression. Recovery in these cases depends on successful treatment of the underlying condition.

Affective Development

Recognition of personal limitations in physical or mental ability, fear of inability to care for oneself, or fear of abandonment can lead to **anxiety** (see Chapter 43: Depressive and Bipolar Disorders, and Chapter 44: Anxiety Disorders). Anxiety can also arise in association with specific conditions such as depression, dementia, and general medical illnesses. Thus, careful evaluation is critical for identifying potentially reversible causes of anxiety. As is true in other conditions, pharmacological treatment of anxiety should be cautious because of the increased incidence of medication side effects in the older patient.

> Individuals who developed insecure or mistrusting relationships early in life with their own parents appear most vulnerable to concerns about being taken advantage of by their children.

Loss plays a role in many life transitions, which older persons increasingly experience with the deaths of spouse and friends. Feelings of loss occur not only in reaction to death but also in reaction to illness. Anger and resentment are early manifestations of concerns about long-term functioning. Later, preoccupation with health status can lead to depression. The grief process comes to closure as the individual adopts a realistic level of concern regarding the long-term consequences of the condition (see Chapter 47: Stress Disorders, Bereavement, and Dissociative Disorders).

Depression is common in older persons and may be due to serious medical conditions, deterioration in functioning, and social losses. Rates of completed **suicide** increase with age in both men and women. In women, the rate plateaus beginning in middle age. In men, it continues to rise slowly through old age (see Chapter 27: Suicide).

The prevalence of **alcoholism** in older persons is estimated to be 10% to 15%. Approximately one third of elderly persons with alcoholism begin drinking excessively later in life. Those individuals who have a lifelong history of heavy alcohol intake may show evidence of *alcoholic dementia*.

Gender and Sexuality

The biological and social differences between men and women result in differences in their level of sexual activity during old age. In men, physiological degeneration of the *seminiferous tubules* causes decreased semen production and sperm quality. Although orgasm occurs, ejaculation is unlikely with every sexual act and retrograde ejaculation is common. The ability to develop an erection continues in old age, although the degree of tumescence is diminished. The concentration of circulating *testosterone* varies widely among elderly men, but, overall, serum levels decrease with age. Testosterone

levels do not correlate well with impotence when it occurs in elderly men because certain medications (e.g., beta blocking agents) interfere with erection. Medications to improve erectile function are generally safe and effective in older men.

Sexual functioning in women is less affected by age than it is in men. Although reproductive function ceases with menopause by the early to mid-50s, this process typically does not affect sexual desire. However, most surveys show that sexual activity is decreased among elderly women. Physiological changes (e.g., atrophy and drying of vaginal mucosa due to decreased estrogen levels) may play a role, but the decrease in sexual activity appears to be due to more *societal influences* than biological changes.

Social Development

The psychosocial challenge of late life was conceptualized by Erikson as ego integrity vs. despair. **Ego integrity** is maintained when the individual has overall positive feelings of self-worth and is able to view life as a series of personal achievements with challenges and failures in appropriate perspective. Those who do not view their life positively are likely to experience **despair**, isolation, melancholia, and depression. **Isolation** is the most significant threat to ego integrity. Stimulus deprivation can result from neurosensory deterioration (e.g., vision or hearing impairments) or from life in an institutional setting where opportunities for tender touch are limited. Older persons who lack a **support network** of familiar people and objects can lose the will to live.

Physical and neurosensory deterioration lead to reliance on others for normal ADLs. Many older persons are acutely aware of their loss of independence and ability for self-care. Family decisions about respite or nursing home care for elderly family members should include a professional assessment of level of functioning, ability to perform ADLs, and available family and community assistance.

Recommended Readings

Cavanaugh, J., & Blanchard-Fields, F. (2015). *Adult development and aging* (7th ed.). Stamford, CT: Cengage Learning.

Robinson, O. C. (2012). *Development through adulthood: An integrative sourcebook*. London, UK: Pelgrave and Macmillan.

Additional Resources

Association for Adult Development and Aging. Available at http://www.aadaweb.org

World Health Organization. (2015). *Dementia fact sheet number 362*. Available at http://www.who.int/media centre/factsheets/fs362/en/

Review Questions

1. Which of the following best describes a typical health-related characteristic of older persons?
   A. Decrease in completed suicides
   B. Decreased ability to eat
   C. Diminished physiological reserve
   D. Higher than 50% prevalence of dementia
   E. Increased pain

2. Among the following, the capability most likely to be spared in a person with dementia is
   A. activities of daily living
   B. communication
   C. comprehension
   D. consciousness
   E. mobility

3. Following are some general statements about old age. Which one is best supported by current evidence?
   A. Decreased independence and isolation are major threats to maintaining ego integrity.
   B. Depression and dementia are inevitable consequences of aging.
   C. Frailty in old age is primarily associated with physical functioning.
   D. Old people typically complain a great deal to their doctors about their health problems.
   E. The physical and mental changes associated with aging follow highly predictable timelines.

Answer Key on p. 465

16 The Family

J. LeBron McBride, PhD, MPH

- What are the varieties of contemporary families?
- What are the implications of viewing families as small social systems?
- What is the value of a genogram in family assessment?
- What are the stages of the family life cycle?
- What are respite care and custodial care?
- What are five types of postdivorce relationship?

As a new health care professional, you begin your practice with enthusiasm but are puzzled that many patients do not make the changes you encourage. During a visit with a patient and his wife, you find they have a traditional marriage. She does all the cooking, but the patient has concealed the need to change his diet "so as not to worry her." Therefore, you explain the goals of treatment directly to her. At his next visit, the patient has lost several pounds, is eating better, and walks daily with his wife.

Families are not just collections of individuals. Powerful interactions, patterns, and dynamics in each family play a significant role in the development and socialization of individuals and have a profound influence on the health and welfare of family members. Families embody *risk* and *protective factors* that can influence the onset and course of disease. Some factors, such as genetic predisposition, shared family trauma, or family ethnic background, are unmodifiable. Others, such as patterns of communication, power sharing, family structure, and belief systems, may be modified to reduce risk. And still other factors may or may not be modifiable, such as environmental circumstances that can place additional strains upon family systems and individual members. For example, the increasing costs of health care and other barriers to accessibility have resulted in families assuming greater responsibility for health care in the home, placing additional pressures on caregivers and family relationships.

Varieties of Contemporary American Families

What are the varieties of contemporary families?

The US Census Bureau defines a **family** as two or more persons who live together and are related by blood, marriage, or adoption. By this definition, 81.2% of households in 1970 were family households as compared with about 66% in the early 2000s. The number of married couples with children in the home has declined from about 40% of all households in 1970 to 20% in the first decade of the 21st century. This change reflects older age at first marriage, declining marriage rates, postponement of childbearing, children born to persons who are not married, and high rates of separation and divorce. The proportion of children living in single-parent households increased from 12% in 1970 to 28% in 2014. The proportion of children living in single-parent homes more than doubled between 1970 and 2014 from 12% to 28%. About 84% of single-parent households are headed by mothers. Living in a *single-parent household* is an important risk factor for poor health outcome for both the mother and her dependents. Mediating variables include limited income, lacking time for medical appointments for themselves or others, the stress of being unable to meet basic needs due to illness, and carrying the burden of another's care without support. However, with adequate external support, the children in single-parent families do as well as those raised by couples or extended families.

US families are changing at a rapid pace. Families may define themselves differently from how they are counted in the census, and patterns of family life are more varied and complex than in the past. By traditional definitions, the **nuclear family** includes spouses and their children living together. An **extended family** includes three or four generations and encompasses not only grandparents but also aunts, uncles, cousins, and unrelated individuals who come together out of affection, obligation, or economic necessity. The **family of origin** is the family into which a person was born, which may differ from the **family of procreation** or another current household.

Incorporating children from a previous marriage results in a **blended family**. Varying loyalties to the divorced biological parents, anger about the dissolution of the previous family, blame directed at some or all of the adults involved, and guilt about personal responsibility for causing the divorce can foster confusion and conflict in the children. In addition, if the newly formed couple has biological children between them, the complexity of the pattern of relationships and loyalties is increased. Most parents and children are unprepared for the reorganization and adaptation required in a blended family structure.

The US Supreme Court decision of 2015 that made same-sex marriage legal in all states was a recognition that the numbers of same-sex unions and **same-sex families** are increasing and need legal protection. Historically, both society and the families of origin focused on the couple's sexuality, ignoring their social, financial, and emotional needs, which are similar to those of heterosexual couples. In general, children raised in gay and lesbian families do not experience negative effects due to the parents' sexual orientation, nor are they more likely to be gay or lesbian themselves.

The presence or absence of children does not define a family. The availability of safe contraception has made it possible for couples to choose *childlessness*. Reasons for this choice include dedication to career, concerns about personal resources or overpopulation, illness, and developmentally related desires not to be a parent. When young, such couples often face considerable social pressure to have children. For couples unable to have children, treatment for infertility, even if ultimately successful, may produce significant strains, making the couple's sexual life mechanistic and unsatisfying, and imposing large financial burdens.

Families as Social Systems

> What are the implications of viewing families as small social systems?

Considering the family as a small social system involves the concept of **boundaries,** both *external* boundaries between family and nonfamily, and *internal* boundaries between members. *Diffuse external* boundaries allow individuals to come and go at will. In such families, dependent members, especially children, may not have adequate protection and security. *Closed* boundaries make entering and exiting the family difficult. This compromises the eventual emancipation of adolescent or adult children and prevents the acceptance of outside help, including even medical care. The open boundary around a healthy family can change, according to members' immediate needs. For example, a cousin or a friend can step in to care for a child who is ill and out of school, or the family may provide housing to an older member who can no longer manage alone.

Internal family boundaries, especially the boundaries between generations, significantly influence health and behavior. Emotional closeness or bonding among family members is termed **cohesion.** It ranges from *disengagement* (closed boundaries between individuals and low emotional reactivity) to *enmeshment* (diffuse boundaries between individuals and high emotional reactivity). Either extreme can affect family members' emotional well-being and self-regulation. In well-functioning families, adults support one another in setting expectations, applying age appropriate limits on behavior, and transmitting cultural values.

Boundary violations, for example, when a child allies with one parent against the other or when one parent relies on their relatives and excludes a spouse, contribute to a range of behavioral and health-related problems. An adolescent boy who lives with his mother and hears constant disparagement of his father may struggle with self-esteem. A grandmother who undermines her son's relationship with his wife may complicate the couple's ability to manage their child's diabetes. The grossest violations of boundaries, intra-family violence or incest (adult against child or within a generation), can contribute to unstable chronic disease, functional somatic disorders, violent behavior (including homicide or suicide), substance abuse, and psychiatric disorders.

Communication among family members can be *functional* (clear and direct) or *dysfunctional* (confused and indirect). Communication occurs on verbal as well as nonverbal levels. The actual words of verbal communication are modified by *prosody* (i.e., tone, volume, pitch of the voice) and *nonverbal behavior* (e.g., gestures, facial expressions, touches). Healthy families demonstrate congruent verbal and nonverbal communication, express emotion and caring, and share feelings and thoughts (see Chapter 10: Cognition, Communication, and Social Interaction).

Overall, family functioning determines **familial power relationships**. Different family members may exert power in different domains: elders may establish cultural norms, while other members provide emotional comfort, and still others control how the family manages its time, where they live, and how they meet financial obligations. Like boundaries, power arrangements within families may be chaotic, rigid, or flexibly adaptive to changing circumstances.

Changes within society and the place of the family within the **family life cycle** are normal modifiers of family systems. The need for two incomes and women's desires for broader social roles have led many families in the US to abandon traditional patriarchal configurations for more egalitarian structures. As children grow, family rules evolve to reflect changing capacities. Unexpected demands, such as job loss or providing care for a severely or chronically ill member, may require changes in who has power to do what and can induce both emotional distress and unstable behavior. Flexibly adaptive family structures allow families to adjust rather

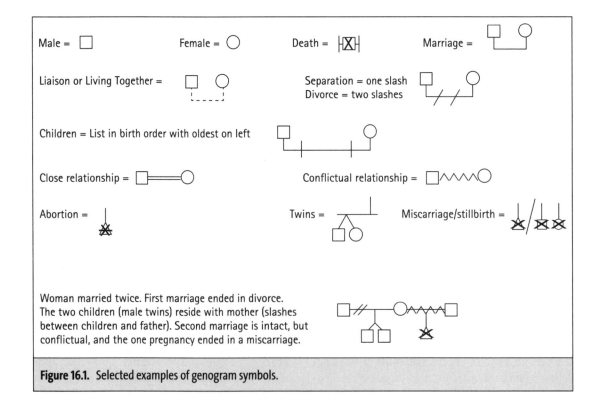

Figure 16.1. Selected examples of genogram symbols.

than become stuck in patterns that no longer work.

Family researchers assess families by interacting with them over time, eliciting different points of view, directly probing relationships, and observing patterns of interaction and communication. Most medical care providers assess families based on the descriptions provided by an individual patient or by a parent–child or spouse–patient dyad. In either case, construction of a family genogram uncovers and efficiently presents a wealth of information about family history, structure, and functioning.

Genograms

> **What is the value of a genogram in family assessment?**

Genograms (see Figure 16.1) are a type of family tree that can be used to diagram life events, illnesses, and interpersonal relationships. They may communicate ethnic, religious, and relationship histories as well as the patterns of occurrence of certain problems (e.g., substance abuse, marital conflict, a hereditary disease).

The Family Life Cycle

> **What are the stages of the family life cycle?**

The concepts of the family life cycle derive from the study of nuclear families, although these concepts can be applied to other family constellations as well. Health care providers must recognize the diversity of life trajectories, outdated assumptions about family life, and increased complexity in families today. We cannot assume that our own family is the norm by which others are measured; our concept of family must be broad enough to include variety and multiple formations. However, the traditional family life cycle can provide a foundational understanding of family transitions over time. It is important to realize that stages are rarely clear-cut and can merge more with one another than in past eras.

The traditional family life cycle involves six stages: (1) being between families: the single young adult; (2) joining: the newly married couple; (3) incorporating: the family with young children; (4) letting go vs. holding on: the family with adolescents; (5) launching children: the empty nest; and (6) withstanding time: the family in later life (see Table 16.1).

Transitions between life cycle stages require adaptation to new ways of functioning (e.g., changing the marital relationship to accommodate a child; accepting the independence of a child who graduates from high school). Well-functioning families that have anticipated these transitions and use effective coping strategies are most likely to maintain good individual and family health.

Between Families: Single Young Adults

This phase involves the young adult establishing independence and autonomy; separating from parents; establishing new relationships; and assuming responsibility for financial management, place of residence, and health care. Cohabitation has become a part of the process into marriage in the US; 69% of first marriages are preceded by living together. In many societies, especially those that promote early arranged marriage, young people never live "between families" because they either bring a spouse into their family of origin or marry into their partner's family without living independently.

Joining: Newly Married Couples

The median age at first marriage in the US has increased since the late 1900s from 23 to 27 years for females and from 25 to 29 years for males. Although illegal in this country, child marriages, often between a young girl and an older man, are common elsewhere. Such arrangements can have negative psychological and social consequences for the girls, who rarely complete their education and never develop the skills to support or protect themselves or their children. Child marriage customs also foster the transmission of sexually transmitted infections and maternal disability or death from early and frequent pregnancy.

Table 16.1. Stages of the family life cycle

Family Life Cycle Stages	Key Features of the Associated Emotional Processes	Changes Required for Evolution
Between families: Single young adults	Accepting emotional and financial responsibility for self	a. Differentiation of self in relation to family of origin b. Development of intimate peer relationships c. Establishment of vocational and financial independence
Joining: Newly married couple	Committing to a new system	a. Formation of marital system b. Realignment of relationships with extended family/friends to include spouse/partner
Incorporating: Families with young children	Accepting new members into the system	a. Adjusting marital system to accommodate children b. Sharing childrearing, financial, and household tasks c. Realignment of relationships with extended family to include parenting and grandparenting roles
Letting go/holding on: Families with adolescents	Increasing flexibility of family boundaries to permit children's independence and grandparents' dependence	a. Shift in parent/child relationships to permit adolescents movement into/out of the system b. Refocus on midlife marital and vocational issues c. Beginning shift toward caring for older generation
Launching children: Empty-nest couples	Accepting exits from and entries into the family system	a. Renegotiation of marital system as a dyad b. Development of adult-to-adult relationships between children and their parents c. Realignment of relationships to include in-laws and grandchildren d. Dealing with disability and death of parents (grandparents)
Withstanding time: Couples in later life	Accepting shifting generational roles	a. Maintenance of functioning and interests despite physiological decline b. Support for central role of middle generation c. Adjustment to loss of spouse, siblings, and peers and preparation for death

Adapted from Carter, B., & McGoldrick, M. (Eds.) (1999). *Expanded family life cycle: The individual, family, and social perspectives* (3rd ed.). Boston, MA: Allyn and Bacon.

The glossing over of conflicts or difficulties common in the early stages of a new relationship between adults is called *romantic idealization* or the "utopia syndrome." Eventually, the new couple must integrate the expectations they bring from their respective families. As it evolves, a relationship requires communication, negotiation, compromise, and conflict resolution to remain healthy. This stage often involves negotiation about contraception and childbearing, which may involve consultation with health care professionals.

Incorporating: Families With Young Children

With the arrival of children, the partners (or extended family) must adjust to meeting the child's needs, the resultant disruption in family routines, and decreased time alone. Differences in childrearing practices, thresholds for exhaustion and privacy, and balancing demands for time and attention required by the children must be negotiated. As children grow and develop, they interact with larger systems such as peer groups and schools. These experiences bring new ideas and energy into the family, but may lead the child to challenge the family's belief system and routines. Children of immigrants often function as cultural interpreters for their parents, which may be both a stress and a source of enhanced self-esteem for them.

Letting Go Versus Holding On: Families With Adolescents

The major issue of Western adolescence is **autonomy**. If the family has been authoritarian, rigid, or enmeshed, this life cycle transition may be difficult. Parents and adolescents who avoid extreme positions and negotiate compromises make the most successful transitions. Adolescents' difficulty assessing risk may require families to impose reasonable rules about acceptable behavior, especially about driving and substance use. Some adolescents react to the self-consciousness that comes with the bodily changes of puberty or to rejection or nonacceptance by peers by retreating into the family, and may need encouragement to seek out new experiences and better peer relationships. Compared with Europeans, US families appear to have particular difficulty talking openly with their adolescents about sex, leading to higher rates of teenage pregnancy and sexually transmitted infections.

Launching Children: Empty-Nest Couples

While many couples derive satisfaction and relief from knowing that the phase of rearing dependent children is past, others experience feelings of uselessness (**empty nest**). Because of educational, financial, career, or marital considerations, adult children may return to their parents' home repeatedly, the so-called *boomerang effect*. There can be a delayed onset of fully assuming the adult role called *emerging adulthood*. Young adults today are not reaching the traditional adulthood markers such as launching from the parental home, starting a family, and becoming established in a career as early as prior generations. This is a prime example of why the family life cycle is best viewed as a flexible series of stages and transitions, some of which are extended or repeated.

As parents enter middle age, they become aware of *health problems* in peers and experience their own *physical changes* (e.g., increased weight, decreased metabolic rate). This motivates many to initiate better health practices. Age-related bodily changes occurring at this stage typically signal decline. Coping with these reminders of mortality may adversely affect well-being and marital adjustment. Struggles with personal identity can produce a **midlife crisis**.

This is also the period when most couples experience the loss of their parents and assume the roles of matriarch or patriarch for younger generations. The addition of grandchildren may bring the generations closer together as the new parents come to appreciate the contributions their parents made to their own care and upbringing. Grandparents can enjoy their grandchildren without the demands of parenthood, but must respect and support their adult children as parents.

Withstanding Time: Couples in Later Life

Adjustments during this period of life include retirement and shifting generational roles. *Physical and intellectual decline, custodial care, loss*, and *bereavement* become major issues. For some, the later stage of life involves enjoying accomplishments and finding satisfaction in the freedom to pursue new interests. For others, the transitions and adjustments are negative. With the aging of baby boomers in the US, we are seeing an increase in older persons divorcing, which has been termed the **gray divorce revolution**. In 1990, only 8% of people who divorced were over 50 compared with 25% in 2013.

Retirement requires significant adjustment if the couple has difficulty tolerating the amount of time they now have together, or if the partners disagree about how to divide their time between outside interests and each other. Those who have derived their identity from their vocation miss the satisfaction of their job and may become isolated. Retirement can strain financial resources if income drops as assisted living and medical expenses increase.

The most significant loss experienced during this stage is the death of the spouse (25% of adults 65 or older are widowed). When a death occurs, the extended family must realign and adjust to new relationships. If death followed chronic illness, burnout among caregivers may complicate the adjustment process, limiting support for the grieving spouse.

What are respite care and custodial care?

Many persons function well in old age but physical and intellectual declines eventually concern both the individual and the family. Some dependent individuals can be cared for within their family with periodic **respite care**. Others need partial or full **custodial care** in an **assisted living facility** or **nursing home**.

Assessing the attitudes of each family member about custodial care, the family's emotional and logistical resources without placement, the financial resources for placement, and timing of the placement is vital. Options such as home nursing care, bringing a full-time caretaker into the home, and accessing community services should be explored. Some individuals relocate to be near adult children, oftentimes after a long period of resistance. Even when the individual is living independently, this change can be precarious. Losing long-established friendships and routines and trying to establish new relationships and habits may make such changes extremely stressful and poorly tolerated.

Special Issues of Contemporary Families

Occupation and Career

Two-career families must balance childrearing, household chores, and careers. Women generally retain the major responsibility for running the home even if they have other employment. Despite the added stress, women who work outside the home report enhanced self-esteem, but letting career obligations routinely take precedence over family life can produce tension in both marital and parental relationships.

More than 64% of mothers with children younger than 6 years and about 75% of mothers with children 6 to 17 years old work outside the home. Comparisons between children raised by *stay-at-home mothers* and children placed in *child care* reveal that the effect of early child care on infant development reflects many factors such as group size, child to caretaker ratio, and consistency of the child care provider.

Latchkey children are youngsters younger than 13 years who care for themselves at home while their parents work. Although parents may be concerned about children at home alone, many have few alternatives. Lack of appropriate supervision increases the risk of behavioral problems as well as the risk of accidents, mistreatment, or exploitation. Recognizing this, many schools and community agencies provide after-school programs, but cost may be a limiting factor for many families.

Geographic Mobility

Geographic mobility often results in separation from extended family that might otherwise provide support and nurturance. Due to the ready-made network of the workplace, the one who accepts a job transfer may have less difficulty with the change than other family members who do not have the positive reinforcement of a promotion or other career advancement. Indeed, they are likely to lose the community status they have achieved and the support provided by long-term relationships with friends and others, including health care providers. Recent moves and isolation from extended family are recognized risk factors for the incidence and perpetuation of domestic violence. New patient visits provide an excellent opportunity for the health care provider to assess emotional health as well as physical health as the family acclimates to its charged environment just by asking: "How are things at home?" However, truly screening for domestic violence requires more specific probes (see Chapter 25: Interpersonal Violence and Abuse).

Divorce

It is estimated that almost 50% of all US marriages will end in **divorce.** The family life cycle of divorcing families has different phases (see Table 16.2). As a result of family instability and disrupted parenting, children of divorced parents are at increased risk for depression and conduct problems, although not all children of divorce experience these difficulties. Family scholars have called divorce a "detour" for the family, with most eventually rejoining the "main road" of family development, although with greater complexity. Parents need to assure their children that the divorce is not their fault and to maintain as much stability as possible in their children's lives during the process. Ideally, they should refrain from criticizing or devaluing the divorced partner; children identify with both parents and having to divide loyalties is frequently troubling and disruptive for them until they reach a new equilibrium.

Litigation in court is the most common approach to divorce settlements and to child custody. It is typically costly, time-consuming, and

Table 16.2. Phases of the family life cycle for divorcing families

Phase		Emotional Process of Transition: Prerequisite Attitude	Developmental Issues
Divorcing	Decision to divorce	Accepting the relationship must end	a. Accepting personal responsibility for the failure of the marriage
	Planning the break-up of the system	Supporting viable arrangements for all parts of the system	b. Working cooperatively on problems of custody, visitation, and finances
			c. Dealing with extended family about the divorce
	Separation	Coparenting cooperatively Beginning dissolution of attachment to spouse	a. Mourning loss of the intact family
			b. Restructuring marital and parent–child relationships
			c. Realigning of relationships with own and spouse's extended family
	Divorce	Overcoming hurt, anger, and guilt	a. Mourning loss of the intact family; giving up fantasies of reunion
Postdivorce	Single parent (custodial household or primary residence)	Maintaining cooperative coparenting	a. Making flexible visitation arrangements with ex-spouse and family
			b. Rebuilding own social, financial, and emotional resources
	Single parent (noncustodial)	Maintaining cooperative coparenting Fulfilling financial responsibilities Maintaining parental contact and supporting custodial parent's relationship with children	a. Finding solutions to problems of visitation and distance parenting
			b. Fulfilling financial responsibilities to ex-spouse and children
			c. Rebuilding own social, financial, and emotional network

Adapted from Carter, B., & McGoldrick, M. (Eds.) (1999). *Expanded family life cycle: The individual, family, and social perspectives* (3rd ed.). Boston, MA: Allyn and Bacon.

adversarial. **Divorce mediators** function as neutral parties in negotiating divorce settlements, seeking a mutually acceptable division of assets and authority. Successful mediation is contingent on both partners' willingness to negotiate without intimidation. The resulting agreement is usually reviewed by the attorney and financial consultant representing each party.

Legal custody can be *sole* (i.e., one parent has the legal right to make decisions regarding the child) or *joint* (i.e., both parents have the legal right to share in decisions). **Physical custody** can be either sole or joint. In sole physical custody, the child lives with one parent, and the other parent may have visitation rights as determined by the court or the parents. In joint custody, the amount of time the child spends at each home is negotiated.

Health care professionals sometimes participate in custody negotiations. Joint custody may not be in the best interests of the child when one parent is clearly abusive, addicted, or unstable. Also, when caring for children of divorced parents, providers must know who has legal authority to consent to medical care.

Reduced standard of living is a major problem for the children of divorced parents. True financial hardship is a common result of the need to maintain two households. Nonpayment of child support is also a problem. Unresolved conflict between the former spouses is a primary motivation for nonpayment. Withholding child support is used to punish the former spouse, often without regard for how nonpayment affects the child. From the children's perspective, financial support can be perceived as a measure of how much the noncustodial parent loves and cares for them.

> **What are five types of postdivorce relationship?**

People adjusting to divorce typically vacillate between relief and depression (see Chapter 47: Stress Disorders, Bereavement, and Dissociative Disorders). Unless aware that this emotional turmoil is normal, they may feel they are becoming mentally ill. Rapid movement into another relationship provides escape from emotional pain. Such "rebound" relationships are usually short term, but typically act as conduits to the next phase of relationship building.

Postdivorce Relationships

Perfect Pals: Disappointment about the failed marriage does not impair positive elements of the relationship. Share decision making. Spend holidays together and maintain relations with extended families. Many feel they are better parents divorced than married.

Cooperative Colleagues: Work together around concerns of children and family, but are not close friends. Able to manage conflicts and separate spousal from parental issues.

Angry Associates: Like cooperative colleagues but not able to compartmentalize anger. Often tense, hostile, or in open conflict with former spouse.

Fiery Foes: Intensely angry and litigious years after the divorce. Unable to recall anything good about the marriage. Cling to very old wrongs. Still attached, but quick todeny it.

Dissolved Duos: After the divorce, have no further contact.

Adapted from Ahrons, C. R. (1990, June). Divorce: Not the end, but a change in a relationship. In D. Bishop (Ed.), *The Brown University Family Therapy Letter* (p. 4). Providence, RI: Manisses Communication Group.

Although highly educated women are less likely to do so, most divorced persons remarry. Some persons experience feelings of loss when their former spouse marries, because they must confront disavowed fantasies of reconciliation.

Surrogate Mothering

Surrogacy refers to bearing a child for someone else, usually in return for payment. Reasons for choosing a surrogate include infertility, repeated miscarriages, hysterectomy, or other health conditions. Whenever possible, the *commissioning couple* supply both sperm and egg, which, when fertilized *in vitro,* is implanted in the surrogate mother's uterus *(gestational carrier surrogate).* This procedure circumvents the issue of whose child the woman is carrying, because all genetic material derives from the couple. In some situations, the sperm or egg may be provided by an anonymous donor bank. Potential confusion regarding parental rights, still debated in the court system, makes a gestational carrier the least desirable egg donor.

Moral, ethical, and legal issues raised by surrogate mothering include arguments that it is exploitative, particularly of poor women. "Renting" a woman's uterus places her at risk for pregnancy- and delivery-associated complications, for which financial gain seems inadequate benefit. Some surrogates, however, derive great satisfaction from helping infertile couples. For the couple seeking surrogacy, this technologic advance significantly lessens the emotional pain of infertility by allowing them to have a biological child.

Family Interventions in Contemporary Health Care

Recent trends in early hospital discharge have stimulated the growth of *home health agencies.* Agency personnel assist family members with caretaking responsibilities including home dialysis, home chemotherapy, and ventilator management. The patient may recover more function more quickly than in an institutional setting, and the family may experience a heightened sense of accomplishment. Parents of children undergoing treatment, in particular, may feel in better control of the care and comfort their child receives. Even with good resources and the ability to give adequate care, however, **caregiver burnout** is common.

Families embodying relatively unmodifiable risk factors such as recent losses or highly dysfunctional structure may be referred to mental health providers for **family therapy**. However, all clinicians should learn simple family interventions, particularly how to educate family members about the medical conditions and needs of individual patients. They may enlist families directly for patients < 18 years (except for **emancipated minors**, or where confidentiality is protected by law, as in the provision of reproductive health services in some US states). Adults should always be asked to consent for physician communication with family members, who should be specifically identified by the patients.

Sophisticated clinicians intent on changing modifiable risk factors learn to identify and ally themselves with family members who have the respect and authority to arbitrate cultural boundar-

ies, relieve others' emotional distress, and allocate resources. Different family members may have influence in different domains. For example, if a patient mistrusts the scientific explanation of a symptom, it may be most effective to engage the family member who is sympathetic to or shares the patient's concerns. Integrating competing medical and cultural perspectives within the family reduces conflict and facilitates treatment adherence (see Chapter 17: Culture and Cultural Competence in Health Care). When the patient and family share a pathological behavior or belief, such as abnormal eating or substance abuse, failure to involve family members inevitably undermines treatment, whereas including family members can enhance healing.

Recommended Readings

Benokraitis, N. (2014). *Marriages and families: Changes, choices, and constraints* (8th ed.). Upper Saddle River, NJ: Pearson Education.

Knox, D., & Schacht, C. (2013). *Choices in relationships: An introduction to marriage and the family* (11th ed.). Belmont, CA: Wadsworth.

McDaniel, S., Doherty, W., & Hepworth, J. (2014). *Medical family therapy and integrated care* (2nd ed.). Washington, DC: American Psychological Association. http://doi.org/10.1037/14256-000

Thomlison, B. (2016). *Family assessment handbook: An introductory practice guide to family assessment* (4th ed.). Boston, MA: Cengage Learning.

Thoburn, J., & Sexton, T. (2015). *Family psychology: Theory, research, and practice.* Santa Barbara, CA: Praeger.

Additional Resources

National Council on Family Relations. Available at: https://www.ncfr.org/

American Association of Marriage and Family Therapists. Available at: https://www.aamft.org/iMIS15/AAMFT

Review Questions

1. What is the average age at first marriage for males and females in the US?
   A. 21, 20
   B. 23, 22
   C. 25, 26
   D. 26, 28
   E. 29, 27

2. Which percentage is the closest estimate of single-parent households in the US that are headed by mothers?
   A. 25%
   B. 35%
   C. 55%
   D. 75%
   E. 85%

3. A family that isolates from the larger society would have what kind of boundaries?
   A. Chaotic
   B. Closed
   C. Diffuse
   D. Open
   E. Solid

4. The traditional family life cycle model is to be understood as
   A. a basic structure for understanding family constellations
   B. a way to keep family life simple
   C. an example of the desired normal
   D. the goal of all healthy families
   E. the most common family process

5. The *boomerang effect* is
   A. adult children returning to live in the parental home
   B. the impact of sickness on the couple's relationship
   C. the off-again, on-again status of many early relationships
   D. the tendency of old family patterns to be perpetrated
   E. the way violence is transmitted in the family

Answer Key on p. 465

Section VI
Social and Cultural Issues

17 Culture and Cultural Competence in Health Care

Marlene Camacho-Rivera, ScD, MPH

- How do the changing demographics of the US population influence the need for "culturally competent" care?
- What are three ways in which provider diversity can contribute to reducing health care disparities?
- What are the five constructs that make up Campinha-Bacote's process of cultural competence in the delivery of health care services?
- What are the health, social, and financial benefits of cultural competence in health care settings?
- How has the construct of culture-bound syndromes changed within the DSM-5?

The Importance of Culturally Competent Care

> How do the changing demographics of the US population influence the need for "culturally competent" care?

The US is becoming an ever more racially and ethnically diverse nation. Studies by the Pew Research Center show that, by 2060, White Americans will make up 43% of the nation's population, while Hispanic and Black Americans will, together, make up 45% of the population. Furthermore, it has been projected that nearly one in five persons will be foreign born. Over the next several decades, the number of Americans who identify as being of two or more races is expected to increase substantially (Table 17.1).

These demographic changes in the US population will have significant implications for the health care system and the well-being of the people it serves.

In 2013, according to the Association of American Medical Colleges (AAMC), Black or African Americans and Hispanics or Latinos made up 4.1% and 4.4%, respectively, of all active physicians in the US, with American Indians or Alaska Natives accounting for 0.4%, and Asians for 11.7%.

Under these circumstances,

- individuals from racial and ethnic minority backgrounds suffer from greater health problems than their White counterparts;
- racial and ethnic minorities have been found to have different patterns of health care use compared with nonminorities; disparities in access to health care contribute to these differences; and
- although there has been increased representation of minorities in the health professions, minorities continue to be underrepresented among physicians and nurses, relative to their proportion of the general population.

> What are three ways in which provider diversity can contribute to reducing health care disparities?

It is anticipated that the demographics of the health care workforce will change in the second half of the 21st century. Research has demonstrated that provider diversity can contribute to reducing disparities in health care in at least three ways:

1. *Improved access:* Minority providers are more likely to treat minority patients and to practice in underserved communities.
2. *Increased patient satisfaction:* Studies indicate that when minority patients can select a health care professional, they are more likely to

Table 17.1. Population by race and Hispanic origin: 2014 and 2060 (population in thousands)

Race and Hispanic Origin[1]	2014		2060		Change 2014 to 2060	
	No.	%	No.	%	No.	%
Total Population	**318,748**	**100.0**	**416,795**	**100. 0**	**98,047**	**30.8**
One Race	310,753	97.5	390,772	93.8	80,020	25.8
White	246,940	77.5	285,314	68.5	38,374	15.5
Non-Hispanic White	198,103	62.2	181,930	43.6	−16,174	−8.2
Black or African American	42,039	13.2	59,693	14.3	17,654	42.0
American Indian and Alaska Native	3,957	1. 2	5,607	1. 3	1,650	41. 7
Asian	17,083	5.4	38,965	9.3	21,882	128 .1
Native Hawaiian and Other Pacific Islander	734	0.2	1,194	0.3	460	62.6
Two or More Races	7,995	2.5	26,022	6.2	18,027	225.5
Race Alone or in Combination[2]						
White	254,009	79.7	309,567	74.3	55,558	21. 9
Black or African American	45,562	14.3	74,530	17.9	28,968	63.6
American Indian and Alaska Native	6,528	2.0	10,169	2.4	3,640	55.8
Asian	19,983	6.3	48,575	11. 7	28,592	143 .1
Native Hawaiian and Other Pacific Islander	1,458	0.5	2,929	0.7	1,470	100.8
Hispanic or Latino Origin						
Hispanic	55,410	17.4	119,044	28.6	63,635	114.8
Not Hispanic	263,338	82.6	297,750	71.4	34,412	13.1

Note. [1] Hispanic origin is considered an ethnicity, not a race. Hispanics may be of any race. Responses of "Some Other Race" from the 2010 Census are modified. For more information, see https://www.census.gov/popest/data/historical/files/MRSF-01-US1.pdf
[2] "In combination" means in combination with one or more other races. The sum of the five race groups adds to more than the total population, and 100 percent, because individuals may report more than one race.

Reprinted from Colby, S. L. & Ortman, J. M. (2015). *Projections of the size and composition of the U.S. population: 2014 to 2060. Population estimates and projections.* Washington, DC: U.S. Census Bureau. Retrieved from https://www.census.gov/content/dam/Census/library/publications/2015/demo/p25-1143.pdf

choose someone of their own racial and ethnic background. Relationships between providers and patients of the same racial or ethnic background have also been found to entail higher levels of respect, trust, and recommendation of the provider to other patients.

3. *Support of culturally competent care:* Health professions education research has demonstrated that exposure to racial and ethnic diversity during training contributes significantly to the cultural competence of future providers by broadening the learning environment, helping students challenge racial and ethnic assumptions, and expanding students' perspectives regarding cultural differences.

Recruiting a diverse health care workforce is necessary, but insufficient by itself to provide quality care for patients of various groups. The AAMC has identified cultural competence education and training as a key strategy to reduce health disparities, and promote health equity and the practice of culturally responsive care. Furthermore, the Liaison Committee on Medical Education (LCME) and the Accreditation Council for Graduate Medical Education (ACGME) now require cultural competence education and training.

Definitions and Conceptual Frameworks for Cultural Competence

A number of frameworks and guidelines have been proposed to help health care providers consider patients' cultural context and conduct cultural assessments. These models acknowledge that, while awareness of, and respect for, different cultural traditions are valued, familiarity with all cultural perspectives a health care provider might encounter in clinical practice is impractical. Additionally, viewing patients as members of ethnic or cultural groups, rather than as individuals with unique experiences and perspectives, might lead providers to stereotype patients and make inappropriate assumptions about their beliefs and behaviors.

Early Models of Cultural Competence

Pioneers in cross-cultural medicine outlined the general attitudes and skills that form the foundation for cultural competence. These include (1) cultural awareness and respect for diversity of individuals and groups; (2) cultural knowledge of health believes and behaviors as well as understanding of similarities of biological, psychological, and sociopolitical causes of illness; (3) ability to care for all individuals with trust, empathy, respect, and cultural appropriateness; and (4) recognition of cultural competences as a continuous process.

Culture is shaped by multiple factors including race, ethnicity, nationality, language, gender, socioeconomic status, physical and mental ability, sexual orientation, and occupation that together result in integrated, recognizable patterns of human behavior. **Cultural competence** implies having the capacity to function effectively as an individual and organization within the contexts of the various cultures of specific patients and their communities. According to the AAMC, cultural and linguistic competence is a set of congruent behaviors, knowledge, attitudes, and policies that enables effective work in cross-cultural situations.

Cultural Competence in Health Care Settings

Cultural competence in health care describes the ability of systems to provide care to patients with diverse values, beliefs, and behaviors, including tailoring delivery to meet patients' social, cultural, and linguistic needs. Cultural competence has been recognized as integral to the reduction and elimination of disparities in health care, and combines the tenets of patient- and family-centered care with an understanding of the social and cultural influences that affect the quality of medical services and treatment.

> What are the five constructs that make up Campinha-Bacote's process of cultural competence in the delivery of health care services?

In an article titled "Process of Cultural Competence in the Delivery of Health Care Services," Campinha-Bacote develops a culturally conscious model of care. This model views cultural competence as composed of five constructs:

- *Cultural awareness* is examining one's biases toward other cultures through exploration and self-examination of one's own cultural and professional background.
- *Cultural knowledge* is obtaining a sound educational base about culturally diverse groups, while focusing on the integration of health-related beliefs, practices, and cultural values, and disease incidence and prevalence.
- *Cultural skill* is collecting relevant cultural data regarding the patient's presenting problem and performing a culturally based physical assessment.
- *Cultural encounter* is personally engaging in interactions (face-to-face and other types) with individuals from diverse backgrounds to develop an informed understanding about a cultural group and to prevent stereotyping.
- *Cultural desire* is engaging in the process of becoming culturally aware, culturally knowledgeable, culturally skillful, and motivated to seek cultural encounters.

Campinha-Bacote considers cultural competence to be a process that health care providers should continuously engage in, and improve upon, to provide the best possible care for each patient.

Benefits of Cultural Competence in Health Care Settings

> What are the health, social, and financial benefits of cultural competence in health care settings?

Culturally competent care promotes health and social benefits as well as financial benefits for health care organizations. A report from the Equity of Care Initiative and the American Hospital Association highlights 16 benefits to an organization that meets the health care needs of a diverse patient population (Box 17.1).

Barriers to Cultural Competence in Health Care Settings

There is confusion about what cultural competence means, and different ways in which it is conceptualized and operationalized. This confusion leads to

---

Box 17.1. Benefits of meeting the health care needs of a diverse patient population

Health Benefits	Social Benefits	Financial Benefits
• Improves patient data collection	• Increases mutual respect and understanding between the patient and the organization	• Incorporates different perspectives, ideas, and strategies into the decision-making process
• Increases preventive care	• Increases trust	• Decreases barriers that slow progress
• Reduces health care disparities	• Promotes inclusion of all community members	• Moves toward meeting legal and regulatory guidelines
• Increases cost savings from a reduction in medical errors and number of treatments	• Increases community participation and involvement in health issues	• Improves efficiency of care services
• Reduces the number of missed medical visits	• Assists patients and families in their care	• Increases the market share of the organization
	• Promotes patient and family responsibilities for health	

Based on Health Research & Educational Trust. (2013). *Becoming a culturally competent health care organization.* Chicago, IL: Author. Retrieved from http://www.hpoe.org/becoming-culturally-competent

disagreement regarding the topic areas and practices in which a provider should be trained to attain cultural competence. The populations to which the term cultural competence applies are also poorly defined. Cultural competence is often seen as encompassing only racial and ethnic differences. This definition omits other marginalized population groups that are ethnically and racially similar to a provider but at risk for stigmatization or discrimination because of differences in other identities. These differences may lead to unrecognizable and unmet health care needs, resulting in health disparities.

Strategies for Achieving Cultural Competence in Health Care Settings

The American Medical Association (AMA) has highlighted policies and activities to reduce racial and ethnic health disparities through

- increasing awareness of racial and ethnic disparities in health care among the general public, key stakeholders, and health care providers;
- avoiding fragmentation of health plans along socioeconomic lines and strengthening the stability of patient–provider relationships in publicly funded health plans;
- increasing the proportion of underrepresented racial and ethnic minorities among health professionals;
- applying the same managed care protections to publicly funded health maintenance organization (HMO) enrollees that apply to private HMO enrollees;
- promoting consistency and equity of care;
- supporting the use of interpreter services;
- supporting the use of community health workers and implementing multidisciplinary treatment and preventive care teams;
- implementing patient education programs to increase knowledge about accessing care and participating in treatment decisions;
- collecting data on health care access and utilization by race, ethnicity, and socioeconomic status, and monitoring progress toward the elimination of disparities; and
- conducting research to identify sources of disparities, barriers to eliminating disparities, and to assess promising intervention strategies.

In 2013, the US Department of Health and Human Services (HHS) released enhanced national standards for Culturally and Linguistically Appropriate Services (CLAS) in health and health care, which serve as a blueprint for health organizations to improve the quality of health care delivered in our nation's diverse communities. These standards, developed by the HHS Office of Minority Health, provide a comprehensive update of the 2000 National CLAS Standards and are grounded in a broad definition of culture – one in which health is recognized as being influenced not only by race and ethnicity or language, but also by factors such as spirituality, disability status, sexual orientation, gender identity, and geography.

Several organizations have instituted cultural competence guidelines for their membership. For example, the AMA provides information and resources on policies, publications, curriculum and training materials, and relevant activities of physician associations, medical specialty groups, and state medical societies. As another for example, the Society of Teachers of Family Medicine has developed guidelines for curriculum material to teach cultural sensitivity and competence to family medicine residents and other health providers.

Cultural Competence Within Provider–Patient Interpersonal Communication

Within health care settings, there are numerous opportunities where cultural competence (or lack thereof) can influence the provider and patient encounter, as well as clinical decision making. Examples include (1) patient and provider recognition of personal biases against people of different cultures; (2) awareness of the social, political, and economic influences provider and patient personal biases exert against people of different cultures; (3) respect and tolerance for cultural differences; and (4) willingness to make clinical settings more accessible to patients.

A provider who is culturally competent explores and respects patient beliefs, values, meaning of illness, preferences, and needs; builds rapport and trust and establishes common ground with the patient; and is aware of personal biases and how structural inequities can create health disparities among minority groups.

> Mai Nguyen, a 29-year-old refugee from Vietnam, was being seen for a physical exam prior to starting a new job. She had numerous somatic complaints but was hesitant to talk about emotional, familial, or intimate matters, and refused a gynecological exam. Her physician consulted more experienced colleagues who advised accepting her complaints as consistent with Vietnamese "culture." However, after several encounters with the patient, the physician learned that the patient had escaped from Vietnam in a small overcrowded boat and had undergone significant trauma and sexual abuse while at sea. He came to realize her complaints were not just "cultural" but related to posttraumatic stress disorder that required social and psychiatric intervention.

This example highlights the numerous complex political, social, and psychological factors that may influence a patient's presentation of illness, provider–patient interaction and communication, and the provider's diagnosis and subsequent treatment plan. Provider training in the explicit use of effective cross-cultural communication might have uncovered underlying factors in earlier encounters with the patient, thus reducing the patient's anxiety and improving the quality of the health care provided. Frameworks that can be used to improve the provider–patient encounter are highlighted in Table 17.2.

Strategies for improving patient–provider interaction and institutionalizing changes in the health care system include recruiting and retaining a diverse clinical staff; providing training to increase cultural awareness, knowledge, and

Table 17.2. Models of effective cross-cultural communication and negotiation

Model	Source
Learn Listen with sympathy and understanding to the patient's perception of the problem Explain your perceptions of the problem Acknowledge and discuss the differences and similarities Recommend treatment Negotiate treatment	Berlin, E. A., & Fowkes, W. C. (1983). A teaching framework for cross-cultural health care. *Western Journal of Medicine, 139,* 934–938.
Eliciting Patient Information and Negotiating Identify core cross-cultural issues Explore the meaning of the illness Determine the social context Engage in negotiation	Carrillo, J. E., Green, A. R., & Betancourt, J. R. (1999). Cross-cultural primary care: A patient-based approach. *Annals of Internal Medicine, 130*(10), 829–834.
Ethnic Explanation (How do you explain your illness?) Treatment (What treatment have you tried?) Healers (Have you sought any advice from folk healers?) Negotiate (mutually acceptable options) Intervention (agreed on) Collaboration (with patient, family, and healers)	Levin, S. J., Like, R. C., & Gottlieb, J. E. (2000). ETHNIC: A framework for culturally competent ethical practice. *Patent Care, 34*(9),188–189.
Model for Cultural Competency in Health Care Normative cultural values Language issues Folk illnesses Patient/parent beliefs Provider practices	Flores, G. (2000). Culture and the patient-physician relationship: Achieving cultural competency in health care. *Journal of Pediatrics, 136,* 14–23.

skills; using community health workers and interpreters as appropriate; and incorporating institutional policies that can address social, economic, and political barriers to health care.

Metrics for demonstrating cultural competence within health care settings include tracking the quality of care across racial, ethnic, and cultural subgroups; including community members in setting priorities and planning, delivering, and coordinating care; ongoing training regarding delivery of appropriate services; and recruiting and retaining a diverse workforce that reflects the patient population.

Cultural Constructs as a Foundation for Cultural Competence

Andrews and Boyle developed a system for understanding health belief models that cultural groups use to explain health and illness. Those relevant to health literacy include, among others, *magicoreligious, biomedical,* and *deterministic* beliefs.

- *Magicoreligious* refers to belief in supernatural forces that inflict illness on humans, sometimes as punishment for sins, in the form of evil spirits or disease-bearing foreign objects. This view may be found among Latin American, African American, and Middle Eastern cultures.
- *Biomedical* refers to the belief system generally held in the US in which life is controlled by a series of physical and biochemical processes that can be studied and manipulated by humans. Disease is seen as the result of the breakdown of physical parts of the body due to stress, trauma, pathogens, or structural changes.
- *Determinism* is the belief that outcomes are externally preordained and cannot be changed. Those holding to this belief system ask questions such as, If illness is bestowed by God, why try to prevent it or seek treatment?

Cultural Concepts of Distress in the DSM-5

> How has the construct of culture-bound syndromes changed within the DSM-5?

Table 17.3. Examples of cultural concepts related to Eurowestern concepts of mental illness

Concept	Ethnic Group	Description
Ataque de nervios	Latino	Intense emotional upset; uncontrollable crying/screaming; trembling; heat sensation in the chest, neck, head; verbal or physical aggression or suicidal behavior; depersonalization/ derealization symptoms; a sense of being out of control
Maladi moun	Haitian	Also known as "sent sickness": interpersonal envy and malice cause people to harm their enemies by sending illness (psychosis, depression), or social or academic failure
Khyâl cap	Cambodian	Symptoms similar to panic attacks; dizziness, palpitations, shortness of breath
Shenjing shuairuo	Chinese	The syndrome is composed of several of nonhierarchical symptom clusters including: weakness, emotions, excitement, nervous pain, and sleep. This syndrome is often called *neurasthenia* in the West
Susto	Latino	Cultural explanation for distress and misfortune prevalent among Latinos in the US and among Mexicans, Central Americans, and South Americans
Taijin kyofusho	Japanese	Anxiety about and avoidance of interpersonal situations due to the thought, feeling, or conviction of personal inadequacy

Historically, the **culture-bound syndrome** construct has been of key interest in cultural psychiatry. In the 5th edition of the *Diagnostic and Statistical Manual of Mental Disorders* (DSM-5), this construct has been replaced by three concepts that offer greater clinical utility, as shown in Table 17.3 (see also Chapter 38: Introduction to Psychopathology):

1. *Cultural syndrome* is a cluster or group of co-occurring, relatively invariant symptoms found in a specific cultural group, community, or context (e.g., *ataque de nervios*). The syndrome may or may not be recognized as an illness within the culture, but may, nevertheless, be recognizable by an outside observer.
2. *Cultural idiom of distress* is a linguistic term, phrase, or way of talking about suffering among individuals of a cultural group referring to shared concepts of pathology and ways of expressing, communicating, or naming essential features of distress.
3. *Cultural explanation* or *perceived cause* is a label, attribution, or feature of an explanatory model that provides a culturally conceived etiology or cause for symptoms, illness, or distress. Causal explanations may be salient features of folk classifications of disease used by laypersons or healers.

Cultural concepts arise from local folk or professional diagnostic systems for mental and emotional distress, but they may also reflect the influence of biomedical concepts. Cultural concepts have four key features:

- There is seldom a one-to-one correspondence of any cultural concept with a DSM diagnostic entity; the correspondence is more likely to be one-to-many in either direction.
- Cultural concepts may apply to a wide range of illness severity, including presentations that do not meet DSM criteria for any mental disorder.
- In common usage, the same cultural term frequently denotes more than one type of cultural concept. A familiar example may be the concept of *depression,* which may be used to describe a syndrome (e.g., major depressive disorder), an idiom of distress (e.g., as in the common expression, "I feel depressed"), or a perceived cause (similar to "stress").

- Like culture and the DSM itself, cultural concepts may change over time in response to both local and global influences.

Cultural Formulation Interview

The Cultural Formulation Interview (CFI) is a set of 16 mental health assessment questions that providers may use to obtain information about the impact of culture on key aspects of an individual's clinical presentation and care. In the CFI, culture refers to

- the values, orientations, knowledge, and practices that individuals derive from membership in diverse social groups (e.g., ethnic groups, faith communities, occupational groups);
- aspects of an individual's background, developmental experiences, and current social contexts that may affect their perspective; and
- the influence of family, friends, and other community members (the person's social network) on the individual's illness experience.

The CFI emphasizes four domains of assessment: Cultural Definition of the Problem (questions 1–3); Cultural Perceptions of Cause, Context, and Support (questions 4–10); Cultural Factors Affecting Self-Coping and Past Help Seeking (questions 11–13); and Cultural Factors Affecting Current Help Seeking (questions 14–16). The CFI may be used in its entirety, or components may be incorporated into a clinical evaluation as needed. The CFI may be especially helpful when there is

- difficulty in diagnostic assessment owing to significant differences in the cultural, religious, or socioeconomic backgrounds of the health care provider and the patient;
- uncertainty about the fit between culturally distinctive symptoms and diagnostic criteria;
- difficulty in judging illness severity or impairment;
- disagreement between the provider and the patient on the course of care; or
- limited engagement in and adherence to treatment by the patient.

(CFI is available at www.psychiatryonline.org, https://doi.org/10.1176/appi.books.9780890425596. CulturalFormulation)

Recommended Readings

Andrews, M. M., & Boyle, J. S. (2008). *Transcultural concepts in nursing*. New York, NY: Wolters Kluwer/ Lippincott, Williams & Wilkins.

Betancourt, J. R., Green, A. R., Carrillo, J. E., & Ananeh-Firempong, O. (2003). Defining cultural competence: A practical framework for addressing racial/ethnic disparities in health and health care. *Public Health Reports, 118*(4), 293–302. http://doi.org/10.1016/S0033-3549(04)50253-4

Butler, M., McCreedy, E., Schwer, N., Burgess, D., Call, K., Przedworski, J., ... Kane, R. L. (2016). *Improving cultural competence to reduce health disparities* (Comparative Effectiveness Review No. 170. AHRQ Publication No. 16-EHC006-EF). Rockville, MD: Agency for Health Care Research and Quality. Available at https://www. effectivehealthcare.ahrq.gov/index.cfm/reports/final/

Campinha-Bacote, J. (2002). The process of cultural competence in the delivery of health care services: A model of care. *Journal of Transcultural Nursing, 13*(3), 181–184. http://doi.org/10.1177/10459602013003003

Hark, L. A., & DeLisser, H. M. (Eds.). (2009). *Achieving cultural competency: A case-based approach to training health professionals*. Singapore: Wiley-Blackwell. http:// doi.org/10.1002/9781444311686

Kleinman, A., Eisenberg, L., & Good, B. (1978). Culture, illness, and care: Clinical lessons from anthropologic and cross-cultural research. *Annals of Internal Medicine, 88*(2), 251–258. http://doi.org/10.7326/0003-4819-88-2-251

US Department of Health and Human Services. (2000). *National standards on culturally and linguistically appropriate services (CLAS) in Health Care*. Rockville, MD: Department of Health and Human Services, Office of Minority Health, Federal Register. Available at https:// www.thinkculturalhealth.hhs.gov/clas

Review Questions

1. Explanatory models (EMs) are concepts that patients, family members, and healers form about a specific sickness. Which of the following statements is true about EMs?
   A. EMs are based primarily upon the pathophysiology of the disorder.
   B. EMs do not change once they are formed.
   C. EMs do not typically address the natural history of the disease.
   D. Eventually, patients, family members, and healers have the same EMs about the sickness.
   E. Greater agreement between people's EMs leads to fewer conflicts.

2. Which of the following is true about classification of diseases by different ethnic groups?
   A. A standard system of disease classification exists.
   B. All ethnic groups classify disease by physiological systems and etiologies.
   C. All ethnic groups classify disease in similar ways.
   D. Classification systems are static.
   E. Different disease classification systems contribute to miscommunication.

3. The primary reason the use of professional translators is preferred over family members or friends for provider–patient interactions is that they
   A. add background information they believe helps explain symptoms
   B. clarify or interpret questions and answers
   C. embellish answers to provide additional information
   D. translate conversations word for word
   E. withhold information they feel may be too distressing

4. Which of the following is not a construct within Campinha-Bacote's process of cultural competence?
   A. Cultural knowledge
   B. Cultural desire
   C. Cultural skill
   D. Cultural assessment
   E. Cultural encounter

5. Which of the following is a key feature of a cultural concept as described within DSM-5?
   A. There is often a one-to-one correspondence of any cultural concept with a DSM diagnostic entity.
   B. The same cultural term frequently applies to more than one type of cultural concept.
   C. Cultural concepts are static over time and context.
   D. Cultural concepts apply to illnesses that are minor in severity only.
   E. Cultural concepts are solely applied to mental and emotional distress.

Answer Key on p. 465

18 Health Care in Minority and Majority Populations

Michael C. Hosokawa, EdD

- What are some causes of population differences in health status?
- What accounts for differences in infant mortality, life expectancy, and cause of death among minority and majority populations?
- How does racism affect health outcomes?

Examination of health data reveals significant variations in mortality and morbidity among different populations.

What are some causes of population differences in health status?

Health status is determined by many factors such as race and ethnicity, education level, socioeconomic status, and sexual orientation. Those who are at highest risk of a poor quality of health and lower quality of health care are most often the poor and racial minorities.

In recent years, sexual orientation and gender identity have also been noted as important variables in assessing the quality of care. For example, data indicate that groups with a different sexual orientation than the majority receive lower quality of care. Although lesbian, gay, bisexual, and transgender (LGBT) individuals encompass all races and ethnicities, religions, and social classes, research suggests that LGBT individuals have health disparities related to societal stigma and discrimination (see Chapter 20: Health Care Issues Facing Lesbian, Gay, Bisexual, and Transgender Individuals).

Racial and Ethnic Minorities

Although the overall population of the US is growing more slowly than in the past, certain sub-groups are growing rapidly. The US Census occurs each decade, so population projections are made by estimating changes. In 2020, the projected population will be 335 million; in 2030, the population is expected to have increased to 359 million; and in 2060, the population is projected to be 417 million. These changes represent an increase of about 2 million people per year. Individuals living in the US, but born in another country, make up 14.3% of the population as of the second decade of the 21st century and will increase to 18.8% in 2060.

The US population is becoming more racially and ethnically diverse. In 2015, the non-Hispanic White population made up about 62.2% of the total population. People of Hispanic or Latino origin made up 17.4% of the population, Black or African Americans 13.2%, Asians 5.4%, American Indians or Alaska Natives 1.2%, and Native Hawaiians and Pacific Islanders 0.5%. It should be noted that the term *Hispanic* denotes an ethnicity, and Hispanic people may be of any race. Currently, 2.5% of individuals identify themselves as being of two or more races. In 2044, it is projected that the non-Hispanic White population will no longer be the majority; instead, the proportion of the population represented by the various racial and ethnic groups will be a plurality.

These projected population dynamics foretell interesting discussions of health care when, in 2044, there will no longer be a racial or ethnic majority or minority. Already, the non-White population in cities such as Los Angeles, New York

City, Washington, DC, Cleveland, Detroit, Atlanta, Miami, Dallas, Houston, Oakland, and Chicago is larger than the White population.

There are many factors contributing to the quality of health care and morbidity and mortality. Race and ethnicity, economic status, poverty, education, employment, sexual preference, and access to health care services are essential components in determining the overall health of the US. As single entities, these factors do not necessarily predict disparities in morbidity and mortality, but combined, they have a synergistic and profound effect on health, disease, and access to health care services. It must be noted that race may actually be a proxy for class, and race and class should be considered as codeterminants of disparities in health.

Black Americans

While most immigrant groups relocated to the US in search of better political, social, or economic circumstances, most Black Americans are descendants of individuals imported as slaves. The rates of poverty, crime, and inadequate education are higher among the Black population than among the majority population, in part due to state and federal laws that denied equal access to educational and social benefits until the mid-20th century.

Despite changes in the laws, discrimination and bias persist. Although other immigrant groups have encountered these problems, most groups have been able to at least partially assimilate after one or two generations. In contrast, discrimination, prejudice, and the segregation of Black Americans have been more easily imposed and sustained because of skin color differences and stereotypes. Many of the stereotypes are perpetuated by the media and even by language. Terms such as *black moods, black sheep, black market, blackball,* and *blackmail* have strong negative connotations. Villains and cowboys with black hats and clothing are evil, as is the black cat.

Millions of Black Americans have moved up the socioeconomic ladder to create a stable and growing Black middle class. There are many highly successful Black leaders in government, the sciences, business, and entertainment. However, Black Americans still predominate in the lower socioeconomic classes.

Hispanic Americans/Latinos

Most of the more than 55 million Hispanic/Latino Americans living in the US trace their ancestry to Mexico; the remainder to Puerto Rico, Cuba, and Central and South America. Many individuals who trace their ancestry to Mexico are descendants of seasonal laborers who came to the US and worked in agriculture, often under deplorable conditions.

About 90% of Hispanic/Latino Americans live in metropolitan neighborhoods where some language and customs are preserved. Many do not seek complete assimilation at the expense of relinquishing their culture. As the first Hispanic immigrants were able to gain citizenship and have families, the success of later generations often came at the expense of learning to succeed in an educational system structured for the dominant culture.

In many parts of Florida, New Mexico, Arizona, Texas, Colorado, and California, the Hispanic/Latino culture is dominant. In fact, many Hispanic/Latino Americans have resisted giving up language and cultural traditions and bilingual (English-Spanish) signage is used in many government offices and other public accommodations throughout the US, although House Resolution (H.R.) 3898 declares English as the official language of the US and mandates that official governmental and legal business be conducted in English.

Asian Americans

China and Japan were major sources of indentured laborers for mining during the Californian Gold Rush and the building of the railroads. Nearly 200,000 Chinese laborers were brought to the western US to build railroads. Anti-Asian sentiment grew when the railroads were completed and the gold rush declined.

Some Chinese left the US in response to discriminatory practices, but the majority remained and established self-contained Chinatowns in larger cities. Economically, the Chinese developed a robust tourist industry offering food and commodities. They transformed work camp services such as cooking and laundry into lucrative businesses.

The Japanese were hired as field hands and workers for the railroads, canneries, lumber mills, and mines. They were particularly vulnerable to discrimination because they were scattered over the West, did not form an effective sociopolitical group, and were successful in competing with majority farmers. Anti-Japanese sentiment peaked after the bombing of Pearl Harbor. Approximately 120,000 men, women, and children, both Japanese aliens and Americans of Japanese ancestry, were sent to 10 concentration camps for the duration of World War II. Although released at the end of the war, many Americans of Japanese ancestry lost their homes, farms, and businesses while in the camps. The dissolution of the Japanese American communities that had been centered along the West Coast forced those leaving the camps into the mainstream as they sought education and opportunity. While Chinese Americans were more limited in their assimilation by the development of Chinatowns, the Japanese were launched into a more rapid acculturation process.

By the end of the 20th century, Hispanics/Latinos and Asians had become the *fastest growing minorities* in the US. The three largest US Asian groups are Chinese (except Taiwanese); Filipino and Asian Indian; followed by Vietnamese, Korean, and Japanese. Many of the more recent immigrants came from Vietnam, Cambodia, Laos, Thailand, and Indonesia during and after the war in Vietnam. Many families were helped to settle in the US by churches and community groups. The children of these families are well assimilated into American culture.

The increase in the Hispanic/Latino population has been largely by birth in the US. The increase in the Asian population has been mostly through immigration.

American Indians and Alaska Natives

Between 1990 and 2006, the native American Indian and Alaska Native populations increased from 2 million to 3.3 million, although some estimates put this figure at 4.4 million including individuals of mixed race. Most of these individuals are members of one of the more than 500 federally recognized tribes with distinctive cultures and histories.

Contrary to popular stereotypes, only about one fourth of American Indians and Alaska Natives live on federal reservations. The Bureau of Indian Affairs encouraged American Indians to leave the reservations and relocate in urban areas to find economic opportunities. However, poor education and lack of skills have resulted in high rates of unemployment. As a result, most urban American Indians have dispersed rather than remain in groups or ethnic neighborhoods to obtain better education, health care, and social services.

The Indian Health Service and Tribal Council Health Care Administrations provide tribes with outpatient and inpatient medical services. Tribes have three options for receiving health care: (1) from the Indian Health Service (IHS), (2) contracting with the IHS to have administrative control and funding transferred to tribal governments, or (3) an agreement with the IHS for the tribe to have autonomy in the provision of health care services. About 600 IHS and tribal health care facilities are spread over 35 states, most often in rural and isolated areas.

For many Native Americans, IHS or tribal health care facilities are the only accessible services. Unfortunately, many of the needed health care services, including specialty care and laboratory, imaging, and pharmacy services, are not available through IHS or tribal facilities and must be purchased under contracts with private sector health providers. While the IHS and tribal health services are often inadequate and underfunded, they also serve only 56% of the American Indian and Alaska Native population, leaving 44% of this group to receive health services through other means or not at all. Of particular concern are the rural poor and urban groups without access to services.

The Poor

A discussion of health disparities must include the poor. In 2014, 14.8% of the US population lived in poverty, representing almost 50 million people. Of those poor, 10% are White, 24% Hispanic, and 26% Black.

Poverty is the biggest determinant of health status and access to care. Poverty is present in all racial groups and negatively affects health, regardless of racial classification. In 2016, the poverty threshold was US $11,770 for a single person and US $24,250 for a family of four. The risk for sickness, death, unhealthy behaviors, exposure to environmental hazards, reduced access to health care, and poor quality of care increases with lower socioeconomic status. Income can also influence health by its direct effect on living standards (e.g., access to better quality food and housing, leisure time activities, and health care services, including preventive care).

There were almost 47 million people living in poverty in the US in 2016. About one in five children under the age of 18 and one in 10 people 65 and older live in poverty. It is estimated that a family of four needs at least twice the federal poverty level of US $24,250 to cover basic expenses. Most of the children living in poverty have parents who work, but for low wages in unstable employment and without health insurance. Poverty contributes to impeding children's ability to learn as well as to behavioral problems, poor physical health and poor mental health. Growing up in poverty compromises children's ability to move out of poverty as adults.

Health Status and Health Determinants

Infant Mortality

> What accounts for differences in infant mortality, life expectancy, and cause of death among minority and majority populations?

Infant mortality is defined as the number of deaths occurring in the first year of life per 1,000 live births. It is an important indicator of health, as it reflects maternal health and health care resources. Infant mortality in the US has improved dramatically over the last 100 years. In 1900, 100 in 1,000 infants died during the first year of life. Currently, about 6 in 1,000 infants die during the first year of life. Although maternal and child health care has improved, the US ranks 27th in the world for infant mortality. Finland, Japan, Portugal, and Sweden have infant mortality rates of less than 3 per 1,000 live births.

There is a striking disparity between the infant mortality for non-Hispanic White mothers of 5.6 deaths per 1,000 live births and the non-Hispanic Black population of 11.1 deaths per 1,000 live births. Thus, the infant mortality rate among African Americans is twice as high as that of White mothers. As a group, Hispanic mothers have an infant mortality rate of 5.0 per 1,000 live births and Asian Pacific Islanders a rate of 4.07 per 1,000 live births.

These differences are due in part to African Americans often having lower incomes, lower education levels, and less access to medical care – all risk factors for infant mortality. The stress of minority group status and racism may also be factors that contribute to infant mortality. Supportive cultural and family environments among Hispanic groups likely contribute to lower infant mortality rates despite low income, low education, and low health insurance levels.

Preterm births are another indication of health status. Babies born preterm (before 37 completed weeks of gestation), are at increased risk of immediate life-threatening health problems as well as long-term complications and developmental delays. Preterm birth is a leading cause of infant death and childhood disability. Overall, 9.6% of babies are born preterm. The preterm birth rate varies by race and ethnicity with 13.2% of babies born to non-Hispanic Black women compared with 8.9% of babies born to non-Hispanic White women. The causes of preterm birth are not well understood, but are linked to access to health care, poor living environments, substance abuse, nutrition, infection, and medical conditions such as diabetes and hypertension.

Life Expectancy and Causes of Death

Life expectancy continues to increase, but significant racial differences remain. Overall, a male baby born today can expect to live 76 years and a female baby 81 years. However, there are racial disparities. A White male baby can expect to live 6 more years than a Black male baby and the disparity between White and Black female babies is 4 years. Heart disease and malignant neoplasia are the two leading causes of death for males and females of all races except American Indians. Among American Indian males, unintentional injuries are second to heart disease and claim more lives than malignancies. Heart disease and stroke are not only leading causes of death in the US but also account for the largest proportion of disparities in life expectancy between Whites and Blacks despite the existence of low-cost, highly effective, preventive treatment.

Cancer incidence and death rates are generally declining for men, women, and children. For all men, the incidence of colorectal, lung, and prostate cancer have decreased, and melanoma has increased. For all women, the breast cancer incidence rate has remained level; cervical, colorectal, lung, and ovarian cancer incidence rates have decreased; and the melanoma incidence rate has increased. Cancer incidence and mortality vary considerably among racial and ethnic groups. For all cancer sites combined, Black men have the highest rate of developing cancer, followed by White, Hispanic, Asian/Pacific Islander, and American Indian/Alaska Native men. Among women, White women have the highest rate of developing cancer followed by Black, Hispanic, Asian/Pacific Islander, and American Indian/Alaska Native women. The rate of dying from cancer also varies depending on race and ethnicity. Black men and women are more likely to die from cancer than any other group.

Stomach and liver cancer incidence and death rates are twice as high in Asian American and Pacific Islanders compared with Whites, reflecting an increased prevalence of chronic infection with *Helicobacter pylori* and hepatitis B and C viruses in this population. Compared with Whites, minority populations are more likely to be diagnosed at a later stage of disease. Decreased cancer survival is associated with being poor and less educated, and with lack of access to health care and high-quality screening leading to later diagnosis and treatment of cancer. Poor quality treatment and higher risk of exposure to occupational and environmental carcinogens also contribute to higher death rates.

Disparities in health status are related to income, education level, insurance coverage, access to health care, and racism. People who are negatively affected by one or more of these factors are more likely to live in environments with increased exposure to disease and limited access to health care.

Uninsured Health Care

In 2006, the estimated number of *uninsured* US residents was 47 million and was projected to reach 52 million by the end of 2010. Census data in 2014 showed the number of uninsured Americans declined by 8.8 million as more Americans bought their own coverage or enrolled in Medicaid as the Affordable Care Act (ACA) took effect in 2014. For Black Americans, the uninsured rate decreased from 17.2% in 2013 to 12.7% in 2014. For Latinos, the uninsured rate decreased from 25.6% in 2013 to 20.9% a year later. People in the near-poor group are often part-time employees and are not provided with health insurance by their employers. In particular, department stores, fast-food chains and restaurants, small businesses and convenience stores, and agriculture often do not provide benefits such as health insurance and pensions. Also, small employers such as cafes, florists, and cleaners do not have benefits programs. Thus, an individual might hold two or three jobs and not have health insurance, but have an income too high to qualify for Medicaid or services at a low-income community clinic. The political thrust to repeal and replace the ACA in 2017 has created an uncertain future for health care finance over the next several years.

Access to Health Care in Minority Groups

How does racism affect health outcomes?

Access to care is an important factor in determining health status, especially preventive care and timely treatment of illness and injury. Many of the poor do not have access to regular preventive care and often seek care in the emergency room, the most expensive place to receive medical care. The poor often do not seek care when they are ill and are less likely to get prescription drugs if they do get care because they frequently have to choose between buying food and buying medicine. Thus, their illnesses are often more serious, care is delayed until hospitalization is necessary, and the hospital stay is longer. Rates of preventable hospitalizations increase as incomes decrease. Eliminating these disparities would prevent approximately 1 million hospitalizations and save US $6.7 billion in health care costs each year. There also are large racial and ethnic disparities in preventable hospitalizations, with Blacks experiencing a rate more than double that of Whites.

Surveys have shown that Black Americans are less likely to receive fair treatment when obtaining health care. A report from the Institute of Medicine stated that Blacks often get inferior care, and there is disparity between care that racial and ethnic minorities receive and the quality of care for Whites. However, discrimination and bias can be very subtle, yet important factors in obtaining health care.

Discrimination is often not overt. **Microaggression** is a term coined by Chester Pierce, a psychiatrist at Harvard University in 1970. He described microaggressions as insults and dismissals Whites inflict on Blacks. Today, microaggressions are the everyday verbal, nonverbal, and environmental slights, snubs, or insults, whether intentional or unintentional, that communicate hostile, derogatory, or negative messages to target persons based solely social standing such as race or ethnicity, education, employment status, and sexual preference.

Education Level

Education is an important determinant of future employment and income. Higher education usually leads to higher socioeconomic status and less poverty. The high school graduation rate for the population is 81%, but for Black students, it is 68%, for Hispanic students it is 76%, and it is 68% for American Indian and Alaska Native students. The Asian graduation rate is 93%. A great deal can be done to increase educational attainment and progress toward decreasing health disparities.

Racism can have significant implications for overall health outcomes in low-income minority populations due to its effects on social and economic life. Communities with substantial health disparities often have disproportionately large racially divided populations and have fewer resources including good schools, health services, and a safe, clean environment. These disadvan-

tages increase health problems, delay care, offer inferior care, and increase stress.

Stress

Stress is especially problematic when extreme or prolonged and has a significant influence on both physical and psychological health. It can also lead to increased incidence, earlier onset, and greater severity of diseases and illnesses such as hypertension and depression, as well as to early death. Experiences and environmental influences affect genetic predisposition to disease, emerging brain architecture, and long-term health in children. Substandard housing, debt, crowding, violence, family dysfunction, unemployment, and discrimination are underlying factors in what is now termed *toxic stress*. Toxic stress was the topic of a technical report published by the American Academy of Pediatrics in 2012, stating that adult disease should be viewed as a developmental disease that began early in life (see Chapter 2: Predisposition, and Chapter 7: Stress, Adaptation, and Stress Disorders).

Sexual Orientation

Sexual orientation, like race and socioeconomic status, is an important sociocultural factor when evaluating health disparity. LGBT individuals include all races and ethnicities, religions, and social classes. Research suggests that LGBT individuals face health disparities linked to societal stigma, discrimination, and denial of their civil and human rights. Discrimination against LGBT persons has also been associated with high rates of psychiatric disorders, substance abuse, and suicide. They are at higher risk of violence and victimization (see Chapter 20: Health Care Issues Facing Lesbian, Gay, Bisexual, and Transgender Individuals).

Health Equity

Health disparities are the problem. **Health equity** is the goal. Health equity will be achieved when every person has the opportunity to reach full health potential and no one is disadvantaged by social standing, race, ethnicity, religion, or sexual orientation. The US Department of Health and Human Services website *Healthy People 2020* defines *health equity* as the "attainment of the highest level of health for all people." Everyone deserves a fair chance to lead a healthy life and no one should be denied this chance by factors that are avoidable, unfair, or unjust.

Recommended Readings

Colby, S., & Ortman, J. M. (2015). *Projections of the size and composition of the US population: 2014 to 2060. Population estimates and projections.* Washington, DC: US Census Bureau. Available at http://www.census.gov/content/dam/Census/library/publications/2015/demo/p25-1143.pdf

DeNavas-Walt, C., & Proctor, B. D. (2015). *Income and poverty in the United States: 2014* (Current population reports, P60-252). Washington, DC: US Census Bureau. Available at http://www.census.gov/library/publications/2015/demo/p60-252.html

Shonkoff, J. A., & Garner, A. S. (2012). The lifelong effects of early childhood activity of toxic stress. *Pediatrics*, 129. http://doi.org/10.1542/peds.2011-2663

Smith, J. C., & Medalia, C. (2015). *Health insurance coverage in the United States: 2014* (Current population reports, P60-253). Washington, DC: US Census Bureau. Available at https://www.census.gov/content/dam/census/library/publications/2015/demo/p60-253.pdf

Additional Resources

Brown, A. (2014). *US Hispanic and Asian populations growing, but for different reasons.* Washington, DC: Pew Research Center. Available at http://www.pewresearch.org/fact-tank/2014/06/26/u-s-hispanic-and-asian-populations-growing-but-for-different-reasons

Hamilton, B. E., Martin, J. A., Osterman, M. J. K., Curtin, S. C., & Mathews, T. J. (2015). Births: Final data for 2014. *National Vital Statistics Reports, 64*(12). Available at http://www.cdc.gov/nchs/data/nvsr/nvsr64/nvsr64_12.pdf

National Center for Health Statistics. (2015). *Health, United States, 2015.* Available at http://www.cdc.gov/nchs/data/hus/hus15.pdf

US Census Bureau. (2014). *Projecting majority-minority: Non-Hispanic Whites may no longer comprise over 50 percent of the U.S. population by 2044.* Available at https://www.census.gov/content/dam/Census/newsroom/releases/2015/cb15-tps16_graphic.pdf

US Department of Health and Human Services. *Healthy people 2020.* Available at http://www.healthypeople.gov/2020/topics-objectives/topic/lesbian-gay-bisexual-and-transgender-health

Review Questions

1. By the mid-21st century, it is predicted that no single group will represent an absolute racial majority in the US. When this occurs, it is likely that
   A. access to and quality of health care will improve because of larger numbers of providers of color
   B. health equity will be achieved because all persons will have access to the same level of health care
   C. racial plurality will not immediately change health care because the social determinants of health care include many factors
   D. the quality of health care will likely deteriorate as the proportion of the White population declines
   E. there will be less disparity in income, access to health care, and quality of health care shortly afterward

2. The American Academy of Pediatrics recognizes substandard housing, debt, crowding, violence, family dysfunction, unemployment, and discrimination as underlying factors in what is now termed
   A. generational poverty
   B. generational welfare
   C. genetic variation
   D. persistent poverty
   E. toxic stress

Answer Key on p. 465

19 Sexuality and Sexual Disorders

Charles P. Samenow, MD, MPH, and Kaliris Y. Salas-Ramirez, PhD

- What is considered healthy sexual behavior?
- How do specific health situations affect sexuality?
- How do age, gender, and culture affect sexual health?
- How does normal sexual behavior differ from problematic sexual behavior?

Sexual Health

Sexual health is defined as a state of physical, mental, and social well-being in relation to sexuality. Sex is a basic physiological need that can be driven by the psychological and social need for intimacy which will increase sexual motivation and drive.

What is considered healthy sexual behavior?

The term **healthy sexual behavior** implies a positive and respectful approach to sexuality, the enhancement of life and personal relationships, and the possibility of having pleasurable and safe sexual experiences that are free of coercion, discrimination, and violence. Reproductive or sexual health services should provide basic information about biological and psychological aspects of sexual development, human reproduction, and the variety of sexual behaviors, dysfunctions, and disorders. The provision of such services requires health care professionals who possess positive attitudes toward sexuality, provide opportunities for discussion of sexual matters, and show understanding and objectivity in providing advice, information, and treatment.

Human Sexual Response

The phases of the human **sexual response** include a cycle of *desire, excitement, plateau, orgasm,* and *resolution.*

- The *desire phase* involves spontaneous thoughts, fantasies, and biological urges to self-stimulate or initiate sexual activities with a partner.
- The *excitement (arousal) phase* is induced by sensory stimuli or mental imagery. Physical response includes male penile erection and female vaginal lubrication, erect nipples in both genders, and engorged clitoris and testicles. Respiration increases up to 60 breaths per minute and heart rate up to 180 beats per minute, and blood pressure may rise by 40 to 80 mmHg systolic and 20 to 50 mmHg diastolic. In males, arteriolar dilation causes penile engorgement and obstruction of venous outflow. Engorgement is limited by the fascial sheath, causing rigidity. Other responses include scrotal engorgement, testicular retraction, and pre-ejaculatory secretion by the Cowper's glands. In females, vasocongestion elevates the uterus, and increases the depth of the vagina, the upper two thirds of which expands while the lower third becomes engorged and narrowed.
- With the *plateau phase*, arousal levels off; it may be of varying duration depending on the experience of the individual.
- The *orgasmic phase* is a brief physiological response involving involuntary motor activity.

Ejaculation occurs in males, as muscular contractions of the prostate, urethra, and perineum propel seminal fluid through the urethral opening. Up to 15 vaginal and perineal muscular contractions occur in females.

- In the *resolution phase*, physiological parameters return to normal. In males, repeated orgasm is impossible until after completion of the *refractory period*, which lasts minutes to hours depending on various factors, including age.

Women's Sexual Health

There are important differences between men and women regarding the sexual response cycle. A *new view of women's sexual health* is based on a *circular model* of sexual response for women and postulates that the sexual response cycle differs for men and women. For example, sexual desire is not always necessary for, nor does it always occur before, arousal in women; whereas in men, sexual libido or desire is critical for sexual performance. Females are also capable of multiple successive orgasms. Other models explore the role of emotional experience, intimacy, relationship, and closeness in triggering women's sexual arousal. Relationship problems, cultural conflict, sexual inexperience, and trauma may also play more of a role in sexual complaints than pure physiological response. This has important implications for how practitioners view normal female sexual responses.

Common Sexual Concerns of Patients

While some patients may present their concerns and problems explicitly, in many cases, these concerns may arise only when an astute clinician listens to the subtext of the patient's dialogue. The most common concerns include:

- Am I normal? How do I compare?
- Sexual identity: lifestyle, orientation, preference.
- Psychosexual development: over the life cycle.

- Reproduction: infertility, family planning, contraception, pregnancy, abortion.
- Sexual desire, satisfaction, and dysfunctions; couple's differences in desire; problems with vaginal lubrication, erections, orgasm, pain.
- Sexual changes due to age, physical disability, medical illness, treatment.
- Sexual trauma resulting from molestation, incest, rape.
- Safe sex practices: HIV/AIDS, sexually transmitted infections (STIs).
- Paraphilias and sexual compulsions.

The **PLISSIT model** offers a good guide to discussing sexual health with patients. The health care provider first gives the client Permission (P) to discuss sexual health topics. The health care provider then gives limited information (LI) that addresses the concern of the client but does not overwhelm them with extraneous information. After educating the client, the health care provider offers specific suggestions (SS) to help improve sexual satisfaction and health. If these suggestions do not meet the client's needs, the health care provider offers referral to a specialist trained in intensive therapy (IT).

Situation-Specific Sexuality Issues

Contraception

Determining the best method of **contraception** (Table 19.1) for a particular person depends on (a) type and frequency of intercourse (a woman having infrequent intercourse may prefer a barrier to a continuous method); (b) number and type of partners (a woman with several partners is better protected using condoms and spermicide with oral contraception than using oral contraception alone); (c) health history of the partner (the female partner of a man with genital herpes should use condoms rather than a diaphragm); (d) timing of a future desired pregnancy (a barrier method may be preferred to a long-term method such as injectable progesterone); (e) number of previous pregnancies (an intrauterine device [IUD] or relatively permanent contraception such as tubal ligation may be appropriate for a female in a mutually monogamous relation-

Table 19.1. Advantages and disadvantages of different types of contraception

Type of Contraception	Examples/Class	Advantages	Disadvantages
Hormonal	Progesterone implants/injections	Long lasting Safer with hypertension and diabetes	Delayed return of fertility Irregular bleeding
Combined pill	Estrogen/progesterone	Protects against cancers and osteoporosis Regulates menses No long-term effects	Contraindicated in women >35 with smoking, hypertension, or diabetes Side effects
Mini pill	Progesterone only (oral)	Good for women with contraindications to combined pill Safest during breastfeeding	Must be taken at the same time each day
Condom (male or female)	Barrier	Easy to use Helps prevent STIs	Dulling of sensation Potential for failure
Intrauterine device (IUD)	Barrier	No effect on hormones Works immediately	Risk of pelvic inflammatory disease
Diaphragm/cap	Barrier	Inserted prior to sex No hormones	Can cause cystitis Potential for failure
Rhythm/fertility awareness	Natural	No side effects	Restrictions on timing of sex Least effective method

ship); (f) degree of discomfort with touching one's body (oral contraceptives may be preferred to a diaphragm); and (g) concurrent medical conditions (oral contraceptives may be contraindicated).

Pregnancy

During early pregnancy, *fatigue, nausea,* or *breast tenderness* may interfere with sexual desire. In the second trimester, bothersome symptoms decrease, but issues of *body image* often arise. Some women feel unattractive; others feel more sexual due to the fluctuation of hormones during gestation. Some men are concerned about "hurting the baby" and avoid intercourse. Late in pregnancy, conditions such as a high-risk pregnancy may require abstaining from vaginal intercourse. Sexual activi-ty during gestation increases level of oxytocin and prostaglandins, which can result in contractions, inducing vaginal labor. However, in most cases, other forms of sexual intimacy are possible.

The discomfort of the healing perineum after episiotomy can interfere with resumption of sexual activity after childbirth. Sleep deprivation caused by an infant who awakens during the night can decrease libido.

Some women find breastfeeding to be sexually stimulating because of increases in oxytocin, prolactin, and dopamine in the brain; others feel ambivalent about their partner touching or stimulating their lactating breasts. Both men and women can suffer from postpartum depression (PPD) decreasing sexual desire and activity. Marital strain can occur when a husband feels displaced by an infant who receives much of the mother's attention. Conflict can arise over the distribution of infant-related chores, parenting styles, or the financial pressures of an expanded family.

Chronic Illness

How do specific health situations affect sexuality?

Medical conditions associated with changes in sexual functioning include arthritis and joint disease, diabetes mellitus, endocrine problems (including fertility-related disorders like polycystic orvary syndrome [PCOS]), injury to the autonomic nervous system by surgery or radiation, liver or renal failure, mood disorders (including depression, anxiety, and panic), multiple sclerosis, peripheral neuropathy, radical pelvic surgery, respiratory disorders (e.g., chronic obstructive pulmonary disease [COPD]), spinal cord injury, and vascular disease.

Supportive therapy may be needed for patients experiencing physical limitations or changes in physical appearance or sexual functioning. Information about reproductive options such as electroejaculation is important for men with spinal cord injury. Patients may be embarrassed about appliances such as catheters, ostomies, or artificial limbs, or about surgical scars. A postmastectomy patient's body image and relationship with her partner help determine whether reconstruction or a prosthesis should be considered. Antihypertensive drugs frequently cause erectile dysfunction, and although alcohol, sedatives, and narcotic analgesics may reduce inhibitions, they may also interfere with normal physiological functioning.

Infertility

Infertility and difficulty getting pregnant can cause conflict and concern. Monitoring, scheduling intercourse, taking medications, and undergoing testing are stressful. Respecting concerns, informing, counseling, and minimizing blame and guilt are essential components of managing infertility. Most couples have success using "low tech" options with a minority requiring *in vitro fertilization*. Success rates depend on type of therapy and age of the partners. Two thirds of couples being treated for infertility will conceive a baby.

Fertility treatment options include:
- *Fertility drugs*: Clomiphene, letrozole (ovulation induction), anastrozole (ovulation induction), and gonadotropins.
- *Surgery*: Hysterosalpingogram (HSG) to determine blockage of the fallopian tubes, followed by laparoscopic surgery, if needed.
- *Intrauterine insemination*: Artificial insemination, where sperm are placed into the uterus.
- *In vitro fertilization (IVF):* Fertility drugs are used to produce eggs. Eggs are removed, inseminated outside of the female body until fertilization occurs, and then placed back into the uterus.

Termination of Pregnancy

Unwanted pregnancy is most common at the extremes of a woman's reproductive life. While political, religious, and ethical controversy surrounds this issue, providing information about alternatives is considered essential by most people, even if that means referral to another provider. Thus, familiarity with community resources and separating personal bias from the care of the patient are fundamental to good care. Current options include the *morning after pill*, a high dose of an oral contraceptive (levonorgestrel) taken within 72 hr after sexual intercourse; an *abortifacient* like mifepristone, methotrexate, or misoprostol (to induce spontaneous abortion); and *vacuum aspiration*. *Adoption* should be presented as an option as well.

Sexually Transmitted Infections

Common **sexually transmitted infections** (STIs) are usually treatable with antibiotics and include gonorrhea, syphilis, and chlamydia. *Viruses* that cause STIs include human immunodeficiency virus (HIV), human papillomavirus (HPV), cytomegalovirus (CMV), and herpes simplex virus (HSV). Some of these viral STIs present risk of transmission to the child during childbirth or through breastfeeding. Although mainly transmitted by mosquitoes, the Zika virus, which can cause severe birth defects, may also be sexually transmitted.

Some strains of HPV have been associated with genital warts and with cervical cancer.

Currently, it is recommended that the HPV vaccine be administered to all females and males between the ages of 9 and 26. For optimal results, the vaccine should be administered before the individual becomes sexually active. Public debate about immunizing young, prepubescent individuals against an STI is ongoing as a primarily social rather than medical issue, especially in states like Texas where immunization has been mandated. Other sexually transmitted conditions such as trichomonas, molluscum contagiosum, pubic lice, scabies, and monilial vaginitis are bothersome, but rarely cause serious long-term problems. *Bacterial vaginosis*, frequently caused by *Gardnerella*, *Haemophilus*, or group B streptococcus, has been implicated in premature labor and small-for-gestational-age infants.

Prevention of STI requires candid communication between patient and partner and effective protection. Condoms, although not perfect, provide the best mechanical protection when combined with an appropriate spermicide. Latex gloves, finger cots, or condoms can be used for manual stimulation. Dental dams can be used during oral sex. In cases of latex allergy, nonlatex skins can be applied over or under other coverings depending on which partner is allergic.

Least risky behaviors include gentle kissing, mutual masturbation, fellatio with a condom, and nonshared sex toys. *More risky behaviors* include oral sex on a male (fellatio) without a condom; oral sex on a female (cunnilingus) without a dental dam; and vaginal or anal intercourse using a condom and spermicide and withdrawing prior to ejaculation. *Most risky behaviors* include anal or vaginal intercourse without a condom, with or without ejaculation, and fellatio without a condom and with ejaculation. Correct techniques for condom use should be taught, and reasons for not using condoms discussed. Role-playing situations in which patients find themselves confronted by a partner who does not want to use a condom are helpful, particularly for adolescents.

Postexposure prophylaxis (PEP) may be available for individuals exposed to HIV. Candidates are individuals who are HIV-negative, but have been in contact with a HIV-positive individual, or an individual of unknown status in high prevalence areas. Such individuals must have engaged in a high-risk sexual behavior and present for treatment within 72 hr of exposure. The course of therapy, lasting 28 days, usually involves two or three classes of antiretroviral therapy. Individuals who repeatedly engage in high-risk behaviors are not good candidates for this treatment.

Preexposure prophylaxis (PreP) can be effective in reducing the transmission of HIV in serodiscordant couples and high-risk populations (men who have sex with men [MSM]). Individuals take a combination antiretroviral emtricitabine/tenofovir daily as a means of reducing risk. As with any **harm reduction strategy**, there is controversy about whether PreP encourages risk-taking behavior. While highly effective against HIV transmission, PreP does not protect against other STIs. Current research is exploring the effectiveness of intermittent administration of PreP.

Age and Culture Specific Sexuality Issues

> How do age, gender, and culture affect sexual health?

Childhood and Adolescence

Adolescent sexual behavior often includes masturbation and noncoital stimulation with partners of the same or opposite gender. Adolescents today engage in intercourse at an earlier age than their parents. By age 15, the majority of African American males and more than a quarter of African American females and White males and females have had coitus. By age 18, most adolescents have had sexual experiences including intercourse. Same-sex behavior in adolescence is not uncommon and does not necessarily predict future sexual orientation or behavior.

Adolescents know little about the risks of not using contraceptives or the types of contraceptives available. About 35% do not use contraceptives during their first sexual experience. Unfortunately, 20% of all pregnancies occur during the first 2 months of sexual activity. Adolescents are also at increased risk for STIs for biological (lower estrogen, immature lining of the cervix) or psychosocial (risky behaviors, embarrassment about contraception) reasons.

When interviewing adolescents, use language and terms appropriate to their developmental age and provide a safe, nonjudgmental environment to talk about sexual issues. This may involve time without a parent present.

Many adolescents avoid consultation on sexual issues for fear of parental disapproval. Some states require parental permission, while others allow treatment of minors for possible STIs without parental permission.

Aging

Although sexual desire does not necessarily diminish with age, physiological function does change (see Chapter 21: Geriatric Health and Successful Aging). Postmenopausal women not taking *hormone replacement therapy* experience decreased vaginal lubrication, mucosal thinning, diminished vaginal expansion, and reduced vasocongestion. Ultra-low doses of topical (vaginal) estrogen may be sufficient to treat sexual dysfunctions involving thinning of vaginal mucosa. Older men require longer to achieve penile erection and, if interrupted, may not gain full tumescence; ejaculation is less intense and forceful. Women typically cease to reproduce at *menopause*, but men have been reported to reproduce into their 90s. While older couples do not necessarily have less satisfaction from intimate experiences, perceived diminution in function may inhibit activity. Medical conditions, medications, and physiological change can interfere with sexual functioning at any age, but these problems become more prevalent with age. Other issues for older persons include embarrassment, family disapproval, lack of privacy, and the illness or death of a partner. Given that older adults continue to engage in sexual practices, it is important to remember safer sex counseling and STI screening (including HIV) in this population.

Social and Cultural Expectations

Every culture has *norms* regarding sexual behavior. Sex may be acceptable only for procreation or only after a postmenstrual ritual cleansing bath.

Extramarital sex or polygamy may or may not be acceptable. Some religions prohibit contraception unless the mother's life is at risk. In some cultures, unwed mothers are accepted; in other cultures, they are ostracized or killed. In 1999, the World Association of Sexual Health adopted a **Declaration of Sexual Health** that included the right to

- sexual freedom, excluding all forms of sexual coercion, exploitation, and abuse;
- sexual autonomy and safety of the sexual body;
- sexual pleasure, which is a source of physical, psychological, and spiritual well-being;
- sexual information: generated through unencumbered yet scientifically ethical inquiry;
- comprehensive sexuality education; and
- sexual health care, which should be available for prevention and treatment of all sexual concerns, problems, and disorders.

The declaration is not meant to impose upon cultural traditions, but certain customs, such as female genital circumcision (also known as female genital mutilation [FGM]), may be challenged under such a declaration. In the last several years, nonprofit organizations, such as Intact America, have advocated an end to circumcision in male babies as well, since empirical evidence does not clearly demonstrate that circumcision of boys provides sufficient health benefits to justify universal recommendation of the practice.

Sexual Orientation and Identity

Sex is the designation given at birth based on observed anatomy (genitalia) or biology (e.g., chromosomes). **Gender** denotes the role assigned by society based on behavior and expression, and can typically be differentiated by toddlers around the age of 2 years. **Gender identity** is the personal perception of oneself as male, female, or nongender binary. This is sometimes manifested by someone's outward presentation of themselves. **Sexual orientation** denotes the physical, romantic, or emotional attraction to another person (homosexuality, heterosexuality, bisexuality). **Sexual identity** describes the person's subjective experience of sexual orientation. Sexual behavior does not always indicate orientation or identity, since individuals may be involved in same-sex activity, but not identify themselves as homosexual. However, the majority of people are consistent with self-identification, behavior, and attraction throughout their adult lives.

Homosexuality and Bisexuality

Most individuals develop a behavioral preference for same- or opposite-sex partners during adolescence. While neuroscience and genetic research suggest a role for genes and neurobiological factors in determining sexual orientation, the actual biological determinants of sexual orientation remain unclear. Several hypotheses suggest that gonadal hormones during gestation affect neural organization of the brain, which can also lead to differential hormonal regulation and responses of physiological systems associated with sexual motivation and performance as well as other sexually dimorphic behaviors.

About 40% of males will have at least one *homosexual experience* leading to orgasm in their lifetime, but only about 10% of men practice homosexuality at any given time, and about 4% are exclusively homosexual for > 10 years. **Homosexuality** appears to be less prevalent in women than in men, but women are less genitally focused than men, and definitions related to the number of homosexually induced orgasms may not accurately reflect a person's perception of their own sexual orientation. Although 10% to 13% of women have had sexual experiences with other women, only 3% of all women describe themselves as lesbian.

Persons who identify themselves as **bisexual** are sexually attracted to members of both sexes. Although only a few people describe themselves as bisexual, many members of both genders have had sexual experiences with members of the same and the opposite sex in their lifetime.

Transgender

Transgender individuals feel an incongruity between their anatomic gender and their gender identity, often describing their problem as being "trapped in the wrong body." For some, this realization occurs during childhood; for others, it occurs during adolescence or later. **Gender dys-**

phoria refers to the discomfort or unhappiness experienced in the biologically assigned gender role. Some individuals choose to undergo hormone therapy or surgical correction; others live their lives in the opposite role without any anatomical changes. The term **transsexual** has been used to refer to an individual who desires gender-changing procedures to acquire a physical appearance consistent with their gender identity. There are many health disparities for individuals who identify as transgender. (see Chapter 20: Health Care Issues Facing Lesbian, Gay, Bisexual, and Transgender Individuals).

Intersexed

Intersexed is a term that refers to individuals who are born with physical characteristics that make it difficult to determine their biological sex (male or female). This can be the result of chromosomal abnormalities (sex chromosomes), hormonal abnormalities, or anatomical abnormalities that lead to deformations or the presence or absence of certain reproductive organs. Surgery is usually performed if the condition threatens normal physiological functioning (e.g., passing urine) or for aesthetic reasons. The Intersexed Society of North America is an advocacy group and resource for such individuals with the primary goal of preventing sexual trauma by the medical profession.

Sexual Disorders

> How does normal sexual behavior differ from problematic sexual behavior?

Definitions of "normal" vs. "abnormal" sexual behavior vary across cultures and time. For example, homosexuality was considered a sexual disorder until 1973 when it was eliminated from the *Diagnostic and Statistical Manual of Mental Disorders* (DSM). Currently, there are five categories of sexual disturbance: sexual response dysfunction, sexual pain, gender identity disturbances, paraphilia, and disorders due to a medical condition (see Table 19.2). In brief, each individ-

Table 19.2. Sexual and gender identity disorders: definitions and estimated frequency

Disorder	Estimated Frequency	Definition
Sexual desire disorders		
Male hypoactive sexual desire disorder	20% adult males	Reduced desire for sexual contact or total aversion to sexual activity
Sexual arousal disorders		
Female sexual arousal/interest disorder	33% married females	Inability to attain or maintain sexual arousal sufficient to initiate or complete sexual acts
Male erectile disorder	2–4% < 35 years old 75% > 80 years old	
Orgasmic disorders		
Female orgasmic disorder	5% adult females	Excessive orgasmic delay, absence of orgasmic response, or premature orgasm
Premature (early) ejaculation	30% adult males	
Sexual pain disorders		
Genito-pelvic pain/penetration disorder	Unknown	Pain in sexual organs during sexual activity that interferes with or prevents sexual activity
Gender identity disorders	Unknown	Discomfort with or nonacceptance of primary sexual identification and desire to change sexual identification to the opposite gender

Based on American Psychiatric Association. (2013). *Diagnostic and statistical manual of mental disorders* (5th ed., pp. 440–443). Washington, DC: American Psychiatric Association. And Maurice, W. (2007). Sexual desire disorders. In S. Leiblum (Ed.), *Principles and practice of sex therapy* (4th ed.). New York, NY: Guilford Press.

ual will have a sexual identity (male or female), orientation (homosexual, bisexual, heterosexual), intensity of desire (hypo, "normal," hyper), object of desire (solo, partner, group, inanimate), and behavior (consenting, nonconsenting). These domains can be fluctuating or fixed for an individual. Problems in how the individual accepts each of these domains or how their identity in these domains conflicts with societal morals, laws, and values can all lead to problems.

Disorders of Desire and Arousal

Decreased libido is the most common complaint of women (**female sexual interest/arousal disorder**) and may also be experienced by men (**male hypoactive sexual desire disorder**). Decreased libido may be person-specific (a particular partner) or global, or reflect a discrepancy between partners' expectations of frequency or activity. Etiologies include dissatisfaction with a relationship, underlying medical or psychiatric problems, medications, substance abuse, stressors, and normal differences in desire. Sudden change in desire unrelated to a specific stress suggests an underlying medical or psychiatric problem. **Flibanserin** is the first approved pharmacological treatment for female sexual interest/arousal disorder in premenopausal women.

Erectile disorder is the inability to attain and maintain a penile erection sufficient to permit satisfactory intercourse. Up to 30% of men with erectile dysfunction have no identifiable organic basis for the problem. Differentiation of *psychogenically* based erectile dysfunction from *organically* based erectile dysfunction is critical to appropriate treatment. Individuals with psychogenic erectile dysfunction often have spontaneous nocturnal erections, whereas those with organic etiologies do not. History and physical examination should identify medications (e.g., antihypertensive or antidepressant agents) or medical conditions (e.g., diabetes) that might cause dysfunction. Vascular studies can uncover arterial or venous outflow problems. Oral medications that increase blood flow provide effective treatment in many cases. Surgical intervention may be necessary in more severe cases. Phosphodiesterase inhibitors such as sildenafil are usually effective. Endocrinological evaluation may indicate that administration of testosterone or alpha-adrenergic receptor antagonists, penile self-injections, or use of urethral suppositories containing a vasodilator would be helpful. Vacuum pumps that provide negative pressure to obtain an erection that is maintained by an elastic band at the base of the penis, and various malleable or rigid penile implants are other options.

Nonorganically based, or combined, erectile dysfunction in the male and disorders of arousal in the female often benefit from **sensate focus therapy**. This therapy includes having couples engage in progressive, sensual touching exercises with focus on the patient's sexual sensations. *Performance anxiety* is removed by initially excluding intercourse from the exercises.

Disorders of Orgasm

Premature (early) ejaculation is defined as ejaculation without sufficient voluntary influence over timing. For some men, ejaculation is considered rapid if it occurs within the first 2 min of vaginal intercourse; for others, it may be defined as ejaculation before $\geq$ 10 min of vaginal intercourse. Treatments to control the timing of ejaculation include the *stop-and-start technique* (repeated cycles of withdrawal of stimulation before ejaculation becomes inevitable) and the *squeeze technique* (application of pressure below the coronal ridge or at the base of the penis for 5–10 s until the urge to ejaculate ceases).

Men generally find vaginal intercourse an effective method of stimulation. Intercourse, however, is not the most effective means of stimulation for the female because the vagina is less sensitive to stimulation than the clitoris. Consultation for women who cannot achieve satisfactory orgasm includes learning direct methods of clitoral stimulation either by the patient or the partner, or use of appliances such as vibrators.

Psychological issues contributing to disorders of arousal include conflicts between an individual's level of sexual interest and perceived social "norms" (e.g., "nice girls don't have sex for orgasm"). Sometimes couples describe a change in their ability to "let go" when their role changes from date to spouse or from partner to parent. Sensate focus exercises may have the benefit of increasing the frequency of orgasm since less emphasis is placed on achieving it.

Sexual Pain Disorders

The **sexual pain disorders** affect women primarily. Onset may follow sexual trauma or gynecological surgery, or have other physical or psychological origins. Discomfort during intercourse (**genito-pelvic pain disorder**) can occur at all times or only in certain situations or with certain partners. Discomfort due to inadequate foreplay, pain because of insufficient lubrication, or involuntary muscular contractions can all contribute.

Pain on intromission may be due to vaginal infection, irritation, anatomic abnormalities, changes resulting from irradiation, inelasticity, or trauma. Pain on deep penetration can be caused by infection or other conditions such as endometriosis. True vaginismus, or involuntary spasm of the perineal muscles, can be treated with graduated vaginal accommodators to a point where intercourse is possible. **Sexual trauma** must be ruled out as an etiological factor in any case of dyspareunia, but especially in suspected vaginismus.

Paraphilic Disorders

Paraphilia is defined by the presence of intense sexually arousing fantasies or sexual urges or behaviors to induce sexual excitement that occur over at least 6 months (see Table 19.3 for a list of common paraphilias). A paraphilic disorder is only diagnosed when it causes the person significant distress or impairment, as, for example, when it is apparent the individual feels the behavior cannot be controlled or the behavior is taking away from more healthy intimate relationships. Sexual play or even sexual behaviors that are less "permissible" in society (e.g., bondage, striptease, role play, camming/sexting) are not considered paraphilic disorders, because they often are between consenting adults and are used to enhance intimacy and sexual pleasure. It is also essential to distinguish between occasional behaviors and behavior that is repetitive or necessary for sexual arousal, and between consent vs. nonconsent by the partner. Lastly, certain paraphilias such as exhibitionism, pedophilia, and frotteurism are considered crimes

because they involve a nonconsenting person.

The expression of paraphilias has been associated with increased levels of androgen in the male; therefore, chemical castration that directly decreases androgen levels has been proposed to inhibit what some consider aberrant sexual behaviors. Although antiandrogens can effectively inhibit sexual consummatory behaviors, they cannot decrease sexual thoughts or sexual fantasies. Thus, some authorities recommend that treatment for paraphilic disorders include cognitive behavior therapy in addition to inhibitors of the neurohormones and neurochemicals responsible for regulating sexual behaviors.

Sexual addiction (also known as hypersexuality, compulsive sexual behavior, out-of-control sexual behavior, and problematic sexual behavior) is sexual activity that temporarily alleviates anxiety, loneliness, and depression and that continues despite negative consequences to the individual. According to some authorities, when the need to have sexual experiences interferes with normal activities and relationships, the condition should be viewed as similar to any addiction, because sexual behaviors are physiological needs and increase the levels of dopamine in the neural structures associated with reward. That is, for some individuals, sexual interactions can result in a sig-

---

Table 19.3. Common paraphilic disorders

Paraphilia	Behavior
Exhibitionistic disorder	Genital exposure to an **unsuspecting** person or stranger
Fetishistic disorder	Use of **nonliving objects** (e.g., pieces of apparel of the other sex) for arousal
Frotteuristic disorder	Touching and rubbing against a **nonconsenting** person
Pedophilic disorder	Attraction to or behavior involving a **prepubescent** boy or girl
Sexual masochism disorder	Intense fantasies, urges, or behaviors, whether real or simulated, of **being humiliated** or made to suffer
Sexual sadism disorder	Arousal is achieved from the real psychological or physical **suffering of the victim**
Transvestic disorder	**Cross-dressing** by a male in women's attire that produces sexual arousal
Voyeuristic disorder	Arousal while viewing nudity or sexual activity of **unsuspecting others** who have not given permission

For DSM-5 criteria see American Psychiatric Association. (2013). *Diagnostic and statistical manual of mental disorders* (5th ed). Washington, DC: American Psychiatric Association.

nificant increase of dopamine in the brain, creating a "rush" or " high" similar to that produced by drugs of abuse. Individuals who identify as sexual addicts often feel unworthy and ashamed. Sexual addiction can present within the context of a committed relationship, as extramarital activity, or as a primary mode of sexual relations.

Sexual Exploitation

Sexual offender is a criminal justice term and is not considered a mental diagnosis. A sexual offender can be seen as any individual whose sexual activity either violates others or violates current rules of society. **Rape** is also a legal rather than medical term. It is defined as penile penetration of the vagina without mutual consent or with a person who is less than a certain age (**statutory rape**). Although rape involves a sexual act, it is primarily an expression of violence or power (see Chapter 25: Interpersonal Violence and Abuse).

Incest

It is estimated that one in four girls and one in five boys experience sexual abuse. Most perpetrators are known to the victim. **Incest** between siblings or child relatives is more common but less often reported than incest perpetrated by an adult relative. In some families, only one child may be victimized; in other families, many children may be abused. Although most sexually abused children are between 8 and 12 years of age, younger children, including infants, have been assaulted. Some children experience incest as a one-time event; others may experience it on an ongoing basis for years.

Long-term *sequelae of incest* include difficulty establishing intimate relationships, sexual dysfunction during adulthood, and increased genitourinary complaints in later life. *Dissociation* is a common coping mechanism used by children while being assaulted. As a result, some victims never have memories of the events; others remember them years later either spontaneously or during the course of psychotherapy. While the effects of incest and child sexual abuse can be extremely traumatic, it is important to note that most indi-

viduals with trauma histories are able to live fulfilling, stable, and healthy lives.

Sexual Harassment

The legal definition of **sexual harassment** in the workplace includes sexual advances or conduct that interferes with the employee's working environment, performance, or conditions of employment. A study of federal employees found that 44% of women and 19% of men had felt sexually harassed at work during the preceding 24 months. Although regulations exist to prevent sexual harassment in the workplace, it is often subtle and difficult to prove. Most cases involve male perpetrators and female victims, although successful suits have been brought by men against women. Recent court cases have broadened the definition of sexual harassment to include unwanted sexual contact between members of the same sex.

Sexual Abuse in Intimate Relationships

Women who experience physical violence in an intimate relationship often experience being forced to have sex against their wishes. In fact, most women who have their first intercourse experience before age 15 report that the act was not voluntary. Women in such coercive situations may be at risk if they leave the relationship precipitously. Although reported less commonly, men can have similar experiences and are also at risk. Couples in a violent relationship should not be referred for conjoint counseling since the victim may not disclose information at all or the batterer may retaliate physically or emotionally if the victim does disclose. Referring the victim and the perpetrator individually to counseling services is imperative.

Prostitution

Prostitution involves the exchange of sex with another person for the explicit purpose of receiving immediate payment. Female prostitution for heterosexual activity is more prevalent than male prostitution, which is usually homosexual.

Prostitution puts the individual at risk of an STI, assault or injury by customers, exploitation by pimps or other agents of organized crime, involvement of minors, and arrest for illegal activity.

Recommended Readings

Balon, R., & Seagraves, R. (2009). *Clinical manual of sexual disorders*. Washington, DC: American Psychiatric Press.

Batur, P., Bowersox, N., & McNamara, M. (2016). Contraception: Efficacy, risks, continuation rates, and use in high-risk women. *Journal of Women's Health, 25*(8), 853–856. http://doi.org/10.1089/jwh.2016.5942

Clayton, A. H., & Harsh, V. (2016). Sexual function across aging. *Current Psychiatry Reports, 18*(3), 28. http://doi.org/10.1007/s11920-016-0661-x

Corona, G., Isidori, A. M., Aversa, A., Burnett, A. L., & Maggi, M. (2016). Endocrinologic control of men's sexual desire and arousal/erection. *Journal of Sexual Medicine, 13*(3), 317–337. http://doi.org/10.1016/j.jsxm.2016.01.007

Komisaruk, B. R., & Rodriguez Del Cerro, M. C. (2015). Human sexual behavior related to pathology and activity of the brain. *Handbook of Clinical Neurology, 130*, 109–119. http://doi.org/10.1016/B978-0-444-63247-0.00006-7

Perry, D., Walder, K., Hendler, T., & Shamay-Tsoory, S. G. (2013). The gender you are and the gender you like: Sexual preferences and empathetic neural responses. *Brain Research, 1534*, 66–75. http://doi.org/10.1016/j.brainres.2013.08.040

Review Questions

1. A proposed treatment for paraphilias among males is
   A. amphetamines
   B. antibiotics
   C. antidepressants
   D. antipsychotics
   E. castration

2. In women, which phase is characterized by vaginal lubrication and breast enlargement?
   A. Arousal
   B. Desire
   C. Orgasm
   D. Plateau
   E. Resolution

Answer Key on p. 465

20 Health Care Issues Facing Lesbian, Gay, Bisexual, and Transgender Individuals

David W. Pantalone, PhD, Douglas C. Haldeman, PhD, and Christopher R. Martell, PhD

- What is the difference between sexual orientation, sexual behavior, and sexual identity?
- Why are there limited research data on the health care problems of LGBT individuals?
- What are the major areas of LGBT health care concerns?
- What are the potential risk factors for cancer among LGBT individuals?
- What are the rates of anxiety and depression among LGBT individuals?
- What are the guidelines for providing informed care for LGBT individuals?

People who identify as sexual (i.e., gay, lesbian, bisexual) or gender (i.e., transgender) minorities face many of the same health care problems as the population in general. However, some such individuals – we often use the umbrella term **lesbian, gay, bisexual, and transgender** (LGBT) – have additional unique health concerns resulting from the societal discrimination they face because of their sexual minority status. These health issues may result from directly overt or explicitly enacted discrimination (e.g., ignorance or hostility on the part of the health care providers, physical assault via hate crimes) or result indirectly from the psychological stress associated with being LGBT (e.g., realistic fears about disclosure and coming out, societal messages about the immorality of same-sex sexual behavior, lack of faith in the health care system). The competent, ethical provision of physical and mental health care services to LGBT patients requires a basic understanding of these unique stressors and their health consequences. Empirical data indicate that many LGBT individuals have had negative experiences with health care providers in the past, and rate their overall health as significantly poorer than do heterosexuals. Thus, it is critical that providers learn about this group of patients, so they can deliver culturally competent medical care in a professional and respectful manner (see Chapter 17: Culture and Cultural Competence in Health Care, and Chapter 18: Health Care in Minority and Majority Populations).

Sexual Orientation and Sexual Identity

What is the difference between sexual orientation, sexual behavior, and sexual identity?

Sexual orientation is the most widely accepted term for referring to the way in which individuals define their sexual identity. Examples of sexual orientation are *opposite sex* or *heterosexual* and *same sex* or *lesbian, gay,* or *bisexual*. Note that transgender individuals may have a sexual orientation that is same sex or opposite sex. **Gender identity** and **sexual orientation** are independent constructs even though *gender nonconforming* behavior is often linked to later identification as a sexual minority, and gender is reflected in some of the common sexual orientation labels (e.g., *lesbian* implies both same-sex attraction and female gender identity). It is also important to mention that terms like *same sex* and *opposite sex* reflect a strict gender binary of male/female, despite increasing acceptance of the view that gender (like sexual orientation) is more accurately considered a continuum instead of a category. In recent years, research has noted an increase in sexual orientation labels that are uncoupled from gender identity, including the terms *queer* and *pansexual*. For terminology, *sexual orientation* is typically viewed more favorably than terms such as *sexual preference* or *gay lifestyle,* which are seen as invalidating or trivializing an individual's sexual identity. It is also important to note that *sexual identity* and *sexual behavior* are not always synonymous. Behavior is what people do; identity is how people view themselves and how they present themselves to the world. For example, a woman may engage in same-sex sexual behaviors but not identify as lesbian, or she may indeed self-identify as lesbian without engaging in same-sex sexual behaviors. Providers should respect and affirm whatever sexual orientation or gender identity is reported by a patient.

Historically, homosexuality was included in the roster of mental illnesses, reflecting prevailing beliefs and biases on the part of society and the health care establishment during that era. However, in 1973, as a result of activism within the professional organization, the American Psychiatric Association removed homosexuality from the Diagnostic and Statistical Manual of Mental Disorders (DSM), and all other major medical associations followed suit.

Despite the general reduction in cultural stigma against LGBT individuals over the past 35 years, prejudice still persists in numerous social arenas. LGBT individuals who have internalized negative attitudes about their sexual orientation from their families or from religious or other cultural groups may seek to change their sexual orientation through, for example, psychotherapy. Such "reparative therapies" have no credibility among mainstream mental health organizations, given their demonstrated lack of success and potential to actually harm individuals. These "treatments" are viewed by most providers as scientifically unfounded and professionally inappropriate attempts to oppress sexual minority individuals. All of the major mental health and medical organizations have condemned their use as unethical. Further, several jurisdictions have prohibited mental health professionals from conducting such "treatments" with minors.

Many providers are uncomfortable working with patients whose cultural background (e.g., race, ethnicity, or sexual orientation) is different from their own. As a result, a provider may avoid asking sensitive questions that are most important to the patient. Providers should become aware of this reluctance, and strive to act in the best interests of the patient. To be respectful of patients who may be LGBT, providers should assess behavior and identity separately, and use appropriately inclusive language when questioning patients about their background, relationships, or sexual history. For example, it would be heterosexist (assuming heterosexuality universally) to say to every female patient, "Do you have a boyfriend?" and inclusive to ask, "Are you in a significant relationship right now?" Also, when a patient reports sexual activity, one could ask, "Have your sex partners been male-bodied, female-bodied, or both?" in order to identify people who engage in same-sex sexual behavior but who do not necessarily identify as LGBT.

Why are there limited research data on the health care problems of LGBT individuals?

Epidemiologic research on LGBT populations, as hidden minority groups, is limited because large-scale surveys typically omit explicit questions about sexual orientation. Even when such questions are included, many LGBT individuals are reluctant to answer truthfully or, in forced-choice questions, do not find their preferred sexual orientation label listed (e.g., pansexual) and either skip the question altogether or choose another option that does not genuinely apply to them. Thus, the field lacks accurate estimates of the size of the LGBT population overall, as well as for relevant health and mental health factors. Because of the relatively small proportion of LGBT people, and the societal **stigma** attached to identifying as such, any data yielded by population-based studies must necessarily be viewed as an underrepresentation of the true figures. The most widely accepted prevalence figures for LGBT individuals indicate that about 3.5% of adults in the US identify as LGB and 0.3% as transgender; around 8% report that they have engaged in same-sex sexual behavior, and about 11% acknowledge some same-sex sexual attraction. Also, it is misleading to group together all LGBT individuals or, for example, to assume homogeneity within the *L* or *G* categories. It is more accurate to speak about LGBT "communities" (always in plural) since there is substantial diversity in, for example, cultural background, ethnic and racial identity, age, education, income, and place of residence. Individuals who engage in same-gender romantic or sexual experiences may not identify as LGBT (especially young people whose sexual orientations are not yet solidified) and would, therefore, be lost to researchers asking questions about this population in particular.

> Patients who identify as LGBT can vary in the degree to which sexual orientation is central to their identity. Many LGBT individuals have other identity labels that they feel are more important to them, such as being Latino, being a father, or being Christian. Some young LGBT people may eschew identity labels altogether. To the extent that it is relevant to patient care, providers are encouraged to ask LGBT patients about their identity and its importance using open-ended questions and a curious, non-judgmental stance. Similarly, providers are discouraged from making assumptions based on an individual's physical appearance, mannerisms, or even the behavioral elements of their history.

Major Health Care Concerns for LGBT Communities

> What are the major areas of LGBT health care concerns?

The political climate of the early 21st century put a chill on funding for LGBT research, thus making the question of major health concerns for LGBT individuals more difficult to answer. More recently, the attitudes of providers and policy makers have undergone an evolution with respect to LGBT health concerns. Federal funding has supported some research and treatment interventions specific to the health needs of LGBT individuals. The Institute of Medicine (IOM) issued a landmark report in 2011 that identified both risk and protective factors for LGBT individuals, assessed the epidemiology of various health problems across generational LGBT cohorts, and outlined strategies for improving access to health care for LGBT individuals. Low socioeconomic status (SES), lack of connection with the health care system, and dealing with societal reactions to one's sexual minority identity (otherwise known as **minority stress**) all appear to contribute to LGBT health disparities. For LGBT individuals, good health, fewer illnesses, and positive health behaviors have been shown to be associated with positive self-esteem, although these data are still debated. Population-based research has found that bisexual individuals may fare more poorly than either heterosexuals or their gay and lesbian counterparts, as unemployment, lack of a primary health care provider, and having no health or dental insurance are more common among this group. According to the IOM, transgender individuals also face the difficulty of having few providers that have had the training to treat them in a culturally competent manner.

> Six specific areas of LGBT health concerns to which providers should be especially attentive are: (1) physical fitness and cardiovascular health; (2) sexual risk behaviors leading to HIV and other sexually transmitted diseases; (3) alcohol and substance use, including tobacco dependence; (4) interpersonal violence; (5) cancer; and (6) mental health, including depression and suicidality.

Physical Fitness and Cardiovascular Health

Emerging areas of interest among public health researchers are the health behaviors of LGBT individuals related to *physical fitness*, including *diet, exercise*, and overweight or *obesity*. Compared with heterosexual men, sexual minority men appear to have higher rates of body image problems and disordered eating, including purging behavior and binge eating episodes, in addition to clinically diagnosable eating disorders. Important consequences include blood pressure changes, osteoporosis, dehydration and electrolyte imbalance, muscle loss, and tooth decay. Paradoxically, gay men are generally more dedicated to physical fitness than their male heterosexual counterparts, and do not show significantly different rates of disorders related to lack of exercise.

In contrast, sexual minority women tend to report more satisfaction with their **body image** than heterosexual women do. However, sexual minority women report less exercise than heterosexual women and are more likely to be overweight or obese. The consequences of these weight problems include increased risk of hypertension, heart disease, and diabetes. Qualitative studies suggest that the possible reasons for lesbian obesity are complex, and may include rejection of heterocentric norms of "thin females," or overeating as a symptom of depression and reaction to stress. One recent study linked binge eating on the part of lesbians with internalized negative attitudes about sexuality. Although the specific causes of obesity may vary from person to person, it is consistently identified as the top health concern for lesbians.

Importantly, *heart disease* is the most frequent cause of death among women, and thus, risk factors should be monitored closely because lesbian and heterosexual women have similar risk profiles. Indeed, it may be especially important to be attentive to the cardiovascular health (including hypertension) of sexual minority women, given the higher rates of overweight, smoking, and elevated stress levels due to their sexual minority status. Sexual minority men, by virtue of their higher rates of smoking and alcohol and substance use, may also be at increased risk of heart problems. Transgender individuals may be at higher risk for heart disease due to hormone use and the high prevalence of risk factors like smoking and obesity. Because cardiovascular disease is highly prevalent among African Americans in the US, sexual and gender minority African Americans may be at particularly high risk and may require especially vigilant screening.

Health Issues Related to Sexual Risk Behaviors

Since the initial clinical presentation of *HIV/AIDS* in 1981, it is estimated that up to 78 million people have been infected worldwide, with 37 million HIV-infected people living today. There are more than 1.1 million people living with HIV in the US today. More than half of those people are thought to be men who acquired the virus through sex with other men (men who have sex with men [MSM]) irrespective of their sexual orientation or sexual identity. Transgender women are also at substantial risk (see the IOM report of 2011). Early in the epidemic, most affected men were White.

However, the demographics of the US epidemic have shifted, and beginning in 1998, most people living with HIV/AIDS have been Black or Latino MSM. Recent prevalence rates continue to show that White, Black, and Latino MSM are at highest risk for new infections. Recent data also indicate that many MSM of color do not identify as gay or bisexual. This is a crucial point, as most HIV prevention programs have tacitly equated behavior with identity by specifically targeting programs toward men who identify as gay or bisexual (e.g., by recruiting people from predominantly gay neighborhoods or bars). The use of recruitment venues populated primarily by men who identify as gay makes it difficult to generalize findings to MSM who do not identify as gay, and has likely served as a barrier to effective HIV prevention efforts for that group.

The advent of *combination antiretroviral therapy* (cART) has made it possible for HIV/AIDS to be a condition with which many individuals can live productive, satisfying lives. Nevertheless, HIV continues to spread among gay men of all generations. A number of factors may play a role: Some, especially younger, gay men may view HIV as a manageable condition and erroneously minimize their likelihood of exposure. In the literature, this is termed *HIV optimism.* Some gay men eschew the use of condoms because substance abuse impairs judgment or because of an unwillingness to relinquish the pleasure associated with condomless anal sex, the primary high-risk sexual behavior within this group; and some men attach symbolic meaning to unprotected sexual behavior (i.e., having a trusting relationship with a partner). Advances in cART have meant that, for many men infected with the virus, their HIV viral load can be controlled by taking one or two pills once per day.

HIV prevention programs have, in aggregate, shifted the trend in sexual behavior toward the use of barrier protection for anal sex by gay or bisexual men. Successful prevention programs use targeted interventions focused directly on the behaviors of condom use that are *culturally appropriate* (i.e., tailored to the unique barriers and strengths of a given subgroup). Several psychosocial factors that influence sexual risk taking are self-esteem, social support, mood prior to sexual encounter, overall optimism or fatalism, age, education, and alcohol or drug use before or during sex. The majority of patients do not discuss sexual activity with health care providers, which is a missed opportunity for education and intervention. One recent, dramatic advance in HIV prevention has been the use of some of the prescription medications typically used for cART (emtricitabine/tenofovir or Truvada) as prophylaxis against acquiring HIV. As a preventive agent, this practice is referred to as *preexposure prophylaxis* (PrEP). In 2010, the US Food and Drug Administration approved daily PrEP for MSM at high-risk for acquiring HIV, after trials showed this method to be more than 90% effective at preventing new infections.

The US Centers for Disease Control and Prevention (CDC) estimate that gay men are 17 times more likely than heterosexual men to develop anal cancer, and significantly more likely to develop prostate cancer. Rates of some sexually transmitted infections (STIs) are higher among MSM than among men who only engage in sex with women. MSM are also at risk of acquiring other STIs, including urethritis, proctitis, pharyngitis, prostatitis, hepatitis A and B, syphilis, gonorrhea, chlamydia, herpes, and human papillomavirus (HPV). Transgender individuals appear to be at higher risk for some STIs than their **cisgender** peers (i.e., people who have a gender identity matching the sex assigned at birth). Increasing rates of HIV infection parallel the rising rates of unprotected sex and other STIs. Lack of education is only part of the problem: Many men who engage in sexual risk behaviors do not identify as "gay" and, as such, are outside the reach of customary educational efforts targeting the gay community. Further, shame and mistrust often cause sexual and gender minority individuals to delay or avoid medical treatment because of a realistic fear of mistreatment by culturally insensitive health care staff or providers.

There are no data showing that women who have sex with women have any higher rates of STIs; indeed, the opposite appears to be true. However, while sexual minority women are at lower risk for acquiring HIV, the risk is not zero. HIV could be spread through even occasional condomless sex with a male partner (for women who have sex with male- and female-bodied individuals) or through sharing sex toys.

Alcohol and Substance Use

Early research on *alcohol use* found LGBT individuals reporting significantly higher rates of problem drinking. However, these studies relied on sampling methods that may have artificially inflated prevalence estimates (e.g., recruiting participants at bars or gay pride events). More recent research has presented some conflicting findings including studies showing similar rates of problem drinking across sexual orientation and gender identity groups. For example, some studies have found no significant differences in rates of problem drinking (gay men, lesbians) or frequency of bar-going behavior (lesbians) compared with same gender, heterosexual counterparts. A few studies have found higher rates of abstinence from alcohol (but not social drinking) among gay men, possibly related to the individual's past history of alcoholism or in response to a family history of alcoholism. Some studies have reported a higher incidence of binge drinking among bisexual women. Despite the equivocal findings in the literature, it appears that, for some sexual and gender minority individuals, problematic alcohol use and significant alcohol related problems are crucial predictors of health status and worthy of routine assessment and more intensive intervention.

Research on substance use other than alcohol indicates higher rates of *smoking* among sexual minority men and women and gender minority individuals. In fact, these individuals are up to 200% more likely to be smokers than their heterosexual and cisgender peers, respectively. Lesbians are the only demographic subgroup whose rate of smoking actually increases with age. Rates of *marijuana* and *cocaine* use are also higher in lesbians compared with heterosexual women. Compared with heterosexual men, gay men have higher rates of use of *inhalants* (e.g., amyl or butyl nitrite, also called "poppers," and usually used during sex), *hallucinogens,* and *illicit drugs* overall. Gay men and lesbians 18 to 25 years old report higher rates of substance use compared with older cohorts and with heterosexual peers.

Gay men are significantly more likely than heterosexual men to abuse drugs: They appear to be 3.5 times more likely to abuse marijuana and 9.5 times more likely to abuse heroin. Drug use among gay men is often associated with condomless anal sex, especially the use of *ketamine*

("Special K"), *MDMA* ("ecstasy"), and crystal methamphetamine ("meth" or "Tina"). Gay men, in particular, may abuse crystal methamphetamine at high rates, especially in urban areas, because it increases the drive for sex over a period of many hours while simultaneously delaying orgasm, a behavior which facilitates HIV transmission. Nonjudgmental inquiry about drug use, and the combination of drug use and sexual behavior, should be standard assessment practice for all gay men, even if these are not identified a priori by the patient as a concern.

Interpersonal Victimization

The psychological and physical health consequences of **interpersonal victimization** are well documented (see Chapter 25: Interpersonal Violence and Abuse), and include emotional distress and mental disorders (depression, posttraumatic stress disorder [PTSD]), acute health problems (fractures, lacerations), and chronic health problems (lower back pain, fibromyalgia). Rates of traumatic victimization appear higher among sexual minority individuals both during childhood (psychological, physical, and sexual abuse) and adulthood (psychological or physical coerced sexual experiences, rape). It is possible that sexual and gender minority individuals are targeted by perpetrators because of their perceived sexual orientation or gender nonconforming behaviors. Indeed, current trends indicate that there is sometimes a backlash against LGBT individuals, in terms of increased violent victimization, in the time period after legislative or policy changes favoring LGBT protections.

Screening for a history of gender identity-related victimization, such as bullying or hate crimes, as well as interpersonal abuse across the lifespan, such as partner violence, is critical. Data regarding violence perpetrated by a romantic partner suggests that the rates may be comparable in male–male, female–female, and male–female couples. Patients are often uncomfortable or fearful about disclosing abuse. However, in same-sex relationships, there is also another barrier to reporting: Sexual minority women tend not to perceive their female partners as abusive, and sexual minority men tend not to perceive themselves as victims. For this reason, it is essential to ask behaviorally based questions (e.g., "Has your partner ever slapped, hit, or kicked you?") rather than perception-based questions (e.g., "Has your partner ever abused you?"). Providers report a great deal of discomfort and avoidance in assessing for partner abuse overall, and thus, they should engage in whatever training and supervision is needed to facilitate making such inquiries standard practice.

Cancer

> **What are the potential risk factors for cancer among LGBT individuals?**

Like all women, sexual minority women should be screened routinely for both *breast* and *colon cancer*. Like all men, sexual minority men should receive routine screening for *prostate, testicular, colon*, and *anal cancer*. Transgender men who still have a uterus, ovaries, or breasts are at risk for cancer in these organs. Transgender women are at risk for prostate cancer, though this risk is low. Cancers related to the use of hormones appear to be rare; however, screening is still recommended.

In general, LGBT and heterosexual individuals are at equal risk for developing cancer. In some cases, however, individual health behaviors such as smoking or alcohol consumption may increase risk. Other potential problems may be lack of preventive health care, since delayed detection and diagnosis are associated with negative outcomes; fear and distrust of health care providers based on previous negative experiences; and implicit or explicit discomfort among providers about working with sexual minority patients around topics like sex and reproduction.

Sexual minority individuals, especially men, do have an increased risk of anal cancer, possibly because of higher rates of HPV infection. Anal cancer can be detected through a pap smear-like test performed rectally.

Mental Health Issues

> **What are the rates of anxiety and depression among LGBT individuals?**

Typically, major, large-scale studies of the prevalence of mental disorders in the general population have not included sexual orientation as a demographic variable, thus limiting information about mental health disparities among sexual or gender minority individuals. Most of the work that has been done has looked at sexual orientation or gender identity within populations meeting criteria for specific disorders or has used symptom scales that may be correlated with mental disorders at a diagnostic and criterion level. With these caveats, rates of mood and anxiety problems among LGBT individuals appear to be higher than among heterosexuals and cisgender individuals, respectively. This is most likely due to the phenomenon of *minority stress,* or the individual's internalization of the social stigmatization, prejudice, and fear of violence that many sexual minority individuals encounter. Recent studies identify minority stress as the foremost compromising health factor for LGBT individuals.

Rates of *anxiety* and *depression* among LGBTs are especially high if they are not "out" about their sexual orientation or gender identity and thus lack adequate social support targeted to their unique stressors. The situation is likely compounded for younger LGBT individuals, who may lack role models and may fear abandonment by their family of origin, and for LGBTs of color, who face the additional stress of managing another stigmatized identity. The result is higher rates of health and mental health care utilization and, in some subgroups, higher rates of suicidal and other self-harm behaviors. Screening for mental health problems, suicidal or self-harm behaviors, and psychosocial stressors should be part of routine health care for LGBT individuals, with referral for culturally competent mental health services as needed. In fact, mental health concerns and stress can be lethal: Researchers have found that the life expectancy of LGBT people living in communities with high levels of antigay prejudice is 12 years less than that of those living in more tolerant areas.

Unique Issues Related to Treating Transgender Patients

The term **transgender** refers to a variety of identities and behaviors indicative of gender expression that does not conform to an individual's anatomically assigned gender, or to rigid societal norms about what it means to be "male" or "female." Unlike the same-sex attraction experienced by gay and lesbian individuals, transgender refers to a potential crisis of gender identity about the experience of being male or female. Further, some transgender individuals find that neither the male nor the female gender identity feels comfortable for them and thus question the notion of a binary gender categorization altogether.

There is frequently confusion about the term *transgender* that must be clarified. The term *transgender* is distinct from **transvestite**, which refers to individuals who derive pleasure, sometimes erotic, from **cross-dressing** (wearing attire of the opposite gender). Such behaviors may be episodic or regular; typically, they are chronic and are most often experienced by heterosexually identified persons, usually men. In and of themselves, transvestic behaviors do not pose unique health-related concerns, although sometimes the secrecy and shame associated with the behaviors can affect interpersonal relationships.

The transgender category does include **intersex** individuals, whose biological sex is ambiguous. These individuals are born with a reproductive or sexual anatomy that does not seem to fit the typical definitions of female or male based on chromosomal, anatomical, or other variations. Intersex individuals may or may not claim a primary male or female identity in adult life, and may have had surgery during their youth to "correct" their ambiguous secondary sex characteristics. Adult intersex individuals may thus have positive, negative, or mixed feelings about their body and the decision-making process of their families and physicians in the past.

True transgenderism, or **transsexualism**, is characterized by a persistent sense of having been "born in the wrong body." This means that the individual likely exhibited gender-atypical play interests in youth, feels most comfortable when attired in the manner of another gender, and seeks to evolve toward a stable life and presentation as the opposite gender. Transgender individuals may be either "M to F" (MTF; biological males seeking to live as females) or "F to M" (FTM; biological females seeking to live as males). Some, but certainly not all, transgender individuals have as their goal eventual sex reassignment through surgery.

Prior to this, a series of medical and social prerequisites must be met (see Chapter 19: Sexuality and Sexual Disorders).

The transgender individual seeking *sex reassignment* – as it has been called historically, or *gender affirmation* or *gender confirmation* in more recent years – must be under the care of a psychologist or psychotherapist in advance of initiating any changes in hormonal state or physiognomy. The first medical step for transgender individuals is usually hormone therapy, initiated after a 6- to 12-month period of psychological counseling. In the case of MTF transgender individuals, the person may seek removal of body hair through electrolysis or laser treatments, facial feminization surgery, and a number of other procedures prior to seeking sex reassignment surgery (SRS). According to the Standards of Care of the World Professional Association for Transgender Health (WPATH), the person should be living full time in the role of their desired gender for a period of 1 year prior to being eligible for surgery. This usually includes living and working in-role, as well as coming out to family and friends about one's thoughts and feelings. The process can be challenging, but the determination with which most transgender individuals approach it is testament to the deeply felt nature of the syndrome. The actual medical and psychological management of transgender cases usually requires specialized competence and training.

Tips for Providers Working with LGBT Patients

> What are the guidelines for providing informed care for LGBT individuals?

Providers interested in more in-depth discussion of research findings related to LGBT health issues are directed to the IOM's 2011 report. Those interested in more details about how to work with LGBT patients should consult *The Fenway Guide to Lesbian, Gay, Bisexual, and Transgender Health* or the Gay and Lesbian Medical Association's *Guidelines for Care of*

Lesbian, Gay, Bisexual, and Transgender Patients. There are also guidelines for mental health providers working with LGB clients, and guidelines for working with transgender clients, each published by the American Psychological Association and freely available from their website (https://www.apa.org/practice/guidelines/). The following suggestions will help providers screen for problems and better understand these patients that may have certain vulnerabilities because of their sexual orientation:

- Always take a thorough sexual history regardless of the partner or marital status of the patient. For example, ask a cisgender man married to a cisgender woman if he only has sex with his wife and if he only has sex with women. Patients who identify as heterosexual may sometimes engage in same-sex sexual behavior (this situation is sometimes referred to in the popular literature as being "on the down low" or "DL").

- Ask about the patient's understanding regarding condom use practices and how successfully they follow their own sexual risk limits. Are there circumstances (certain places, certain partners, when feeling sad, when drinking or using drugs) in which they are more likely to engage in condomless sex or otherwise cross their sexual risk limits? Referral to a mental health professional or community clinic focusing on how to reduce sexual risk may be warranted. In any case, ask about behaviors or conditions for which LGBT patients are at higher risk.

- Sexually active patients should be screened regularly for STIs and encouraged to receive appropriate vaccinations (e.g., for hepatitis A and B, HPV).

- Inquire thoroughly about health-related habits: patterns of exercise, diet, smoking, alcohol and drug use, and general levels of stress, and intervene directly or through appropriate referral, as required.

- Be aware that LGBT individuals may be more vulnerable for certain psychological problems such as depression and anxiety disorders, including panic. LGBT adolescents may have higher rates of suicidal ideation than heterosexual adolescents. Understand the protective factors and strengths and resilience factors available to the patient. Inadequate social support is related to higher suicidality in LGBT adolescents, and good social support can serve as a protective factor.

Important Questions to Ask About Social Support

- Who knows about your sexual orientation and gender identity?
- What has their reaction been?
- What people are in your life that you trust and with whom you can share concerns? Who are they, and how often do you have contact with them?
- Whom do you consider to be family? Are they biological relatives or a network of friends with whom you share a particular bond?
- What substances (alcohol, tobacco, other drugs) do you use regularly? Are there others that you use only occasionally? Does your use of a "substance" ever make you nervous or feel like it's difficult to control?
- How do you resolve conflicts with your romantic partner? Do arguments or fights ever become violent?
- What best describes, for you, a successful working relationship with a health care provider?

Many LGBT individuals have good reason not to trust the medical establishment. LGBT individuals have often been viewed as mentally disordered, and may currently be treated as sexually out of control. Transgender patients are often treated with intolerance or labeled as having a mental disorder. The LGBT patient's reluctance to be forthcoming with personal information may not be a sign of uncooperativeness or "resistance," but rather, based on anti-LGBT attitudes from society at large. Providing high-quality, culturally competent care to this socially and medically vulnerable group requires skill, objectivity, and compassion.

Recommended Readings

Hatzenbuehler, M., McLaughlin, K., Keyes, K., & Hasin, D. (2010). The impact of institutional discrimination on psychiatric disorders in lesbian, gay and bisexual populations: A prospective study. *American Journal of Public Health*, *100*, 452–459. http://doi.org/10.2105/AJPH.2009.168815

Institute of Medicine. (2011). *The health of lesbian, gay, bisexual and transgender people: Building a foundation for better understanding*. Washington, DC: National Academies Press.

Makadon, H. J., Mayer, K. H., Potter, J., & Goldhammer, H. (Eds.). (2008). *The Fenway guide to lesbian, gay, bisexual, and transgender health*. Philadelphia, PA: American College of Physicians.

Meyer, I. H., & Northridge, M. E. (Eds.). (2007). *The health of sexual minorities: Public health perspectives on lesbian, gay, bisexual and transgender populations*. New York, NY: Springer. http://doi.org/10.1007/978-0-387-31334-4

Review Questions

1. Of the following, HIV/AIDS is most prevalent among
   A. Black and Latino lesbians
   B. Black and Latino men having sex with men
   C. Black and Latino transgendered people
   D. White lesbians
   E. White men having sex with men

2. Sexual minority men are at risk for which of the following conditions?
   A. Anal cancer
   B. Drug abuse
   C. Eating disorders
   D. Suicidal death
   E. All of the above

3. Among the following, the major reason LGBT people receive less-than-optimal preventive health care is
   A. appropriate care requires specialized training
   B. gays and lesbians hide their sexual orientation
   C. insurance does not cover atypical sexually transmitted diseases
   D. practitioners are uncomfortable discussing sexual orientation and behavior
   E. routine surveillance or screening tests are inadequate

Answer Key on p. 465

21 Geriatric Health and Successful Aging

Patricia M. Lenahan, LCSW, LMFT, BCETS

- What are some of the physiological changes of aging?
- What are common mental health problems of aging?
- What harmful substances are older people most likely to use?
- How does chronic illness affect sexual functioning?
- What living arrangement options exist for older people?

The world is experiencing an unprecedented increase in the aging population. China alone will have about 270 million people > 60 years of age within the next 20 years. Census data reveal that the greatest advances in aging will be among people of color and in underdeveloped regions of the world. In the US, as the first wave of *baby boomers* reaches the age of 65, the number of individuals > 65 in 2030 will be approximately twice the number of those > 65 in the year 2000.

The Aging Process

What are some of the physiological changes of aging?

Aging produces variable physiological changes leading to gradual loss of functional abilities. Changes in connective tissue and the *fat to muscle ratio* lead to decreased flexibility, motor strength, and endurance, and affect how medications are distributed in the body. Aging-related changes such as decreased sensory system functioning, decreased sensitivity to touch and to pain, hearing loss especially in high frequencies (presbycusis), diminished visual acuity (presbyopia), and greater sensitivity to light are common. Impaired visual acuity and mobility have an impact on an individual's ability to perform the **instrumental activities of daily living** (IADLs) such as shopping and cooking, and can lead to falls, fear of falling, and

loss of fitness due to reduced activity. Changes in taste occur as a result of illness, smoking, pollution, or medications. Dentures can make chewing food difficult, and loss of appetite is not unusual. Undetected, these changes can lead to malnutrition, decreased strength, functional disabilities, and mood disorders.

Most individuals experience the onset of some chronic health condition during the fifth and sixth decades of life. Women, in particular, are at risk for hypertension, arthritis, diabetes, and osteoporosis. Heart disease, cancer, and stroke are the leading causes of death overall, but pneumonia, influenza, and chronic obstructive pulmonary disease are also significant causes of death among older people.

Sleep disturbances and changes in sleeping patterns are common in older adults. Insomnia and daytime naps disrupt the normal circadian rhythm (see Chapter 6: Chronobiology and Sleep Disorders). This age group uses the highest percentage of sedative-hypnotic drugs, even though long-term usage of these medications is often ineffective and can even exacerbate insomnia. Caregiving responsibilities, chronic illness, mood disorders, caffeine, nicotine, and sedative-hypnotic drug and alcohol use all contribute to sleep disturbances.

The prevalence of **Alzheimer's disease** (AD) is 1% among 65- to 74-year-olds, but increases to at least 25% in people > 85. Currently, about 5 million people suffer from AD, and the projections for the future are staggering. With the advent of aging baby boomers, it is expected that more than 14 million people will be diagnosed with AD by the year 2030. At the same time, it is projected that more than 3 million individuals in the US aged 85 and older will have AD. This means 1 in 45 persons will develop AD. While the probability of developing this disease is a function of advancing age and heredity, factors that mitigate the onset and severity of AD include education and diet. It is essential to raise this issue with patients during middle adulthood so that they can adopt lifestyle habits that reduce their risk.

Individuals with a *thinner margin of health* (e.g., genetic predisposition to certain diseases) and lower income experience higher rates of disability due to greater exposure to risk factors and limited access to health care. Individuals who rely upon governmental insurance programs that pay only a fraction of health care costs receive less than optimal care. Members of minority groups typically receive fewer diagnostic tests and surgical procedures, thus subjecting them to greater risks of disability and premature death (see Chapter 18: Health Care in Minority and Majority Populations).

Diagnostic Assessment of Cognitive Functioning

Comprehensive assessment is required to differentiate among brain disease, substance-related disorders, delirium, and "masked depression." Co-occurring dementia and depression is common, especially in the early and middle stages of dementia. It is important to treat any existing depression during this time to help clarify the diagnosis. The **Mini–Mental State Examination** (MMSE) is among the most commonly used diagnostic tools for assessing cognitive decline, but newer tools such as the Mini-Cog and the **Montreal Cognitive Assessment** (MoCA) may have broad applications in screening for dementia and milder cognitive impairments. Also, the St. Louis University Mental Status (SLUMS) exam has been found helpful in identifying mild cognitive changes. Making appropriate distinctions is

critical when considering the changes in classifications in the *Diagnostic and Statistical Manual of Mental Disorders, 5th edition* (DSM-5) related to cognitive disorders.

The *Cornell Scale for Depression in Dementia* has been validated for use with older individuals with and without dementia. Both the *Geriatric Depression Scale* and the *Center for Epidemiological Studies Depression Scale* are reliable tools for assessing depression in older adults; the latter has also been validated with Spanish-speaking groups and has been studied with American Indian and Alaska Native populations. However, there may be significant limitations to the use of these instruments in minority populations, due to language ability, translation issues, education levels, cultural concepts, and culturally appropriate expressions of mental health disorders. It is important to recognize how these factors may influence the results of testing and to develop alternative assessments. Clinicians should always familiarize themselves with the cultural variations in expression of symptoms characteristic of the ethnic group populations they serve (see Chapter 17: Culture and Cultural Competence in Health Care).

Psychiatric Disorders

What are common mental health problems of aging?

The term **successful aging** is used frequently by the baby boomer generation and is synonymous with US cultural norms that emphasize the importance of maintaining independent functioning, continued physical mobility, social interactions with family and friends, ongoing interest in activities, and a sense of well-being. Successful aging describes an individual's ability to balance self-acceptance of who they are and "what" they are, with a sense of engagement with life; it is not related to age, ethnicity, or marital status. Other factors that promote successful aging include adoption of healthier lifestyles, early detection of disease through screening, injury prevention techniques, and development of self-management strategies. The reality, however, is that many individuals may not be able to age well, due to poverty, losses, lack of access to care, or lack of appropriately supportive neighborhoods and communities. Individuals who are frail may need another set of standards to be deemed as "aging well."

The postretirement period is sometimes referred to as the *Third Age,* and is characterized by self-determination, fulfillment of life goals, and enjoyment. The physical changes and realities of aging such as wrinkles, graying or loss of hair, and decreased height – while signs of normative aging – may affect the psychological perception of the individual about themselves and result in loss of self-esteem.

In contrast to the concept of successful aging and the Third Age, older adults become more vulnerable to depression and other mental disorders as their physical and adaptive abilities decline. These changes may present many challenges and needed adaptations for older adults and their families. This time period characterized by declining health often is referred to as the *Fourth Age.*

These life transitions and unmet expectations may contribute to feelings of depression or anxiety. At the same time, many elderly patients take multiple *over-the-counter* (OTC) and prescription medications for chronic conditions. The side effects of these medications may contribute to depressive symptoms. Individuals who have suffered myocardial infarctions, strokes, hip fractures, or chronic illnesses such as arthritis and diabetes are especially at risk for depression.

The presence of stress or stressors represents other factors associated with aging that can exacerbate lifelong behavioral or mental health problems. For example, some older people experience increased stress in family relationships if they become the primary caregiver for grandchildren or are affected by the successes or failures of children or grandchildren. Assimilation and acculturation stresses are common for foreign-born seniors who experience communication difficulties with grandchildren, whom they may believe have abandoned traditional values, including respect for older people.

The experience of real or perceived **losses** (physical abilities, social status, relationships, income, pets) heightens vulnerability, and can result in isolation, withdrawal from usual activities, and loneliness. The loss of role and status associated with retirement also may contribute to a lowered sense of self-esteem and personal competence. Bereavement is complicated by practical necessi-

ties, such as decisions to keep or sell one's home or distribute assets. If the deceased spouse was the primary caregiver, relocation can precipitate other losses (e.g., the neighborhood, support networks, sense of safety, transportation, health care).

> The US Department of Health and Human Services (DHHS) estimates that 20% of older adults will experience a mental disorder not associated with normal aging. It is also estimated that the prevalence of mental health problems in older people will double during the next 25 years, including significant increases in mood disorders, dementia, substance abuse, and schizophrenia.

Depression

Depression is one of the most common mental disorders in later life, especially among women. Bereavement, accumulated loss, and alcohol and medication abuse are contributing factors. *Masked depression* occurs when an individual or family member attributes symptoms of depression (e.g., memory problems) to the onset of cognitive impairment due to, for example, dementia. In fact, severe depression can be associated with sufficient cognitive impairment to raise the question of dementia. *Subthreshold depression* is associated with a perceived sense of worsening physical health as well as decreased emotional functioning. Symptoms include increased anxiety and a history of mood disorders. Individuals with this symptom constellation have a pessimistic outlook and lowered sense of personal mastery and self-efficacy.

> Depressive disorders are common in patients with a wide variety of chronic medical and neurological diseases. *Masked depression* or *depression without sadness* is a variant of late-life depression with clinically significant cerebrovascular compromise. Characteristics include mild mood symptoms and prominent psychomotor retardation and executive cognitive dysfunction (poor insight, inability to plan, cognitive inflexibility).

Anxiety

Anxiety is underdiagnosed in older people due to overlapping symptoms with depression as well as some physical disorders. Many practitioners assume the symptoms are associated with the "normal" worries of aging (see Chapter 44: Anxiety Disorders, and Chapter 47: Stress Disorders, Bereavement, and Dissociative Disorders). The underlying basis for somatic expressions of anxiety, such as somatoform disorders and hypochondriasis, can go unrecognized and be attributed to the aging adult's physical health status. However, approximately 10% of older adults, mostly women, appear to have some type of anxiety disorder. Older patients with both major depression and generalized anxiety have a worse prognosis than individuals who have either diagnosis alone. Patients with comorbid disorders are more likely to have chronic functional impairments, higher utilization of health care services, and increased suicide risk. Aging individuals develop social phobias more frequently than younger people. These phobias can be related to self-consciousness about appearance, health conditions, and social fears (e.g., worrying about becoming incontinent in a social situation).

Posttraumatic stress disorder (PTSD) is seen in some older adults, including individuals who have served in military conflicts. Immigrants who came to the US from war-torn regions meet criteria for this diagnosis at 3 times the rate of the general population. Older individuals who have witnessed or experienced torture or physical or sexual trauma as a result of political uprisings often present with multiple somatic complaints or culture-bound syndromes (see Chapter 17: Culture and Cultural Competence in Health Care).

High **suicide** rates exist for both older women and men. Individuals at particular risk are women, White males > 85 years old, and those with limited social supports, lower socioeconomic levels, and significant medical disability. High rates are also found among older Chinese women, older Japanese men, American Indians, and Alaska Natives. Suicide is generally associated with depression related to poor health.

> In assessing suicide risk in older people, providers should be sensitive to behavioral changes such as disregard for personal hygiene or giving away prized possessions. Verbal expressions of suicidal thought ("You won't have me around much longer" or "I won't burden you much longer") should prompt an assessment of suicidality (see Chapter 27: Suicide).

"**Rational suicide**" and **physician-assisted suicide** appear to be particularly attractive for some older adults who reflect upon their desire for death with dignity and without pain, a need to preserve some degree of financial security especially for the remaining spouse, and a desire to avoid becoming incapacitated.

Violence and Abuse

Elder abuse includes *physical, emotional, psychological,* and *financial abuse,* as well as *self-neglect* or *neglect by caregivers.* Forms of self-neglect include failure to take medications, cluttering and hoarding, pet collecting, and poor hygiene. Fiscal or financial abuse includes Internet scams, solicitations for home repairs, and collections for charitable donations as well as stealing social security or pension checks by family and friends. Agencies working with victims of elder abuse include financial abuse specialist teams (FAST) that assess and intervene in such cases. The incidence of intimate partner violence and sexual abuse decreases in aging populations, although the rates of psychological and emotional abuse do not decline with age. Chronic pain and depression are common diagnoses among victims of violence.

Substance Abuse and Addictive Behaviors

> What harmful substances are older people most likely to use?

Nicotine has been the most frequently used substance among seniors, with approximately 15% of older adults smoking. While nicotine use correlates with leading indicators of cause of death in older people, there is evidence to suggest that the current cohort of seniors is smoking less.

Alcohol problems and **prescription drug misuse** are seen more commonly than illicit drug use. However, it is anticipated that the use of marijuana, heroin, and cocaine will continue to rise among older adults as the next generation ages. The belief that illicit drug use will decrease in older populations due to premature death, incarceration, or a switch to "legitimate" drugs such as prescription medications or alcohol is proving to be inaccurate. The legalization of medical marijuana and the proliferation of medical marijuana dispensaries may lead to increased marijuana use among the older population.

Older people appear to drink *less alcohol* than the general population but the physiological changes of aging promote intoxication at lower levels of intake. The prevalence of alcoholism or *problem drinking* among older adults in the general community appears to be about 10%, but the rate of current or prior alcoholism among individuals in hospitals, nursing homes, and other health care settings ranges from 15% to 58%. Alcohol-related symptoms are often difficult to diagnose and may be confused with medical or psychiatric problems. Some studies have found that up to 88% of nursing home residents have alcohol-related problems. Two thirds of older *early-onset* drinkers (those who developed problem drinking behaviors before age 40) are men. Women are more likely to be *late-onset* drinkers, whose drinking seems related to stressful life events. Some studies suggest that baby boomers may have a higher prevalence of alcohol-related problems since alcohol consumption has been more socially acceptable than in previous generations.

> The National Household Survey on Drug Abuse (NHSDA) and the National Survey on Drug Use and Health (NSDUH) predict that illicit drug use will increase significantly as baby boomers age, due to the higher rate of lifetime use among that generation.

Older adults consume approximately one third of all *prescription drugs* and nearly two thirds of all OTC medications. It is not unusual for an older person to regularly take seven or more prescription medications along with OTC medications, supplements, and herbal products. Alcohol consumption can potentiate or diminish the effects of medications and result in overprescribing or underprescribing. Ideally, all adults should be screened for **substance use disorders**. The presence of severe cognitive impairment can complicate the assessment process. It is important to obtain a history of alcohol use since even relatively small quanti-

ties of alcohol can have a negative effect on health and functioning. The *Geriatric Michigan Alcohol Screening Test* (**G-MAST**) is a valid screening instrument.

Treatment should be encouraged if problem drinking or drug misuse is detected. The screening brief intervention and referral to treatment (**SBIRT**) model may be used in addressing treatment concerns.

Age-specific group therapy is recommended as a part of an overall approach. Programs such as Project Guiding Older Adult Lifestyles (Project GOAL), Project BRief Intervention and Treatment for Elders (Project BRITE), and Alcoholics Anonymous offer helpful approaches to treatment. Harm reduction techniques are generally successful with older alcoholics (see Chapter 24: Substance-Related and Addictive Disorders).

Gambling has emerged as an area of concern for older adults, as lotteries, bingo, casinos, and online gaming have grown in popularity. Many senior centers and assisted living facilities offer day trips to local casinos. This form of recreation includes a social aspect, relieves tension, provides an escape from day-to-day problems, and alleviates boredom. However, increased gambling may lead to problem or even pathological gambling disorders, depending on the frequency of gambling, the number of gambling activities an individual engages in, and the amount of money spent on gambling.

The South Oaks Gambling Screen (**SOGS**) and the Revised SOGS (**SOGS-R**) are widely used to assess gambling problems. Another tool, the Gambling Motivation Scale (**GMS**), examines three aspects of gambling: for rewards, for release of tension and guilt, and for social recognition. While the rates of problem gambling among older adults appear to be lower than among younger adults, gambling disorders remain a concern for people with fixed incomes/limited resources.

Psychiatric Treatments

Few clinicians would agree with Freud who stated that older patients were not appropriate candidates for therapy because they do not have enough life left to complete the process; yet, many clinicians are reluctant to treat what they regard as a difficult and challenging population. Lack of adequate reimbursement through Medicare for practitioners and lack of appropriate training and experience are concerns contributing to the limited number of therapists treating older adults (see Chapter 29: The US Health Care System).

Patient sensitivity to the stigma of mental disorders, the belief that personal problems should be solved within the home and family, sociocultural factors, and limited accessibility (transportation, mobility) contribute to low utilization of mental health services by older adults. Individuals in rural environments have limited access to qualified therapists, while those from other cultural backgrounds often lack confidence in the value of therapy. The advent of telemedicine may bring additional services to physically and linguistically isolated older adults who seek counseling.

Older adults are appropriate candidates for a variety of therapeutic interventions including: short-term, problem-focused individual counseling; cognitive behavioral therapy (CBT); dialectical behavior therapy (DBT); group therapy; self-help groups; support groups; reminiscence groups; life review groups; book clubs and reading groups; couples' counseling; and family therapy. *Life review therapy* is especially beneficial to older patients because the primary goal is to facilitate the integration of past and present experiences through structured reminiscence, constructive reappraisal of the past, and recollection of successful coping mechanisms used previously. Life review therapy can include both individual and group activities such as writing a life history, sharing photo albums, or listening to music.

Medications in combination with psychotherapy, when administered by an experienced clinician, may produce results equal to, or better than, treatment regimes relying on medications or psychotherapy alone. Electroconvulsive therapy (ECT) is generally only considered in older adults who have unremitting depression despite adequate antidepressant and psychotherapeutic treatment, or those individuals whose complex medical conditions make ECT the safer choice for treating comorbid depression.

> Psychotropic medications can be beneficial if applied judiciously. In general, older patients are more physiologically sensitive to medication effects and require adjustment of standard dosages.

Nontraditional Treatments

Community mental health centers located in ethnic communities often offer *culturally sensitive treatments* that may not be offered in the general therapeutic community (e.g., a community mental health center in Chinatown that offers acupuncture as a treatment for depression). Other alternative therapies include music, art, dance, and drama therapy. The health and mental health benefits of exercise (walking, tai chi, chi gong, longevity stick), touch, and aromatherapy are being studied. Many of these therapies embrace cultural values and forms of expression familiar to elders from varying backgrounds.

Studies of the therapeutic value of *companion animals* have demonstrated decreases in blood pressure and agitation among patients with AD when animals are present. However, not all individuals or all animals should be included in a pet-facilitated therapy program. Organizations such as the Delta Society (which certifies a variety of animals other than dogs), Therapy Dogs International, Paws for Life, and Bright and Beautiful Therapy Dogs offer comprehensive testing of animals before they are approved as "therapists."

Sexuality and Sexual Health

Physiological changes in the sexual response cycle of aging women include decreased estrogen level, reduced elasticity and muscle tone, atrophy of the uterus, and loss of vulvar tissue. Vaginal lubrication is decreased, which may result in pain on intercourse and even bleeding. Changes in the intensity of orgasm and painful spasms during orgasm may occur. Aging women may need more direct manual stimulation to become aroused. Men may require more direct genital and mental stimulation, experience increased time to achieve an erection, and have decreased tumescence during penetration, decreased volume of ejaculate, and increased refractory time.

Chronic illness, disability, medications, mobility, psychosocial issues, and ageist beliefs can affect the sexual functioning of older adults. It is important to discuss sexual functioning in an open and sensitive manner, including the sexual orientation of the patient. There is an increasing recognition and research on the sexual needs and health care concerns of aging gay, lesbian, bisexual, and transgender persons (see Chapter 19: Sexuality and Sexual Disorders, and Chapter 20: Health Care Issues Facing Lesbian, Gay, Bisexual, and Transgender Individuals).

Sexuality and Chronic Disease

How does chronic illness affect sexual functioning?

Individuals who have had a heart attack, or stroke, or who have a chronic illness such as diabetes, pulmonary disease, or arthritis can maintain healthy and satisfying sexual lives. However, many of the medications used to treat these conditions can contribute to sexual dysfunction. For example, selective serotonin reuptake inhibitors (SSRIs) used to treat mood disorders can have a significant negative sexual side effect. Despite these barriers, older adults, who are counseled about adapting their sexual activities and are open to suggestions about timing and positional changes, can maintain satisfying sexual lives. Organizations (e.g., the Arthritis Foundation) often have information on disorder-specific sexual issues.

Sexual Expression in Dependent-Living Facilities

Fears of liability (e.g., falls, other health consequences) along with biases of family, staff, and health care personnel contribute to constraints on privacy and sexual expression in congregate living environments such as assisted living and nursing home facilities. Barriers to sexual expression include unavailability of a socially sanctioned partner, physical and cognitive decline, inability to control the environment, lack of privacy, and body image concerns. Some facilities may consider sexual behavior to be acceptable as long as the individual understands what they are doing and respects the rights of others.

Sexuality and Dementia

Elderly residents with AD can participate in and even initiate sexual activity as long as certain criteria are met (e.g., an MMSE score of 15 or more). Sexual behavior should be consistent with lifelong sexual behaviors. Patients should also be cognitively able to engage in sexual activities, and be able to recognize the partner. However, patients and partners may experience conflict about continuing the sexual relationship. For example, role changes may take place in that the previously passive partner now becomes the initiator of sexual behavior, or a caregiving spouse is no longer able to see the partner as sexually attractive. The clinician should explore the sexual wishes and needs of the patient and partner and determine whether a sexual relationship is mutually beneficial. The provider must be alert to the possibility of abuse should one of the partners no longer consent to engage in sexual activities.

HIV/AIDS

The current cohort of older people has been neglected with regard to prevention of sexually transmitted infections (STIs) leading to a steady rise in the diagnosis of HIV and other STIs in the > 60 age group. Up to 15% of all new cases of AIDS and 25% of overall cases of HIV occur among people > 50. Many older individuals do not consider unprotected sex to be a high-risk behavior since they are no longer concerned about the need for contraception. Therefore, they are less likely to use condoms. However, postmenopausal women are at greater risk for both HIV infection, and reinfection, during heterosexual intercourse because estrogen depletion results in fragile vaginal mucosa. Diagnosis of AIDS is complicated by early symptoms (fatigue, confusion, loss of appetite) that are common in other age-related illnesses. AIDS stigma among older people contributes to their underutilization of health and mental health services. Individuals are living longer with HIV and, as a result, are more likely to develop diseases associated with aging, perhaps at an earlier age. Recent evidence suggests that neurocognitive disorders may be increasing among older adults who have HIV.

Retirement and Volunteerism

Many baby boomers plan to continue working after they reach the traditional retirement age of 65. Although some will make this decision because of personal preference, the recent downturn in the economy has had a significant impact on older adults who saw the value of their retirement savings diminish. These financial factors as well as the decline in employer-sponsored pensions are causing many older adults to reexamine the feasibility of retirement. Some will alternate between periods of working and leisure time, while others will embark on a second career. Still others, who have adequate resources but want to maintain the mental stimulation and challenges associated with working, will volunteer. Currently, baby boomers have the highest rates of volunteer participation and volunteer for longer hours than any age group except the current older generation. Agencies as demanding as the Peace Corps are seeing an increase in volunteer applications from seniors.

Long-Term Care: Conservative Care or Creative Options

> What living arrangement options exist for older people?

Studies of older adults have found that most older people prefer to "age in place" – that is, to remain in their own homes and environments for as long as possible. It is important to consider the person–environment fit when assessing the appropriateness of the living situation.

The continuum of care that is **long-term care** includes home and community-based services along a spectrum of specialized health, rehabilitative, and residential care. These services focus on the biopsychosocial, spiritual, residential, rehabilitative, and supportive needs of individuals and their families. Contrary to the belief of many older people, long-term care services are not all synonymous with nursing homes; they may be delivered in a person's home, in the community (senior centers, mental health facilities, cultural clubs, churches, schools),

or in residential care facilities (assisted living or nursing homes). A variety of factors determine the kinds of services needed, including income, type of housing and level of safety and ease of access, health status (including self-rated health), age and frailty, and availability of community resources.

Advances in medical treatment and the advent of managed care have complicated access to health care for seniors. A recent AARP survey indicated that 70% of its members believed that *long-term care insurance* was a good thing, yet only 17% had purchased any form of coverage, due in part to the high cost.

Community and In-Home Services

Changes in public policies granting greater access to affordable community services are needed to alleviate the burden of long-term care borne by family caregivers. Governmental agencies such as the Veterans Health Administration will be called upon to develop new approaches to service delivery to meet the burgeoning aging population. The *National Family Caregiver Support Program* (NFCSP) was established in 2000 to help provide education, information, support groups, and some limited services such as respite care in local communities (e.g., support to grandparents who are raising grandchildren).

Long-term care services in the home and community provide many older adults with their first experience with aging-related services at a senior center where they attend exercise classes, participate in congregate meal programs, or select from a variety of other activities.

Home health care services provide a wide range of health-related services in the client's home including skilled nursing care, psychiatric nursing, physical therapy, occupational therapy, speech therapy, home health aides, and social work services. *In-home supportive services,* a part of home health care, include help with meal preparation, shopping, light housekeeping, money management, personal hygiene, laundry, and chore services.

Adult day care/adult day health programs provide functionally impaired adults with daytime community-based programs in a protective setting. Therapeutic interventions can be adapted to focus on the behavioral and mood-related problems associated with psychiatric disorders, AD, and other health maintenance issues. Such programs support and provide respite for family caregivers of cognitively or physically disabled elders. Some of these services may be included in long-term care insurance benefits but most are not covered by general health insurance plans.

Respite Care

Respite care is short term and can be provided in the home or a facility. It allows family caregivers to take some time off to rest and relax and regain perspective on what they have chosen to undertake. Respite care services that acknowledge the significance of culture and provide volunteers or trained staff who speak the language of the patient are most likely to be used.

Types of Long-Term Residential Services

Long-term care options for individuals no longer able to live at home include *congregate housing* (including Section 8 rent-subsidized housing), *assisted living, board and care, intermediate care,* and *extended care* facilities. Residents in extended care facilities are subject to preadmission screening and annual reviews under the Omnibus Budget Reconciliation Act (OBRA) of 1987. OBRA closely regulates the quality of care in these facilities, including the use of psychotropic and other medications. This oversight is especially important since as many as 88% of nursing home residents exhibit symptoms of mental health problems.

The transition from living independently, to life in an extended care facility is fraught with emotion for both the older person and the family. It amplifies the older person's fears of being abandoned and may trigger feelings of loss, anger, helplessness, and despair in the older person, who is now viewed as old, sick, and frail. The older adult must also confront mortality, the reality of declining health, and realization that this may be the final move. Family reactions include guilt, anger, resentment, and, in some cases, relief.

Hospice Care

Hospice care is based on the philosophy that death is a natural event and should be treated as a normal phase of life. It recognizes that through the provision of palliative care and pain management, individuals can be spared the pain of terminal illness and accorded death with dignity. Creative approaches to symptom control include acupuncture, massage, and exercise. Hospice care can be provided in the patient's own home or in a comfortable home-like setting. Hospice care is focused not only on the dying person, but also on the family. A team of physicians, nurses, social workers, therapists, and pastors provide services that include assistance with funeral and burial preparations and help with the disposal of personal items. Ongoing bereavement counseling after the death of the family member is also an integral part of hospice care (see Chapter 33: Palliative Care).

Special Populations

Lesbian, Gay, Bisexual, and Transgender Older People

There are an estimated three million older gays and lesbians in the US. This number is expected to double by 2030. This has been a largely invisible group, and little research has been devoted to aging in this population. Many of today's older gays and lesbians grew up when being homosexual was illegal and often considered immoral or sinful. Although societal acceptance is growing, discrimination and stigma have resulted in marginalization from the health care and mental health sectors and disenfranchisement from aging organizations, housing, employment, and long-term care facilities (see Chapter 20: Health Care Issues Facing Lesbian, Gay, Bisexual, and Transgender Individuals).

Future Outlook for Older Minorities

Minority elders are expected to account for 24% of the > 65 population in the US by the year 2020. Health care disparities, including access to care and lack of culturally appropriate services, are major concerns in addressing health outcomes and disease prevention (see Chapter 18: Health Care in Minority and Majority Populations).

Extended care facilities have been underutilized by minority populations due largely to cultural concerns (traditions of family care, lack of ethnic meals, few bilingual staff, inattention to traditions), social isolation, and access issues. *Medicare* and *Medicaid* are the primary payers for nursing home services, yet many minority families may not qualify for these programs. The Indian Health Service has never provided nursing home care although the Bureau of Indian Affairs has been charged with providing nursing home care. The first American Indian and Alaska Native nursing home was founded in 1969. Today, there are fewer than 20 such facilities on tribal lands and reservations with extended care facilities located at great distances from reservations. This has prompted tribal groups to contemplate building their own facilities using money acquired from tourism or gaming.

While advancements are being made, the status of older minority members is not likely to improve significantly in the immediate future. In addition, the factors that determine quality of life (education, employment, income, health care) are not likely to vary much among any of the minority populations now approaching retirement age. More research is needed about ethnogeriatric issues and training of culturally competent health care clinicians.

Recommended Readings

Cené, C. W., Dilworth-Anderson, P., Leng, I., Garcia, L., Benavente, V., Rosal, M., ... Cochrane, B. (2016). Correlates of successful aging in racial and ethnic minority women age 80 years and older: Findings from the Women's Health Initiative. *Journal of Gerontology, Series A: Biological Sciences and Medical Sciences, 71*(Suppl. 1), S87–S99.

Minkin, M. J. (2016). Sexual health and relationships after age 60. *Maturitas, 83*, 27–32. http://doi.org/10.1016/j.maturitas.2015.10.004

Moore, R. C., Eyler, L. T., Mausbach, B. T., Zlatar, Z. Z., Thompson, W. K., Peavy, G., ... Jeste, D. V. (2015). Complex interplay between health and successful aging: Role of perceived stress, resilience and social support. *American Journal of Geriatric Psychiatry, 23*, 622–632.

Padesky, C. A., & Mooney, K. A. (2012). Strengths-based cognitive-behavioural therapy: A four-step model to build resilience. *Clinical Psychology and Psychotherapy, 19*, 283–290. http://doi.org/10.1002/cpp.1795

Park, S., Han, Y., Kim, B., & Dunkle, R. (2015). Aging in place of vulnerable older adults: Person-environment fit perspective. *Journal of Applied Gerontology.* Advance online publication. http://doi.org/10.1177/0733464815617286

Reichstadt, J., Depp, C. A., Palinkas, L. A., Folsom, D. P., & Jeste, D. V. (2007). Building blocks of successful aging: A focus group study of older adults' perceived contributors to successful aging. *American Journal of Geriatric Psychiatry, 15*, 194–201. http://doi.org/10.1097/JGP.0b013e318030255f

Scheibe, S., & Carstensen, L. L. (2010). Emotional aging: Recent findings and future trends. *Journal of Gerontology, Series B: Psychological Sciences and Social Sciences, 65B*, 135–144. http://doi.org/10.1093/geronb/gbp132

Review Questions

1. Which of the following therapies is most effective in treating mood disorders in older adults?
   A. Combined drug and short-term psychotherapy
   B. Drug therapy
   C. Electroconvulsive therapy
   D. Problem-solving psychotherapy
   E. Psychoanalysis

2. Which of the following best describes HIV/AIDS in older adults?
   A. Aging heterosexual men are at greater risk of developing HIV than are older women.
   B. It occurs infrequently because of significantly decreased sexual intimacy.
   C. It occurs less frequently because older adults use safe sex practices reliably.
   D. Symptoms of HIV/AIDS may mimic symptoms of other age-related disorders.
   E. The diagnosis of HIV/AIDS increases in persons 60 and older.

3. Intimate partner abuse among older adults
   A. is less common than among younger populations
   B. is perpetrated most frequently by the female partner

C. is routinely addressed as part of
   health care screening
D. occurs more commonly among those
   with few resources
E. occurs more frequently than psychological
   or emotional abuse

Answer Key on p. 465

Section VII
Societal and Behavioral Health Challenges

22 Obesity

Stephen R. Cook, MD, MPH, and Kristin A. Evans, PhD

- How is obesity defined?
- What health consequences can result from obesity?
- How do individual and environmental factors interact to cause obesity?
- What can be done to reverse the current obesity epidemic?

The current national obesity epidemic is likely being driven by a combination of genetic and psychosocial factors occurring in an environment rife with calorie-dense/nutrient-poor foods. Efforts to reverse the trends in overweight and obesity in the US must include interventions at many levels, ranging from individual behavior modification to national policy changes.

What is Obesity?

How is obesity defined?

Simply defined, **obesity** refers to an excess accumulation of body fat that results in a body mass exceeding a recommended level. An individual's weight status is typically quantified by calculating their **body mass index** (BMI), which is a ratio of body mass (kilograms) to height (meters squared). Adults with a BMI ranging from 25.0 to 29.9 kg/m2 are classified as overweight, whereas those with a BMI ≥ 30.0 kg/m2 are considered obese. Adults with a BMI ranging from 35.0 to 39.9 kg/m2 and those ≥ 40.0 kg/m2 are referred to as *severely obese* and *morbidly obese,* respectively.

Children and adolescents are classified clinically as either normal weight, overweight, or obese, based on age and sex-specific growth charts developed by the Centers for Disease Control and Prevention (CDC). Children in the ≥ 85th but < 95th BMI percentile for their age and gender are classified as *overweight* and those ≥ 95th percentile are considered *obese*. There are also more severe degrees of obesity among children and adolescents. Class II obesity is a BMI > 120% up to 140% of the 95th percentile. It was found in 6.3% of children and teens in the US in 2013–2014. Class III obesity or weight > 140% of the 95th percentile was found in 2.4% of US teens in 2013–2014.

The Epidemic

According to the CDC's most recent estimates (2013–2014), more than two thirds (70.7%) of the US adult population (≥ 20 years) was overweight or obese, with about one third of those (37.9%) falling into the obese category. Among children and adolescents (2 to 19 years), nearly one third (31.8%) were overweight or obese, with more than half of those (16.9%) already falling into the obese category. These data reflect a 46% increase in adult overweight or obesity prevalence in the past 4 decades, and a greater than threefold increase in child overweight or obesity over that same time period (Figure 22.1).

The proportion of Americans who are overweight and obese varies by race or ethnicity and gender. For example, a greater proportion of Blacks and Hispanics are overweight or obese compared with Whites (76.3% and 78.4% vs. 68.5%). Prevalence of a BMI ≥ 25 kg/m2 is 73%

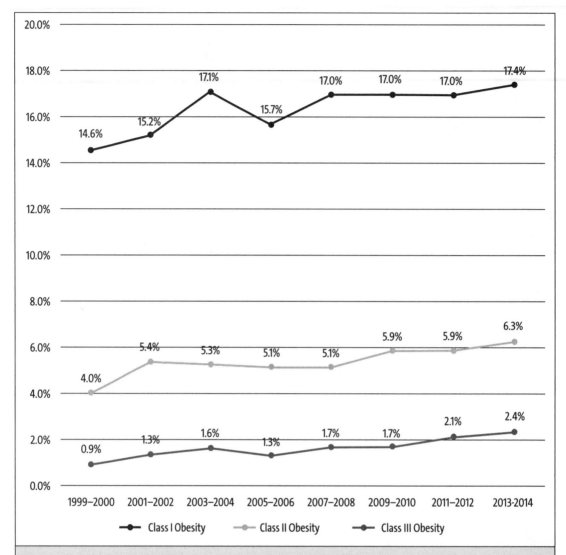

Figure 22.1. Prevalence of Class I, Class II, and Class III obesity among US children aged 2 to 17 years, from 1999 to 2014. Reprinted by permission from Skinner, A. C., Perrin, E. M., & Skelton, J. A. (2016). Prevalence of obesity and severe obesity in US children 1999–2014. *Obesity, 24*(5), 1116–1123. © John Wiley and Sons

and 66.2% among adult men and women, respectively, although this gender difference also varies with racial or ethnic group. Among Whites, a higher percentage of men than women are overweight or obese; the opposite is true among Blacks. More Hispanic men than women are overweight or obese, but the difference is less pronounced than among Whites, and the pattern seems to shift with increasing age.

Among children (aged 2 to 19 years), approximately the same proportion (31% to 32%) of girls and boys have a BMI ≥ 85th percentile, and the

racial or ethnic differences are similar to those seen in adults (Whites 28.5%, Blacks 35.2%, Hispanics 38.9%).

Health Consequences of Obesity

What health consequences can result from obesity?

Over the past several decades, it has become increasingly evident that overweight and obesity are much more than just aesthetic problems. Excess body weight and fat significantly increase an individual's risk for a number of other diseases and conditions including insulin resistance, type 2 diabetes, heart disease, osteoarthritis, reproductive complications, and certain cancers including breast, uterine, colon, and kidney cancer. The risk of premature death from any cause is estimated to be 50% to 100% greater among overweight or obese individuals compared with those who are normal weight. For many diseases, the relative distribution of body fat is a more significant risk factor than BMI. Individuals with excessive *abdominal adiposity*, as opposed to more fat in the lower body (measured via the waist to hip ratio), are at greater risk of developing type 2 diabetes or suffering a heart attack.

Economically, the costs associated with obesity in the US are substantial. The most recent government estimates indicate that medical spending attributable to overweight or obesity (including inpatient and outpatient services and prescription drug costs) is nearly US $150 billion per year, with a substantial portion of that being paid by government-funded insurance programs (Medicare, Medicaid). This total accounts for nearly 10% of all medical expenditures in the US.

What Causes Obesity?

How do individual and environmental factors interact to cause obesity?

At the most fundamental level, overweight and obesity result from an excess intake of food calories in relation to calorie expenditure (basal metabolic rate + physical activity). Although debated in the current literature, the prevailing evidence supports the idea that, on a population level, the positive energy balance associated with the high prevalence of overweight and obesity is due more to an increase in caloric intake than to a substantial decrease in physical activity. The following sections will describe the individual and social factors that influence this energy imbalance, as well as how these forces interact to create the population's weight crisis. Current evidence also supports the notion that obesity is the result of a complex interplay of genetic, environmental, and psychosocial factors.

Genetic Factors

Determining the precise contribution of genes to an individual's body weight and to the obesity epidemic has proven difficult. In only the rarest cases can any single gene explain obesity in a given individual – a phenomenon known as *monogenic obesity*. For the rest of the population, body weight and body fatness are regulated by complex gene–gene and gene–environment interactions. Estimates of the *heritability* of BMI and body fat range from 16% to 85%, and 35% to 63%, respectively. To date, more than 100 single genes have been positively associated with the development of obesity; many of them are involved in the regulation of energy metabolism, fat deposition, and hormone signaling. The most compelling evidence supports a role for genes encoding peroxisome proliferator-activated receptors involved in nutrient metabolism, melanocortin-4 receptors involved in feeding and metabolism, β_3-adrenergic receptors regulating lipid metabolism and thermogenesis, and uncoupling proteins involved in oxidative phosphorylation.

Genes associated with neurotransmitter action have also been linked to food intake and body weight or BMI (see Chapter 5: Energy Homeostasis). It has been proposed that, for some obese people, eating is a form of addiction in which food intake is reinforced by the pleasurable or positive feelings that follow. The action of the neurotransmitter dopamine is known to be associated with reinforcing and addictive behaviors, and individuals with a certain variant (A1 allele) in a gene that determines the density of dopamine receptors are more likely to experience the reinforcing value of food. Furthermore, obese individuals carrying that allele are more likely than nonobese people with the allele to receive positive reinforcement from food intake. In combination, high food reinforcement behavior and the presence of the A1 allele result in significantly greater food intake than either variable alone.

Research has shown that physicians and medical students who themselves engage in regular physical activity are more successful at motivating their patients to do so.

Psychosocial Stress in an "Obesogenic" Environment

Several conceptual theories have been used to explain the health behaviors that have led to the current obesity epidemic. One often-cited theory is the **social ecological model** of behavior (Figure 22.2), which posits that individual health behaviors (e.g., eating, exercise) occur within a multilayered context encompassing interpersonal relations within a community governed by public policies. In the past decade, much research has focused on the *built environment* (the man-made surroundings in which human activity takes place) regarding its effects on energy intake and expenditure.

In particular, the *retail food environment*, or the availability and types of food in a community, has received much attention as it relates to an individual's dietary practices and obesity risk. The main contention is that residents of communities with greater access to cheap calorie-dense/nutrient-poor foods (e.g., those available at convenience stores and fast food restaurants) com-

pared with affordable healthy foods (e.g., fresh produce available in grocery stores and supermarkets) consume less healthful diets and are, therefore, at greater risk of obesity and its comorbidities. Large population studies have found that the presence of supermarkets in a community is positively associated with fruit and vegetable consumption, and a relatively greater number of convenience stores and fast food restaurants are associated with a greater prevalence of obesity and diabetes. These associations may partly explain the *racial* and *socioeconomic disparities* in obesity prevalence, as communities with larger minority populations and greater poverty rates often have less access to supermarkets and grocery stores. Paradoxically, the cost of available healthy food in low-income communities is often greater than the cost of the same food in more affluent areas, mainly due to the lack of supermarkets, which tend to have lower prices than smaller grocery stores.

Elements of the built environment have also been associated with physical activity levels.

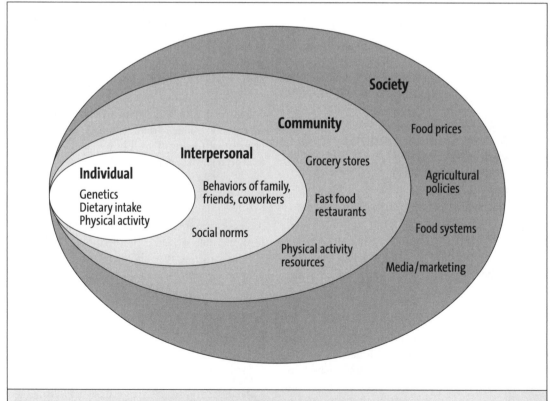

Figure 22.2. Examples of factors related to obesity at each level of the social ecological model.

Environmental studies often categorize neighborhoods and communities based on their "walkability" – that is, the extent to which the design of a community allows residents to walk to conduct their daily activities such as shopping. Highly walkable neighborhoods are generally densely populated, have commercial areas, and have grid-like street patterns. Studies have shown that residents of such neighborhoods tend to engage in more physical activity compared with those living in less walkable areas. There is also some evidence that overweight and obesity are less prevalent in neighborhoods of higher walkability and that neighborhood "greenness" and residential density are negatively associated with children's odds of becoming overweight.

But it sounds healthy...

Did you know...?

Applebee's Pecan Crusted Chicken Salad packs a gut-wrenching 1,310 calories and 81 grams of fat – that's the equivalent of eating more than ½ dozen Krispy Kreme doughnuts!

Beware!

Restaurants often drown an otherwise healthy dish of fresh veggies in a fat- and calorie-laden sea of dressings, cheeses, and fried meats.

Try this...

Ask for grilled instead of fried meats, less of the "extras," and your dressing on the side. Many restaurants will also let you order a ½ size salad, automatically saving you ½ the fat and calories (and maybe even leave room for a *sensible* dessert)!

Although overweight and obesity are ultimately a result of individual behaviors, other factors contribute as well. For example, technological changes in the food industry have decreased the time cost of food for consumers. Developments in areas such as food processing, preservation, and packaging allow manufacturers to produce an increasing variety of foods (often high fat and calorie meals and snacks) that require minimal at-home preparation. Proponents of this **technical change theory** point to two main facts to support it: (1) the consumption of calories from *snacks* (the "meal" in which the most technological changes have occurred) has approximately doubled since the 1970s with

no compensatory decrease in calories from regular meals, and (2) the greatest increase in BMI and proportion of obese individuals has occurred among married women, the group for whom the time cost of food has decreased the most (see Wisman & Capehart, in Recommended Readings).

This increase in the variety and quantity of cheap, ready- (or nearly-ready)-to-eat, unhealthy foods has occurred in tandem with a nationwide increase in everyday psychosocial stressors and economic insecurity. Studies have found several types of *psychosocial stress* to be associated with weight gain, including job demands, difficulty paying bills, depression, generalized anxiety, and perceived constraint in life. Chronic psychosocial stress may contribute to weight gain in two ways: by increasing pleasure-seeking behaviors that include the consumption of highly palatable but unhealthy foods, and by affecting the production of hormones involved in energy metabolism, namely cortisol and other glucocorticoids. *Acute and chronic stress* lead to elevated glucocorticoid levels, which, in turn, stimulate insulin secretion, promoting both emotionally induced food intake ("comfort feeding") and fat deposition. Abdominal adipose depots are particularly sensitive to the combination of these hormones.

The socioeconomic gradient in obesity observed in the US may be due in part to the chronic stress and insecurity experienced at lower income levels. The growing gap between the richest Americans and the rest of the country supports the notion that social and economic pressures are contributing to the obesity epidemic.

Curbing the Epidemic

What can be done to reverse the current obesity epidemic?

On the individual level, preventing overweight and obesity is conceptually simple: Excessive weight gain can be avoided by maintaining energy balance through a healthy diet and regular physical activity. This advice, however, can be difficult to adhere to in an obesogenic environment. Although healthy eating and physical activity remain the mainstays of public health messages, higher-level interventions are needed to promote the nationwide change in individual behaviors that can curb and reverse the obesity epidemic. Recent community initiatives include improving healthy food options and physical activity in childcare and school environments, passing laws to limit sales and marketing of unhealthy foods and beverages to children, and making healthy foods more widely available in corner stores of low-income communities. Taxation of sugar-sweetened beverages and other unhealthy items has become a topic of national debate. Ending the country's weight problem must become a national priority, but it will require collaboration among many sectors of society to achieve.

To burn off...	You would have to...
A McDonald's Big Mac	Run for 56 min @ 5 mph (or only 26 min @ 10 mph!)
Six Oreo cookies	Do 4,440 jumping jacks
A large movie theater popcorn	Dance for 2½ hr
A Grande Caramel Frappuccino	Shovel snow for 1 hr
Three Olive Garden breadsticks	Mow the lawn for 1½ hr (with a push mower!)

Recommended Readings

Hu, F. (2008). *Obesity epidemiology*. New York, NY: Oxford University Press. http://doi.org/10.1093/acprof:oso/9780195312911.001.0001

Sallis, J. F., & Glanz, K. (2009). Physical activity and food environments: Solutions to the obesity epidemic. *Milbank Quarterly, 67*, 123–154. http://doi.org/10.1111/j.1468-0009.2009.00550.x

Skinner, A. C., Perrin, E. M., & Skelton, J. A. (2016). Prevalence of obesity and severe obesity in US children 1999–2014. *Obesity (Silver Spring), 2415*, 1116–1123. Available at http://onlinelibrary.wiley.com/doi/10.1002/oby.21497/full http://doi.org/10.1002/oby.21497

White House Task Force on Childhood Obesity, Report to the President. (2010, May). *Solving the problem of childhood obesity within a generation.* Available at https://letsmove.obamawhitehouse.archives.gov/sites/letsmove.gov/files/TaskForce_on_Childhood_Obesity_May2010_FullReport.pdf

Wisman, J. D., & Capehart, K. W. (2010). Creative destruction, economic insecurity, stress, and epidemic obesity. *American Journal of Economics and Sociology, 69*, 936–982. http://doi.org/10.1111/j.1536-7150.2010.00728.x

Yang, W. J., Kelly, T., & He, J. (2007). Genetic epidemiology of obesity. *Epidemiologic Reviews, 29*, 49–61. http://doi.org/10.1093/epirev/mxm004

Review Questions

1. Children are classified as obese if they are at or above what age- and gender-specific BMI percentile?
   A. 50th
   B. 66th
   C. 75th
   D. 85th
   E. 95th

2. Which BMI would classify an adult as overweight?
   A. 23.0
   B. 24.9
   C. 27.5
   D. 30.1
   E. 35.5

3. Which of the following has been identified as a contributing factor in the development of overweight and obesity?
   A. Environment
   B. Genes
   C. Hormones
   D. Stress
   E. All of the above

4. Which of the following is true about the retail food environment?
   A. Access to convenience stores and fast food restaurants is associated with lower risk of diabetes.
   B. Fresh produce and other healthy foods are generally more affordable than unhealthy foods.
   C. Low-income communities often have greater access to cheap unhealthy foods than to nutritious foods.
   D. Supermarket availability is associated with greater obesity risk.

    E. Technological advances have made healthy foods more affordable and easier to prepare.

Answer Key on p. 465

23 Eating Disorders

Richard E. Kreipe, MD, and Taylor B. Starr, DO, MPH

- How are eating disorders defined?
- What are the characteristic features of affected individuals?
- What are the causes of eating disorders?
- In assessing eating disorders, what other medical conditions must be ruled out?
- How are eating disorders treated?
- What is the prognosis for patients with eating disorders?

Definitions

In the last 8 months, Brittany, a 14-year-old high school freshman, has joined the cross-country team, lost 9 lb (4 kg) in an attempt to "get in shape," become a vegetarian, and not menstruated after having normal periods for a year. Although her body mass index (BMI) is at the 10th percentile, she reports feeling fat and needing to lose more weight. On examination, she is thin, cold with bluish hands and feet, and a low supine heart rate that almost doubles on standing. She notes feeling sad and worried that she will not be allowed to lose more weight. She also worries about her grades, although she is at the top of her class. Laboratory findings are all normal. She sleeps about 6 hr per night, and does not eat breakfast because she needs to prepare for school and has "no time."

> How are eating disorders defined?

The predominant eating disorders (EDs) are **anorexia nervosa** (AN) and **bulimia nervosa** (BN). AN is characterized by overestimation of body size and shape, with a relentless pursuit of thinness that typically combines excessive dieting and compulsive exercising. AN is divided into a *restrictive* subtype in which caloric intake is severely limited, and a *binge-purge* subtype featuring intermittent overeating followed by acts to rid the body of calories by vomiting or taking laxatives. BN is characterized by episodes of eating large amounts of food in a brief period (binge eating), followed by acts intended to eliminate or reduce the effects of ingested calories by vomiting, laxative use, exercise, or fasting. The *Diagnostic and Statistical Manual of Mental Disorders, 5th edition* (DSM-5) classification of mental disorders includes criteria for severe and less severe degrees of AN and BN, allowing for the early identification of individuals at a stage when the conditions are more responsive to treatment. In addition, two disorders have been included as stand-alone disorders: **binge-eating disorder** (BED), in which binge eating is not followed by compensatory behavior and results in varying degrees of obesity with profound behavioral and mental health morbidity; and **avoidant/restrictive food intake disorder** (ARFID), which is marked by behaviors to avoid or limit intake of foods, not because of body image problems but, rather, in response to the sensory qualities of, or adverse experiences associated or anticipated with, certain foods.

Characteristic Features

> What are the characteristic features of affected individuals?

The distribution of EDs in the population is not uniform. AN typically is seen in White, early to middle adolescent females of above-average intelligence and socioeconomic status, who are conflict-avoidant, risk-aversive, anxious, and perfectionist, and who often have depressed mood or obsessive-compulsive traits. BN tends to emerge in later adolescence, sometimes following AN, and is typified by impulsivity, difficulty maintaining stable relationships, and depression. The 0.5% to 1% and 3% to 5% incidence rates among younger and older adolescent females for AN and BN, respectively, most likely reflect ascertainment bias in sampling and underdiagnosis in cases not fitting the typical profile. The same may be true of the significant gender disparity noted in affected individuals: Females account for 90% of patients diagnosed with EDs. Among men, gay males are at increased risk due to the cultural emphasis on thinness and appearance. Other groups at risk include athletes, models, and dancers, regardless of gender. Male body builders are also at risk and can develop muscle *dysmorphia* or "reverse AN" in their desire to increase muscle and "get bigger." Depending on the sensitivity of the criteria used in diagnosis and the particular demographic features of the specific groups, ≥ 10% of some adolescent female populations may have some form of ED. BED is more commonly seen in adults and is often associated with depression, whereas ARFID is more common in pediatric age groups, but can persist into adulthood as "picky eating."

Causes of Eating Disorders

What are the causes of eating disorders?

Eating disorders are best viewed as a final common pathway, with a number of *predisposing* factors that increase the risk of developing an ED; *precipitating* factors often related to developmental processes of adolescence triggering the emergence of the ED; and *perpetuating* factors that cause an ED to persist.

Predisposing Factors

The range of heritability estimates for AN is 48% to 76% and for BN is 54% to 85%. **Genetic vulnerability** may be activated in girls at early and midstage puberty due to neuroendocrine changes. Speculations about what is inheritable include eating regulatory mechanisms, temperament and character styles, and biological predispositions such as ovarian hormone activity and serotonin system functioning that help regulate hunger, satiety, and mood. For example, the dysregulation of **serotonin** systems appears to be involved in the development and maintenance of EDs. Recent studies also suggest that in AN there may be a dysfunction in the cortico-striatal-insular neural network, wherein the insula fails in its role as a connection and regulator between cortical and subcortical structures involved in AN. BN and BED tend to be more closely associated with anxiety traits, whereas AN and ARFID tend to occur in individuals with depressive traits.

Family influence in the development of EDs is complex because of the interplay of genetic, environmental, and developmental factors. Genetic research suggests that shared elements of the family environment and immutable genetic factors account for about equal variance in disordered eating. The emergence of EDs coinciding with the processes of adolescence (e.g., puberty, identity, autonomy, and cognition) indicates the central role of development in pathogenesis. Inherited genetic factors influence the emergence of EDs during adolescence, but only indirectly. A genetic predisposition to anxiety, depression, or obsessive-compulsive traits, modulated through puberty, appears to mediate the risk of developing an ED.

There is little evidence that parents "cause" an ED in their child or adolescent. However, parental involvement in treatment is essential to successful recovery. Likewise, adults with eating disorders benefit from strong social support from partners, peers, and family.

Research indicates a complex interplay of culture, ethnicity, gender, peers, and family on disordered eating. The gender dimorphism is presumably related to female perception of a relationship between body image and self-evaluation. Numerous studies demonstrate the influence of the Western cultural "thin body ideal" on the development of EDs. Race and ethnicity appear to moderate the association between risk factors and disordered eating, with African American and Caribbean females reporting lower body dissatisfaction and less dieting than Hispanic and non-Hispanic White females.

Peer acceptance is central to healthy adolescent growth and development, especially in early adolescence when the prevalence of AN initially peaks. Indeed, numerous studies, including with experimental designs, support causal relationships among peer pressure, body image, and eating. Teasing by peers or by family members (especially males) may be a contributing factor for overweight girls. Studies showing associations among parent and child eating behaviors, dieting, and physical activity levels suggest parental reinforcement of body-related societal messages.

> A history of sexual trauma is not significantly more common in individuals with eating disorders than in the population at large, but when present, it makes recovery more difficult.

Precipitating Factors

Dieting is an especially significant precipitating factor in the development of disordered eating behavior. The causal relationship between dieting and EDs is unclear but may involve the physical effects of relative starvation and internalization of a "thin ideal," the experience of negative social comparisons, family or peer pressure to be thin, or peer teasing, all of which can create body dissatisfaction leading to dieting. ARFID is often associated with a traumatic event, either experienced or anticipated, such as choking, vomiting, or tasting something noxious.

Perpetuating Factors

When persistent, the biological effects of significant starvation and malnutrition (e.g., true loss of appetite, hypothermia, gastric atony, amenorrhea, sleep disturbance, fatigue, weakness, or depression) combined with the psychological boosts that come from an increased sense of mastery and

reduced emotional reactivity, actually "reward" and maintain pathological ED behaviors. This positive reinforcement of behaviors and consequences, generally viewed by parents and others as "negative," helps to explain why affected individuals characteristically deny that a problem exists and resist treatment. Though noxious, purging can be reinforcing due to a reduction in the anxiety triggered by overeating; purging also can result in short-term, but reinforcing, improvement in mood that is related to changes in neurotransmitter levels. Recent studies indicate that an imbalance in neurotransmitters, most notably serotonin and dopamine, and possibly ghrelin and leptin, support the concept of EDs as both brain and behavioral disorders. However, the cause–effect relationship between central nervous system (CNS) alterations and EDs is not clear, nor is reversibility. ARFID can be associated with persistent sensory experiences in which the color, appearance, smell, taste, or consistency of food can trigger aversive responses, often attributed to "wiring" of gustatory circuits in the brain.

Assessment

> In assessing eating disorders, what other medical conditions must be ruled out?

A careful history and thorough physical exam sometimes supplemented by self-report questionnaires help to target health care interventions. Thus, symptoms of excessive weight loss (feeling tired, cold, lacking energy, dizziness, and difficulty concentrating) can be linked to hypothermia with acrocyanosis and slow capillary refill, loss of muscle mass, and bradycardia with orthostasis. Table 23.1 details common eating and weight control behaviors and associated symptoms and signs that should be addressed in providing treatment.

In BED, a large amount of food is consumed in a short period of time, usually in the latter part of the day, and followed by feelings of shame, guilt, or remorse. Health problems of obesity are not different from those seen in individuals who do not binge eat. In ARFID, body image is not affected, but the loss of weight and malnutrition that can result can be the focus of medical attention.

Table 23.1. Eating and weight control habits, symptoms, and signs associated with eating disorders

	Anorexia Nervosa	Bulimia Nervosa
Habits		
Intake	Inadequate calories; low calorie and nonfat foods predominate	May restrict during the day, then binge at night on "forbidden" food
Food	Monotonous "healthy" food/ beverages of low caloric density	Aware of calories and fat, but less regimented than anorexia nervosa
Beverages	Water or other low/no calorie drinks; nonfat milk	Variable, diet soda common; may drink alcohol to excess
Meals	Rigidly consistent schedule and structure to meal plan	Impulsive and unregulated binges followed by purging
Snacks	Reduced or eliminated	Large amounts common in impulsive or planned binges
Dieting	Initial habit that becomes progressively restrictive	Initial habit that gives way to chaotic eating and binges
Binge eating	Essential feature in binge/purge subtype	Essential feature, often secretive, followed by shame/guilt
Exercise	Compulsive, ritualistic, often linked to sport (dance, track)	Less predictable; may be athletic or avoid exercise
Vomiting	More common in binge/purge subtype; may chew, then spit out food	Most common means used to eliminate effects of eating/overeating
Laxatives	Restrictive subtype for constipation; binge/purge subtype for catharsis	Second most common habit to reduce or avoid weight gain
Diet pills	Very rare except in binge/purge subtype	Used to reduce appetite or increase metabolism
Symptoms and Signs		
Body image	Distorted, feels fat/fears getting bigger; strong drive for thinness	May be overweight; desire to avoid weight gain predominant
Metabolism	Hypometabolic (cold, tired, weak, lacking energy)	Variable, depending on balance of intake and output and hydration
Skin	Cold, cyanotic extremities; dry, delayed healing, easy bruising	Self-injurious behavior (cutting, scratching) may occur
Hair	Lanugo-type hair on face/upper body; alopecia of scalp hair	–
Eyes	–	Subconjunctival hemorrhage from vomiting
Teeth	–	Enamel erosion with tooth decay/fracture/loss due to stomach acid
Salivary glands	–	Enlargement of parotid and/or submandibular glands
Heart	Dizziness, fainting, palpitations	Dizziness, fainting, palpitations
Abdomen	Full, bloated, discomfort after eating small amounts; constipation	Discomfort after a binge; cramps/diarrhea with laxative abuse
Mental status	Depression, anxiety, obsessive/compulsive symptoms	Depression, anxiety; borderline personality traits; substance use

Differential Diagnosis

Weight loss can occur in increased catabolism (e.g., malignancy or occult infection) or malabsorption (e.g., regional enteritis or celiac disease), but these illnesses are usually associated with other findings and are not typically associated with decreased caloric intake. However, the distinctions are not always clear-cut. For example, patients with inflammatory bowel disease (IBD) experience abdominal cramping, and patients with AN may experience abdominal discomfort because of gastric atony.

Endocrinopathies can also share features with EDs. In BN, voracious appetite in the face of weight loss might suggest diabetes mellitus, but blood glucose levels are normal or low in EDs. Thyroid disorders or adrenal insufficiency may be associated with weight loss and other symptoms of EDs.

In the CNS, craniopharyngiomas (Rathke pouch tumors) can mimic some of the findings of AN, such as weight loss and growth failure, and even some body image disturbances. However, the latter are less fixed than in typical EDs and are associated with other findings, including evidence of increased intracranial pressure. Any patient with an atypical presentation of an ED, based on age, sex, or other factors, deserves a scrupulous search for an alternative explanation. Finally, individuals may have both an underlying illness and an ED.

Laboratory Findings

Laboratory abnormalities, when found, are due to malnutrition, weight control behaviors, or medical complications; studies should be chosen based on history and physical examination. A routine screening battery typically includes a complete blood count, an erythrocyte sedimentation rate (should be normal), and a biochemical profile. Common abnormalities associated with EDs include (1) low white blood cell count with normal hemoglobin and differential; (2) hypokalemic, hypochloremic metabolic alkalosis if there is severe persistent vomiting; (3) mildly elevated liver enzymes, cholesterol, and cortisol levels; (4) low gonadotropin and blood glucose levels with marked weight loss; and (5) generally normal total serum protein, serum albumin, and renal function. An electrocardiogram (ECG) may be useful when profound bradycardia or arrhythmia is detected; the ECG typically has low voltage, with nonspecific ST or T wave changes. Although prolonged QT_c has been reported, prospective studies have not found any increased risk associated with this finding.

Treatment

Health Care Monitoring

How are eating disorders treated?

While explicitly linking ED behaviors to symptoms and signs may increase some patients' motivation to change, unresolved psychosocial conflicts in both the *intra*personal (self-esteem, self-efficacy) and *inter*personal (family, peers, school) domains may impede change. Weight control practices initiated as coping mechanisms become reinforced because of positive feedback. That is, *external rewards* (e.g., compliments about improved physical appearance) and *internal rewards* (e.g., perceived mastery over what is eaten or what is done to minimize the effects of overeating through exercise or purging) are more powerful in maintaining behavior than negative feedback (e.g., conflict with parents, peers, and others about eating) in changing it. Thus, definitive treatment requires the development of more productive means of coping.

Health care visits should focus on behaviors, symptoms, and signs. Daily journals can be reviewed at each visit: caloric intake (food/drink, amount, time, location), physical activity (type, duration, intensity), and emotional state (e.g., angry, sad, worried). Focusing on recorded data helps to identify dietary and activity deficiencies and excesses as well as behavioral and mental health patterns.

Patients with AN tend to overestimate their caloric intake and underestimate their activity level. Thus, prior to reviewing journal entries, it is important to measure: (1) weight, without underwear, in a hospital gown after voiding, (2) urine specific gravity, (3) temperature, and (4) blood pressure and pulse in supine, sitting, and standing positions to provide objective data about health status. In addition, a targeted physical examination focused on hypometabolism, cardiovascular stability, and mental status, as well as any related symptoms should occur at each visit to monitor progress (or regression).

Patients with BN tend to underestimate their caloric intake and overestimate their activity level. Compensatory behaviors such as vomiting or laxative abuse can lead to volume depletion and as well as to cardiac arrhythmias related to electrolyte disturbance. Individuals with BN are also at risk of developing alcoholism or substance abuse or of engaging in high-risk sexual behavior and self-injury. Lisdexamfetamine dimesylate, a stimulant used to treat attention-deficit disorder, is now approved for use in BED, as part of a comprehensive treatment plan.

Nutrition and Physical Activity

The most important element of treatment for EDs is emphasizing that "*food is medicine.*" Framing food as fuel for the body and the source of energy for daily activities emphasizes health. For patients with low weight, the nutrition prescription should be designed to gradually increase weight at the rate of about ½ to 1 lb/week (0.23–0.45 kg/week). This can be accomplished by increasing energy intake by ~200 kcal every few days toward a target of approximately 90% of average body weight for gender, height, and age. Weight gain will not occur until intake exceeds output. Intake for continued weight gain may exceed 3,500 kcal/day, especially for patients who are anxious and have high levels of nonexercise activity thermogenesis. Stabilizing intake is the goal for patients with BN, with a gradual introduction of "forbidden foods" while also limiting foods that may "trigger" a binge.

Dysfunctional cognitions include "all-or-none" thinking (related to perfectionism) with a tendency to overgeneralize and jump to catastrophic conclusions. Affected patients also believe that their body is governed by rules that do not apply to others. These tendencies lead to dichotomization of foods into "good" or "bad" categories, having

a day "ruined" because of one unexpected food-related event, or choosing foods based on rigid self-imposed restrictions. These cognitions may be associated with neurotransmitter abnormalities related to executive function and rewards.

Patients with AN tend to follow highly structured routines with markedly restricted intake; in contrast, patients with BN tend to lack structure, which results in chaotic eating patterns and binge/purge episodes. Patients with AN, BN, BED, or ARFID all benefit from a structured plan for healthy eating that includes three meals and at least one snack distributed evenly over the day and based on balanced meal planning. Breakfast deserves special emphasis because it is often the first meal eliminated in AN and is frequently avoided the morning after a binge/purge episode in BN. In BED, nutritional excess is more common than deficiency, and a sedentary lifestyle is typical. In addition to structuring meals and snacks, patients should structure their activities. If appropriate, monitored exercise (≤ 45 minutes daily, at no more than moderate intensity) can improve mood and make increasing calories more acceptable.

Mental Health

Selective serotonin reuptake inhibitors (SSRIs) have minimal effect until weight is restored. With weight restored, however, SSRIs are effective in reducing binge/purge behaviors regardless of depression and are considered a standard element of therapy in BN. The dose of SSRI in the treatment of BN may require the equivalent of 60 mg of fluoxetine or more to maintain effectiveness.

Evidence-based studies indicate that *cognitive behavioral therapy* (CBT), which focuses on restructuring "thinking errors" and establishing adaptive patterns of behavior, is more effective than interpersonal or psychoanalytic approaches. *Dialectical behavior therapy* (DBT), a form of CBT in which distorted thoughts and emotional responses are challenged, analyzed, and replaced with healthier responses, requires adult thinking skills and is useful for older patients with BN. *Group therapy* can provide support, but requires skilled leadership because of the risk that group members at different stages of recovery may teach each other how to evade treatment or compete on remaining thin or losing weight. As a general principle, the younger the patient, the more intimately the parents need to be involved in therapy. The only approach with evidence-based effectiveness in the treatment of AN in children and adolescents is *family-based treatment*, exemplified by the Maudsley approach (http://www.maudsleyparents.org). This three-phase intensive outpatient model (1) helps parents play a positive role in restoring their child's eating pattern and weight to normal, then (2) returns "control" of eating to the child who has demonstrated the ability to maintain healthy weight, and then (3) encourages healthy progression in the other domains of adolescent development. Features of effective family treatment include an "agnostic" approach in which the cause of the disease is irrelevant to weight gain, emphasizing that parents are NOT to blame for EDs. Parents are taught to model healthy eating behaviors by sharing many meals with their affected child. They are also encouraged to be actively nurturing and supportive of their child's healthy eating while reinforcing limits on dysfunctional habits, rather than assuming the role of authoritarian "food police" or maintaining a completely hands-off approach. Finally, parents are the best resource for recovery for almost all patients, and their positive role should be reinforced by professionals who serve as consultants and advisors.

Supportive Care

Support groups are often designed primarily for parents. Because their daughter or son with an ED typically resists the diagnosis and treatment, parents may feel helpless and hopeless. Because of the historical precedent of blaming parents for causing EDs (only recently recognized in the psychiatric literature as neither accurate nor useful), parents frequently express feelings of shame and isolation. Support groups and multifamily therapy sessions bring parents together with other parents whose families are at various stages of recovery from an ED in ways that are both educational and encouraging. Because of residual body image or other issues, patients often benefit from support groups after intensive treatment or at the end of treatment.

Prognosis

> What is the prognosis for patients with eating disorders?

With early diagnosis and effective treatment, $\geq 80\%$ of youths with AN recover physiologically (i.e., develop normal eating and weight control habits, maintain average weight for height, and function well in school, work, and relationships), although some still have residual body image distortions. In females, when weight is restored to normal, fertility appears to return as well, although the weight for resumption of menses (about 92% of average body weight for height) may be lower than the weight for ovulation.

Unfortunately, up to 10% of severely affected patients die. The prognosis for youth with BN is less well established, but may be better than the prognosis for youth with AN. Because BED and ARFID were only officially recognized in 2013, data about prognosis are still being gathered. Death is a major risk, especially in BN and AN binge/purge subtype, when electrolyte abnormalities lead to cardiac arrhythmias or when vomiting leads to severe esophageal tears. Outcome improves with multidimensional treatment that includes SSRIs and attention to mood, past trauma, impulsivity, and psychopathology, if it exists.

Recommended Readings

Culbert, K. M., Slane, J. D., & Klump, K. L. (2008). Genetics of eating disorders. In S. A. Wonderlich, J. E. Mitchell, M. de Zwaan, & H. Steiger (Eds.), *Annual Review of Eating Disorders Part 2* (pp. 27–42). New York, NY: Radcliffe Publishing.

Fisher, M. (2006). Treatment of eating disorders in children, adolescents, and young adults. *Pediatrics in Review, 27*, 5–16. http://doi.org/10.1542/pir.27-1-5

Montano, C. B., Rasgoni, N. L., & Herman, B. K. (2016). Diagnosing binge eating disorder in a primary care setting. *Postgraduate Medicine, 128*, 115–123. http://doi.org/10.1080/00325481.2016.1115330

Rosen, D. S. (2010). American Academy of Pediatrics Committee on Adolescence. Identification and management of eating disorders in children and adolescents. *Pediatrics, 126*, 1240–1253. http://doi.org/10.1542/peds.2010-2821

US Department of Health and Human Services, National Institutes of Health, National Institute of Mental Health. (2016). *Eating disorders.* Available at https://www.nimh. nih.gov/health/topics/eating-disorders/index.shtml

Review Questions

1. A 9-year-old male choked on a potato chip at a family picnic and is now unwilling to eat anything except milkshakes that his mother makes for him. He is losing weight and feels tired, cold, and hungry. Which of the following is the most likely diagnosis?
    A. Anorexia nervosa
    B. Attention-seeking behavior of middle childhood
    C. Avoidant/restrictive food intake disorder
    D. Esophageal diverticulum
    E. Food refusal associated with autism spectrum disorder

2. A 17-year-old male with bulimia nervosa has been vomiting 3 times a day for the past 2 weeks so he can wrestle at a lower weight class. Of the following, which is the most common pattern of electrolyte disturbance that would be expected?
    A. Chloride high; sodium high; carbon dioxide high
    B. Chloride low; sodium low; carbon dioxide low
    C. Potassium low; chloride high; sodium high
    D. Potassium low; chloride low; carbon dioxide high
    E. Sodium low; potassium high; carbon dioxide low

3. A 14-year-old female cross-country runner with restrictive anorexia nervosa and a BMI below the 3rd percentile presents for a sports pre-participation evaluation. Which of the following would most likely be found on physical examination?
    A. Alopecia and tachycardia
    B. Dental enamel erosion and salivary gland enlargement
    C. Gingival hypertrophy and cervical lymphadenopathy
    D. Hypothermia and bradycardia
    E. Knuckle calluses and self-inflicted cuts

4. A 34-year-old male is being evaluated for hypertension associated with weight gain and depression. Dietary intake history uncovers binge-eating disorder. Which one of the following medications is approved for use in binge-eating disorder?
    A. Cyclobenzaprine
    B. Fluoxetine
    C. Lisdexamfetamine dimesylate
    D. Methylphenidate
    E. Phentermine

Answer Key on p. 465

24 Substance-Related and Addictive Disorders

María F. Gómez, MD, and João V. Nunes, MD

- Which drugs are most likely to be abused?
- What dangerous health behaviors are associated with substance abuse?
- What physical and psychological factors contribute to substance abuse or dependence?
- What are some treatment approaches and how do they work?
- What is a "network intervention "program?"
- What is a "harm reduction" program?

Substance Use Disorder

The American Psychiatric Association published criteria for substance-related and addictive disorders in the *Diagnostic and Statistical Manual of Mental Disorders, 5th edition* (DSM-5). The new category that combines the prior diagnoses of substance abuse and dependence into a single disorder called **substance use disorder** (SUD) exists on a continuum from mild to severe. While each specific substance may provoke a specific use disorder term (e.g., alcohol use disorder, stimulant use disorder) all use disorders conform to similar criteria. SUD, as a general category, can be described as maladaptive use that disrupts or impairs functioning at work, school, home, or leisure. It often causes or precipitates physical and psychological harm and persistent legal, social, and interpersonal problems. In the US, 40% of the population uses illicit substances in their lifetime. SUD is more common in men than in women, and unemployed persons and members of minority groups show higher rates. More than 75% of men and 65% of women with SUD have a comorbid mental disorder dual diagnosis such as *antisocial personality disorder, major depressive disorder,* or *persistent depressive disorder*.

SUD locks persons into cyclical, disturbed, and destructive patterns of behavior preventing them from exercising the sound judgment that would enable them to resist such behavior. This leaves such persons vulnerable to risky behaviors such as sharing used syringes and needles, often engaging in communal drug injecting ("shooting galleries"). Such practices result in frequent microtransfusions accompanied by disease transmission. Persons who inject heroin alone or in combination with cocaine "shoot up," on average, 3 to 5 times a day. Intravenous cocaine users may inject themselves every 15 min to maintain a "high." The frequency of syringe- and needle-sharing injections multiplies the risk.

Diagnostic Categories

DSM-5 provides criteria for the diagnosis of clinical presentations directly related to substance use, or substance-induced disorders. **Substance intoxication** develops soon after intake of a drug and reverses once the drug is metabolized and excreted. Its psychological signs and symptoms and maladaptive behavioral changes are due to the effects of the substance on the central nervous system (CNS). **Tolerance** is the state in which a person requires increasing doses of a substance to achieve the same effects. **Withdrawal** comprises the physical and psychological signs and symptoms that occur when a person stops using a substance for a period of time, typically abruptly. Withdrawal symptoms can be reversed if the drug or a suitable substitute is administered. Although neither tolerance nor withdrawal is required for a diagnosis of SUD, withdrawal is usually associated with SUD. **Substance/medication-induced mental disorders** refer to disorders that are usually temporary and likely to resolve within a month of resolution of acute withdrawal, intoxication, or use of the medication or substance. Substance/medication-induced mental disorders are considered in the differential diagnosis of independent psychiatric disorders, but to be actually included, there must be evidence that the disorder is not better explained by an independent mental disorder.

Gambling disorder has been added to the Substance-Related and Addictive Disorders category given that there is evidence that it is similar to the other substance-related disorders in clinical expression, brain reward system activation, comorbidity, physiology, and treatment. Research is ongoing about whether or not to include Internet gaming disorder, although considered an addictive behavior, in this category.

Commonly Abused Substances

> Which drugs are most likely to be abused?

Alcohol, which is used by about 50% of the world's adult population, is the most commonly used psychoactive substance, and alcoholism is the most common SUD worldwide. In 2014, approximately 88% of Americans $\geq$ 18 years of age had used alcohol at least once in their lifetime and 52% of Americans > 12 reported being current drinkers of alcohol. About 15% of the US health care dollar goes to treating alcohol-related disorders. In fact, alcohol and other substance-related deaths rank third behind heart disease and cancer, both of which can be induced or exacerbated by smoking tobacco, another highly prevalent addictive substance.

Although use of most drugs has stabilized or declined over the past decade, marijuana use has increased in most areas of the US, and is expected to rise further as states legalize medical marijuana. Use of crack cocaine has decreased over the last few years, but use of both heroin and pre-

Commonly Abused Psychoactive Substances
• Alcohol
• Nicotine
• Caffeine
• Cannabis
• Hallucinogens: lysergic acid diethylamide (LSD), mescaline
• Phencyclidine (PCP)
• Inhalants: nitrous oxide or volatile hydrocarbons)
• Opioids: morphine, meperidine, methadone, oxycodone, heroin
• Sedatives, hypnotics, anxiolytics, CNS depressants (barbiturates, methaqualone, benzodiazepines)
• Stimulants: amphetamine, methamphetamine, 3,4-methylenedioxymethamphetamine (MDMA), cocaine
• Belladonna alkaloids: atropine, scopolamine
• Designer/"Club" drugs: synthetic cannabinoids, MDMA, ketamine, gamma-hydroxybutyric acid (GHB), flunitrazepam (Rohypnol)

Effects of Alcohol on Selected Organ Systems	
Cardiovascular:	Arrhythmias, cardiomyopathy
Gastrointestinal:	Gastritis, bleeding, hepatitis, fatty liver, cirrhosis
Neurological:	Neuropathy, dementia (major and minor neurocognitive disorders), cerebellar degeneration, Wernicke-Korsakoff syndrome
Immune system:	Suppression leading to increased infection
Neuroendocrine:	Erectile dysfunction, testicular atrophy, feminization
Gynecological/reproductive:	Infertility, fetal alcohol syndrome, other teratogenicity

scription opiates is increasing as is the number of fatal overdoses. Heroin is available on the street in close to pure form, which makes the high conferred by inhalation (which is especially appealing to women) similar to that obtained by injection. The purer forms of both heroin and crack are often sprinkled on marijuana and serve as an introduction to the harder drugs of abuse.

> What dangerous health behaviors are associated with substance abuse?

Intravenous (IV) drug use is an important vehicle for the acquisition and transmission of blood-borne infectious diseases (e.g., hepatitis B and C, HIV/AIDS), and ranks immediately behind unsafe sex practices as the most common risky behavior in which individuals with HIV/AIDS engage. More than 45,000 cases of AIDS in the US have been attributed to IV drug use. Although the rate of infection among IV drug users nationwide stabilized at approximately 40% to 45% in 2001, the rate of HIV infection among injecting drug users in New York City is estimated at 50%.

Etiological Factors

> What physical and psychological factors contribute to substance abuse or dependence?

Understanding the bio-behavioral mechanism of alcoholism contributes to the disease model of addiction and greatly reduces the stigma attached to affected individuals. Although imitation of peers is a potent factor in drug use, children and adolescents often first experiment with drugs as a way of coping with tension in the family. In such situations, drug use must be understood in the context of family dynamics. Adolescents sometimes use drugs to attract their parents' attention, as if to communicate that it is preferable to receive negative attention and punishment from parents than it is to be ignored. Conversely, drug use by acting-out adolescents may be encouraged covertly by the family so it can focus on the drug using behavior instead of focusing on underlying problems that threaten the integrity of the family.

Children may perceive parental substance use (alcohol included) as tacitly condoning use by their children. If the parents prohibit and punish their children for behaviors the parents themselves exhibit, the children may dismiss the parents as hypocritical. Alcohol use poses an especially difficult challenge for adolescents. Because it is pervasive in all segments of society, adolescents may view drinking alcohol as an

Patterns of Substance Use and Misuse

- Experimental (may abate, intensify, or turn into other types of use)
- Social-recreational (may remain as such, intensify, or become compulsive)
- Circumstantial-situational (opportunistic; may intensify, or become compulsive)
- Compulsive (maladaptive)
- Intensified (often a quality of the other patterns)

Note: While all patterns of substance use *may* become maladaptive and impair functioning, a compulsive pattern is *always* maladaptive.

aspect of identity formation and as a marker of adulthood.

Family problems associated with substance abuse include neglect, marital discord, job loss and frequent relocations, disrupted family dynamics and peer relationships, and social instability. Children of substance abusers may be stigmatized in school and the community. To cope with the resulting stress, some resort to abusing substances themselves. The children may understand this behavior as cognitively and emotionally maladaptive, but they may be unaware of resources that could allow them to break the behavioral cycle or they may not be in a position to access such resources without parental assistance.

Bio-Behavioral Mechanisms of Addiction

Certain persons appear to be at increased risk for developing alcohol misuse disorders. This risk presumably reflects genetic variability of the brain's reward system. Cross-fostering studies have revealed that genetic risk may be greater than social risk in offspring of alcohol abusers. Genes that influence the metabolism of alcohol (as in aldehyde dehydrogenase deficiency) may be protective because they induce a negative reaction (nausea, vomiting) to drinking alcohol. This gene is particularly prevalent among, for example, Asian populations.

The brain *reward circuit* includes dopaminergic neurons located in the ventral tegmental area

(VTA). VTA neurons project to and modulate neuronal activity in the nucleus accumbens (NAcc) via the medial forebrain bundle. The NAcc has extensive connections with the prefrontal association cortices and basolateral amygdala. These connections give this circuit wide influence over behavior, including behavioral responses to stimuli that promote feelings of pleasure, reward, and motivation. Most drugs of abuse (e.g., cocaine, amphetamine, nicotine) produce marked episodic increases in dopamine levels in the NAcc, which disrupt the reward system. For example, psychoactive substance stimulation or disinhibition of VTA neurons whose projections release dopamine in the NAcc initiates what is perceived as a rewarding experience. Such reward positively reinforces the behavior. Reinforcement also occurs when the physical and psychological discomfort triggered by substance withdrawal is relieved by use of the same or similar substances.

The reward circuit is considered the final common pathway for reward and the regulation of motivation. The pleasurable signal drugs of abuse create in the brain reinforces their continued use, leading to further drug seeking, which displaces more adaptive behaviors.

Substance Abuse Treatment Programs

Principles of Treatment

> What are some treatment approaches and how do they work?

Three principles guiding the development of treatment for substance abusers are:
1. Adverse physical symptoms must be minimal (few people knowingly put themselves in a position where discomfort and pain are likely).
2. The motivation for giving up the substance must be greater than the motivation for continued use.
3. Places, activities, and other situations strongly associated with using the substance (smoking while drinking a cocktail or coffee) must be avoided.

Treatment cannot begin until the patient takes initial steps toward recovery by voluntarily entering a program and developing a therapeutic relationship with a counselor. Recidivism is high even for those who take these steps, but it approaches 100% among those who are involuntarily enrolled in treatment unless they eventually agree to participate voluntarily.

Supportive care during withdrawal depends on the type of drug the patient used and the patient's place within the withdrawal cycle. For example, *supportive care* for patients who are experiencing a "bad trip" from LSD may entail only a quiet space and a warm reassuring person to "talk them down." While hallucinogens, marijuana, and caffeine are exceptions, most drugs of abuse are associated with significant withdrawal symptoms. These may not be life threatening, but they do require prompt recognition and proper treatment. Withdrawal from cocaine may have serious emotional and psychological consequences including risk for suicide.

Treatment Approaches

> **Treatment Approaches**
> 1. Detoxification (acute; 5–21 days)
> 2. Rehabilitation (short-term; 28 days)
> 3. Residential treatment (long-term; 6–24 months)

Detoxification, employed to treat the acute physical effects of withdrawal from opiates, alcohol, and sedative-hypnotics, is provided in medical units. On average, length of stay for detoxification ranges from 5 days for alcohol and 14 days for opiates to 21 days for benzodiazepines. Detoxification programs are designed to prevent potentially life-threatening withdrawal syndromes through treatment prescribed by protocol. Affected patients are usually given a substance for which they have a cross tolerance that is administered in tapered doses over a defined number of days. As a rule, "detox" treatment teams include physicians, nurses, social workers, rehabilitation and occupational counselors, and certified alcoholism and substance abuse counselors. Most offer 12-step and other *relapse prevention* programs.

After detoxification, many patients enter 28-day *short-term* **rehabilitation programs** that offer a full schedule of structured activities to divert attention away from wanting or needing drugs, motivate continued progress toward recovery, and prevent early relapse. Typical activities include health education, HIV counseling, individual supportive or insight-oriented counseling, acupuncture, rehabilitation and vocational services, and groups that focus on support, spirituality, relaxation, meditation, and activities of daily living (personal grooming, housekeeping, recreational and gym activities).

Some patients enter **residential programs** for 6 months to 2 years of intense therapy and limited contact with the outside world. The goal is life-long sobriety and abstinence from drugs through improvement in emotional state and belief system, while providing employment and education. Success requires commitment and adherence to strict rules. Many enroll in such programs as court-ordered alternatives to incarceration. Those who are poorly motivated or who enroll only to satisfy others may be unable to engage in the required self-reflection or to tolerate continuous scrutiny. Like most substance abuse programs, residential programs rely on peer counselors and role models.

Adjunctive pharmacological treatments are available to facilitate abstinence from alcohol. These include **disulfiram** which induces aversive symptoms like nausea and vomiting after drinking; naltrexone, which reduces craving and the reward experience; and acamprosate, which reduces craving. The 12-step self-led program of Alcoholics Anonymous has been adapted to the treatment of other addictions. Such programs require persons to participate in groups where members work through a hierarchy of psychological and behavioral steps to accept the reality of their loss of control and eventually recommit to a non-using lifestyle.

Network Intervention

> What is a "network intervention" program?"

Network intervention generally occurs in treatment settings (residential, nonresidential; short- or long-term). The therapist recruits and engages the addicted patient and enlists the assistance of significant others (family, friends) to provide support, encouragement, and monitoring. Significant others provide accurate assessment of progress in recovery (e.g., quantity and pattern of use), while their involvement reinforces the message that the patient has not been abandoned and others are invested in the program and its success.

Harm Reduction Strategies

> What is a "harm reduction" program?

Harm reduction programs attempt to minimize the consequences of any psychoactive substance misuse. In particular, harm reduction is more successful than abstinence-based approaches for opiate addicts. For others substances, while abstinence is the best outcome, demanding an all-or-nothing commitment may not be possible for persons who fall into transition categories in their movement toward change. Encouraging and reinforcing smaller steps makes the ultimate goal – stopping usage – more attainable (see Chapter 36: Motivating Healthy Behaviors).

If the individual wants to continue IV drug use, then stopping drugs by injection becomes the goal. If injection is desired, then not sharing injection equipment is the goal. If sharing will continue, using a decontaminating agent between users is the goal. In harm reduction, any positive steps are reinforced.

Needle exchange programs (NEPs) are an example of a harm reduction method. At an NEP, addicts are given a supply of sterile needles in return for dirty used needles. At some NEPs, bleach kits are distributed for cleaning needles between injections. Condoms may also be distributed. These programs often operate out of mobile centers that travel to high drug use areas on a regular schedule. To engage their clients, these centers also may provide medical care, program referrals, and food.

Recovery readiness programs are similar to harm reduction programs. Program goals include outreach to users that are not yet responsive to overtures from drug treatment programs.

Methadone Maintenance Programs

Methadone is a synthetic narcotic that has pharmacological effects similar to those of heroin and morphine although it inhibits the euphoric effects of narcotic agents.

Methadone maintenance programs provide daily doses of methadone to heroin addicts at a regular time and in a safe place, as they reinforce the person's steps toward recovery. The intent is to reduce the need to participate in criminal acts to fuel the addiction. Success is defined as reduction or cessation of heroin use, cessation of criminal activity, and appropriate productive functioning in the community. Recently, general medical practitioners have become authorized to prescribe buprenorphine, which is a partial opioid agonist that can be used without a structured social program.

Buprenorphine and Naloxone for Opioid Use Disorders

Recently **buprenorphine**, a mixed opiate agonist/antagonist, has become available as an alternative to methadone both for detoxification and maintenance treatment. Providers with brief special training can use it in general or psychiatric settings without a structured social program, enhancing the privacy and convenience of treatment. Because of its antagonist properties, buprenorphine conveys less risk of respiratory depression and death than heroin or methadone. It may be mixed with a non-absorbed form of the antagonist naltrexone, to prevent diversion for intravenous use.

Naloxone, a complete opioid antagonist, quickly reverses the effect of overdose. In light of a sudden rise in the diversion for illicit use of highly potent opioids, especially the prescribed narcotic fentanyl and its metabolites (norfentanyl), some jurisdictions are distributing naloxone injection kits to emergency responders and even drug users, to rescue people who have misjudged their dose and are in or about to be in respiratory arrest.

Smoking

Smoking Cessation Programs

Smoking cessation programs follow the same tenets as programs designed to treat other drug addictions, emphasizing recovery and relapse prevention. Nicotine withdrawal produces uncomfortable symptoms that, like those from other drugs, need specific therapeutic attention. To aid recovery and prevention relapse, many smoking cessation programs use transdermal nicotine patches and nicotine gum as replacement therapy in addition to social support and motivational counseling. Adjuvant pharmacological treatment with bupropion or varenicline is frequently used to help reduce nicotine withdrawal and the urge to smoke. Programs also provide psychoeducational sessions designed to counter media messages promoting smoking. Many programs are located in schools and are directed toward children and adolescents. Since peer pressure and curiosity are the most common reasons young people begin smoking, prevention is the key to successful antismoking programs for this age group.

Acupuncture in the Treatment of Addictive Behaviors

Auricular acupuncture, with needle insertion limited to defined antiaddiction points on the ear, is a popular therapy for alcoholism, smoking, and obesity. In Oregon, for example, where no methadone treatment programs are available, addicts receive regular periodic auricular acupuncture treatments. Anecdotal and small-scale case reports have described good success rates that are comparable to pharmacological and cognitive behavior treatments. However, few randomized controlled trials have been carried out.

Evidence for the effectiveness of various treatment approaches may be found in the evidence-based medicine literature. Unfortunately, the recidivism rates for *all* treatment approaches remain relatively high.

Recommended Readings

Galanter, M., Kleber, H. D., & Brady, K. (Eds.). (2015). *American Psychiatric Publishing textbook of substance abuse treatment* (5th ed.). Arlington, VA: American Psychiatric Publishing.

Levounis, P., & Herron, A. (Eds). (2014). *The addiction case-book*. Arlington, VA: American Psychiatric Publishing. http://doi.org/10.1176/appi.books.9781585625352

Levounis, P., Zerbo, E., & Aggarwal, R. (2016). *Pocket guide to addiction assessment and treatment*. Arlington, VA: American Psychiatric Publishing. http://doi.org/10.1176/appi.books.9781615370726

Ries, R. K., Fiellin, D., Miller, S. C., & Saitz, R. (Eds.). (2014). *The ASAM principles of addiction medicine* (5th ed.). Philadelphia, PA: Lippincott Williams & Wilkins.

Additional Resources

Alcoholics Anonymous. (2001). *Read the Big Book and twelve steps and twelve traditions.* Available at http://www.aa.org/pages/en_US/read-the-big-book-and-twelve-steps-and-twelve-traditions

Review Questions

1. Among the following, which condition must be met for substance abuse treatment to be successful?
   A. Counselor must be available at all times of crisis.
   B. Family must insist on therapy.
   C. Individual must be motivated to change.
   D. Pain associated with abuse must be greater than the pleasure.
   E. Threat of legal action must be substantial.

2. The basic goal of harm reduction programs is
   A. development of supportive peer and family networks
   B. improved education about the negative effects of drugs
   C. minimization of the consequences of drug use
   D. provision of assistance to recovering addicts
   E. substitution of a less addictive drug

3. A 40-year-old man tells his doctor that he has been using cocaine. Which of the following symptoms is most likely to be seen as a result of cocaine withdrawal?
   A. Flushed face
   B. Hypertension
   C. Dysphoric mood
   D. Tachycardia
   E. Tremors

Answer Key on p. 465

25 Interpersonal Violence and Abuse

Roland D. Maiuro, PhD, and Nancy K. Sugg, MD, MPH

- What are four major forms of abuse?
- Which children are at risk for abuse?
- What are the clinical signs of intimate partner violence and abuse?
- What are common characteristics of a perpetrator?
- What is the trauma syndrome?
- Which external or situational factors contribute to violence?

Interpersonal violence and abuse refers to behavior that occurs within or outside a family setting involving physical, coercive, or intimidating acts to instill fear or gain control over another person. This behavior may result in both physical and psychological trauma responses such as fear, anxiety, depression, guilt, learned helplessness, or sense of worthlessness.

What are four major forms of abuse?

There are four major forms of abuse:
1. **Interpersonal violence** should be considered in any case of unexplained injury, as evidenced by bruises, welts, burns, lacerations, abrasions, fractures, or bites. Incidents may involve pushing, slapping, punching, kicking, choking, assault with an object or weapon, or forced restraint. It should be suspected and investigated when the patient's account is inconsistent with the observed pattern of injury.
2. **Psychological/emotional abuse** is defined as intimidating or controlling behavior where the perpetrator exercises power over another person or violates the person's rights and freedom through fear, degradation, threats of harm, extreme jealousy and possessiveness, deprivation, or humiliation.
3. **Sexual abuse** includes acts of exposure, sexual exploitation (including childhood prostitution), and forced, coerced, or any other unwanted sexual contact.
4. **Social/environmental abuse** is defined as behaviors that directly or indirectly limit or monitor a victim's activities (e.g., physical restraints, electronic monitoring) including contacts with family and friends, access to transportation or work, or withholding financial or basic support as a method of control.

Types of Abusive Relationships

Family violence includes spouse or partner abuse, child abuse, child sexual abuse or incest, sibling abuse, marital rape, and elder abuse. Family or intimate partner violence is characterized by a *continuing relationship* between the victim and the perpetrator. There is a high risk of repeated or increasingly violent encounters because of common living quarters or ongoing contact that provides easy access to a vulnerable victim. Such violence can occur between current, estranged, or former spouses or romantic partners; girlfriends; boyfriends including same-sex partners; and cohabiting couples. Power dynamics involving one partner controlling the other through threatened or actual violence can render the victim dependent, fearful, and ambivalent about leaving the relationship or seeking and accepting help.

Although some cases involve mutual violence, there is commonly a predominant aggressor and instances of self-defense by the victim. Because many episodes of family violence or intimate partner violence occur in private, they are often undetected or go unreported to authorities.

Child Maltreatment and Abuse

> Which children are at risk for abuse?

Child maltreatment includes neglect as well as physical, sexual, and psychological abuse. It was the first type of domestic violence to be legally defined, legislated against, and designated as a violent act. Reporting to appropriate authorities (police, Child Protective Services [CPS]) by providers serving in health or educational capacities (physicians, nurses, social workers, teachers) is mandated throughout the US.

> In suspected cases, standards of care not only require attention to immediate injuries and trauma, but also notification of child protective authorities who may perform a comprehensive investigation and assessment of future risk to the child.

Child maltreatment refers to any act of omission or commission that endangers or impairs the child's emotional or physical heath and development. Typically, it is the intentional, nonaccidental, and injurious use of force by an adult caretaker that is reported to authorities. About 80% of reported perpetrators are parents of the abused child. However, sibling abuse (violence perpetrated by full siblings, half siblings, and adopted siblings) is very common and often underreported because usually the perpetrator is not a caregiver and, therefore, does not fall under the purview of CPS.

Sexual abuse refers to sexual acts perpetrated on children by adults or on any individual below the age of consent by another individual who is at least 4 years older. Incest refers to acts perpetrated specifically by a family member on a child. It is estimated that each year more than 250,000 children in the US are subjected to various acts of incestuous contact.

Children are especially vulnerable to abuse because of their physical and emotional dependence and inability to protect themselves. Children < 5 years of age are at particular risk for **shaken baby syndrome** (SBS), a subtype of *abusive head trauma*. The US Centers for Disease Control and Prevention (CDC) identifies SBS as "an injury to the skull or intracranial contents of an infant or young child or inflicted blunt impact and/or violent shaking." There is a diagnostic triad of medical findings including subdural hematoma, retinal bleeding, and brain swelling caused by violent shaking. In a majority of cases of SBS, there is no externally visible sign of injury.

Emotional abuse, although more difficult to identify and quantify than physical abuse, may be more profoundly damaging. Definitions of neglect (inadequate food, shelter, clothing, supervision) vary by state and may be mitigated by circumstances including intentionality, ignorance, poverty, and mental illness of the adult caretaker. In some states, children witnessing violence in the home is considered reportable child abuse since a growing body of evidence points to the long-term emotional damage experienced by children who witness violence, a form of "toxic stress."

Risk Factors for Child Abuse
- Difficult/unwanted pregnancy
- Traumatic delivery
- "Difficult" child
- Colic
- Hyperactivity
- Congenital abnormalities
- Chronic illness
- Physical disabilities
- Inadequate parental bonding or attachment

In 2014, the Children's Bureau surveyed CPS offices throughout the US and estimated that 702,000 children were victims of maltreatment, with approximately 75% of those being neglected, 17% physically abused, and 8% sexually abused. This number represents only children brought to the attention of CPS and, therefore, is considered to represent a significant underestimate of the real prevalence (US Department of Health and Human Services, Administration on Children, Youth and

Families. Child Maltreatment 2014. Washington DC: US Government Printing Office; 2016: Available at http://www.acf.hhs.gov/programs/cb/resource/child-maltreatment-2014).

Clinical Signs Suggestive of Child Abuse

- Multiple injuries in different stages of healing
- Fractures caused by pulling, twisting, shaking
- Rib fractures in the absence of a plausible history of accidental trauma
- Multiple skull fractures suggesting repeated blows to the head
- Cerebral edema and retinal hemorrhages suggesting violent shaking
- Burns to the hands, buttocks, feet, and legs
- Scalding of the feet, or lower legs, or in a stocking/glove pattern suggesting immersion in hot water
- Grip marks on thighs, bite marks on breasts or buttocks, perineal lacerations or scars
- Bruising of genitalia or anus suggesting sexual abuse
- Any unexplained injury

Discipline Versus Abuse

Determining when parental discipline is severe enough to be child abuse is sometimes complicated by sociocultural and ethnic factors. Severe physical punishment was acceptable discipline to many parents in the US until the 1950s. Current standards of childcare, however, require the parent or guardian to meet the child's basic needs for shelter, nutrition, safety, and hygiene. These standards also require the parent or guardian to refrain from physical acts that may result in welts, bruises, or other enduring physical marks on the child. Even in cases in which enduring marks are not observed, it is generally appropriate to discourage the use of spanking and other forms of physical discipline, due to possible longer-term psychological trauma and because such practices model aggressive behavior as acceptable.

Intimate Partner Abuse

Intimate partner abuse includes marital, nonmarital, and same-sex adult partners and former partners. Although psychological and verbal abuse are the most common types of abuse in partner

relationships, physical and sexual maltreatment as well as property damage are also included. Child abuse and pet abuse may occur concomitantly. Many states now have legal statutes that include pet abuse as a form of domestic violence.

Although the majority of serious injuries occurring in cases of partner or spouse abuse are perpetrated by the male partner, a significant number of women are also verbally and physically aggressive in domestic settings. Furthermore, men often have difficulty asking for help when they are victims, resulting in underestimation of female-to-male or male-to-male intimate partner violence. In some instances, abuse is bidirectional, further complicating the definitions of victim and perpetrator.

Intimate Partner Abuse

- 26% of women and 16% of men experience intimate partner violence in their lifetime (CDC data)
- 41% of rapes or sexual assaults against females were committed by an intimate partner (Bureau of Justice statistics)
- 45% of murdered women and 5% of murdered men were killed by an intimate partner (Bureau of Justice statistics)

Marital Rape and Date Rape

Marital rape and **date rape** are sexual acts forced on an individual without their consent. Marital rape definitions vary by state depending on whether, and to what extent, intention to have sexual relations is implicit in longer-term consenting adult relationships. It is estimated that 10% to 14% of married women in the US have been raped by their husbands. Intimate partner rape can also be perpetrated by unmarried, long-term partners and former partners. The term *date rape* describes forced sexual acts perpetrated on an individual in a short-term, noncommitted relationship. Almost 41% of all rapes are committed by an intimate partner, compared with 39% committed by an acquaintance and 21% committed by a stranger.

What are the clinical signs of intimate partner violence and abuse?

> **Physical Signs of Partner Abuse**
> - Multiple bruises, cuts, blackened eyes
> - Defensive trauma to the hands, wrists, arms
> - Cerebral concussion
> - Strained or torn ligaments
> - Fractures
> - Blunt injuries to the chest or abdomen or back
> - Loss of hearing, ruptured ear drum
> - Loss of vision
> - Burns or bites
> - Knife or gunshot wounds
> - Vaginal, perianal, and cervical tears and lacerations
> - Recurrent sexually transmitted infections
> - Chronic pain syndrome
> - Miscarriage, placental hemorrhage, fetal fractures, rupture of the uterus, and premature labor

Many victims may mask interpersonal violence injuries as "accidents" or justify being hurt by blaming themselves. Attempting to avoid further threats and violence, some women restrict their activities and become less assertive. They accept apologies by their partner, hoping the situation will improve. They may be reluctant to report battering because of financial dependency, immigration status, fear of police or the judicial system, religious or cultural constraints, or fear of retribution by the abuser including further violence or death. Consequently, repeated injury is likely. It is essential to examine *the patient's entire medical history* for indications of previous abuse and to document findings and suspicions in those cases in which the patient's diagnosis cannot be made. Domestic violence cases can also present as stress, anxiety, posttraumatic stress disorder (PTSD), or depressive disorders and be characterized by overutilization of medical services to treat vague, recurring complaints (see Chapter 50: Somatic Symptom and Related Disorders). Ending the relationship does not necessarily end the violence. Up to 40% of women without a current relationship are at risk of violence by a past partner as a result of persistent threatening behavior or stalking.

Elder Abuse

Elder abuse statistics generally involve adults > 60 years of age. There are approximately 500,000 to 1,000,000 victims of elder abuse each year. The National Center on Elder Abuse estimates that more than two thirds of elder abuse perpetrators are spouses, children, or other relatives (https://ncea.acl.gov/). Thus, although some abuse of older persons occurs in institutional settings, the majority of abuse takes place in the home. Evidence of physical assault is often not visible to the casual observer and may become apparent only when assisting with bathing or performing a physical examination. Physical abuse must be differentiated from accidental falls and mishaps resulting from infirmity. Physical abuse is often coupled with neglect and can occur in the context of caregiving challenges (e.g., dementia, handicaps, self-care limitations) that the family member is poorly prepared to handle.

> **Types of Elder Abuse**
> - Failure to provide adequate food, clothing, shelter, hygiene, or medical care
> - Verbal or nonverbal threats or acts that inflict pain, humiliation, or distress, including isolating or infantilizing the person
> - Misuse or illegal use of a person's money or property, including cashing checks without permission or deceiving them into signing documents
> - Physical violence such as slapping or beating as well as inappropriate use of restraints or drugs to control the person
> - Any nonconsensual touching or sexual act
> - Abandonment or threats of abandonment by a caregiver

As is the case for children in child abuse, older persons may be unable to report maltreatment because they are dependent on the perpetrator. Wrongdoing may be denied by the victimized older person and attempts made to cover for the offending family member.

> Self-disparaging comments made by the victim regarding being old or of no value, communicating a sense of resignation, or acceptance of low self-worth may be signs of emotional abuse. Clinical signs of elder abuse include multiple bruises or fractures at different sites and of different ages; genital and urinary tract infections; bleeding; malnutrition; excessive or inadequate medication; and poor hygiene.

Perpetrators of Interpersonal Violence

> **What are common characteristics of a perpetrator?**

Interpersonal violence and abuse is a complex public health problem with multiple determinants affecting a broad and diverse segment of the population. Although there is no evidence to support a single typology, common characteristics of perpetrators of domestic violence include exposure to family violence during childhood, drug or alcohol abuse, rigid assumptions about gender roles, denigrating attitudes toward women, exaggerated need to control, jealousy or paranoia, low self-esteem or depression, difficulty communicating feelings, being prone to anger and hostility, and use of aggressive tactics to deal with interpersonal conflict.

There is growing evidence of health risks associated with chronic anger and hostility that go beyond the victimization of others. In a large ($N = 3,126$) prospective, population-based study of men and women followed since 1985 by the National Institute on Aging, high levels of hostility and difficulty coping with stress at age 25 were associated with the emergence of a variety of health problems in later life. These health problems not only included previously documented cardiovascular risk factors (CVRFs), but lower cognitive functioning during midlife. These risks were enduring, independent of demographic characteristics, educational level, depression, negative life events, midlife smoking and alcohol habits, and lifelong exposure to other CVRFs.

> Perpetrators of interpersonal violence are found in every socioeconomic, educational, racial, ethnic, religious, and political group and are of all ages and both genders.

Perpetrators of child abuse commonly have a history of violent treatment or neglect by their parents during their childhood, which then serves as their model for parenting behavior. As a result, there may be impaired bonding to the child, deficits in child-rearing skills, or developmentally inappropriate expectations for the child's behavior. Stressors, such as socioeconomic pressure, lack of adequate family support, spousal discord, and conflicts over childcare responsibilities, are common in abusing families.

Stranger Violence

Stranger-to-stranger violence includes acts of workplace violence, gang violence, domestic and international terrorism, violent hate crimes targeting specific groups, and random violence associated with criminal activity. The Bureau of Justice statistics show that stranger-to-stranger violence accounts for 52% of male and 31% of female victims. Although stranger assault carries a lower risk of repetition and escalation than intrafamily assault, its physical and psychological effects can be greater. Victims may become emotionally disabled by the apparently senseless and unpredictable quality of the violence and withdraw from what they perceive as an unsafe world.

Violence-Related Trauma Syndrome

> **What is the trauma syndrome?**

The psychological effects of violence closely parallel those experienced by victims of other traumatic events. The psychophysiological distress of the **trauma syndrome** is characterized by pervasive fear and anxiety and accompanied by sleep deprivation, early morning awakening, and recurrent nightmares. Diminished resiliency, inability to concentrate, and emotional instability are common. Somatic complaints may result from actual physical injuries, but more often are related to stress. Suspiciousness, anger, and rage can evolve into morbid hatred of the perpetrator. Grief, depression, and suicidal ideation, especially following multiple traumatic events, can occur. Avoidance, denial, emotional numbing or blocking, and, in some cases, detachment or psychogenic amnesia, may also occur.

Cognitive Signs of the Trauma Syndrome

Signs of **cognitive distress** in traumatized people include viewing the world as unsafe, insane, and devoid of meaning; viewing themselves as damaged; expressing feelings of guilt and self-blaming; developing a sense of personal powerlessness and limited hope for the future (learned helplessness); and believing in the inevitability of violence and abuse. Disturbances in interpersonal relationships include pathological detachment or dependency on the perpetrator after family violence; loss of emotional connection with loved ones after stranger assault; inability to trust or be intimate; emotional instability; avoidance of opportunities for new or more satisfying relationships; difficulty setting limits or establishing boundaries with others; and repetition of previous patterns of interaction.

Posttraumatic Stress Disorder

Although the diagnosis of **posttraumatic stress disorder (PTSD)** was initially given to survivors of natural disasters or war, the disorder is prevalent among individuals who experience interpersonal violence. In fact, while previously categorized as an anxiety disorder, the latest diagnostic schema in the *Diagnostic and Statistical Manual of Mental Disorders, 5th edition* (DSM-5) now regards PTSD as a *trauma- and stressor-related disorder* (see Chapter 47: Stress Disorders, Bereavement, and Dissociative Disorders). PTSD can occur as a result of personal exposure to a traumatic event involving actual or perceived threat of death, serious injury or sexual violation, or knowledge of a similar event affecting an intimate or family member. Victims of violence can experience a range of symptoms ranging from acute stress reactions and more limited emotional disorder (anxiety, depression) to more persistent and profound PTSD. Of note, PTSD can not only result from interpersonal violence and abuse, but also precipitate episodes of such behavior in the form of externalized reckless or destructive behavior. There are gender differences in the expression of PTSD.

DSM-5 also includes a new developmental subtype of PTSD called posttraumatic stress disorder for children 6 years and younger. As the developmental subtype of an existing disorder, this diagnosis acknowledges recent work which focused on the vulnerability of young children

in violent households. Given limitations in self-report, children < 6 years of age can now be assessed with more developmentally sensitive and behaviorally observable indicators that focus on both direct abuse and the witnessing of abuse committed by parental and other adult figures.

Common Features of PTSD

- Intrusive memories or flashbacks of the original trauma
- Nightmares
- Heightened arousal or reactivity such as exaggerated startle response
- Hypervigilance to potential danger
- Numbness or dissociation
- Disturbances in interpersonal relationships (mistrust, inability to become intimate, aggression)
- Negative alterations in cognitions and mood involving fear, anger, depression
- Use of avoidant strategies and lifestyle changes designed to prevent rekindling of reactions to trauma-related stimuli
- Sexual dysfunction

There can also be differences associated with the type of trauma experienced. Some researchers have suggested the term *complex PTSD* to denote trauma symptoms that develop due to prolonged and recurring forms of inescapable psychological abuse or intermittent exposure to lesser, but still intimidating, forms of physical threat by an intimate or controlling family member. Recent data lend support to the notion that *severe psychological forms of abuse* can have an equal or even greater impact on the development of PTSD than many forms of physical assault.

Etiological Factors in Violent Abusive Behaviors

Societal and Situational Factors

Which external or situational factors contribute to violence?

Violence is sanctioned and modeled in sports, the military, law enforcement, certain situations such as self-protective acts by regular citizens, and in various forms of popular media. Institutional acts of violence also exist as sexism, sexual harassment, ageism, and racism. Violence is often precipitated by social and environmental events such as interpersonal conflicts with intimate family members, by territorial disputes between strangers, and by domineering and unjust authority figures. Recent job loss and relationship loss (due to separation or divorce) or being denied access to children can be major events and risk factors for intimate partner violence. Family-related stressors such as pregnancy, the addition of children, or caregiving burden in relationships with older family members have been documented as important correlates in a variety of cases. Psychological factors such as acceptance of aggression as a means of resolving conflict, unrealistic expectations regarding certain types of relationships, prejudicial sentiments toward groups of people, and learned responses to stress and challenge also increase the risk of violence.

Influence of Drugs and Alcohol

Drug and alcohol intoxication increase the risk of violence. The severity of an assault is correlated with the use of alcohol or drugs by either the perpetrator or the victim or both. In some instances, individuals who have no history of violence but who are taking benzodiazepines can become violent, especially following the ingestion of alcohol or abrupt withdrawal from the medication. Taking a careful history about current prescribed and over-the-counter drugs can help detect potential chemical interactions and diagnose atypical reactions to medication. Abuse of illicit drugs such as cocaine, LSD, amphetamines, and phencyclidine hydrochloride (PCP) heightens the risk of violence by increasing arousal, irritability, and the possibility of inducing psychosis or paranoia. Most authorities regard the presence of substance abuse as an exacerbating and compounding problem rather than a cause in most cases of interpersonal violence, indicating the need for intervention for both problems.

Damage to the Central Nervous System

Damage to the hypothalamus or frontal and temporal lobes of the brain increases the likelihood of aggressive and assaultive behavior. The individual who has brain damage may have limited ability to assess degree of threat, or to manage frustration or anger. Rarely, a seizure disorder (e.g., temporal lobe epilepsy or complex partial seizures) can elicit violence, but this type of behavior is usually diffuse, disorganized, and stereotyped. The number of people who perpetrate violent acts due to neurological impairment is relatively small, but this etiology should be considered because it represents a potentially treatable cause of aggressive behavior. Specialized anger management treatment protocols developed for *traumatic brain injury* populations have shown promising results (see Hart, Fann, Brockway, & Maiuro, 2016, in Recommended Readings).

Psychiatric Conditions

Violent behavior is not specific to certain psychiatric conditions. With the exception of *intermittent explosive disorder*, which includes violent behavior by definition, many diagnostic categories list aggressive behavior as one of many possible manifestations of emotional instability and impaired impulse control (see Chapter 49: Disruptive, Impulse-Control, and Conduct Disorders). Thus, psychopathology is best viewed as a vulnerability factor that makes anger and assaultive behavior more likely, rather than as a causal factor per se. Furthermore, the presence of a psychiatric illness is neither necessary nor sufficient for violence and victimization to occur. That said, some forms of psychiatric disorder (e.g., intermittent explosive disorder, antisocial and borderline personality disorders, bipolar and paranoid schizophrenia) may be associated with an increased risk for violent behavior, if the condition is poorly managed or if the individual is experiencing an acute emotional breakdown.

Violence as a Crime

The types of violence discussed above are crimes in most states. Elder and child abuse are considered crimes in all states. Although these behaviors are crimes, current professional policy dictates that the perpetrator receive attention from both the criminal justice and health care systems. Health care providers must become familiar with local reporting requirements to ensure compliance with these laws. The Joint Commission on Accreditation of Health Care Organizations requires the identification of interpersonal violence and abuse in clinical settings and the implementation of protocols for identification, assessment, and diagnosis. Health care providers must be able to recognize cases of violence, assess the risk for further harm, and make reasonable efforts to protect the patient, family members, and potential victims from physical and emotional harm. Except for cases involving threats to life, serious bodily injury, lasting or disfiguring trauma, broken teeth and bones, or use of a weapon, most states do not require mandatory reporting of spouse abuse. Such decisions are usually best made in collaboration with victims to preserve trust, to empower them to take action as they feel appropriate, and to avoid inadvertently exposing them to increased risk.

Intervention

The CDC has adopted the **RADAR** system to encourage health providers to intervene in case of interpersonal violence:

R = Routinely screen for violence- and abuse-related injury and symptoms during the course of customary care.

A = Ask direct questions about violence and abuse in private, in a nonjudgmental manner. (See HITS below as an example of a screening tool.)

D = Document findings in the chart, with use of body maps and photos for evidentiary purposes.

A = Assess the patient's immediate safety and develop a safety plan.

R = Review options and refer the patient to in-house and community-based resources.

HITS is a four-question screening instrument validated for both female and male patients. Over the last 12 months, how often did your domestic partner (or anyone else):

1. Hurt you physically?
2. Insult you?
3. Threaten you with harm?
4. Scream or curse at you?

Points: 1 = *never,* 2 = *rarely,* 3 = *sometimes,* 4 = *fairly often,* 5 = *frequently*

Scores > 10 for female patient indicate victimization
Scores > 11 for male patient indicate victimization

From Sherin, K. M., Sinacore, J. M., Li, X. Q., Zitter, R. E., & Shakil, A. (1998). HITS: A short domestic violence screening tool for use in a family practice setting. *Family Medicine, 30*(7), 508–512. Reproduced with permission of first author, Kevin Sherin. For further reproduction contact him at sherinkmj@gmail.com.

Education and Prevention

Men and women from all socioeconomic strata and lifestyles can be victims and perpetrators of violence. Repeated exposure to less severe forms of interpersonal violence can still be associated with serious risk for physical and mental health problems in both adults and children. However, recent studies indicate that patient screening and resource information protocols alone have limited impact upon immediate physical and mental health. It is often necessary to have a follow-up protocol that requires tertiary levels of intervention

Tertiary prevention of violence and abuse requires referral to social work staff, as well as access to specialized crisis intervention programs, women's shelters, emergency response and safety planning, legal advocacy, and perpetrator interventions. A recent controlled trial among African American women has demonstrated that a brief psychobehavioral intervention can be effective in reducing recurrent intimate partner violence during pregnancy and postpartum. Most states now have guidelines and standards of care for counseling programs that can be offered to perpetrators of domestic abuse. Most communities offer low-cost positive parenting classes that can also be recommended as part of the overall care and wellness counseling offered by a health care provider.

Secondary prevention requires education, particularly among health care professionals, and effective public service campaigns. Primary prevention involves eradicating sexism, power imbalances, racism, ageism, and elitism, and increasing individual responsibility for promoting zero tolerance for violence. It also requires beginning early to educate children about healthy, nonviolent relationships and conflict resolution and their parents about positive parenting practices and prosocial modeling.

Recommended Readings

Dillon, G., Hussain, R., Loxton, D., & Rahman, S. (2013). Mental and physical health and intimate partner violence against women: A review of the literature. *International Journal of Family Medicine,* 313909. http://doi.org/10.1155/2013/313909

Hart, T., Fann, J. R., Brockway, J. A., & Maiuro, R. D. (2016). Treatment of anger and aggression following acquired brain injury. In P. Sturmey (Ed.), *The Wiley handbook of violence and aggression.* New York, NY: Wiley.

Kiely, M., El-Mohandes, A. A. E., El-Khorazaty, M. N, & Gantz, M. G. (2010). An integrated intervention in pregnant African Americans reduces postpartum risk: A randomized trial. *Obstetrics and Gynecology, 112*(3), 611–620.

Maiuro, R. D. & Eberle, J. A. (2008). State standards for domestic violence perpetrator treatment: Current status, trends, and recommendations. *Violence and Victims*, *23*, 133–155. http://doi.org/10.1891/0886-6708.23.2.133

Wallace, H., & Roberson, C. (2013). *Family violence: Legal, medical, and social perspectives* (7th ed.). New York, NY: Routledge.

World Health Organization. (2013). *Responding to intimate partner violence and sexual violence against women: WHO clinical and policy guidelines*. Geneva, Switzerland: Author.

Review Questions

1. The *diagnostic triad* for shaken baby syndrome commonly includes which of the following medical findings?
   A. Bruises around the neck, subdural hematoma, and brain swelling
   B. Contusions to the front and back of the head, subdural hematoma, and brain swelling
   C. Evidence of prior bone fractures, retinal bleeding, and brain swelling
   D. Grip marks on the upper torso, subdural hematoma, and brain swelling
   E. Subdural hematoma, retinal bleeding, and brain swelling

2. PTSD can be characterized by which of the following statements?
   A. It can be associated with both victimization and perpetration.
   B. It can occur in adults and children.
   C. It can result from severe psychological abuse in the absence of life-threatening physical assault.
   D. It is typified by persisting behavioral, cognitive, emotional, and physiological reactivity.
   E. All of the above

3. In most states, it is mandatory to report which of the following?
   A. Child abuse
   B. Elder abuse
   C. Gunshot wounds
   D. Life-threatening intentional injuries
   E. All of the above

Answer Key on p. 465

26 Poverty and Homelessness

K. Ramsey McGowen, PhD

- How is poverty defined?
- How many people are poor?
- What is life like when living in poverty?
- What are the medical implications of poverty?
- Who is without a home?
- What is it like to be homeless?
- What are the medical implications of homelessness?
- What are effective interventions in working with the poor or homeless?

Social factors are major influences on health and disease: Approximately 60% of premature deaths are attributable to nonbiological causes. The network of **social determinants of health** include a variety of complex and interacting phenomena such as education, economic stability, social status, and social cohesion. These factors are not static but, instead, can be aggravated or mitigated by other circumstances. Poverty and homelessness are two important factors in this network that have profound medical consequences.

Poverty

Definition

How is poverty defined?

The US Census Bureau establishes **poverty thresholds** based on data reflecting the amount of cash income that is required to support families of various sizes. The thresholds are used primarily for statistical purposes to track poverty rates. This amount is adjusted annually for inflation, but not for geographic variations in living costs. The US Department of Health and Human Services (HHS) issues simplified versions of the poverty thresh-

Table 26.1. 2017 Poverty Guidelines for the 48 Contiguous States and the District of Columbia

Persons in Family/ Household	Poverty Guideline
1	US $12,060
2	US $16,240
3	US $20,420
4	US $24,600
5	US $28,780
6	US $32,960
7	US $37,140
8	US $41,320

For families/households with more than 8 persons, add US $4,180 for each additional person.
Retrieved from https://aspe.hhs.gov/poverty-guidelines

olds, termed **poverty guidelines**. The guidelines establish separate figures for the mainland US and for Alaska and Hawaii. The HHS guidelines are used for administrative purposes such as determining eligibility for various programs including Head Start, food stamps, school lunch and other nutritional supplement programs, Legal Services for the poor, and the Job Corps. In addition, many state and local governments and nonprofit organizations use these guidelines to determine program eligibility. These guidelines are published each year in the *Federal Register*. The 2016 guidelines for the mainland US are listed in Table 26.1.

Distribution of Poverty by Age, Location, Race, and Ethnicity

How many people are poor?

In 2014, the US Census Bureau reported that 14.8% of all persons in the US lived in poverty. Poverty rates have remained relatively static in recent years (see Figure 26.1). The 2014 poverty rate for Blacks was 26.2%, Hispanics 23.6%, Asians 12.0%, and non-Hispanic Whites 10.1%. Although the percentage of those in poverty is much higher for Black and Hispanic individuals, the absolute number of individuals in poverty is much greater for Whites since Whites make up the largest segment of the population. Therefore, the typical person living in poverty is White. The

2014 poverty rate for children under the age of 18 was 21.1% (see Figure 26.2).

There are significant variations in poverty in different geographic areas of the US. For example, poverty is more prevalent in the Sunbelt (southern states in the US), although pockets of high poverty exist throughout the country. Figure 26.3 shows the regional distribution of poverty across the US.

Poverty is a multifaceted phenomenon that has both objective and subjective dimensions. Objectively, poverty is defined in economic terms by one of two means. Definitions using **absolute poverty** specify an income threshold considered the minimum amount necessary for survival (basic shelter, food, and clothing). **Relative poverty** defines poverty in comparative terms and stipulates poverty as a proportion of the median income in a society, below which people are effectively excluded from attaining the average standard of living in their society (e.g., below 60% of annual median income). The US uses an absolute standard; the UK and EU use a relative standard to define poverty.

Poverty also has a subjective dimension that should be incorporated into a more complete definition. **Subjective poverty** includes the sense of

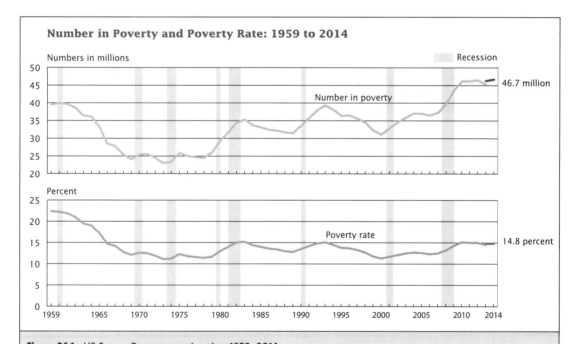

Figure 26.1. US Census Bureau poverty rates, 1959–2014.
From US Census Bureau, *Income and Poverty in the United States: 2014*. Retrieved from https://www.census.gov/content/dam/Census/library/publications/2015/demo/p60-252.pdf

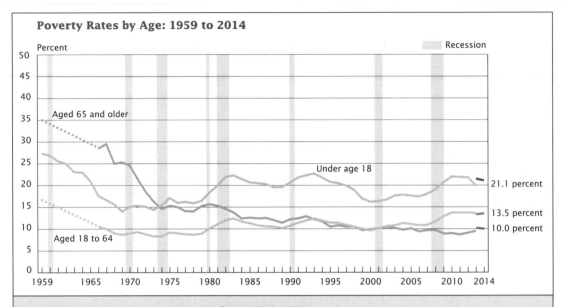

Figure 26.2. US Census Bureau poverty rates by age, 1959–2014.
From US Census Bureau, *Income and Poverty in the United States: 2014*. Retrieved from https://www.census.gov/content/dam/Census/library/publications/2015/demo/p60-252.pdf

well-being (or its opposite, a compromised quality of life), social setting, cultural values, psychological resources, and context of an individual's experience. It includes the extent to which people believe they are empowered or deprived in a society based on the resources available to them.

What is life like when living in poverty?

Poverty is not the same for everyone. Different forms of poverty are associated with different attitudes, beliefs, and outcomes. **Generational poverty** occurs when at least two generations of a family have lived on limited financial and other resources (e.g., psychological, educational, relational) and never owned property. Generational poverty is often accompanied by a family history of low educational attainment, a focus on survival, and **learned helplessness**. It is the form of poverty people are least likely to escape. **Situational poverty** results from an event such as being laid off or divorced, or experiencing chronic illness. People in situational poverty often have experienced stability and have a middle-class perspective. Situational poverty also is associated with having more resources in domains other than finances,

such as prior educational attainments, supportive relationships, and an attitude that poverty is escapable. Situational poverty is more common than generational poverty. The 2014 census reports that during the 4-year period from 2009 to 2012, 34.5% of the population had at least one period of poverty lasting 2 or more months but that 2.7% of the population lived in poverty during all 48 of those months. **Working class poverty** refers to those who are in the workforce but whose income falls below the cutoff for poverty (Figure 26.4). Working class poverty involves never having extra money, living from paycheck to paycheck, and focusing on survival. Dealing with unexpected expenses, medical care, or emergencies presents major difficulties in this situation. According to the Bureau of Labor Statistics, 7% of those in the workforce fall into the working poor category, but this percentage varies significantly by race.

Poverty and Biopsychosocial Health

What are the medical implications of poverty?

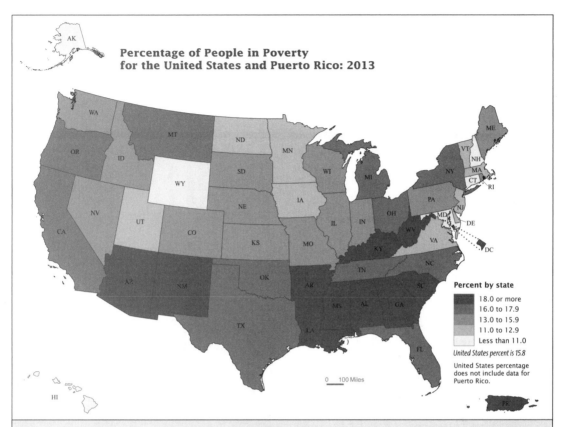

Figure 26.3. US Census Bureau: regional variations in poverty.
From US Census Bureau, *2013 American Community Survey and 2013 Puerto Rico Community Survey*. Retrieved from
https://www.census.gov/content/dam/Census/library/publications/2014/acs/acsbr13-01.pdf

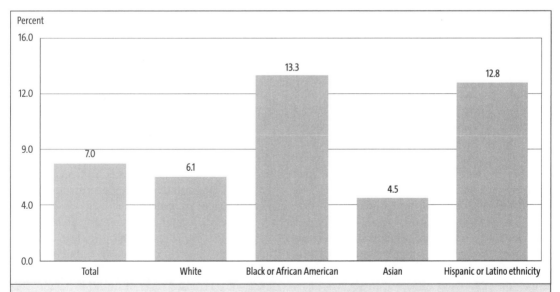

Figure 26.4. Working class poverty rates by race and ethnicity, 2013. *Note*. People whose ethnicity is identified as Hispanic or Latina may be of any race.
From US Bureau of Labor Statistics, *Current Population Survey (CPS), Annual Social and Economic Supplement (ASEC)*.

Income is a significant determinant of both physical and mental health. Low income is associated with increased morbidity and mortality from a variety of conditions, especially those that are chronic. The Centers for Disease Control (CDC) and National Center for Health Statistics (NCHS) have reported that the medical consequences for individuals living in poverty compared with those whose income was at least four times the poverty level include:

- a fivefold higher rate of poor or fair health (not good or excellent);
- being twice as likely to have multiple health problems;
- having 93% higher utilization of emergency department care; and
- being more likely to forego needed prescription drugs due to cost.

Children and adolescents are particularly adversely affected by poverty. They experience higher rates of:

- chronic conditions such as asthma, anemia, and pneumonia;
- acute health problems such as multiple ear infections;
- exposure to environmental contaminants such as lead paint and toxic waste;
- exposure to violence that can cause injury or death; and
- having no usual source of health care.

A **life course perspective** suggests that children who grow up in poverty experience lifelong detrimental effects in physical, mental, and social functioning. In addition to the increased frequency of various health problems, children who experience **toxic stress** (extreme stress during development) may show structural changes in their central nervous system and neurobiological damage resulting in emotional dysregulation (see Chapter 7: Stress, Adaptation, and Stress Disorders). These adversities not only disrupt childhood but may also sow the seeds for chronic health problems in adulthood. The means by which this occurs may be through exposure to extreme stress during sensitive periods (e.g., nutritional deprivation, violence), the cumulative effects of stress over many years of exposure, or living in circumstances that create a social trajectory of disadvantage and limited options.

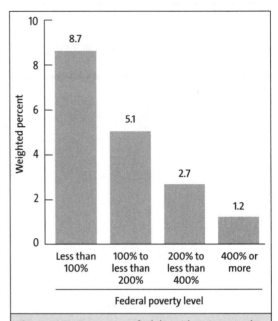

Figure 26.5. Percentage of adults with serious psychological distress, by income relative to federal poverty level: US, 2009–2013.
From CDC/NCHS, *National Health Interview Survey, 2009–2013.* Retrieved from https://www.cdc.gov/nchs/products/databriefs/db203.htm

Poverty also is linked to poorer mental health. Rates of mental illness are higher among the poor; those in the lowest income brackets have a twofold to threefold increase in diagnosable psychiatric conditions. Those below the poverty level are almost 8 times more likely to report serious psychological distress (see Figure 26.5). Depression is 4 or more times more likely to occur among those living in poverty across all life stages (Figure 26.6).

The **social drift hypothesis** speculates that the presence of mental illness leads to declines in socioeconomic status. However, data suggest that poverty is more likely to precede mental illness than to be a consequence.

The relationship between poverty and health is complicated. Those living in poverty face exposure to multiple sources of **stress**, including violence and chaotic life circumstances. Poverty is associated with increased rates of health behaviors that increase medical risk such as smoking and poor dietary patterns. Adults living in poverty, however, do not necessarily differ significantly in some mal-

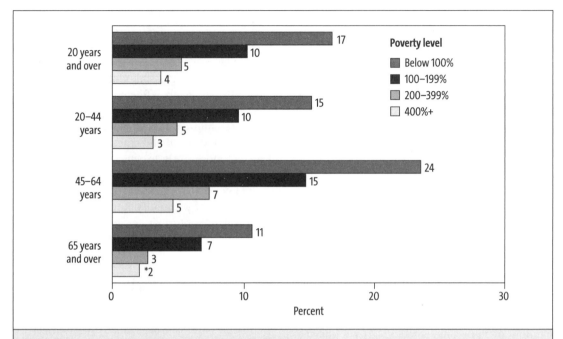

Figure 26.6. Depression by age and poverty level, 2005–2010.
From CDC/NCHS, *Health, United States, 2011* (Figure 33). Data from the National Health and Nutrition Examination Survey. Retrieved from https://www.cdc.gov/nchs/data/hus/hus11.pdf

adaptive health behavior. For example, they are no more likely to engage in heavy or binge drinking. Individual health behaviors are also affected by certain societal constraints such as reduced access to health care and limited interventions suited to low-income circumstances. In addition, low-income housing areas typically have limited resources for healthy food choices, are characterized by unsafe surroundings, are situated in areas of increased exposure to environmental hazards such as air pollution, and offer few accessible green spaces, all of which combine to create barriers to healthy lifestyles. **Food insecurity** is a common occurrence among the poor. Individuals not only often skip meals but they also have limited, typically nonnutritious food choices when they are able to purchase food. The **hunger–obesity paradox** describes the finding that although the poor have limited access to food, they are more likely to be obese. This may be in part because inexpensive foods are more likely to be high calorie, low nutrition selections. It may also reflect the fact that the stress and inconsistent access to food associated with poverty produce physiological changes that affect fat storage. Finally, the poor may use maladaptive mechanisms

such as smoking to cope with stressors. Thus, the relationship between poverty and health is bidirectional, with poverty leading to poorer health and poorer health contributing to poverty.

Homelessness

Definition

Who is without a home?

Homelessness occurs when an individual lacks a regular and adequate nighttime residence and has a primary nighttime residence that is either a supervised temporary shelter, an institution that provides a temporary residence for individuals intended to be institutionalized, or a place not designed or ordinarily used for sleeping by humans. The exact number of homeless individuals is difficult to document. The US Department of Housing and Urban Development (HUD) obtains data on homelessness by collecting a point-in-time count from communities, usually conducted on a single night in late January. According to HUD, 564,708 people were homeless in the US in January 2015. Of that number, 36% were people in families with children, while 64% were individuals; 15% of homeless individuals were considered "chronically" homeless; and 8% were military veterans.

What is it like to be homeless?

In the US, homelessness is usually temporary, although those who experience homelessness are more likely to have unstable housing over the long term, causing disruption in social, educational, and health domains. Chronic homelessness is often the public face of homelessness despite being a relatively small proportion of the homeless population. Families often become homeless after a financial setback such as a medical emergency. Youths frequently become homeless after family disruptions such as divorce, abuse, or neglect, or leaving home because of conflict over issues like coming out as lesbian, gay, bisexual, or transgender (LGBT).

Veterans may experience long-term adjustment problems leading to homelessness as a result of service-related disabilities. The ethnic make-up of the homeless population varies according to geographic location. HUD reports that among individuals using shelters in cities, 40.4% are African American; among individuals using shelters in rural areas, 25.9% are African American.

Etiological Factors

Multiple factors lead to homelessness, including poverty, unemployment, mental illness, domestic violence, and a lack of affordable housing. Affordable housing is a common problem, and many individuals working in low-wage earning jobs earn insufficient income to afford reasonable housing.

The biggest risk factor for homelessness is poverty, and the factors associated with poverty are common in the homeless population, such as stress and unstable social environments. Homelessness also is associated with high rates of traumatic events. The typical homeless family is headed by a single mother with young children, who has experienced physical or sexual assault. Being homeless places families in situations in which they are at greater risk of family dissolution, assault, or witnessing violence. Children are especially adversely affected by homelessness. They are sick and hungry twice as often as non-homeless children. Frequent moves disrupt their education and social and emotional development. They are more likely to repeat a grade as well as have a learning disability. **Food insecurity** and the hunger-obesity paradox and the life course implications of accumulating risks are relevant to those who are homeless as well as those who live in poverty.

Homelessness and Health

What are the medical implications of homelessness?

Homelessness has numerous health implications. The National Health Care for the Homeless Council summarizes these concerns as exposure to the elements (e.g., frostbite, hypothermia), violence, stress, malnutrition, and unsanitary conditions. They state that "healing and recovery are nearly impossible without a home." The risk for mortality is 2 to 5 times higher for homeless individuals. Increased rates of infectious diseases (HIV, tuberculosis, pneumonia), chronic diseases (cardiovascular disease, chronic obstructive pulmonary disease), trauma, and skin disorders are documented among the homeless. Homeless individuals are less likely to have a place for routine care, to receive standard preventive and health screening procedures, and to access prescription medications, dental care, eyeglasses, and surgery. In addition, keeping up with medications and appointments is complicated by not having a reliable address or phone number.

Mental health and substance abuse problems are frequent among the homeless. About 25% of the homeless population is estimated to have some form of severe mental illness, and a higher percentage experience other forms of psychiatric disorders. Serious mental illness is associated with impairments in functional abilities such as self-care and in maintaining supportive social relationships. The homeless often tend to misinterpret efforts to assist them or provide treatment. Attempts to cope by using street drugs or alcohol are common. Substance abuse and dependence also are common. The combination of mental illness, substance abuse, and physical health problems makes it difficult for these individuals to obtain employment, let alone stable housing.

Interventions

> What are effective interventions in working with the poor or homeless?

Providing health care for poor or homeless individuals is challenging and highlights the importance of an *integrated services model*. Improving care for these populations requires individual and systems innovations.

On a systems level, *integrated and collaborative care networks* that simultaneously address physical and mental health may be especially helpful for individuals facing obstacles such as poverty and homelessness. The National Health Care for the Homeless Council has proposed innovative approaches such as **medical respite care** for the homeless who are too frail to recover from medical problems on the street, but too well to remain in the hospital. An evaluation of medical respite care demonstrated cost savings and success in reducing readmissions. The Agency for Healthcare Research and Quality (AHRQ) has documented that innovations such as mobile or shelter-based clinics and programs that reduce barriers to supportive housing are associated with cost savings and reduced utilization of emergency care. Screening for social factors such as poverty and food insecurity would enable physicians to develop more appropriate interventions for their patients in these circumstances.

Addressing systems biases and obstacles is also important. Incorporating public health perspectives into the design of social policy can help mitigate the many health issues of those who are poor or homeless. The norms, unwritten rules, and priorities for daily life that function to help the poor and homeless survive complicate their ability to participate in the standard medical interventions that are based on middle class life circumstances. For example, recommending exercise such as

walking around the neighborhood is ineffective for someone living in a high crime area. Thus, working collaboratively to find practical interventions for patients who are homeless or financially limited is critical.

Health care providers are susceptible to the **fundamental attribution error**: minimizing the role of external factors and ascribing the cause of an individual's behavior or situation to their character or personality. This implicit cognitive disposition can lead to blaming individuals for the hardships they experience and create barriers to the effective care, empathy, and patient-centered attitudes that are essential to professionalism. Developing cognitive strategies to counteract this implicit tendency is crucial to working effectively with members of these populations. Ultimately, creative and comprehensive approaches will be required to intervene effectively in resolving these multifactorial problems.

Recommended Readings

Braveman, P. (2007). Do we have real poverty in the United States? *Preventing Chronic Disease, 4*(4), A84.

Conroy, K., Sandel, M., & Zuckerman, B. (2010). Poverty grown up: How childhood socioeconomic status impacts adult health. *Journal of Developmental and Behavioral Pediatrics, 31*(2), 154–160. http://doi.org/10.1097/DBP.0b013e3181c21a1b

Fazel, S., Geddes, J. R., & Kushel, M. (2014). The health of homeless people in high-income countries: Descriptive epidemiology, health consequences, and clinical and policy recommendations. *Lancet, 384*(9953), 1529–1540.

Galea, S., Tracy, M., Hoggatt, K. J., DiMaggio, C., & Karpati, A. (2011). Estimated deaths attributable to social factors in the United States. *American Journal of Public Health, 101*(8), 1456–1465. http://doi.org/10.2105/AJPH.2010.300086

O'Connell, J. (2005). *Premature mortality in homeless populations: A review of the literature.* Nashville, TN: National Health Care for the Homeless Council.

Schanzer, B., Dominguez, B., Shrout, P. E., & Caton, C. L. (2007). Homelessness, health status, and health care use. *American Journal of Public Health, 97*(3), 464–469. http://doi.org/10.2105/AJPH.2005.076190

Schroeder, S.A. (2007). We can do better – Improving the health of the American people. *New England Journal of Medicine, 357,* 1221–1228. http://doi.org/10.1056/NEJMsa073350

Stringhini, S., Sabia, S., Shipley, M., Brunner, E., Nabi, H. Kivimaki, M. & Sing-Manoux, A. (2010). Association of socioeconomic position with health behaviors and mortality. *Journal of the American Medical Association, 303*(12), 1159–1166. http://doi.org/10.1001/jama.2010.297

Additional Resources

National Child Traumatic Stress Network. Available at http://www.nctsnet.org/nccts/nav.do?pid=hom_main

National Health Care for the Homeless Council. Available at http://www.nhchc.org/

National Poverty Center. Available at http://www.npc.umich.edu/

Robert Wood Johnson Foundation-Social Determinants of Health. Available at http://www.rwjf.org/en/our-topics/topics/social-determinants-of-health.html

Substance Abuse and Mental, Health Administration – Homelessness Resources Center. Available at http://homeless.samhsa.gov/default.aspx

Review Questions

1. Which segment of the population has the highest percentage living in poverty?
   A. Asian
   B. Black
   C. Hispanic
   D. Non-Hispanic White
   E. Pacific Islander

2. Among the factors listed, a person experiencing homelessness most commonly
   A. is a military veteran
   B. is in a family with children
   C. lacks an established place for routine medical care
   D. lives in homelessness as a chronic condition
   E. participates in the labor force

3. The Edwards family lives in Morehead, Kentucky, and consists of Jane and her 4-year-old twins, Jared and Janelle. Jane works 30 hr per week in a minimum wage job. The annual family income is US $11,430. The Edwards family
   A. is less likely than the general population to be exposed to environmental contaminants
   B. is living in subjective poverty
   C. is not considered poor because Jane is working
   D. might be eligible for social services, if their income is < 60% of the national median income
   E. would be eligible for social services such as Head Start for the children

4. Someone in generational poverty is more likely to have
   A. a belief that poverty is inescapable
   B. a reduced likelihood that the children will be adversely affected
   C. an average level of educational attainment
   D. better access to social services than someone in situational poverty
   E. resources to enable escaping poverty such as educational attainments

Answer Key on p. 465

27 Suicide

Alexander L. Chapman, PhD, RPsych, Jessica F. Ferreira, BA, and Keyne C. Law, MA

- How many people die by suicide each year?
- Why do people die by suicide?
- What are the major risk and protective factors related to suicidal behavior?
- When and how do I conduct a thorough risk assessment?
- What treatments or interventions are recommended for suicidal patients?

Definitions and Incidence of Suicide

How many people die by suicide each year?

Suicide claims over 45,000 lives annually in the US and Canada and more than 1 million lives worldwide. For every suicide, six other people are closely affected, for an estimated total of 270,000 people in North America. Both attempted and completed suicides place a heavy cost burden on the health care system, which is estimated to be about US $51 billion annually in direct medical costs and in indirect costs such as loss of productivity.

Not all self-injurious behaviors are suicidal acts. **Nonsuicidal self-injury** involves the direct and deliberate destruction of body tissue without the intent to die. **Suicidal behavior** encompasses related yet distinct behaviors, including *suicidal ideation* (e.g., thoughts, beliefs, or images that involve the intention of ending one's own life); *suicide attempts*, or nonfatal self-inflicted harmful behaviors that involve the intent to die as a result of the behavior; and *suicide*, or fatalities caused by self-inflicted harmful behaviors with the intent to die.

Suicide is a very common cause of death in the US among individuals 15 to 34 years old, and the 10th leading cause of death overall. In recent years, more people have died by suicide than homicide, and the number of suicides in the US and Canada appears to be increasing. Thirty times more people attempt suicide each year than those who complete suicide. Death by suicide is approximately 4 times more common among males than females; however, *attempted* suicide is 3 times more common among females than males. These gender differences are associated with the use of more lethal, violent means among men vs. women. For example, men are most likely to use firearms whereas poisoning (e.g., medication or drug overdose) is most common among females.

Other demographic patterns are noteworthy. Whites die by suicide more frequently than non-Whites, with the exception of individuals aged 15 to 24. Among late adolescents and young adults, American Indians have the highest rate of suicide per 100,000 people. Suicide rates are the lowest among the married and highest among the divorced, separated, and widowed. Approximately 90% of those who die by suicide have a diagnosable psychiatric disorder at the time of death. Suicidal behavior, however, occurs across all demographic groups and, thus, suicidality should be routinely and systematically evaluated with patients suffering from mental health problems as well as those with serious physical health concerns.

Theories of Suicide

Why do people die by suicide?

Thomas Joiner's **interpersonal theory of suicide** proposes that feelings of thwarted belongingness (the unmet human need to belong), perceived burdensomeness (belief that one is a burden to others), and the capability to attempt suicide predict suicidality. This theory posits that desire (caused by thwarted belongingness and perceived burdensomeness) and capability of engaging in suicidal behavior are not the same, and that individuals possessing both factors are at greater risk than those with desire or capability alone.

The **three-step theory** suggests that the development of suicidal ideation and the progression from thinking about suicide to acting involves distinct processes. Specifically, suicide ideation arises from a combination of pain and hopelessness and becomes serious when pain outweighs feelings of connectedness to others. Dispositional, acquired, and practical factors that increase the ability to inflict lethal self-injury then facilitate the transition from ideation to action. The **strain theory of suicide** is a sociological theory suggesting that four competing pressures or strains in an individual's life usually precede suicide: value strain (conflicting values), aspiration strain (discrepancy between aspiration and reality), deprivation strain (e.g., poverty), and coping strain (lack of effective coping skills). **Diathesis-stress models of suicide** postulate that people with certain biological predispositions (e.g., serotonergic system dysfunction, elevated cortisol levels, and hyperactive hypothalamic-pituitary-adrenocortical axis [HPA] axis) may have a lower threshold for suicidal behavior. According to these models, biological precursors are necessary but insufficient conditions for suicide. Precipitating stressors must be present for an individual to attempt or die by suicide.

By combining these theories, a transactional *biopsychosocial model* conceptualizes suicidal behavior as the result of complex transactions among biological (e.g., genetics, brain and neurotransmitter functioning), psychological (e.g., hopelessness, depression), social, and environmental (e.g., deprivation, thwarted belongingness) factors. In this model, risk factors and suicidal behavior influence each other in a dynamic interplay. In a diathesis-stress model, an individual with elevated cortisol levels may be vulnerable to, or have a lower threshold for, suicide but does not engage in suicidal behavior unless faced with psychological or environmental precipitants. However, a biopsychosocial model assumes a *transactional* relationship such that social or environmental factors increase psychological and physiological (e.g., cortisol) manifestations of stress and set the occasion for actions that may increase or reduce risk through the generation of additional stress (e.g., crises) or the deployment of effective coping methods, respectively. An interplay of environmental, behavioral, and physiological factors influences the likelihood of suicidal behavior at any given time. Over the longer term, suicidal behavior may result in negative changes in the environment (withdrawal of support, conflict), neurobiological changes, and reduced capacity for effective problem solving, all further increasing the risk of eventual suicide. This framework acknowledges the reciprocal relationship among risk factors and recognizes that understanding the interaction among these factors is necessary to explain the complexity of suicidal behavior.

Risk Factors

Acute Risk Factors

> What are the major risk and protective factors related to suicidal behavior?

The probability that an individual will make a suicide attempt generally increases with the number of risk factors present. However, not all factors confer equal levels of risk. The most robust predictor of suicide attempts is a history of previous suicide attempts, especially within the past 2 years. About one third of individuals who have made a suicide attempt will make another attempt within a year. The presence of a plan, availability of means, and preparatory behaviors (e.g., acquiring or researching means for suicide, preparing a will) are also indicators of elevated acute suicidal risk. As such, restricting access to means (e.g., removing any guns from the home) is an important step in suicide risk management.

Acute risk factors indicate an imminent danger of suicide. When combined with other personal and biological predisposing factors, environmental stressors significantly increase the likelihood of suicidal acts in the near future. Many stressors are intuitive, such as a recent loss or the diagnosis of a terminal condition. Suicide attempts are highest within the first year following these stressors. Some seemingly positive changes (e.g., improvement in depressive symptoms, release from a psychiatric hospital) also can increase acute suicide risk. In patients with schizophrenia, one third of suicides occur during admission or within 1 week of discharge from the hospital. *Individuals presenting with acute risks warrant immediate risk assessment.*

Acute and Imminent Risk Factors

Unmodifiable

Recent or past year:
- Suicide attempt
- Major life stress (e.g., divorce, job loss, death of a friend or family member)
- Discharge from a psychiatric hospital or abrupt clinical change
- Diagnosis of a terminal condition
- Severe weight loss
- Imprisonment – *especially first night of incarceration*

Modifiable

Current:
- Suicidal ideation, intent, or self-harm
- Specific suicide plans and preparation for suicide
- Availability and ease of access to preferred or lethal means
- Feelings of hopelessness and burdensomeness
- Social withdrawal
- Excessive or increased alcohol or drug consumption
- Sleep disturbances including insomnia and nightmares
- Severe affective states including marked agitation, irritability, or panic
- Increased recklessness, impulsivity, or risk-taking – *especially if out of character*

Chronic Risk Factors

Chronic risk factors are ongoing and put the individual continually at risk for suicidal behavior. In the absence of other influences, these individuals are typically not in immediate danger, but a thorough risk assessment and referral for treatment to help manage suicide risk is still pertinent.

Chronic Risk Factors

Unmodifiable

A history of:
- Suicidal behavior or previous attempts
- Psychiatric treatment
- Parental psychiatric disorders, violence, divorce, or substance abuse
- Numerous or severe prior negative life events
- Childhood maltreatment
- Traumatic brain injury
- Reduced neurotrophic signalling – *especially the serotonin pathway*
- Hyperactivity in the hypothalamic-pituitary-adrenocortical (HPA) axis
- Genetic predisposition (protein kinase A dysfunction, BDNF 66MET allele)
- Old age

Modifiable
- Lack of social support
- Diagnosable psychiatric disorder, especially mood, personality, psychotic, and substance abuse disorders – *risk increases 90 fold if ≥ 1 coexisting psychiatric and medical disorder is present*
- Feelings of hopelessness
- Unemployment
- Unmarried/single

As with acute risk factors, some chronic factors are static, while others can be modified through intervention. Negative life events are often predisposing risk factors but differ from acute stressors in the amount of time that has passed since the event (i.e., > 1 year). Individuals who experienced maltreatment or abuse during childhood or whose parents were violent, abused substances, had psychiatric disorders (especially psychotic or mood disorders), or were divorced are also more likely to engage in suicidal behaviors.

Individuals with *chronic medical disorders* are also at increased risk of suicide, especially if the condition causes functional impairment or pain. Individuals with cancer, HIV, parkinsonism, or amyotrophic lateral sclerosis (ALS) typically have higher suicide rates than healthy individuals or individuals with less debilitating disorders such as diabetes. Furthermore, there is evidence that hyperactivity in the HPA axis, through non-suppression of the cortisol response, may cause vulnerability to suicidal behavior. Hyperactivity of the HPA axis may occur in response to chronic stressors that lead to elevated cortisol levels, which, in turn, may inhibit neuroprotective brain trophic factors and neurogenesis (see Chapter 2: Predisposition). There is also evidence that genetic vulnerabilities contribute to reduced neurotrophic signaling, especially in the serotonin pathway, which can contribute to suicidal vulnerability.

Protective Factors

Identifying and strengthening **protective factors** can facilitate assessment and intervention. Having a strong social support system, feeling hopeful, having goals and reasons for living, and engaging in effective coping skills are strong protective factors and should be encouraged in suicidal patients. The majority of people contemplating suicide are ambivalent about dying and wish to escape the pain of their current circumstances. Therefore, hope that the current situation will change, expectations that they will be able to cope and overcome difficulties in the future, and commitment to solving their current problems are crucial protective factors.

Key Protective Factors

- Adherence to effective treatment
- Strong social support
- Hopefulness/goals/reasons for living
- Coping skills
- Stable relationships or responsibility to others
- Fear of suicide, death, or dying
- Fear of social disapproval/belief suicide is immoral
- Willingness to follow crisis plan
- Access to material resources (e.g., food, clothing, shelter)

Suicide Risk Assessment

When and how do I conduct a thorough risk assessment?

The majority of health professionals will interact with a suicidal patient at least once during their career. Underestimating a patient's risk can have tragic consequences; thus, it is essential that all clinicians be well-informed about how to assess suicide risk.

Warning Signs

All patients seeking treatment for, or complaining of, life stresses or mental health symptoms should be screened for suicide risk. This can be as simple as asking the patient if they have been having any thoughts about suicide. Often providers are hesitant to raise the topic of suicide for fear of giving someone the idea, but there is no evidence that asking the question raises suicide risk. On the contrary, inquiring about suicide informs the patient that suicidal thoughts are appropriate to discuss. Questions should be direct and specific and include the words "suicide" and "death."

Err on the Side of Caution

A **suicide risk assessment** should be conducted whenever someone threatens self-harm or suicide, talks openly about suicidal ideation, or gives any indication of imminent or long-term risk. Some individuals contemplating suicide will engage in behaviors to prepare for death, such as talking or writing about death, acquiring firearms or stock-

---

I	Ideation
S	Substance abuse
P	Purposelessness (saying things like "what's the point" or "it doesn't matter")
A	Anxiety (agitation)
T	Trapped (feeling like there is no way out)
H	Hopelessness
W	Withdrawal (from friends and family, as well as activities or commitments)
A	Anger
R	Recklessness (with personal safety or finances)
M	Mood changes (including suddenly seeming calmer and "better")

piling medications, writing a will, giving away possessions, purchasing insurance, or talking with loved ones or treatment providers in a way that sounds like a goodbye. While some individuals may not talk about or demonstrate any preparatory behaviors prior to a suicide attempt, there are often other signs that a patient may be at risk. The American Association of Suicidology has an acronym to help remember key warning signs: **IS PATH WARM?**

Conducting a Suicide Risk Assessment

When conducting a suicide risk assessment, remain calm, open, and supportive, asking questions in a nonjudgmental and matter-of-fact manner. The goal is to obtain as much information as possible by asking follow-up questions and prompting details. Use the risk factors to guide questioning. The risk assessment procedure can also be used to help lower or manage risk by helping patients find other solutions to their problems and pointing out or strengthening any protective factors.

Risk Assessment

- Have you thought about killing yourself recently/currently?
  - If YES: When? How often do you think about it? Do you think you can cope with or control these thoughts? How do you think you would do it? Do you have a specific plan? Can you carry out your plan (e.g., Do you have access to a gun? Are there bullets in it?) Have you written a suicide note or have one in progress? Have you taken any action toward carrying out this plan? Do you have a timeline in mind?
  - If NO: Have you *ever* had thoughts about killing yourself? (Then ask all the same questions listed above.)
    - ■ *The more detailed the plan the higher the risk*
- Have you ever done anything to kill yourself?
  - ■ *The more numerous, recent, and lethal the previous attempts, the higher the risk*
- Have you ever intentionally hurt yourself? Have you ever cut, burned, or punched yourself or intentionally inflicted pain in another way?
  - If YES: When? How often/how many times have you done this? How did you hurt yourself?

- What did you use to ___ (use patient's own words, e.g., cut, burn)? Why did you ___ (use patient's own words, e.g., cut, burn) yourself? Where were you? Were you alone?
    - ■ *The greater the frequency, severity, and recency of these self-injurious acts the higher the risk*
- Do you drink alcohol? Do you use drugs (illicit or prescription)?
  - IF YES: What do you drink? What kind of drugs do you use? Why do you take them? How often/how many times a week do you drink alcohol/use drugs? How many drinks/how much ___ do you take per occasion? Has substance use increased or decreased recently? Why?
    - ■ *Sudden increases in substance use habits or chronic substance abuse increase risk*
- Have you ever had a time when you thought a lot about suicide but did not do anything to kill yourself?
  - If YES: What helped get you through that time? Why did you decide to choose life? What did you do to keep yourself safe while coping with that difficult time?
    - ■ *The greater the number of strengths and attachments to life, the lower the risk*
- How do you feel about the future? Do you have personal goals?
    - ■ *Help identify at least one reason for living. Goals and hopefulness about the future are strong protective factors*

Determining Level of Risk

Relying on a single measure or source of information can lead to erroneous risk assignment. For example, the **SAD PERSONS Scale** would yield a higher score for a 50-year-old divorced male with diabetes and no suicidal ideation than for a 35-year-old woman with severe depression and an organized suicide plan. Clinical judgment is, therefore, essential. It is important, however, to recognize the limitations of clinical judgment and to use a variety of assessment methods that have empirical utility in suicide risk assessment. Individuals with a history of multiple suicide attempts are at greater risk for suicidal behaviors compared to those with a history of one attempt

Suicide Risk Rating Classification

Very Mild or Nonexistent
- No identifiable suicidal symptoms
- No past suicide attempts
- No or very few other risk factors

Mild
- Multiple attempter with absolutely no other suicidal risk factors
- Nonmultiple attempter with suicidal ideation of limited intensity and duration,
- No or only general plans or preparation, and no or few other risk factors

Moderate
- Multiple attempter with any other notable risk factor
- Nonmultiple attempter with well-developed plans and some preparation
- Nonmultiple attempter with no or mild general plans, but moderate to severe suicidal ideation and ≥ 2 other notable risk factors

Severe
- Multiple attempter with ≥ 2 notable risk factors
- Nonmultiple attempter with well-developed plans, some preparation, and ≥ 1 other notable risk factor

Extreme
- Multiple attempter with well-developed plans and preparation
- Nonmultiple attempter with well-developed plans and preparation, with strong or uncontrollable suicidal ideation, and ≥ 2 other notable risk factors

Adapted from Chu, C., Klein, K. M., Buchman-Schmitt, J. M., Hom, M. A., Hagan, C. R., & Joiner, T. E. (2015). Routinized assessment of suicide risk in clinical practice: An empirically informed update. *Journal of Clinical Psychology, 71*(12), 1186–1200.

tion. Acute risk factors including severe affective states, sleep disturbances, and pronounced weight loss, should be considered in the context of other risk factors in order to determine more imminent risk. The sample profiles below provide an idea of what might be appropriately classified at each level of risk.

Next Steps

Consultation with colleagues regarding suicide risk and related interventions is essential. After appropriate interventions or actions have been undertaken, suicide assessments should be well documented so that the practitioner can make use of this information to coordinate with other professionals or future professionals involved in the patient's care. Clinicians should provide specific information (i.e., not just a general statement about risk level) about the factors considered in determining risk. Document the patient's own words as well as record any actions, consultations, and plans to follow up with the patient. Suicide assessment is ongoing and must be readdressed regularly over the course of treatment, particularly following significant changes or times of stress.

General Steps in Conducting a Suicide Risk Assessment
1. Ask direct questions
2. Collect as much information as possible
3. Review history, current risk, and protective factors to determine level of risk
4. Consult when appropriate
5. Develop and implement an action plan appropriate to current level of risk
6. Document decisions and actions
7. Follow up and reassess

Intervening or Lowering Suicide Risk

What treatments or interventions are recommended for suicidal patients?

After determining a patient's level of suicide risk, steps may be necessary to lower that risk. Move from the least invasive forms of intervention to

or those who think about suicide but have never attempted suicide. More recent attempts within 2 years often indicate relatively greater suicide risk. However, half of individuals who die by suicide do so on their first attempt, so it is important to assess suicidal thoughts and desire along with plans and preparation for suicide. When determining risk level, it is important to consider significant risk factors such as stressful life events, social isolation, feeling like a burden, nonsuicidal self-injury, and other psychopathology that may contribute to a patient's overall clinical presenta-

more restrictive prevention methods as warranted by level of risk. Make every effort to have the patient actively participate in lowering or minimizing risk. Steps may include disposing of any lethal means, generating a crisis plan involving coping skills or strategies to modify or tolerate distress, encouraging the communication of suicidal thoughts to a trusted friend, family member, or therapist, or having the patient stay with a friend or family member until the crisis has passed. If the patient is unable or unwilling to take these actions, or if the situation involves imminent risk and the patient is unable to collaboratively minimize risk, more invasive steps may be needed, such as informing family members, calling the police to conduct a welfare check, or instituting restrictive approaches, such as hospitalization.

A **crisis response plan** (CRP) should be the next step after a thorough risk assessment. A CRP provides specific directions to a patient on steps to take during a crisis. Write the plan down (e.g., on a 3x5 index card), have patients carry a copy with them, and put a copy in their home, car, and anywhere else they might need to access this information. Some patients may prefer to store this plan in their phone; some even program alarms that remind them to read their crisis plan or use their coping skills.

There is no evidence that traditional "no suicide contracts" reduce the risk of suicide to the patient or liability to the practitioner.

The first steps in the CRP involve self-management by the patient to identify stressors and constructive coping options. If, after instituting self-management strategies, the patient is still feeling suicidal, they should act on accessing external interventions, such as identifying an emergency contact person, making note of that person's contact information, and including a backup plan such as going to an emergency department if the support person is unavailable.

Ways to Reduce Suicide Risk

1. Instruct the patient not to do it. (Now is the time to be firm and directive!)
2. Ask the patient to remove or stay away from lethal means.
3. Get the patient connected to a mental health provider, as well as trusted family and friends.
4. Have the patient stay with a friend or family member if possible or appropriate, based on level of risk.
5. Get the patient to brainstorm ways they can cope with distressing thoughts or emotions. Simple suggestions include:
   - distracting activities, such as spending time with other people, getting out of the immediate environment, or engaging in intense physical exercise;
   - progressive muscle relaxation, diaphragmatic/paced breathing;
   - removing or lowering stressful events (e.g., vacation from work); and
   - making a plan for one small step toward solving the problem.
6. Develop a detailed plan of the strategies the patient will use to keep themselves safe (a CRP) including both things they can do by themselves and whom they can call or where they can go to get help if they need it.
7. Obtain a commitment to this plan of action. This differs from a "no suicide contract" in that it involves a commitment to a personal plan to reduce suicide risk.
8. Troubleshoot this action plan. (What could go wrong or get in the way of this plan?)
9. Follow up or get the patient to check in with someone as they implement the plan.

Psychotherapy Interventions

The most effective *interventions* for patients in acute suicidal crisis are short-term, directive, and crisis-focused, emphasizing problem solving and skill building. An intensive behavioral approach to therapy, combined with ongoing outreach, has been shown to be effective for reducing future hospitalizations among suicidal patients. In this approach, patients are given greater access to a therapist or crisis mental health worker than in most standard forms of care (e.g., access to after-hours phone support). Effort is made to maintain contact with patients for an extended period of time (3 to 12 months), even if they are not receiving formal ongoing treatment. This may take the form of phone calls following missed appointments, or sending patients postcards at regular intervals to wish them well and remind them that help is available.

Cognitive behavioral therapy (CBT), the goals of which are to manage immediate risk by inducing hope, helping the patient to problem solve, creating a crisis intervention plan, and encouraging treatment compliance, is a brief but effective therapy for treating acutely suicidal patients.

For patients who are more chronically suicidal, the immediate danger is lower and, therefore, may allow for relatively longer-term therapy, focusing more on the underlying issues of the individual's psychopathology (e.g., interpersonal communication, emotion regulation). *Dialectical behavior therapy* (DBT) is a specialized form of treatment, originally developed to treat suicidal women that has now become a well-established treatment for borderline personality disorder. This intensive treatment includes individual therapy, group skills training, and telephone access to a therapist for crisis support and skills coaching. DBT has demonstrated efficacy among both adolescents and adults, and may be useful for patients struggling with emotional dysregulation, impulsivity, or self-destructive behaviors (see Chapter 40: Principles of Psychotherapy).

Recommended Readings

Chu, C., Klein, K. M., Buchman-Schmitt, J. M., Hom, M. A., Hagan, C. R., & Joiner, T. E. (2015). Routinized assessment of suicide risk in clinical practice: An empirically informed update. *Journal of Clinical Psychology, 71*(12), 1186–1200. http://doi.org/10.1002/jclp.2221

Gould, M. S., Marrocco, F. A., Kleinman, M., Thomas, J. G., Mostkoff, K., Cote, J., & Davies, M. (2005). Evaluating iatrogenic risk of youth suicide screening programs: A randomized controlled trial. *Journal of the American Medical Association, 293*(13), 1635–1643. http://doi.org/10.1001/jama.293.13.1635

Granello, D. (2010). The process of suicide risk assessment: Twelve core principles. *Journal of Counseling & Development, 88*, 363–371. http://doi.org/10.1002/j.1556-6678.2010.tb00034.x

Jobes, D. A., Rudd, M. D., Overholser, J. C., & Joiner, T. E. (2008). Ethical and competent care of suicidal patients: Contemporary challenges, new developments, and considerations for clinical practice. *Professional Psychology: Research and Practice, 39*, 405–413.

Joiner, T. (2005). *Why people die by suicide.* Cambridge, MA: Harvard University Press.

Klonsky, E. D., May, A. M., & Saffer, B. Z. (2016). Suicide, suicide attempts, and suicidal ideation. *Annual Review of Clinical Psychology, 12*(1), 14.1–14.24. http://doi.org/10.1146/annurev-clinpsy-021815-093204

Meichenbaum, D. (2005). 35 years of working with suicidal patients: Lessons learned. *Canadian Psychology/Psychologie Canadienne, 46*, 64–67. http://doi.org/10.1037/h0087006

Review Questions

1. Among the following, the strongest predictor of completed suicide is
   A. diagnosis of a terminal illness
   B. discharge from a psychiatric hospital
   C. major life stress
   D. previous suicide attempt
   E. suicidal ideation

2. Which of the following statements about suicide is true?
   A. Death by suicide is more common among males.
   B. It is the 10th leading cause of death in the US.
   C. More people die by suicide than homicide.
   D. Suicide in the US appears to be increasing.
   E. All of the above

3. Which of the following are modifiable risk factors?
   A. Feelings of hopelessness
   B. Gender
   C. Lack of social support
   D. A and C
   E. All of the above

Answer Key on p. 466

28 Understanding and Improving Health Literacy

José L. Calderón, MD

- What are literacy levels in the US?
- What is functional literacy?
- What is health literacy?
- How is health literacy measured?
- How can health literacy be improved?

Give it to them briefly so that they will read it, clearly so they will appreciate it, picturesquely so they will remember it, and above all accurately so they will be guided by its light.

Joseph Pulitzer

Literacy

In the 19th century, if you could sign your name, you were considered literate. Today, literacy means having the ability to read and write as well as having the knowledge that relates to a specified subject. This means that use of the term *literacy* is multidimensional and not limited to reading and writing, although they are important skills and measures of text literacy.

Assessment of Literacy

What are literacy levels in the US?

In 1992, data from the National Adult Literacy Survey (NALS), estimated that about 90 million people lack sufficient literacy skills to function optimally in American society. Most professionals scored at NALS Level 3: They could make low-level inferences, integrate information from lengthy text, and generate a response based on easily identifiable information. Less than 5% of adults scored at Level 5, which indicates the ability to search for information in dense text, make high-level inferences, use specialized knowledge, and use background knowledge to determine quantities and appropriate numerical operations. Importantly, the NALS was not administered in Spanish. This means it did not include any information about Latino immigrants who speak Spanish preferentially.

National Adult Literacy Survey (1992)

- 48% of the US population could only read simple text and perform simple calculations
- 12% of adults had proficient literacy skills
- 90% of adults lacked the skills to manage their health and prevent disease
- 14% of adults (30 million) scored below the basic literacy level

In 2003, the National Assessment of Adult Literacy (NAAL) introduced the current method of reporting literacy using four levels from *below basic* to *proficient*. Below basic, the lowest level of performance, means a person may only be able to sign a form or add the amounts on a bank deposit slip. *Basic* means a person can perform simple everyday tasks such as comparing the ticket price of two sporting events or understanding a pamphlet that describes how a person is selected for jury duty. *Intermediate* means that a person can do moderately challenging tasks such as calculating the cost of an order from an office supply catalog or identifying a specific location on a map. *Proficient* means performing complex activities such as comparing viewpoints in two editorials or interpreting a table about blood pressure and physical activity. The results for these levels in the NAAL survey of 2003 are shown in Table 28.1.

Table 28.1. Literacy levels in 2003		
NAAL Level	**Capacity**	**Percentage of US Adults**
Below basic	Very simple, concrete tasks	14%
Basic	Simple everyday tasks	29%
Intermediate	Moderately challenging tasks	44%
Proficient	Complex tasks	13%[1]

Note. NAAL = National Assessment of Adult Literacy.
[1] Significant drop from National Adult Literacy Survey estimates in 1992.

The NAAL found the 2003 literacy levels to be essentially unchanged in the 10 years since the NALS except for a statistically significant drop in the percentage of adults proficient enough to complete complex literacy tasks. Importantly, unlike the NALS, the NAAL was administered in Spanish. In part, the drop in the percentage of people scoring at the proficient level may have resulted from the inclusion of authorized Latino immigrants, who tend to have limited educational attainment such as a grade school education in their country of origin. For the estimated 12 million unauthorized immigrants, literacy skills may be more limited.

Research in several countries has repeatedly documented the negative effect of limited literacy on virtually all aspects of health, including the prevalence of accidents and a wide range of diseases such as diabetes, cardiovascular disease, and rheumatoid arthritis. Hospital utilization by children is highest in communities with a high prevalence of limited literacy.

Literacy affects health both directly and indirectly. Persons with less than proficient literacy

skills (approximately 85% of the population) find it difficult to access, understand, and use health information and services from completing forms to providing informed consent and interacting with providers. They are less likely to seek timely intervention, administer medication, follow treatment regimens, engage in self-care, and care for others. Parents with limited literacy skills face significant barriers to fostering healthy development and school readiness in their children.

Functional Literacy

What is functional literacy?

Literacy may develop by increasing specific knowledge of a subject though social interactions and is influenced by cultural and socioeconomic factors such as class, race, ethnicity, language, gender, and the value placed on education by any given community of people. This makes literacy context-specific and brings to bear the concept of *multiple literacies*, such as technological literacy (computer and digital media literacy), social literacy (financial and social media literacy), and general health literacy (primary and secondary disease prevention) as well as disease-specific health literacy (about diabetes, mental illness, breast cancer).

In 1991, the National Literacy Act established the concept of *functional literacy*. In this broader view, adult literacy is determined by the extent to which a person's cognitive and functional capacities enable them to *do* as well as know.

Functional literacy varies with circumstances and social contexts. Most people function at a high level in day-to-day and familiar surroundings such as at home or work even when facing literacy barriers. For example, a person may have had very good educational attainment in their country of origin but be unable to read an operator's manual in English. If that person was able to learn how to perform their job by demonstration and practice, the person is said to be *functionally literate* in that social context. However, in a new environment, such as that of a hospital, they may become less functional.

A person may have diminished reading and writing skills from aging, chronic disease, or the use of prescription drugs, all of which are known barriers to attaining good-*health literacy*, but still be able to board a bus and get to a hospital or clinic using landmarks. They are said to be *functionally literate* in that specific social context. However, that same person may encounter difficulty within the hospital system at various levels, from completing forms to understanding tests and treatment instructions. In this context, they are said to have *limited functional health literacy*.

The National Literacy Act cites proficiency in English as a measure of literacy. Although English is the most commonly spoken language and lingua franca for business, education, and commerce, Congress has never ratified English as the nation's official language. The importance of this is that Spanish is the second most commonly spoken language and is spoken preferentially by millions of Latinos, who make up the fastest growing population in the US. In today's complex health care environment, a person with limited English proficiency may not have full access to information about opportunities and benefits available to them and may, therefore, experience functional limitations in American society.

Literacy in America is Measured by the Ability to:
- Read, write, and speak in English
- Compute and solve problems
- Function on the job and in society
- Achieve one's goals
- Develop one's knowledge and potential

From National Literacy Act (1991.) Retrieved from https://www.govtrack.us/congress/bills/102/hr751

Despite laws mandating health communication in languages other than English, millions of US residents continue to experience language and cultural barriers to improving their health literacy. This contradicts the 1983 *Report of the Task Force on Black and Minority Health* (Heckler Report) convened by the secretary of the Department of Health and Human Services that mandated health care delivery systems to:

"Develop new health information and educational materials suitable for specific minority groups where none already exist. New materials should be formulated to be acceptable to the cultural and language needs of each targeted population."

From the Report of the Secretary's Task Force on Black & Minority Health by the US Department of Health and Human Services, 1983, p. 12. Retrieved from https://minorityhealth.hhs.gov/assets/pdf/checked/1/ANDERSON.pdf

Health Literacy

What is health literacy?

Health literacy has been defined by many institutions in various ways.

Definitions of Health Literacy

Institute of Medicine
"The degree to which individuals have the capacity to obtain, process and understand basic health information needed to make appropriate health decisions."

AMA Council of Scientific Affairs
Functional health literacy is "the ability to read and comprehend prescription bottles, appointment slips, and the other essential health related materials required to successfully function as a patient."

The Patient Protection and Affordable Care Act ("health reform"), Title V, Section 5002
"Health literacy is the degree to which an individual has the capacity to obtain, communicate, process and understand health information and services in order to make appropriate health decisions."

World Health Organization
"The cognitive and social skills which determine the motivation and ability of individuals to gain access to, understand and use information in ways which promote and maintain good health."

What these definitions have in common is that they are based on the consumer's ability to acquire and understand health information. However, it is generally known that health-related information, whether presented on paper or electronically, can be difficult to read and understand by the average health care consumer, and even more so by persons from vulnerable populations (the elderly, race/ethnic minorities, the homeless).

These definitions are limited by placing the onus on the health care consumer. They say nothing about the responsibility of health care delivery systems and providers to make health information accessible, comprehensible, and reflective of the sociocultural factors that influence health literacy in the communities they serve.

The source of most health care communication problems is a mismatch between providers' and patients' logic, language, and experience. Consequently, work to improve health literacy has focused on enhancing information delivery. Due to special training and vocabulary, physicians and other health care professionals think and talk about health, illness, and treatment in unique ways. Even among native-born patients, who are not only proficient in English but also highly educated professionals in their own field, the culture and language of medicine can be barriers to efficient, effective care. To address this in the context of taking a medical history, psychiatrist and anthropologist Arthur Kleinman developed a set of interview questions to elicit a patient's experience and perception of a condition and its treatment. Practitioners can use these questions to close gaps between a patient's logic, language, and experience and their own (see Chapter 17: Culture and Cultural Competency in Health Care).

Health literacy is a type of functional literacy. Like computer literacy, it develops with need, opportunity, and experience. Regardless of literacy skills, nearly everyone has limitations in functional health literacy; that is, they typically lack background knowledge, medical vocabulary, and experience with health care delivery systems. For example, few people have the need, opportunity, or take the time to learn and talk about diabetes until they or a significant other is diagnosed. It is only at diagnosis that their health literacy or, more specifically in this example, their "diabetes health literacy" begins to develop. Similarly, many people lack the background knowledge and vocabulary to navigate health care delivery systems effectively until they are in need of health care. With experience their health literacy, in par-

ticular their health care literacy, may improve, and they may progress toward higher levels of functioning.

Skills Needed to Negotiate Health Care Delivery Systems
- Locating health information, providers, and services
- Evaluating information for credibility and quality
- Analyzing risks and benefits
- Calculating dosages & interpreting test results
- Understanding graphs or other visual information
- Understanding spoken advice or directions and articulating health concerns
- Engaging in self-care and chronic disease management

Assessment of Health Literacy

How is health literacy measured?

Over the past 2 decades, studies have focused on individual patient scores on health literacy screening tests administered for clinical and research purposes. Researchers have adapted reading and comprehension tests from the field of education, to identify patients with limited health literacy and to guide providers in drafting health information that is understandable to most patients. Currently, four tests are commonly used to measure health literacy (Table 28.2): Newest Vital Sign, Rapid Estimate of Adult Literacy in Medicine (REALM), the Short Assessment of Health Literacy for Spanish-Speaking Adults (SAHLSA), and the Short Test of Functional Health Literacy in Adults (S-TOFHLA). However, none of these tests measure health literacy directly. Instead, they test ability to decipher a nutrition label, word recognition, word meaning, and comprehension of a paragraph, respectively.

Using Plain Language

How can health literacy be improved?

More recently, federal and state law, Medicare and Medicaid regulations, and accreditation standards

Table 28.2. Tests commonly used to measure health literacy			
Newest Vital Sign NewestVitalSign.org	**REALM** Rapid Estimate of Adult Literacy in Medicine	**SAHLSA** Short Assessment of Health Literacy for Spanish-speaking Adults	**S-TOFHLA** Short Test of Functional Health Literacy in Adults
Use Clinical	Clinical and Research	Clinical	Research
Tasks Review nutrition label Respond to 6 questions	Read 66 words (Scored on correct pronunciation of words)	Selected meaning of 50 words (Scored on number of words defined correctly)	Fill in missing words in 4 numerical items and 2 prose passages
Languages English Yes Spanish Yes	English Yes Spanish Yes	English No Spanish Yes	English Yes Spanish Yes

have placed responsibility for patient understanding squarely with the provider. For example, the Plain Writing Act of 2010 requires that government documents be written in "plain language," defined as "writing that is clear, concise, well-organized, and follows other best practices appropriate to the subject or field and intended audience." This law applies to health and medical information used in health care organizations that receive *any* federal funding.

There are many definitions of plain language. Simply, it is communication that the audience will understand first reading or when first heard. The utility of plain language is mediated by the literacy skills of the audience or the *oracy* skills (use of the spoken word) of the communicator. The term *oracy* was coined in the 1960s as an analogy to literacy and numeracy to draw attention to the neglect of oral skills in education. This is an important concept since a person with limited literacy, who hears a message read from text written in complex language, may not understand the message.

The Plain Language Association International states that "a communication is in plain language if the language, structure, and design are clear so that the intended audience *can easily find what they need, understand what they find, and use that information.*" This definition mirrors the definition of health literacy adopted by the Department of Health and Human Services (HHS): "Health literacy is the degree to which individuals have the capacity to *obtain, process, and understand basic health information and services needed to make appropriate health decision.*"

Information about plain language and resources to aid drafting plain language text is available on the Internet (see Additional Resources). Basically, five principles guide drafting plain language text: (1) understanding the audience's information needs; (2) using appropriate and familiar text formats; (3) using visual appearance (layout, information graphics) to clarify the message; (4) choosing words and sentence structures that are short, simple, active voice, and which avoid jargon; and (5) evaluating against a checklist or field testing.

Improving Readability of Written Materials

Numerous guidelines have been published to improve the readability of written health information (see Recommended Readings and Additional Resources). Most formulas estimate readability based on the number of syllables in a word and the number of words in a sentence. Using polysyllabic words and complex sentences (having more than one thought or idea) makes reading more difficult.

The reading level of text can be estimated using the Flesh-Kincaid Formula (F-K) and its synergistic Flesh Reading Ease Formula (FRE). The F-K provides an estimate of the grade level skills needed to read and comprehend a sample of text. The FRE estimates readability on a scale from 0 to 100, with 100 being the easiest text to read and 0 the most difficult (see Table 28.3).

Estimating readability can help establish whether a piece of text matches the literacy skills of its audience. However, a very easy-to-read text is not necessarily comprehensible.

The underpinning of simplifying the readability of text is to covert long complex sentences (two or more thoughts per message) into shorter simple sentences (one thought per message): This can be accomplished by avoiding connector words (coordinating conjunctives). These can be remembered by the mnemonic *FONBAYS BOOTS*. FONBAYS are commonly used words (*for, or, nor, but, and, yet, so*) and BOOTS less commonly used (*be, often, on, to, since*). Simplification is demonstrated in Figure 28.1 and Figure 28.2 using a sample of text from a consent form.

In this example, two complex sentences were simplified into four simple sentences. The text is

Table 28.3. Difficulty raings of FRE and F-K readability estimates

Reading Ease Score	Reading Difficulty Rating	Grade Level Difficulty
Less than 40	Very difficult	Graduate school
41–50	Difficult	College
51–60	Fairly difficult	10th–12th
61–70	Standard (average)	7th–9th
71–80	Fairly easy	4th–6th
81–90	Easy to read	1st–3rd
91–100	Very easy to read	Kindergarten

also more readable because there is ample white space within the document, and the font and font size provide space between letters and words. This lowers the cognitive access cost of engaging a document and makes text easier to read for persons with limited literacy. This may also benefit persons with visual impairment such as older

Anticipated Benefits to Society

Sentence 1: The researchers believe that the information collected will contribute to documenting the first aid preparedness of inner city school employees, and to identifying their learning needs and attitudes toward acquiring and providing first aid skills.

Sentence 2: Furthermore, this information will serve as a basis for developing a curriculum for providing first aid skills to school employees.

[Times New Roman 11]

Mean Flesh-Kincaid score		17th grade
Mean Flesh Reading Ease score 22		Very difficult to read
Sentence 1	F-K score	20th grade
	FRE score 12	Very difficult to read
Sentence 2	F-K score	13th grade
	FRE score 34	Difficult to read

Figure 28.1. Readability of an original consent form sample.

Possible Good For Others

The information tells us how ready school workers are to give first aid. It also helps us know their learning needs. This will help us to develop a first aid course for school workers. We will also know their feelings about learning and teaching first aid.

[High Tower Text 12]

Average F-K score		5th grade	
Average FRE score		83	Easy to read
Sentence 1	F-K score	6th grade	
	FRE score	77	Easy to read
Sentence 2	F-K score	2nd grade	
	FRE score	93	Very easy to read
Sentence 3	F-K score	4th grade	
	FRE score	90	Easy to read
Sentence 4	F-K score	6th grade	
	FRE score	75	Easy to read

Figure 28.2. Readability of the simplified consent form sample.

---

readers. As shown above, the font High Tower 12 is used instead of Times New Roman 11.

Health Literacy Universal Precautions

Universal precaution is defined by the Occupational Safety and Health Administration as "an approach to infection control to treat all human blood and certain human body fluids as if they were known to be infectious for HIV, HBV and other blood borne pathogens" (Blood borne Pathogens Standard 29 CFR 1910.1030(b) definitions).

Given this definition, **health literacy universal precautions** may be defined as "approaches to health literacy that assume that all persons have limited literacy skills and limited health literacy."

The Agency for Healthcare Research and Quality (AHRQ) hosts a Health Literacy Universal Precautions Tool Kit on its website for use in the clinical setting, such as the Brown Bag Review of medications and the Teach-Back Method to assess a patient's understanding of what they need to do to improve and maintain good self-management (see Additional Resources).

In the consent form example above, the written health information was made simpler to read by improving the cognitive and visual design aspects (readability) of the difficult-to-read original sentences. This allows more people, including those with limited literacy, to read and comprehend the intended message. However, there are populations with very limited literacy skills. As a consequence, interventions and platforms that do not rely on written information may represent the most universal of health literacy precautions.

Nonwritten Venues for Improving Health Literacy

Nonwritten interventions such as novellas, live action videos, and animation have been used successfully to improve health literacy. Animated videos have great potential since they are nonthreatening and have the advantage of being entertaining as well as educational. In addition, information is a powerful social marketing tool that is engaging and familiar from television, video games, slot machines, movies, and cell phones. The cost effectiveness of animation lies in its long shelf-life, ease of use, adaptability to multiple languages, and universal acceptance as a media venue. This is in contrast to the cost of developing and implementing strategies to improve reading proficiency for millions of persons with limited reading skills, especially in multicultural populations.

Improved information delivery alone, however, is not likely to mitigate the relationship between limited literacy and poor health outcomes. New studies suggest it is possible to promote functional health literacy through specific health education strategies and direct assistance to a specific patient to personalize the information and demonstrate how to apply it in context. Support from family, friends, or social services providers can buffer the negative effects of low health literacy by enabling a person to understand information, enter and navigate the health system, and adhere to treatment regimens. Collaboration between health care organizations and literacy enhancing community services, such as adult basic education and English-language learning classes, may also prove beneficial.

To Facilitate the Use of Information to Maintain or Enhance Health:

- Focus on behavior (what to do to cope, recover, or enhance health)
- Ask the patient to repeat how and when to take the medicine include caregivers in the discussion
- Connect the patient with institutional and community interpreter or case management or home health services
- Follow up visits by phone to check how the patient is implementing the treatment plan
- Be more concerned about what a patient does than about what a patient understands

To Facilitate Understanding of Information You Provide:

- Become aware of the culture and language of medicine and of your institution
- Become aware of your patients' culture and language
- Use plain language (say "walk" instead of "ambulate")
- Ask the patient to "teach back" to confirm understanding
- Repeat the most important patient instructions as needed (repetition aids learning)
- Invite patients to read important treatment instructions aloud, then ask what they read about
- Do not assume a patient understands your instructions or printed information
- Use health literacy universal precautions

Recommended Readings

Calderón, J. L., Norris, K. C., Shaheen, M., Baker, R. D., Fleming, E., & Hays, R. D. (2014). Improving diabetes health literacy by animation. *The Diabetes Educator, 40*(3), 361–372. http://doi.org/10.1177/0145721714527518

Calderón, J. L., Smith, S., & Baker, R. (2007). "FONBAYS": A simple method for enhancing readability of patient information. *Annals of Behavioral Science and Medical Education, 14*(1), 20–24.

Cho, Y. I., & Crittenden, K. S. (2008). Effects of health literacy on health status and health service utilization amongst the elderly. *Social Science & Medicine, 66*(8), 1809–1816. http://doi.org/10.1016/j.socscimed.2008.01.003

Jordan, J. E., Osborne, R. H., & Buchbinder, R. (2011). Critical appraisal of health literacy indices revealed variable underlying constructs, narrow center content and psychometric weakness. *Journal of Clinical Epidemiology, 64*, 366–379.

Lee, D. (2009). Health literacy, social support and health status among older adults. *Educational Gerontology, 35*, 191–201.

Nutbeam, D. (2008). The evolving concept of health literacy. *Social Science & Medicine, 67*, 2072–2078. http://doi.org/10.1016/j.socscimed.2008.09.050

Additional Resources

Agency for Healthcare Research and Quality. *Health literacy universal precautions tool kit* (2nd ed.). Available at http://www.ahrq.gov/professionals/quality-patient-safety/quality-resources/tools/literacy-toolkit/healthlit-toolkit2.html

European Center for Disease Prevention and Control. (2012). *A rapid evidence review of interventions for improving health literacy.* Available at http://ecdc.europa.eu/en/publications/_layouts/forms/Publication_DispForm.aspx?ID=620&List=4f55ad51-4aed-4d32-b960-af70113dbb90#sthash.qRrO7Y6u.dpuf

Ontario Ministry of Health, Literacy and Health Project. (1989). *Phase one: Making the world healthier and safer for people who can't read.* Available at http://www.eric.ed.gov/ERICWebPortal/search/detailmini.jsp?_nfpb=true&_&ERICExtSearch_SearchValue_0=ED346338&ERICExtSearch_SearchType_0=no&accno=ED346338

Plain Language Action and Information Network. (2011). *Improving communication from the federal government to the public.* Available at: http://www.plainlanguage.gov/

US Department of Health and Human Services, Centers for Medicare and Medicaid Services. (2012). *Toolkit for making written material clear and effective.* Available at https://www.cms.gov/WrittenMaterialsToolkit

Review Questions

Is each of the following statements True or False?

1. Enhancing health literacy is the sole responsibility of health care consumers.

2. Estimating readability of a document is sufficient to draft easy-to-comprehend text.

3. A 40-year-old Latina immigrant reads at the third-grade level. Her 7-year-old daughter's immunizations are up-to-date, and the girl sees her pediatrician annually, is meeting developmental milestones, and is doing well in school. This parent demonstrates functional health literacy in the context of her daughter.

Answer Key on p. 466

Section VIII
The Health Care System, Policy, and Economics

29 The US Health Care System

Tingyin T. Chee, MD, MPA, and Jillian S. Catalanotti, MD, MPH

- What are the components of the US health care system?
- What is continuity of care?
- How do we ensure competency of health care providers?
- How does the third party payment system work?
- What are the different forms of public health insurance?
- What reforms are included in the Patient Protection and Affordable Care Act?
- How does the US health care system rate when compared internationally?

The US health care system is characterized by *decentralization* and *fragmentation*; its components are uncoordinated and operate mainly independently. Compared with other developed countries, the US has consistently ranked the most expensive in health care expenditures, yet it is among the poorest in several health outcomes. Decades of attempts at health care reform with the aim of containing costs while improving quality culminated in the passage of the 2010 Patient Protection and Affordable Care Act (ACA), which introduced steps toward a more integrated and value-based health care system as well as expanded access to health insurance.

sizes the treatment and cure of disease, targeting individual patients. The medical health care system includes infrastructure for *health care delivery* and *health care payment*. The US health care system has traditionally emphasized treatment and acute care rather than prevention, both in its financial reimbursement practices and in its delivery of care models. Public health and medical care are frequently viewed as parallel, nonintegrated systems, although recent innovations recharacterize population health as squarely within the domain of health care providers. This chapter will briefly describe the public health infrastructure, then focus on the components of the medical health care system.

Components of the US Health Care System

> What are the components of the US health care system?

The US health care system spans the spectrum from public health to medical care. The public health system emphasizes population-based health, targeting disease prevention and health promotion, while the medical care system empha-

Public Health Infrastructure

Public health population-based efforts, such as implementing vaccination campaigns, banning tobacco use in public spaces, and constructing sanitation systems, have been instrumental in increasing life expectancy and decreasing mortality from infectious and neoplastic diseases. The US public health infrastructure involves all levels of government: federal, state, and local. The federal infrastructure consists of the following agencies housed within the **Department of Health and Human**

Services (HHS): Centers for Disease Control and Prevention (CDC); National Institutes of Health (NIH); Food and Drug Administration (FDA); Health Resources and Services Administration (HRSA); Agency for Healthcare Research and Quality (AHRQ); Substance Abuse and Mental Health Services Administration (SAMHSA); and Indian Health Service (IHS). These agencies perform and fund health research; provide guidance for local health delivery; coordinate interstate surveillance efforts; ensure the safety of food, drug, and durable medical equipment; and oversee the Federally Qualified Health Center (FQHC), IHS, and nationwide organ transplantation programs.

> Whereas federal public health agencies perform research and coordinate public health activities for the nation, most public health services (e.g., vaccination services, health promotion campaigns, data collection) occur on a state or local level. Each state has a health department or board of health, and most states have one or more local health boards at the city or county level.

Continuity of Care

> What is continuity of care?

Ideal health care should be continuous – that is, characterized by a seamless transition of the patient and their health information between different settings and providers over time. The most continuous care possible would be provided by one health care provider with intimate knowledge of the patient's health history. Unfortunately, in an era of medical specialization, **continuity of care** depends on good communication between multiple health care providers.

There are three main levels of health care that may introduce different health care providers: primary, secondary, and tertiary care. *Primary care* consists of preventive, diagnostic, and treatment services for common, uncomplicated medical problems (80% of health problems) and is typically delivered in an outpatient or home-based setting. *Secondary care* requires specialist physicians and is either delivered in an outpatient setting or

through short hospital stays, typically in smaller community hospitals. Secondary care addresses about 15% of health problems. *Tertiary care* involves complex medical management and newer medical technology delivered in large, specialized medical centers. Although tertiary care accounts for the bulk of health care costs, it addresses less than 5% of health problems. There is also *post-acute* care, which includes rehabilitation.

Breakdowns in communication between settings and providers have been identified as a common source of medical errors leading to unnecessary patient harm. A barrier to continuity of care in the health care system is the degree to which care is fragmented among different providers, in different settings, affiliated with different hospitals or health care organizations, and different payers for health care with different priorities or contractual obligations. Each of these entities has its own system for record keeping and variable availability of records to others. Even electronic medical records, which may improve completeness, accuracy, and legibility over paper charts, do not ensure accessibility of records to others. The frequent result is a lack of coordinated care, characterized by duplication and waste.

Health Care Delivery Settings

Medical care may be classified by the delivery setting (e.g., inpatient care, outpatient/ambulatory care, long-term care, or home-based care). *Inpatient care* involves admission to a hospital or extended care facility for more than 1 day, mainly for major physical or mental health problems that are potentially life threatening or require services that cannot be provided at home. *Outpatient* or *ambulatory care* is provided in office settings, ambulatory surgery centers (for procedures that do not require overnight observation), and urgent care clinics. *Long-term care* serves individuals who cannot care for themselves and is generally provided in extended care facilities with skilled nursing or residential staff, such as assisted living facilities or nursing homes. *Assisted living* facilities may provide support for shopping, food preparation, household chores, or medication management. *Home-based care* occurs along a continuum depending on the needs, disability, and infirmity of the patient. For disabled or homebound patients, who cannot easily travel but require services that can be provided outside of an institutional setting, nursing and other specialized care can be provided in the home.

Health Care Providers

> How do we ensure competency of health care providers?

Health care providers include physicians, nurse practitioners, podiatrists, physician assistants, dentists, nurses, clinical psychologists, social workers, providers of ancillary services (e.g., physical and occupational therapists, speech therapists, respiratory therapists, dietitians, optometrists, chiropractors, dental hygienists, pharmacists, case managers), and other allied health professionals (e.g., laboratory technicians, radiology technicians, phlebotomists, medical assistants, emergency medical technicians). In the 19th century, health professionals were variably trained with no system to ensure quality education and training. The 1910 *Flexner Report* standardized medical education and training, giving rise to modern medical schools.

To ensure minimal competence among health care providers and quality among health care settings, there are three main types of regulation: **accreditation**, **licensing**, and **certification**. Educational and training programs, health care delivery organizations, and health insurance plans must be *accredited* as meeting certain set criteria. Accrediting agencies for educational and training programs include the *Liaison Committee for Medical Education* (LCME) for allopathic medical schools; the *Accreditation Council for Graduate Medical Education* (ACGME), for allopathic residency programs; and the *American Osteopathic Association* (AOA) for osteopathic medical schools and residency programs. Criteria for these programs include required courses, duration of training or study, resource availability, and faculty qualifications. Accrediting agencies also include the *Joint Commission* for health care delivery organizations such as hospitals, medical offices, and nursing homes and the *National Committee on Quality Assurance* (NCQA) for health insurance plans.

In contrast, individual health care providers must be *licensed*, which requires completion of training at an accredited institution and meeting competency requirements to be granted legal permission to deliver clinical care. *Certification* is not a requirement for practice, but rather recognizes achievement of a higher standard of competency by a professional organization (*Board Certification*). In addition to meeting other requirements, certification typically requires passing an examination, and maintenance of certification may require reexamination at set intervals (e.g., annually or every 10 years) or completion of continuing medical education activities.

> Licenses are granted by states. Health care providers can only practice in states in which they are licensed, although competency requirements often include meeting national benchmarks such as passing the US Medical Licensing Examination (USMLE) for allopathic physicians.

Health Care Payment

> How does the third party payment system work?

Payment for health care comes directly from individual patients (*out-of-pocket*) or by health insurance plans (private insurance or public government-subsidized plans). A health insurance plan is a contract between the patient (*beneficiary*) and the insurer stipulating how much the individual must pay and what services the health insurance plan will cover. The purpose of health insurance is to protect individuals from bankruptcy in the face of a medical catastrophe by pooling risk (i.e., collecting payments from many beneficiaries in the hope that only some of them will incur health care expenses). Health insurance has evolved to become the primary mechanism to pay for health care. This **third party payment system** adds to the complexity of the health care payment system, as there are many different health insurance companies, each offering different plans to their beneficiaries. The fragmented administrative requirements of this system alone significantly increase health care costs.

The evolution of the third party payment system started during the Great Depression, when the economic vulnerability of hospitals and the population led to the formation of private health insurance plans, in which participants paid monthly or annual premiums in exchange for a set amount of hospital days or medical care. In response to employee injuries and the desire to maintain a healthy and efficient work force, Henry J. Kaiser of Kaiser Steel teamed with a local physician, Dr. Sidney Garfield, to provide medical care for his employees at a local hospital. Thus began the prominent role of the employer in the provision of health care.

The role of the employer expanded during World War II (WWII), when the federal government imposed nationwide salary freezes but permitted increases in benefits packages, including health insurance. Employer-sponsored health insurance plans allowed workers to subsidize the cost of purchasing health insurance. After the war, returning veterans became entitled to a number of benefits, including federal government–insured health care, thus creating the first government-subsidized health program, under the Department of Veterans Affairs (VA).

The years leading up to and during WWII brought advances in the treatment of infectious diseases with the discovery of penicillin. Subsequently, the burden of care shifted from infectious diseases to chronic diseases such as heart disease and cancer. Chronic diseases proved not only difficult to prevent, but costly to treat, and health care expenditures increased dramatically. The central role of the employer in providing health insurance limited access to health care for those who were not employed. In 1965, two programs were created to address this issue for three particular groups: older persons, the disabled, and the poor. **Medicare** is a federally funded health insurance plan for older persons and the permanently disabled, and **Medicaid** is a joint federal and state funded health insurance plan for the poor. The creation of these programs increased the federal government's role in paying for and monitoring the provision of health services.

Even with health insurance, beneficiaries are responsible for significant cost-sharing. A *premium*

is a beneficiary's monthly or annual payment for health insurance. Premiums used to vary based on preexisting health conditions, age, gender, or health behavior (e.g., smoking), wherein individuals deemed at higher risk of using health care resources were charged higher premiums. However, the ACA in 2010 outlawed this practice, as well as outlawing denial of insurance coverage based on preexisting conditions. A *deductible* is money the beneficiary must pay out of pocket for a health care service before their health insurance plan kicks in. In general, health insurance plans with lower premium rates tend to have higher deductibles, and those with higher premium rates tend to have lower deductibles. Most health insurance plans require beneficiaries to pay a *co-pay* when they receive certain health care services. A co-pay is a set amount paid out of pocket for a medical service. In addition to cost-sharing, co-pays were designed to influence the behavior of beneficiaries to prevent unnecessary use of health care resources and influence a beneficiary's choice of health care providers (e.g., charging a lower co-pay for care in a physician's office than in an emergency room, or for a visit with a primary care provider rather than with a specialist). When a co-pay is charged as a percentage of total cost rather than a set amount of money (e.g., 20% rather than $20), it is called *co-insurance*.

Private Health Insurance

About two thirds of Americans are enrolled in private health insurance plans, the majority of which are *employer-sponsored plans. Individual private health insurance* allows a person to select a plan better suited to individual needs; however, the entire premium must be paid by the beneficiary alone. The advantages of employer-sponsored plans are: (1) part of the premium is paid by the employer; (2) employers purchasing a health plan on behalf of many beneficiaries have more bargaining power than individuals; and (3) for a large group of employees, it is highly likely that the financial burden of one person's preexisting medical condition, new medical problem, or risk factors will be absorbed by the pool without dramatically increasing premiums. The main disadvantages are: (1) a beneficiary can only select between plans offered by the employer, which may or may not suit individual needs; (2) the burden of cost may be significant for employers; and (3) employment changes may affect insurance coverage.

Many health insurance plans are **managed care plans**, designed to control costs while still providing high-quality medical care. The most common forms of managed care plans are **health maintenance organizations** (HMOs) and **preferred provider organizations** (PPOs). Traditional HMOs are both the insurer and provider of medical care, and beneficiaries may only see physicians employed by the HMO plan. If beneficiaries choose to see providers outside the HMO, they will have to pay for the service out of pocket. PPOs, in contrast, enroll physicians to become *in-network* providers with whom the PPO has a contract for services at a lower rate. Beneficiaries are given incentives, such as lower co-pays, to choose in-network providers. A beneficiary may choose to see an *out-of-network* provider, but will have to pay any charges beyond the amount paid by their insurance.

Government-Funded Health Insurance

> What are the different forms of public health insurance?

Public (government-funded) health insurance is provided through five principal programs: Medicare, Medicaid, State Children's Health Insurance Plan (SCHIP), Tricare, and VA. Medicare and Medicaid are administered by an agency under the HHS called the Centers for Medicare & Medicaid Services (CMS).

Medicare is an insurance plan that covers citizens or permanent residents who are older or disabled (see Table 29.1 for eligibility criteria). It is financed by a combination of general revenue, payroll tax, and beneficiary premiums. Eligibility criteria, prices, and coverage are set by the federal government for the entire country. Medicare has annual limits on certain types of services for each beneficiary. In 2010, about 54 million Americans were covered by Medicare, about 84% of whom were aged 65 or older.

Medicare is divided into four "Parts" (A, B, C, and D) for coverage of different health services. *Medicare Part A* covers inpatient hospital care, limited skilled nursing home and inpatient rehabilitation services, and hospice care. It is available

Table 29.1. Eligibility criteria for Medicare

US Citizens or Permanent Residents Who Are/Have:	Year Eligibility for Medicare Began
1. Age 65 or older, and the person or spouse has paid income tax for at least 40 quarters (10 years)	1965
2. Permanently disabled (any age)	1972
3. End-stage renal disease requiring dialysis or kidney transplant (any age)	1972
4. Amyotrophic lateral sclerosis, also called Lou Gehrig's disease (any age)	2001

to every Medicare beneficiary without a premium but does have deductibles and co-insurance payments. *Medicare Part B* covers outpatient physician visits, home health care, medical equipment, and ancillary services. Any Medicare beneficiary may choose to purchase Part B for a premium, which is determined, along with deductibles and co-pays, by the federal government. It is important to note that long-term care services are not covered by Medicare. *Medicare Part C* allows beneficiaries to choose to have their Medicare benefits administered through certain private insurance HMO or PPO plans called Medicare Advantage Plans. *Medicare Part D*, established in 2003, covers prescription medications and is administered through various private insurance companies.

The Part D coverage gap (the *"donut hole"*) refers to a gap in coverage set by the original legislation (see Figure 29.1). After paying the annual deductible, beneficiaries pay co-insurance (typically 25% for generic medications) up to a specified limit (total of US $3,310 paid by the beneficiary and the insurance plan in 2016). Above this limit, beneficiaries enter the coverage gap, in which co-insurance increases to 58% (as of 2016, for generic drugs) until reaching a second "catastrophic" out-of-pocket spending limit. Above this second limit, beneficiaries pay very little (5% co-insurance on average) for additional medications. Prior to passage of the ACA, co-insurance in the coverage gap was 100% (hence its nickname "donut hole"). The ACA ordered a phased decrease in co-insurance until the coverage gap is eliminated; as of 2020, the donut hole will close and beneficiaries will pay 25% co-insurance on prescriptions without a coverage gap.

Medicaid was established in 1965 as an insurance plan for the poor who meet certain criteria (see Box 29.1). Medicaid is jointly funded by both federal and state tax dollars. Eligibility, prices, and coverage are set by states in accordance with federal criteria. Thus, individuals may qualify in one state but not another, and eligibility may vary from year to year with state budget changes. Since passage of the ACA, states may opt to expand Medicaid eligibility criteria to include all adults with incomes at or below 133%

of the federal poverty level (FPL). As of 2016, 31 states and the District of Columbia have chosen to expand Medicaid eligibility and approximately 62 million people are covered by Medicaid.

Medicaid generally covers hospital care, outpatient care, skilled nursing home services, and dental care, and, depending on the state, may or may not cover ancillary services, inpatient rehabilitation services, medical equipment, and prescriptions. Deductibles and co-pays are relatively small and determined by state governments, and no co-pay may be charged for emergency services. Beneficiaries can see any providers who accept Medicaid, but the level of payment by Medicaid is often less than what is charged by providers, with the result that many providers will not accept Medicaid, and beneficiaries may have limited access to care.

The **State Children's Health Insurance Program** (SCHIP) is an insurance plan covering poor children who do not qualify for Medicaid. It

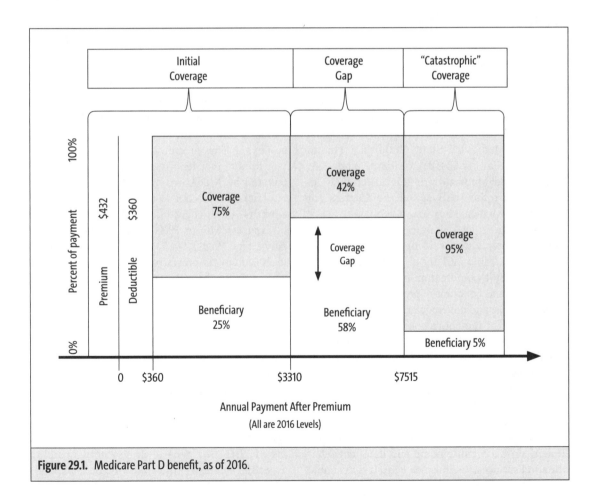

Figure 29.1. Medicare Part D benefit, as of 2016.

Box 29.1. Eligibility criteria (minimum federal requirements) for Medicaid for US citizens or permanent residents

Children

< Age 6	< 133% FPL (optional expansion to < 185% FPL for children aged 0–1 with federal matching funds)
Age 6–19	< 100% FPL
Foster care children	Any income level
Pregnant women	< 133% FPL (optional expansion to < 185% FPL with federal matching funds)
Parents < 65 with dependent children	If qualify for Aid to Families with Dependent Children (AFDC) program
Certain poor Medicare beneficiaries	Varied criteria but generally if qualify for SSI or 75% FPL (Medicaid would pay for Medicare premium, deductible, and co-pays)
Poor, blind, or temporarily disabled	If qualify for Supplemental Security Income (SSI) or 75% FPL
"Medically needy" (those who have incurred large medical expenses)	Defined differently by each state (optional, with federal matching funds)
Other non-disabled adults < 65	< 133% FPL

Note. FPL = federal poverty level for family or individual income as calculated by the US Census Bureau.

---

is funded by federal and state governments, but administered by the state. Children whose families earn up to 200% FPL (or 250% FPL in 24 states) qualify for SCHIP. Cost-sharing limits are, generally, no more than 5% of the family's annual income. Many states combine their SCHIP and Medicaid programs.

Tricare is a health insurance plan for active and retired members of the military and their dependents. It is similar to an employer-sponsored health insurance plan, and offers PPO and HMO options, but the employees are military service members and the employer is the federal government. It is both a health payment plan and a health delivery system. Tricare beneficiaries can see any health care providers that accept their coverage, or can see health care providers directly hired by the military health system.

The **Department of Veterans Affairs** (VA) is a government-operated health benefit and fully integrated health care delivery system with locations distributed across the country. Honorably discharged active-duty veterans are eligible for VA services. The VA directly hires its own health care providers and owns and operates its own ambulatory care centers and hospitals. Serving 8.76 million veterans yearly, the VA is the largest integrated health system in the US. Payment is internal via budgeting under the Department of Defense.

Health Care System Reform

> What reforms are included in the Patient Protection and Affordable Care Act?

In addition to the changes described in the previous sections, the Patient Protection and Affordable Care Act (ACA), signed by President Obama on March 23, 2010, is a comprehensive plan to overhaul the health care system with a focus on increasing access to health care and improving health care quality and coordination. The ACA focuses on several objectives with staggered implementation over 10 years (see Box 29.2).

As of 2015 (5 years after the ACA was passed), the effect of the ACA on access to health insurance was clear, with an estimated 30 million more Americans having health insurance. The greatest gains have occurred among young adults, Hispanics, Blacks, and low-income populations. Health Insurance Exchanges allowed 11.7 million people to obtain individual private insurance, Medicaid expansion covered an additional 10.8 million Americans, 3 million young adults obtained coverage via extension of their parents' policies, and an estimated 8 to 12 million people benefited from regulations on coverage for preexisting conditions and policy termination.

Box 29.2. Goals of the Patient Protection and Affordable Care Act (ACA) 2010

Reduce the number of uninsured
- Allows states to expand Medicaid eligibility to all citizens and residents up to 133% of FPL
- Requires US citizens and legal residents to have health insurance coverage
- Provides health insurance subsidies to the poor (those who do not qualify for Medicaid) and establishes Health Insurance Exchanges – virtual marketplaces selling insurance plan options
- Requires employers with ≥ 50 employees to offer health insurance coverage

Reform health insurance industry
- Outlaws pre-existing condition exclusions
- Requires all plans to cover dependent children up to age 26
- Prohibits rescissions of coverage or dollar value limits (lifetime)
- Sets minimum coverage requirements for all health plans
- Requires insurance companies to justify premium increases
- Established Health Insurance Exchange marketplaces allowing individuals and small businesses to purchase insurance
- Requires insurance companies to spend 85% of premium income on clinical services and quality improvement

Improve preventive care
- Requires all health plans to cover a minimum level of preventive care, for free
- Requires Medicare and Medicaid to cover preventive services with no cost-sharing
- Established the Independence at Home program to provide home-based primary care services for high-need Medicare beneficiaries

Improve health care quality
- Established the Center for Medicare & Medicaid Innovation (CMMI) to develop, test, and scale new health care delivery models
- Requires physician reporting on certain quality and outcome measures
- Provides incentive payments for improving health care quality and lowering costs through Accountable Care Organizations
- Reduces Medicare payments for hospital-acquired infections and preventable hospital readmissions
- Funds comparative effectiveness research for direct comparisons of treatments and medications

Decrease health care costs
- Increases oversight to reduce waste, fraud, and abuse in Medicare and Medicaid
- Decreases co-insurance rate in the "donut hole" from 100% to 25% over 10 years
- Established the Independent Payment Advisory Board to reduce growth in Medicare spending

Increase access to care
- Increases Medicaid payment rates for primary care services to Medicare rates for 2 years
- Increases funding for the Federally Qualified Health Center program
- Recruits providers to primary care: loan repayment and training incentives, especially for rural/underserved areas; 10% bonuses on Medicare payments for 5 years

Decrease administrative overhead
- Streamlines and standardizes health insurance claims processing

Pay for health care reform
- Increases Medicare payroll taxes, reduces tax relief from health savings and flexible spending accounts
- Imposes fees on health insurance and pharmaceutical companies
- Levies tax on certain employer-sponsored health plans with very high levels of coverage

Improve public health
- Created the Prevention and Public Health Fund, the largest public health fund in US history
- Requires restaurants and vending machines to publish calorie information

Note. FPL = federal poverty level.

To improve health care quality and coordination, efforts began to move away from fee-for-service models toward value-based payments for health care. One such approach is financial penalties for suboptimal care, such as hospital readmissions and hospital-acquired infections and injuries. A second approach, Accountable Care Organizations (ACOs), are groups of providers or institutions who assume responsibility for the total quality and cost of care to the Medicare patients they serve. ACOs must report quality data and, through the Medicare Shared Savings Program, are eligible to share in the savings they achieve for Medicare in proportion to the level of quality they achieve. ACOs may also share in losses incurred for Medicare if the care they provide is too costly. In January 2015, HHS Secretary Sylvia Burwell announced the ambitious goal of tying 90% of all health care payments to value by 2018.

Since its passage in 2010, there have been repeated attempts by Republicans in the House of Representatives to repeal and/or replace the ACA. At the time of this writing, shortly after the election of President Donald Trump, the American Health Care Act was proposed to replace significant parts of the ACA. The fate of this bill remains uncertain but readers are directed to the Henry J. Kaiser Family Foundation websit as a trusted source of up-to-date information.

With the increasing role of state and federal policy in the provision of and payment for health care, it is critical for physicians to become actively engaged in adovocating for policies that best benefit patients, providers, and the overall health care system.

Safety Net for the Uninsured or Underinsured

Despite the accomplishments of the ACA, at least 32 million Americans were uninsured in 2014. Many cite the high cost of health insurance as the main reason for being uninsured. Although the ACA mandates that all individuals have health insurance, some choose not to purchase insurance because they perceive their personal risk as low compared with the cost of health insurance or the penalty for remaining uninsured.

The uninsured have worse health outcomes. According to the Institute of Medicine (IOM), 18,000 persons die prematurely each year because they lack health insurance. The **Emergency Medical Treatment and Active Labor Act** (EMTALA), passed in 1986, stipulates that all hospitals that receive Medicare payments and have emergency rooms must treat all patients

Table 29.2. Eligibility criteria for and benefits of designation as a Federally Qualified Health Center (FQHC)

Eligibility Criteria	Benefits
1. Located in or serves a community with limited access to health care	1. Federal grant money and federal loans for capital improvements
2. Provides comprehensive primary health care services and support services topromote access to care	2. Improved reimbursement rates for Medicaid and Medicare payments
3. Provides health care to all with sliding-scale fees based on ability to pay	3. Ability to hire National Health Service Corps providers
4. Governed by a board, at least 51% of whom are patients who represent the target population	4. Medical malpractice for providers paid by the Federal Government
5. Meets certain clinical, administrative, and financial performance and accountability requirements	5. Special price discounts for pharmaceutical products for patients of the center

with emergency medical problems, regardless of ability to pay. Unfortunately, due to difficulty accessing health care in ambulatory settings, the uninsured tend to use emergency rooms unnecessarily for health care that could be delivered more cheaply and with greater continuity in an outpatient setting. Not surprisingly, the uninsured are also less likely to receive recommended screening tests.

The **Federally Qualified Health Center** (FQHC) program was established in 1969 as part of President Johnson's War on Poverty to improve access to health care for the uninsured. FQHCs target high-need communities and deliver culturally appropriate comprehensive primary health services. They include Community Health Centers, Migrant Health Centers, Health Care for the Homeless programs, and Public Housing Primary Care programs. Designation as an FQHC means that the center meets program criteria and receives several benefits (outlined in Table 29.2). In 2002, President George W. Bush's President's Health Center Initiative doubled funding for the FQHC program from US $1 billion to US $2 billion and created 1,200 new health centers. The 2008 American Recovery and Reinvestment Act (ARRA) designated an additional US $2 billion for investment in FQHCs over 2 years. The ACA designated US $11 billion for investment in FQHCs over 5 years. As of 2013, there were 9,170 FQHC sites serving over 21.7 million patients across the country. The FQHC program is estimated to help save US $24 billion in total health care costs by helping patients access preventive medical services, avoiding unnecessary emergency room visits, and preventing hospitalizations.

Health System Performance

> How does the US health care system rate when compared internationally?

The US spends far more than any other country on health care. In 2014, spending for health care reached US $3.0 trillion or approximately 17.5% of the nation's economy. Health care costs have outpaced inflation. The largest shares of this expenditure were spent by the federal govern-

ment (28%), households (28%), private businesses (20%), and state/local governments (17%). Unfortunately, high costs have not guaranteed high quality. In the landmark report, *To Err Is Human*, the IOM reported that medical errors cause 98,000 deaths in the US annually. In a subsequent report, *Crossing the Quality Chasm*, the IOM defined quality care as safe, timely, effective, efficient, equitable, and patient centered. Although there are no universal standards for evaluating health care systems, in 2000, the World Health Organization (WHO) used criteria including *infant mortality* (the US ranked 19th worldwide), *maternal mortality* (ranked 32nd), and *life expectancy* (ranked 24th) to determine that *the US health care system ranked 37*th *in the world in overall quality*.

The quality of the health care system depends on which outcomes are valued. The US health care system performs well on outcomes such as survival after myocardial infarction and traumatic injuries. In its rankings, the WHO highly valued *equal access* to health care services, a criterion on which the US health care system performs relatively poorly because access to health care is uneven and closely related to insurance status. Studies have repeatedly shown that those without health insurance forgo needed medical care and have higher mortality rates for many conditions than those who are insured. Additionally, health care providers and facilities are not evenly distributed across the country; common shortage areas include both rural and inner city localities. The Commonwealth Fund compares 11 industrialized nations on health outcomes and quality annually. Since 2010, and most recently in 2014, the US was ranked the most expensive and worst performing on quality of care (effective, safe, coordinated, patient-centered), access to care, efficiency, equity, and healthy lives.

Recommended Readings

Institute of Medicine. (1999). *To err is human: Building a safer healthcare system. November 1, 1999. Brief report.* Available at http://www.iom.edu/Reports/1999/To-Err-is-Human-Building-A-Safer-Health-System.aspx

Institute of Medicine. (2001). *Crossing the quality chasm: A new health system for the 21st century. Brief report.* Available at https://www.ncbi.nlm.nih.gov/pubmed/25057539

Sultz, H. A., & Young, K. M. (2010). *Health care USA: Understanding its organization and delivery* (7th ed.). Boston, MA: Jones and Bartlett.

US Department of Health and Human Services, Center for Medicare and Medicaid Services. (2016). *Accountable care organizations: What providers need to know.* Retrieved from https://www.cms.gov/medicare/medicare-fee-for-service-payment/sharedsavingsprogram/downloads/aco_providers_factsheet_icn907406.pdf

Additional Resources

Commonwealth Fund. *Mirror, mirror on the wall, 2014 update: How the U.S. health care system compares internationally.* Available at http://www.commonwealthfund.org/publications/fund-reports/2014/jun/mirror-mirror

Henry J. Kaiser Family Foundation. *Health reform source.* http://healthreform.kff.org/

US Department of Health and Human Services. *About the Affordable Care Act.* Available at http://www.hhs.gov/healthcare/about-the-aca/index.html

US Department of Health and Human Services. Official US Government Site for Medicare. http://www.medicare.gov/

Review Questions

1. The amount of money that health insurance beneficiaries must pay regardless of whether or not they seek health services is called a(n)
   A. co-insurance
   B. co-pay
   C. deductible
   D. out-of-pocket cost
   E. premium

2. Which of the following groups of US citizens or permanent residents is *not* eligible for Medicare?
   A. Individuals > 65 who have paid income tax for 10 years
   B. Individuals with amyotrophic lateral sclerosis
   C. Individuals with end-stage kidney disease requiring dialysis
   D. Permanently disabled individuals
   E. Poor pregnant women

3. The Patient Protection and Affordable Care Act (ACA)
   A. allows states to expand Medicaid eligibility to all adults under age 65 with income < 133% of the FPL
   B. offers limited bonuses to primary care physicians treating Medicare patients
   C. requires all health plans to cover a minimum level of preventive care
   D. requires all individuals to have health insurance
   E. all of the above

Answer Key on p. 466

30 Theories of Social Relations and Interprofessional Collaboration

Barret Michalec, PhD, and Frederic W. Hafferty, PhD

- How might theories of social relations help explain important issues in interprofessional collaboration (IPC)?
- How does structural/functionalism theory differ from conflict theory with regard to IPC?
- How does the study of complexity facilitate our understanding of social relations and IPC?
- How does punctuated equilibrium theory differ from diffusion of innovation theory?
- How are the processes of unfreeze-change-(re)freeze similar to the concept of *knotworking*?
- Why might expectation states theory be a useful approach to explore occupation-related status differentials among health care providers?

Introduction

How might theories of social relations help explain important issues in interprofessional collaboration (IPC)?

Interprofessional collaboration (IPC) refers to health professionals from differing disciplines working together to provide health care. The implementation of IPC has been associated with improved patient safety, decreased medical costs, enhanced job satisfaction, and reduced job turnover. All of these factors are essential to delivering high-quality patient care in a complex medical environment. Interprofessional education (IPE) refers to the instruction- and practice-based training that prepares students of diverse health care occupations to familiarize themselves with the knowledge, skills, and approaches of others' disciplines, to facilitate effective integrated collaboration.

Research about IPC is based on a range of theoretical perspectives from sociology, psychology, education, mathematics, and business to better understand the structure and dynamics of interpersonal and group relations. In the following sections we will first present a brief synopsis of three overarching and conceptually dominant theoretical perspectives (conflict, structural functional-

ism, and symbolic interactionism), from which the more specialized and focused theories described in the subsequent section have evolved.

Overarching Theoretical Perspectives

Conflict Theory

A prominent example of **conflict theory** is Karl Marx's theory of class struggle in industrialized societies: Those who control the means of production exercise social control and dominance. The unequal distribution of authority shapes, among other things, patterns of social class. Other examples include conflict between the sexes (part of the focus of feminist sociological theory), and among racial, ethnic, political, and religious groups. *Poststructuralism* is a more recent version of *conflict theory* and focuses on the scientific and cultural institutions in society (such as law and medicine) and the power struggles that emerge as a function of how these institutions seek to structure daily existence. An example from medicine is *medicalization,* where certain "conditions" (e.g., alcoholism, drug addiction) are considered "diseases" rather than problems of a personal (e.g., lack of character or moral fiber), social (e.g., criminal), or religious (e.g., sinful) nature. *Conflict theory*, however, focuses more on issues of *inequities* and how the definitions of problems, and the solutions offered, serve the vested interests of "a few" (e.g., management and capital) rather than those of "the many" (e.g., workers and employees). A case in point is how the use of addictive drugs was more likely to be considered a crime rather than a disease (drug addiction) until drug use moved from the inner cities to the suburbs and began to threaten the social stability and self-identities of the middle and upper classes. Theories that address the inequalities within the hierarchy of health care professions (i.e., "resource-based" differences between, and general perceptions of, doctors and nurses, and others with different roles in the system), and how these differences affect team-based, collaborative care, or influence interactions between different types of health professionals in an IPC setting stem from a conflict perspective.

Structural Functionalism

> How does structural/functionalism theory differ from conflict theory with regard to IPC?

Structural functionalism (SF) emphasizes how change in one part of a group or social system has implications for other parts of that group or system. SF arose from an attempt to apply models of biological functioning to social action as SF sociologists attempted to appear "more scientific" by modeling themselves after the dominant scientific paradigm of the time (see Chapter 1: Evolving Models of Health Care). Society is considered analogous to the biological organism, which is composed of various parts, each of which contributes to the functioning of the whole, and where all are needed to function in a state of homeostasis. Depending on the unit of analysis (e.g., individual, community, state, nation), the object is viewed as composed of interdependent and coordinated parts and, in turn, is itself part of some even larger interdependent and coordinated system. Change in one part generates reactive and/or adaptive change in another. As a rule, individuals who apply a SF perspective to the analysis of social issues focus more

on outcomes and consequences (e.g., homeostasis or its absence) than on causes. From an SF perspective, a pattern of social action is more likely to endure if a given social phenomenon contributes more to achieving system goals than to impeding them. Conversely, if the consequences are considered negative, then that pattern is likely to change. Thus, systems tend toward a pattern of dynamic equilibrium in which change is "met" by system adaptation in a manner designed to preserve stability and balance. Theories stemming from this perspective tend to examine how IPC initiatives serve to enhance respect and understanding among the health professions, cultivate role blurring, and restore or maintain a general homeostasis within the care delivery system. Such theories also examine how a balanced health care delivery system, in turn, affects other social systems such as education, employment, and families.

Symbolic Interactionism

Symbolic interactionism and its related areas of inquiry (pragmatism, phenomenology, and ethnomethodology) begin with three assumptions: (1) people react to the world based on their understandings of it, (2) these understandings come from the interactions people have with others, and (3) people make these understandings by filtering them through their own experiences. *Symbolic interactionism* gives microsocial relations a more powerful role in the construction of social reality. Not only does society shape the individual, but individuals shape society as well. As such, symbolic interactionism illustrates how individuals create and use the social structures of which they are a part. Put simply, shared understandings and meanings (of social symbols) enable social actors to successfully interact in a variety of social settings. Symbolic interactionists focus on the microsocial relations within the health care system, specifically the interactions among providers, and the struggles between providers and the health care systems in which they work. Symbolic interactionists would be concerned with the effect on team functioning and quality of care of differing styles of interaction, use of language, and understandings of roles and responsibilities between team members (e.g., doctors, nurses, health psychologists, social workers), and how these differences are initially learned and how they are most effectively shared.

Having provided an overview of general sociological perspectives, including how these broad theoretical frameworks may be applied within IPC research, we now discuss specific theories that have been explicitly showcased in the IPC and IPE literature. In addition, we will review other theories that have been proposed as practical, informative, and more user-friendly but which are only referred to implicitly within these research domains.

Specific and Focused Theories

Organizational Learning Theory

Organizational learning theory (OLT), a macro-to-meso level theory, is often utilized to explore how knowledge is created, maintained, and transferred within and between organizations. Over time, and through various organizationally based experiences and general maturation, an organization gains knowledge. This knowledge is then used to increase efficiency, promote productivity and reliability, and improve relations among stakeholders within and surrounding the organization. In short, the organization *learns* (from experience) how to improve. From this approach, knowledge is created at four different units of analysis: individual, group, organizational, and interorganizational. Of course, different organizations learn at different rates, and these learning rates are influenced by various aspects of the organization, including participating workers' abilities, available technology, and organizational policies and practices. In this sense, organizational learning serves as an adaptive function in a highly competitive environment.

Within the context of IPC, OLT can be used to better understand how health care delivery institutions (i.e., hospitals and clinics, departments within hospitals) "learn" from other health care institutions, as well as their own collaborative care delivery practices, to promote more efficient and effective comprehensive care with regard to variables such as cost, safety, and quality. Aspects of OLT are often employed in IPC research to exam-

ine a variety of quality of patient care issues such as programs to expedite patient care transfers between the emergency department and medical intensive care unit.

Complexity Theory

> How does the study of complexity facilitate our understanding of social relations and IPC?

Complexity theory has evolved from earlier systems theories in sociology, such as structural functionalism. Its main theoretical lineage, however, is tied to recent interdisciplinary advances made in the study of complex systems, including such phenomena as *six-degrees of separation* (everyone in the world is connected by six or fewer people) and *swarm behavior* (complex group behaviors, such as large crowds leaving a baseball stadium, can be modeled using simple rules, such as those followed by swarming bees). Within *complexity theory*, systems are variously defined as self-organizing, adaptive, emergent, comprising a large number of elements, and network-like in structure. According to IPC scholars, complexity theory addresses complicated adaptive systems that are unpredictable, often paradoxical, and feature a number of "unknowns." IPC studies engaging this model focus on health care delivery as an elaborate system comprising several intricately interacting and competing disciplines. These studies explore the adaptive nature and emergence of care delivery teams as well as the intrinsic and extrinsic factors that have an impact on team formation and team processes.

Contingency Theory

Contingency theory focuses on the constraints and demands (i.e., "contingency factors") an environment makes on an organization and the resulting interactions and processes within that organization designed to accommodate these factors. The theory contends that it is essential to examine the interplay between contingency factors and the structure(s) of the organization to best understand the depth and nature of various organizational attributes such as explicit and implicit procedures and practices and how authority is structured. On a broader level, contingency theory can also be used to examine organizational leadership and how various internal and external constraints (i.e., size of the organization, available resources and resource allocation, perceptions of employees) may affect how a given leadership strategy will "fit" the needs of the organization. From this approach, the needs of an organization (i.e., IPC in a health care delivery institution or IPE in a health professions education institution) are more likely achieved when programs and practices are effectively designed and the leadership style is appropriate to both the group and its task(s).

Punctuated Equilibrium Theory

Punctuated equilibrium theory (PET) provides another method for understanding change (especially policy-related change) in complex social systems. PET suggests that most social systems exist in extended periods of stasis (i.e., equilibrium), but at some point, these systems are *punctuated* by sudden shifts, forcing a change of course in order to recover and respond to the environment. This model suggests that the policy change stemming from this punctuated shift generally only happens incrementally due to restraints such as the imbedded nature of institutional culture, varied stakeholder interests, and the limits of individual decision makers. Regarding IPC, PET could be used to examine the progressive onset and impact of IPC on health care delivery, and of IPE on training.

Diffusion of Innovation Theory

> How does punctuated equilibrium theory differ from diffusion of innovation theory?

Whereas PET may be best used to examine the onset of, and initial engagement with, IPE and IPC, **diffusion of innovation theory** (DIT) would be an appropriate tool to determine the acceptance and continued implementation of IPE and IPC programs and practices. DIT seeks to explain how, why, and to what extent new directives and initiatives spread through organizations and institutions. The theory contends that the spread of a new initiative relies heavily on buy-in from social actors (particularly those in power) for it to be sustained. It is important to note, however, that the "diffusion" of the innovation (e.g., IPC team-based care and practices nested therein) differentially manifests itself in various institutional cultures, and thus is highly subject to the social actors within that institution and the practices and processes already in existence. Although this particular theory has not yet been heavily utilized in IPC research, DIT has extensive potential to provide better understanding of the "sticking" and "staying" power of IPC and IPE.

Activity Theory

Activity theory, and its offspring, **cultural-historical activity theory** (CHAT), provides a lens to view micro- and macro-level interactions and their impact on interpersonal, interprofessional, and even interdepartmental and interagency relations. CHAT was developed to showcase the value of exploring the sociohistorical and cultural aspects of communities of practice. Within this theory, *activity* refers to the happenings among interacting individuals (as opposed to individually based activities) where such happenings are characterized by instability and contradiction. The outcome of such interactions affects the social actors themselves, the surrounding environment, and perhaps even the social structure. Some researchers have applied a particular conceptual element of activity theory, *knotworking* (a term originally coined by Engeström, who originally developed CHAT), whereby individuals tie, untie, and re-tie separate threads of activity, to provide a more in-depth understanding of IPC in the hospital setting.

Unfreeze-Change-(Re)Freeze

> How are the processes of unfreeze-change-(re)freeze similar to the concept of knotworking?

Somewhat similar to the tie, untie, and re-tie processes of *knotworking* (although knotworking examines activity at a group level), an approach was proposed by Kurt Lewin for a three-stage model commonly referred to as *unfreeze, change, freeze* (or *refreeze*). Although often criticized for being overly simplistic, this model works at all levels (individual, group or organization, state or country). The first stage, *unfreezing*, refers to anticipating change and coming to understand the necessity for change. Motivation for change is influenced by both internal and external factors (i.e., Lewin's notion of *force field analysis*). The second stage, which Lewin refers to as the *change* process, basically involves an "unfreezing" of the status quo whereby individuals are more open to making changes that are deemed necessary. Interpersonal support for, as well as role modeling of, new attitudes and behaviors play a significant role at this stage. The third stage, *freezing* (or *refreezing*) is perhaps the most controversial, especially in contemporary times, as it is difficult to understand the benefit of "re-freezing" a routine (even if it is a "new" routine). Therefore, scholars have suggested that this stage should be viewed in the modern area as more flexible in nature. The key, however, to this three-stage model is that the change be accepted, practiced, and sustained. Unfreeze-change-(re)freeze theory can be used to explore how health care organizations can overcome issues that arise over changes in management and confront institutional (and profession-specific) cultures and embedded practices to embrace IPC and IPE effectively.

Role Theory

Role theory highlights the expectations attached to particular social positions and examines the interplay and outcomes of such expectations. Put simply, a *role* is a set of expectations about what one *should* do in a particular social position (e.g., the values, norms, and practices associated with being a particular provider). From a more social-psychological perspective, role theory examines if, how, and to what extent social actors work at and within roles, and the dynamism of these roles within the larger social structure. Researchers have explored various aspects of role theory in relation to IPC and IPE, paying special attention to role specificity (i.e., discipline-specific responsibilities and expectations) and role blurring (the overlapping and sharing of roles between occupations), and exploring how students in IPE may navigate the apparent tension between role specificity and role blurring.

Contact Hypothesis

Contact hypothesis suggests that "contact" between in- and out-groups will, in turn, reduce prejudice and stereotypes held by and between those groups. Gordon Allport is often credited as the forefather of the *contact hypothesis* as it was he who first presented four key, positive conditions in which intergroup contact could reduce prejudice and stereotypes between the group members: (1) equal status between groups – both groups must perceive equal status in the situation; (2) common goals – groups must work together toward a shared goal; (3) intergroup cooperation – groups must work interdependently, not competitively, toward the shared *goal*; and (4) the support of authorities, law, or custom – intergroup contact must be explicitly supported by the institution(s) and authorities of those institutions.

The contact hypothesis is often applied in evaluation-based research to assess the outcomes of IPE programs (e.g., shifts in students' attitudes and perceptions of other health profession groups). Three principal models of how intergroup contact can have an impact on cognitive representations of group membership and dissolve stereotypes have evolved from Allport's original theory: *personalization*, *common in-group identity*, and *mutual intergroup differentiation*. These models suggest intergroup contact can be structured to break down the deleterious effects of categorization and alter cognitive representations of group membership. All three models suggest mechanisms by which group members cognitively reconceptualize their memberships from one that is mutually exclusive to one that is more interactive (which will, in turn, promote intergroup cooperation).

Social Identity Theory and Social Categorization Theory

Social identity theory asserts that people define and evaluate themselves in terms of the groups to which they belong – that is, the group provides people with a collective self-concept or social identity. People can have as many social identities as the groups to which they feel they belong. The theory emphasizes group membership and belongingness and their consequences for interpersonal and intergroup relations. Preferring a positive rather than a negative identity, people perceive their group (the in-group) more positively than the out-group. Researchers have used social identity theory to explore interprofessional socialization and the development of an interprofessional identity among health professions students. Findings have revealed key tenets of social identity theory in the examination of "relative distancing" practices among health professions students navigating their professional identity.

Social identity theory actually stems from *social categorization theory*, which highlights the propensity of social actors to perceive self and others as members not only of particular groups but also of social categories, often to the disadvantage of others. Groups into which people categorize others (i.e., cognitive representations) have the intended effect of minimizing perceived differences among in-group members and accentuating differences between the in-group and out-groups. Furthermore, this in- and out-group classification is a superimposed category distinction with emotional and social identity significance. Despite the ties between social categorization theory and social identity theory, as well as the contact hypothesis, there has been little attention paid to social categorization theory in the IPC literature to date.

Expectation States Theory

> Why might expectation states theory be a useful approach to explore occupation-related status differentials among health care providers?

Expectation states theory (EST), a more micro-level theory (although affected by group and societal level beliefs), examines how key social categories (e.g., gender) are linked to status beliefs (e.g., men are more competent) and how those status beliefs organize social interaction in a way that replicates and maintains disparities. Status is a central concept in EST and assigns "worth" to different categories of people based on shared cultural beliefs or stereotypes. Status inequalities result when some social groups are deemed higher status or have more respect, esteem, or prestige than other groups of people. EST is ideally suited for understanding phenomena such as IPC

because the theory is concerned with the influence of status differences in goal-oriented situations. For example, it examines how individuals interact around some collective task using each other's different attributes (e.g., gender, race, age) to form certain judgments, expectations, and perceptions. According to EST, status is important to interactions, and the maintenance of social inequalities is due to its connection to performance expectations. Performance expectations are exactly that: They are the way we expect individuals to perform based on stereotypic assumptions of their status. For instance, men are typically thought of as more competent, assertive, and task-oriented than women. These status characteristics are then activated within interactions (e.g., IPC) in the form of performance expectations – that is, we expect men to fulfill these characteristics. Researchers use EST to spotlight how status differences related specifically to gender may negatively impact the implementation and influence of IPE and IPC, and even general interactions within the health care delivery workplace.

Learning Theories

Various learning theories have been featured in IPC research. These include evaluation-based studies nested within the behaviorist perspective, which focuses on learning outcomes such as changes in students' behavior and attitudes, as studies grounded in the constructive approach, which focuses on learning processes (i.e., reflexive, problem-based, and collaborative), "scaffolds" (i.e., learning support structures or agents), and the influences of social and environmental factors.

Often referred to as a bridge between behaviorist and cognitive learning theories, Albert Bandura's *social learning theory* contends that individuals learn behavior from one another through such mechanisms as observation and imitation. According to Bandura, learning from modeled behavior not only promotes understanding of how a particular behavior is performed, but also provides templates for the observer to guide future similar actions. In this sense, social learning theory provides an excellent framework for examining health profession students' perceptions of behavior modeled by practitioners in the clinical setting. Within IPE and clinical training, behavior and attitudes modeled by professional practitioners are particular mechanisms by which students implicitly "learn" (as compared with explicit, formal instruction) various aspects of their future professional position. Researchers have used elements of Bandura's theoretical principles (e.g., people act on their environment and learn through experience as well as through their observations of others) in their development of self-reporting instruments and assessment of team-based training programs (see Chapter 11: Selected Theories of Development).

Summary

Various theoretical approaches can be used to develop, explore, and examine the efficacy of IPC. A number of these theories are explicitly showcased in IPC research, while others have only been proposed implicitly. The models presented in this chapter are judged to be more user-friendly compared with others featured in some of the more comprehensive reviews cited below and, therefore, more likely to be applied in future research.

Recommended Readings

Barr, H. (2013). Toward a theoretical framework for interprofessional education. *Journal of Interprofessional Care, 27*, 4–9. http://doi.org/10.3109/13561820.2012.698328

Hall, P., Weaver, L., & Grassau, P.A. (2013). Theories, relationships and interprofessionalism: Learning to weave. *Journal of Interprofessional Care, 27*, 73–80. http://doi.org/10.3109/13561820.2012.736889

Lutfiyya, M. N., Brandt, B. F., & Cerra, P. (2016). Reflections from the intersection of health professions education and clinical practice: The state of the science of interprofessional education and collaborative practice. *Academic Medicine, 91*, 766–771. http://doi.org/10.1097/ACM.0000000000001139

Suter, E., Goldman, J., Martimianakis, T., Chatalalsingh, C., DeMatteo, D. J., & Reeves, S. (2013). The use of systems and organizational theories in the interprofessional field: Findings from a scoping review. *Journal of Interprofessional Care, 27*, 57–64. http://doi.org/10.3109/13561820.2012.739670

Thistlethwaite, J., Moran, M., & The World Health Organization Study Group on Interprofessional Education and Collaborative Practice. (2010). Learning outcomes for interprofessional education (IPE): Literature review and synthesis. *Journal of Interprofessional Care, 24*(5), 503–513.

Review Questions

1. The person who believed that all societies are controlled by the bourgeoisie that own the means of production and who can be considered the "grandfather" of the conflict perspective is
   A. Emile Durkheim
   B. Georg Simmel
   C. Herbert Spencer
   D. Karl Marx
   E. Talcott Parsons

2. The idea that society is a system with parts that work together to promote stability is the main perspective of which theoretical paradigm in sociology?
   A. Conflict
   B. Feminist
   C. Neoconflict
   D. Structural functionalism
   E. Symbolic interactionist

3. Allport's four key, positive conditions in which intergroup contact could reduce prejudice and stereotypes between the group members include each of the following except
   A. common goals
   B. equal status between groups
   C. intergroup cooperation
   D. space to interact
   E. support of authorities

Answer Key on p. 466

31 Moral, Ethical, and Legal Issues in Patient Care

Margie H. Shaw, JD, PhD

- What is the relationship between morals, ethics, and the law?
- What is the role of moral theories and principles in bioethical decision making?
- What are the four principles of bioethics?
- What is conscientious objection?
- What are capacity and competency?
- What are advance directives, and what is the difference between substituted judgment and best interest?
- What are ways to resolve ethical conflicts that occur in patient care?

Introduction

Taking care of patients is both a moral endeavor and one regulated by state and federal laws. Successful practice in health care requires legal and ethical knowledge, the skills necessary for ethical decision making, and behaviors consistent with good ethical judgment. Legal and ethical knowledge includes an understanding of (1) the relationship between morals, ethics, and the law; (2) moral theories and principles, including one's own personal moral beliefs; (3) professional obligations; (4) common legal and ethical issues that arise in patient care as well as those specific to one's practice; and (5) a process for resolution of ethical conflict. Skills necessary for ethical decision making include self-reflection, critical thinking, and communication. Behaviors consistent with good ethical judgment follow from attitudes of respect and humility, including a willingness to learn about different perspectives and frames of reference. This chapter focuses on the knowledge foundational to good ethical decision making in clinical practice.

What is the relationship between morals, ethics, and the law?

A **moral theory** is a system of categorical judgments of right and wrong. **Ethics** is the philosophical study of moral theories. *Normative ethics* is the study of moral decisions and action. Whether or not an individual studies philosophy, they will have beliefs about what is right and wrong. These moral beliefs influence thinking about complex patient care, including morally complex patient care. It is important to understand one's own moral beliefs and how those relate to *professional ethics* and legal obligations. Professional ethics is the moral standard specific to a profession or professions. In addition to teaching professional codes of ethics, clinical educational programs teach the *four principles of bioethics* (*beneficence*, *nonmaleficence*, *autonomy*, and *justice*) popularized by Beauchamp and Childress in the 1970s. **Laws** are governmental codifications of regulations imposed on citizens that may be enforced. Laws create negative rights or positive rights. Negative rights are rights to prohibit action (i.e., the right to refuse medical treatment). Positive rights are rights that compel action (i.e., the right of every patient in an emergency department to be screened and, if necessary, stabilized by medical staff). Basic moral values of a society inform these regulations and set limits on acceptable behavior. To understand the relationships, consider a case.

The patient is a 21-year-old woman who has a diagnosis of persistent vegetative state. The parents come to a difficult decision and request that the attending physician remove their daughter from the ventilator. Believing death would result, the physician refuses, citing his moral and professional obligation to avoid harming a patient (the principle of nonmaleficence) and his obligation to do what is good for the patient (the principle of beneficence). The physician might also have considered potential legal liability and criminal prosecution. Seeking legal recourse, the parents petition the court to appoint the father as the personal guardian with the authority to determine his daughter's medical treatment (the principle of autonomy exercised through surrogate authority). Eventually, the highest court in the state, relying on a Constitutional right of privacy, grants the petition and the parents take the order to the attending physician, again requesting removal of the ventilator. The physician, again, refuses. In this case, known as *In the Matter of Karen Quinlan*, the Supreme Court of New Jersey appointed Karen's father as guardian with full authority over her health care decisions, and held that the removal of the ventilator would not result in civil or criminal liability. The physician would not violate any laws by removing the ventilator from the patient, yet he still refused. It was not standard practice at the time for physicians to remove supportive treatment, and his refusal rested on principles of professional responsibility and personal morals.

Knowing one's own moral values and tendencies as well as the obligations of the profession is as important in patient care as knowing laws that affect practice. It is also important to appreciate that professional values evolve over time, as this case illustrates. Personal values also evolve over time and with experience.

Approaches to Normative Ethics

> What is the role of moral theories and principles in bioethical decision making?

There are three major approaches to normative ethics: deontology, consequentialism, and virtue ethics. **Deontological ethics** considers the rightness or wrongness of an action when determin-

ing moral obligations. This ethical theory is duty based. An example of a duty one might value is the duty to not act in such a way as to result in the death of another person. The health care providers in the Karen Quinlan case may have focused on such a duty.

Consequentialist theories consider the outcome of the actions in determining moral obligations. These theories vary on the particular outcome that is valued (e.g., most happiness, most pleasure, best welfare). A provider with consequentialist tendencies may focus on the overall outcome of a decision to remove patients that are in a persistent vegetative state from ventilator support. Does permitting or facilitating such a decision result in the best outcome for all? Consequentialist theories consider the risks and benefits of any decision to determine which action leads to the best outcome.

Virtue ethics considers the moral characteristics of the actor. This provider would ask: What would the virtuous provider do under these circumstances? This question requires the identification of the particular virtues that one values in the particular role.

Providers may have tendencies that incorporate one or all of the approaches from the three major moral theories. In addition, most health professional education programs teach the four principles of bioethics. These principles provide a common language to facilitate discussion about morally complex patient decisions; however, the principles neither provide a decision-making process nor do they include all principles that influence ethical decision making. Clinicians with consequentialist tendencies may balance these and other principles in an attempt to determine the best outcome. Clinicians with deontological tendencies may value a particular principle in a specific case.

Principles of Bioethics

> What are the four principles of bioethics?

The **principle of respect for autonomy** is the right of individuals to decide how to live their own life. The legal **doctrine of informed consent** rests on the principle of respect for autonomy. The doctrine of informed consent requires providers to give patients that have the capacity to understand full information about the diagnosis, the prognosis, and the risks and benefits of any treatment options, including the option of no treatment. Patients with the capacity to make medical decisions can decide what they believe is the best decision for themselves and can refuse any or all treatment, including life-sustaining treatment.

The **principle of beneficence** requires health care providers to promote the welfare of the patient and always strive to do what is right for the patient. This principle requires the balance of risks and benefits. Historically, physician providers determined the beneficent course using medical criteria.

The **principle of nonmaleficence** requires health care providers to avoid harm to the patient. Clinicians must balance beneficence with nonmaleficence and avoid inflicting harm that is not justified by the benefit. Most rights in health care are negative rights: Patients cannot compel a health care provider to act in such a way that the provider believes will cause more harm than benefit.

The **principle of justice** has multiple meanings generally concerned with the fairness of decision making. In research, the principle of justice requires that the burdens of research do not fall on one patient population while the benefits accrue to another; and all research must be equally distributed among all members of society. The principle of justice also requires the fair allocation of resources in research and clinical settings. Finally, it requires providers to have a fair decision-making process in all encounters.

Professional Obligations

Professional organizations adopt ethical principles as standards of conduct intended to define the profession. While multiple professions populate health care teams, the codes of ethics are comparable: They each focus on the responsibilities to the patient, family, larger community, the profession, other health professionals, and society. Obligations include respecting persons, protecting patients' privacy, ensuring honesty and integrity, respecting property and laws, and behaving with appropriate professional deportment. Providers

need to examine personal values in light of professional obligations and specifically to identify any conflicts, and, in the event of conflict, develop a process for reconciling the differences so as to avoid both interference with patient care and moral distress. Understanding the professional obligations of other team members also benefits collaboration and enhances patient care.

Health care professionals have a **fiduciary duty** to patients. This is a special relationship between a person of power and a vulnerable person. Because of the imbalance of power, the fiduciary has an obligation to put the interests of the other first. This relationship requires loyalty to the interests of the other. As Justice Cardozo explained: "Many forms of conduct permissible in a workaday world for those acting at arm's length, are forbidden to those bound by fiduciary ties. A trustee is held to something stricter than the morals of the market place. Not honesty alone, but the punctilio of an honor the most sensitive, is then the standard of behavior."

What is conscientious objection?

There are instances when professional obligations may conflict with the personal moral beliefs of a health care provider. In these instances, very importantly, health care providers have the professional obligation to never abandon a patient. If a provider has a **conscientious objection** to a treatment decision, that provider must transition the care of the patient to a provider who does not have the same conscientious objection. The transition must occur in such a way as to cause minimum disruption of care to the patient and also must minimize any burden to other professionals.

A **conscientious objector** is an individual with deeply held moral or religious beliefs about the rightness or wrongness of an act in all circumstances (e.g., all war, not a specific war). To qualify for conscientious objector status for purposes of military service, individuals must satisfy conditions set by the federal government. Despite recommendations to the contrary, conscientious objector status in health care does not currently require satisfaction of conditions by a licensing board or medical tribunal. Absent oversight, health care professionals must self-regulate to ensure the right of all patients to access standard health care in a timely fashion.

Common Legal Issues That Arise in Patient Care

Self-regulation is a critical feature of professions, and many professional obligations have corresponding legal obligations. Legal obligations affecting patient care come in the form of federal and state statutes (legislation), federal and state case law (court decisions), and federal and state administrative law (regulation). Like professional obligations, legal obligations address issues in public health as well as issues in individual decision making.

There is no one overarching body of law affecting patient care; rather, the federal government and states have each passed laws to address specific issues. For example, following the Supreme Court decision upholding a constitutional right for a physician to provide termination of pregnancy interventions under certain circumstances, the federal government and most states adopted legislation addressing conscientious objection to certain medical treatments. States have an interest in protecting the life and health of citizens, and most health law is state law. States license health care professionals, to protect the public by ensuring minimal levels of competence and providing oversight. State medical malpractice laws hold providers to a standard of care determined by the profession and provide civil remedy for negligent practice. The federal Emergency Medical Treatment and Active Labor Act (EMTALA) extends the professional obligation to never abandon a patient, to requiring emergency departments to screen and stabilize any person who comes to the facility and requires stabilization. While the federal Health Insurance Portability and Accountability Act (HIPAA) imposes privacy standards on patient health information, state laws have mandatory reporting of certain kinds of information. For example, based on case law, providers must report when a patient is a danger to others (e.g., if a patient makes a credible threat to kill another person). Health care providers must also report suspected child or elder abuse as well as domestic violence. State laws mandate reporting of specific diseases to the local health officer. Most are communicable diseases, but mandatory reporting laws may also include diseases that could affect public health in other ways (e.g., disorders characterized

by lapses in consciousness). Hospitals are required to make sure patients have a safe plan before discharge, and members of the health care team work together to help the patient make as smooth a transition as possible.

Determining Capacity and Competency

> What are capacity and competency?

As discussed above, the decision *In the Matter of Karen Quinlan* extended the right of refusal to health care to surrogate decision makers. Some of the most common ethical questions in patient care are (1) whether the patient has capacity to make a decision; (2) when the patient lacks capacity, who is the appropriate surrogate; and (3) what is the standard upon which the surrogate ought to rely in making a decision.

All adults are presumed to be competent and to have the capacity to make health care decisions. **Competency** is distinguishable from **capacity**. *Competency* is a legal determination and requires a judicial ruling. A court finds an adult incompetent when they are severely impaired and unable to make decisions about finances, property, or health care. In these cases, the court appoints a guardian to make decisions on behalf of the individual deemed incompetent. A competent person may face circumstances that impair decision making, such as a medical event.

The determination of **capacity** is a clinical decision. Determining capacity can be difficult: It requires time and clinical acumen. Nonetheless, helping a patient to voice preferences about medical decisions not only supports the patient's right to self-determination but also relieves the health care team and family of uncertainty. To determine capacity, the clinician makes a functional assessment about the patient's ability to understand the necessary information, to appreciate the significance of the decision, and to provide reasons for a communicated choice. A diagnosis of dementia or cognitive decline (or disability) does not necessarily mean the patient lacks capacity. Capacity evaluations do not require a psychiatric consultation, and evidence of a psychiatric illness does not mean that a patient lacks capacity. Only when the clinician believes a psychiatric condition is affecting the patient's capacity should the clinician consult with psychiatry. The health care provider who knows the patient best, rather than a consultant, is usually the most appropriate person to assess capacity.

Capacity often fluctuates in patients who are hospitalized. It is important for clinicians to maximize the patient's opportunity to demonstrate capacity by making the assessment during the patient's best times, by minimizing distractions, by minimizing medications that could affect the determination (for the duration of the assessment and discussions about treatment choices), and by engaging team members and, potentially, family members in the communication process. Capacity is not a global determination: It is specific to a particular question and a patient can have **partial capacity**. For example, a patient who lacks the capacity to understand the complexities of a difficult medical decision may have the capacity to complete an advance directive naming a health care agent. It is important to help patients express values and preferences about treatment decisions as well as preferences about the decision-making process.

While it may seem counterintuitive to some, patients with capacity can also delegate decisional authority to another. A few patients may prefer that a family member make decisions on their behalf. If this is an autonomous decision made by a patient with capacity, the medical team should respect this decision while continuing to engage the patient as much as possible.

There are some limits to the rights of patients with capacity to make decisions about medical treatments. In *Vacco vs. Quill*, the US Supreme Court unanimously held that a state has an interest in protecting ethical decision making in medicine, preventing euthanasia, protecting vulnerable populations from potential prejudice, and, most importantly, preserving life. These interests, the Court held, were rationally related to the challenged New York State statute that prohibited physicians from assisting terminally ill adults who have capacity from taking action to hasten death other than by withdrawing life-sustaining treatment. New York State law allows an adult patient with capacity to have life-sustaining ventilator

support withdrawn, with the intent that it results in death; but the law does not allow a physician to aid an adult patient with capacity, who is not on life-sustaining therapy, to take a medication with the intent that it results in death. The court held that, regardless of the motives of the health care provider, the example of providing a medication involves the criminal elements of causation and intent, while removing the patient from life support, when requested by the patient, does not. This Supreme Court decision reaffirms the right of states to regulate issues of health, life, and death.

As of the summer of 2016, four states (Oregon, Washington, Vermont, and California) had enacted legislation to allow physicians to aid patients in dying. In another state, Montana, the State Supreme Court had ruled current state law does not prohibit a physician from prescribing medication to hasten death for a patient with capacity. This is an evolving area of state law. Other states have considered, and continue to consider, legislation on this topic. What is consistent across states is continuing support for the ability of health care providers to comfort patients during the dying process, including providing pain medication appropriate to alleviate the patient's suffering. While such pain medication may have effects that hasten death, such as suppression of respiration, as long as the purpose of the prescription is to mitigate pain, the prescription is justified under the **principle of double effect** (a harm is justified if it occurs when attempting to promote a good). That is, the harm would not be permissible except as a "side effect." Thus, health care providers focused on the treatment of symptoms and patient comfort should not feel constrained by fear of the secondary effects of those treatments.

> What are advance directives, and what is the difference between substituted judgment and best interest?

Courts have interpreted the US Constitution and state constitutions to support patient rights in decision making. In 1990, Congress passed the **Patient Self Determination Act** requiring hospitals, nursing homes, home health care agencies, and hospice providers to provide all patients with information about patients' decision-making rights, including the right to create an advance directive. As discussed above, the legal doctrine of informed consent both requires health care providers to inform patients about treatment choices and allows adults with capacity to refuse recommended medical treatments. State laws vary on the exact nature of the required disclosures, but agree that the best decision-making process is shared and includes consideration of the patient's stated values and choices.

Advance Directives

Advance directives are instructions provided by the patient about health care decisions in case of future loss of capacity. Advance directives apply only if and when the patient loses capacity. There are two kinds of advance directives: procedural and substantive. **Procedural advance directives** tell the health care team what procedure to use for decision making when the patient lacks the capacity to do so (e.g., ask my health care agent, Aunt Mary). Procedural advance directives can take different forms (e.g., a *durable power of attorney for health care decisions,* a *health care agent,* or a *health care proxy*). **Substantive advance directives** leave instructions about the substance of patient preferences (e.g., "*do not resuscitate*"). A **living will** is an example of a substantive advance directive (see Chapter 33: Palliative Care). Following the Karen Quinlan case, individuals who wanted to place limits on medical treatment enacted living wills, but these documents can also express wishes for intensive treatment. Substantive advance directives provide information about the patient's values and, if appropriate to the situation, can allow the patient's expressed wishes to inform treatment decisions. A common problem with substantive advance directives, however, is that the imagined scenario does not match the current medical condition. For example, a patient could have an advance directive that includes "*do not intubate*" in the face of a circumstance that requires only temporary intubation to return to baseline. Substantive advance directives may provide an opportunity for patients to consider values and preferences in health care decisions; yet, it is often more helpful for the team if the patient has identified someone trusted to communicate their values and preferences. Public policy presumes a health care agent is better positioned than the health care team to evaluate whether a directive does, in fact, express what the patient would decide under the exact circumstances.

Surrogate Decision Making

There are three **standards for surrogate decision making**: reliance on the previously **expressed wishes of the patient**, substituted judgment, and best interest. Relying on a substantive advance directive is reliance on previously expressed wishes of the patient. The standard used when making the decision the patient would make, absent expressed instructions, is **substituted judgment**. To apply substituted judgment, the surrogate must know the patient well enough to know what the patient would decide. It is important to help a surrogate apply the values of the patient to the decision rather than their own values. The team can help the surrogate understand the substituted judgment standard by asking what the patient would decide if they could wake up for 15 min, understand their condition, and know that they were to return to that condition regardless of the treatment. Application of the substituted judgment standard requires knowledge of the patient's beliefs, values, and attitudes toward medical treatments. If the surrogate does not know these, then the surrogate cannot exercise substituted judgment and must consider what is in the best interest of the patient.

The **best interest standard**, originally adopted in family law to provide the incapacitated (minors) a voice separate from surrogates, is also accepted as an appropriate standard for decision making for incapacitated adult patients who do not have discernible preferences. The support for this approach is that it provides an objective standard, one that weighs the burdens and benefits in light of what a reasonable person would decide. While the best interest standard may provide incontrovertible guidance when there is a preferable treatment choice, it is less clear when there are multiple reasonable treatment options. Factors to consider when determining best interest include the patient's level of understanding; potential outcomes of treatments, including prolonging life; any cognitive, emotional, or sensory pleasure; as well as pain and suffering before, during, and after the treatments.

How one thinks about these factors, however, reflects one's biases, values, and beliefs. First, it is difficult for people who are able-bodied to imagine life with different abilities, and many people who are able-bodied underestimate the quality of life of people with disabilities. This bias risks undervaluing the life of a patient facing future disabilities. Second, this standard relies on concepts that are connected to the patient's consciousness. How does one consider risks and benefits when a patient is understood to have no awareness and feel no pain? Courts disagree whether it is in the patient's best interest to remain on a ventilator when diagnosed as permanently unconscious. The general population appears to disagree as well: A 2013 survey by the Pew Research Center found that about a third of Americans believe health care providers should attempt to save lives "in all circumstances," regardless of the resulting quality of the life saved.

Third, it can be uncertain what the reasonable person would choose when offered two equally unappealing options. Fourth and finally, while some suggest decisions about what is in the best interest of the patient must also consider external factors (e.g., the effect of the decision on primary care providers and available social supports for the care of persons with disabilities), others argue it is unfair to deny, or remove treatment from, individuals because of either effects on primary care givers or failures in social structures. Given these challenges to the best interest standard, it is preferable to find a surrogate with some knowledge of the patient's values and wishes. If that is not possible, the health care team and decision maker should be transparent about the factors influencing the decision, to ensure reasonableness.

Surrogate Decision Making for Children

When applying the best interest standard in **decision making for pediatric patients**, these same issues apply. This may account for efforts to facilitate reliance on either the substituted judgment standard or, when possible, the stated wishes of the patient. Unlike adults, however, the law does not recognize a broad right of minors to make decisions. The age of majority in most states is 18,

and states recognize expansive rights in parental authority over children who have not reached the age of majority. States do, however, recognize limited circumstances under which minors are considered to have attained adult status (i.e., are **emancipated minors**) and, therefore, are granted the authority to make health care decisions. In most states, the criteria for considering minors emancipated include marriage, military service, living independently from parents, and self-sufficiency. States have also identified some medical interventions minors can access for certain medical conditions, without parental involvement (e.g., sexually transmitted diseases, contraception, desire to terminate pregnancy, substance abuse). In these instances, states allow minors to access services to facilitate treatment, but not as a recognition of maturity of the minor patient.

Thus, in most instances, parents are the appropriate surrogates for children, even children who are close to the age of majority. However, coinciding with the growing numbers of chronically ill pediatric patients, health care providers have increasingly recognized the importance of involving pediatric patients in treatment decisions. While pediatric patients lack capacity under the legal doctrine of informed consent, this doctrine rests on the moral principle of respect for persons and the right of self-determination. As a result of the advocacy and leadership of health care professionals, a few states have adopted the **mature minor doctrine** either through legislation, case law, or regulation. Even in states where decisional authority rests with the parents, health care teams encourage pediatric patient involvement appropriate to the level of the child's development. This demonstration of respect for the pediatric patient as a person has the potential to encourage emotional development and other forms of growth and maturity. Involving pediatric patients in discussions and decisions about treatment improves patient and provider communication, which affects the patient's experience with the disease and the health care team. When pediatric patients participate in discussions and decisions, it improves the patient's participation in the treatment plan, again directly affecting the patient (and provider) experience. Facilitating a positive patient experience is likely to have an impact on all members of the health care team, including the family.

While most health care providers recognize the benefits of involving pediatric patients in discussions and decision making, it is important to consider complicating factors. First, parents may disagree with the providers' assessment of their child's ability to comprehend and participate. Second, even when agreement exists about the patient's abilities, parents may disagree with the appropriateness of involving a pediatric patient. Third, parents and health care team members may have different understandings of the diagnosis or prognosis, or what it means to live with the disease and various treatment choices. Thus, health care providers must work with parents to establish an agreed-upon level of pediatric patient involvement. Health care providers and parents should discuss how much information is appropriate to give the patient (e.g., what the team can tell the patient about the diagnosis, prognosis, or treatment) and how those conversations should occur. Parents may want to protect their child from "bad" information, and providers may have to educate the parents about the evidence supporting pediatric patient involvement. Overall, it is critical to establish trust and good communication among the patient, family, and health care team. This can be challenging when the health care team perceives parental values or decisions as jeopardizing the patient's well-being. Because states also have a legitimate interest in protecting minors and will intervene when parents are abusive or negligent, health care providers must report suspicion of abuse or neglect. The state agency charged with protecting the welfare of minors is the appropriate authority to determine whether state intervention is warranted.

Resolving Ethical Conflicts

> What are ways to resolve ethical conflicts that occur in patient care?

When a conflict arises, health care providers should attempt to resolve the conflict before seeking assistance from institutional or governmental resources. Yet, most clinical education does not include sufficient material on ethical decision-making processes. The principles of bioethics provide a common language and a starting point for ethical deci-

sion making in clinical practice, and the principle of justice requires that providers have a fair process for patient encounters and decision making. Providers need to decide how to respond to ethical questions and dilemmas. The bioethics literature provides useful guidance on how to approach ethical decision making. For example, Jonsen, Siegler, and Winslade created the Four Topics Chart for this purpose (see their *Clinical Ethics,* cited in Recommended Readings). In addition, providers may find the approach of **narrative medicine** helpful. Narrative medicine values the role of the patient's story in clinical practice, and **narrative ethics** prioritizes the patient's values in decision making. Ethical conflicts are often characterized by conflicts between the principles of bioethics and differences of opinion as to which principle should have priority in a particular situation. Narrative medicine provides the framework for the ordering of the principles – that is, the order is determined by the values of the patient. Narrative medicine requires providers to understand the patient's experience with illness – including the relational, emotional, and psychological dimensions – and the patient's values and preferences. Providers need to ask patients about what is important to them, what they value, how they want to live, and how the illness is affecting how they live.

Good approaches to ethical conflict resolution in clinical practice have common features. First, it is important to get the medicine right. Good medicine facilitates good ethical decision making. It is important to reflect upon personal and professional values and how those values may be influencing how one perceives the salient features of a case. Health care providers should consider ethical dilemmas from multiple perspectives, remembering that a person's experiences and values determine how one sees the case. Walking into a patient's room, a veteran health care provider likely will see something very different from what a novice health care provider sees, or what a family member sees. As Nancy Sherman explains in *The Fabric of Character,* "It is that our judgments of particular cases and our knowledge of how to 'compose the scene' is itself a part of the moral response…. In this sense, character is expressed in what one *sees* as much as in what one *does.* Knowing how to discern the particulars, Aristotle stresses, is a mark of virtue" (emphasis in the original; see Sherman, in Recommended Readings).

Once one considers personal and professional influences on how one composes the scene, the next step is to communicate with other team members and identify differences in perception. The skills needed to communicate effectively about emotionally charged and complex moral matters allow access to alternative frames and facilitate understanding.

Many ethical dilemmas are resolved through mutual understanding of the medical condition and identification of the salient features of the case and relevant ethical principles, combined with good communication. If the ethical issues remain unresolved, the health care team can ask for help from the hospital ethics committee. Good consultants are skilled in ethical reasoning, and a function of hospital ethics committees is to help clinicians think through and resolve ethical dilemmas. Teams may need help identifying relevant laws, professional obligations, or moral theories and principles. On occasion, teams may need the ethics committee to facilitate communication between team members or between the team and the patient and family.

As a last resort, the law may provide a dispute resolution process. Courts do provide a process for adjudication of some matters affecting health, but, as the Court explained *In the Matter of Karen Quinlan*, "We consider that a practice of applying to a court to confirm such decisions would generally be inappropriate, not only because it would be a gratuitous encroachment upon the medical profession's field of competence, but because it would be impossibly cumbersome." In other words, good patient care, including resolution of moral and ethical conflicts in decision making, is the responsibility of health care professionals.

Recommended Readings

Armstrong, A. E. (2006). Toward a strong virtue ethics for nursing practice. *Nursing Philosophy, 7*(3), 110–124. http://doi.org/10.1111/j.1466-769X.2006.00268.x

Beauchamp, T. L., & Childress, J. F. (2012). *Principles of biomedical ethics* (7th ed.). New York, NY: Oxford University Press.

Card, R. F. (2016). In defense of medical tribunals and the reasonability standard for conscientious objection in medicine. *Journal of Medical Ethics, 42*, 73–75. http://doi.org/10.1136/medethics-2015-103037

Charon, R. (2001). Narrative medicine: A model for empathy, reflection, profession, and trust. *Journal of the American Medical Association, 286*(15), 1897–1902. http://doi.org/10.1001/jama.286.15.1897

Charon, R. (2006). *Narrative medicine: Honoring the stories of illness*. New York, NY: Oxford University Press.

Jonsen, A. R., Sieglar, M., & Winslade, W. J. (2010). *Clinical ethics: A practical approach to ethical decisions in clinical medicine* (7th ed.). New York, NY: McGraw-Hill.

Montello, M. (Ed.). (2014). Narrative ethics: The role of stories in bioethics. *The Hastings Center Report, 44*, S7–S11. http://doi.org/10.1002/hast.260

Pellegrino, E. D., & Thomasma, D. C. (1993). *The virtues in medical practice*. New York, NY: Oxford University Press.

Sherman, N. (2004). *The fabric of character: Aristotle's theory of virtue* (pp. 3–4). Oxford, UK: Clarendon Press.

Additional Resources

Pew Research Religion & Public Life Project. (2013). *Views on end-of-life treatments*. Available at http://www.pewforum.org/2013/11/21/views-on-end-of-life-medical-treatments/

Review Questions

1. The principle of bioethics that supports the legal doctrine of informed consent is
   A. autonomy
   B. beneficence
   C. fidelity
   D. justice
   E. nonmaleficence

2. What is a conscientious objector in the context of health care?
   A. An individual who disagrees with a patient's decision
   B. An individual who does not want to get involved in controversial medical care
   C. An individual with deeply held moral or religious beliefs about the rightness or wrongness of an act in all circumstances

    D. An individual with deeply held moral or religious beliefs about the rightness or wrongness of an act under certain conditions

    E. There is no conscientious objection in medicine, only in war

3. A determination of incapacity would be unnecessary if the patient
    A. has bipolar disorder
    B. has cognitive decline
    C. has dementia
    D. has schizophrenia
    E. is a minor

4. In surrogate decision making, it is best to rely on
    A. substituted judgment
    B. the best interest of the patient
    C. the medical team's recommendation
    D. the patient's expressed wishes
    E. none of the above

Answer Key on p. 466

32 Complementary and Integrative Medicine

Hilary H. McClafferty, MD, FAAP, and Olle Jane Z. Sahler, MD

- How are conventional, complementary, and integrative medicine defined?
- How does integrative medicine differ from complementary and alternative medicine (CAM)?
- How are complementary therapies classified?
- Why is the popularity of integrative medicine increasing?
- Which complementary medicine practices are licensed in the US?
- What distinguishes behavioral science-based treatments from complementary medicine treatments?
- Why do some proponents of complementary medicine reject accepted scientific standards for research?
- How should complementary therapies be evaluated for usefulness?

Conventional, Complementary, and Integrative Medicine

How are conventional, complementary, and integrative medicine defined?

Conventional medical practice in the US is based on the biomedical model that had its origins in the 1910 *Flexner Report,* which called for an increased focus on scientifically based training and practice for physicians. Complementary therapies, as defined by the National Institutes of Health (NIH) National Center for Complementary and Integrative Health (NCCIH), include a wide range of non-mainstream practices with demonstrated evidence of safety and effectiveness that are used together with conventional medicine.

How does integrative medicine differ from complementary and alternative medicine (CAM)?

Integrative medicine has been defined by the NCCIH as an approach that brings together conventional and complementary approaches as part of a coordinated plan of health care.

In response to accumulating evidence for the efficacy of many complementary therapies, the term **complementary and alternative medicine** (CAM) is increasingly being replaced by the terms *complementary and integrative medicine,* or simply *integrative medicine.* This renaming is designed to differentiate complementary therapies from alternative therapies, which are therapies used *in place of* conventional medicine, but which are unsupported by scientific evidence. An important example of this trend is reflected in the name change in 2014 of the National Center for Complementary and Alternative Medicine (NCCAM) to the National Center for Complementary and Integrative Health (NCCIH).

Classification of Complementary Therapies

How are complementary therapies classified?

Box 32.1 gives examples of how the NCCIH has organized complementary therapies into the two broad subgroups of (1) *natural products* and (2) *mind and body practices.* Natural products include botanicals and other products taken internally that are commonly known as dietary

---

Box 32.1. Examples of complementary therapy classifications

Mind and Body Practices	Meditation	**Natural Products**	Botanicals
	Relaxation techniques		Vitamins
	• Breath work		Minerals
	• Guided imagery		Probiotics
	• Clinical hypnosis		
	• Progressive muscle relaxation	**Other**	Whole medical systems
	• Therapeutic massage		• Traditional Chinese
	Manipulation		medicine
	• Osteopathic		• Ayurveda
	• Chiropractic		• Homeopathy
	• Acupuncture		• Naturopathy
	Yoga		Creative arts therapies
	Tai chi		• Music
	Chi gong		• Art
	Healing touch		• Dance
	Movement therapies		Journaling
	Alexander technique		
	Rolfing structural integration		
	Trager psychophysical integration		

---

supplements. Mind and body practices encompass a wide range of therapies including meditation and/or relaxation, manipulation, and movement. Complementary health approaches that fall outside these two main categories (*other*) include whole medical systems and creative arts therapies.

Many traditional health care systems and complementary practices share several basic holistic assumptions such as that (1) individuals possess a life force and seek balance among physical, spiritual, emotional, social, mental, and environmental factors through diet, family and other relationships, lifestyle, spirituality, and culture; (2) illness is a complex manifestation of imbalance within the person's life experience; and (3) restoring and maintaining balance among mind, body, and spirit induces wellness. The holistic practitioner's goal is to assist patients in creating and maintaining well-being by educating, encouraging personal responsibility, and enhancing innate strengths to maximize their own healing potential.

Why is the popularity of integrative medicine increasing?

Increased interest in integrative medicine has been attributed to a variety of factors including the high cost, invasive nature, and potential noxious side effects of many conventional treatments. Greater interest in prevention, reduced need for prescription medications, and appreciation for the more user-friendly, palliative nature of complementary care practices are additional compelling reasons for its appeal.

National health statistics reports show that the use of complementary and integrative therapies has remained at about 33% for adults and 12% for children aged 4 to 17 years since Eisenberg and colleagues published their 1993 landmark study in the *New England Journal of Medicine*. The typical annual expenditure for complementary therapies is about US $34 billion.

Complementary and Integrative Medicine, Public Policy, and Academic Progress

The NIH established the Office of Complementary and Alternative Medicine (OCAM) in 1991 with a budget of US $2 million to support research on various complementary medicine treatment approaches. In 1998, the office was upgraded to and renamed the **National Center for Complementary and Alternative Medicine** (NCCAM) with a budget of $110 million (which, as mentioned in the opening section of this chapter, became the NCCIH in 2014).

In 2000, the White House Commission on Complementary and Alternative Medicine Policy was established to review this body of medical care and develop administrative and legislative proposals aimed at educating health care professionals and creating safe and effective complementary medicine opportunities for the public. In 2005, the Institute of Medicine recommended that health profession schools incorporate complementary medicine subject matter into training curricula. A year later, the American Medical Association (AMA) also recommended that complementary medicine education be included in medical school curricula. As a result of these recommendations, most medical schools now include instruction in some aspects of complementary medicine. Continuing medical education offerings are common, and a growing number of programs offer specialized fellowship training in integrative medicine nationally. Board certification has been available for physicians in the US through the American Board of Integrative Medicine since 2014.

Although relatively few allopathic physicians are formally trained to deliver complementary care, many are interested in integrative medicine, and seek to offer patient information or referrals, especially in situations where biomedical therapies have not been successful, or when patients are motivated to explore nonpharmacological or nonsurgical approaches to treatment.

A 2016 report by Eisenberg and colleagues reflects the ongoing momentum in the field noting that in 2015, 62 well-respected academic health centers are listed as members of the Academic Consortium for Integrative Medicine and Health in the US and Canada. Work is active in the field to determine best clinical practices and appropriate reimbursement and insurance models, and how to incorporate integrative therapies into a wide variety of clinical settings.

Licensed Complementary Medicine Practices

> Which complementary medicine practices are licensed in the US?

A comprehensive review of all complementary and integrative therapies is beyond the scope of this chapter. Therefore, we will focus on currently licensed complementary practices in the US.

As of the summer of 2016, four complementary medicine practices were recognized as *licensed professions* by many, if not all, states in the US: chiropractic, acupuncture, naturopathy, and massage. To be licensed as a professional in one of these four areas, the provider in most states is required to be a graduate of an accredited school recognized by the US Department of Education and pass a standardized national examination. In addition to these four professions, there are a number of other complementary treatment approaches that are *certified* by states or professional interest groups. Of note, certification requirements vary considerably between individual complementary approaches, and from state to state.

Acupuncture

Acupuncture is a component of **traditional Chinese medicine**, which classically consists of a broad spectrum of interventions including herbal therapy, dietary therapy, chi gong exercises, tui na massage, and acupuncture or moxibustion. Acupuncture treatment involves the insertion of fine needles (typically 0.25 mm in diameter) into defined acupuncture points at specific anatomic locations. These points lie along 14 main *meridians* (energy pathways) that are thought to run parallel to, but distinct from, the circulatory and nervous systems. There are 361 primary points corresponding to different organ systems and functions of the body. **Acupressure** is a variant of acupuncture. In this case, pressure, rather than skin puncture, at the primary points is used to obtain the effects.

The goal of acupuncture is to promote the smooth flow of energy, or *chi* (pronounced "chee"), throughout the body to restore balance and good health. Needles placed in the appropriate acupuncture points are presumed to facilitate energy flow along the meridians. In certain cases, **electroacupuncture**, the application of a weak electric current to an inserted needle to strengthen the degree of stimulation, is used. Tui na massage is a form of hands-on body treatment used to move chi. Moxibustion is burning mugwort herb on or near the skin's surface, close to or at acupuncture points, to stimulate movement of chi.

Efficacy: In November 1997, the NIH convened an expert, multidisciplinary panel to determine the effectiveness of acupuncture as medical treatment. The panel determined that there was evidence of treatment effectiveness for nausea associated with chemotherapy, pregnancy, postoperative recovery, and motion sickness; analgesia for dental pain, headaches, menstrual cramps, fibromyalgia, osteoarthritis, and low back pain; and anesthesia for certain surgical procedures. The NCCIH review on acupuncture cites a lack of consistent clinical practice guidelines, but suggests sufficient evidence exists for consideration of its use in those living with chronic pain from a variety of sources including low back pain, knee pain related to osteoarthritis, and tension and migraine headaches (see https://nccih.nih.gov/health/acupuncture/introduction#hed3).

Mechanisms underlying pain relief appear to involve the activation of the body's own response systems. Research has shown acupuncture-stimulated changes in opioid receptor binding in brain networks associated with the sensory and affective aspects of pain, especially the right medial orbitofrontal cortex (see Chapter 8: Pain, and Chapter 50: Somatic Symptom and Related Disorders). How acupuncture affects other disorders is unknown.

Training and licensure: Some states include acupuncture in MD and DO licensure, but most require additional training or an examination. *Physician acupuncturists* take a 300-hr structured acupuncture course that provides a measure of standardization, and there is now an American Board of Medical Acupuncture, established in early 2000, that provides physician acupuncturists with the opportunity to obtain board certification. The American Academy of Medical Acupuncture is a physician organization that supports the integration of acupuncture with Western medicine and promotes an all-encompassing approach to health care.

For *nonphysician acupuncturists*, licensing requirements are set by individual states, but usually include graduation from an accredited school (typically 3- to 4-year master's level programs) and passing a national standardized exam. As of 2016, there were approximately 50 accredited nonphysician acupuncture schools in the US, and all states and the District of Columbia license acupuncturists. Most states require successful completion of the National Certification Commission for Acupuncture and Oriental Medicine (NCCAOM) written examination, or a state written exam. Some states also require the Practical Examination of Point Location, or a state practical exam.

Chiropractic

Chiropractic was founded in the late 1800s by a layman, Daniel Palmer. It is concerned with the relationship between the structure and function of the spine, and how it affects the nervous system and body functioning. Loss of structural integrity, termed *subluxation,* is presumed to result in loss of normal physiology or function. The goal of chiropractic therapy is the correction of subluxation with resulting restoration of function. This goal is accomplished primarily through the use of *adjustment* (joint manipulation), which involves a high velocity, low amplitude maneuver to restore normal joint alignment and mobility. The site of adjustment is determined by symptoms, clinical examination (e.g., palpation), or diagnostic assessment (e.g., thermographic patterns, radiological imaging).

Biological basis: The biological basis for the structural and physiological effects of chiropractic is not entirely understood. Reported responses to manipulation include elevation of serum beta-endorphin levels, increased joint mobility, enhanced neutrophil activity, and attenuation of spinal electromyographic activity.

Efficacy: Most conditions treated by chiropractors involve low back complaints. Non–low back complaints are usually musculoskeletal conditions involving neck pain, mid back pain, arm or leg pain, and headache. Uncomplicated low back pain is the most widely researched condition commonly treated by manipulation. Nonmusculoskeletal complaints such as asthma, otitis media, and gastrointestinal distress account for less than 3% of all patient visits to chiropractors, and evidence for the efficacy in these conditions is insufficient for routine recommendation, especially in children.

The Agency for Health Care Policy and Research has recommended spinal manipulation in its published guideline on the management of acute low back pain. A 5-year pilot program, initiated by Congress in 1995 to assess the effectiveness of chiropractic care in the military concluded that patients with neuromuscular complaints had (1) better outcomes with chiropractic care, (2) increased satisfaction with medical care, (3) less lost duty time, and (4) reduced hospitalization time and costs. NCCIH and the National Institute of Arthritis and Musculoskeletal and Skin Diseases have provided funding for chiropractic research.

Contraindications: Contraindications to chiropractic care include conditions caused by serious underlying disease (cancer and cardiac disease), previous unfavorable response to manipulation, fractures, ligament injury, inflammatory arthritis, ankylosing spondylitis, bone disease, osteoporosis, infection, disc prolapse, and bleeding disorders.

Complications: The most serious complication of cervical manipulation is injury to the vertebrobasilar artery resulting in a cerebrovascular accident (CVA). The incidence of developing a CVA after cervical manipulation is estimated at 1 in 500,000 to 1 in 2 million manipulations. Lumbar manipulation carries a lower risk for serious complication than cervical manipulation.

Training and licensure: Chiropractic is licensed in all states, but there is significant variation in the scope of practice. Some states allow only spinal manipulation (adjustment), and restrict the use of clinical examination procedures. Other states permit chiropractors to perform certain laboratory procedures (e.g., venipuncture), practice acupuncture, give nutritional advice, and dispense supplements.

Chiropractic training requires 4 years. All schools currently have at least a 2-year undergraduate requirement that includes prescribed hours in the sciences and humanities. A bachelor's degree is becoming an increasingly common requirement for admission. As of 2016, there are 18 chiropractic colleges in the US accredited by the Council on Chiropractic Education (CCE), the accrediting agency recognized by the US Department of Education. Thirteen colleges are also accredited by regional accrediting agencies for secondary and postsecondary colleges. At least one college offers a 7-year combined BA-DC program. Following the completion of educational requirements, the chiropractor must pass state and national examinations to become licensed. Postgraduate level studies that lead to specialty certification include sports chiropractic, rehabilitation, chiropractic sciences, orthopedics, neurology, and nutrition.

Naturopathy

While **naturopathy** had its origins in the natural healing movements of the 18th and 19th centuries, its establishment in the US is associated with the work of Dr. Benedict Lust. Dr. Lust, an immigrant from Germany, came to the US in the 1890s, completed his own medical training (studying allopathic [conventional Western], chiropractic, osteopathic, and homeopathic medicine), and established the first school of naturopathic medicine in New York City. About the same time, Dr. James Foster established a school of naturopathic medicine in Idaho. These two individuals subsequently collaborated in establishing the new profession of naturopathy, which drew on an array of natural healing interventions derived from traditional Chinese, Ayurvedic, and Greek medicine, American Indian healing systems, and modern scientific principles and technology.

Six Basic Principles of Modern Naturopathy

1. Nature has the power to heal, and it is the physician's role to enhance the self-healing process.
2. Treat the whole person so that every aspect of a patient's natural defenses and function is brought into harmonious balance.
3. "First, do no harm" reflects the Hippocratic creed that the physician should utilize methods and substances that are nontoxic and noninvasive.
4. Identify and treat the cause, in contrast to suppressing symptoms.
5. Prevention is an important aspect of care that the physician should promote.
6. Doctors should be teachers and educate the patient about their personal responsibility to maintain health.

Naturopathic Modalities

Clinical nutrition and the therapeutic use of diet, including drug–nutrient interactions

Physical medicine procedures such as hydrotherapy, exercise, massage, manipulation, immobilization, braces, splints, ultrasound, diathermy, heat therapy, electrical stimulation, and balneology (therapeutic use of thermal/mineral baths)

Homeopathic treatments that simulate the body's own natural forces

Botanical medicine including the use of herbs and other natural substances to maximize desirable effects and minimize undesirable side effects, including drug–herb interactions

Natural childbirth

Traditional Chinese medicine including the use of Chinese herbs and acupuncture

Ayurvedic medicine

Mind–body techniques that emphasize the facilitative effects of counseling, psychotherapy, behavioral medicine, hypnosis, stress management, and biofeedback

By the 1920s, there were approximately 20 colleges of naturopathy in the US, and naturopathy was licensed in most states. As a result of the increasing influence of biomedicine, however, naturopathy declined in popularity until the 1970s, when it experienced a resurgence due in part to the high costs of biomedicine and changes in health care financing. Currently, there are six recognized colleges and universities of naturopathic training accredited by the Council on Naturopathic Medical Education and recognized by the US Department of Education. Drawing on effective treatments from a wide range of healing approaches, naturopathy has been shown to be an effective *complement to biomedicine* in disease prevention, the treatment of acute illnesses, and supportive treatment of chronic and degenerative conditions. Naturopathic physicians recognize that conventional medicine is essential in addressing more complex medical crises such as acute trauma, childbirth emergencies, fractures, corrective surgery, and acute life-threatening illnesses. Recognition of their relative strengths and limitations has led to increasing collaboration between biomedical and naturopathic physicians.

According to the 2007 National Health Interview Survey, an estimated 729,000 adults and 237,000 children had used a naturopathic treatment in the previous year.

Training and licensure: There are three categories of naturopathic practitioners: naturopathic physicians, traditional naturopaths, and other health care providers who offer naturopathic services as part of their practice.

Naturopathic physicians complete a 4-year graduate level program. Admission requirements generally include a bachelor's degree and standard premedical courses. Naturopathic physician students receive training in anatomy, cell biology, physiology, pathology, neuroscience, histology, genetics, biochemistry, pharmacology, clinical and physical diagnosis, laboratory diagnosis, biostatistics, and epidemiology. Graduates receive the degree of ND (Naturopathic Doctor) or NMD (Doctor of Naturopathic Medicine) depending on where the degree is issued. Although it is not required, some graduates pursue residency training.

As of 2016, 18 states, the District of Columbia, and two US territories (Puerto Rico and the Virgin Islands) had licensing requirements for naturopathic physicians. In all of these places, naturopathic physicians must graduate from a 4-year naturopathic medical college and pass the naturopathic licensing exam (NPLEX). A graduate's scope of practice is variable and defined by law in the state or territory in which they practices. For example, a naturopathic physician may or may not be allowed to prescribe drugs, perform minor surgery, practice acupuncture, or assist in childbirth. It is estimated by the Association of Accredited Naturopathic Medical Colleges that, in 2015, there were approximately 3,500 naturopathic physicians practicing in the US.

Traditional naturopaths emphasize naturopathic approaches to a healthy lifestyle, strengthening and cleansing the body, and noninvasive treatments. Prescription drugs, injections, X-rays, and surgery are not included in their scope of practice. Several schools offer training for this type of naturopathy, but the programs are highly variable, and are not accredited by organizations recognized by the US Department of Education. Admission requirements for these schools can range from minimal to a high school diploma to specific degrees and coursework. Traditional naturopaths are not eligible for licensing.

Efficacy: Naturopathy appears to be increasingly integrated into conventional medicine due to cost effectiveness and the relatively less distressing nature of its natural treatment alternatives. It has received increasing respect from the health care consumer, government bodies, and the biomedical community. There is positive evidence for the effectiveness of some of the common naturopathic interventions. However, because of its wide-ranging nature (i.e., drawn from a large number of healing systems), it cannot be assumed that this provides conclusive evidence of the efficacy of all naturopathic or associated complementary healing systems. Well designed and controlled research is required to determine the efficacy of specific techniques for specific disorders.

Massage Therapy

Massage therapy is defined as the systematic, therapeutic stroking, rubbing, or kneading of the skin and underlying muscle and other soft tissue of the patient for the purpose of physical and psychological relaxation, improvement of circulation, relief of sore muscles, and other therapeutic effects. There are multiple forms including *relaxation*, *Swedish*, *sports*, *deep tissue*, and *trigger point massage*. According to the 2012 National Health Interview Survey, an estimated 15.4 million adults and 385,000 children received massage therapy in the previous year.

Efficacy: Although data are limited, studies support the effectiveness of massage therapy in reducing anxiety, blood pressure, and heart rate; relieving pain; and reducing stress and feelings of depression. In 2008, a review of 13 clinical trials showed massage to be useful in the treatment of low back pain. The *gate control theory* of pain perception suggests that massage stimulation may help to block pain signals sent to the brain. Massage is known to release endorphins and serotonin that can positively affect mood. Massage is commonly used in hospice settings and is increasingly used in neonatal intensive care unit settings.

Licensure and training: In 2016, 43 states and the District of Columbia offered licensure in massage therapy. Training requirements ranged from 100 to 1,000 hr, with most states requiring ≥ 500 hr. Some states require graduation from a training program approved by the Commission on Massage Therapy Accreditation (COMTA) or an equivalent program, or training in a specific area such as anatomy. Most states that license massage therapists require successful completion of the Massage and Bodywork Licensing Examination (MBLEx), or one of two exams provided by the National Certification Board for Therapeutic Massage and Bodywork.

Complementary Therapies and the Behavioral Sciences

> What distinguishes behavioral science-based treatments from complementary medicine treatments?

In his book *The Best Alternative Medicine,* Pelletier states: "Of all the CAM interventions, mind–body medicine is supported by the greatest body of scientific evidence for the greatest number of conditions for the largest number of people. It has also gained the widest acceptance within the conventional medical system" (p. 59). He then traces the evolution of **mind–body medicine** from its origins in the revolt against the reductionism of biomedicine, through the shifts in focus from infectious diseases to lifestyle- and public health–based disorders, to the increasing recognition of the interplay of environmental, psychological, social, and lifestyle factors in health. What Pelletier is describing is, in fact, the emergence of the **biopsychosocial model**, although he does not use that term. Since its inception, the biopsychosocial model has gained increasing acceptance, largely through the supporting empirical evidence accumulated via research on the role of the behavioral sciences in medicine. These research efforts have given rise to the emerging fields of behavioral medicine, health psychology, and psychoneuroimmunology, all of which have focused on identifying the mechanisms of bio-behavioral interaction. Many psychiatrists, especially those with particular interest and training in psychosomatic medicine, also take a integrative medicine approach to care (see Chapter 38: Introduction to Psychopathology, and Chapter 39: The Psychiatric Evaluation).

Empirically based treatment modalities developed out of these research efforts include relaxation, meditation, hypnosis, imagery and visualization, cognitive behavior therapies, and biofeedback. All are forms of treatment based on research into the role of behavioral and cognitive factors in the etiology of select medical and psychiatric disorders. As Pelletier points out, they are now widely accepted within the conventional biomedical system, so he argues, by definition, they should not be subsumed under the complementary medicine rubric.

Complementary Therapies and the Scientific Method

> Why do some proponents of complementary medicine reject accepted scientific standards for research?

Some proponents of complementary medicine argue that accepted standards of scientific investigation are not appropriate for evaluating complementary and integrative methods and treatments. The argument is based on two assumptions:

1. Complementary treatments are individualized and, therefore, cannot be fairly assessed by large-sample randomized controlled trials. The argument is not unique to complementary medicine adherents, as biomedical researchers, in general, realize that large-scale studies do not enable the clinician to make predictions about individual case responses, especially those requiring individualized treatment. At the same time, biomedical researchers believe that the efficacy of any treatment approach must first begin with demonstrated effectiveness within population samples.
2. Complementary approaches are based on explanations fundamentally different from those of conventional biomedical approaches and, therefore, should not be judged by the same biomedical criteria. This argument implies that the theoretical causal explanations

of complementary medicine actions are not biological, cognitive, behavioral, sociocultural, or environmental in nature, but rather attributed to phenomena that lie outside the realm of generally accepted scientific explanations for human functioning, disease, and disorder. Not all adherents of complementary practice agree with this position. Naturopathic physicians and chiropractors, for example, recognize and undergo stringent training in the biomedical and behavioral sciences.

While there is evidence that certain complementary therapies can be effective in the treatment of selected disorders and can serve palliative and supplementary roles with biomedical approaches, continued research into the efficacy of specific treatments for specific disorders and their mechanisms of effect is required. In 2005, the Institute of Medicine report on complementary and alternative medicine in the US stated that health care should be both comprehensive and evidence based, with biomedicine and complementary medicine following the same research principles, but recognizing that new research methods need to be developed to test some therapies in *both* conventional and complementary medicine.

Part of the answer to the dearth of scientific evidence is due to the limited financial support earmarked for complementary medicine research. Between 1998 and 2010, the NCCAM budget grew from US $121 million to US $127 million, or an increase of 0.7%. In 2015, funding was actually reduced to US $124 million. The total NIH budget during those years grew from US $28.7 billion to US $30.4 billion, or an increase of 8%. Although many of the individual institutes (e.g., National Cancer Institute, National Institute of Nursing Research) also help support complementary medicine research, the overall funds available are still extremely small. Unlike pharmaceutical industry research, which can lead to financially lucrative patents, there is little or no financial reward associated with, for example, finding a better way to teach self-hypnosis, especially if it results in less need for anxiolytic or antidepressant medications, mainstays of drug sales.

Thus, lack of good data for or against efficacy is the result of many factors, some based in theoretical and methodological differences about what constitutes "good" data and how to obtain it, and some based on the very practical issues of financing credible research in an era of dwindling resources.

The new initiative of **Precision Medicine** announced by President Obama in his 2015 State of the Union Address, in which individual differences and preferences are given ascendency, may hold promise for our future understanding of what works well or better for a given individual and how best to target conditions and symptoms to provide maximal benefit. Most complementary therapies are targeted and personalized, the very definition of precise intervention. This feature, however, is exactly what makes it extremely difficult to study using randomized controlled trials.

Integrative Medicine

> R.J. is a 41-year-old construction worker who injured his back 8 months ago, falling off a roof. Although disabled for a month, he has been working full time since then despite moderate back pain that has been minimally responsive to over-the-counter analgesics. He does not want to take any stronger medication. He asks you about chiropractic adjustment, weekly massage, and using a TENS unit. How do you respond?

As research into complementary therapies has demonstrated evidence of efficacy, a wider variety of treatment options are beeing incorporated into health care plans. Concurrently, more training in complementary modalities for practitioners and students has become available. The planned incorporation of complementary therapies into a patient's health care plan is now referred to as *integrative medicine*. This model of care will be facilitated by

- improvements and innovations in research methods;
- increased federal and state funding for research;
- expanded education about integrative medicine for conventional health care professionals;
- improved standardization of training, credentialing, and licensing of complementary therapists; and
- improved insurance reimbursement for complementary therapies and integrative medicine approaches.

> How should complementary therapies be evaluated for usefulness?

Providers must address the following questions:
- What is the evidence?
- What is the potential harm?
- Does the therapy resolve the underlying problem or merely suppress symptoms?
- Is the therapy consistent with the patient's culture and belief system?
- What is the cost?
- Will receiving a complementary therapy interfere with receiving necessary conventional treatment?
- Is the treatment clinically responsible, ethically appropriate, and legally defensible?

This risk to benefit table is appropriate for evaluating *any* treatment, including both complematary therapies and conventional treatments.

		Benefit	
		Y	N
Risk	N	Use	Use if patient strongly desires
	Y	Use cautiously and monitor carefully	Do not use

Recommended Readings

Clarke, T. C., Black, L. I., Stussman, B. J., Barnes, P. M., & Nahin, R. L. (2015). *Trends in the use of complementary health approaches among adults: United States, 2002–2012*. (National Health Statistics Reports: No. 79). Hyattsville, MD: National Center for Health Statistics.

Eisenberg, D. M., Kessler, R. C., Foster, C., Norlock, F. E., Calkins, D. R., & Delbanco, T. L. (1993). Unconventional medicine in the United States. Prevalence, costs, and patterns of use. *New England Journal of Medicine, 328*, 246–252.

Eisenberg, D. M., Davis, R. B., Ettner, S. L., Appel, S. Wilkey, S., Van Rompay, M., & Kessler, R. C. (1998). Trends in alternative medicine use in the United States, 1990–1997. *Journal of the American Medical Associa-*

tion, *280*, 1569–1575. http://doi.org/10.1001/jama.280.18.1569

Eisenberg, D. M., Kaptchuk, T. J., Post, D. E., Hrbek, A. L., O'Connor, B. B., Osypiuk, K., ... Levy, D. B. (2016). Establishing an integrative medicine program within an academic health center: Essential considerations. *Academic Medicine*, *91*, 1223–1230. PMID:27028029

Faass, N. (2001). *Integrating complementary medicine into health systems*. Gaithersburg, MD: Aspen.

Institute of Medicine. (2005). *Complementary and alternative medicine in the United States*. Washington, DC: National Academics Press.

Pelletier, K. R. (2000). *The best alternative medicine*. New York, NY: Fireside.

Rakel, D. (2012). *Integrative medicine* (3rd ed.). Philadelphia, PA: Elsevier.

Wisneski, L., & Anderson, L. (2009). *The scientific basis of integrative medicine* (2nd ed.). Boca Raton, FL: CRC Press. http://doi.org/10.1201/b10166

2. According to Pelletier, the efficacy of which of the following complementary therapies is supported by the most evidence?
   A. Chiropractic
   B. Homeopathy
   C. Mind–body medicine
   D. Music therapy
   E. Traditional Chinese medicine

3. Which of the following questions is considered the **LEAST** important in assessing the usefulness of a complementary therapy?
   A. How often must the patient be treated?
   B. Is the therapy culturally appropriate?
   C. What is the cost?
   D. What is the evidence?
   E. What is the potential harm?

Answer Key on p. 466

Additional Resources

Academic Consortium for Integrative Medicine & Health. (2016). *Member listing*. Available at: http://www.imconsortium.org/members/members.cfm

National Center for Complementary and Integrative Health. (2016). *Complementary, alternative, or integrative health: What's in a name?* Available at https://nccih.nih.gov/health/integrative-health

American Board of Integrative Medicine. Available at http://www.abpsus.org/integrative-medicine

Review Questions

1. Which of the following is **NOT** included in the National Center for Complementary and Integrative Health (NCCIH) classification of complementary therapies?
   A. Chelation therapy
   B. Dietary supplements
   C. Energy therapies
   D. Mind–body medicine
   E. Whole medical systems

33 Palliative Care

Timothy E. Quill, MD, and Erin M. Denney-Koelsch, MD

- What are palliative care and hospice care?
- When is palliative care appropriate?
- What are the four main end-of-life trajectories?
- What are common events during the dying process?
- What is complicated grief?

Introduction

The role of **palliative care** is to provide patients with relief from physical, psychological, spiritual, and social suffering. Unlike hospice, which is reserved for patients in the last months of life and focused exclusively on comfort, palliative care can be initiated at any point in the illness and given in tandem with disease-directed treatment.

What are palliative care and hospice care?

Inpatient palliative care services consult with the patient's attending physician and treatment team in one or more of four domains: (1) symptom management, (2) assistance with medical decision making, (3) added patient and family support, and (4) end-of-life issues. Some hospitals have designated inpatient units for patients receiving predominantly palliative treatments, and most others offer consultation wherever the patient resides in the hospital. **Outpatient palliative care clinics** also provide consultation and follow-up care for those who need ongoing palliative treatment and support outside of the hospital. **Home visit programs** provide palliative care for patients in their own homes and are often the best option for those who cannot physically tolerate being transported to and from an outpatient clinic. Ideally, the **palliative care team** is interdisciplinary and, at a minimum, includes physicians, nurses, social workers, mental health professionals, and pastoral caregivers providing coordinated multifaceted care (Figure 33.1).

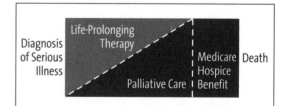

Figure 33.1. The place of palliative care in the course of illness. Adapted from National Consensus Project for Quality Palliative Care (2004). Clinical practice guidelines for quality palliative care. *Journal of Palliative Medicine, 7,* 611–627. Reprinted with permission.

Hospice

If cure is not possible or disease-directed treatment too burdensome, palliative care may become the sole focus of treatment. In such cases, the patient may be a candidate for **hospice** programs funded by Medicare and most private insurances. In adult medicine, hospice is designed to provide exclusively palliative care services for terminally ill patients. To qualify for hospice coverage, a patient must have an expected survival of less than 6 months, and be willing to forego disease-directed therapies. The situation for pediatric patients is sometimes different, and continued disease-directed therapy may be permitted (see "Special Considerations in Pediatric Palliative Care," below).

For many patients, **home hospice** is their first choice. However, home hospice provides only a few hours of hands-on professional patient care each day. For many families unable to shoulder the remaining caregiving requirements, hospice houses and hospice care at nursing homes are alternatives. **Hospice houses** are available in only a few parts of the country. They are staffed by trained volunteers and provide a home-like environment free of charge to the patient. **Nursing home hospice care** provides custodial care paid for by patients or other sources, as well as daily extra aide service and multidisciplinary team support covered by the hospice benefit. **Acute hospice units** provide intensive nursing care and physician oversight for patients with severe, recalcitrant symptoms, many of whom are imminently dying.

Case Vignette – Part 1

Mr. A. is a 71-year-old man with idiopathic pulmonary fibrosis. Prior to his diagnosis 4 years ago, he was an avid golfer, but increasing shortness of breath has meant he can no longer play. Mr. A. has been maximally treated with corticosteroids and immunosuppressant therapy with only marginal benefit. He has not discussed his prognosis with his doctor, but has remarked to his wife, "When my time comes, just let me go." Mr. A. goes to his pulmonologist for a routine follow-up. The physician reports that "nothing's really changed" since the last visit and gives a relieved Mr. A. medication refills. Mr. A. remains "full code" (i.e., he is a candidate for resuscitation should he suffer a cardiac or respiratory arrest), and has significant shortness of breath but believes that nothing can be done about it.

When is palliative care appropriate?

Unlike hospice, patients receiving palliative care can have a normal life expectancy, and may pursue any and all disease-directed treatments. Early palliative care can be appropriate for a patient with a wide range of illnesses. In fact, some studies have shown that early involvement of palliative care consultation alongside traditional medical therapy may prolong life compared with traditional

medical care alone. All seriously ill patients need palliative care, but not all will need a formal palliative care consultation, provided the other treating providers are able and willing to address the patient's fundamental palliative needs (basic pain management, goals-of-care discussions, basic support of patient an family). Specialist palliative care would then become involved for difficult-to-treat symptoms, conflict around the goals of treatment, or very challenging end-of-life decision making.

The Palliative Care Interview

In preparing for an initial palliative care interview, information is gathered from members of all involved medical teams regarding the disease process, treatment options, and prognosis. Making note of areas the teams agree on and determining what information has already been shared with the patient limits miscommunication and enables the provider to synthesize information with the patient and family.

If the interview is being done by a palliative care specialist, after introductions, an explanation of palliative care should follow, such as "We help relieve pain and other uncomfortable symptoms, provide added support for you and your family, and assist with difficult decision making." The patient (and family) should be asked to tell their story about how the illness is affecting them, including a careful review of potentially uncomfortable symptoms. Their understanding of the prognosis and treatment options should also be explored and clarified. After the interview and physical examination, the discussion should be summarized, options described, recommendations shared, and a follow-up meeting arranged. Any new recommendations made by a consulting palliative care specialist that could potentially change the direction of a patient's overall treatment should also be shared and negotiated with the referring team before presenting them to the patient and family.

Delivering Bad News

One of a physician's most daunting tasks is **delivering bad news**, such as when a serious illness is first diagnosed or with each decline in the patient's condition. Before meeting with the patient, facts about the patient's illness, prognosis, and treatment options must be reviewed to ensure understanding. The meeting should be held in a quiet, private setting, and everyone the patient desires should be present if possible. If the patient's health status impairs understanding, the health care proxy or other surrogate should be present.

Case Vignette – Part 2

Two months later, Mr. A. is hospitalized with pneumonia. He requires supplemental oxygen and desaturates with minimal exertion after 2 weeks of treatment. During a conversation with his primary care physician, Mr. A. talks about his plans to attend his granddaughter's college graduation in 6 months, and his physician keeps silent about the low likelihood of Mr. A.'s surviving until then. After the visit, a palliative care consultation is requested to clarify prognosis and treatment options.

During the consultation, it is clear that Mr. A. does not know his prognosis, thinking instead that his illness is "not that serious." When asked if he would like to hear about his prognosis, he indicates that he does and is given a "typical" scenario of worsening dyspnea and fatigue. When then asked if he would like to hear an expected timeframe, he again says "yes" and is told it is most likely 3 to 6 months, although it could also be longer or shorter

Mr. A. seems stunned. The patient, physician, and family sit quietly for several seconds. The physician says that she "wished things were different." Mr. A. asks for time alone with his family. The doctor, patient, and family agree to talk again that afternoon. The physician tells Mr. A. how to reach her in the interim, should he have questions.

Begin by assessing what the patient and family understand about the area to be discussed (e.g., test results, treatment options, prognosis). *Ask – Tell – Ask* is a good strategy for assessing readiness and for ensuring understanding. *Ask* – "Are you ready to hear about the test results?" This both solicits the patient's permission to give the news and also provides a "warning shot" that something difficult to hear is coming. *Tell* – "The biopsy showed cancer." Tell information in small amounts using clear language to avoid overwhelming the patient

or family with details. Again *Ask* – "I want to be sure you have gotten the information correctly, so I am going to ask you to tell me what you have heard." Be prepared for an emotional response, be it grief, anger, denial, anxiety, or acceptance. No matter what response the news elicits, acknowledge and legitimize emotions: "This must seem so unfair." Encourage questions. Repeat the *Ask, Tell, Ask* cycle as often as needed to provide key points and assess for understanding. Before concluding the meeting, determine if the patient is at risk for self-harm. Ensure a safe ride home, as patients can be too distracted to drive safely. Offer to call relatives or friends to provide support. Establish a clear follow-up plan, such as another visit or a phone call the next day. If any appointments for subspecialists, tests, or procedures are needed, offer to arrange them. Finally, reassure the patient that you will continue to work with them no matter what the course of the disease.

Giving a Prognosis

Patients and families generally value a *balance of realism and compassion.* A realistic understanding of the disease course and timeline can aid patients in prioritizing family visits, vacations, financial issues, spiritual and religious needs, or guardianship arrangements. Before giving a prognosis, it is critical to determine the likely course of the patient's disease, including the average length of survival. Certain illnesses, such as cancer, congestive heart failure, and dementia, have distinct trajectories that, if understood, can lead to a better understanding of the prognosis. Some patients, upon hearing their initial diagnosis, may ask, "How much time do I have?" Others may want little or no information. Again, use *Ask – Tell – Ask* to make sure the patient and family are interested in hearing prognostic information, and then assuring that the information given was heard correctly. If a prognostic timeline is requested, give averages and allow for outliers in both directions: for example, "The average person with your illness will live 3 to 9 months. It could be longer if treatment is successful but, unfortunately, it could also be shorter...." Note the possibility for longer survival than average, which allows for hope, but also the possibility of shorter survival than expected, which encourages preparation: "Let's hope for the best but prepare for the worst."

Disease Trajectories

> **What are the four main end-of-life trajectories?**

The four main end-of-life trajectories for adults are (1) terminal cancer, (2) organ failure, (3) frailty, and (4) sudden neurological impairment (see Figure 33.2). Palliative care is appropriate in all four of these trajectories. The first trajectory is one that many cancers follow: a relatively rapid predictable decline over weeks to months. This trajectory best fits the hospice option, since once the decline begins, death is likely within 6 months. The second trajectory, sudden decline with intervening periods of relative stability, is more characteristic of organ failure such as congestive heart failure or pulmonary fibrosis. For these patients, one cannot reliably predict if the prognosis is 1 day or 6 months. Exacerbations tend to come suddenly, and the patient either recovers or dies, or potentially becomes dependent on mechanical ventilation. The third trajectory, gradual progressive decline resulting in an often lengthy period of frailty, is characteristic of Alzheimer's dementia. Here the prognosis can be years, depending on how aggressively illnesses and complications are treated. The fourth trajectory is for patients with acute central nervous system injury from trauma and bleeding. Such patients sometimes die suddenly; if they survive the initial phase, they may have variable degrees of neurological recovery over days to weeks and sometimes longer. It is critical that patients and families understand which trajectory applies to their illness, and use that information in decision making.

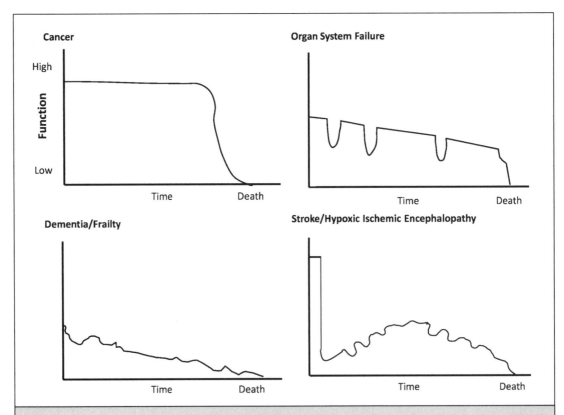

Figure 33.2. The four typical end-of-life trajectories. Adapted from Lynn, J., & Adamson, D. M. (2003). *Living well at the end of life: Adapting health care to serious chronic illness in old age.* Santa Monica, CA: RAND Corporation. © 2003 by The RAND Corporation. All rights reserved. Reproduced with permission.

Do-Not-Resuscitate Orders

Responsible care for seriously ill patients requires a candid discussion of **do-not-resuscitate** (DNR) and **do-not-intubate** (DNI) orders. Misconceptions about the effectiveness of cardiopulmonary resuscitation (CPR) have been fueled by media depictions of miraculous, highly successful interventions. In fact, < 5% of cardiac arrest victims survive to hospital discharge. Of those who do survive, many have subsequent neurological impairments and are not able to live independently. In the setting of severe chronic illness(es), CPR is much less effective than it is for those with pure cardiac disease. If the patient survives the initial event, the underlying disease process still progresses. Similarly, patients with serious chronic illness who are intubated and on a ventilator have difficulty being weaned.

When discussing *resuscitation status* for patients with serious chronic or terminal illness, physicians should inform the patient if CPR is likely to result in outcomes most patients would find unacceptable. The patient should understand that a decision to withhold CPR or intubation does not preclude other more efficacious, aggressive medical interventions. The provider should offer recommendations and experience as they apply to the patient's clinical situation: for example, "Given your desire to live as long as possible, but not to lose your independence, I suggest we continue to try all potentially effective treatments, but I also recommend that you avoid CPR and breath-ing machines. They are harsh treatments and are unlikely to work in your circumstance."

Presenting the Hospice Option

Since a hospice patient must have a prognosis of < 6 months (more likely than not to die in that timeframe) and be willing to forgo disease-directed treatment, when a question of hospice care is raised, the patient is often confronting the prospect of impending death for the first time. The physician should emphasize that choosing hospice is not "giving up." Rather, the goal of care shifts from disease-driven treatments that may add to a patient's suffering, to maximizing quality of life. This means aggressive symptom control and giving patients the opportunity to gain emotional, spiritual, existential, and social closure. The physician promises to not abandon the patient and to use all of their expertise to maximize the patient's quality of life; the physician–patient partnership is maintained, and sometimes even strengthened in this process. In many cases, disease-directed therapies are also palliative (e.g., bronchodilators, steroids, heart failure treatment), and these treatments can be continued on hospice as long as they contribute to the patient's well-being.

Case Vignette – Part 3

Mr. A. is ready for discharge. He has decided to continue disease-driven treatment so he can have his "best shot" at seeing his granddaughter graduate. In the hospital, he began treatment with low-dose around-the-clock opioids to help relieve dyspnea, which helped him feel considerably better. Outpatient palliative care follow-up was arranged. Prior to discharge, Mr. A. agrees to a DNR order since he understands such efforts would likely be futile. He considers a trial period of intubation, then decides against it after his physician explains that the most likely outcome would be lifelong mechanical ventilation. Although he is now DNR and DNI, they did agree to a trial period of noninvasive ventilation if there is a chance of response, since he still hopes to make his granddaughter's graduation in 6 months if possible.

Case Vignette – Part 4

Mr. A. returns to the hospital several times over the next few months because of respiratory insufficiency. He and his doctor continue to talk about the benefits and burdens of disease-directed treatment vs. hospice. Mr. A. holds firm to his goal of seeing his granddaughter graduate, so together they work aggressively to reduce his dyspnea with opioids and bronchodilators while searching for reversible elements of the underlying disease. Mr. A.'s appetite has been poor, and a feeding tube is considered, but after a discussion of risks and benefits with a nutritionist and the palliative care clinician, Mr. A. decides against tube placement.

Experimental Treatments

Academic centers and other institutions occasionally offer qualified patients *experimental therapy* as part of clinical trials, when standard therapies are no longer effective. For patients unlikely to do well with conventional treatments, such opportunities offer the possibility of improving the patient's condition and prolonging life. However, potential downsides to experimental therapy must also be carefully considered. First, what is the *toxicity* of the treatment? Many patients will not want to pursue treatments that have severe side effects if the benefit is small or unknown. Second, *time* is precious for seriously ill patients, who may not want to spend it in medical settings. Third, what *outcome* does the therapy offer? If the treatment extends survival for a small percentage of patients by a few months if successful, those months may or may not be worthwhile if quality of life is poor. On the other hand, if side effects, time commitment, and possible benefits are acceptable, experimental treatment can be compelling. Experimental therapy may be important to patients who have invested hope in the possible efficacy of medical treatments. Such patients prefer to "go down swinging" and would experience stopping disease-directed treatment as potentially giving up. Patients need realistic information about the potential benefits and burdens of treatments available, and what their physician recommends. Those who put their hope in experimental therapy should also be given the opportunity to prepare for the possibility that the treatment will not work, and make back-up plans accordingly.

Case Vignette – Part 5

Mr. A.'s son, while searching the Internet, finds several clinical trials for patients with pulmonary fibrosis. After he reviews the information with his doctors, it becomes apparent that Mr. A. is not a good candidate because he has late-stage disease, and the side effects of the experimental therapy would be beyond his tolerance.

The Family Meeting

Family meetings should be conducted in a quiet conference room or the patient's room if they are too ill to be moved. Ensure critical family members are present, especially the health care proxy in the event the patient is, or is likely to become, unable

to make their own decisions in the near future. Other important figures (e.g., clergy, matriarch, patriarch, primary care physician) whose input would be valued by the family should be invited with permission from the patient and family.

Case Vignette – Part 6

During Mr. A.'s last admission, hypoxia renders him drowsy and unable to participate in medical decisions. The palliative care team meets with his family and primary care physician (PCP), whose opinion the family trusts. The PCP explains that the frequent hospitalizations, delirium, and hypoxia are all indicators of approaching death. Mr. A.'s wife, who is his health care proxy, and their children review Mr. A.'s goals. Attending his granddaughter's graduation is no longer possible. Recalling his statements at the time of his brother's death, his wife is sure her husband would "just want to be made comfortable." His PCP recommends hospice, a recommendation echoed by the palliative care team. Reassured that Mr. A. will receive diligent attention to his symptoms and quality of life, the family chooses a home hospice program.

All who attend should be encouraged to contribute their perspective of the patient's present situation, and develop a collective understanding of the illness and its prognosis. If the patient is unable to make their own medical decisions, surrogates should be encouraged to think in terms of *what the patient would want* rather than what they want for the patient. This can be challenging if the patient never expressed any wishes regarding end-of-life care, such as in the case of young children. Sometimes a patient's wishes must be inferred from prior health decisions or personal values. Sometimes patient preferences clash with those of the proxy or family. It is important to remind decision makers to make decisions as they imagine the patient would (using **substituted judgment**), and not decide based on their own wishes or values. "What would you do, doctor?" is a common question. If the practitioner believes that certain choices are best for the patient, given what is known of the patient's clinical circumstances and values, the proxy and family should be so informed. Often a physician's recommendation is not only welcome but can also ease the uncertainty and guilt that can accompany end-of-life decisions.

Pain Management

Pain is rated on a scale of 0 to 10, with 0 being no pain and 10 the worst pain imaginable. *Mild pain* (1 to 3) can be treated with nonopioid medications such as acetaminophen and nonsteroidal anti-inflammatory drugs (NSAIDs). *Moderate to severe pain* (4 to 10) is often treated with opioids, with doses titrated according to pain intensity, especially in the presence of serious, potentially terminal illness. Adjuvant pain medications (drugs not usually used for analgesia that have a benefit for specific types of pain) can be used at any level of discomfort. Often, an alert patient with mild or intermittent pain can be treated with *prn (as-needed) analgesics.* However, patients with moderate to severe constant pain require a combination of *scheduled pain medication* as well as prn dosing.

Opioids are also effective at reducing the sensation of shortness of breath in those with potentially terminal illness. Providers may hesitate to schedule opioid medications fearing respiratory depression. However, since sleepiness almost always precedes respiratory depression, the next scheduled dose can be withheld if lethargy develops and the doses following adjusted accordingly.

Potential prescribers of opioids need to understand the differences between tolerance, dependence, addiction, and pseudoaddiction. **Tolerance** means that increasing doses of opioids may be required over time to achieve the same analgesic effect; this should give prescribers pause about prescribing opioids for chronic illness. **Physical dependence** is an expected result of chronic opioid use and means the body has adapted to its opioid use. In the physically dependent patient, abruptly decreasing the opioid dose can result in a withdrawal syndrome. Both tolerance and dependence are expected parts of chronic opioid use, and should be anticipated and compensated for. **Addiction** is characterized by impaired control over drug use, craving, erratic behaviors, and continued use over time despite harm. Risk factors for addictive behavior include preexisting alcohol or substance abuse problems, and poverty. If such problems coexist in patients who can potentially benefit from opioid treatment, involvement of a pain or palliative care specialist is advised. **Pseudoaddiction** appears similar to addiction, but is, in fact, a result of inadequate pain relief from suboptimal prescribing. The behavior disappears when the patient's pain is properly treated.

Case Vignette – Part 7

Mr. A.'s doctor receives a call from the home hospice aide 1 week after Mr. A. is discharged. The aide reports that the patient is complaining of severe pain in his lower back and anxiety. After examining Mr. A. to ensure there are no acute neurological deficits, his doctor suspects a compression fracture and increases the opioid dose. The increased opioid dose reduces both his pain and his anxiety without having to add a benzodiazepine. They jointly discuss having Mr. A. go for an X-ray if the pain does not respond, or if he develops weakness in his legs, but together decide to hold off for now.

Finding the right regimen of pain medications can be a complex task. Chronically ill or dying patients often require dose titration and adjuvant therapies. Converting from one opioid to another is frequently necessary to minimize side effects or to optimize the dosing regimen. Calculating the **equianalgesic dose** of a strong opioid with a variable, dose-dependent half-life such as methadone, requires considerable expertise. Enlisting the aid of palliative care or other pain management specialists is advisable in more complex cases (also see Chapter 8: Pain).

Special Issues in Terminal Care

Balancing Aggressive Management and Alertness

If a dying patient experiences increasing pain, strong opioids in increasing doses may be necessary, although such treatment may be accompanied by decreased mental status. Since some patients prefer to be as alert as possible, even if it means they experience more discomfort, it is important to ascertain the patient's preferences. Such preferences often evolve over time, and may need to be frequently reassessed, especially as the patient is approaching death. The patient and family should be reassured that, should suffering become severe, the team will seek solutions that keep the patient in charge of pain relief.

Artificial Nutrition and Hydration

In many cultures, preparing and serving food is an expression of caring. Withholding food can seem unforgivable, even though many dying patients experience anorexia. Providing the family with information about the natural aspects of diminished need for food and fluids as death approaches, while exploring and empathizing with their concerns, can help with decisions regarding *feeding tubes* and *intravenous fluids*. First, feeding through a gastric tube has not been shown to prolong the life of most patients, except those with select cancers (e.g., oropharyngeal or esophageal). Second, tube feeding and intravenous fluids can increase the discomfort of actively dying patients as they lose the ability to mobilize fluids and handle respiratory secretions, resulting in significant generalized edema and increasing respiratory distress and congestion. Third, delirious patients often pull at intravenous lines and feeding tubes, potentially necessitating the use of restraints. Finally, the taste and texture of real food even in small amounts and the social engagement that occurs at mealtime make eating enjoyable; artificial feeding offers none of these benefits.

Patients and families should be reminded that not eating or drinking much toward the end of life is a *natural process,* and does not result in increased suffering. People who have voluntarily fasted have reported that, as long as their mouth was kept moist, the experience was not unpleasant. Some describe an almost euphoric state after a few days without food. Furthermore, dying patients who do not receive tube feeds or intravenous fluids can still take small amounts of whatever food or beverage they desire. The mouth of a patient who is unable to eat or drink at all can be kept clean and moist with diligent mouth care.

Delirium and Agitation

Delirium is generally addressed by an extensive metabolic and anatomic work-up, as well as a careful review of medications. Toward the end of life, however, delirium can be a natural phase in the dying process, and should be handled more symptomatically. For example, aggressive symptomatic treatment may be necessary if delirium and agitation are extremely distressing for both the patient and the family. In the later stages of disease, symptoms can be handled with *antipsychotics* or *benzodiazepines*. Environmental modifications, such as a quiet atmosphere with limited interruptions and the regular presence of family and staff, can also decrease agitation. The removal of any equipment such as intravenous lines, telemetry, or nasogastric tubes can help calm the patient. Physical restraints should almost never be used; instead, if possible, use continuous staff or family presence with gradually increasing sedation, if needed.

On rare occasions, delirium is intractable and requires **palliative sedation**. The administration of proportionately dosed sedatives can relieve extreme degrees of suffering by reducing the patient's level of consciousness and is used as a *last resort* once conventional management has failed. Before implementation, informed consent is obtained from the patient (if capable) or the patient's proxy decision maker(s). The patient, proxy, family, and medical staff should develop a clear plan that includes the reasons and end points for sedation. The patient is generally sedated until restlessness and agitation cease, and then is maintained at that level of sedation. Frequent reassessment is needed to ensure the level of sedation is adequate to relieve distress. Support should be provided to the family throughout the process. Heavy palliative sedation should generally be used with consultation and guidance from a palliative care specialist.

Case Vignette – Part 8

According to his daughter, Mr. A. will no longer take any food or drink and "looks like a skeleton." She is concerned that he is suffering from thirst and hunger, and asks if tube feeds can be started. Mr. A.'s doctor reassures her that her father is likely not experiencing any discomfort as a result of not eating or drinking. She also explains that starting tube feeds may actually cause discomfort through fluid overload, resulting in edema and worsening shortness of breath. The daughter feels more at ease after these reassurances. She increases the use of moist mouth swabs and puts balm on her father's lips, which becomes one of the ways she expresses her love for him.

Case Vignette – Part 9

After a week of home hospice, everyone in Mr. A.'s family is exhausted. He has become increasingly agitated despite medication, attempting to strike his caregivers and occasionally injuring himself. He appears to be "seeing things" in his room that frighten him. Antipsychotic medication is added with directions for regular around-the-clock dosing and as-needed ("breakthrough") doses for persistent agitation. The family is asked to call with a progress report in 24–48 hr, and the possibility of admission to an acute hospice unit for symptom management is considered.

Requests for Physician-Assisted Death

Patients, families, clinicians, and the general public are divided on the ethics of **physician-assisted death (PAD)**. Requests for such assistance often result from intolerable symptoms or fear of future (physical, emotional, spiritual, or psychological) suffering. The patient's request should be explored, and triggering symptoms aggressively managed. The possibility that underlying delirium, depression, or anxiety are contributing to the

Case Vignette – Part 10

Mrs. A asks the hospice nurse, "Can't we just end it all? I can't stand to see him like this." His doctor speaks at length with Mrs. A. and learns that she is most bothered by her husband's extreme agitation, which has not responded to increasing doses of antipsychotics and anxiolytics. The family decides that Mr. A.'s needs can no longer be met at home despite their efforts. He is admitted to an acute inpatient hospice unit. Although the family is relieved, they feel guilty that they were unable to let him die at home. The hospice team reassures them that they have made the most loving decision in bringing him to the inpatient unit where he can be made as comfortable as possible. In the acute hospice unit, his antipsychotic regimen is proportionately adjusted so that he is calmer, but also more sedated. All agree that this is acceptable. Aggressive symptom management brings Mr. A.'s agitation and delirium under control. Opioids provide good relief of his dyspnea. Mr. A. dies quietly a few days later surrounded by members of his family and the medical team.

request should be carefully evaluated. After careful evaluation, most suffering can be addressed within the bounds of standard palliative care. However, the patient should be informed that, if suffering becomes intolerable, palliative sedation or voluntary cessation of eating and drinking are legal options of last resort available throughout the Western world. The legal availability of physician-assisted death is in flux in the US, Canada, and Western Europe. Clinicians should have a clear awareness of the status of the law where they are practicing, and also should pay attention to their own moral views on this subject as they decide how to respond. Many patients find comfort in knowing they have some control over the manner and timing of their death with such options, which, in fact, most never choose to activate even in environments where PAD is legal. (see Chapter 31: Moral, Ethical, and Legal Issues in Patient Care).

What to Expect during the Dying Process

What are common events during the dying process?

Because many people have not witnessed death, they may be anxious and uncertain about what to expect as it approaches. Preparing the family can help alleviate their concern. The family should be reassured that the palliative care or hospice team will do everything in their power to minimize suffering. The family should be told that dying patients frequently become more somnolent, and may develop congested breathing prior to death because of secretions they are too weak to mobilize. The family should be told that these are anticipated signs that death is approaching, and they should be reassured that such signs are usually more distressing for onlookers than for the patient.

Grief and Bereavement

Grief is the emotional response to loss (see Chapter 47: Stress Disorders, Bereavement, and Dissociative Disorders). A dying patient not only experiences loss of life but loss of employment, family, self-image, and independence. During

anticipatory grief (prior to death), some patients review their life experiences with their close family members – a time that many experience as very meaningful for all who participate. There is an opportunity to ask for, give, and receive forgiveness or to express thanks and love. Some have described this as a time of personal growth.

Case Vignette – Part 11
A few days after the death, the hospice bereavement counselor contacts Mrs. A. Although she feels some lingering doubts about the decisions she made on behalf of her husband, her overall sense is one of relief, especially that her husband is no longer suffering. His doctor also calls Mrs. A. the following week, which she appreciates and which also helps the doctor to achieve some closure about the experience.

Grieving survivors usually move, eventually, toward accepting their loss. Their sense of self returns to feeling intact, life retains meaning, and relationships with others are resumed.

What is complicated grief?

In comparison, **complicated grief** is characterized by feelings of purposelessness, disbelief, and emotional detachment. Emotions such as unrelenting loneliness, anger, and bitterness become prominent. The bereaved may experience intrusive thoughts of the deceased. While complicated and uncomplicated grief can both demonstrate these features, in complicated grief, the symptoms last longer and cause a high degree of impairment. *Risk factors* for complicated grief include unexpected or traumatic death, a history of mental illness, family dysfunction, low self-esteem, prior dependency on the deceased, and isolation.

Bereavement, the state of loss that occurs after death, is a health risk, and can result in increased use of medical services. Most palliative care teams and all Medicare-certified hospice programs include bereavement specialists who monitor families for complicated grief and use preventive measures such as counseling, for survivors at risk. Expressions of condolence from the medical team (sending a card, making a phone call, attending the funeral) can be powerful gestures that are appreciated by the bereaved. Clinicians may need

to grieve after they have lost a patient with whom they were very close, or for whom they provided care through a medically complex illness. It is useful to find safe places (e.g., talking with colleagues or a counselor, participating in a team meeting) to express and explore such feelings. Leaving such feelings unaddressed may lead to isolation and problems for the clinician as time passes.

Special Considerations in Pediatric Palliative Care

Many of the same principles of palliative care developed primarily for adults also apply to infants and children. Pediatric palliative care teams assist with symptom management and decision making for infants and children with life-limiting conditions such as prematurity, congenital anomalies, genetic syndromes, cancer, or critical illnesses or injuries. Pediatric palliative care consultation is available at an increasing number of hospitals as well as through home care agencies and in outpatient settings. While medication doses vary according to age and weight, symptom management principles are similar to those applied to adult patients. However, there are significant differences in expected disease trajectory. Many pediatric palliative care patients are not terminally ill, having a potential for good outcomes after long and sometimes difficult treatment courses (e.g., neonatal intensive care unit [NICU] stay for prematurity or intensive chemotherapy for leukemia). In other cases, they may have symptomatic chronic diseases with prognoses that last many years (e.g., muscular dystrophy, cystic fibrosis). Because of this, there is a much higher likelihood that children will need to receive disease-directed treatments alongside palliative treatments much later in the disease course and, therefore, rarely use hospice programs that do not permit concomitant care. Intensive symptom management and psychosocial support should be provided at all stages of disease.

Perinatal palliative care can be offered to families who learn of a life-limiting condition prenatally, such as complex congenital heart disease, chromosomal disorders such as trisomy 13 and 18, and other congenital disorders. This is a growing field of palliative care, with many new programs being formed across the country. Families coping with prenatally diagnosed conditions often describe being faced with numerous challenging decisions about the type of care they want during the pregnancy, birth, and newborn period, while they are also coping with the loss of their expected pregnancy and baby. Perinatal palliative care teams can assist with preparation of an interdisciplinary birth plan as a perinatal *advanced directive*. If the diagnosis or prognosis is uncertain, the team can follow families through initial neonatal stabilization and evaluation in the NICU, and assist with decision making about goals of care as more information is gathered. When a family desires only comfort measures for their baby at birth, palliative care programs can assist with ensuring the newborn stays with the family, avoiding invasive testing and treatments, and aggressively treating any symptoms.

Minors, by definition, lack capacity for medical decision making. However, as they mature, they are increasingly able to express their wishes and should be included in discussions about care, even though the final choices for treatment remain with the parents or guardians. Older children may contribute their opinions and can assent to treatments. When parents are asked to make a difficult decision on behalf of a young child, there are usually no prior health decisions or lifestyle values to guide substituted judgment ("What would Johnny say to do?"). Guardians, therefore, most often make decisions based on a *best interest* ethical standard. Some parents feel burdened by being asked to make decisions about withholding or withdrawing life-sustaining treatment for a beloved child, and appreciate guidance and recommendations from trusted medical providers (see Chapter 31: Moral, Ethical, and Legal Issues in Patient Care).

Communicating about illness, death, and dying with children (and, in some cases, siblings) must take into consideration the child's developmental age. Younger children (< 6 years) may not understand that death can actually happen to them. They also often believe death is reversible (i.e., someone who has died may simply wake up). They also tend to infer cause and effect, such as believing that they caused the illness or death because of a thought or wish (*magical thinking*). In middle childhood (7 to 12 years), children are generally

aware that death is irreversible and they could die themselves, and may be better able to weigh the risks and benefits of their own treatments. Adolescents are generally very clear about the universality of death and may have sophisticated explanations about it. They may grieve future losses (college, marriage), express anger, need to exercise their independence, and crave peer support. Because many children are not able to verbalize their feelings, expressive therapies (art, music) can be very helpful in uncovering what a child is thinking or fearing. As with adults, an interdisciplinary team approach involving physicians, nurses, creative arts therapists, child life specialists, chaplains, and social workers is most able to address the complex needs of the pediatric population.

Recommended Readings

Back, A. L., Arnold, R. M., Baile, W. F., Tulsky, J. A., & Fryer-Edwards, K. (2005). Approaching difficult communication tasks in oncology. *CA: A Cancer Journal for Clinicians*, *55*, 164–177. http://doi.org/10.3322/canjclin.55.3.164

Casarett, D. J., & Quill, T. E. (2007). "I'm not ready for hospice": Strategies for timely and effective hospice discussions. *Annals of Internal Medicine*, *146*, 443–449. http://doi.org/10.7326/0003-4819-146-6-200703200-00011

Morrison, R. S., & Meier, D. E. (2004). Clinical practice: Palliative care. *New England Journal of Medicine*, *351*, 1148–1149. http://doi.org/10.1056/NEJM200409093511120

Quill, T. E., Bower, K. A., Holloway, R. C., Shah, M. S., Caprio, T. V., Olden, A., & Storey, Jr., C. P. (2014). *Primer of palliative care* (6th ed.). Chicago, IL: American Academy of Hospice and Palliative Medicine. (see Table 10.4: Stages of Development and Supportive Interventions on pp. 236–237)

Quill, T. E., Lo, B., & Brock, D. W. (1997). Palliative options of last resort: A comparison of voluntarily stopping eating and drinking, terminal sedation, physician-assisted suicide, and voluntary active euthanasia. *Journal of the American Medical Association*, *278*, 2099–2104.

Storey, Jr., C. P. (Series Ed.) (2008). *UNIPAC Eight: The hospice and palliative medicine approach to caring for pediatric patients* (3rd ed.). Chicago, IL: American Academy of Hospice and Palliative Medicine. (see Table 3: Well Child's Concepts of Death, Implications, and Recommended Supportive Interventions)

Temel, J. S., Greer, J. A., Muzikansky, A., Gallagher, E. R., Admane, S., Jackson, V. A., ... Lynch, T. J. (2010). Early palliative care for patients with metastatic non-small-cell lung cancer. *New England Journal of Medicine, 363,* 733–742. http://doi.org/10.1056/NEJMoa1000678

Additional Resources

National Consensus Project for Quality Palliative Care. (2013). *Clinical practice guidelines for quality palliative care* (3rd ed.). Available at http://www.nationalconsensusproject.org/guideline.pdf

Review Questions

1. A patient with cancer has bone metastases and 8 to 10 out of 10 pain. According to the World Health Organization (WHO), the best pain management is likely to result from the administration of
   A. adjuvant modalities
   B. weak opioids alone
   C. weak opioids and adjuvant modalities
   D. strong opioids alone
   E. strong opioids and adjuvant modalities

2. Which of the following people is **MOST** likely to experience complicated grief?
   A. 31-year-old woman whose third child has a known severe cardiac anomaly and is not resuscitated in the delivery room according to the family's birth plan
   B. 58-year-old woman whose husband dies peacefully at home after a 2-year battle against cancer
   C. 62-year-old mother of two young adults who participates in a bereavement support group
   D. 75-year-old man whose 99-year-old mother dies in a nursing home
   E. 86-year-old childless man whose wife of 60 years dies suddenly of a stroke

3. Palliative care is appropriate for which of the following patients?
   A. 20-year-old woman with relapsed leukemia being treated with chemotherapy and bone marrow transplantation, who has uncontrolled pain and nausea
   B. 55-year-old man in the ICU following a car accident, who it not improving despite maximal treatments, and whose family is undecided about continuing ventilator support
   C. 73-year-old woman with advanced heart failure requiring frequent admissions to the hospital, who is considering hospice care
   D. 88-year-old woman with moderate Alzheimer's dementia, living in a nursing facility, who is slowly losing weight and spending more time in bed
   E. All of the above

Answer Key on p. 466

Section IX
The Clinical Relationship

34 The Provider–Patient Relationship

Dennis C. Russo, PhD, Marissa E. Carraway, PhD, and Lars C. Larsen, MD

- What are the responsibilities and rights of providers?
- What are the rights and responsibilities of patients?
- What is the difference between transference and countertransference?
- What are patients' two main fears?
- What are six methods for supporting participatory decision making?
- What influences adherence to treatment recommendations?

The **Hippocratic Oath** required physicians to be responsible for the patient's well-being, but did not require the physician to inform the patient or follow the patient's wishes. In fact, the physician could deceive the patient if the deception was intended to offer hope. By the end of the 18th century, Benjamin Rush, a physician and signer of the US Declaration of Independence, was urging physicians to share information with patients, while John Gregory, of the University of Edinburgh, proposed that patients be more responsible for their own health education and that physicians aid their efforts.

Today, the provider–patient relationship is changing such that the patient is at the center of a health care delivery system that seeks to not only manage illness but also identify morbidity early and provide multidisciplinary, team-based care. Thus, the provider–patient relationship is based on a *mutual exchange of information* and *participatory decision making*. The patient's right to determine their care is a core element of the implicit provider–patient contract. The patient's values and preferences are to be discussed and incorporated into the treatment plan that the clinician and patient share responsibility for developing and implementing. Patient-centered care emphasizes the active role of the patient in maintaining health or managing illness. Effective communication is an integral part of providing patient-centered care and has been demonstrated to improve patient outcomes, satisfaction, and adherence to treatment.

While the dominant culture of the US emphasizes patient autonomy, active involvement, and independent functioning, patients from more family-oriented cultures may find this type of provider–patient relationship offensive or discourteous. In many of these cultures, the family is viewed as the agent of decision making, although negotiating treatment is still a major element of determining care. Hence, the provider should be especially sensitive to cultural differences and the effect they will have on patient expectations and practices (see Chapter 17: Culture and Cultural Competence in Health Care).

Responsibilities and Rights of Providers

Provider Responsibilities

What are the responsibilities and rights of providers?

Provider responsibilities include *informing* the patient regarding the nature of the disorder, probable course if untreated, and available and recommended treatments. The provider also has an obligation to *elicit and listen* to the patient's concerns, *address* them objectively and sensitively, and *respect* the patient's decisions even though the provider may disagree with them. Above all, the provider has a responsibility to *use their authority* in the best interest of the patient and *avoid the abuse of this authority,* which can result when there are conflicts of interest (see Chapter 31: Moral, Ethical, and Legal Issues in Patient Care).

Recommending Appropriate Treatments

Although treatment costs must be considered in medical decisions, the most important principle is that patients receive *appropriate care*. For example, a 60-year-old, otherwise healthy patient who has suspected pneumonia expects, and should receive, appropriate diagnostic studies and medication. Among terminally ill patients, whose feelings regarding prolongation of life vary, however, the same situation may raise complex ethical dilemmas that require balancing expectations for cure against the realities of quality of life.

Provider Rights

Refusal to Perform Certain Procedures

The provider may refuse to perform any act that conflicts with personal moral or ethical principles (e.g., performing an abortion or withdrawing life support). However, the provider has the responsibility to *respect the patient's wishes* and make a referral to another provider who is more comfortable and responsive to the patient's wishes.

Rights and Responsibilities of Patients

Patient Rights

> What are the rights and responsibilities of patients?

In 1972, the American Hospital Association developed the **Patient's Bill of Rights,** which details the patient's right to receive complete information, to refuse treatment (unless the patient is incompetent or the decision poses a threat to the community), and to know about a hospital's possible financial conflicts of interest. **Informed consent**

is the patient's right to know all treatment options and to decide which care is appropriate for them. To empower the patient to make a rational decision, the provider must afford the patient full information including accurate and understandable explanations. Until the late 1970s, decisions regarding life-sustaining treatment were considered the domain of clinicians. Respect for patient participation in such decisions led to the passage of the **Patient Self-Determination Act** in 1991.

Informed Consent

The *Patient Self-Determination Act* requires health care institutions to advise patients that:

1. they have the right to refuse or accept medical care; and
2. they have the right to execute an advance directive concerning their care or to designate a person (proxy) to make decisions for them if they are unable to do so.

Informed consent is an *open communication process* between the patient, the clinician, and other health care team members, which results in the patient understanding and approving or not approving a medical intervention or course of action. Under most circumstances, care can be withdrawn at a patient's request. However, it is illegal in most states for a health care worker to actively hasten death even at the patient's explicit request (e.g., **provider-assisted suicide**). Parents are empowered to make legal decisions for their children, but over the past 30 years, there has been a movement to allow children to participate more actively in medical decision making. In the case of experimental protocols, it is mandated by some institutions that children as young as 7 years of age must give **informed assent** prior to being accepted as a participant, and their parents must give *informed consent*. Adolescents may make their own decisions regarding sexual matters (e.g., contraception, treatment of sexually transmitted infections, abortion), although some states require parental notification or involvement.

Patient Responsibilities

Defining **patient responsibilities** is less straightforward than defining the responsibilities of providers, because the latter typically have responsibilities dictated by the guidelines of their respective professions. Patients, in contrast, are often faced with considerable challenges and barriers, making even the most seemingly reasonable "responsibilities" hardly applicable. For example, attending appointments may seem like a reasonable responsibility until one considers a patient living in a rural community 45 min from the provider's office with no transportation and limited financial resources. Still, many practices do choose to present patients with a list of responsibilities. Common themes found in such lists include requests that, whenever possible, patients should make their best effort to

1. fully participate in decisions involving their health care and to accept the outcomes of these decisions;
2. report whether they clearly understand their health conditions and the planned course of treatment;
3. ask questions to ensure understanding, and communicate a need for more information when necessary;
4. give health care providers the most accurate and complete information regarding their present complaints, medical history, medications, and changes in any of their health conditions;
5. comply with the treatment plan by attending appointments, taking medications as prescribed, and asking questions when clarification is needed;
6. inform their provider if they did not, cannot, or plan not to, follow the treatment plan for any reason; and
7. respect and be considerate of health care providers, staff, other patients, and the facility, by their words and actions.

These idealistic responsibilities should be considered goals for patients to strive to achieve to the best of their ability and not grounds for patient dismissal, unless the patient is persistently uncooperative or disruptive. Even in these circumstances, it is incumbent on the provider to seek to understand the patient's circumstances and to help remove as many barriers as possible to promote adherence.

Establishing Limits of Confidentiality

Except in situations where the provider is concerned that the patient will harm themselves or others, or in situations that involve mandatory reporting (child abuse, communicable diseases), patient information may not be shared with others without the patient's expressed consent. Patient information may be discussed without explicit patient consent only with professional individuals who are involved in the patient's care, or with members of a teaching group (all of whom have been instructed in the principles of confidentiality) in a controlled environment away from areas where the discussion could be overheard.

The **Health Insurance Portability and Accountability Act (HIPAA)**, which took effect in 2003, provides standards to protect patients' written and electronic medical records and other health information that is provided to health plans, practitioners, hospitals, and other health care providers. These standards give patients access to their medical records and more control over how their personal health information is used and disclosed. With the development of the integrated model of team-based health care (e.g., the *patient-centered medical home,* PCMH), access to patient records is available to the team and to the patient as well.

Guidelines for Protecting Confidentiality
- Conduct the interview in private
- Tell patients with whom and under what circumstances information will be shared
- Teach or consult about patients in private
- Override confidentiality when safety of the patient or others is a concern

With the development and promulgation of *electronic health records* (EHRs), **protected health information** (PHI) is more available to members of the patient's health care team but, at the same time, more vulnerable to access by a variety of individuals and organizations. Communications between providers or between provider and patient, both verbal and written, must comply with HIPAA regulations. HIPAA requires that individually identifiable health information be protected and includes all written, numeric, or pictorial information related to physical or mental health that would allow a patient to be identified.

Factors Influencing the Provider–Patient Relationship

Effective communication is by far the most essential component of a collaborative relationship between practitioner and patient. Effective communication leads to improved quality of care, improved physiological health, improved emotional health, increased patient compliance, increased patient satisfaction, and improved health outcomes. The fundamental components of effective provider–patient communication include gathering information, understanding the patient's perspective, sharing information, agreeing on problems, and collaborating on a treatment plan. To effectively achieve these elements, providers must employ accurate empathy.

Accurate empathy is the ability to understand the patient's illness experiences from the patient's perspective, to communicate this understanding to the patient, and to have this understanding confirmed by the patient. Patients list kindness, understanding, interest, and encouragement as primary expectations they have of their providers. They want their physical, interpersonal, and emotional needs met in a mutually understood, courteous, warm, and personal manner that permits them to feel they are partners with the provider. **Nonverbal skills** that can facilitate empathy include eye contact (when culturally appropriate), pleasant and/or concerned facial expression, relaxed posture, congruent affect, and modulated tone of voice.

While empathy is pivotal, other factors influence the provider–patient relationship. These include mutual trust, respect, genuineness, acceptance, and warmth (see Chapter 40: Principles of Psychotherapy). Expectation management also plays an important role. Providers must understand and recognize factors that influence expectations of both patients and themselves as clinicians, including transference and countertransference.

> What is the difference between transference and countertransference?

Transference refers to the beliefs, expectations, and perceptions from previous relationships that influence current life experience. For example, take the case of a woman with insulin-dependent diabetes who has not complied well with dietary restrictions. The patient grew up in a household with a harsh, critical parent. If the provider attempts to counsel her about proper dietary habits and expresses these recommendations in a firm fashion, the patient may become angry and feel belittled because the patient feels the provider has not appreciated her efforts to control her diet. In this instance, the patient is reacting as if the clinician were a parent (transference).

Countertransference refers to inappropriate reactions the provider has to a patient. If the provider perceives the patient as a "nice little old lady" who is just like a favorite aunt, the provider may find it difficult to ask her questions that seem intrusive (e.g., about how frequently she voids or if she has urinary incontinence). Effective medical care involves being objectively vigilant and aware that the patient *and* provider may bring past emotional experiences to each encounter.

Impediments to Communication

Language and Cultural Differences

Virtually every provider will need to communicate with a patient through a *translator* or an *interpreter* at some time. Because of differences in language structure, literal translations may not be possible or accurate. Efforts should be made, however, to ensure that the patient's complaints and condition are clearly communicated. An interpreter, in contrast to a translator, brings their own cultural and ethnic background values, knowledge, and belief system to the exchange. In effect, the role of the interpreter *triangulates the encounter*. For example, if the patient is angry, but the interpreter feels that displaying anger is inappropriate, the provider will not be told, and the patient's answers will be softened or references to anger, blame, or guilt removed. If the translator or interpreter is a child or family member of the patient, issues such as confidentiality become especially important.

The time needed for an interview involving a translator or interpreter is usually twice as long as one solely between practitioner and patient. The provider should acknowledge to the patient that there may be difficulty in arriving at a diagnosis and management plan as a result of the language difference but that they will work together to overcome these problems.

Cognitive differences include the disparity between how the patient and the provider *conceptualize experiences*, and how they understand and explain the world, including the disease and its treatment. Misconceptions, often made at first glance, can affect subjective assessments of the patient's race, ethnic origin, cultural values, appearance, demeanor, and reason for seeking care. This profile, possibly due to a lack of cultural awareness and poor communication, may lead to misdiagnosis and inappropriate care of the patient. Awareness of personal bias and prejudice, coupled with attention to the patient and a willingness to listen and understand their concerns, is requisite for providing quality treatment for every individual (see Chapter 10: Cognition, Communication, and Social Interaction, and Chapter 17: Culture and Cultural Competence in Health Care).

Age Effects

Because age is associated with increased experience, younger providers are sometimes challenged for being too young and may need great patience to win a patient's confidence. Seeing themselves as children or even grandchildren, younger providers sometimes have difficulty advising older patients.

Sensory Impairment

Communication is likely to be inhibited to some degree by impaired hearing, sight, or verbal expression. *Hearing-impaired individuals* may need to use sign language, require an ASL translator to translate, or be able to read the lips of a provider who must speak clearly and slowly. For patients with hearing impairment who are literate, the interview may be facilitated by the use of written material. The *visually impaired* patient's need for verbal explanation and description exceeds

that of all other patients. The patient who is mute may be able to sign and, therefore, may require a translator. When any patient has an impairment, the provider must inquire about the extent to which physical or cognitive assistance will be required to adhere to the therapeutic plan and if that assistance will be available.

Gender Effects

Gender differences in communication style may impact the provider–patient relationship. Research evidence demonstrates that female providers engage in more positive talk and rapport building behavior with patients such as encouragement, attentive silence, and nonverbal communication (nodding, smiling). Female providers also demonstrate less dominance during consultation and are rated as more empathic than male providers. Female providers have been found to ask more psychosocial questions and spend two minutes more on average consulting with patients than male providers. Overall, there is no difference in the amount of information or directives given by male and female providers although male providers tend to give more biomedical information and female providers engage in more emotionally focused talk.

Provider Factors

Providers may inadvertently create barriers to effective communication, which can hinder the provider–patient relationship. One potential barrier is provider avoidance of any discussion of emotional or social aspects of problems due to time constraints or perceived inability to adequately address these concerns. In addition, providers who discourage patients from expressing concerns or from requesting further information may disempower patients and thwart the creation of a collaborative working relationship and treatment plan.

Technology

Increased use of technology in medical settings, including EHRs and documentation, has resulted in more streamlined and improved medical care for patients. In many ways, technology has expedited many required tasks for providers. However, technology may hinder the clinician–patient relationship. Effective communication requires active listening, undivided attention, and accurate empathy. Technology often creates a distraction that disrupts verbal and nonverbal communication. Clinicians who use technology while interacting with patients should take exceptional care to position themselves so that all team members, including the patient, can clearly see one another. Providers should also be careful to focus on the patient (not the computer screen) while the patient is talking and to remain actively engaged, with eye contact and other nonverbal signs.

Other Factors

Psychosocial stresses and *psychiatric disorders* may pose an impediment to the interview. Psychosis, paranoia, and some personality disorders may hinder the provider from forming a therapeutic relationship with the patient. Children or individuals with developmental or cognitive disorders may have difficulty understanding complex issues and decisions related to their health care. Also, patients with various types of *dementia*, especially in the early stages, may confabulate or provide unreliable or inaccurate medical information. In these cases, having family members involved in the interview to confirm information and assist in the care plan for the individual can be valuable. In trauma situations, such as rape or domestic violence, the provider must be aware of the need for privacy and support. The patient should be given clear guidance concerning the process of the physical examination and other data collection, and should not be left alone in the exam room.

Understanding Patient Fears

What are patients' two main fears?

A patient typically has two main fears: **losing bodily integrity** and **becoming dependent**. The degree to which these fears affect the patient

depends on the patient's age and stage of development, personality, and life experiences. Young athletes are usually able to tolerate injury and pain, yet they have little tolerance for discomfort or inconvenience if an illness limits their activities or makes them dependent on others. In contrast, older persons with a chronic illness may accept limited independence, being more concerned about maintaining at least the basic functioning essential for remaining in their own home.

Acceptance of Dependency Is Influenced by Life Stage

1. Young children are used to being dependent on others, but may be fearful because they do not understand illness.
2. Adolescents struggle to establish their identity and may find any threat to independence difficult to accept.
3. Adults may find it difficult to tolerate absence from work or isolation from friends, especially if they define themselves in terms of their work or relationships.
4. Older patients may experience illness as a signal that their healthy life is jeopardized and that there may be no hope of recovery.

Evolving Provider–Patient Relationships and Changes in Medical Care Models

Changes in the provider–patient relationship are likely with the implementation of the PCMH. Within this model, the practitioner becomes the primary health care provider and the primary agent for preventing illness, promoting wellness, and managing chronic conditions. The model assumes a strong relationship between an active patient and a primary care provider who, like the family doctor of the past, will be responsible for promoting overall health and well-being, empowering the patient, and working collaboratively with other health care professionals. This model requires an expansion of communication skills to include the ability to understand the whole person, find common ground, incorporate prevention, enhance the provider–patient relationship, and develop realistic goals.

Many practices implementing the patient-centered medical home are using an **integrated primary care model** to assist patients with, or who are at risk for, chronic diseases. This has resulted in a new partnership between provider and patient, in which patients are increasingly being seen as active members of their own health care team. The goal of integrated primary care is to provide team care at the point of care by including members of other health professions, such as behavioral medicine, nutrition, and pharmacy, during the encounter, with the goal of engaging the patient in multidisciplinary, active care of their illness. This paradigm shift allows a focus on preventing the development of further morbidity in patients who have conditions such as diabetes, hypertension, and cardiovascular disease. It is increasingly recognized that patient actions, understanding of illness, and maintenance of healthy lifestyles have significant impact on their ability to maintain improved health.

In this model, patients who arrive for medical visits are seen at the time and place of care not only by the primary provider but also other team members. Visits are brief, integrated with the clinical encounter, and involve documentation in a shared medical record to which the patient has access. The goals are to increase patient ability to manage and care for illness, and to reduce significant comorbidities that lead to decreased health and increased cost of care. This approach must involve frequent and regular screening for behavioral health issues, recognizing that patients with chronic illness, particularly multiple chronic illnesses, are at increased risk. While the provider manages the team, the patient is always a member and sits at the center of the clinical process. Providers and patients find this results in an improved relationship producing positive health outcomes and reduced morbidity.

Provider Flexibility in Rapidly Evolving Health Care Systems

Models of health care delivery and payment are rapidly changing. Current methods of primary care delivery and payment are shifting the focus of care upstream with the goal of early identification of illness and behavioral health comorbidities. For providers, this requires flexibility and partnership with the patient as an active team member in prevention and management of health conditions.

Participatory Decision Making

> What are six methods for supporting participatory decision making?

Patients who participate in decisions regarding their care are more likely to adhere to the treatment plan. Successful **participatory decision making** requires that the patient be fully informed about the clinical findings (i.e., the nature of their condition), the treatment options available, and the efficacy and risks associated with each option.

Effective participatory decision making inevitably depends upon the provider's presentation of the effectiveness of available treatments. How the information is interpreted will be influenced by:

Patient knowledge, fears, and prioritized treatment goals. It is imperative that the provider be familiar with the patient's level of knowledge, concerns, and treatment goals, and be prepared to inform and advise the patient when necessary.

Methods for Supporting Participatory Decision Making

1. Present options for how the patient can participate in the decision-making process.
2. Present options for how clinical detail is presented to the patient.
3. State information regarding clinical procedures in terms of absolute risk, since relative risk reduction statements may be confusing and misleading.
4. Carefully weigh the order in which information is presented.
5. Carefully present the time frame of treatment outcome.
6. In presenting outcome rates, use proportions rather than percentages, especially with less educated or older patients.

Provider knowledge, resources, biases. The provider should ensure that their knowledge base is current, resources are available, and personal biases are openly discussed and fairly presented.

External resources, accessibility to facilities, limitations in time and practice. The provider should ensure in advance that external resources and facilities are available, and that practice constraints and demands will not impede patient care.

Ensuring Treatment Plan Success

The success of any intervention depends on the provider and patient reaching agreement about the nature of the problem and its proper treatment (see Chapter 17: Culture and Cultural Competence in Health Care). The patient's explanation of the illness, or **explanatory model**, influences beliefs about causation and determines what assistance they will seek and accept. Therefore, every effort should be made to explain the nature of the illness, its etiology, and its treatment accurately, but in terms that are in keeping with the patient's explanatory model, culture, and treatment expectations.

Maximizing Adherence

> What influences adherence to treatment recommendations?

It is rare for patients to follow treatment recommendations rigorously. The adherence rate for prescribed medications is about 50% even in the treatment of acute illness, and the proportion of patients completing treatment decreases as the duration of treatment increases. Thus, higher-dose but shorter-course treatments are used for a wide variety of infections.

Patient **adherence** to therapy recommendations typically depends upon (1) the complexity of the regimen, (2) the persistence of symptoms, (3) the frequency and quality of contact with the provider, and (4) patient beliefs. In cases of chronic illness, the provider can help to ensure that patients have the proper skills to manage the "prescription" through a careful explanation of the agreed-upon care plan, the specific behaviors required by the patient, and an ongoing assessment of patient adherence as a regular part of repeated clinical encounters. Providing specific benchmarks for patient compliance, frequent feedback, and praise for success in meeting adherence goals should replace general statements of support (see Chapter 28: Understanding and Improving Health Literacy).

Adherence to Treatment Will Depend on the Patient's Belief that:

1. The illness warrants treatment.
2. The treatment is effective.
3. The cost of treatment is reasonable given the benefits.
4. The treatment is feasible.
5. The patient's behavior will make a difference in outcome.

Recommended Readings

Cummings, C. (2013). Communication in the era of COWs: Technology and the physician-patient-parent relationship. *Pediatrics Perspectives*, *131*, 401–403. http://doi.org/10.1542/peds.2012-3200

Ishikawa, H., Hashimoto, H., & Kiuchi, T. (2013). The evolving concept of "patient-centeredness" in patient-physician communication research. *Social Science & Medicine*, *96*, 147–153. http://doi.org/10.1016/j.socscimed.2013.07.026

Kelly, J. M., Kraft-Todd, G., Schapira, L., Kossowsky, J., & Riess, H. (2014). The influence of the patient-clinician relationship on healthcare outcomes: A systematic review and meta-analysis of randomized controlled trials. *PLoS ONE, 9*(4), e94207. http://doi.org/10.1371/journal.pone.0094207

Riess, H., & Kraft-Todd, G. (2014). E.M.P.A.T.H.Y.: A tool to enhance nonverbal communication between clinicians and their patients. *Academic Medicine*, *89*, 1108–1112. http://doi.org/10.1097/ACM.0000000000000287

Vidaeff, A. C., Kerrigan, A. J., & Monga, M. (2014). Cross-cultural barriers to health care. *Southern Medical Journal, 108*(1), 1–4. http://doi.org/10.14423/SMJ.0000000000000221

Additional Resources

American College of Obstetricians and Gynecologists. (2014). *Effective patient-physician communication.* Available at http://www.acog.org/Resources-And-Publications/Committee-Opinions/Committee-on-Health-Care-for-Underserved-Women/Effective-Patient-Physician-Communication

Dingley, C., Daugherty, K., Derieg, M. K., & Persing, R. (n.d.). *Improving patient safety through provider communication strategy enhancements.* Available at http://www.ahrq.gov/downloads/pub/advances2/vol3/advances-dingley_14.pdf

HHS.gov. *Effective communication in hospitals.* Available at http://www.hhs.gov/civil-rights/for-individuals/special-topics/hospitals-effective-communication/index.html

The Patient Provider Communication Forum. Available at http://www.patientprovidercommunication.org

Weir, K. (2012). *Improving patient-physician communication.* Available at http://www.apa.org/monitor/2012/11/patient-physician.aspx

Review Questions

1. Dr. Johnson works as a primary care physician in a large federally qualified health center that operates using an integrated primary care model. Today, he sees a patient with uncontrolled diabetes, heart disease, and many reported psychosocial stressors. Dr. Johnson suspects that depression may be present and that symptoms are a barrier to adequate management of chronic illness. Which of the following providers might Dr. Johnson consult at the point of care within an integrated primary care model?
   A. Behavioral health provider
   B. Nutritionist
   C. Pharmacist
   D. All of the above
   E. None of the above

2. Which of the following best describes the basic requirement of informed consent?
   A. The clinician must be well informed before consenting to perform a procedure.
   B. The patient must have a designated proxy to make decisions if the patient becomes incompetent.
   C. The patient must have all necessary information before agreeing to medical treatment.
   D. The patient's family must be advised before medical procedures are undertaken.
   E. The patient's primary care provider must be informed before a subspecialist performs a procedure.

3. The presence of empathy is crucial in the development of the provider–patient relationship. The core element in establishing empathy focuses on
   A. avoiding excessive emotional detachment
   B. mastering active or reflective listening
   C. modeling how to remain in calm self-control
   D. providing reassurance about a positive outcome
   E. using exclusively open-ended questioning

4. Encouraging patients to participate in the clinical decision-making process
   A. complicates and impedes the treatment course
   B. decreases patient confidence in provider competence
   C. increases patient adherence to treatment regimens
   D. increases the risk of poor outcomes and litigation
   E. raises ethical issues with regard to clinical responsibility

Answer Key on p. 466

35 The Medical Encounter and Clinical Decision Making

Jonathon M. Firnhaber, MD, Dennis C. Russo, PhD, and Lars C. Larsen, MD

- What is rapport?
- What kinds of questions should be avoided during an interview?
- What are seven data-gathering techniques?
- What is included in a comprehensive medical history?
- What is the mental status examination?
- What are two types of clinical reasoning?
- What are the six steps in the clinical decision-making process?
- What are 10 sources of error in clinical decision making?

The Medical Encounter

Setting, time constraints, and purpose determine the structure of each provider–patient medical encounter. In an emergency or triage situation, the interview is limited to essential information sufficient to initiate care. In contrast, in a new patient office visit, data collection is more thorough and comprehensive, requiring sufficient time to accomplish the goals of the visit. In a continuing care encounter, addressing issues to keep the patient healthy or managing chronic illness become important parts of the agenda. Whatever the circumstance, every patient encounter should be documented in writing to facilitate communication and consistency of care.

Introductions

The interviewer should always introduce themselves, even if wearing a name tag. The patient should be addressed using a formal title (i.e., Mr., Mrs., Ms.) and the patient's last name, unless the patient is a child or has asked to be addressed in another way. Many providers shake hands with the patient and anyone accompanying the patient. However, care should be taken to respect differences in social practices and expectations if the patient is from another culture.

Developing Rapport

What is rapport?

Rapport is a state of mutual confidence and respect between two people. Because the provider is perceived as being in a position of authority, developing rapport is essential to establishing a mutually respectful relationship. The development of trust comes when the patient believes the provider understands and respects their concerns.

Sensitivity to Emotions

Responding appropriately to an expression of emotion by the patient can be reassuring and facilitate the interview. It is important for the provider to be comfortable with emotion to allow the patient to be comfortable expressing it. When a patient cries, showing respect and caring by waiting or offering a tissue can be comforting even if nothing is said. With an angry or hostile patient, acknowledging the anger, remaining calm and listening reflectively, and encouraging the patient to discuss what is causing the anger are likely to diffuse the situation. Above all, care should be taken to avoid taking the patient's display of anger as personal.

Cultural Appropriateness

Every patient has a set of culturally based *health beliefs*, *illness behaviors*, and *explanatory models* for what is normal or abnormal. Understanding and respecting the patient's cultural context increases the likelihood of full participation in developing and adhering to an effective treatment plan.

Establishing Limits of Confidentiality

The medical encounter involves the patient sharing large amounts of personal information with the provider. The patient must feel confident that the provider will treat that information in a manner consistent with accepted standards and guidelines for confidentiality (see Chapter 34: The Provider–Patient Relationship).

Attentive Listening

Attentive listening communicates interest, concern, and understanding about what the patient is saying and feeling. The provider's interest enhances the patient's impression of professional competence, which, in turn, facilitates trust and prompts the patient to be more open and candid.

To Promote Attentive Listening

1. The setting should be comfortable.
2. The provider should face the patient with an erect but relaxed posture.
3. Eye contact should be frequent, if culturally appropriate.
4. The provider should use gestures and facial expressions that are congruent with what is being said, and speak in a pleasant voice.
5. The provider should address the topic the patient has introduced and encourage the flow of information by using occasional facilitative words and phrases.

Observation

Careful observation is an important part of evaluating the patient and should begin the moment the provider first sees the patient. How is the patient groomed? Does the patient appear comfortable? Relaxed? Impatient? Frightened? When the patient is accompanied by others, what information on interpersonal or family relationships does this interaction provide? Initial hypotheses begin to form as the provider notes apparent age, gender, race, dress, affect, and whether the patient appears healthy, ill, or in distress.

Touching

Touching between the provider and the patient in the interim between shaking hands during introductions and the physical examination may or may not be appropriate. Although touching can be interpreted as empathetic by some patients, others can construe it as intrusive or seductive. Backing away, stiffening, or becoming silent are clues that a patient prefers not to be touched. Most experienced providers use measured, appropriate physical contact to reassure patients and enhance rapport unless the patient signals that this is unwelcome.

Conducting the Interview

Interviewers usually begin with open-ended questions, follow with more focused questions, and end with closed-ended questions to confirm data. *Open-ended questions* ("How have you been getting along?" "How can I help you?") signal the provider's interest in the patient, and allow the patient to present issues they wish to address. Although it may seem paradoxical, open-ended questions elicit the maximum amount of information in the minimum amount of time because they impose few values or expectations, involve the patient in the interview and problem-solving process, and allow the patient to reveal information not apparent from the presenting complaint or medical history.

Focused questions narrow the area to be explored, but still give the patient latitude in answering (e.g., "What is your understanding of your situation?" or "How do you think this happened?"). Questions to help *clarify certain points* are "What do you mean when you say ...?" or "What are some examples of ...?"

Closed-ended questions prompt specific responses and are appropriate for further clarifying details, facilitating decision making in triage or emergency situations, or directing the interview. Questions that elicit *specific information* are "Where does it hurt?" or "What did you eat today?"

Open-Ended Questions Can Quickly Elicit:

1. Major concerns or most pressing or potentially serious problems
2. Triggering events that led the patient to seek help now
3. Attributions or explanatory models for the symptoms
4. Expectations about what can or should be done

What kinds of questions should be avoided during an interview?

Questions to be *avoided* include *compound questions*, which are several questions asked together (e.g., "Tell me what happens when you have chest pain, does it come after you've eaten something, or when you're feeling anxious?") and *leading questions*, which prompt the patient to give a specific response (e.g., "You haven't been drinking alcohol again, have you?").

What are seven data-gathering techniques?

Seven Successful Data-Gathering Techniques

1. *Nonverbal techniques:* head-nodding and verbal cues ("Tell me more about that") prompt the patient to expand and report what they feel is most important.
2. *Checking:* reviewing or repeating to ensure accuracy ("You think this started last Thursday?").
3. *Clarification:* asking the patient to restate or give examples, or paraphrasing what the patient has said ("So, your headaches occur both day and night, but are the absolute worst when you wake up. Is that correct?").
4. *Interruption:* breaking the flow if the patient is rambling. Acknowledge the importance the patient attaches to the information being given, then pro-

vide a transition to another topic ("Mrs. Jones, your son's school problems are certainly worrying you, but how about you? How's your arm healing?").
5. *Transition:* linking what the patient has been saying with a change in direction ("What you've been talking about reminds me to ask you....").
6. *Reflection:* paraphrasing what the patient has said to demonstrate attention ("You've told me a lot of things. Let's see if I've understood them all.").
7. *Information sharing:* interpreting and explaining the problem to clarify goals and expectations for outcomes. Written information should be culturally appropriate and suitable for the patient's literacy level.

Defining the patient's condition and concerns requires two kinds of information: **subjective data**, such as the description and history (chronology) of the symptoms; and **objective data**, such as observations during the interview, the physical examination, and results from laboratory tests and studies.

The History

What is included in a comprehensive medical history?

A Comprehensive Medical History Includes:

1. *Identifying data:* name, age, gender, occupation, and a brief statement of the major presenting problem in one or two sentences.
2. *Reliability of the source of data:* patient, family member, chart records, letter of referral.
3. *Chief complaint:* the reason for seeking care in the patient's exact words.
4. *History of the present illness:* narrative account of each current problem including its beginning, course, diagnosis, and management; the patient's explanation for the problem and how it has affected their life ("Diabetes runs in my family"; "I can't sleep at night"); characteristics of each symptom: timing or chronology, quality or character, quantity or severity, location, aggravating or alleviating factors, associated manifestations.
5. *Past medical history:* medical, surgical, obstetrical, and psychiatric problems not currently active, including injuries and hospitalizations.

6. *Current health status and habits:* prescriptions, over-the-counter, and herbal or supplemental medications; allergies; habits (including substance use); environmental exposures; travel; diet; immunizations; and exercise and health maintenance and prevention.

7. *Family history:* narrative and genogram of the family, including as many generations as possible, with dates of birth and death, causes of death, and illnesses.

8. *Social history:* biographical sketch including birthplace, parents, education, places of residence, work, marital status and relationships, children, hobbies, satisfactions and stresses.

9. *Review of systems:* standard set of questions about common symptoms associated with each organ system that help to disclose any disease not yet discussed.

Mental Status Examination

What is the mental status examination?

The **mental status examination** (MSE) bridges the history and physical examination. It begins with observation and assessment throughout the encounter and concludes with a more formal evaluation of the cognitive status of the patient. The formal evaluation of mental status includes assessment of level of consciousness; attention; memory (short- and long-term); orientation to time, place, and person; thought processes; thought content, insight, and judgment; affect; mood; language; vocabulary; fund of knowledge; and ability to abstract, calculate, and copy.

In primary care, increasing emphasis is being placed on the integration of behavioral health services at the point of care to identify behavioral health comorbidities. Brief screening tools such as the Patient Health Questionnaire (PHQ-9), Generalized Anxiety Disorder Screener (GAD-7), and Montreal Cognitive Assessment (MoCA), can support the health care team in identifying preventive and treatment strategies to modify chronic health conditions through behavior change and patient empowerment. Early intervention may identify depression, anxiety or other behavioral health problems, and also provide prescriptive

information to assist the patient in becoming a better manager of their own illness. Chronic illness, such as diabetes, is often associated with depression, and development of an integrated care plan can reduce morbidity and mortality. Team care also allows other disciplines, such as nutrition and pharmacy, to develop and integrate simultaneous care plans in partnership with the primary provider and patient (see Chapter 30: Theories of Social Relations and Interprofessional Collaboration).

The Physical Examination

The physical examination elicits *signs* (observable objective data) indicative of disease. Signs primarily confirm hypotheses that have been generated during the interview process. The physical examination, like the history, may be complete or focused. When a patient has *symptoms* (subjective complaints) that are limited to a specific region or organ system, the examiner may decide to limit the examination to that area. The risk is that a significant finding will be undetected (e.g., a heart murmur in a child with acute rheumatic fever who presents complaining only of a limp). Physical alterations can occur over the natural course of a disease, and can be detected by observation, palpation, percussion, or auscultation.

Generally, a complete physical examination is conducted by region, starting with the head and neck and concluding with the extremities. The recording of the findings should begin with a descriptive general statement followed by a listing of the vital signs. The remainder of the data is usually organized under the following categories: skin, head, eyes, ears, nose, mouth and pharynx, neck, lymph nodes, thorax and lungs, cardiovascular system, breasts, abdomen, genitalia, rectum, peripheral vascular system, musculoskeletal system, and neurological system.

Laboratory Investigation

Necessary laboratory studies may be ordered after data from the history and physical examination have been collected and an initial *differential diagnosis* (list of diagnostic possibilities with their relative probabilities) has been generated. Diagnostic laboratory studies are likely to be most helpful when the probability of a particular disease is in the intermediate range, although some diagnostic tests are obtained to confirm a highly likely diagnosis. Tests should be ordered based on *predictive value* (likelihood of providing diagnostic help) as well as *cost benefit*. It is poor medical practice to order tests automatically, or to order an entire panel of tests merely because they can be processed simultaneously.

Ending the Clinical Encounter

Before ending the clinical encounter, the provider should review the relevant clinical information, the diagnosis and explanation of the patient's problem, and the mutually agreed upon step-by-step plan for treatment, ending with scheduling the next appointment.

Clinical Reasoning

> What are two types of clinical reasoning?

Central to the clinical decision-making process is the provider's expertise in clinical reasoning. Psychologists and other researchers describe two types of decision-making processes: *nonanalytic* or *intuitive*, where previous experience and other frequently unconscious factors drive the clinician to make decisions, and *analytic*, where controlled, deliberate, and thoughtful consideration of all aspects of the patient's case is used to reach a decision. From a conceptual standpoint, these two modes of decision making are substantially different, even to the extent that they involve different areas of the brain. In practice, both are used in the clinical decision-making process, although often to varying degrees. Most failures in clinical reasoning stem from overreliance on the quick, automatic, and reflexive intuitive process. Analytic reasoning is typically more reliable, and is employed in cases where the provider has less experience, the clinical presentation is more complex, or the case does not fit a characteristic disease pattern.

The Six Steps in the Clinical Decision-Making Process

> What are the six steps in the clinical decision-making process?

The provider's role in the clinical decision-making process begins before the patient's appointment. It is initiated through a self-made appointment or a professional referral seeking answers to questions about the patient's condition. These questions determine the parameters of the provider's role in dealing with the patient, and the decisions the provider will be asked to make. *Referral questions*, either from the patient or from a referral source, such as another provider, define the initial problem. The provider develops a set of hypotheses that determine what information will be required and how it will be obtained. For example, if the patient is a hyperactive child being seen because a teacher has expressed concern to the parent, the clinician may seek assessment of school performance, gather data about behavior at home, and meet with the child's parents and teachers in addition to examining the child in the office.

The Six Steps of the Clinical Decision-Making Process

1. *Defining the problem:* clarifying the nature of the problem, including an appreciation of the patient's cognitive context (i.e., beliefs, assumptions, expectations).
2. *Defining outcome goals:* defining the desired resolution of the problem in attainable terms.
3. *Generating alternative solutions:* identifying possible alternative solutions to resolve the problem.
4. *Selecting the best solution:* conducting a cost-benefit analysis based on the merits of each alternative solution (probable consequences; good vs. adverse effects; approximation to desired outcome), developing a strategic plan for the implementation of each solution (how much will it cost in time, money, energy), and then choosing the solution not only most likely to produce health but also most likely to be followed.
5. *Implementing the solution:* carrying out the plan.
6. *Evaluating the outcome:* determining if the goal was achieved and the problem solved. If not, reformulating the plan to reach a desirable end. Sometimes, as in chronic illness, the patient must redefine "health" to reach an accessible end point.

Defining the Problem

The *problem list* serves as an organizing point for clinical problem solving. The list is a compilation of all the symptoms, signs, problems, and issues (e.g., family history of breast cancer) of concern. As the list is developed, symptoms and signs may cluster under a single diagnosis, hypotheses become better defined, and certain problems may be eliminated as new data are acquired.

Case Vignette – Part 1

A 41-year-old female engineer who has had increasingly severe headaches with shoulder and jaw pain is referred to the Behavioral Medicine Clinic by a neurologist because no medication has been helpful in reducing her symptoms. History and physical examination reveal no other current or past medical problems. The patient experiences headaches most frequently midmorning, Monday through Friday, and occasionally in the evening. Personal and social history reveals the patient is married to another engineer, a "Type A workaholic." They both leave for work at 6 a.m. and return home at 6 p.m., at which time the patient prepares dinner. After dinner, they prepare construction materials for two cabins they are building on weekends. The patient reports no personal time, no recreational activities, and feeling pressured to work as hard as her husband. Her job as a middle manager in a large firm requires her to manage contract negotiations between the company and government agencies. Her office is in a large manufacturing plant, with continuous exposure to production noises that can interfere with concentration (e.g., metal saws, riveting), and to dust and debris. The initial referral hypothesis, that her headache problem may be stress related, is supported by the fact that: (1) she is working in a physically stressful work environment; (2) she is working in a psychologically stressful work environment; (3) her home environment is stressful; (4) she reports that she experiences pain in her shoulders and jaw, and difficulties concentrating; and (5) she has no private or personal time or recreation.

Tentative hypotheses generated by the referral question are tested and refined in light of the information obtained from history taking and physical examination. These, in turn, are subjected to verification through the selection of appropriate tests. The provider should be knowledgeable about the validity and reliability of each potential test to ensure that the selected test measures what needs to be measured, and does so in a consistent, accurate, reproducible, and conceptually meaningful way.

Defining Outcome Goals

Initial diagnostic impressions based on referral questions, history, and examination may rule out some diagnoses but raise questions about others. Further data gathering and laboratory and other tests will produce a limited set of problems and diagnoses. Building a clinical partnership allows the provider and patient to carefully weigh realistic and attainable *outcome goals* – what is the patient's desired health condition at the conclusion of treatment? Once these goals have been negotiated and agreed upon, the provider and patient work together to generate one or more alternative solutions in the form of various treatment modalities.

Case Vignette – Part 2

Outcome goals for the patient's defined problems were discussed and agreed to as follows: (1) reduce work environment stress; (2) reduce work-related psychological stress; (3) reduce stress at home; (4) increase personal and private time and recreation.

The provider should be cautious to not overestimate the patient's ability to understand basic health information (see Chapter 28: Understanding and Improving Health Literacy). An effective provider assumes patients may *not* understand, and is proactive in verifying successful communication. For example, asking, "What questions do you have?" rather than "Do you have any questions?" resets expectations and can reassure the patient that having questions is normal.

Prevention and Early Intervention as Targets of Care

Upon initial examination, some patients may exhibit physical and laboratory findings consistent with imminent or early chronic illness. Careful observation of patients with chronic illness may reveal significant emotional distress (depression, anxiety) and somatic symptoms that reflect the patient's reaction to their medical illness as opposed to a primary psychological disorder. In such cases, the physician should consider prevention or early intervention as a primary goal of treatment. Point-of-care assessment and identification of lifestyle factors such as poor diet, lack of exercise, or somatic complaints such as headache or insomnia should alert the practitioner to add these issues to the problem list with specific consideration about their treatment.

Generating Alternative Treatment Solutions

Given the symptom complaints and diagnosis, what solutions or *intervention strategies* can the patient use to remediate the problem and achieve their outcome goals? The decision-making process focuses on how to (1) modify behavior or cognitions, (2) alter biological functioning, (3) facilitate changes in the environment, and (4) identify and use social resources. This stage of the decision-making process is critical to the eventual treatment outcome. The provider's training and experience, command of a repertoire of treatment alternatives, intellect, clinical-reasoning skills, and pragmatic creativity are brought to bear on helping the patient find favorable cost–benefit solutions to the problems inherent in their situation. Early identification of these problems and the provision of integrated services can enhance outcomes and increase patient participation in managing their own care.

Case Vignette – Part 3

The provider and patient together decided on the following solutions for each of the patient's outcome goals: (1) develop a scenario for requesting enclosed sound and dust-proof office space; (2) develop a scenario for requesting staff support to help manage government contracts; (3) meet with the patient and her husband to discuss reducing stress at home by limiting the number of evenings devoted to cabin preparation work, and planning one "no work" weekend a month for getting away together; and (4) assist the patient in arranging to attend aerobics class after work two nights a week, and allowing sufficient time for a relaxing bath before bedtime.

Selecting the Best Solution

In developing the treatment plan, the provider must review the defined problems with the patient and together determine the *best methods* for resolving these problems and the order of *priority* in which various problems should be addressed. An advanced approach to selecting the best solution involves **shared decision making** (SDM). Whereas many providers are accustomed to *informing* patients of their various treatment options, the SDM process is more formal, involved, and evidence-based. Importantly, not all medical decisions are appropriate for the SDM process. Progressively greater degrees of shared decision making include: (1) choice talk: the physician makes sure that the patient knows reasonable options are available; (2) option talk: the provider offers more detailed information about options, often by integrating the use of decision support tools; (3) decision talk: the provider helps the patient explore their personal preferences and make the actual decision.

Case Vignette – Part 4

After discussion with a behavioral medicine specialist, the patient decided her home situation was the most critical problem. Hence, she made the implementation of solutions 3 and 4 top priority. She further decided that because solutions 1 and 2 would require time to develop, prepare, and rehearse, she would take time to give some thought to how to approach her supervisor and planned to do so in about a month. This process led to regular integrated care behavioral medicine follow-up aimed at assisting the patient to meet her goals.

Implementing the Solution

The treatment plan, thus formulated, is ready to be implemented. It is important that the provider and patient understand the various tasks, their respective responsibilities, and check for mutual understanding. The various steps should unfold in logical sequence (i.e., each step setting the stage for the next step). The strategy is to have the treatment course build to a final resolution of the patient's problem.

Evaluating the Outcome

The decision about whether treatment has been successful and the outcome goal achieved will be determined by the selection and assessment of appropriate *outcome criteria*. Optimally, outcome criteria should be observable and quantifiable (e.g., symptom reduction; measurable changes in biological function, behavior, or cognition). However, qualitative assessments are also legitimate (e.g., assessing changes in quality of life, feelings of self-control, competency, or perceived intensity of pain). A fully successful outcome, including the resolution of the original problem and the termination of treatment, is the final goal. However, if assessment reveals that treatment has not been successful, the treatment plan must be modified, or alternative solutions developed. The revised solutions are then implemented, and the outcome again assessed. This "back to the drawing board" process continues until the treatment goals are attained.

Sources of Error in Clinical Decision Making

> What are 10 sources of error in clinical decision making?

More than 100 biases affecting clinical decision making have been described in the literature. Each can influence the provider's thinking and introduce error into the decision-making process. Ten common sources of error are listed below:

1. **The provider's theoretical and personal biases:** Gathering medical information through the filter of a provider's personal orientation can distort the interpretation of clinical data. The traditional biomedical model biases judgments toward (a) reduction of clinical phenomena to anatomic structure and biological function; and (b) mind–body dualism, which draws a distinction between the physical and the nonphysical, the observable and the subjective, the material and the spiritual, and the "medical" and the "psychiatric" (see Chapter 38: Introduction to Psychopathology). In reality, cognitive, emotional, and sociocultural factors are tightly interwoven with biological factors in determining disease and illness. The recognition of this interplay is the cornerstone of the biopsychosocial model.

2. **Diagnosis by formula:** Trying to fit patients into preconceived categories, even when data are not fully congruent.

3. **Optimism vs. pessimism:** The provider's desire to seek the best for the patient may result in explaining problems and their treatment too optimistically. Conversely, perhaps fearing litigation, providers may overemphasize the worst-case scenario.

4. **Too many hypotheses:** Only a limited number of hypotheses can be adequately examined simultaneously. The provider should systematically rule out the most improbable hypotheses as soon as possible to allow focus on more likely hypotheses.

5. **Oversimplification:** The provider may assume that all the patient requires is a simple explanation and treatment plan, when, in fact, the patient's concerns are more complex, emotionally based, and resistant to intervention.

6. **Reorganizing the abnormal:** The provider should avoid dismissive judgments about "minimally abnormal" test values, the behaviors or beliefs of patients from different sociocultural backgrounds, or patients with an unusual genetic history.

7. **Provider–patient interactions:** Dislike, distrust, and disdain – on both sides of the provider–patient relationship – can breed distortion, and result in defective decisions. Patients who question the provider are sometimes labeled as "crocks" or deemed uneducated. Such attitudes and labels sabotage objective clinical judgment.

8. **Mistaking correlation for causation:** Clinical phenomena are rarely straightforward, linear, cause-and-effect processes. Rather, patients live within complex interactive systems (see Chapter 1: Evolving Models of Health Care).

9. **Search satisficing:** Neglecting to search for additional problems or potential explanations for a patient's symptoms once the provider deems that a likely explanation has been found.

10. **Framing:** Approaching the patient's symptoms from the perspective of an initial description by a colleague or referring physician, rather than from a more global perspective.

Recommended Readings

Croskerry, P. (2013). From mindless to mindful practice — cognitive bias and clinical decision making. *New England Journal of Medicine*, *368*, 2445–2448. http://doi.org/10.1056/NEJMp1303712

Custers, E. (2013). Medical education and cognitive continuum theory: An alternative perspective on medical problem solving and clinical reasoning. *Academic Medicine*, *88*, 1074–1080. http://doi.org/10.1097/ACM.0b013e31829a3b10

Koh, H., & Rudd, R. (2015). The arc of health literacy. *Journal of the American Medical Association*, *314*, 1225–1226. http://doi.org/10.1001/jama.2015.9978

Norman, G., Monteiro, S., & Sherbino, J. (2013). Is clinical cognition binary or continuous? *Academic Medicine*, *88*, 1058–1060.

Review Questions

1. Which one of the following statements is consistent with the guidelines for protecting confidentiality?
   A. Conduct interviews in a setting where privacy can be maintained.
   B. Hallway discussions are preferable to talking in front of an anxious patient.
   C. Keeping confidentiality overrides any other agreement between patient and physician.
   D. Only family members should have the opportunity to review files without patient consent.
   E. The patient should be protected from knowing who has access to their medical record.

2. Which of the following is an open-ended question?
   A. Are you sexually active?
   B. Do you have any questions?
   C. How can I help you this morning?
   D. Where is the pain?
   E. You don't smoke, do you?

3. Of the questions below, which one would you use to begin a clinical encounter?
   A. Do you get the pain when you eat or when you walk?
   B. Just give me the short list of your problems.
   C. What brings you in to see me today?
   D. Where does it hurt?
   E. You haven't been drinking, have you?

4. An assessment of the patient's attention, memory, orientation, and judgment is part of the
   A. examination of the head
   B. mental status examination
   C. past medical history
   D. review of systems
   E. social history

5. Which of these steps comes first in the clinical decision-making process?
   A. Acting on the proposed solution
   B. Defining outcome goals
   C. Defining the problem
   D. Evaluating the outcome
   E. Selecting the best solution

6. The differential diagnosis is a list of
   A. all the patient's active and inactive
      medical problems
   B. diagnostic possibilities and their
      probabilities
   C. diagnostic tests to be ordered
   D. reasons the patient is being seen at
      this visit
   E. symptoms present for at least a month

Answer key on p. 466

36 Motivating Healthy Behaviors

Richard J. Botelho, BMedSci, BMBS

- What are the leading lifestyle causes of preventable death?
- How can you use a decision balance to explore patients' ambivalence and resistance to change?
- How can you assess a patient's perceptions and readiness to change?
- How can you motivate healthy behavior change?
- How can you enhance a patient's self-efficacy and positive outcome expectancies?
- How can you strengthen a patient's motives to change?

Unhealthy Lifestyles

What are the leading lifestyle causes of preventable death?

The American College of Lifestyle Medicine promotes using nondrug modalities (e.g., whole food, plant-based diets; exercise; stress management; tobacco and alcohol cessation) to prevent, treat, and reverse all lifestyle-related diseases. Lifestyle medicine is also about planetary health. We cannot have healthy people without a healthy planet. Thus, providers must learn how to motivate healthy behavior and to support movements for a healthy planet.

In 2000, about 50% of the causes of preventable death in the US were related to lifestyle behaviors. Almost a decade later, an international collaborative group determined that deaths attributable to tobacco (467,000) and high blood pressure (395,000) each accounted for one fifth of all mortality associated with lifestyle. Obesity (216,000) and physical inactivity (191,000) each accounted for one tenth of preventable deaths. Thus, despite considerable attention being focused on the risks of unhealthy habits in the professional literature and public media, information alone is often insufficient to change a patient's behavior.

Providers typically report that they have limited time to address patients' unhealthy habits, other than to give information and advice about the reasons to change. They appeal to patients' rationality and good intentions to pursue healthier lifestyles, without addressing their emotional resistance. Good intentions, like New Year's resolutions, usually fail. This traditional health education or "fix-it" role helps only the minority of patients who are *ready to change*.

Good intentions are often short lived because the short-term emotional rewards of unhealthy habits (e.g., smoking to relax) outweigh the rational, long-term benefits (e.g., avoiding preventable diseases and living longer). Being knowledgeable about the risks of unhealthy habits and the benefits of change is insufficient for helping most people to change. In fact, the vast majority of knowledgeable patients are ambivalent or even resistant to change. To work with these patients, providers should adopt a motivational role to guide them through a series of learning experiences that

1. shift patient perceptions toward healthy change;
2. maximize the harms and minimize the benefits of their risk behaviors;
3. minimize the risks and maximize the benefits of change;
4. lower resistance and enhance patient motivation;
5. enhance patient self-efficacy;
6. strengthen motives to change; and
7. address discrepancies between what they say and what they do.

Decision Balance

How can you use a decision balance to explore patients' ambivalence and resistance to change?

Providers can adopt a motivational role and activate patients to take charge of their decision-making process using **decision balance** methodology. This strategy provides a structure that can help them clarify their perceptions about the status quo vs. change in order to discuss their "pros" (change talk) and "cons" (sustain talk) of behavior change.

Case Vignette – Part 1

Mrs. S., a 45-year-old woman, went to her family physician, Dr. M., to follow-up on her HIV test. Two years ago, she remarried after being divorced for many years. She had recently moved back to her home town after her husband broke his parole and was returned to jail. Mr. and Mrs. S. had regularly attended an HIV clinic because Mr. S. was HIV positive. Mrs. S. deferred to her husband's wishes to not wear a condom, and, fortunately, she remained HIV negative even without practicing safe sex. The doctor at the HIV clinic advised Mrs. S. to have an HIV test done every 3 months. Dr. M. ordered the HIV test and asked her to fill out a decision balance form to better understand why she did not want to use condoms. She agreed and provided the following:

Reasons Not to Use Condoms

What are the benefits of not using condoms?
- Not make him feel he is failing at being sexually competent
- He feels secure that I will stay with him

What are your concerns about using condoms?
- He will have erection problems, and it will make him sad
- He will wish he were with his ex-girlfriend (who is HIV positive) so he won't have to use them

Reasons to Use Condoms

What concerns you about not using condoms?
- Don't want HIV
- Don't want my family hurt
- Maybe people will think he doesn't care to protect me

What are the benefits of using condoms?
- Won't get HIV so won't upset family
- Won't get sick myself so I can take care of him when he gets sicker
- Will feel that he cares enough about me and will not allow me to get sick

Case Vignette – Part 2

Assessing resistance and motivation
Dr. M. asked her to use a scale from 0 to 10 (0 = *not important*, 10 = *very important*) to rate her reasons for not using condoms. Mrs. S. had a *resistance score* of 9. Dr. M then asked her to rate her reasons for using them. She had a *motivation score* of 4.

Assessing thoughts and feelings about change
Mrs. S. stated that her scores were based on her feelings. In other words, she was an *emotional decision maker* on the issue of condom use; her scores represented how she *felt* about change, rather than what she *thought* about it. Dr. M. then asked her to rate her overall reasons to stay the same *versus* her reasons to change based on what she thought. Mrs. S. had a score of 6 for cognitive resistance and a score of 8 for cogni

tive motivation. This process helped her understand how much her emotions ruled her decision making. Emotionally, she felt she should stay the same, but rationally, she thought she should protect herself.

Understanding emotions and values
Reviewing her decision balance, Dr. M. said that Mrs. S. must really love her husband. Mrs. S. expressed devotion to her husband, stating that she wanted to care for him when he gets terminally ill. Dr. M. asked her how she valued her relationship with her husband compared with her own welfare and her relationship with her children. Mrs. S. loved her husband so much that she was willing to sacrifice her life for him, but admitted to having mixed feelings when thinking about her children.

Stages of Change Model

How can you assess a patient's perceptions and readiness to change?

Typically, patients maximize the benefits of their risk behaviors and minimize the risks. Conversely, providers minimize the benefits of the risk behavior and maximize the risks (see Figures 36.1 and 36.2).

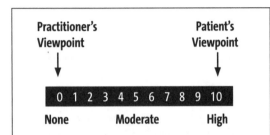

Figure 36.1. Benefits continuum. Reproduced with permission from Botelho, R. (2004). *Motivational practice: Promoting healthy habits and self-care of chronic disease.* Rochester, NY: MHH Publications. © 2004 MHH Publications.

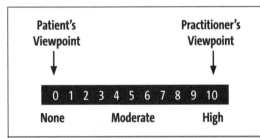

Figure 36.2. Risk continuum. Reproduced with permission from Botelho, R. (2004). *Motivational practice: Promoting healthy habits and self-care of chronic disease.* Rochester, NY: MHH Publications. © 2004 MHH Publications.

Given these discrepancies in perceptions, providers and patients are often at different stages in terms of their responsiveness to the need to take action. Thus, unless practitioners make appropriate accommodations, they can run the risk of making patients more resistant to change (see Figure 36.3)

The **stages of change model** is a framework to understand how patients' perceptions about the pros (motivation) and cons (resistance) of behavior change can shift in favor of healthy change.

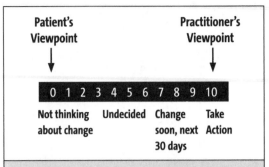

Figure 36.3. Readiness for change continuum. Reproduced with permission from Botelho, R. (2004). *Motivational practice: Promoting healthy habits and self-care of chronic disease.* Rochester, NY: MHH Publications. © 2004 MHH Publications.

Stages of Change Model

1 **Precontemplation:** Patient has no intention of changing within the next 6 months
2 **Contemplation:** Patient intends to make change within the next 6 months
3 **Preparation:** Patient intends to change within the next 30 days
4 **Action:** Patient has changed, for < 6 months
5 **Maintenance:** Patient has changed, for > 6 months

Stage 1: Patients are in the *precontemplation stage* when the cons (reasons to stay the same) far outweigh the pros (reasons to change). Some precontemplators, such as diehard smokers, are fully aware of the risks, but disregard them, while others are unaware of the risks (heart disease) of a particular behavior (smoking).

Stage 2: Patients are in the *contemplation stage* when the strengths of the pros and cons are about the same. They are ambivalent about change but they intend to quit within 6 months. However, many smokers think about quitting for 2 years or more before making a serious quit attempt. Providers can often help these patients make a serious attempt to quit much sooner.

Stage 3: Patients are in the *preparation stage* when the pros far outweigh the cons, and patients are willing to change within 1 month.

Stage 4: Patients are in the *action stage* when they put their goals into action.

Stage 5: Patients are in the *maintenance stage* when they have achieved their goal for more than 6 months. A "lapse" at this stage is a temporary setback, such as smoking a couple of cigarettes over a few days, whereas a "relapse" is complete reversion to a previous pattern of behavior, such as smoking a pack of cigarettes daily. When patients relapse they often recycle through these stages.

Case Vignette – Part 3

The *stages of change model* facilitates understanding provider–patient differences in perceptions about the risk, benefit, and harm of change. Mrs. S. was cognitively in favor of change but emotionally against it. The provider did not fall into the trap of responding to her cognitive inclination but responded instead to the emotional factors that were holding Mrs. S. from protecting herself. Dr. M. used motivational interviewing techniques to address Mrs. S.'s ambivalence and shift her perceptions in favor of change.

Motivational Interviewing

> How can you motivate healthy behavior change?

Motivational interviewing (MI) is "a collaborative, person-centered form of guiding designed to help patients elicit and strengthen motivation for change." Patient motivation is a "change-able" state that is influenced by the nature of the provider–patient interaction and the provider's interviewing style. An empathetic and nonconfrontational style can facilitate change, whereas a controlling or confrontational style can make patients regress and become more resistant to change. Providers use five basic strategies for enhancing the patient's motivation and commitment to change:

1. Expressing empathy through listening rather than telling.
2. Identifying discrepancies between where patients are now (i.e., risk behavior) and where they want to be.
3. Avoiding argumentation (i.e., trying to convince patients by force of argument).
4. Rolling with the patient's resistance rather than challenging it head-on.
5. Supporting self-efficacy, instilling hope, and encouraging patients' belief that they can change.

MI is divided into two major phases: (1) *building motivation* to change and (2) *strengthening commitment* to change. MI techniques include **o**pen-ended questions, **a**ffirmations, **r**eflections, and **s**ummaries (OARS). Providers can effectively implement OARS by using the spirit of MI. This spirit includes *empathy*, *collaboration*, *autonomy-supportiveness*, *directness*, and *evocation*.

With a nonjudgmental, genuine stance of positive regard, providers are more likely to empathize with patients' emotional experiences and *cognitive dissonance*. This engagement process involves respecting patients' autonomy to choose. Providers are directive in focusing patients' attention on their health decisions, but without persuading, coercing, or forcing any commitment. Evocation involves exploring patient ambivalence about change, with the goal of shifting the dialogue from *sustain talk* to *change talk*. Providers can elicit change talk about desires, abilities, reasons, and need to change. The amount of change talk predicts patient outcomes. This collaborative process enhances patients' commitment to change.

Case Vignette – Part 4

Dr. M. adopted a nonconfrontational stance with Mrs. S. He empathized with her decision-making process, even though he disagreed with her decision. Rather than confronting her, he "rolled with" (did not challenge) her resistance and began to explore her ambivalence about change, based on how she felt about not using condoms and what she thought about using them.

Self-Efficacy

> How can you enhance a patient's self-efficacy and positive outcome expectancies?

Self-efficacy is confidence in being able to achieve a behavioral goal. When patients have low self-efficacy, providers seek to boost their confidence in their ability to change through empowerment strategies such as setting incremental goals with achievable outcomes, identifying and linking patients' strengths and past successes to goals, blocking self-defeating thoughts, and focusing on solutions rather than problems.

Outcome expectancy reflects the patient's belief that a given behavior (e.g., a low-calorie diabetic diet and physical exercise) will produce a particular outcome (e.g., normal glucose levels and weight reduction). Patients may have high self-efficacy about sticking to a low-calorie diabetic diet and exercise program but doubt that these lifestyle changes will produce the desired change (40-lb [18-kg] weight loss and normalized blood glucose levels). Thus, patients with low outcome expectancies may not bother making lifestyle changes, even when they have high self-efficacy. Conversely, patients with high outcome expectancies may not make lifestyle changes when they have low self-efficacy.

Case Vignette – Part 5

Self-efficacy is a key predictor of behavior change. Mrs. S. knew how to use condoms. She believed that condoms would protect her from getting HIV from her husband, but her reasons for not using condoms arose from chronic low self-efficacy and her fear of losing her husband if she used condoms.

Motives

> How can you strengthen a patient's motives to change?

Providers benefit from understanding the variety of factors (stresses, competing priorities, and life circumstances) that influence patients' blend of motives over time.

- *Indifferent motives* – "I don't care if I live or die." Indifference may be due to factors such as stress, depression, or environmental or social barriers.
- *External (controlled) motives* – "I'm only changing because my family wants me to." A patient may only comply because they do not want to upset their spouse or provider. Relapse may occur when external reinforcement is absent or insufficient to maintain the behavior desired by others.
- *Introjected (controlled) motives* – "I ought to quit smoking." Individuals act out of a sense that they should change their behavior. Out-

wardly, they appear to have autonomous motives (see below), but inside they feel conflicted because of ambivalence. They initiate and maintain change by internally prompting themselves. Relapse may occur in the absence of such internal reinforcement.

- *Integrated (autonomous) motives* – "I love to exercise. It makes me feel great." With autonomous motives, individuals experience a true sense of volition about their behavioral choice.

Box 36.1. Motivational principles

A Support and respect autonomy
- Invite participation
- Gain consent
- Be nonjudgmental
- Offer choice

B Understand patient's perspective
- Develop empathetic relationships
- Clarify roles and responsibilities
- Clarify patients' issues about change
- Work at a pace sensitive to patients' needs
- Understand patients' perceptions, motives, and values

C Adopt a positive stance
- Focus on strengths rather than weaknesses
- Focus on health rather than pathology
- Focus on solutions rather than problems
- Provide constructive feedback
- Help patients believe in healthy outcomes
- Encourage patients to do emotional work

D Elicit patient's problem-solving skills
- Enhance patients' confidence and ability
- Increase supports and reduce barriers
- Negotiate reasonable goals for change
- Develop plans to prevent relapses
- Use "failures" as learning opportunities

E Maintain long-term engagement
- Maintain a learning partnership
- Monitor resistance and motivation
- Negotiate frequency of follow-up
- Adjust goals to changing circumstances

Reproduced with permission from Botelho, R. (2004). *Motivational practice: Promoting healthy habits and self-care of chronic disease.* Rochester, NY: MHH Publications. © 2004 MHH Publications.

The initiation and maintenance of behavior change is self-regulated and driven by the patient's values and freely chosen motives, as opposed to being influenced by others.

When egalitarian providers use motivational principles (see Box 36.1), patients are more likely to develop autonomous motives for change. Conversely, when paternalistic providers act in authoritarian ways, patients are more likely to experience controlled motives, indifference, or resistance to change.

Case Vignette – Part 6

Mrs. S. came from an abusive family and suffered from chronic low self-esteem. As an adult, she became an alcoholic and raised her children with her first husband. She divorced, recovered from her alcoholism without treatment, and remarried. Mrs. S. has felt overwhelmed most of her life and has had chronic anxiety and recurrent bouts of depression. She cares about her second husband and was willing to help him until his death from AIDS, but she had little time and energy left to address her own needs.

Mrs. S. was not indifferent about the prospects of getting HIV. She did not want to get AIDS, but did not use condoms, deferring to her husband's wishes. She felt conflicted and knew her children would disapprove, but she did not tell them about this situation. Mrs. S. lacked self-esteem. Her decision was greatly influenced by her valuing her husband's wishes more than her own health. Her external motives were more powerful than her introjected (controlled) or integrated (autonomous) motives.

Dr. M. asked Mrs. S.'s husband to attend a session to discuss her HIV status, but he did not respond. Soon after, Mrs. S. separated from her husband and had an alcoholic relapse for several months following the separation. She stopped drinking without professional help, and became involved with another man who was also HIV positive. This time, however, she insisted on using condoms with her new partner.

Recommended Readings

Alvarom, S., Grandes, G., Cortada, J. M., Pombo, H., Balague, L., & Calderon, C. (2009). Modelling innovative interventions for optimising healthy lifestyle promotion in primary health care: "Prescribe Vida Saludable" Phase I research protocol. *BMC Health Services Research, 9*, 103.

Johnson, B. T., Scott-Sheldon, L. A. J., & Carey, M.P. (2010). Meta-synthesis of health behavior change meta-analyses. *American Journal of Public Health, 100*, 2193–2198. http://doi.org/10.2105/AJPH.2008.155200

Miller, W. R., & Rollnick, S. (2013). *Motivational interviewing: Helping people change* (3rd ed.). New York, NY: Guilford Press.

Prochaska, J. J., & Prochaska, J. O. (2011). A review of multiple health behavior change interventions for primary prevention. *American Journal of Lifestyle Medicine, 5*, 208–221. http://doi.org/10.1177/1559827610391883

Schwarzer, R. (2008). Modeling health behavior change: How to predict and modify the adoption and maintenance of health behaviors. *Applied Psychology: An International Review, 57*, 1–29. http://doi.org/10.1111/j.1464-0597.2007.00325.x

Additional Resources

To join a learning community about developing a peer health coaching movement for motivating healthy habits, go to http://www.healthcoachingbuddies.com

To become a student member of the American College of Lifestyle Medicine, go to http://www.lifestylemedicine.org/Membership-Application

To learn more about the new discipline of *planetary health,* go to https://www.rockefellerfoundation.org/planetary-health/

Review Questions

1. Warning an obese patient about the risks and consequences of an unhealthy diet and lifestyle is generally not effective unless the
   A. health care provider is willing to offer an effective treatment plan
   B. health care provider specializes in nutritional and lifestyle counseling

C. patient has health insurance that covers preventive care
D. patient has social support from friends and family
E. patient is ready to change their behavior

Directions: The items below consist of lettered headings followed by numbered descriptions. For each numbered description, choose the *one* lettered heading to which it is *most* closely associated. Each lettered heading may be used *once, more than once,* or *not at all.*

In items 2–5, match the scenario with the stage of change

A. Action
B. Contemplation
C. Maintenance
D. Precontemplation
E. Relapse

2. A 29-year-old woman who smokes a pack of cigarettes per day tells her doctor that her grandfather smoked cigars all his life and lived to be 95.
3. A 30-year-old man arrested for a driving under the influence (DUI) offense reports he had not had a drink in more than a year prior to his arrest.
4. A 40-year-old woman checks herself into a residential detoxification program.
5. A 62-year-old woman who lost 40 lb (18 kg) in the past 8 months is now down to her target weight of 160 lb (72.5 kg) but continues to attend weight a management support group.

Answer Key on p. 466

37 Physician Health, Impairment, and Misconduct

Charles P. Samenow, MD, MPH

- What are the major types of impaired physician behaviors?
- What are the common traits that predispose physicians to unhealthy behaviors?
- What substances are most commonly abused by physicians?
- What are the most common psychiatric problems found in physicians?
- What physical illnesses can lead to impairment?
- How does misconduct differ from impairment?
- What responsibility do colleagues have to report an impaired physician?
- What resources are there for the treatment and monitoring of impaired physicians?

While this chapter focuses on physician health, impairment, and misconduct, the issues and concerns raised are actually relevant to all health care professionals. Although each discipline has its own set of specific professional principles and sanctions for misconduct, careful review will reveal that definitions of proper and improper behavior and the grounds for revocation of licensure or certification are virtually identical and focus on providing prompt, appropriate, and prudent patient care.

Physician Impairment

> What are the major types of impaired physician behaviors?

While *alcohol* and *substance abuse* remain major public health problems among practicing physicians, **impairment** actually encompasses a wide variety of behaviors and conduct. According to the Federation of State Medical Boards' (FSMB) *Essentials of Modern Medical Practice Act* (p. 26):

"Impairment should be defined as the inability of a licensee to practice medicine with reasonable skill and safety by reason of: (1) mental illness; or (2) physical illness or condition, including, but not limited to those illnesses or conditions that would adversely affect cognitive, motor, or perceptual skills; or (3) habitual or excessive use or abuse of drugs defined by law as controlled substances, or of alcohol, or of other substances that impair ability."

Simply having a disability, mental disorder, or alcohol or drug use does not automatically imply impaired physician behavior. In fact, many physicians who are under treatment for such conditions, or who may have mild variants, are known as exceptional practitioners. Rather, the underlying disorder must jeopardize the safety of medical practice to be considered true impairment.

It is believed that 7% to 12% of practicing physicians are impaired at some point in their careers. About 75% of cases are due to alcohol or drug use. Up to 20% of physicians report impairment due to mental health problems. In many instances, mental health problems and substance use are present as comorbid conditions. The remaining cases are due to cognitive impairment and physical disability. The number of reported cases of behavioral problems (e.g., anger outbursts, sexual harassment, misprescribing controlled substances) that straddle the line between professional misconduct and markers of potentially impaired functioning has risen over the years.

Physician impairment presents a direct risk to patient safety. Furthermore, physicians are valuable human resources deserving of good health and well-being. Finally, the public places great trust in the hands of physicians. Hence, even the appearance of impropriety should be avoided because it detracts from the overall confidence people have in the profession.

Risk Factors for Impairment

> What are the common traits that predispose physicians to unhealthy behaviors?

Often, traits that the public values most are what place physicians at greatest risk. The public demands *meticulousness* and *perfectionism*. At healthy doses, these traits can lead to exceptional clinical care. However, when these traits are inflated or out of control, they place physicians at risk of isolation and feelings of inadequacy.

Gabbard has defined the compulsive traits among physicians, who commonly present with problems as *self-doubt*, *guilt*, and an *exaggerated sense of responsibility*. These physicians often struggle with rigidity, stubbornness, inability to delegate tasks, and neglect of self and family. Given the complexity of medical systems, and the inevitability of sickness and death, such physicians set themselves up for failure because of unrealistic expectations. Shame, guilt, and feelings of failure can predispose certain physicians to anxiety and depression, which they self-medicate with alcohol and other substances.

Multiple biological, psychological, and social factors can contribute to physician impairment. Similar to the general population, risk factors such as family history, gender, or a history of trauma can predispose a physician to certain psychiatric disorders. There is evidence that those who select a career in medicine may have certain psychological vulnerabilities. The culture of medicine may exacerbate these vulnerabilities by modeling unhealthy behaviors, abusive relationships, and financial, emotional, and physical demands and expectations.

An important risk factor for physician impairment, particularly depression, is **burnout**. This syndrome is marked by emotional exhaustion, cynicism, ineffectiveness, and depersonalization in relationships. Up to 60% of physicians have reported experiencing burnout during their

careers; women appear to be especially at risk. Burnout has been associated with poor health behaviors and changes in practice behaviors such as ordering more tests, writing more prescriptions, having less empathy, and receiving more patient complaints.

Alcohol and Drug Abuse

> What substances are most commonly abused by physicians?

The rate of physician *alcohol abuse* and dependence is equal to the general population when matched for age, sex, and socioeconomic status, with an estimated lifetime prevalence of 8% to 15%. However, physicians are overrepresented in terms of *opiate addiction* and other prescription drugs, probably because they have easier access to these drugs. Substance-related and addictive disorders cross all medical specialties, although anesthesiologists, emergency medicine physicians, and surgeons tend to have a higher rate of opiate dependence than other physicians.

The use of *psychostimulants* (e.g., amphetamine salts, methylphenidate) is increasing among physicians, particularly trainees. What little data exist suggest that use is mostly situational (e.g., around examinations) and not at a level causing impairment.

Finally, there is increasing recognition of *behavioral addictions* including pathological gambling and sexually compulsive behaviors such as viewing pornography. Both of these behaviors are facilitated by access to the Internet throughout the hospital or in medical offices. In their most severe form, sexual compulsions can lead to *sexual boundary violations*.

Mental Health

> What are the most common psychiatric problems found in physicians?

Mental health problems can lead to impairment through multiple mechanisms. *Depression* can lead to difficulty concentrating, and inability to complete tasks due to low energy, poor memory, and problematic judgment. *Mania* can lead to distractibility, impulsiveness, irritability, and grandiosity that can compromise patient care and relationships with the health care team (see Chapter 43: Depressive and Bipolar Disorders).

Recent studies have found that almost 25% of medical students report having been depressed. Among practicing physicians, the rate of depression is similar to the general population. Anxiety disorders are common. Psychotic disorders are less common, probably because the initial presentation of such disorders typically occurs during the second decade of life, and it is unlikely that someone with a serious mental disorder would meet the requirements for admission to medical school.

Suicide

Physicians have an elevated rate of **suicide** compared with the general population. Unlike the general population, where men are more likely to complete suicide, the sex distribution among physicians is approximately equal. This equates to a fourfold risk for female physicians when compared with the general population. Other risk factors include older age (> 45 years for women, > 50 years for men), White race, decreased social support, presence of psychiatric or physical illness, and access to lethal means, as well as physician-specific factors such as professional isolation and coping with malpractice suits and licensure investigations. While physician suicide crosses all medical specialties, recent studies report that psychiatrists, anesthesiologists, and general practitioners have the highest rates. Overdose of a prescription drug is the most common method of suicide.

Physical Illness

What physical illnesses can lead to impairment?

In general, *physical illness* does not limit a physician from practicing for prolonged periods of time. Certain illnesses, however, may prevent a physician from practicing safely. Examples include neurological degeneration (e.g., Parkinson's disease, multiple sclerosis) or traumatic injuries that affect manual dexterity or cognitive functioning. Of particular concern with the aging workforce is the onset of dementia and other cognitive disorders (see Chapter 46: Neurocognitive Disorders: Dementia). Such cases can be particularly difficult to recognize because of physician denial or compensatory behaviors by loyal staff, who may have worked with the physician for years.

Physician Misconduct

How does misconduct differ from impairment?

Over the past several decades, increasing numbers of physicians have been summoned by medical licensing boards due to disruptive behaviors, misprescribing controlled substances, and sexual boundary violations. Similar to physician impairment, these behaviors stem from a complex interaction of physician factors and environmental factors. While many of these physicians have underlying mental health issues including depression and personality disorders, the profession, to date, has not viewed these as traditional forms of physician impairment (see Chapter 51: Personality Disorders).

Disruptive physician behavior is defined by the American Medical Association (AMA) as "personal conduct, whether verbal or physical, that negatively affects or that potentially may negatively affect patient care." Examples can be verbal (foul, intimidating, belittling, or demeaning language) and nonverbal (facial expressions or other body language). They are classified as aggressive (throwing objects, striking out), passive (chronically late, failure to write chart notes), or passive-aggressive (hostile or inappropriate notes, derogatory comments about colleagues or institutions).

Misprescribing controlled substances is a form of physician misconduct. It may be the result of poor education about pain management or being the victim of drug-seeking patients. In other cases, it may be indicative of personality issues (inability to say no), family of origin issues (addiction history), or poor practice organization.

Box 37.1. Examples of sexual boundary violations by subtypes

Sexual Impropriety	**Sexual Violation**

Sexual Impropriety

Making sexually demeaning comments to or about a patient

Not using appropriate disrobing or draping techniques

Subjecting a patient to intimate examination in front of students without informed consent

Performing an intimate examination without explaining the need for the examination

Requesting details of the sexual history when not clinically indicated

Using sexually suggestive expressions

Using the physician–patient relationship to solicit a date

Discussing personal sexual problems, preferences, or fantasies

Sexual Violation

Frank physical contact of a sexual nature:
- Oral sex
- Penetration
- Sexualized kissing
- Touching of the breasts or genitals for any purpose other than a clinical exam

Encouraging the patient to masturbate in front of the physician or masturbation by the physician in front of the patient

Exchanging practice-related services (e.g., drugs) for sexual favors

---

Adapted from Federation of State Medical Boards (FSMB). (2006). *Addressing Sexual Boundaries: Guidelines for State Medical Boards.* Retrieved from https://www.fsmb.org/Media/Default/PDF/FSMB/Advocacy/GRPOL_Sexual%20Boundaries.pdf

---

Sexual boundary violations are defined by the AMA as "sexual contact or a romantic relationship concurrent with a physician-patient relationship." Such behavior is considered unethical. Sexual relationships with former patients are also generally unethical but depend on specialty, type of medical encounter, and jurisdiction. The FSMB subdivides sexual relationships into two categories: *sexual violation* and *sexual impropriety* (see Box 37.1). These behaviors often begin with nonsexual boundary violations such as accepting gifts from patients, engaging in business affairs, and excessive self-disclosure.

Sexual harassment, according to the US Equal Employment Opportunity Commission, is any unwanted and repeated verbal or physical advances, derogatory statements or sexually explicit remarks, or sexually discriminatory comments made by someone in the workplace. Such behavior or comments are considered harassment if the recipient (patient, employee, trainee) is offended or humiliated or their job performance suffers. In almost all cases of physician misconduct, it is the physician who is held accountable for the behavior due to the inherent inequity in power in the physician–patient relationship.

Physician misconduct does not only cause potentially serious harm to the physical and mental health of both patients and staff, but it can also cause serious repercussions for the physician, including loss of licensure, restriction in practice, loss of relationships, and even public humiliation. While mental health issues may underlie certain unprofessional behaviors, these are usually seen as mitigating factors and areas for rehabilitation, as opposed to excuses or reasons not to discipline the physician. A comprehensive evaluation by trained professionals can help determine to what extent misconduct may stem from impairment or a clinical disorder.

Reporting Impaired Colleagues and Unprofessional Conduct

What responsibility do colleagues have to report an impaired physician?

The AMA is explicit in stating that it is the **duty of colleagues to report** any suspected impaired behavior. The primary goal is to protect the safety of the public from dangerous clinical practice. With that said, the AMA and other regulatory agencies also recognize the importance of rehabilitation and nonpunitive approaches toward fostering a culture of health and wellness. Hence, both the AMA and the Joint Commission (formerly, the Joint Commission on Accreditation of Healthcare Organizations [JCAHO]) require that hospitals have a mechanism in place to detect, handle, and rehabilitate impaired physicians that avoids disciplinary procedures except when absolutely necessary.

> **AMA Ethical Principle 9.031**
> "Physicians have an ethical obligation to report impaired, incompetent, and unethical colleagues in accordance with the legal requirements in each state...."
>
> **JCAHO MS 2.6**
> "Medical Staff implements a process to identify and manage . . . physician health that is separate from Medical Staff disciplinary function."

Resources for Identification, Treatment, and Monitoring

> What resources are there for the treatment and monitoring of impaired physicians?

Most impaired physicians can return to clinical practice after rehabilitation. In fact, the recovery rate for physicians with substance-related and addictive disorders is 85% to 90%, which far exceeds that of the general population. Physicians tend to be a highly motivated group, and there are multiple incentives that can be used to facilitate recovery, including restriction of clinical practice and licensure, which has serious personal, career, and financial implications.

Most states have professional organizations that can help intervene, refer, advocate for, and monitor impaired physicians. These organizations, known as **physician health programs** (PHPs), may be administered by boards of licensure, branches of state medical societies, or independent agencies. A physician who is referred or self-refers to such organizations will generally receive a comprehensive evaluation by an objective multidisciplinary team of individuals that can provide a clinical diagnosis and treatment plan. In some cases, hospital **employee assistance programs** or **physician wellness programs** can serve as a referral or monitoring resource.

The PHP can use the information from the comprehensive exam to refer an impaired physician to a local professional for monitoring and treatment. In the case of a physician with a substance-related problem, this may include *residential treatment* in a program that specializes in treating impaired professionals, followed by *random urine drug screens*, psychotherapy, and participation in a **Caduceus group** (a 12-step recovery program specifically for health care professionals). A physician with mental health problems may be required to see a psychiatrist or therapist, and to have a **360-degree behavioral evaluation**, which involves colleagues, staff, and sometimes patients providing an anonymous report on the physician's behavior. A physician with physical disability or cognitive impairment may be required to undergo an intensive retraining program to ensure clinical proficiency.

Generally, a physician will sign a 5-year contract to work with a PHP. By doing this, the physician's medical record and treatment plan remain confidential from the licensing board and employer. The PHP may advocate on the physician's behalf so that the physician may return to practice as soon as possible and avoid restrictions or other disciplinary action. A physician who is noncompliant with treatment, relapses without seeking help, or demonstrates unsafe behavior will ultimately be reported to the medical board and employer for disciplinary action.

Many physicians fear seeking help because of concerns about their medical career. Physicians in a number of states have challenged questions asked by licensing boards that seem to stigmatize individuals with mental health problems; some have prevailed in lawsuits under antidiscrimination clauses in the Americans with Disabilities Act. In theory, licensing boards may only ask questions that assess for impairment of function. Hence, a physician who is undergoing treatment or who has had treatment in the past should not be at risk of having their license restricted. Finally, given the tremendous success PHPs have had in assisting physicians to reenter practice, the risks associated with impairment far outweigh the risks of seeking help.

Physician Health and Patient Care

In recent years, physicians have shown an overall improvement in their own healthy behaviors. They have been found to exercise more, eat better, and smoke less than the general population. Yet, physicians still lag behind the general population in terms of not going to work when sick, having their own personal doctors, and not self-treating rather than seeking professional help.

Instilling healthy behaviors in physicians is important, not only for the individual physician, but for society at large. There are data to suggest that physicians' own health behaviors affect their professional behaviors. Physicians who have better personal health practices tend to recommend better health practices to their patients. Furthermore, patients who perceive that their physician is healthy are more likely to implement healthy lifestyle changes when their doctor recommends them.

Recommended Readings

Brooks, E., Gendel, M. H., Gundersen D., Early, S. R., Schirrmacher, R., Lembitz, A., & Shore, J. H. (2013). Physician health programmes and malpractice claims: Reducing risk through monitoring. *Occupational Medicine, 63*(4), 274–280. doi:10.1093/occmed/kqt036

Earley, P. R. (2014). Physician health programs and addiction among physicians. In R. K. Ries, D. A. Fiellin, S. C. Miller, & R. Saitz (Eds.), *The ASAM principles of addiction medicine* (5th ed., pp. 602–603). Chevy Chase, MD: American Society of Addiction Medicine.

Myers, M. F., & Gabbard, G. O. (2008). *The physician as patient: A clinical handbook for mental health professionals*. Arlington, VA: American Psychiatric Publishing.

Shanafelt, T. D., Boone, S., Tan, L., Dyrbye, L. N., Sotile, W., Satele, D., ... Oreskovich, M. R. (2012). Burnout and satisfaction with work-life balance among US physicians relative to the general US population. *Archives of Internal Medicine, 172*(18), 1377–1385. http://doi.org/10.1001/archinternmed.2012.3199

Tschan, W. (2014). *Professional sexual misconduct in institutions*. Boston, MA: Hogrefe Publishing.

Review Questions

1. Compared with the general population, physicians are at greater risk for which of the following conditions?
   A. Alcohol abuse
   B. Anxiety
   C. Cocaine abuse
   D. Depression
   E. Suicide

2. Which of the following behaviors is an example of sexual violation according to the Federation of State Medical Boards?
   A. Making sexually suggestive comments
   B. Not using proper robing techniques
   C. Performing an unnecessary exam
   D. Touching a patient's genitals outside the physical exam
   E. Using a clinical encounter to solicit a date with a patient

3. Which of the following is a form of physician impairment?
   A. Engaging in sexual relations with a patient
   B. Making sexually suggestive comments to staff
   C. Prescribing too many narcotic drugs
   D. Tremulousness
   E. Yelling profanity at nurses

4. Among the following, which organization can help with the treatment of an impaired physician?
   A. National practitioner data bank
   B. Specialty society
   C. State medical board
   D. State medical society
   E. State physician health program

Answer Key on p. 466

Section X
Psychopathology

38 Introduction to Psychopathology

Julia B. Frank, MD

- Is psychopathology a medical science?
- How are psychiatric disorders defined in the US and worldwide?
- How does psychiatric diagnosis relate to etiology, pathophysiology, and patient experience?

Psychopathology

Is psychopathology a medical science?

Psychopathology is the scientific study of psychiatric disorders and the factors that influence their onset, course, and treatment. The term *pathology* in this context is in part a metaphor. It analogizes the study of mental phenomena to pathology in biomedicine, a field that explores organ systems defined by anatomical structure and physiological function. Medical pathology assumes that symptomatology reflects the effects of some process or lesion within the body. This assumption applies to some elements of psychopathology, though not all. Functional neuroimaging has made it possible to associate aspects of thought, emotion, or behavior with areas of brain activity. Neuroendocrine factors, and the homeostatic systems they regulate, malfunction in a variety of psychiatric disorders. Together with the immune system, the brain and neuroendocrine system coordinate and regulate all mental and bodily functions for the purpose of meeting challenges to survival of the individual and the species.

Psychopathology is, however, more than brain science. Even severe disorders may occur in people with no discernible neurological lesions. The brain integrates, organizes, and regulates responses to experience as an individual develops, learns, and adapts. Early experience, typical patterns of thought, and even language and culture shape behavior. The processes of adaptation produce both normal behavior and symptoms such as inability to perceive or interpret reality (psychoses, delirium), extreme moods (elation, fear, rage, sadness) disrupted vegetative functions (sleep, arousal, appetite, capacity for pleasure, sexual interest), difficulty processing bodily experiences (pain, somatic symptoms), and seriously maladaptive behavior, especially social behavior. These elements of mental illness are organized, somewhat arbitrarily, into the categories of *psychiatric disorders*, described below.

The scientific study of complex human behavior is a relatively modern enterprise. From ancient through medieval times, some problems of thought, emotion, or behavior were understood as manifestations of organic disease, but others were attributed to divine or demonic influence, moral weakness, or social processes. Historically, forces governing aberrant individual behavior included malevolence and witchcraft. Supernatural explanations defy scientific exploration.

The philosopher **René Descartes (1596–1650)** laid the foundation for psychopathology as a scientific discipline by positing the existence of an immaterial mind connected to the mechanistic functioning of the body. Termed mind–body **dualism**, Descartes' separation of self or soul from the body promoted the development of general medical science, while still leaving many mental and behavioral functions within the domain of philosophy and religion. Descartes' work stimulated the development of biological and social sciences as separate approaches to understanding human experience.

Psychoanalysis was the first widely disseminated, systematic, post-Enlightenment attempt to explain subjective human experience and erratic or irrational behavior in scientific terms. Its founder, **Sigmund Freud (1856–1939)**, studied neuroembryology and evolutionary science early in his career. In constructing his theory, he made often unrecognized leaps from verifiable fact (e.g., consciousness represents only a fraction of brain activity) to sheer speculation (e.g., all children develop a conscience by mastering sexual and murderous impulses toward their parents – the "Oedipus complex").

Despite its weaknesses and limited empirical base, psychoanalysis made enduring contributions in highlighting the regularity of behavior change during development and in exploring how childhood and adolescent experience shapes the normal and pathological aspects of adulthood. Genetically regulated adaptation or maladaptation begins before birth and progresses most rapidly during infancy, childhood and adolescence, and senescence. Not coincidentally, many psychiatric disorders or prodromes first appear in these periods of rapid physical and neurological development or change.

Psychoanalysis also recognized that the irrational aspects of human behavior may serve identifiable purposes in stabilizing personal adaptation and general social organization. The psychoanalytic focus on humans' unique capacities for symbolic thought and language contributed substantially to the development of **psychotherapy** as a legitimate medical activity.

Taking a more standard medical approach, **Emil Kraepelin (1856–1926)** and his followers studied the natural history of psychiatric conditions in institutionalized patients. They identified patterns linking bodily function, behavior, and psychological experience and described how these patterns change in predictable ways over time. Kraepelin recognized the cycles of mood that characterize *manic-depressive* (now *bipolar*) *disorder*. He and other investigators hoped to correlate observed symptoms with brain lesions on postmortem examination, but lacked methods that could identify the complex genetic, neurochemical, and submicroscopic derangements contributing to the behavioral patterns they identified. The patterns themselves, however, strongly influence the current nosology of psychiatric disorders.

A number of mid-20th century psychiatrists, especially **Adolf Meyer (1866–1950)** and **George Engel (1913–1999)**, advocated particular ways of integrating the sciences that explain disordered behavior. Meyer's **life history method** highlighted the interplay of psychological, biological, and cultural forces in structuring mental life and its expression in behavior. Engel's **biopsychosocial model** called attention to the multiple factors that contribute to psychiatric and medical disorders, without laying out in detail how these factors interact (see Chapter 1: Evolving Models of Health Care).

The discipline of psychopathology belongs within the domain of evolutionary science, in which knowledge of the evolving interaction of genetic, physiological, environmental, and social factors explains how behavior is built from its simplest elements. The biopsychosocial model provides clinical shorthand for identifying the interaction between multiple psychosocial factors and biological processes, resulting in the genesis of symptoms and disorders.

Like general pathology, psychopathology increasingly highlights the role of genes that structure and restructure tissues and organs, and then regulate the activity of these organs over time. Genetic influence does not work in one direction. The brain continuously registers and responds to homeostatic challenges from within and without, constructing meaning, storing knowledge, and learning from experience at both the psychological and cellular level. Such interactions affect the expression or suppression of gene activity throughout life, influencing the structure and function of all bodily systems. Whether these processes are adaptive or maladaptive will determine the individual's psychiatric status and physical health.

In Part I of this book, we defined an **integrated sciences model** and the diverse variables that may contribute to pathogenesis when adaptation fails. At its best, psychopathology applies modern scientific methods and tools to the investigation of adaptive failures, with the ultimate aim of promoting evidence-based (or evidence-informed) approaches to treatment.

Older perspectives on mental illness, however, coexist with scientific ones. Harsh moral and social judgments leading to exclusion or punishment are recurring themes in the general understanding of problems of psychopathology.

However defined, mental illnesses or psychiatric disorders involve experiences and behaviors that escape conscious control or violate social norms, causing the person to act inappropriately or nonrationally. These qualities may be judged as evidence of sin or weakness, evoking negative **stigma**. Many psychiatrically disordered individuals are overtly mistreated or rejected by family, prospective employers, and others. Stigma is institutionalized in how the media portray psychiatric problems and in the rampant incarceration of the mentally ill. Wittingly or unwittingly, medical professionals perpetuate stigma by practicing in a system that discriminates and raises barriers between medical and mental health care. These attitudes, as well as the limitations of technology and the difficulty of relating human experience to animal and cellular processes, continue to shape the field of psychopathology and to limit its scope as a biomedical science.

How are psychiatric disorders defined in the US and worldwide?

Contemporary classifications of psychopathology grew out of sciences, traditions, and methodologies that often contradicted one another. In the 1970s, the World Health Organization (WHO) and the American Psychiatric Association (APA) embarked upon parallel efforts to unify the profession and standardize diagnoses. The APA brought together researchers and clinicians to produce a catalog of psychopathology based solely upon shared observations (descriptive psychopathology). This effort has produced successive editions of the *Diagnostic and Statistical Manual of Mental Disorders* (DSM). The current version, DSM-5 (2013), defines psychiatric disorders as *syndromes,* patterns of symptoms, and measurable behaviors that have a characteristic onset, course, and duration.

The signs and symptoms that make up the DSM syndromes include both unusual experiences and ones that are normal – but excessive in degree or inappropriate to context. The criteria for a disorder may include extreme or unduly persistent *emotional states* (sadness, anxiety, euphoria, irritability), *thoughts* (helplessness, hopelessness, guilt, low self-esteem, obsessions, suicidal or aggressive thoughts), *beliefs* (delusions), *percep-*

tions (hallucinations), *vegetative functions* (sleep, appetite, pleasure), and *patterns of behavior* (avoidance, impulsivity, compulsivity, aggression). To receive a *diagnosis*, the patient's signs and symptoms must reach a critical threshold of duration and severity. This information must then be matched against stated criteria for a particular disorder.

DSM-5 has been criticized for pathologizing or medicalizing problems that are normal, even adaptive, responses to typical situations or stressors. Occasional excessive drinking does not automatically indicate an alcohol use disorder. Even hallucinations may be nonpathological, as for example, when a recently bereaved person hears the voice of someone who has died. To draw a clear boundary between normal difficulties and psychiatric disorder, DSM-5 requires that a condition must cause distress or functional impairment to merit a formal diagnosis.

Because some symptoms or patterns of symptoms may be manifestations of other medical disorders or the effects of psychoactive substances, the DSM further requires that medical etiologies be considered, and, where possible, ruled out, as part of refining a psychiatric diagnosis. Substance use must also be ruled out or ruled in as a contributory factor in all of the more common disorders.

Elements of a Diagnosis in DSM-5

- Name of condition
- Characteristic symptoms (sets of criteria which may specify duration and course)
- Statement that the condition must cause significant distress or impairment
- Statement that the symptoms are not attributable to the effects of substance use or another medical condition, unless the disorder is defined as secondary to one of these

The descriptive approach has allowed for studies of the incidence, prevalence, comorbidities, and course of the defined syndromes, a critical element of contemporary psychiatric research. Findings from such research have in turn influenced the underlying organization of successive editions of the DSM. Each version clusters individual disorders into broader domains. Where possible, these domains go beyond grouping disorders by similar symptoms to reflecting their shared epidemiology or underlying pathophysiology – that is, shared genetics or elements of development or function.

DSM-5 largely aligns with the behavioral disorders section of the *International Statistical Classification of Diseases and Related Health Problems* (ICD-10), published by the WHO. The two differ in that ICD-10 contains sets of criteria for many disorders, but also provides a variety of undefined terms for typical clinical problems that do not meet specified criteria. ICD-10 requires ratings of the severity of many conditions, but unlike DSM-5, it does not define the border between normal and abnormal by the presence of impairment. Different versions of ICD-10 are available for use in general clinical settings and for research.

DSM-5 is a proprietary product that must be purchased individually or accessed through a subscription to the database (http://www.psychiatry-online.org). ICD-10 is available online for free. The online versions of both are regularly updated, and a new edition, ICD-11, is in development. Most insurers now require ICD-10 codes, rather than DSM diagnoses, for billing and payment.

> How does psychiatric diagnosis relate to etiology, pathophysiology, and patient experience?

The DSM replaced an earlier classification of mental disorders that often involved unproven assumptions about the effects of early experience or unconscious processes as the drivers of patients' symptoms and behaviors. Basing diagnoses upon shared observation, rather than on assumptions driven by theory, vastly improved their reliability. Reliable description, however, does not equal validity. By design, the disorders defined in the DSM-5 (or ICD-10) are not linked to any etiological or pathophysiological factors. Disorders that look alike may result from very different underlying processes, or one process may result in symptom clusters that look more different than they are. For example, depressed mood may result from trauma to the frontal lobes, deficient neurochemical activity in the pleasure-regulating areas of the limbic system, metabolic imbalances, or a learned response to adversity in an otherwise grossly normal brain. All fall under the descriptive umbrella "major depressive episode." Conversely, the same or closely related imbalances in the inter-

play of serotonin and norepinephrine in the brain can cause either mood or anxiety disorders or both. These fall into separate domains, complicating the task of researching their shared causes and obscuring their common responses to treatment.

> A 17-year-old girl has a body mass index (BMI) of 17 kg/m2. She expresses a motivation to stay thin and is unconcerned, even pleased, that she looks emaciated. Her BMI and excessive desire for thinness merit the diagnosis of *anorexia nervosa*, but the term does not provide any information about developmental experiences (bullied? criticized by her parents?), psychological qualities (perfectionism?), social factors (media images of thinness?), or pathophysiology (effects of starvation on thought and behavior?) that may have contributed to the disorder. These factors suggest avenues of treatment that the diagnosis itself does not.

Several alternative ways of looking at psychiatric disorders have emerged to compensate for the deficiencies of both DSM-5 and ICD-10. The Research Domain Criteria (RDoC) characterize the phenomena of mental illness as qualities and behaviors that can be related to gene expression and studied in animals as well as humans. This system does not attempt to classify the full range of conditions seen in clinical settings. It is not currently available to clinicians, although it promises to lead to advances in the science of behavior.

The *Johns Hopkins Perspectives of Psychopathology* provide an alternative scheme. The Hopkins method divides recognized patterns of maladaptation into a *disease perspective,* a *dimensional perspective,* a *behavioral perspective,* or a *life story perspective.* A disease would be a condition reflecting known brain dysfunction (schizophrenia, dementia). The dimensional perspective covers extremes of normal behavior (anxiety that becomes crippling). Substance-related disorders and disorders of impulse control fall under the behavioral perspective. The life story perspective focuses attention on problems that might benefit from the reframing of experience through psychotherapy. This way of classifying disorders comes closer than either DSM-5 or ICD-10 to capturing both pathogenesis and the lived experience of mental illness. It is thus more phenomenological. Though not universally accepted, the Hopkins perspectives are especially useful for deciding where to focus when prioritizing approaches to research and treatment.

Most educational institutions in the US base their psychiatric curricula on the DSM-5, which provides the organizing structure for the psychopathology section of this book. National exams now use DSM-5 terms exclusively, but terms and definitions from the earlier editions of the manual still appear in research articles and some clinical settings and may be noted in some chapters. DSM-III and IV and IV-TR were "multiaxial" systems. Syndromes with discreet onset appeared on Axis I. Lifelong conditions, especially personality disorders and developmental disorders in children, were on Axis II. Medical conditions were specified on Axis III, contributory stressors on Axis IV, and a global assessment of function (GAF) on Axis V.

DSM-5 abandoned the multiaxial system. Personality disorders are coded like other disorders. Disorders seen in children and adolescents appear in the same sections as their adult forms. (Our text continues to present some of these within a separate domain.) Following ICD-10, many DSM-5 diagnoses require the observer to categorize conditions as mild, moderate, or severe. This dimension replaces the GAF scale.

The following chapters present several of the most common DSM categories against the backdrop of the integrated sciences model presented in Chapter 1, emphasizing how multiple perspectives take the field beyond descriptive psychopathology and empirical therapies. Ultimately, the scientific study of behavior, however imperfect, is a compassionate attempt to make disorders less mysterious and reduce stigma by finding common mechanisms underlying normal and abnormal mental phenomena.

Recommended Reading

American Psychiatric Association. (2013). *Diagnostic and statistical manual of mental disorders* (5th ed.). Arlington, VA: American Psychiatric Publishing. http://doi.org/10.1176/appi.books.9780890425596

Frances, A. (2013). *Essentials of psychiatric diagnosis: Responding to the challenge of DSM-5* (Rev. ed.). New York, NY: Guilford Press.

Lamb, S. D. (2014). *Pathologist of the mind: Adolf Meyer and the origins of american psychiatry*. Baltimore, MD: Johns Hopkins University Press.

McHugh, P., & Slavney, P. (2011). *The perspectives of psychiatry* (2nd ed.). Baltimore, MD: Johns Hopkins University Press.

World Health Organization. (1992). *The ICD-10 classification of mental and behavioural disorders: Clinical descriptions and diagnostic guidelines*. Geneva, Switzerland: Author. Available at http://www.who.int/classifications/icd/en/bluebook.pdf

Review Questions

1. A 45-year-old man with well-controlled schizophrenia is denied housing because of his history of a mental disorder. This is an example of
   A. a life problem that would be coded on Axis V
   B. faulty appreciation of material reality
   C. the effect of genetic vulnerability in generating maladaptive behavior
   D. the functional impairment required for all DSM diagnoses
   E. the impact of stigma

2. The main advantage of the DSM-5 over other systems of classification is
   A. its clear separation of mental and physical disorders
   B. its simplicity of application
   C. its wide availability
   D. the reliability of its diagnoses
   E. the validity of its diagnoses

3. DSM-III and DSM-IV included a separate domain for disorders of infancy, childhood, and adolescence. Based on longitudinal studies that demonstrate how particular early problems do or do not evolve into the syndromes identified in adults, DSM-5 reclassified child and adolescent disorders within adult domains. This reflects acknowledgement of the underlying principle that
   A. age is not a meaningful variable in the definition of psychiatric disorders
   B. an individual's stage of development will affect how symptoms of a disorder are manifested

C. different observers cannot reliably apply the criteria of disorders and arrive at similar conclusions

D. genetic endowment dictates all phenotypic manifestations of disorders

E. recognition of symptoms in children requires special skills that adult diagnosticians may lack

Answer Key on p. 466

39 The Psychiatric Evaluation

Julia B. Frank, MD

- How does the purpose of an evaluation determine its elements?
- Which histories are required to make a diagnosis?
- What are the components of the mental status examination?
- What is a case formulation?

Purposes of a Psychiatric Evaluation

How does the purpose of an evaluation determine its elements?

The specific purposes of a psychiatric evaluation are to

1. gather the information needed to make a provisional *diagnosis* according to DSM-5 or ICD-10;
2. assess the patient's *risk* for violence or self-harm, in order to determine the appropriate level of care (outpatient or inpatient; voluntary or involuntary); and
3. arrive at a *formulation* of the causes, development, and perpetuating or protective elements of the patient's difficulties in order to identify appropriate treatments.

Even brief psychiatric assessments touch on all of these areas. A full assessment typically takes 60 to 90 min or may be conducted over several sessions. Every assessment should conclude with some explicit response that expresses genuine understanding of the patient's concerns. The process should establish rapport and initiate a trusting provider–patient relationship.

Beyond these basic principles, evaluations vary depending on their purpose. Assessing decision-making capacity requires particular focus on a person's current mental status, with some specific probes about the decisions that need to be made (see Chapter 31: Moral, Ethical, and Legal Issues in Patient Care). When a patient is being evaluated for psychotherapy, the interviewer will look for patterns of thought, or experiences during development, or capacity for emotional regulation that are likely to respond to a particular treatment (see Chapter 40: Principles of Psychotherapy).

Elements of the Psychiatric Evaluation

History of the Present Illness

Which histories are required to make a diagnosis?

Assessment begins with the concerns of the person who requests the evaluation, usually but not always the patient. This may be a simple statement about depression, or stress, or some problem behavior, or it may be a narrative of several minutes when the patient has a story they need to tell. After acknowledging the chief complaint or the initial story, the evaluator asks follow-up questions related to the diagnoses that the initial statements suggest. It is essential to determine the *onset, quality, duration, intensity,* and *ameliorating and aggravating factors* of any criterion symptom or behavior. As many mental disorders are chronic, dating the onset of the present illness often involves asking when was the last time the person felt well, rather than the first time symptoms ever appeared. The sequence and environmental context of symptoms contributes to diagnosis. For example, if a middle-aged person describes sadness, sleep problems, social withdrawal, delusion of guilt, and hallucinations that have evolved over 3 months following a major tragedy in the person's life, *major depression with psychotic features* will be a more likely diagnosis than *schizophrenia*.

Even if the presenting problem clearly fulfills diagnostic criteria for a recognized disorder or the patient has a long established psychiatric condition, the evaluation must answer the crucial question: Why now? Patients may seek help, as medical patients do, for sudden worsening or for new symptoms, but many come because of some crisis that affects their general adaptation, including interruptions in access to treatment, recent life changes, losses, disappointments, and traumatic experiences.

Regardless of presenting symptoms or precipitating events, every patient should be asked about *vegetative signs, mood, risk factors for suicide and aggression*, and *recent behavior*. The interviewer also probes for commonly comorbid symptoms (e.g., anxiety in the course of depression). Because psychiatric patients may lack insight and because memory of emotional states is unreliable, soliciting information from someone close to the patient improves the accuracy of diagnosis. Gaining third party information requires the patient's explicit consent, except for rare exceptions as when the patient is uncooperative and the case raises concerns about danger to self or others.

Diagnostic assessment includes a *past psychiatric history* covering previous psychiatric diagnoses and treatment as well as untreated or unrecognized prior episodes of illness or dangerous behavior. Although past diagnoses may differ from the present one, the best predictor of any patient's likely response to treatment is their past response.

Other Histories

A **general medical history** covers physical conditions that may account for, or influence the course of, a psychiatric condition. This includes current health status; previous serious illnesses and surgeries; use of prescribed, over-the-counter, and herbal medicines; and allergies to medication. Pain and disability are important contextual factors for understanding current and past psychiatric illness. In women, the relationship between symptoms and menses, pregnancy, the postpartum period, and menopause may be important clues to pathogenesis. Suspected medical conditions may require neurological or laboratory testing.

Functional neuroimaging (functional magnetic resonance imaging [fMRI], single photon emission computed tomography [SPECT], and positron emission tomography [PET] scans) are commonly used in research but only rarely in clinical psychiatric assessments. When a neurological lesion is suspected (e.g., when an adult develops epilepsy or when depression or mania begins after head injury), magnetic resonance imaging (MRI) is best. MRIs can reveal masses, vascular abnormalities, and inflammatory or demyelinating processes that may cause psychiatric symptoms. Other objective methods, including studies of *sleep architecture* (sleep electroencephalography [EEG]) and *genetic profiling*, may answer specific questions in selected patients.

Family history involves asking patients about family members with diagnosed mental illness or substance abuse, and their treatment. This information offers clues about possible genetic **predisposition,** both for a particular psychiatric disorder and for behaviors that contribute to risk assessment (e.g., poor impulse control or suicidal acts in family members).

Social and developmental histories provide information about the patient's current life circumstances and important experiences, patterns of behavior, social networks, and personality characteristics. The developmental history covers major events including trauma; the attainment of expected developmental stages (milestones); past academic and occupational performance; and brief descriptions of the person's past relationships with parents, siblings, friends, colleagues, intimate partners, and children. Ethnic identification, religious practices and affiliation, other spirituality, legal involvement, and military service should also be covered. Current social circumstances include financial status, housing, supportive or destructive relationships, occupational or educational resources, and stressors.

By convention, medically trained providers typically include use of drugs, alcohol, or tobacco in the social history. In a psychiatric evaluation, a *detailed substance use history* may be listed separately, included in the social history, or incorporated into the history of the present illness. The medical and behavioral consequences of the person's use of substances should be noted, along with the pattern and amount of use. The **Alcohol Use Disorders Identification Test** (AUDIT) is a 10-item questionnaire used nationally and internationally by public health and research organizations (e.g., National Institute on Drug Abuse [NIDA] and the World Health Organization [WHO]). See https://www.drugabuse.gov/sites/default/files/files/AUDIT.pdf.

Developmental and social histories elicit factors relevant to diagnosis, formulation, and treatment planning. Early loss of a parent, for example, is a recognized risk factor for depression. Deprivation, disorganization, or overt mistreatment in a patient's family of origin can contribute to many psychiatric disorders. Themes that emerge from the patient's description and interpretation of events and circumstances will generate hypotheses about underlying qualities of personality as well as possible grounds for psychotherapy. Current problems with material resources or conflicted relationships may explain why the patient seeks treatment at a particular time. Past history is also crucial for assessing the person's *resources* and *resilience*. Skillful investigation of these very personal issues fosters rapport.

Mental Status Examination

> What are the components of the mental status examination?

In addition to multiple histories, a psychiatric evaluation includes a systematic assessment of the patient's state at the time of the interview, which is assessed with the **mental status examination** (MSE). The MSE combines recorded observations of the patient's self-presentation and behavior, mood, and capacity for coherent communication, along with answers to standardized probes that measure the specific cognitive functions, of attention, concentration, immediate memory, judgment, and capacity for abstract thought. Many clinicians use the **Mini–Mental State Examination**

Mental Status Examination Format

Appearance:	Grooming, appropriateness of dress
Attitude:	Degree of cooperativeness, trust
Motor behavior:	Level of activity, posture, gait, eye contact, body language, abnormal movements
Mood:	Patient's description of emotional state
Affect:	Observer's assessment of patient's expression of emotion
Speech & language:	Rate, prosody, modulation of tone and volume, articulation, spontaneity
Thought content:	Amount of thought, themes, abnormal content (e.g., delusions, obsessions, preoccupations, overvalued ideas)
Thought form:	Rate and flow of ideas, organization of thought
Perception:	Nature and quality of perceptual disturbances in any of the five senses (illusions and hallucinations)
Insight:	Awareness of where symptoms come from, understanding one's own motivations (inferred from history)
Judgment:	Capacity to make decisions (tested by standardized probes or inferred from history)
Cognitive functioning:	Level of arousal, attention and concentration, working memory, language comprehension and production, calculation, abstraction. (The MMSE and MoCA test these functions, plus sequencing and praxis)
Risk assessment:	Ideation, motivation, intention, and planning of suicidal or violent behavior

(MMSE) or the **Montreal Cognitive Assessment** (MoCA; http://www.mocatest.org) to test and record cognitive function. Although the MSE is reported as a distinct section of the psychiatric evaluation, assessment of mental status is continuous throughout the interview.

The patient's posture, motor activity, general state of health, body weight, grooming, and dress may provide clues to diagnosis (e.g., the exhausted demeanor and poor grooming of a severely depressed patient; the odd, eccentric dress of the patient with schizophrenia) and social circumstances (e.g., professional vs. casual clothing). Activity level, eye contact, gait, abnormal movements (e.g., *tremors*, *tics*, *dyskinesias*, *choreoathetoid movements*) relate to the function of subcortical brain areas implicated in the pathophysiology of some disorders.

The patient's *body language* may suggest mood, attitude toward the examination, or cultural identification. Attitude toward the examiner (open and cooperative, reserved, defensive, mistrustful) may be recorded under appearance or as a separate category.

Mood and affect: Mood is a sustained subjective emotional state as reported by the patient. Moods commonly reported in psychiatric disorders include euphoria or excitement, sadness, worry or fear, anger, and disgust. Some people have little subjective emotion and describe only indifference. **Affect** is an observed emotional state; it is more immediate and transitory than mood. Facial expression and rate and tone (prosody) of speech convey affect, which is rated as being *full range, constricted, blunted* or *flat*. The examiner should specifically note *incongruence*, when mood and affect are not consistent with the patient's expressed thought.

Speech and language: The amount, rate, tone, volume, fluency, articulation, and spontaneity of the patient's speech also may provide clues to diagnosis. Deviations from normal include the slow, monotonic answers and lack of spontaneity seen in major depression; the loud, rapid, difficult-to-interrupt (pressured) speech of mania; and the types of aphasia seen in dementias.

Thought form and content: Normal thought is "logical and goal directed," flowing easily from one idea to the next and communicating ideas clearly. Disorders of thought form include *tangentiality* (wandering from a topic), *circumstantiality* (providing excessive detail), rapid jumps from one idea to the next (*"flight of ideas"*), and lack of logical connectedness (*"derailment"* or *"loose associations"*). Some patients with psychosis link words by sound (*clanging*) rather than meaning. Others create new words (*neologisms*). More subtle abnormalities include *blocking* (going blank) and *perseveration* (the inability to move from one idea to the next). While many people have mildly disorganized thought that does not seriously impede communication, significant disorders of thought form are prominent in psychosis, mania, severe depression, delirium, and dementia.

Abnormalities of *thought content* include **rumination** (preoccupation with distressing thoughts), **obsessions** (unwanted concerns, ideas, images, or impulses intruding into consciousness), and **delusions** (false beliefs foreign to the individual's sociocultural or religious background that persist despite contradictory evidence). Delusions may be *fixed* (unshakeable and consistently present) or *fluctuating* (changing in response to circumstances). Delusions are also rated as *mood congruent* or *incongruent, plausible*, or *bizarre*. Schizophrenic delusions are often bizarre as, for example, belief that an alien force has turned others into robots. Mood congruent delusions may reflect (and justify) an underlying pathological mood. For example, delusionally depressed patients may believe they are poverty stricken, or dying of some unknown disease, or guilty of a terrible crime. *Mood congruent manic delusions* include the belief that one has special powers, can control others, or has unlimited resources. *Delusions or ideas of reference* include the belief that general input is directed personally (e.g., feeling personally targeted or controlled by something on television). Ideas of reference occur in various psychotic states.

Perception: *Perceptual disturbances* occur in any sensory modality. **Illusions** are misinterpretations of actual stimuli (e.g., thinking a coat on a hook is a threatening person). **Hallucinations** are sensory experiences that occur without external stimulation (e.g., hearing voices when alone). **Insight** is subjective awareness and understanding, both about the sources of other experiences (e.g., "I know the voices come from inside my head") and about the connections between one's thoughts and actions. **Judgment** is the capacity to organize and manipulate information to make appropriate decisions and regulate behavior. Lack of insight fosters poor judgment, but intact insight does not guarantee good judgment. Many psychiatric conditions impair both insight and judgment.

Risk assessment: While risk of suicide or violence relates to many factors (e.g., diagnosis, recent stressors, capacity for impulse control as revealed in other parts of the assessment, prior risky behavior, intoxication; see Chapter 25: Interpersonal Violence and Abuse), some elements of risk are recorded as part of the mental status exam. These include answers to questions about *feelings*, *attitudes*, *ideas*, *motives*, and *intentions* to harm self or others. It is also essential to ascertain whether the patient has means and opportunity to execute the behavior and the extent of planning that the patient has already done. The availability of a gun should be noted specifically (see Chapter 27: Suicide).

Cognitive functioning: While taking the history, the examiner will note the adequacy of a patient's orientation, memory, concentration, and capacity for abstraction. These observations are then supplemented by standardized probes. Before assessing cognition, the evaluator notes the patient's level of arousal, consciousness, or *sensorium*. Patients must be fully alert for cognitive tests to be valid. Fluctuating level of consciousness is the cardinal sign of **delirium**.

Most of the probes frequently used to assess cognition come from the **Wechsler Adult Intelligence Scale** (WAIS or IQ test). This test gives normal ranges for various functions, just as systematic measurement determines the normal limits for blood pressure and pulse. The MMSE or MoCA have been standardized on populations of people who are ill with delirium, dementia, or other serious psychiatric disorders (see Table 39.1, for a comparison of the two tests). In all cognitive assessments, patients are asked to tell who they are; where they are; and the day, date, season, or time of day (*orientation*). They are given the names of three (or five) objects to repeat (*registration*) and then asked to restate them a few minutes later (*recall*). They perform serial subtractions of 7 from 100 (test of *concentration*), remember increasingly long strings of numbers forward and backward (*digit span*; a test of *attention*), identify similarities and interpret common proverbs

Table 39.1. Comparison of specialized cognitive measures, MMSE and MoCA

	MMSE	MoCA
Orientation	Person, place, date, situation	Time, day, month, year, place, city
Visuospatial (praxis)	Copy overlapping pentagons	Copy a cube, draw a clock, Connect alternating numbers and letters (trails test)
Aphasia	Name two objects Repeat a sentence Read and follow a command Write a sentence	Name three objects Repeat two sentences Spontaneously give words beginning with *F* for 1 min
Attention	Subtract 7 from 100 and count backwards by 7s to 65	Subtract 7 from 100 and count backwards by 7s to 65 Tap every time the letter A occurs in a string of letters
Registration and recall	Repeat 3 objects Recall 3 objects after distraction	Repeat 5 objects Recall 5 objects after distraction
Abstractions		Identify similarities in two pairs of objects

Note. MMSE = Mini–Mental State Examination; MoCA = Montreal Cognitive Assessment.

(*abstraction*), and describe the best response to particular situations (*judgment*).

The maximum score on either test is 30, with a high score indicating a good level of cognitive capacity, and a low score indicating cognitive impairment. Scores above 25 on the MMSE or 26 and above on the MoCa are generally considered normal. Both tests may be affected by culture and present state. They are better for measuring change from a baseline score than for providing an absolute threshold for pathology. Both tests have been abstracted from more extensive psychological test batteries described in the Appendix. The MoCA is available in several versions and is in the public domain.

Questionnaires often used in psychiatric evaluation include the **Beck Depression Inventory** (BDI I and II; http://www.beckinstitute.org), Symptom Checklist (SCL90-Revised), and the Patient Health Questionnaire (PHQ9). These are research instruments modified for use in general medical and clinical psychiatric settings (note: some instruments are in the public domain, and others are proprietary). By themselves, questionnaires only screen for the possible presence of a psychiatric disorder. Making a diagnosis requires a face-to-face interview and other investigations covering all of the elements above. Written tests can be used to quantify the severity of different conditions, and are often used clinically and in research to assess response to treatment over time ("measurement-based care").

> Taken together, different forms of information gathering should lead to a diagnosis or diagnoses that conform to the criteria of DSM-5 or ICD-10. The evaluator records information not as the patient expressed it, but in a standard form that leads to a particular conclusion or assessment.

Assessment

In support of a likely diagnosis, the evaluator draws on epidemiology and indicators from genetics and past history, along with defining criteria. The written note records the presence or absence (pertinent positives or negatives) of phenomena in the major categories of psychopathology including mood, anxiety, psychosis, somatic, cognitive, substance use, and personality. Systems for recording data often include a **symptom filter** based on these categories, which helps the clinician recognize co-occurring conditions and avoid making diagnoses that are too narrow or too broad.

Except in the instances where an objective test can confirm the diagnosis (e.g., a positive urine toxicology screen in substance-induced disorders, or finding a medical or neurological condition that explains the psychiatric presentation), all initial psychiatric diagnoses are provisional and may be incomplete. Information from future interviews or from other sources may reveal new elements. The future course of the person's condition may require revision of the original assessment, as when a depressed person becomes manic and is re-diagnosed as suffering from bipolar disorder. When symptoms could result from various disorders, the diagnostic plan should be to "consider also" rather than "rule out" related conditions. Many patients will meet criteria for more than one disorder, either concurrently or at different points in time.

Format for Documenting a Psychiatric Evaluation

- Chief complaint or reason for visit
- History of present illness (HPI)
- Past psychiatric history (PPH)
- Medical history
- Family psychiatric history
- Developmental and social history
- Substance use history
- Mental status exam
- (Symptom filter)
- Diagnosis
- Assessment and formulation (including risk assessment)
- Plan

The assessment should be recorded in the format required in a particular setting (shared or separate chart or electronic medial record [EMR]). The particular DSM-5 or ICD-10 diagnosis will be used for billing and coding, and should be adequately supported in the accompanying notes. In settings that use the EMR, at least the diagnostic terms will be visible to providers in other specialties.

> What is a case formulation?

The tasks of evaluation go beyond provisional diagnosis. Thus, a **case formulation** should be constructed to concisely summarize *pathogenesis*. It highlights the elements that may be addressed in treatment, as illustrated in the following example.

> **Diagnosis**: Mrs. R. is a 54-year-old married woman with diabetes, who now describes symptoms of a *major depressive episode with anxiety*: 3 months of depressed mood, poor sleep, increased appetite, apathy, hopelessness, and periods of agitation and uncontrollable worry, but with no suicidal thoughts. She also has night sweats and irregular menses, indicating she is perimenopausal.
>
> **Formulation** (based on a full medical and mental status assessment): Mrs. R. has a family history of depression (mother and sister) that suggests genetic predisposition. She has disturbed sleep and tearfulness, which may reflect the imbalances of neurotransmitter activity seen in depression, exacerbated by perimenopausal hormone flux and possibly unregulated blood sugar. She was abused as a child and now describes generally low self-esteem and difficulty making friends. These longstanding traits have made it hard for her to cope with her recent move and possibly unregulated blood sugar. She was abused as a child and now describes generally low self-esteem and difficulty making friends. These longstanding traits
>
> and possibly unregulated blood sugar. She was abused as a child and now describes generally low self-esteem and difficulty making friends. These longstanding traits have made it hard for her to cope with her recent move to a new city because of her husband's job promotion and being, herself, out of work. The move has precipitated a recurrence of a prior depressive illness. Her strengths include generally mature psychological defenses and the capacity for reflection and self-awareness.
>
> **Plan**: In addition to *antidepressant medication*, Mrs. R. would benefit from either individual or group *psychotherapy* to help her cope with recent changes. Mrs. R. has good social skills and a supportive husband. Outpatient care is appropriate, given her low risk for suicide. She should consult with a primary health provider as soon as possible to discuss management of her diabetes and perimenopausal symptoms.

A schematic recording of information provides a template to organize the written formulation (Table 39.2). This method separates modifiable and unmodifiable elements of the person's situation, distinguishing pathogenesis from current symptoms and identifying possible avenues of treatment.

In the course of psychiatric education, trainees learn to apply different perspectives of psychopa-

Table 39.2. Schematic case formulation

	Predisposing or Background (Unmodifiable)	Precipitating (Unmodifiable)	Perpetuating (Modifiable)	Protective (Modifiable)
Biological	Genetic vulnerability (FH) Female gender Chronic medical condition (DM)		Monoamine transmitter imbalances Menopausal symptoms ? blood sugar control	Generally good health
Psychological	Early trauma Poor parenting Loss of work identity	Similarity to prior losses Change was unwanted	Low self esteem Rejection sensitivity Internalizing tendencies Negative predicting	Generally realistic Good impulse control No suicidal ideation
Social	Move to new city	Loss of former job and relationships	No meaningful daily activity (job) Lack of friends	Adequate material support Good social skills Supportive marriage

Note. DM = diabetes mellitus; FH = family history.

thology, or different theories of pathogenesis, to case formulation. The simple methods presented here, however, are applicable in many clinical settings, including those of general medicine, nursing, and social work.

Recommended Readings

APA Work Group on Psychiatric Evaluation. (2016). *Practice guidelines for the psychiatric evaluation of adults* (3rd ed.). Arlington, VA: American Psychiatric Association. Available at http://psychiatryonline.org/doi/pdf/10.1176/appi.books.9780890426760

Campbell, W. H., & Rohrbaugh, R. M. (2006). *The biopsychosocial formulation manual: A guide for mental health professionals*. New York, NY: Routledge.

Review Questions

1. A 20-year-old woman who seems excited and unrealistic in her thinking is brought to the Emergency Department after making a scene in a store because she felt the sales clerk was rude to her. She denies that she has any problems and demands to be discharged. While waiting for the results of a toxicology screen, the evaluator should
   A. administer medication and interview her again when she is calmer
   B. order a brain scan
   C. place her in restraints
   D. request psychological testing
   E. review available records; get permission to obtain information from third parties

2. The MMSE or MoCA screens for which of the following conditions?
   A. Cognitive impairment
   B. Movement disorders
   C. Personality disorders
   D. Psychotic symptoms
   E. Risk of violence or suicide

3. Among the following, the neuroimaging study most useful in the clinical evaluation of patients with psychiatric complaints is
   A. computerized axial tomography
   B. magnetic resonance imaging
   C. positron emission tomography
   D. single photon emission computed tomography
   E. ventriculography

Answer Key on p. 466

40 Principles of Psychotherapy

Julia B. Frank, MD, and John E. Carr, PhD

- What is psychotherapy?
- Who provides psychotherapy?
- What distinguishes first-, second-, and third-generation psychotherapies?
- What elements characterize the therapeutic alliance?

Psychotherapy

What is psychotherapy?

Psychiatry aspires to be a branch of medicine that addresses disorders that are linked in some fashion to measurable symptoms and outcomes (see Chapter 38: Introduction to Psychopathology). However, just as people consult medical professionals for symptoms and distress unrelated to disease, they seek mental health care for problems that may or may not be connected to a diagnosable syndrome. The principles of psychotherapy provide guidance on how to respond to such distress.

Throughout evolution, the human species has survived because of uniquely complex social capacities. Humans have extraordinary tools for understanding, supporting, nurturing, teaching, empathizing, and caring for one another. A neurological disorder that affects social cognition, a life event involving loss or defeat, or a lack of the resources needed to shape rudimentary inborn traits into age-appropriate qualities, are among a host of factors that may affect an individual's self-concept and social adaptation. Eurowestern cultures, like many others, have developed complex roles and methods that produce specialized healers. These are people who learn to cultivate relationships that improve the ability of distressed people to regulate their internal states. Under the broad umbrella of health care, such healing practices are deemed **psychotherapy**.

All forms of psychotherapy involve *structured interpersonal influence*. Given the power of close relationships to shape human life, character, and society over time, relational processes can be as powerful as, or even more powerful than, medication or social engineering in changing the behavior and experience of individuals. Psychotherapy training teaches practitioners to use empathy, overt persuasion, encouragement of positive emotions, and prescribed behavior change to mobilize intrinsic social capacities and improve the adaptation of troubled people. It differs from other healing relationships by hewing to the ethical principles of medicine, especially *beneficence* and *respect for autonomy* (see Chapter 31: Moral, Ethical, and Legal Issues in Patient Care). Regardless of technique, psychotherapy should be performed for the good of the person seeking help, and its effect depends on the person's willing belief in the process.

Each form of psychotherapy draws upon the values, symbols, and mores of the culture in which it develops. In our era, science has unique power to help people understand and control troubling phenomena. Contemporary methods of psychotherapy trace their origins to the mid-19th century, when science first matched and then surpassed other culturally specific belief systems, especially religion, as the source of healing practices. As medical science has applied knowledge of the *biology* of social processes to the development of *biological* interventions, so have medicine, anthropology, psychology, and other health professions applied knowledge of *social* processes to develop more effective *social* and *behavioral* interventions. Religious healing and other approaches coexist with science and continue to exert psychotherapeutic influence. These practices may exist independently, as in faith healing, or by allying with the scientific pursuit of measurable proof of mechanisms and outcome, as in integrative medicine. Many self-help programs also apply basic principles of psychotherapy, sometimes straddling the boundary between formal medical care and the rest of society, as, for example, in the integration of programs like Alcoholics Anonymous into some formal treatment settings.

Who provides psychotherapy?

Because psychotherapy may be applied to people who are not suffering from a diagnosable condition, and because of its relation to various other methods of healing, considerable confusion exists about whether psychotherapy is or should be considered (and supported) as a medical treatment. This confusion is institutionalized in the separation of mental health care from general medical care in many insurance schemes, at least in the US. This separate but unequal treatment has reduced the number of physicians, even psychiatrists, who practice psychotherapy after training. Other professions help fill the gap.

In addition to some psychiatrists, accredited practitioners of psychotherapy include clinical or counseling psychologists, psychiatric social workers, and psychiatric nurse practitioners, all of whom undergo postgraduate training to develop broad expertise, grounded in fundamental principles. Generalist physicians, nurses, physician assistants, physical therapists, and many other health care providers learn basic relational skills that facilitate care of those with medically recognized conditions, without formal acknowledgement that this activity may be a form of psychotherapy. Addiction specialists, pastoral counselors, and various other licensed professional counselors are trained in particular therapeutic skills, with more limited scope of practice, typically targeting specific issues or populations.

Evolution of Psychotherapeutic Systems

What distinguishes first-, second-, and third-generation psychotherapies?

All systems of psychotherapy are based on developmental, psychological, interpersonal, behavioral, and existential or humanistic concepts and principles. Each embodies a system for understanding how normal human functioning goes awry, characterizing the phenomena of psychopathology in relation to the particular system's techniques and methods of treatment. Three stages of development characterize the evolution of contemporary therapies: first-generation therapies that provided theoretical models of human function and dysfunction, second-generation therapies whose procedural innovations reflect conceptual advances in the underlying theories, and third-generation therapies that integrate the more effective contributions of major therapeutic systems into complex amalgams of empirically validated treatments.

First-Generation Therapies

Psychoanalysis

Psychoanalysis was the earliest, quasi-scientific effort to explain human behavior in secular and evolutionary terms. The theory postulates that all behavior, but especially irrational or maladaptive behavior, is deeply influenced by **unconscious processes**. These processes, in turn, are shaped by childhood experiences. Within this theoretical domain, the psychoanalyst recognizes unconscious processes by making inferences based on the free flow of a person's thoughts, memories, dreams, and fantasies. Patients in classic psychoanalysis "free associate," talking with ever-lessening self-censorship about their distress, symptoms, inability to achieve psychologically important goals, self-defeating behaviors, or failures to adapt. The therapist responds in ways that gradually elicit and reshape the patient's ways of perceiving and responding to the world. Sudden shifts of understanding, or **insight**, are often part of the process.

Psychodynamic Psychotherapy

Psychodynamic psychotherapy is the contemporary derivative of psychoanalysis. The term captures both the fluid (dynamic) nature of patient's thoughts and emotions, and the back-and-forth quality of the relationship between therapist and patient or client. The therapist looks for patterns of interactions between the patient and others, including the therapist, that derive from the person's early experience (**transference**), and evidence that the patient is using unconscious psychological operations (**psychological defenses**) that impair adaptive coping (see Chapter 10: Cognition, Communication, and Social Interaction). Patients learn to identify past maladaptive efforts, modify them, and develop more realistic, present-focused ways of understanding and reacting to their life circumstances. Although psychodynamic therapists often withhold direct advice, they encourage patients to explore and experiment with changes in beliefs and behavior to help them identify coping strategies and to test and reflect on new ones.

Elements of Psychodynamic Psychotherapy

- Focus on affect and underlying emotion
- Exploration of avoidance of distress
- Identification of recurring themes
- Discussion of past experience as shaper of the present
- Focus on relationships
- Attention to therapeutic relationship
- Acceptance and exploration of fantasies, dreams, desires, and fears

---

Adapted from Wells, L. A. & Frank, J. B. (2012). Psychodynamic psychotherapy: From psychoanalytic arrogance to evidence-based modesty. In R. D. Alarcon and J. B. Frank (Eds.), *The psychotherapy of hope: The legacy of persuasion and healing* (pp. 190–214). Baltimore, MD: Johns Hopkins University Press.

Behavioral Therapy

Behavioral therapy had its beginnings in the early 20th century when **academic psychol-**ogy evolved separately from psychoanalysis. Its methods involved research into the determinants of behavior and behavioral change in animals, specifically the principles of classical and operant conditioning. This activity prompted the study of what initiates and sustains changes in human behavior, taking unique human capacities for language and thought into account to a limited degree. Behavioral modification techniques were applied to carefully delineated human problems as early as the 1920s, with behavioral therapy emerging as a significant therapeutic modality in the early 1950s. Strict behavior therapists apply learning theory to modifying maladaptive behaviors, such as substance misuse, sexual problems, and aggression (see Chapter 9: Emotion and Learning).

Contemporary behavioral therapy involves selecting a target maladaptive behavior, identifying the stimulus cues that trigger the behavior, and making the behavioral changes required to achieve a more desired outcome. A behavioral therapist might instruct the patient with insomnia to avoid texting or watching TV in the bedroom, and to go to or stay in bed only when drowsy.

Since the outcomes they seek are measurable activities, behavioral therapists have been able to demonstrate convincingly when their methods work and also to realize when they fail. Behavioral techniques such as *graduated exposure* are especially effective for phobic avoidance. However, the technique of aversive conditioning does not reliably induce lasting change in behaviors with more complex determinants, including substance misuse. The misapplication of behavioral techniques to change sexual orientation is also ineffective, and is now considered fundamentally unethical.

Second-Generation Therapies

Gestalt Therapy

Gestalt therapy, originating in in the late 1940s, was, in part, a reaction against the extensive exploration of the unconscious and past experience that is typical of psychoanalytic psychotherapy. Experiential and humanistic in nature, Gestalt therapy focuses on the immediate life experience of the individual. Patients are prompted to subjectively feel and objectively observe experience without interpretation. Insight is facilitated by awareness focused on how a person experiences a situation and how they react to it, rather than by the interpretations of the therapist. Change is encouraged by experimenting with different types of dialogue and behavior in problematic situations. **Psychodrama**, in which patients role play different personal situations from multiple points of view, is one of several derivatives of Gestalt therapy still in common practice. In a sense, Gestalt therapy is an existential or phenomenological behaviorism that recognizes the influence of cognition on behavior, yet incorporates the behavioral principles involved in maintaining or changing some part of a person's experience.

Client-Centered Therapy

In the early 1950s, Carl Rogers developed **client-centered therapy**, highlighting the importance of the therapist–client relationship. He was among the first to attempt to identify the essential qualities of an effective therapist: *congruence* (i.e., authenticity, genuineness), *respect* for the client, and *empathy*. Empathy as demonstrated to the client by the therapist's reflective responses was especially important. Later researchers refined the definition to stress *accurate empathy*, where the therapist communicates their understanding of the client, and the client then confirms that the therapist understands the client's communication. *Mentalization*, a feature of several contemporary therapies, builds on understanding of the client, in the client's own terms. It encourages the therapist to enter deeply into a patient's frame of reference, cognitively as well as emotionally. Doing so requires continual checking with the patient to assess the accuracy of the process. This method may gradually induce shifts in the patient's perspective toward less distorted, rigid, or otherwise dysfunctional responses to others.

Cognitive Therapy

Partly in reaction against strict behavior therapy, in the mid-1950s, some psychologists began to emphasize the importance of cognitive processes in influencing human behavior. In developing **rational emotive therapy** (RET), Albert Ellis affirmed that how an individual responded to a stimulus or challenging event depended upon the beliefs the individual held about such events. If those beliefs were distorted, then the respondent behavior would be maladaptive. RET focuses on identifying and correcting those distorted belief systems through encouraging and teaching patients to make rational choices about beliefs and behaviors.

Building upon Ellis's work, in the 1960s Aaron Beck developed **cognitive therapy**, which focuses on how repetitive, conscious but fleeting thoughts (cognitions) shape behavior. Cognitive therapy locates the source of most distress in the patient's distorted beliefs about self, the present, and the future. These beliefs, moreover, reflect latent *schemas* or linked beliefs related to such basic processes as perceiving threats (anxiety) or filtering out positive perceptions so that immediate experience and expected outcomes are consistently negative (depression). Being physicians, Beck and colleagues related these schemas to medical definitions of psychopathology, especially anxiety and depressive disorders. This work realigned psychotherapy with other medical treatments, reversing the isolation that characterized psychoanalytically based treatments.

Cognitive Behavioral Therapy

Beck expanded his initial work to develop **cognitive behavioral therapy** (CBT). CBT posits a circular process in which distorted cognitions and schema result in behaviors that reinforce and perpetuate the person's dysfunctional thoughts. For example, people who are depressed make inaccurate *appraisals* of the challenges they face, systematically underestimate their ability to handle stress, overpersonalize negative information, and make negative assumptions about the future and significant others in their lives. These inaccurate appraisals lead to *maladaptive coping behavior* and *dysfunctional social relations*, which become *self-fulfilling prophecies* that contribute to the persistence of the person's depressed mood. The cognitive behavioral therapist guides the person to recognize distorted thinking, interpret situations and relationships more accurately, and learn from experience by trying out new strategies and behaviors. After evaluating the outcome, the individual further modifies cognitions and behaviors and tries out new behaviors.

The focus on targeted problems, the specific situations in which they occur, and the factors that determine them has led to many CBT variants, each designed to address a specific disorder, syndrome, or patient population. Many forms of CBT are "manualized" and involve detailed data collection, readily lending themselves to systematic evaluation. As a result, the CBT research literature improves upon other literature about the outcomes of treatment, and allows for cost–benefit analyses.

Although CBT was initially propounded as an alternative to medication, more recent research explores the relation between the effects of medication and therapy. While medications may be equally helpful in relieving symptoms (including changing depressive cognitions and normalizing behavior), the benefits of cognitive self-examination and behavioral practice last beyond the initial period of treatment. CBT provides patients with skills for consciously managing and anticipating challenges. It constitutes a "toolbox" that may improve adaptation to many situations, beyond those that originally prompted a person to seek help.

Interpersonal Psychotherapy

Interpersonal psychotherapy (IPT), initially developed as a treatment for depressive disorders, evolved from psychodynamic therapy, but focuses less on past experiences and more on *current social relationships*, which are seen as the primary area of dysfunction in depression. Like CBT, IPT is a targeted, time-limited treatment. It is generally used for depression related to one of four interpersonal crises: loss, social conflict, role transitions (job change, graduation, becoming a parent), or developmental deficits (inability to establish rewarding relationships).

Designed to be tested, IPT protocols are well defined in treatment manuals and have empirically supported benefits. By design, the treatment is compatible with the use of medication. As with CBT, the benefits of IPT may persist and even increase after the end of a formal course of therapy

> In early sessions with a man going through a divorce, an interpersonal psychotherapy therapist would take an inventory of his close relationships and educate him about symptoms of depression. The therapist would then encourage him to spend several sessions mourning the loss of his marriage. When his distress has abated, the therapist would help him think about ways to maintain his relationship to his children and perhaps expand his network of personal relationships to include other adults.

Third-Generation Therapies

Research into treatment of any kind often seeks to isolate its effective elements and demonstrate a competitive advantage over other methods. While this has been a productive research strategy, it discourages applying elements of different treatments in the care of individual patients. The value of combining diverse approaches has prompted the development of several eclectic or integrated therapy systems.

Dialectical Behavior Therapy

Marsha Linehan developed **dialectical behavior therapy** (DBT) specifically to treat people with the self-destructive behaviors, emotional lability, histories of personal trauma, and disturbed perceptions of others subsumed in the diagnosis of **borderline personality disorder** (see Chapter 51: Personality Disorders). Linehan incorporated therapeutic concepts from CBT and several other modalities. She stressed that *acceptance* or respect for the patient's perspective and experience are essential. The therapist need not agree with the patient's beliefs, but does need to grasp empathically what the person is experiencing and why (mentalization). Therapy is a *dialectical process* where change or transformation occurs in an iterative fashion involving interpersonal interaction, discussion, and accommodation. The therapeutic targets are to (1) develop self-control, (2) experience and tolerate emotion, (3) learn to problem solve, and (4) enlist these skills in committing to a productive life (existential development). The various elements of DBT are applied in multiple contexts, such as individual therapy sessions, skills training groups, and phone coaching in emergency situations. Research has shown effectiveness of DBT for suicidal and self-injurious patients and has prompted examination of its application in other disorders.

Acceptance and commitment therapy (ACT) is another evidence-informed treatment that applies similar principles to the care of people with intractable or persistent problems, including chronic medical conditions.

Cognitive Behavioral Analysis System of Psychotherapy

In the 1980s, James McCullough incorporated psychodynamic, IPT, and CBT concepts and methodologies into **cognitive behavioral analysis system of psychotherapy** (CBASP) for chronic depression. Drawing on etiological research, CBASP targets the interpersonal problems of chronically depressed individuals (IPT element). Therapists review past significant transference relationships to uncover the sources of deviant and maladaptive interpretations of events and beliefs about significant others (psychodynamic element). Focusing on here-and-now social interactions, patients are guided to (1) adopt an objective view of social interactions, (2) distinguish between maladaptive (distorted) and adaptive interpretations, (3) identify possible behavioral responses, (4) explore realistic and unrealistic expectations about the outcome of interactions, and (5) learn from the analytic process in order to modify future behavior (CBT element).

In a major multisite, double-blind study, CBASP and an antidepressant medication were shown to be equally effective (52% to 55% improvement), but their combination yielded a surprisingly high improvement rate (85%). This finding has stimulated research into other combination therapies and the mechanisms of biobehavioral interaction in the treatment of depressive disorders.

Narrative Medicine

The therapies described above seem to require technical skills beyond the grasp of most health care practitioners. Rita Charon, an internist with a doctorate in literature, has developed an alternative she calls **narrative medicine**. This method addresses distress related to medical illness, including conditions presaging death or deterioration and those occurring in adverse social circumstances such as isolation, conflicted close relationships, or material deprivation. The underlying idea is that in telling a medical story, patients develop self-awareness, find coherence in their suffering, and derive comfort from being understood empathically by the listening medical professional. These processes may occur within the structure of an ordinary history-taking encounter. Professionals develop their skills in responding to patient narratives by reflecting on their own responses in journals, reflective writing, and even in how they record information in the medical record. Although not called psychotherapy, and not formally tested as such, narrative medicine makes intuitive sense. In structuring empathetic encounters with patients, it may produce positive changes in patients' adaptation to disease or disability and increase the satisfaction of helping professionals committed to compassionate care (see Chapter 34: The Provider–Patient Relationship).

The Therapeutic Alliance

> What elements characterize the therapeutic alliance?

While psychodynamic, CBT, IPT, and DBT therapists may view themselves as different, research consistently finds that these and other variants all induce similar improvements, the *equal outcomes phenomenon*. Psychotherapy is not, as some claim, a placebo, but rather a nonspecific remedy like a nonsteroidal anti-inflammatory drug (NSAID) that may relieve pain or fever regardless of its cause. What, then, are the essential elements of all therapies that account for their benefits?

The answer to that question depends on the model of care under investigation, which determines how outcome is defined and measured.

A *medical model* assumes that specific actions in specific therapies are necessary to produce specific results. Research based on the medical model focuses on outcomes such as symptom relief. Such studies tend to favor therapies such as CBT or IPT, when tested against no treatment. However, when these therapies are tested against other therapies without their specific elements, differences in outcome may become insignificant.

In contrast, a *contextual model* assumes that the healing context (the therapist's confidence and the patient's belief in the treatment, the therapist–patient relationship, the rationale for the treatment and actions consistent with that rationale, and the meaning the patient attributes to the therapy) is more powerful than any specific element. Bruce Wampold reviewed the absolute and relative efficacy of different methods, specificity of components, effects due to common factors, effects due to adherence, and differential therapist effects and concluded that, in each case, the evidence supports a contextual model over a medical model (see Recommended Readings).

This conclusion implies that the success of any therapy depends upon a strong **therapeutic alliance** involving (1) *conceptual compatibility* between the patient and the therapist, which facilitates communication and collaboration; (2) the patient feeling *respected* without judgment, by a (3) caring, *empathic, genuine* therapist, and (4) the professional competence of the therapist to administer *empirically validated therapeutic skills and tools*. In addition, the therapist's ability to *instill hope* and *enhance mastery* contributes to the relief of patients' distress. These skills provide the foundation for a therapeutic provider–patient relationship in any health care setting.

Recommended Readings

Alarcon, R. D., & Frank, J. B. (2012). *The psychotherapy of hope: The legacy of persuasion and healing*. Baltimore, MD: Johns Hopkins University Press.

Charon, R. (2012). At the membranes of care: Stories in narrative medicine. *Academic Medicine, 87,* 342–347. http://doi.org/10.1097/ACM.0b013e3182446fbb

Frank, J. D., & Frank, J. B. (1991). *Persuasion and healing: A comparative study of psychotherapy*. Baltimore, MD: Johns Hopkins University Press.

Roth, A., & Fonagy, P. (2005). *What works for whom? A critical review of psychotherapy research*. New York, NY: Guilford Press.

Wampold, B. E. (2001). *The great psychotherapy debate: Models, methods, and findings*. Mahwah, NJ: Lawrence Erlbaum.

Review Questions

1. A therapist treating a depressed man tells him to record his thoughts daily about doing a pleasurable activity, engage in the activity, and record his reactions. This exemplifies which of the following methods of therapy?
    A. Behavioral
    B. Cognitive behavioral
    C. Gestalt
    D. Narrative
    E. Psychodynamic

2. An otherwise healthy woman consults her physician because of insomnia from brooding over disappointments and past mistakes. The physician should recommend a therapist
    A. of her own gender
    B. who inspires trust and demonstrates understanding
    C. who will focus on behavioral change
    D. who will focus on family relationships
    E. with training in a particular discipline

3. The capacity to exert therapeutic influence on patients seems to deteriorate during the course of general medical education. The reason may be that trainees feel it necessary to
    A. consider cultural factors in diagnosis
    B. consider multiple contributors to a dysfunctional state
    C. explain distress in terms that make sense to the patient
    D. focus solely on the objective realities of a disease
    E. respect patient confidentiality

Answer Key on p. 466

41 Disorders of Infancy, Childhood, and Adolescence

Richard R. Pleak, MD, and João V. Nunes, MD

- How is intellectual disability classified?
- What is the definition of a learning disorder?
- How are language disorders related?
- What are some examples of autism spectrum disorder?
- When does oppositional defiant disorder become conduct disorder?
- What is a tic?
- How should enuresis be treated?

The disorders of infancy, coming early in the individual's development, reflect the greater influence of genetic and biological predisposition. The disorders of childhood and adolescence reflect the increasing influence of environmental, social, and experiential factors that comes with age.

Developmental disorders are characterized by limitations in academic, communication, social, motor, and intellectual functioning. The limitations become apparent in infancy or childhood as delays in the acquisition of **developmental milestones**, or developmental gaps, become noticeable. *Diagnostic and Statistical Manual of Mental Disorders, 5th edition* (DSM-5) nosology and diagnostic criteria are used to describe various disorders discussed in this chapter.

Intellectual Disability

William is a 13-year-old boy who lives with his mother. Although pregnancy was normal, as an infant, he did not smile or babble, and had marked speech delays. At age 3, he began to bang his head and flap his hands, sometimes injuring himself. Now he does not play with other children, wants to do the same things repeatedly, and becomes aggressive in school when a new teacher is present or when there are changes in his classroom routine. His IQ is 45. Since he entered puberty and has become larger and stronger, his mother can no longer control his outbursts. She struggles with whether to send him to a residential treatment center.

How is intellectual disability classified?

Intellectual disability (ID), also known as intellectual developmental disorder (and formerly called mental retardation) is characterized by deficits in intellectual functions such as reasoning, planning, judgment, and learning that are confirmed by clinical assessment and intelligence testing (generally IQ < 70). In ID, the effects of a low IQ are compounded by deficits in adaptive functioning and failure to be personally independent and socially responsible, with limitations in communication, social participation, and independent living across home, school, and community environments. The onset is during the developmental period, defined as before age 18. ID is difficult to diagnose in children < 5 years old because test results are less reliable in younger children, and intellectual and adaptive difficulties may not be evident until the child enters elementary school. There are four levels of severity of ID as shown in Table 41.1).

Table 41.1. Intellectual disability severity levels

Severity Level	Conceptual Domain	Social Domain	Practical Domain
Mild	Difficulty in learning; support needed	Immaturity in social interactions	Support needed for complex daily living activities
Moderate	Conceptual skills lag markedly behind; slow language skills; limited academic understanding	Marked deficits in social and communication behavior	Delayed development of personal care skills (eating, dressing, elimination, hygiene)
Severe	Limited attainment of conceptual skills; little understanding of written language	Spoken language quite limited	Support required for all activities of daily living; maladaptive and self-injurious behavior may be present
Profound	Conceptual skills involve physical world rather than symbolic processes; motor and sensory impairments	Very little understanding of symbolic communication; may understand simple instructions or gestures	Dependent on others for all aspects of daily living

For DSM-5 criteria see American Psychiatric Association. (2013). *Diagnostic and statistical manual of mental disorders* (5th ed.). Arlington, VA: Author.

ID is commonly associated with autism spectrum disorders (ASDs), Down syndrome (DS), fragile X syndrome (FXS), cerebral palsy, and exposure to toxic environmental agents such as lead and organophosphate insecticides in early life. Although not all people with ASD have ID, approximately 60% of people with severe ASD also have ID; 95% of DS cases are caused by trisomy of chromosome 21; 4% by fusion of chromosome 21 with chromosome 13, 14, or 15; and 1% by mosaicism (i.e., the presence of both normal and abnormal cells in the same individual). FXS, an X-linked dominant disorder, is the most common inherited neurodevelopmental disorder. It is twice as prevalent in males (1:4,000 births) as in females, and is associated with autistic symptoms. In this disorder, the CGG nucleotide sequence in the FMR1 gene is repeated hundreds of times, which reduces production of the FMRP (protein), resulting in abnormal brain development with cognitive, emotional, behavioral, and neurological impairments. The wide range of impairment in children with FXS may be explained by mosaicism. The distinguishing physical features of the disorder (long face, prominent jaw and forehead, large protruding ears, and large testicles [in males]) become most apparent around puberty, but are not reliable as a basis for diagnosis. Perinatal hypoxia leading to cerebral palsy often results in some degree of ID. Environmental toxins can cause decrements in intelligence. For example, even small amounts of lead from contaminated water, air, or ingested matter (food, paint chips) can permanently decrease intelligence.

The cause of ID remains unknown in a large percentage of cases. Potential causes include maternal abuse not only of alcohol but also of other substances such as drugs during pregnancy; metabolic disruption involving mother or fetus (e.g., hypothyroidism); trauma; and central nervous system infections such as toxoplasmosis, zika, and rubella. ID can also be comorbid with neurological disorders such as epilepsy.

About 85% of persons with ID fall in the mild, educable range. Although no intervention will significantly alter IQ, most people with mild mental retardation can find suitable vocations and function to maximal capacity with proper behavioral management, social support, and education.

Specific Learning Disorders (LD)

What is the definition of a learning disorder?

The diagnosis of LD refers to academic skills that are substantially below what would be expected at the person's age and that significantly interfere with academic progress or occupational performance. The diagnosis of LD is confirmed by scores on standardized tests of reading, mathematics, or written expression, that are low for age, years of schooling, and intellectual ability.

Specific Learning Disorder With Impairment in Reading

Specific learning disorder with impairment in reading (formerly called *dyslexia,* which is now an alternative term) is manifested by slow inaccurate reading characterized by letter reversal, poor word recognition, and comprehension problems in the absence of ID or sensory deficits. Additional diagnoses of *expressive, receptive,* or *mixed language disorders* or *disorder of written expression* may be warranted. This disorder is often apparent by age 6, although recognition may be delayed in children of above average intelligence. About 5% to 10% of school-aged children are estimated to have a reading disorder, with boys affected more often than girls. Although prevalence of reading disorder in families of affected individuals is increased, a genetic link has not been confirmed. Interventions, including remedial education, management of any emotional problems, and parent counseling, should begin by the third grade. Otherwise, reading is likely to remain impaired, with consequent low self-esteem and poor school attendance.

Specific Learning Disorder With Impairment in Mathematics

Specific learning disorder with impairment in mathematics (formerly called *dyscalculia*) is characterized by deficiencies in four arithmetic-related skill areas, not explained by poor education or neurological, sensory, or cognitive impairments: (1) *linguistic skills* – understanding mathematical terms and conversion of verbal instructions

into mathematical symbols; (2) *perceptual skills* – recognition of symbols and ordering of number clusters; (3) *performance skills* – carrying out and appropriately sequencing the four basic arithmetic operations; and (4) *attention skills* – exact copying of figures and performance of operations designated by symbols. Number sense, ability to memorize arithmetic facts, calculations, and math reasoning are impaired. Diagnosis is usually made during or after the second grade. Almost 5% of school-aged children of average intelligence are affected. Remedial education is the treatment of choice. Undiagnosed or inadequately treated children will continue to perform poorly, and may develop poor self-esteem, depression, anger, frustration, disruptive behavior disorders, or school refusal.

Specific Learning Disorder With Impairment in Written Expression

Specific learning disorder with impairment in written expression is characterized by poor spelling; frequent grammatical and punctuation errors; and unclear, disorganized handwriting. The disorder becomes evident around the third grade, appears to be familial, and affects 3% to 10% of school-aged children. Boys are affected more often than girls. The etiology is unknown. Because it often accompanies communication and reading disorder, dysfunction in cerebral information processing areas is suspected.

Communication Disorders

Language Disorder

How are language disorders related?

Language disorder is characterized by persistent difficulties acquiring and using language, with abilities that are substantially below age, including limited vocabulary, difficulty producing properly structured sentences, inability to use correct tenses, and impaired discourse. The diagnosis is confirmed by language test scores. Language disorder affects 3% to 10% of school-aged children; boys are affected 2 to 3 times as frequently as girls. While the etiology is unknown, the disorder is prevalent in families with a history of communication disorders. Language disorder is usually a developmental disorder, but it may also result from a neurological insult (e.g., trauma, seizure disorder). About 50% of affected children recover spontaneously. In severely affected children, a mild to moderate language impairment will remain long term if the language disorder is untreated. Thus, speech and language therapy is essential. Psychotherapy and parental counseling may be warranted to address associated low self-esteem, frustration, performance anxiety, and depression.

Social (Pragmatic) Communication Disorder

Social (pragmatic) communication disorder is impairment in the social use of verbal and nonverbal communication, with deficits in using communication for social purposes, impairment in changing communication to match contexts, difficulty following conversational rules, and difficulty understanding nonexplicit communication such as humor, innuendo, idioms, and metaphors. Social communication and receptive and expressive language test scores are significantly below age and developmental expectations without evidence of autism spectrum disorder, neurological disorder, or sensory defect.

> Audiological evaluation is essential in persons with a language disorder to rule out hearing impairment, the most common sensory defect contributing to disordered language development.

Mild social (pragmatic) communication disorder may not be identified until later childhood or adolescence and may produce minimal long-term language impairment. Although the etiology is unknown, the observation that children with social (pragmatic) communication disorder respond more to environmental sounds than to speech sounds suggests auditory discrimination difficulties. The incidence of ambidexterity and left-handedness is increased among affected individuals.

Speech Sound Disorder

Speech sound disorder (formerly *phonological* or *articulation disorder*) is characterized by speech sounds that are incorrectly produced, omitted, or substituted for appropriate sounds. This limits effective communication, social participation, and school and employment performance. The diagnosis is made in the absence of anatomical-structural, physiological, neurological, or sensory (e.g., auditory) abnormalities. The disorder occurs in 5% of children, although it may be present in up to 10% of children < 8 years old. Boys are affected more often than girls, and first-degree relatives are at increased risk. Although the etiology is unknown, speech sound disorder is probably caused by *maturational delays* in the brain processes underlying speech. Speech sound disorder is correlated with large family size and lower socioeconomic status, suggesting insufficient stimulation of speech development as an etiological factor. Spontaneous remission is common before age 8, but rare thereafter. Speech therapy provides the most successful treatment. Parental counseling and education are helpful adjuncts.

Childhood-Onset Fluency Disorder (Stuttering)

Childhood onset fluency disorder (stuttering) is characterized by speech that lacks fluency and temporal patterning, resulting in repetition and prolongation of sounds and syllables, broken words, speech blocking, word substitutions (circumlocutions), and an excess of physical tension in producing words. Deficits must exceed any disturbance produced by a speech-motor, neurological, or sensory impairment. Stutterers develop anticipatory anxiety and avoid situations in which they expect they will stutter. Many develop tics, eye blinking, or trembling of the lips and jaw in anticipation of speaking. The etiology is probably multifactorial, with significant learning and anxiety components. Spontaneous remission occurs in up to 80% of cases. Children who do not fully recover may experience months of remission but relapse at times of stress. Treatments focusing on stuttering as a learned behavior and restructuring speech fluency are most successful. Children and adolescents recover better than do adults.

Developmental Coordination Disorder

Developmental coordination disorder is manifested by delayed developmental milestones such as sitting, crawling, standing, and walking; clumsiness; accident proneness; and poor fine motor skills such as tossing a ball or fitting puzzle pieces together. The disorder may interfere with academic progress and trigger emotional and behavioral disorders. Standardized evaluations of a child's skill level at a particular age help establish the diagnosis. Boys are affected 2 to 4 times as frequently as girls. The etiology is unclear but risk factors include hypoxia at birth, prematurity, low birthweight, and perinatal malnutrition. Effective treatments include physical therapy to enhance gross motor skills, occupational therapy to enhance fine motor skills, perceptual motor training, neurophysiological exercise techniques, and modified physical education.

Autism Spectrum Disorder

Autism spectrum disorder (ASD; formerly *pervasive developmental disorder* [PDD]) is characterized by disrupted repetitious behaviors and impaired development of language and social skills during childhood. In DSM-IV, there were four separate PDD diagnoses (autistic disorder, Asperger's disorder, childhood disintegrative disorder, and Rett syndrome). In DSM-5, the first three were subsumed into one: *autism spectrum disorder*. Rett syndrome was removed from the DSM-5 and recategorized as a neurological disorder.

> What are some examples of autism spectrum disorder?

ASD usually appears before age 3 and is characterized by
1. impaired social communication and interactions such as delay or lack of verbal skills; repetitive, stereotyped, and idiosyncratic language; lack of eye contact; deficits in developing and maintaining relationships; lack of

social-emotional reciprocity; and absence of spontaneous symbolic play; and
2. restricted, repetitive, stereotyped, and idiosyncratic behaviors, interests, and activities such as insistence on sameness; fixated interests with abnormal intensity or focus; rigid adherence to routines; repetitive motor movements such as hand flapping or head banging; and hyporeactivity or hyperreactivity to sensory input.

Studies suggest that ASD has increased in prevalence to as many as 1 in 110 individuals. Boys are affected more often than girls (1 in 70 boys), but girls are more likely to have a family history of serious cognitive impairment, and their symptoms are more severe. Two thirds of children with more severe ASD have some degree of ID.

Findings Suggestive of Possible Etiologies for ASD

- Prenatal and perinatal complications
- Older parental age at conception
- Maternal exposure to cigarette smoke during pregnancy
- Minor congenital anomalies, abnormal dermatoglyphics, and ambidexterity
- Higher concordance rates among monozygotic twins compared with dizygotic twins
- Fifty times greater risk among siblings
- Temporal lobe lesions, severe tuberous sclerosis, or FXS in some affected individuals
- Decreased numbers of Purkinje cells in the cerebellum
- Grand mal seizures, EEG abnormalities, and ventricular enlargement
- Diminished response to infection and pain

ASD children with IQ > 70 and reasonable language skills by age 5 have the best prognosis. A few ASD children with high IQ improve to the point of no longer meeting criteria for the disorder, even though they retain some manifestations. Up to 2% of affected children become independent and 5% to 20% become semi-independent. Some, termed "high-functioning," can achieve major accomplishments. However, > 70% will require family or institutional care as adults.

Treatment includes educational and behavioral techniques that encourage normal social interactions, discourage bizarre behaviors, and improve interpersonal communication. These interventions are most effective when begun in the preschool years. ASD children function best in structured settings. Psychopharmacological agents are useful for treating severe perseverations, impulsivity, inattention, aggression, and self-injurious behaviors. Parent support and education is essential. Groups such as Autism Speaks are very helpful (http://www.autismspeaks.org).

Attention-Deficit/Hyperactivity Disorder (ADHD) and Other Disruptive Behavior Disorders

Dean is a 9-year-old boy whose parents have been told he cannot return to school until he is evaluated by a physician for disruptive behavior. Dean talks excessively with peers during instruction time, is inattentive to the teacher, and inappropriately calls out answers. He squirms in his seat and frequently asks to go to the bathroom, but once in the hall, he roams around. He has run into chairs and tables sustaining bruises to the extent that a neighbor considered reporting the parents for abuse. His friends no longer wish to play with him because he cannot wait his turn and constantly interrupts them. He is failing several classes because he does not complete projects or homework. A year ago, Dean began having twitching of his mouth, eyes, and neck, and making sudden odd sounds; he reports, "I have to do this – I can't help it."

Attention-deficit/hyperactivity disorder (**ADHD**, in the past also known as **ADD**) is characterized by persistent attention problems and/or motor/verbal over-activity/impulsivity. ADHD has three presentations: combined (the most common); predominantly inattentive (sometimes referred to in the lay literature as *attention deficit disorder* or ADD); and predominantly hyperactive/impulsive (uncommon without significant inattention). Girls are more likely to have the inattentive type; boys are more likely to have the combined type.

ADHD affects 10% to 15% of children, a minority of whom are in treatment. Two thirds have significant symptoms into adulthood. Youth with ADHD are at risk for dropping out of school, substance abuse, motor vehicle accidents, higher rates of emergency room visits, and difficulty remaining employed.

Characteristics of ADHD
- **Distractibility/Inattention** (careless mistakes, missing work, losing things)
- **Fidgeting/Hyperactivity** ("driven by a motor": taps feet, makes noise, leaves seat, excessive running around)
- **Impulsivity/Disruptive behaviors** (blurts out in class, excessive talking)
- **Difficulty following directions and completing tasks without supervision**
- **Trouble taking turns and sharing** (interrupts, intrudes)

Although the etiology of ADHD is unclear, frontal lobe and reticular activating system dysfunction and deficiency of noradrenergic neurotransmitters are suspected. Genetic vulnerability is suggested by evidence that children with ADHD are very likely to have parents, siblings, or close relatives who have ADHD. In fact, heritability may be as high as 80%. Vulnerability is increased by environmental factors such as intrauterine exposure to tobacco smoke or cocaine and advanced parental age at conception. Treatments include parent management training, behavioral incentive programs, limit setting, tutoring, and structured settings and times for school work and chores. Implementing Section 504 provisions of the Rehabilitation Act can be very helpful. These include having the teacher check the child's homework and assignments, providing extra time for tests, and seating the child at the front of the class for closer observation and supervision. Some children will do best when they receive special education services, such as smaller classrooms, school aides, and resource room and in-school tutoring. The most effective treatment is administration of stimulant medication, to which the great majority of children respond well. Additional assistance for parents is available through national support groups such as Children and Adults With Attention-Deficit/Hyperactivity Disorder (CHADD; http://www.chadd.org/).

Oppositional Defiant Disorder

Oppositional defiant disorder (ODD) is persistent (> 6 months), negativistic, defiant behavior in a child ≥ 3 years old. Symptoms include frequent irritability, annoying others, blaming others, arguing with authorities, defiance, spitefulness, vindictiveness, and loss of temper in interactions with at least one person who is not a sibling. ODD should be considered when symptoms impair functioning and are not due to a mood disorder or psychosis. ADHD and LD are common comorbidities.

Suspected etiological factors include inconsistent caretaking, poor limit setting, neglect, abuse, and family dysfunction. Assessment includes a careful history from parents or caregivers focusing on discipline and conflicts within the family. Treatment includes parenting education to enhance management skills, and treatment of comorbid disorders.

Conduct Disorder

> When does oppositional defiant disorder become conduct disorder?

Conduct disorder (CD) is more severe and socially destructive than ODD, with a negative, persistent pattern of violating the rights of others and social rules. Onset may occur during mid to late childhood or adolescence. Symptoms include bullying, threatening, aggression, or cruelty toward people or animals; using weapons; lying; vandalism including destruction of property and fire setting; deceitfulness; forgery; extortion; rape; truancy; and other significant social rule violations. Approximately 6% of children have some degree of conduct disorder; boys are affected 4 times as frequently as girls.

CD is generally comorbid with ADHD or LD. Youths with CD are at risk for substance abuse, homelessness, gang involvement, prostitution, incarceration, suicide, murder, and homicide. If symptoms persist beyond age 18, the person is rediagnosed as having antisocial personality disorder (see Chapter 51: Personality Disorders). The diagnosis of **antisocial personality disorder** is dependent on a history of conduct disorder, but

less than 50% of adolescents who have severe CD will eventually be diagnosed with antisocial personality disorder. Others remit, become less symptomatic, or die as a result of homicide, suicide, or other violent events. Prosocial outcomes can occur as careers in the military, firefighting, and law enforcement.

The etiology of CD is unclear. Fathers are likely to be alcoholic with a history of violence and incarceration. The child may have been abused, grossly neglected, or harshly or inadequately disciplined, and have had no consistent role models for moral behavior. Developmental markers of conduct disorder in boys include low serum levels of dopamine beta-hydroxylase and muted galvanic skin responses to noxious stimuli, but these findings are neither clinically useful nor diagnostic.

Treatment includes management of comorbid disorders such as ADHD, which is best achieved using pharmacological agents such as stimulant medication; unfortunately, stimulants are highly abusable and salable. Affected youth respond best to immediate and concrete rewards. Family support and assistance is essential, and may include social services, intensive case management, in-home aides, big brothers and/or sisters, truancy officers, police, the courts (where person in need of supervision [PINS] petitions can be obtained), and probation. Intensive behavior modification may be transiently effective. Placement in a long-term therapeutic foster home or residential treatment center or facility can be beneficial.

Tic Disorders

> What is a tic?

Tics are recurrent sudden, rapid, nonrhythmic stereotypical movements or vocalizations.

Tourette's Disorder

Tourette's disorder (also known as *Tourette's syndrome*) appears before age 18 and consists of multiple motor tics and at least one vocal tic. Vocal tics can be, for example, words, vocal sounds, sniffling, coughing, or throat clearing. To meet criteria for the diagnosis, the tics must occur numerous times daily for at least 1 year, impair functioning, and be unrelated to medical disorders. They often wax and wane in frequency and severity, and may change from one area or sound to another over time. Tourette's disorder occurs in 2% of the population, and males are affected 3 times more often than females. Motor tics are often evident by age 5 and vocal tics by age 11. *Coprolalia*, or socially inappropriate words or phrases such as swearing and curses, occurs in only a minority of affected persons. People have some control over their tics, which they describe as "compelling" rather than totally involuntary, with a motor premonition leading to the urge to tic. Focusing on alternative strategies to quell this premonitory urge via therapy with **comprehensive behavioral intervention for tics** (CBIT) is the preferred initial intervention. Pharmacotherapy is another effective form of treatment for more persistent and severe tics, usually starting with alpha-2 adrenergic agonists such as *guanfacine* and *clonidine*. The national Tourette Association of America is the major source of information and support for individuals with tics, their families, and clinicians.

Tourette's disorder appears to have a *genetic component* and exists on a continuum with persistent (chronic) motor or vocal tic disorder. It is an autosomal disorder transmitted in a bilinear mode (i.e., between recessive and dominant). Some tics will remit or lessen, while others may persist into adulthood. Although the etiology is unclear, dysfunction of the dopamine system may be involved. The endogenous opiate system is likely involved in cases of comorbidity with obsessive compulsive disorder, and the adrenergic system appears to be involved in cases that respond to alpha-2 adrenergic agonists.

Motor or Vocal Tic Disorder

Persistent (chronic) motor or vocal tic disorder is manifested by either motor or vocal tics, but not both. Onset is before age 18, prevalence is estimated at 1% to 2%, and early school-aged children are at highest risk of developing the disorder. Children who have onset of motor or vocal tics between 5 and 8 years of age are likely to become symptom free an average of 4 years after onset. Youth with facial tics have a better prognosis than those with tics involving larger muscle groups. Treatment depends on severity and degree of academic, social, and emotional impairment.

Behavioral techniques (e.g., CBIT) and pharmacotherapy (starting with alpha-2 adrenergic agonists) can be effective. Supportive psychotherapy is helpful in the management of secondary emotional problems, difficulties coping with peer reactions, and low self-esteem.

Provisional tic disorder consists of one or more vocal or motor tics or both that begin before age 18; the tics can occur many times a day, but last no longer than 1 year. Up to 25% of school-aged children have a history of tics that intensify or reappear transiently at times of stress. If symptoms are mild with little or no functional impairment, no treatment is needed, and parents should be counseled to ignore the tics. If the tics do not remit soon, or the person declines in social, emotional, or academic functioning, behavioral treatment, pharmacotherapy, or both should be considered.

Stereotypic Movement Disorder

Stereotypic movement disorder is manifested by repetitive movements that impair age-appropriate activities and cause injury to the child. Examples include self-biting, self-hitting, rocking, head banging, hand shaking, and hitting the body not explained by drug effects or medical conditions; compulsions; or developmental disorders. The disorder is more common in boys, and up to 20% of children with ID are affected. Prognosis is correlated with the frequency and intensity of self-injurious behavior. Control often requires the use of physical restraint. Pharmacotherapy and behavioral treatment such as reinforcement and behavioral shaping are the most effective strategies available.

Elimination Disorders

Enuresis

Enuresis is repeated involuntary or intentional urination into clothes or the bed by an individual ≥ 5 years old. The behavior must occur at least twice weekly for 3 consecutive months or be accompanied by emotional distress or functional impairment. The behavior cannot be explained as the effect of a substance or a physical dysfunction. Failure to acquire bladder control at the appropriate age, and loss of bladder control after it is acquired, are both defined as enuresis. Enuresis is specified as nocturnal only, diurnal only, or both.

Although there is some *genetic* predisposition, *psychosocial factors* such as family toilet training practices and family distress are also etiological. *Enuresis is unrelated to sleep stages.*

How should enuresis be treated?

Because many cases of enuresis remit spontaneously, prevalence drops to about 1% in young adults. In persistent cases, restricting fluids close to bedtime, encouraging urination at bedtime, waking the child to urinate, and having the child be responsible for cleaning soiled sheets are useful. Operant reward systems (e.g., charting and rewarding dry nights) are also useful, as is classical conditioning, such as using a device that detects urine dampness and triggers an alarm that wakens the child (**enuresis alarm**). Supportive and family therapy can also promote constructive coping. Pharmacotherapy with synthetic vasopressin (desmopressin) may be helpful when the child is sleeping away from home or when starting behavioral therapy in the presence of no or only a few dry nights. However, unless the behavior itself has changed, enuresis often recurs when the medication is discontinued.

Encopresis

In Western cultures, more than 95% of children have acquired bowel control via myelination of the nerves controlling the anal sphincter by age 4. By age 5, 99% have acquired bowel control. **Encopresis** is repeated intentional or involuntary passage of feces into inappropriate places. Diagnostic criteria include ≥ 1 episode per month for at least 3 months, developmental age ≥ 4 years, and no substance or medical condition to account for the behavior.

The etiology is multifactorial and includes power struggles over toilet training and inefficient or ineffective sphincter tone. Most affected children do not have a psychiatric disorder associated with the encopresis. For many, the disorder is *behavioral*. In contrast, persons who can control their bowel but voluntarily deposit feces in inappropriate places should be suspected of having a primary psychiatric disorder. Developmental and maturational difficulties such as distractibility, poor frustration tolerance, and poor motor coordination are common in affected children. After bowel control has been established, regressive reactions to life stressors may precipitate a recurrence of encopresis.

Many encopretic children develop **psychogenic megacolon**, which arises when painful defecation or voluntary withholding leads to fecal impaction. This, in turn, produces colonic enlargement. Loss of colonic tone reduces sensitivity to pressure that signals the need to defecate. In many cases, encopresis remits spontaneously and rarely persists beyond adolescence.

Nonpunitive parental involvement is essential for a favorable outcome. Reward-based behavioral techniques, psychotherapy, and family therapy are indicated. Short-term laxatives may be useful in consultation with the pediatrician.

Other Disorders of Infancy, Childhood, and Adolescence

Separation Anxiety Disorder (SAD)

Separation anxiety disorder (SAD) is the *most common anxiety disorder in children*, occurring with equal frequency in boys and girls (4% of school-aged children and 1% of adolescents), with typical onset at about 7 years of age. It consists of abnormally intense and persistent fears of separation from others, of bodily harm, or of losing the attachment figure (mother), and heightened response to environmental stressors, present for at least 4 weeks. The etiology is multifactorial, the principal factor being *parental modeling* by an anxious or depressed parent.

Treatment includes psychotherapy for the child and family education and therapy addressing the parent's anxiety and/or depression. Pharmacotherapy with anxiolytics can be useful in more refractory cases. The presence of school refusal requires prompt intervention. In such cases, the goal of treatment is to return the child to school immediately even if for only an hour a day, and then gradually increase the time spent in school to achieve full attendance.

Diagnostic Criteria for Separation Anxiety Disorder

At least three of the following behaviors when separation is occurring or anticipated:

- Excessive distress
- Persistent excessive worry about losing the attachment figure
- Persistent fear of separation from the attachment figure
- Reluctance or refusal to go to school or away from home; fear of being alone
- Reluctance or refusal to go to sleep without an attachment figure or away from home
- Nightmares about separation
- Physical complaints (e.G., headache, stomach ache, vomiting)

Selective Mutism (SM)

Selective mutism (SM) is consistent refusal or failure to speak in social situations where speech is expected, although the child is known to speak in other situations and to have age-appropriate language skills. The difficulty must be present for ≥ 1 month and interfere with academic and social functioning. The diagnosis should be reserved for children whose symptoms are not explained by a communication disorder, developmental disorder, or psychotic disorder. SM usually remits within weeks, but may persist for years. Children who do not improve by age 10 have a worse prognosis. Up to one third of children with selective mutism develop other psychiatric disorders, especially anxiety disorder.

Prevalence is estimated at less than 1 per 1,000 children. Girls are affected more frequently than boys, and up to 90% of children with SM have a history of social phobia. Early psychological trauma is a significant risk factor. Treatment includes cognitive behavioral psychotherapy for the child, counseling and supportive therapy for the parents, and pharmacotherapy.

Reactive Attachment Disorder

Reactive attachment disorder (RAD) is evident before age 5 and is associated with moderate to grossly *apathetic caregiving*, such as neglect or deprivation of basic needs by parents or by staff (e.g., in an orphanage). Affected children demonstrate inappropriate social relatedness not fully explained by developmental delay. The child may fail to thrive physically and have delayed motor and psychosocial milestones. People with RAD have consistently inhibited, withdrawn behavior toward caregivers (e.g., not seeking or responding to comfort when distressed; minimal social and emotional responsiveness; limited positive affect; and episodes of unexplained irritability or sadness).

Disinhibited Social Engagement Disorder

Disinhibited social engagement disorder (DSED) results from extremes of insufficient care such as social neglect or deprivation or repeated changes in caregivers. The child must have a developmental age ≥ 9 months to warrant the diagnosis. DSED is marked by a pattern of unselective, undifferentiated, and uninhibited social relatedness. The child actively approaches and interacts with unfamiliar adults with reduced reticence and overly familiar behavior. The child may also show diminished or no checking back with caregivers, venture away in unfamiliar settings, and be willing to go off with unfamiliar adults.

Family disorganization, single parenting, psychosocial deprivation, inadequate institutional staffing, and poverty increase vulnerability to RAD and DSED. Depending on the severity and duration of pathological caregiving, manifestations can progress to inanition and death. Children with RAD and DSED may continue exhibiting symptoms through adulthood or eventually behave normally.

The goal of treatment is normalization of the child–caregiver relationship. Therapeutic management includes hospitalization if the child is at risk; support services (e.g., child care, improved housing, and financial assistance); decreasing social isolation of the family; comprehensive medical and psychiatric care; parent counseling, education, and skills training; and close supportive follow-up. Long-term placement may be in the best interest of the child.

Recommended Readings

Cheng, K., & Myers, K. M. (2010). *Child and adolescent psychiatry: The essentials* (2nd ed.). Philadelphia, PA: Lippincott Williams & Wilkins.

Dulcan, M. (2015). *Dulcan's textbook of child and adolescent psychiatry* (2nd ed.). Washington, DC: American Psychiatric Publishing.

Martin, A., & Volkmar, F. R. (Eds.). (2007). *Lewis's child and adolescent psychiatry: A comprehensive textbook* (4th ed.). Philadelphia, PA: Williams & Wilkins.

Additional Resources

Tourette Association of America. http://www.tourette.org

Review Questions

1. Sara is 9 years old. She was apparently normal at birth. At the age of 2 months, Sara suffered atypical seizures followed by crying spells. Neurological consultation revealed nonspecific static encephalopathy. Sara's development has been slow: she has never been capable of understandable speech and cannot meet her basic needs. Her mother bathes, dresses, and feeds her, although Sara can eat finger foods independently. The primary goal of schooling has been basic socialization. The most likely diagnosis is
   A. attention-deficit/hyperactivity disorder
   B. disinhibited social engagement disorder
   C. intellectual disability
   D. reactive attachment disorder
   E. specific learning disorder

2. Mario is 8 years old. At 18 months, he became isolated, appeared not to enjoy playing with adults, and ignored other children. He played with toys as though he did not understand their purpose. He flapped his hands frequently and had severe temper tantrums. Currently, his speech consists of a few words repeated from television. He has no friends and has become increasingly emotionally unresponsive to his parents and other family members. The most likely diagnosis is
   A. attention-deficit/hyperactivity disorder
   B. autism spectrum disorder
   C. oppositional defiant disorder
   D. reactive attachment disorder
   E. specific learning disorder

3. Rachna is a 10-year-old girl who is the class clown, always joking and talking to peers when the teacher is trying to instruct. She has been suspended for refusing to follow the teacher's directions, urinating in the classroom, and trying to hit the principal. Her IQ is 99, but she failed fourth grade because she rarely wants to go to school, and her mother cannot set limits. Her father, however, is very punitive, especially when drinking. She has been experimenting with cigarettes and alcohol that she finds in the house. The most likely diagnoses are
   A. attention-deficit/hyperactivity disorder and oppositional defiant disorder
   B. autism spectrum disorder and intellectual disability
   C. conduct disorder and developmental coordination disorder
   D. disinhibited social engagement disorder and separation anxiety disorder
   E. Tourette's disorder and enuresis

4. For years, 14-year-old Johnny has shown a pattern of cruelty to animals and aggression toward his siblings and peers. This pattern has intensified over the past year and now includes lying, running away from home, and stealing. Yesterday, he was caught vandalizing and setting a substantial fire in a neighbor's house. Johnny's behavior is most suggestive of
   A. attention-deficit/hyperactivity disorder
   B. conduct disorder
   C. disinhibited social engagement disorder
   D. oppositional defiant disorder
   E. social communication disorder

Answer Key on p. 466

42 Schizophrenia and Other Psychotic Disorders

Sonja M. Lillrank, MD, PhD

- What are the characteristic features of psychotic disorders?
- What are the symptoms of schizophrenia?
- What is the natural history of schizophrenia?
- What factors have been hypothesized to contribute to the etiology of schizophrenia?
- What are four psychotic disorders other than schizophrenia?

Psychotic Disorders

What are the characteristic features of psychotic disorders?

Psychosis is a generic term for a state in which inner processes distort a person's appraisal of the external world ("impaired reality testing"). Psychotic disorders are characterized by *delusions* (fixed false beliefs*), hallucinations* (internally generated perceptions), and varying degrees of *disorganized thought*, *speech*, and *behavior*. These symptoms create *social impairments* that affect the patient's ability to meet the ordinary demands of life.

Psychotic *symptoms*, especially delusions and hallucinations, may occur in mood disorders, drug intoxication, dementia, delirium, various medical conditions, and developmental disorders. *Primary psychotic disorders* are classified by the nature, severity, and pattern of symptoms and behavior, rarely by known etiology.

Schizophrenia

Schizophrenia, the *most common psychotic disorder*, affects about 1% of the world's population. Both genders are equally affected, but the disorder tends to begin earlier in life in males. It can have pervasive effects on the person, including the loss of ability to perceive and express emotion normally (i.e., dysregulation of affect) and deterioration from baseline personality. To varying degrees, schizophrenia compromises motivation, self-care, and the ability to work, occupy oneself, and relate to other people. Schizophrenia is usually chronic, with periods of remission and exacerbation. When not overwhelmed with psychosis, people with schizophrenia may recover significantly and lead gratifying and productive lives.

Worldwide, management of schizophrenia accounts for more inpatient treatment days per year than any other condition. Schizophrenia also accounts for roughly 2.6% of the total *years lost to disability* (YLD) calculated by the World Health Organization. Statistically, persons with schizophrenia have a reduced life expectancy of about a decade and often suffer from comorbid problems including substance use, tobacco use, difficulty

Previously fastidious and outgoing, a now unkempt 20-year-old college sophomore rarely comes out of his room. He is preoccupied with the meaning of life, mumbles to himself, and expresses little emotion, except for bursts of inappropriate speech. He talks about his "vision quest" to find "the inner soul of the patrician monarchy." He becomes hostile when questioned and accuses the interviewer of attempting to "steal my mind to insert your sins." Physical examination and screening laboratory studies reveal no obvious medical problems, and urine drug screen is negative.

accessing primary care, and obstacles to managing chronic health conditions that contribute to early mortality. About 20% of people with schizophrenia attempt suicide on one or more occasions. Death by suicide occurs in 5% to 6% of cases.

Symptoms of Schizophrenia

What are the symptoms of schizophrenia?

The symptoms of schizophrenia are divided into three groups: positive, negative, and cognitive. Each group implicates dysfunction in different brain regions and neurotransmitters.

Positive symptoms include *delusions, hallucinations, thought disorder,* and *movement abnormalities.* **Delusions** are false beliefs that are not changed by reason or evidence that contradicts them. In schizophrenia, these erroneous beliefs are often bizarre and incongruent with mood, and tend to guide how the individual interprets reality and behavioral responses. Examples include beliefs that one's body, mind, or soul has been mysteriously changed and beliefs that supernatural or alien forces are influencing events, inserting or removing one's thoughts, or causing one's thoughts to be broadcast without speaking them. Some delusions are less bizarre and involve themes of persecution, grandiosity, jealousy, illness, guilt, or sin. Convictions that random events (e.g., a man tipping his hat) or general stimuli (e.g., television, radio programs, or religious texts) are directed toward oneself are called *delusions of reference.*

Auditory hallucinations are the most common type of hallucination, although any of the five perceptual senses may be involved. The hallucinations are typically more complex and bizarre than those of other psychoses. Auditory hallucinations may be experienced as conversations between several different voices that talk together about the individual, comment on the person's thoughts, or command the person to behave in a way that is uncomfortable and uncharacteristic. Other odd experiences include perceptions that someone or something is controlling the thoughts, emotions, and behaviors of the patient.

Thought disorder (see Table 42.1) is characterized by the absence of linear and logical connections between ideas. Communication in speech or writing is also disorganized and may become incomprehensible. The classic thought disorder of schizophrenia is characterized by *loose associations (derailment)* where ideas are strung together in a random, convoluted manner such that the listener cannot understand or make sense of the person's conversation. Other named thought disorders observed in schizophrenia include tangential and circumstantial thought.

Movement abnormalities include purposeless movements repeated over and over (stereotypy) and *catatonia* in which both spontaneous and volitional movements are either retarded to the point of stupor or extremely excited.

Negative symptoms are aspects of normal function that schizophrenia impairs. These include

Table 42.1. Typical descriptors of abnormal thought forms in schizophrenia

Thought Disorder	Description
Derailment	Loss of meaning due to random connections or loose associations between ideas
Tangential	Responses to questions are only partially or remotely connected to the topic
Circumstantial	Excessively detailed or circuitous speech, yet still responsive to the question
Neologism	Creation of words with unique meaning understood only by the individual (e.g., "predentity" or "tragement")
Blocking	Losing track of the goal of speech and not being able to return to the topic
Word salad	Complete disregard for conventions of word usage or grammar, incoherence
Clanging	The sounds of words, instead of the meanings or conventions of speech, determine the flow of speech
Perseveration	Repetition of words or phrases

disturbances of affect or emotional tone (e.g., flat, blunted, or labile affect), *poverty of speech* (alogia), *inability to experience pleasure* (anhedonia), *lack of motivation* (avolition), and *social withdrawal* (asociality). Though less dramatic than positive symptoms, negative symptoms are typically persistent and often account for much of the actual disability of schizophrenia.

Cognitive symptoms can be subtle or dramatic deficits in higher intellectual or executive functions. These often impair adaptive function and decision making. They include *impaired focus and attention* and marked *deficits in working memory*, or the inability to use recently learned information. Cognitive symptoms may make tasks of everyday life difficult and affect the patient's ability to work or study.

Natural History of Schizophrenia and Making the Diagnosis

What is the natural history of schizophrenia?

Schizophrenia typically first appears in adolescence or young adulthood, rarely beyond age 40. The usual course proceeds through three distinct phases: *prodromal*, *active*, and *residual* (see Table 42.2). The prodrome of subtle peculiarity of

Table 42.2 Phases of schizophrenia

Phase	Features
Prodromal	Gradual change in behavior that may appear as personality or mood change (aloofness, preoccupation, moodiness, oddities of thought or behavior) lasting weeks to months.
Active	Classic findings of delusions, hallucinations, disorganized thinking and behavior. May include agitation, sleeplessness, and dangerous behaviors.
Residual	Continuing oddities of thinking and behavior, often with prominent negative and cognitive symptoms. Delusions or hallucinations are typically absent.

thought, social oddity, and diminished motivation often begins in adolescence or early adulthood. Most patients begin treatment in the active phase, when psychotic symptoms appear. The residual phase, when negative and cognitive symptoms persist, may be punctuated by recurrences of active psychosis or relapse.

The most recent *Diagnostic and Statistical Manual of Mental Disorders, 5th edition* (DSM-5) did not change the fundamental diagnostic criteria for schizophrenia listed in previous editions. It did, however, eliminate traditional diagnostic subtypes, for lack of validity. Very few patients clearly fall into one of the defined subtypes. The 10th edition of the *International Statistical Classification of Diseases and Related Health Problems* (ICD-10) still lists subtypes (hebephrenic, catatonic, paranoid, undifferentiated), but its other diagnostic criteria overlap with DSM-5.

To receive a diagnosis of schizophrenia, a patient has to describe or display:

I. *Two or more* of the following symptoms in the active phase of the illness (*one of these symptoms is required):
    1. delusions*
    2. hallucinations*
    3. disorganized speech*
    4. grossly disorganized or catatonic behavior
    5. negative symptoms
II. The diagnosis of schizophrenia also requires that the symptom fulfill the criteria of
    1. an active phase with prominent psychotic symptoms lasting > 1 month, unless symptoms are interrupted by effective treatment; and
    2. continuous signs of the disturbance persisting at least 6 months.

In cross section, many types of psychosis can resemble the acute phase of schizophrenia. Various factors including temporal association with mood findings, inciting factors in the history (e.g., active substance use), and family history may differentiate schizophrenia from other conditions with psychotic symptoms. The mental and behavioral effects of persistent endocrine or nutritional deficiencies, neurological disorders, central nervous system infections, drug or alcohol abuse, and structural brain abnormality are some of the possible causes of symptoms appearing as schizophrenia that should be ruled out during initial evaluation.

Etiology of Schizophrenia: Gene–Environment Interaction

> **What factors have been hypothesized to contribute to the etiology of schizophrenia?**

Research implicates both *genetic* and *environmental* factors in the etiology of schizophrenia. The concordance rate for developing schizophrenia is 45% to 65% in monozygotic twins and 10% in first-degree relatives. The genetic factors are thought to be multiple genes of small effect. Known contributing environmental factors include birth injury or intrauterine malnutrition, fetal exposure to cytokines, or infections in the second trimester. Research continues to uncover other possible causal factors – either specific genes or experiences in prenatal and postnatal development.

Although no single biological abnormality is diagnostic, major *neuroanatomical changes* have been observed repeatedly in some or most brains of schizophrenic patients. These include decreased metabolic activity in the *frontal lobes*; thinning of the medial *temporal lobe cortex*, the *frontal cortex*, and small anterior portions of the *hippocampus*; and correspondingly enlarged *lateral and third cerebral ventricles.*

While most cases of schizophrenia begin in early adulthood, longitudinal studies of populations at risk find subtle problems well before classic symptoms appear. These findings suggest that schizophrenia is a *neurodevelopmental* disorder. Various brain regions, especially the human prefrontal cortex, continue to develop into adolescence and early adulthood. A prenatal or perinatal genetic or environmental insult to the still-developing brain could cause a cascade of negative neurobiological effects that do not produce overt symptoms until the person reaches the stage of adult level competencies in cognitive tasks. Some histological findings related to the effects of schizophrenia susceptibility genes support this hypothesis. Problems stemming from faulty neuronal proliferation, migration, or synapse formation in late-maturing areas of the prefrontal cortex and hippocampus or disordered connections in the circuits between them seem part of a neurocognitive system that is impaired in schizophrenia. Abnormal neuronal development in the prefrontal association areas, in particular, may account for the negative symptoms of impaired executive functioning and planning.

While research focuses on brain circuits and genetic vulnerabilities, current treatment targets neurochemical abnormalities. Drugs that relieve positive symptoms all block the dopamine DA-2 receptors. This finding underlies the so called **dopamine hypothesis of schizophrenia**, which suggests that increased activity of dopamine (DA) in subcortical mesolimbic brain regions produces positive symptoms, while hypofunction or alterations of DA and other neurotransmitter systems in the prefrontal cortex correspond to negative and cognitive symptoms. New antipsychotic drugs manipulate serotonin (5-HT) activity to partially correct an imbalance in the complex, interrelated chemical reactions of the brain involving the neurotransmitters 5-HT, gamma-amino-butyric acid (GABA), and glutamate as well as DA. Recent research has suggested that hypofunctioning of the glutamate system in the prefrontal cortex may be an etiological factor in schizophrenia. Low doses of antagonists of the glutamatergic N-methyl D-aspartate (NMDA) receptor given to healthy volunteers produce aspects of schizophrenia, including problems of attention and memory.

The search for biologically defined disease characteristics has promoted novel ways of studying the underlying pathophysiology of psychosis. Such studies look beyond clinical phenomenology to identify specific categories called *biotypes*. Biotypes are based upon genomic patterns, behavioral dimensions, psychological traits, or brain imaging findings. Multiple biological pathways may lead to phenomenologically similar presentations of psychosis, much like fever or congestive heart failure stem from multiple pathologies.

As an example, a recent study found that psychoses in schizophrenia, schizoaffective disorder, and bipolar disorder with psychosis could be divided into three different biotypes using biomarkers of cognitive control and sensorimotor reactivity. Each biotype could be found within the traditional symptom-based diagnostic criteria. Subjects of one biotype had more brain abnormalities and greater functional impairment. The unaffected first-degree relatives of patients with another biotype had similar but fewer abnormalities in cognitive control, sensorimotor reactivity, social function, and brain structure. This suggests that, in the future, structural and functional brain biomarkers may be able to separate patients with psychosis into groups that are neurobiologically distinct.

Treatment of Schizophrenia

Antipsychotic medications relieve positive symptoms but do not improve negative or cognitive symptoms to the same degree. All have significant adverse effects and risks (see Chapter 52: Pharmacological Interventions for Psychiatric Disorders).

Psychosocial interventions remain essential in treating schizophrenia. Empathetic and consistent psychiatric care fosters adherence to medication and treatment of patients' concurrent medical complications and conditions. Evidence-supported psychosocial interventions include teaching illness management skills, addressing co-occurring substance abuse, rehabilitation to preserve or enhance social and vocational skills, family education, and cognitive behavior therapy. People whose schizophrenia has driven them into homelessness, or who are at risk of becoming homeless, need special attention. Well-designed studies show that early provision of individual or group housing ("housing first") coupled with social services, reduces hospitalizations and the overall costs of care. New funding is needed to pay for social interventions that are not covered by health insurance but are critical to recovery, relapse prevention, and limiting chronic disability.

Prognosis Outlook in Schizophrenia

Prior to the development of effective antipsychotic agents, multiple recurrences, unremitting psychoses, and gradual deterioration of mental and social abilities leading to institutionalization were common. Today the acute phase of the illness almost always remits within a few days or weeks after treatment begins. However, periods of acute psychosis recur for most patients unless maintenance treatment with antipsychotic medications continues. The prognosis for recovery, supported or independent community living, and employment is better than it once was. However, sustained recovery occurs in < 4% of patients within 5 years of diagnosis; an additional 16% of patients show late-phase recovery.

Emerging research has focused attention on the time preceding even the prodromal period, in the belief that the earlier at-risk individuals can be introduced to treatment, the better their long-term prognosis. Newly established diagnostic research criteria attempt to identify youth at ultra-high risk for psychosis. While results to date have been somewhat inconsistent, longitudinal studies suggest that within 3 years, a third of those identified as high risk will develop a psychotic disorder or have a psychotic break. The remaining two thirds go on to develop a variety of mental health problems later in life. Given the risks of antipsychotic medications in people who may never become psychotic, research currently supports intensive individual cognitive behavioral therapy as the first line treatment for people at high risk who are not yet ill. The more the criteria for risk can be refined, the greater the possibility for delaying or even preventing the onset of a devastating condition.

Psychotic Disorders Other Than Schizophrenia

> What are four psychotic disorders other than schizophrenia?

People with **schizophreniform disorder** display all of the cardinal manifestations, but recover in less than the 6 months required for the diagnosis of schizophrenia (Table 42.3). Family history of schizophrenia is less common than in patients with schizophrenia, but more common than in the general population. The prognosis for full recovery is better than in schizophrenia.

Schizoaffective disorder mixes elements of schizophrenia and depression or bipolar disorder, each of which can run different courses. The condition is divided into subtypes (1) bipolar type and (2) depressive type. Schizophrenia and bipolar disorder appear to share genetic roots; the overlap in the genetic risk for both disorders may explain this "in-between" diagnosis. The prognosis for functional recovery in schizoaffective disorder is somewhat better than for schizophrenia.

Delusional disorder involves an isolated nonbizarre delusion of a persecutory, jealous, somatic, or

Table 42.3. Differentiating schizoaffective disorder from related conditions

	Schizoaffective Disorder	Bipolar Disorder or Depression With Psychotic Features	Schizophrenia
Mood symptoms	Mania or major depression occur, accompanied by psychotic symptoms	Mania or major depression occur, accompanied by psychotic symptoms	Excitement or dysphoria may occur but not as identifiable episodes of mania or depression
Course of illness	Psychotic symptoms persist > 2 weeks when mood symptoms are not present	Psychotic symptoms remit when mood improves	Mood symptoms occupy less of total illness time
Treatments (all require antipsychotic medication in the active phase and significant psychosocial interventions)	Maintenance with both antipsychotic and mood-stabilizing medication	Maintenance with mood-stabilizing medication or antidepressants	Maintenance with antipsychotic medication

grandiose type. Organization of thought, personality, and social functioning remain relatively unaffected. Onset is typically later in life than with schizophrenia, schizophreniform disorder, or schizoaffective disorder. Antipsychotics and serotonin-specific antidepressants (selective serotonin reuptake inhibitors [SSRIs]) have been used alone and in combination, with variable success. The persecutory subtype is particularly resistant to treatment.

Brief psychotic disorder is a transient psychosis that develops suddenly, usually after a highly stressful life event. It remits rapidly with minimum intervention, and does not typically develop a pattern of recurrence. Treatment is symptomatic, generally including a brief course of antipsychotic or antianxiety medication.

Recommended Readings

Clementz, B. A., Sweeney, J. A., Hamm, J. P., Ivleva, E. I., Ethridge, L. E., Pearlson, G. D., ... Tamminga, C. A. (2016). Identification of distinct psychosis biotypes using brain-based biomarkers. *American Journal of Psychiatry, 173*(4), 373–384. http://doi.org/10.1176/appi.ajp.2015.14091200

Fusari-Poli, P., Borgwardt, S., Bechdolf, A., Addington, J., Riecher-Rössler, A., Schultze-Lutter, F., ... Yung, A. (2013). The psychosis high-risk state: A comprehensive state-of-the-art review. *JAMA Psychiatry, 70*(1), 107–120. http://doi.org/10.1001/jamapsychiatry.2013.269

Lieberman, J. A. (2005). Effectiveness of antipsychotic drugs in patients with chronic schizophrenia. *New England Journal of Medicine, 353*, 1209–1223. http://doi.org/10.1056/NEJMoa051688

Special edition on schizophrenia. (2010). *Nature, 468*(7321).

Torrey, E. F. (2014). *Surviving schizophrenia: A family manual* (6th ed.). New York, NY: HarperCollins e-Books.

Review Questions

1. A 35-year-old man presents with bizarre delusions, auditory hallucinations, disorganized thinking, insomnia, and agitation. These changes in personality and behavior began nearly a year ago when he lost his job. He became obviously ill in the last month, but resisted evaluation until he assaulted his wife. Neurological examination, screening laboratory tests, urine drug screen, and substance use history are negative. The most likely diagnosis is

A. bipolar disorder, manic phase, with psychotic features
B. brief psychotic disorder
C. major depression with psychotic features
D. schizophrenia
E. schizophreniform disorder

2. Which of the following symptoms of psychosis would be most responsive to treatment with antipsychotic medication?
A. Delusions
B. Depressed mood
C. Negative symptoms
D. Social withdrawal
E. Thought disorder

3. In the last 6 months, a 50-year-old, employed woman has become convinced that relatives are swindling her out of her savings. Her bank manager found no evidence to support her contention. A comprehensive medical work-up shows no evidence of medical or neurological disease, dementia, or substance abuse. She has no signs of a thought disorder. Relationships with people other than family are intact. The most likely diagnosis is
A. brief psychotic disorder
B. delusional disorder
C. major depression with psychotic features
D. schizophrenia
E. schizophreniform disorder

4. Which group of symptoms characterizes the prodromal phase of schizophrenia?
A. Agitation, insomnia, negative thinking
B. Delusions, hallucinations, disorganized behavior
C. Disorganized thinking, hallucinations, loss of appetite
D. Odd behaviors, aloofness, preoccupation
E. Posturing, mechanical speech, agitation

Answer Key on p. 466

43 Depressive and Bipolar Disorders

Rory P. Houghtalen, MD, and Ryan F. Houghtalen, BS, RN

- What are the features of depressive disorders?
- What is known about the neurobiology of the depressive syndrome?
- What principles govern the treatment of depression?
- What are the elements of bipolar and related disorders?

Depression

A 25-year-old taxi driver, formerly a model employee, is on probation due to chronic lateness and complaints from customers that he is impatient, surly, and distracted. His urine toxicology screen is negative. He admits to poor sleep, often feeling uncomfortably anxious, and being unable to enjoy anything for months.

A 75-year-old, retired professor in generally good health loses interest in her lifelong field of study. She complains of profound fatigue, loss of appetite, and feeling sad but is unable to cry. She feels useless, and thinks that her husband and children might be better off without her.

The ancients recognized a pattern of intense mood having features of both despair and fear. In the 5th century BC, Hippocrates described "aversion to food, despondency, sleeplessness, irritability, restlessness" and said that "fear or depression that is prolonged means melancholia." Samuel Johnson, an 18th-century lexicographer who suffered two bouts of despair, coined the term *depression* to connote a discrete illness. In the early 20th century, Emil Kraepelin observed that depression could alternate with states of elevated mood or mania, describing manic-depressive illness. The *Diagnostic and Statistical Manual of Mental Disorders, 5th edition* (DSM-5) classifies various forms of these conditions in the domains of depressive disorders or bipolar disorders.

Beyond extreme moods, disruptions in neurobiological homeostatic functions, cognition, and behavior characterize affective disorders. By definition, these conditions lead to considerable distress and functional failures.

What are the features of depressive disorders?

Sadness is a universal human response to loss, defeat, or other adversity. Depression differs from normal sadness in degree and kind. Persistent deprivation and frustration, or a major life stressor (e.g., bereavement, traumatic events, failure, and major transitions such as divorce or unemployment) may predate a first or second episode of depression, but recurrences may develop in the absence of an identifiable stressor. Some controversy surrounds the inclusion of bereavement as a stressor that may precipitate depression, since bereavement is a normal human experience. Criteria in earlier versions of the DSM cautioned against making the diagnosis during the first 2 months of bereavement, but duration alone does not distinguish normal and abnormal responses. DSM-5 allows for the diagnosis of major depression in early bereavement, leaving it to clinical judgment to differentiate normal responses from patterns suggesting illness and potentially justifying treatment (see Chapter 47: Stress Disorders, Bereavement, and Dissociative Disorders).

Once present, the symptoms of a **major depressive episode** are relatively unresponsive to external influence. Depression, as an illness, often results in withdrawal from others and from usual interests. It reduces the ability to experience pleasure (anhedonia). The illness typically disrupts sleep, appetite, and sexual function. It colors thoughts with negativity, guilt, and self-reproach; affects cognition and memory (notably in older persons); and often produces helplessness and hopelessness that may progress to suicidal despair.

DSM-5 offers diagnostic criteria for seven principal mood disorders: *major depressive disorder* (MDD), *persistent depressive disorder* (PDD), *premenstrual dysphoric disorder* (PMDD), *disruptive mood dysregulation disorder* (DMDD), and (in a separate section) *bipolar I, bipolar II,* and *cyclothymic disorder.* Major depressive episodes occur in the course of most of these conditions.

The DSM-5 definition of a major depressive episode specifies the presence of depressed mood and/or anhedonia (or irritability in children or adolescents) for a minimum of 2 weeks, accompanied by additional symptoms. To "meet the criteria," patients must describe at least five of the possible nine criterion features.

Box 43.1. SIG E CAPS

S = Sleep (insomnia or hypersomnia)

I = Reduced interest in usual activities (anhedonia)

G = Guilt (may reach delusional proportions)

E = Energy-Fatigue (most common presenting complaint in primary care settings)

C = Reduced concentration/attention; cognitive slowing and ineffective processing

A = Appetites (loss of interest in eating or sexual activity), may include weight loss. Overeating and weight gain may occur in the atypical subtype

P = Pleasure/Psychomotor change – Reduced capacity for pleasure (anhedonia); psychomotor change may be slowing (retardation, "leaden paralysis"), or agitation

S = Suicidal ideation or behavior

The mnemonic **SIG E CAPS** (see Box 43.1) encapsulates the main criteria for major depression. The same symptoms, coupled with measures of severity, are covered on the Patient Health Questionnaire-9 (PHQ-9), a measure used to

---

Table 43.1. Subtypes of depression and their significance

Specifier	Condition to Which Diagnosis Applies	Characteristics	Significance
Atypical features	MDD or PDD	Hypersomnia, hyperphagia or significant weight gain, marked psychomotor retardation called "leaden paralysis" Relatively preserved reactivity (difficulty initiating pleasurable activity, but may respond to it) Sensitivity to rejection	More common in seasonal depression, depression in the course of bipolar disorder, and in women Many studies support MAOIs as first line treatments for this presentation, but clinically they are harder to use than SSRIs
Psychotic features	MDD	Mood congruent delusions or hallucinations (accusatory voices or voices commanding suicide often a single word or phrase); delusions of poverty, illness, nihilism, guilt	Treatment requires both antipsychotic and antidepressant medication Electroconvulsive therapy (ECT) may be surest and most rapidly effective treatment Psychotherapy not a primary treatment

Table 43.1. (continued)

Specifier	Condition to Which Diagnosis Applies	Characteristics	Significance
Melancholic features	MDD	Minimal if any response to pleasurable events (anhedonia); early morning awakening; diurnal variation, mornings worse Significant psychomotor retardation or activation, loss of appetite and/or weight, excessive or inappropriate guilt	Not responsive to psychotherapy Possibly more predictable response to dual-acting or tricyclic antidepressants Responds to ECT
Catatonic features	MDD, BPD	Prominent psychomotor signs: immobility, odd posturing, dramatic excitement Mutism and negativism	Antipsychotic medication or ECT required; some patients respond briefly to benzodiazepines
Peripartum onset	MDD	Depressive episode occurring during pregnancy or within weeks or few months after Often associated with severe anxiety and obsessive-compulsive symptoms May include psychotic features	Frequently recurrent Mild to moderate forms respond to serotonergic antidepressants, psychotherapy Psychotic features raise the risk of suicide or infanticide and usually require hospitalization, antipsychotic or mood stabilizing medication Responsive to ECT
Seasonal pattern	MDD, BPD	Episodes in fall-winter that often have atypical features; non-seasonal episodes may occur	Bright light therapy effective in uncomplicated, seasonal MDD Responds to SSRIs, bupropion Light may precipitate hypomania or mania
Mixed features	MDD, BPD, PDD	Episodes that have features of the other mood pole during an index mood episode	Mixed features do not require the diagnosis of BPD when present during a depressive episode
Anxious distress	MDD, PDD, BPD	Two or more significant physical or cognitive features of anxiety that are present during the majority of days of the mood disturbance	Suicide risk is heightened when anxiety is severe Treatment with an antianxiety agent can mitigate symptoms before an antidepressant or mood-stabilizing agent takes effect

Note. BPD = bipolar disorder; ECT = electroconvulsive therapy; MAOIs = monoamine oxidase inhibitors; MDD = major depressive disorder; PDD = persistent depressive disorder; SSRIs = selective serotonin reuptake inhibitors.

rate severity and monitor treatment outcome in research and clinical settings.

The mnemonic does not capture other important elements of depression such as the helpless and hopeless thinking that often precedes suicidal ideation or suicidal behavior, or the presence of psychotic symptoms.

More than 100 combinations of symptoms might fulfill the criteria for a major depressive episode. Subtypes coded as specifiers organize the possibilities into recognizable patterns, supported by current research (Table 43.1). To further complicate diagnosis, the presentation of depression varies across the lifespan and between genders. Irritable and fluctuating moods characterize the condition in children and adolescents. Older adults may have prominent complaints of poor concentration and decreased memory (dementia syndrome of depression). When depressed, men are often more irritable and women more anxious. DSM-5 lists three depressive disorders, which may or may not include a discrete depressive syndrome.

Persistent Depressive Disorder

In persistent depressive disorder (PDD), which combines former dysthymic disorder/chronic major depressive disorder, depressed mood has persisted most of the day, for more days than not, for ≥ 2 years in adults and for > 1 year in adolescents. Irritability may replace depressed mood in children and adolescents. In PDD, the core mood is associated with two or more symptoms typical in MDD. Although symptoms are of lower amplitude than those in MDD, the persistent negative mood is distressing and may compromise school or work performance and complicate relationships.

Premenstrual Dysphoric Disorder

Considered a syndrome of research interest prior to DSM-5, the diagnosis **premenstrual dysphoric disorder** (PMDD) now applies to women experiencing ≥ 5 of the 11 characteristic symptoms in the week before menses, along with one or more of the following: rapidly shifting affects, irritability, depressed mood, hopelessness or self-critical thoughts, anxiety, tension, or feeling keyed up and on edge. In addition, the patient must endorse

one or more physical complaints: breast tenderness, muscle or joint pain, bloating, lethargy, sleep disturbance, increase in appetite with excessive eating or cravings. The criteria require 2 months of prospective ratings of mood and associated symptoms.

Such extraordinary rigor in making the diagnosis is meant to avoid pathologizing normal female menstrual experience. Labeling women as having a "mental disorder" has potentially unintended consequences in matters such as professional licensure and credentialing, qualifying for life insurance, and child custody disputes. Nevertheless, the diagnosis of PMDD is based on solid research and has important treatment implications (see below).

Disruptive Mood Dysregulation Disorder

Disruptive mood dysregulation disorder (DMDD), a syndrome in youths aged 6 to 18 years (onset must occur before age 10), is characterized by frequent and severe temper outbursts for 12 months or more, inconsistent with the child's developmental level. In between episodes, the child's mood is irritable or angry. DSM-5 classifies DMDD as a depressive disorder in light of prospective research showing that these symptoms are more likely to evolve into adult depressive or anxiety disorders than into bipolar disorder, as some observers initially predicted.

Controversies continue to surround DMDD. Being relatively new, little can be said about evidence-based treatment. Even if the symptoms do predict adult disorders, medications used in adults may affect children and adolescents differently, as shown by the association between suicidal ideation and the use of selective serotonin reuptake inhibitors (SSRIs) in adolescents. Whether or when young people should receive treatments developed for adults is an important question for future research.

Differential Diagnosis

Beyond subtypes within the diagnosis of depression, current classifications draw boundaries between depression and conditions with related symptoms. Anxiety and anxiety disorders may develop during the course of depression, precede it, or continue after resolution (*anxious distress specifier*). Depressive episodes occurring in the course of bipolar disorders, which by definition also involve mania or hypomania, have distinct treatment implications (see section "Key Issues in the Treatment of Bipolar Disorder").

Bizarre delusions or complex hallucinations occurring outside of an extreme mood state would warrant consideration of the diagnosis of schizoaffective disorder or schizophrenia (see Chapter 42: Schizophrenia and Other Psychotic Disorders). The presence of psychotic symptoms in the course of a mood disorder indicates a condition that requires the use of antipsychotic medication and/or electroconvulsive therapy (ECT).

Depression, bipolar depression, and mania all may be diagnosed as secondary syndromes. DSM-5 provides diagnoses for *substance/medication-induced* mood syndromes and mood syndromes *due to another medical condition*. Prescribed medications, regular alcohol use, and street drugs may produce symptoms and signs of depression, mania, or hypomania. Endocrine disorders, especially elevations or deficiencies of thyroid hormones or corticosteroids, may cause mood episodes or, in some cases, may develop during an episode. Other conditions associated with mood disorders include autoimmune disorders, vitamin D deficiency, systemic infections, head trauma, epilepsy, kidney disease, liver disease, pancreatic cancer, diffuse vascular disease, dementing disorders, and, rarely, inborn errors of metabolism (e.g., porphyria), neurodegenerative disease (e.g., Parkinson's disease), stroke, or space-occupying lesions in the brain.

It is not necessary or cost effective to rule out every possible medical cause in every depressed patient. In many cases, initial evaluation includes a metabolic panel, complete blood count, and thyroid function tests. More specific tests should be considered if the presentation or exam uncovers risk factors or signs or symptoms that suggest other conditions.

DSM-5 provides *other specified* and *other unspecified* depressive and bipolar disorder diagnoses for symptoms that do not meet full criteria for the principal diagnoses but may still be the focus of clinical attention. Adjustment disorder with depressed mood is another related condition (see Chapter 47: Stress Disorders, Bereavement, and Dissociative Disorders).

What is known about the neurobiology of the depressive syndrome?

Neuroanatomical findings in rigorously diagnosed depressive episodes include reduced prefrontal cortical activity (*hypofrontality*), as measured by positron emission tomography (PET) scans, and abnormalities in prefrontal cortex regulation of limbic system structures, including those involved in the retrieval of memory. This may be why seriously depressed people are often flooded with memories of past failures or losses and have trouble accessing memories that counteract their sense of inadequacy or hopelessness.

The hypothalamic-pituitary-adrenal/end organ (HPA) axis also functions abnormally in severe depression, which may be marked by a loss of normal diurnal variation in cortisol secretion (especially in the melancholic subtype). Hypothalamic dysfunction presumably contributes to vegetative symptoms such as changes in appetite, sleep, and sexual interest.

The HPA axis also regulates the normal flux of estrogen and progesterone in women across the menstrual cycle. Estrogen and serotonin activity rise and fall together in the nervous system by a variety of mechanisms. This finding may partly explain the heightened risk for mood disorders in women during the reproductive years (15 to 45), and the vulnerability to mood and anxiety disorders of a minority of women during periods of normal but marked hormonal flux (premenstrually, postpartum, and during the perimenopause). Hormone function is typically normal and not itself a focus of treatment in these conditions.

Neurochemical findings inferred from the response to antidepressants include dysregulated activity of monoamine neurotransmitters, especially serotonin, norepinephrine, and dopamine. Monoamines, especially dopamine, are known to mediate the experience of pleasure or reward, which are often impaired in depression.

Basic and epidemiological research also associates depressive symptoms with nutritional factors, including the balance of omega-6 and omega-3 free fatty acids and vitamin D deficiency. These findings justify the incorporation of free fatty acids and vitamin D replacement in some treatment protocols, particularly those protocols designed to treat mood conditions that do not respond to usual interventions.

Aberrations in biomarkers, such as C-reactive protein, and elevated cytokines, such as interleukin-6, found in some studies, suggest that inflammatory processes may be involved in the pathogenesis of depression. Other neuroactive substances, including gamma-amino-butyric acid (GABA)/glutamate, endorphins, and endocannabinoids and their receptors, may play a role in mood syndromes.

Psychosocial factors interact with biology. Integrative studies have demonstrated that life stressors, such as early parental loss, are associated with epigenetic changes. These modifications of gene expression produce neurobiological alterations that may explain the correlation between an early stressor and the emergence of mood disorders later in life.

Epidemiology of Depression

According to the World Health Organization, MDD and PDD together rank as the second leading cause of disability worldwide. Epidemiological estimates vary, but about 6% of patients in primary care meet current criteria for a depressive episode. One in eight people (about 12%) will need treatment for depression at some point in life. Overall, lifetime prevalence is about 20%. After puberty, cases in women outnumber men by nearly 2:1. Lifetime prevalence of depression is about 25% for women, 15% for men. Having a first-degree relative with a history of MDD elevates lifetime risk twofold.

Depressive disorders are associated with increased morbidity and poorer outcomes in coexisting diabetes and cardiovascular disease, making depression an important driver of health care costs. The costs of depression also include reduced work productivity, in both patients and family caregivers. Furthermore, depression may affect the health and well-being of others in the family, especially dependent children or older persons. At least 10% of women develop depression in pregnancy or the postpartum period; severe maternal depression may affect the developing fetus and postnatal infant development. These findings justify widespread public health efforts to improve case recognition and to promote the use of effective treatments.

The US Preventive Services Task Force recommends screening for depression in adolescents, adults, and people over 65, if resources are available to provide treatment. Universal screening for depression during pregnancy and postpartum is also recommended. Providers may now bill for annual depression screening under Medicare. The PHQ-9 may also be used in monitoring treatment response (measurement-based care). The Edinburgh Postnatal Depression Scale (EPDS) screens for depression in pregnant and postpartum women.

Treatment of Depression

What principles govern the treatment of depression?

Chapter 40 (Principles of Psychotherapy) and Chapter 52 (Pharmacological Interventions for Psychiatric Disorders) describe the use of psychotherapy and medication for depression, respectively. The majority of cases are treated outside of formal mental health settings. Colocation of general medical and mental health services, protocols for stepped care, rapid availability of consultation, good communication among providers, use of rating scales to track response, and monitoring medication adherence improve treatment outcomes.

The treatment of depression in any setting involves careful application of available knowledge to minimize risk and maximize benefit.

1. All patients who present with symptoms of a major depressive episode should be screened for psychotic features and for a history of hypomania or mania. Depression with psychotic or catatonic features does not respond to psychotherapy. An antidepressant and an antipsychotic or ECT are needed. In people with bipolar disorder or a family history suggesting risks for bipolar disorder, antidepressants may precipitate mania or rapid mood cycling, especially in women.

2. Mild to moderate major depression may respond to depression-specific psychotherapies including cognitive behavioral therapy, interpersonal psychotherapy, brief dynamic therapy, and problem-solving therapy.

3. Psychotic depression does not respond to psychotherapy alone, and melancholic features predict responsiveness to somatic treatments (antidepressants and ECT).

4. Some cases of depression are candidates for transcranial magnetic stimulation (TMS), or vagal nerve stimulation (VNS), where available.

5. Treatment with antidepressants typically takes 4 to 6 weeks to establish full effects (response latency). The Sequenced Treatment Alternatives to Relieve Depression (STAR*D) study demonstrated the value of waiting 8 weeks or more after achieving a threshold therapeutic dose, or following an upward dose titration.

6. When an antidepressant trial of maximal dose and adequate duration does not induce remission, augmentation with other medications such as lithium, triiodothyronine, or buspirone may be needed. Some atypical antipsychotics are US Food and Drug Administration (FDA) approved for this indication. Of possible adjunctive treatments, lithium has the lowest number needed to treat (NNT) of 3 to 4. The STAR*D study found that switching antidepressants or using an augmenting medication were essentially equal in achieving remission.

7. Achieving remission, sometimes defined as a PHQ-9 score < 5, is the primary goal of acute phase treatment. The probability of a first antidepressant trial inducing remission is about 30%. Failure to achieve remission has been associated with the development of chronic disability, general health, and heightened suicide risk over time. Patients in medication trials should be followed closely (weekly or every other week) until remission to monitor progress, medication adherence, and suicide risk. Psychotherapy usually involves weekly sessions until remission.

8. Continuation phase: The goal of continuation treatment is to prevent early relapse. The antidepressant that leads to remission should be continued at the same dose for a period of no less than 6 months and optimally a year from remission. Use may continue indefinitely if maintenance is indicated. Less frequent but ongoing sessions of psychotherapy are indicated during the continuation phase.

9. Maintenance phase: MDD is a highly recurrent disorder. The risk of recurrence after a first episode is at least 50%, rising to 70% and 90% after the second and third episodes, respectively. Some patients with two, and all patients with three, episodes are candidates for maintenance antidepressant treatment, using the same antidepressant dose that achieved remission. Psychotherapy "booster" sessions can improve maintenance outcomes.

10. Discontinuation phase: Slow tapering of most antidepressants is recommended to prevent uncomfortable effects: flu-like symptoms, dizziness, and sometimes shock-like sensations in limbs ("zaps"). Seeing a patient several times following treatment may be advisable to assess for relapse or recurrence.

Subjects in all of the studies alluded to above had documented major depressive episodes. Because PDD is a new concept, little can be said confidently about its epidemiology, treatment, or course. When PDD results from insufficiently treated major depression, intensifying efforts to induce remission may be appropriate. Historically, chronic low-grade depression has been treated with both psychotherapy and anti-depressants, with variable benefit. Compared with MDD, the prognosis for full remission is less optimistic, yet remission should still be the goal.

The principle of response latency may not apply in PMDD, which sometimes responds to intermittent or pulsed use of an SSRI. Fluoxetine is FDA approved for such use. Pulsed use of a benzodiazepine anxiolytic such as alprazolam may also be effective.

Bipolar and Related Disorders

What are the elements of bipolar and related disorders?

A 42-year-old nurse seems uncharacteristically cheerful and energetic. He volunteers for extra night shifts and says he does not need sleep anymore. He moves and talks quickly, has multiple ideas for projects but cannot complete them. He tries to direct and control the work of others, but his judgment seems impaired.

Table 43.2. Features differentiating mania from hypomania

Feature	Mania	Hypomania
Duration	7 days, unless effective treatment alters mood state	4 days, unless effective treatment alters mood state
Psychotic features	Yes	No
Severity of functional failures	Greater	Lesser
Hospitalization required during acute episode[1]	Yes	No

Note. [1]This is a problematic criterion because factors other than severity may determine decisions about hospital admission.

While major depressive episodes typically occur in bipolar disorder, episodes of mania or hypomania are required for diagnosis. DSM-5 offers three principal bipolar diagnoses: *bipolar I disorder* (BPD-I), *bipolar II disorder* (BPD-II), and *cyclothymic disorder* (CD).

Mania and hypomania are states of elevated or irritable mood, coupled with excessive speech, thought, and behavioral activity; novelty seeking; and impulsive pleasure seeking (Table 43.2). In diagnosing a bipolar disorder, one must first establish whether the patient's current mood state is manic or hypomanic; or if the person presents with depression, the history must reveal past manic or hypomanic episodes. BPD-I requires a history of at least one manic episode. The diagnosis of BPD-II is based on episodes of depression and hypomania in the absence of mania.

The mnemonic DIG FAST covers the cardinal symptoms and signs of mania and hypomania.

DIG FAST

In addition to markedly elevated and/or intensely irritable mood, these features are typically prominent:

D = Distractibility and easy frustration
I = Irresponsibility and erratic, uninhibited behavior
G = Grandiosity
F = Flight of ideas
A = Activity increased, including sexually
S = Sleep decreased
T = Talkativeness increased

Patients who are manic usually lack insight into their condition. Obtaining consent to gather information from a third party (spouse or parent)

Table 43.3. Selected causes of manic/hypomanic symptoms or syndrome

Disorder or Exposure	Examples
Drugs and other substances	Intoxication with cocaine or other stimulants, hallucinogens, PCP, synthetic marijuana, Ecstasy and other "designer" drugs, corticosteroids, anabolic steroids, baclofen withdrawal, abuse of prescribed stimulants
Endocrine disorders	Hyperthyroidism, hypercortisolism, porphyria
Infectious diseases	Tertiary syphilis, encephalitis and post-encephalitic syndromes, HIV
Neurodegenerative and demyelinating diseases	Dementing disorders, multiple sclerosis, Huntington's disease
Other neurological disorders	Right fronto-temporal stroke, traumatic brain injury, cerebral tumors
Neoplastic syndromes	Carcinomatosis
Other disorders	Systemic lupus erythematosus, vitamin B_{12} deficiency, postdialysis syndrome, acute psychosis postpartum

improves the accuracy of diagnosis. Differentiating mild mania, or dysphoric mania, from severe anxiety is often difficult. Hypomania, and the early phases of mania, may appear like normal positive mood with improved general functioning. Functioning typically deteriorates as mania evolves.

Like depression, mania or hypomania may occur secondary to other medical and neurological disorders or use of prescribed or illicit drugs. The medical evaluation of mania or hypomania is similar to that for depression, with special focus on urine drug screens and thyroid function tests (Table 43.3).

Bipolar I Disorder

BPD-I is diagnosed if the patient has one or more episodes of mania lasting > 7 days, unless the episode is interrupted by effective treatment. Manic mood states without depression are diagnosed as bipolar disorder, but the natural history of BPD-I typically includes one or more episodes of depression.

Psychotic features may develop in the course of a manic episode. Mood congruent psychotic features include delusions of power, influence, special powers (grandiosity), and auditory hallucinations congruent with the mood state.

The annual prevalence of BPD-I in the US is around 0.6%, or one tenth the prevalence of depression. Lifetime prevalence is about 1%, distributed equally between males and females, although females may experience more frequent episodes. Having a first-degree relative with BPD-I elevates lifetime risk to 5 to 10 times that of the general population. Strong genetic influence is indicated by a 60% to 80% rate of concordance between identical twins. In women, acute psychosis in the first week postpartum may turn out to be a first episode of BPD-I.

Depressive episodes in bipolar disorder occur more frequently, are more difficult to treat, and are more challenging to sustain in remission than unipolar depressive episodes. Most suicide attempts occur during depressive episodes. About 50% of bipolar depressive episodes meet criteria for the atypical features specifier (see Table 43.1).

Bipolar II Disorder

BPD-I may be diagnosed based on the presence of mania alone, but the diagnosis of BPD-II requires that patients experience both hypomanic and major depressive episodes. Epidemiological and family studies suggest that BPD-II is a separate disorder, not simply a variant of BPD-I. Only 5% to 15% of patients with BPD-II transition to BPD-I. Antidepressant treatment may be effective for BPD-II, in contrast to BPD-I, in which antidepressants may induce mania or accelerate cycles. International investigations of BPD-II estimate prevalence at 0.3%, while studies in the US set the figure at 0.8%, suggesting inconsistency in the application of diagnostic criteria. The risk for BPD-II disorder is greater in females.

Cyclothymic Disorder

The criteria for CD specify that, over the course of 2 years (1 year in children or adolescents), the person has experienced frequent periods of depressive or hypomanic symptoms but has not experienced a full episode of either syndrome. Symptoms, when present, must be active more than half the time, and cannot be absent for more than two consecutive months

The diagnosis of CD is controversial, because the mood states involved are difficult to distinguish from extremes of normal temperament and from mood fluctuation seen in other conditions, especially borderline personality disorder (see Chapter 51: Personality Disorders). Despite this uncertainty, lifetime prevalence of CD is estimated to be between 0.4% and 1%, equally distributed between males and females. Estimates of rate of progression to BPD-I or BPD-II vary from 15% to 50%. Evidence about treatment outcome is scarce. Empirically, providers may use antidepressants, mood stabilizing agents (such as lithium or valproic acid), and/or psychotherapy.

Controversy exists about assigning bipolar diagnoses to the broad range of moodiness or irritability, and sleep and impulse control problems. Over the last 20 years, the diagnosis of bipolar disorders has tripled in the US. This finding raises concern about how these diagnoses are commonly applied. The tendency to assign bipolar diagnoses in youth, even very young children, and the potentially hazardous overuse of medication that may follow, is of special concern.

Key Issues in the Treatment of Bipolar Disorders

Treatment for bipolar disorder differs depending on whether the goal is to relieve an acute episode of mania or depression, or to prevent recurrence of one or the other. Scientific evidence most strongly supports the use of lithium for all four aspects of bipolar treatment. It is the only agent shown to lower the suicide rate in bipolar disorder specifically (though colzapine may have this affect in the related catergory of schizoaffective disorder). However, lithium's side effects and toxicities limit its use, especially in general medical settings.

Bipolar depression is harder to treat than mania. Antidepressants are of questionable efficacy and may provoke mania or rapid cycling especially in BPD-I.

1. The presence of psychotic symptoms distinguishes mania from hypomania. Psychotic features are associated with increased risk of erratic behavior, aggression, suicide, and hospitalization.

2. Acute mania responds to lithium, valproic acid, or carbamazepine, often in conjunction with an antipsychotic. Benzodiazepines may be added for immediate sedation. The FDA has approved the atypical antipsychotics lurasidone and quetiapine, and a combination for olanzapine and fluoxetine as treatments for bipolar depression. Lithium is also effective, although this use predates the kinds of studies required for FDA approval.

3. Lithium, carbamazepine, and valproic acid all may prevent or reduce the frequency of manic episodes. Lithium and lamotrigine may prevent episodes of bipolar depression; the efficacy of valproic acid or carbamazepine in preventing bipolar depression is less well established.

4. Large-scale studies, such as the Systematic Treatment Enhancement Program for Bipolar Disorder (STEP-BD) support combining psychosocial treatment with medication.

STEP-BD evaluated cognitive behavioral therapy, interpersonal psychotherapy, social rhythm therapy (targeting sleep hygiene, providing daily structure, and reducing stress in relationships), and family-focused therapy that prevents or delays recurrences by reducing tension in close relationships. When combined with medication, psychosocial treatments shorten acute episodes, enhance functional recovery, and may delay recurrence (partly by improving patients' adherence to maintenance medication). Some of these interventions are time limited, but ongoing psychosocial support, including a consistent relationship with a provider or interdisciplinary team, may benefit people prone to regular recurrences.

Recommended Readings

American Psychiatric Association. (2013). *Diagnostic and statistical manual of mental disorders* (5th ed.). Arlington, VA: American Psychiatric Publishing. http://doi.org/10.1176/appi.books.9780890425596

Ketter, T. A., Miller, S., & Golberg, J. F. (2014). Acute and maintenance treatment of bipolar and related disorders. In G. O. Gabbard (Ed.), *Gabbard's treatment of psychiatric disorders* (5th ed., pp. 249–274). Washington, DC: APPI Books.

Niciu, M. J., Sinclair, C. M., Zarate, C. A., & Shelton, R. C. (2014). Pharmacological and somatic treatments for major depressive disorder. In G. O. Gabbard (Ed.), *Gabbard's treatment of psychiatric disorders* (5th ed., pp. 275–302). Washington, DC: APPI Books.

Shelton, R. C. (2007). The molecular neurobiology of depression. *Psychiatry Clinics of North America*, *30*, 1–11. http://doi.org/10.1016/j.psc.2006.12.005

VanMeter, A. R., Youngstrom, E. A., & Findling, R. L. (2012). Cyclothymic disorder: A critical review. *Clinical Psychology Review, 32*, 229–243. http://doi.org/10.1016/j.cpr.2012.02.001

Vohringer, P. A., & Perlis, R. H. (2016). Discriminating between bipolar disorder and major depressive disorder. *Psychiatry Clinics of North America*, *39*, 1–10. http://doi.org/10.1016/j.psc.2015.10.001

Review Questions

1. A woman with a family history of mental illness complains that her 11-year-old son is always in a bad mood. Small frustrations

trigger outbursts of yelling or tears. He has become a picky eater. Based on the behavior of his two older siblings, his mother feels he should have outgrown this kind of behavior long ago. What should the clinician tell the mother?

A. Family therapy would be useful so that the parents and older siblings use similar disciplining strategies.

B. He may benefit from psychotherapy since such children may develop anxiety disorders or depression as adults.

C. Immature behavior is not unusual in a youngest child and should not be of concern.

D. Such volatility predicts that he will develop bipolar disorder as an adult.

E. The mother should institute a program of gradual privilege restrictions to encourage more age appropriate behavior.

2. A 40-year-old woman has been taking antidepressants for 9 months to treat an episode of major depression. She was previously treated for depression at age 18, at age 23 following the birth of her second child, and again at age 25, after her mother died. The most recent episode seems unrelated to any stressor. She dreads being depressed again, but she has been in remission (PHQ-9 < 5) for 4 months and wants to know if she should stop her medication. She should be told that she

A. may stop after she has been in remission for 12 months

B. may stop at any time she feels ready

C. should continue her current medication regimen indefinitely

D. should continue her medication, at half the dose she takes currently

E. should switch to a different antidepressant with a different mechanism of action

3. A 45-year-old man with a previous manic episode now complains of reduced energy, constant regret about past choices and behaviors, and thoughts that life is not worth living. His sleep varies from day to day: Some days he cannot fall asleep at all, other days he cannot drag himself out of bed. He has been taking lithium, somewhat erratically, for about 4 years. Among the following, the treatment most likely to help him is

A. attendance at a self-help support group

B. combination of an anxiolytic and an atypical antipsychotic

C. group psychotherapy

D. prescription of a selective serotonin reuptake inhibitor

E. taking lithium regularly, with periodic blood levels to confirm adequate dosing

Answer Key on p. 466

44 **Anxiety Disorders**

Rory P. Houghtalen, MD, and Julia B. Frank, MD

- How do innate responses to perceived threat relate to anxiety disorders?
- What are the major anxiety disorders in DSM-5?
- What principles underlie the treatment of anxiety disorders?

Anxiety

On multiple unrelated occasions, a 32-year-old woman experiences a feeling of dread, accompanied by pounding heart, shortness of breath, dizziness, and restlessness. She constantly scans her body for symptoms and notes that episodes seem to be coming more often. She now avoids places where she might not be able to get to a hospital, or where she would be embarrassed by fainting or losing control. Repeated emergency room evaluations for cardiac or respiratory disease are normal but do not reassure her.

How do innate responses to perceived threat relate to anxiety disorders?

Humans' responses to adaptive challenges involve generalized arousal that primes the body and the mind to react reflexively to certain threats and to plan a response to others. Responses to external stimuli and internal cues involve brain stem centers that synthesize and release serotonin (5-HT) and norepinephrine (NE), subcortical structures (including the hypothalamus, thalamus, and amygdala), the sensory and frontal and prefrontal cortices, the autonomic nervous system, and the hypothalamic-pituitary-adrenal/end organ (HPA) axis. The activity of these systems induces cognitive, behavioral, and physiological changes.

A reflexive reaction to danger is abrupt, involuntary, and stereotypic – the fight/flight/freeze response. A more measured response involves *differentiated* reactions that allow individuals to avoid or confront perceived physical or psychological threats. The dorsolateral prefrontal cortex (DLPFC), in particular, modulates reflexive fear by assessing the source and degree of the threat.

Moderate arousal influences cortical activity, enhancing motivation and learning, as when anxiety about a pending exam sharpens focus and improves performance. Cortical modulation also prompts the weighing of positive and negative outcomes and planning in anticipation of future circumstances. Exaggerated appraisal of threat or undue preoccupation with the possibility of future danger facilitates excessive and prolonged physiological responses that impair coping, as in disabling test anxiety (see Chapter 7: Stress, Adaptation, and Stress Disorders).

Overwhelming, unduly persistent arousal or arousal in response to incorrectly appraised threats leads to maladaptive, stereotypic cognitive and behavioral responses that constitute the defining characteristics of **anxiety disorders**.

Trait anxiety describes baseline levels of arousal and thresholds for triggering acute anxiety responses. Levels of trait anxiety and the vulnerability to anxious apprehension in the face of provocative or ambiguous stimuli are heritable qualities. Individuals with anxiety disorders tend to have higher levels of trait anxiety, reduced capacity to inhibit their reactions when the anxiety cascade begins, and catastrophic misinterpretations of their anxiety experiences.

Differences in trait anxiety appear early, when unmodified genetic expression is easier to identify.

Some infants are easily soothed after experiencing stress, while the reactions of other infants are prolonged and intense. Experience modulates the expression of trait anxiety over time. Infants and children learn to appraise danger and modulate their own responses as their brain matures, and as they observe the responses and behaviors of others (social learning). Primate studies have shown that early trait anxiety, modified by experience, may foster both highly adaptive qualities (achievement, affiliation, leadership) or the development of anxiety disorders.

State anxiety is the response to a particular stimulus or situation (e.g., unexpectedly encountering a snake or learning one has a serious illness). If the stimulus is a perceived perturbation in somatic experience (e.g. awareness of skipped heartbeats, dizziness) or comes from a source that is not consciously recognized (e.g., a neutral stimulus related to a previous stressor), the manifestations of state anxiety may seem uncued, as though coming "out of the blue."

Even the "normal" bodily manifestations of state anxiety can be alarming. Individuals may develop *anticipatory fear* ("fear of the fear"). Anticipatory anxiety lowers the threshold for intense, acute responses. It is relieved (and so reinforced) by avoidance behaviors. Avoidance may generalize and become more disabling than acute anxiety itself. The criteria of most anxiety disorders include anticipatory fear and behavioral avoidance, in addition to patterns of unpleasant arousal.

The manifestations of anxiety vary by age and gender. Separation anxiety and fear of novel situations or people (stranger anxiety) normally appear around age 8 months and may last until age 2. Not surprisingly, *separation anxiety disorder* is more common in children. Fluctuating levels of anxiety are more common in women during the years of hormonal cycling – that is, women are at increased risk to develop anxiety disorders, especially panic disorder, during the reproductive years.

Major Anxiety Disorders

> What are the major anxiety disorders in DSM-5?

The seven principal anxiety disorders in the *Diagnostic and Statistical Manual of Mental Disorders, 5th edition* (DSM-5) are *specific phobia, separation anxiety disorder, selective mutism, social anxiety disorder (social phobia), panic disorder, agoraphobia,* and *generalized anxiety disorder.* For anxiety that is a recognized symptom of a medical condition such as hypoglycemia or hyperthyroidism, or anxiety related to substance or medication use, DSM-5 provides the terms *anxiety disorder secondary to (condition* or *substance).* The categories of *specified* and *unspecified anxiety disorders* apply to syndromes that do not meet full criteria for the principal diagnoses but may still require clinical attention.

As a group, anxiety disorders are the most common mental disorders. They frequently co-occur with each other and with other mental disorders, especially mood and substance use disorders. Many patients first seek treatment outside of mental health settings. People come to emergency rooms and offices of primary care, cardiology, pulmonology, neurology, and ear-nose-and-throat specialists, seeking help for the physical symptoms of anxiety.

The **symptom clusters** defining anxiety disorders encompass the following elements: (1) undue **arousal** that may be tonic, paroxysmal, or mixed; (2) **negative expectation** and interpretation of situations as ominous or overwhelming; and (3) **anticipatory anxiety** and **avoidance** of situations perceived as physically or psychologically hazardous, or likely to provoke the dreaded anxiety reaction. The focus of the anxiety and resulting pattern of cognitive, behavioral, and physiological responses differentiate one anxiety disorder from another.

Separation Anxiety Disorder

Formerly considered solely a disorder of childhood, DSM-5 now categorizes **separation anxiety disorder** as a syndrome of excessive and developmentally inappropriate fear in the face of real or anticipated separation from a person or persons to whom a person is strongly psychologically and emotionally attached. Patients experience profound worry that significant other(s) will come to harm and be lost, or that something will happen to separate the person permanently from important attachment figures. The person may refuse or resist being alone or leaving the proximity of the other(s), and may experience nightmares about separation. Multiple physical complaints often arise when separation anxiety is stimulated.

Separation anxiety may develop in the wake of persistent or traumatic stress, particularly circumstances that disrupt important relationships (e.g., after a major natural disaster) or which occurred when the person was isolated and unprotected (e.g., child abuse).

Separation anxiety disorder may be diagnosed in youth with persistent symptoms for a month or more. The typical cutoff for adults is 6 months. Strict criteria are applied to avoid pathologizing normal variants in children, although childhood separation anxiety may be the first sign of vulnerability to a future anxiety disorder.

The treatment literature primarily concerns children. The cornerstone of treatment is cognitive behavioral therapy (CBT); the selective serotonin reuptake inhibitor (SSRI), sertraline, has also demonstrated efficacy in randomized trials.

Selective Mutism

Although still largely a behavioral disorder of childhood, DSM-5 groups this condition with other anxiety disorders. Children with **selective mutism** consistently fail to speak when social demands call for it, as in school or when interacting with people outside their immediate social circle. They do, however, speak freely in other situations. To be considered abnormal, the behavior must persist for at least a month. Selective mutism often coexists with shyness, obsessiveness, and negativism. The diagnosis should not be applied to avoidance of speaking due to language problems (especially speaking a second language) or to mutism occurring only during the first month of school attendance.

A rare disorder, selective mutism usually appears before age 5, but may not come to clinical attention until later when academic expectations expose it. The literature provides little information about specific treatments or outcomes.

Specific Phobias

This disorder is characterized by 6 months or more of a predictable fear response to a specific cue, out of proportion to the actual threat. The fear leads to avoidance that can be disabling, as when a person afraid of flying is promoted to a position that requires frequent air travel.

Phobias such as fear of clowns, animals, or health care providers, are common in young children; most subside as development progresses. Specific phobias may occur spontaneously or following a frightening experience. Common phobias involve animals and creepy/crawly creatures that may be dangerous in theory, as well as situations such as heights, air travel, elevators, and water sports (fear of drowning). Exposure to needles, blood, or injury may induce a profound vasovagal response, resulting in presyncope or actual syncope (fainting). Subsequently, the person may develop an injection, blood, or injury phobia. People with this condition may avoid pursuing clinical careers in health care or resist necessary medical procedures (blood draws, flu shots).

The diagnosis of specific phobia should not be applied when a condition such as traumatic stress disorder, agoraphobia, social phobia, or obsessive-compulsive disorder better explains the symptoms.

CBT involving **exposure and response prevention** (ERP) is the most effective treatment for specific phobia. Patients are persuaded to expose themselves progressively to the phobic object or situation, with therapist guidance, until *habituation* of the anxiety response occurs. Recent advances in computer-aided virtual reality allow for carefully gradated exposure to realistic, simulated situations. Medications have shown little utility for specific phobias, but single doses of benzodiazepines may help a phobic patient endure a necessary, dreaded event, like a plane flight. Patients prone to fainting should lie down and look away while having injections or blood drawn. People can become habituated to the sight of blood or needles and pursue medical training.

Social Phobia

Social phobia describes a syndrome of fear lasting 6 months or more related to one or more social situations. The person always or almost always experiences marked or intense anxiety when anticipating or actually being in situations that involve the potential for scrutiny, embarrassment, or rejection. Examples of feared situations include meeting or conversing with a stranger, eating in public, or participating in a meeting. The anxiety is out of proportion to the real risk of negative evaluation or consequences. While the person may desire social activities and relationships, the dread of humiliation leads to avoidance or intense distress, even panic, when exposure cannot be avoided. DSM-5 provides a *performance only* specifier that applies when the anxiety is limited to situations requiring public speaking or performance ("stage fright").

Risk factors include first-degree relatives with the condition, temperamental behavioral inhibition (a genetic trait), social modeling, and childhood maltreatment from parents or peers (bullying). Patients often use alcohol or other substances to cope with the anxiety and "lubricate" social situations, putting them at increased risk of substance use disorders. Avoidant personality disorder is a risk factor for the generalized form of social phobia.

Social phobia is difficult to treat to full remission, but can be significantly improved with medication or psychotherapy, often in combination. Effective medications include SSRIs, venlafaxine, monoamine oxidase inhibitors (MAOIs), and benzodiazepines. Performance anxiety is uniquely responsive to intermittent, low doses of beta blockers. CBT and interpersonal psychotherapy (IPT) are proven psychotherapies for other forms of social phobia. Group therapy for those who can tolerate it may be particularly effective.

Panic Disorder

Panic disorder (PD) involves recurrent panic attacks that may seem unexpected or spontaneous, or expected, meaning cued by a stimulus or situation. Recurrent, unexpected attacks must persist for at least 1 month and result in **anticipatory anxiety** (worry about having a future attack) and *avoidance* of situations where the person believes an attack is likely to occur or help will be unavailable if it does. Box 44.1 summarizes the defining criteria of a panic attack.

About 25% of the general population will have occasional panic attacks without developing PD. The diagnosis requires recurrent attacks, development of anticipatory anxiety, avoidance, and impairment. A *panic attack* specifier can be added

---

Box 44.1. Criteria for panic attack

A discrete period of abrupt, intense fear or discomfort that peaks in intensity within a few minutes, and during which at least 4 of 13 characteristic symptoms from the categories below develop:

Cardiac: Tachycardia, palpitations, intensified heartbeat, chest pain/discomfort

Gastrointestinal: Choking sensation, nausea, other GI distress

Pulmonary: Shortness of breath, sensation of smothering

Neurological and vestibular: Paresthesias, dizziness, faintness

Physiological: Tremor, shaking, chills, flushed/hot

Cognitive and perceptual: Catastrophic interpretation: fear of dying, loss of control, "going crazy;" Sense that self or surroundings are unreal

---

Note. GI = gastrointestinal. For DSM-5 criteria see American Psychiatric Association. (2013). *Diagnostic and statistical manual of mental disorders* (5th ed.). Arlington, VA: Author.

---

to other diagnoses, since attacks may occur in other anxiety disorders, traumatic stress disorders, obsessive-compulsive disorder, bipolar disorder, or during episodes of major depression. Some studies have identified panic in 10% to 65% of patients with major depression. Panic during the course of depression may precipitate suicidal behavior.

Risk factors include first-degree relatives with PD and other anxiety, depressive and bipolar disorders, childhood sexual and physical abuse, and smoking tobacco. Children with "fearful spells" short of actual panic may later develop PD.

Myriad medical conditions can produce elements of panic or a full-blown episode. Many patients undergo extensive, expensive, and unnecessary diagnostic testing, because an evaluator zeroes in on a particular symptom, without applying the full criteria or considering the age and general health of the patient. At the same time, some possible organic causes are significant and should be sought. Panic attacks arising out of sleep do occur in PD, but may indicate that more careful evaluation for possible cardiac, pulmonary, sleep, and seizure disorders should be pursued.

Box 44.2 summarizes the medical evaluation of panic attacks. All patients should undergo a careful medical and family history and physical exam to guide the nature and extent of evaluation.

Early diagnosis and treatment of PD may prevent disabling avoidance, including the development of agoraphobia. Successful treatment also reduces unnecessary medical visits and associated health care costs ("cost offset"). Effective treatment of PD includes serotonin enhancing antidepressants (typically at higher doses than used in the treatment of major depression), benzodiazepines, and CBT, alone or in combination. Slow conscious breathing, which can be taught in general medical settings or in yoga studios, may induce general calming and prevent hyperventilation, allowing patients to prevent or abort attacks on their own.

Combining CBT with medication provides greater likelihood of a complete and durable response than medication alone. With any treatment, most patients can expect symptoms to flare up from time to time, especially in periods of stress. CBT prepares patients to accept recurrences without relapsing into the full-blown disorder.

Agoraphobia

Agoraphobia is a syndrome of marked fear or anxiety related to anticipating or actually being in situations in which escape would be unlikely or help unavailable if panic or other embarrassing or incapacitating symptoms were to occur. Prior

---

Box 44.2. Medical evaluation of anxiety, especially panic attacks

Common Conditions
that present at a typical age (routine tests)

- Asthma (history, physical exam, pulmonary function tests)
- COPD (history, physical exam, chest X-ray, pulmonary function tests)
- Caffeine use (history)
- Stimulant use (history, urine toxicology)
- Alcohol, sedative withdrawal (history, vital signs, physical exam)
- Hyperthyroidism (thyroid function tests)
- Hypocalcemia (CMP)
- Hypomagnesemia (serum magnesium test)
- Hypoglycemia[1]
- Severe anemia (CBC)
- Valvular heart disease (physical exam, echocardiogram)[2]
- Arrhythmia (physical exam, EKG, possibly Holter monitor)
- Eighth cranial nerve dysfunction (history of vertigo – refer to ENT)

Rare, Unusual Conditions
Indicated by atypical onset, particular physical findings, or failure to respond to treatment

- Pheochromocytoma (very rare; ruled out by normal diastolic blood pressure)
- Carcinoid (typically older adults; symptoms of flushing and diarrhea)
- Pulmonary embolus (sedentary, bedridden, hereditary coagulation defects, recent air travel)
- Sleep apnea (history of snoring, other associated symptoms)
- Angina or heart attack (seek other cardiac risk factors)
- Transient ischemic attack (focal physical findings)

Note. CBC = complete blood count; CMP = comprehensive metabolic panel; COPD = chronic obstructive pulmonary disease; EKG = electrocardiogram; ENT = ear nose and throat.
[1]Glucose tolerance test or other search for hypoglycemia generally not needed. Mild hypoglycemia may be an incidental finding. Significant, sudden hypoglycemia does trigger panic or anxiety in people on insulin and oral hypoglycemic agents.
[2]Mitral valve prolapse can be associated with tachyarrhythmia that may produce symptoms.

to DSM-5, this was considered an unfortunate consequence of untreated or inadequately treated PD. Agoraphobia is now applied as a freestanding diagnosis, although current estimates note a previous history of panic attacks or PD in 30% to 50% of cases.

The meaning of the Greek word agoraphobia is "fear of the marketplace." In this disorder, the person experiences intense anxiety in two or more public situations listed in DSM-5 as

- using public transportation;
- being in open spaces (e.g., city streets, markets, outdoor concerts);
- being in enclosed public spaces (e.g., grocery stores, malls, theaters);
- standing in lines or being in crowds;
- being outside of one's home alone.

The anxiety associated with these situations must occur over the course of 6 months or more. These situations are either avoided altogether or endured with great distress. A person may also refuse to enter the feared situation unless accompanied by a trusted companion.

The diagnosis does not apply if the syndrome is better explained by another condition, such as a specific or social phobia, separation anxiety, traumatic stress disorders, or the presence of a particular obsessional concern such as the concerns of *body dysmorphic disorder* (see Chapter 48: Obsessive-Compulsive and Related Disorders).

The treatment literature offers limited guidance. Protocols have included CBT with ERP, with or without antidepressant medication. Medication is most often used if the condition is a consequence of PD. Agoraphobia tends to be chronic and difficult to treat; the prognosis is poor when symptoms are persistent and longstanding.

Generalized Anxiety Disorder

Generalized anxiety disorder (GAD) is a syndrome of uncontrollable worry about everyday situations and possibilities, with symptoms lasting 6 months or more. Typical concerns include health, personal safety, access to resources, and threats to others' safety and well-being. The diagnosis also requires multiple symptoms and/or signs of arousal and autonomic dysfunction (e.g., insomnia or restless sleep, muscle tension, headaches and

backaches, difficulty concentrating). The cardiac, gastrointestinal, pulmonary, and vestibular symptoms of GAD overlap with those of PD, but do not typically cluster in panic attacks. The worries and attendant symptoms lead to behavioral inhibition, avoidance of risk including novelty, and the impulse to warn significant others of risk and appeals to them to avoid it.

Treatment options include SSRIs, dual-reuptake inhibitors (serotonin and norepinephrine reuptake inhibitors [SNRIs]), MAOIs, tricyclic antidepressants (TCAs), buspirone, benzodiazepines, and psychotherapies, including CBT and a modified brief psychodynamic approach called supportive expressive therapy (SET). The US Food and Drug Administration (FDA) has approved venlafaxine and duloxetine for GAD; doses higher than those typically used for depression may be necessary. Even though not FDA approved, pregabalin (and, to a lesser extent, gabapentin) have substantially reduced symptoms in randomized trials. Some patients respond poorly to anything other than benzodiazepines. These are reserved for use when other treatments fail, because of the risk of physiological dependence, although those with GAD do not typically develop abuse of benzodiazepines. Untreated or ineffectively treated GAD contributes to significant disability, as well as compounding the suffering of people with serious medical conditions such as diabetes, cancer, and heart disease. Table 44.1 summarizes the epidemiology of anxiety disorders (based partly on studies using DSM-5 criteria).

Treatment of Anxiety Disorders

Psychotherapy

> What principles underlie the treatment of anxiety disorders?

Anxiety disorders involve characteristic **cognitive distortions** such as overestimating the hazard or the likelihood of a feared event, and underestimating capacity for self-control and coping, as well as often self-fulfilling catastrophic interpretations,

Table 44.1. Onset, course, and epidemiology of anxiety disorders

Disorder	Typical Onset, Course	Epidemiology	Comment
Panic disorder	Begins in late adolescence, early adulthood (especially reproductive years in women)	Prevalence: 2–3% Higher in clinical settings F > M 2:1	May trigger costly, inappropriate medical evaluations; associated with agoraphobia; panic attacks associated with suicide in the course of depression
Social phobia (social anxiety disorder)	Bimodal onset, around age 5 or in mid-adolescence	Prevalence 7% F > M 3:2 in general population but M=F in those seeking treatment	Early adverse experience Increases risk. Risk factor for alcohol use disorders Chronic but may remit with positive social experiences
Specific phobia	May develop spontaneously, including in childhood, or begin in response to frightening experience	Prevalence 10–11% overall (5% in children and older age; 15% in adolescence) F > M for phobias of animals, natural disaster, specific situations M > F blood injury injection phobia	Most common anxiety disorder
Generalized anxiety disorder	Onset in adulthood, may be preceded by anxious temperament in children Duration > 6 months	Prevalence 3% adults Average age of onset 30 F > M 2:1	May complicate chronic medical illnesses, often comorbid with depression, especially if of earlier onset
Selective mutism	Usually in childhood	Unmeasured, probably rare	
Separation anxiety disorder	More common in children, may occur after trauma or severe stress	4% of children; 1–2% in adults F > M in treatment settings	New diagnostic category, treatment outcomes not established
Agoraphobia	Often follows panic disorder (onset mid-20s); average age of spontaneous onset is 17	2% of general population	Associated with depression, substance abuse

Note. F > m = female to male ratio.

anticipatory anxiety, and avoidance, which prevents corrective learning. The techniques of cognitive behavioral therapy (CBT) help patients to tolerate or control arousal and to interrupt and modify the cognitions and avoidance behaviors that perpetuate their symptoms.

CBT begins with explicit education, tailored to the patient's experience, about the usual characteristics of arousal and how anxiety develops and persists (psychoeducation). The therapist then helps identify and confront distorted thinking. Patients learn the techniques of conscious breathing and systematic muscle relaxation, allowing them to tolerate or control arousal and interrupt and modify the cognitions and avoidance behaviors that perpetuate their symptoms. Therapists then guide patients to expose themselves to fear-inducing situations without resorting to avoidance, until the fear subsides. ERP appears to be a key element of the effectiveness of CBT in anxiety disorders, as described earlier, in the section "Specific Phobias."

Pharmacotherapy

Medications that modulate the serotonin/norepinephrine system, especially SSRIs, MAOIs, and SNRIs are useful in tempering arousal, preventing panic attacks, and reducing anticipatory anxiety. A nonantidepressant serotonergic agent, buspirone, may be effective for generalized anxiety symptoms. Given with explicit instruction about the need for exposure, medication also reduces avoidance behavior. Benzodiazepines as a primary treatment should generally be reserved for later in the treatment algorithm because of their potential for inducing physiological dependence and potential adverse effects on memory and motor performance. In spite of these concerns, escalation of dose, abuse, and diversion are very uncommon among patients with anxiety disorders who do not have a comorbid substance use disorder. Benzodiazepines are commonly used to temper anxiety in the initiation phase of antidepressant treatment to give the patient some relief while the antidepressant has a chance to take effect. Completely suppressing symptoms with benzodiazepines reduces the effectiveness of ERP, which must adequately provoke anxiety to mobilize the intrinsic processes that terminate

it. Medications should generally be continued for a minimum of 6 to 12 months after resolution of symptoms before attempting to taper them. It is not uncommon for patients with PD, social phobia, and GAD to require indefinite maintenance medication.

Recommended Readings

American Psychiatric Association. (2013). *Diagnostic and statistical manual of mental disorders* (5th ed.). Arlington, VA: American Psychiatric Publishing. http://doi.org/10.1176/appi.books.9780890425596

Baldwin, D., Ajel, K. I., & Garner, M. (2010). Pharmacological treatment of generalized anxiety disorder. *Current Topics in Behavioral Neurosciences, 2*, 505–525.

Cyranowski, J. M., & Milrod, B. (2014). Separation anxiety disorder. In G. O. Gabbard (Ed.), *Gabbard's treatment of psychiatric disorders* (5th ed., pp. 357–366). Washington, DC: APPI Books. Available at http://doi.org/10.1176/appi.books.9781585625048.gg17

Lipsitz, J. D. (2014). Specific phobia. In G. O. Gabbard (Ed.), *Gabbard's treatment of psychiatric disorders* (5th ed., pp. 393–404). Washington, DC: APPI Books.

Martin, E. I., Ressler, K. J., Binder, E., & Nemeroff, C. B. (2009). The neurobiology of anxiety disorders: Brain imaging, genetics, and psychoneuroendocrinology. *Psychiatric Clinics of North America, 32*, 549–575. http://doi.org/10.1016/j.psc.2009.05.004

Schneier, F. R., Bruce, L. C., & Heimberg, R. G. (2014). Social anxiety disorder (social phobia). In G. O. Gabbard (Ed.), *Gabbard's treatment of psychiatric disorders* (5th ed., pp. 367–380). Washington, DC: APPI Books.

Szkodny, L. E., Jacobson, N. C., Liera, S. J., & Newman, M. G. (2014). Generalized anxiety disorder. In G. O. Gabbard (Ed.), *Gabbard's treatment of psychiatric disorders* (5th ed., pp. 381–392). Washington, DC: APPI Books. http://doi.org/10.1176/appi.books.9781585625048.gg19

Review Questions

1. Walter, a 31-year-old medical student, is mortified by racing heartbeat, shaking voice, and dizziness when he has to make presentations or respond to questions from his superiors. When observed doing procedures, his hands shake. He wonders if he can finish his training. He has

friends and a solid marriage. The simplest and most rapidly effective intervention would be

A. a beta blocker
B. cognitive behavioral therapy
C. daily dose of a benzodiazepine
D. exposure and response prevention
E. reassurance that he is doing well

2. A nursing student is invited to observe the repair of a large laceration. Eager to participate, he glances at the injury and faints. His supervisor should

A. reassign him to an office position
B. reassure him that he likely will get over it with experience
C. recommend that he see a therapist for CBT
D. tell him that he is unsuited for a health care profession
E. suggest that he wear support stockings to prevent fainting

3. A 68-year-old retired woman with insulin-dependent diabetes describes frequent episodes of sweating, trembling, dizziness, and feelings of dread. She calls her provider frequently, with nonspecific complaints, including headaches and concerns about her prescriptions. She now avoids going places alone, or where she might not be close to medical help. Her most likely diagnosis is

A. agoraphobia
B. anxiety disorder secondary to general medical condition
C. generalized anxiety disorder
D. panic disorder with agoraphobia
E. separation anxiety disorder

Answer Key on p. 466

45 Neurocognitive Disorders: Delirium and Secondary Syndromes

Julia B. Frank, MD, and Michael Peroski, DO

- What is altered mental status?
- What are the key clinical features of delirium?
- What causes delirium?
- What brain dysfunctions produce delirium?
- How is delirium managed?
- What are secondary syndromes?

Altered Mental Status

What is altered mental status?

Altered mental status (AMS) is a nonspecific clinical term describing changes in baseline awareness, attention, perception, memory, language, personality, or behavioral responses to various internal and external stimuli. AMS is not itself a diagnosis. It does not distinguish primary psychiatric disorders from psychiatric symptoms secondary to medical or neurological problems (secondary syndromes). While primary psychiatric disorders are not usually life threatening, the conditions that cause delirium and secondary syndromes, including those due to substance use or substance withdrawal, may be. Patients presenting with AMS require careful diagnostic evaluation to differentiate among these possibilities, including times when these changes are superimposed on a primary psychiatric disorder.

Delirium

Mr. B. brings his 74-year-old mother to the Emergency Department because she has been behaving strangely for 3 days. She seems confused and has had trouble with dressing, preparing meals, and using the telephone, things she normally does without difficulty. At times, she seems less confused. She has been in good health, with regular routine medical screening tests. She takes only calcium and vitamin D supplements for osteopenia. In the ED, her temperature is 39 °C. On exam, she is lethargic and answers questions slowly and unreliably. She is disoriented to time and situation and has trouble recalling recent events. Her physical examination is unremarkable. Urinalysis reveals many white blood cells, signs of a urinary tract infection. Following treatment with antibiotics, she gradually returns to her baseline level of functioning.

What are the key clinical features of delirium?

Delirium is characterized by an *acute alteration of mental status* with *fluctuating* disturbances in attention or awareness and at least one other domain: cognition, perception, behavior, affect, or sleep. The disturbance can be traced to an underlying physical cause (see Box 45.1). Symptoms of delirium, subtle or obvious, mark an abrupt departure from baseline functioning. Associated symptoms such as agitation, mood lability, or perceptual disturbances (illusions and hallucinations) are also seen. The brain dysfunction of delirium is objectively verifiable by electroencephalography (EEG). In addition, patients may have physical signs associated with the etiological condition

---

Box 45.1. Characteristics of delirium

Acute onset: Symptoms develop over hours to days and represent a clear change from baseline functioning.

Fluctuating course: The quality and intensity of disturbances may vary within a 24-hr period and on consecutive days. Periods of transient improvement may be mistaken for resolution. Patients suspected to have delirium should be examined multiple times in a day.

Impaired attention: Difficulty in focusing, sustaining, and shifting attention is present. Marked distractibility is a hallmark of delirium.

Altered level of consciousness: Often described as a change in consciousness, more accurate descriptors are impaired awareness or "abnormal levels of arousal" connoting states ranging from somnolence to hypervigilance.

Memory deficits: Impairment in the registration, consolidation, retention, and retrieval of information appears as poor performance on tasks that assess immediate, short-term, and remote memory. Verbal and nonverbal memory are affected; severe cases may impair procedural memory. Autobiographical memory is usually preserved, but retrieval may vary, leading patients to provide misleading or inaccurate information ("confabulation").

Disorientation: Delirious patients are usually disoriented to time, place, and situation but rarely to self. Marked impairment in tracking the passage of time may be one of the earliest signs.

Thought disorder: Thoughts may be tangential, circumstantial, or disorganized, or may demonstrate an illogical flow of ideas. Severe cases include paucity of thought content and lack of spontaneous speech. Patients' communication may be incoherent or hard to follow.

Perceptual disturbances: Initially, delirious patients may perceive sizes, shapes, and colors abnormally. Misperception may develop into illusions or gross misinterpretations of external stimuli in any sensory modality, most often vision and hearing. Misperceptions of internal stimuli are termed *hallucinations*. These are typically auditory or visual, although tactile, gustatory, and olfactory hallucinations may occur. The presence of vivid and bizarre visual hallucinations is more common in delirium and other secondary syndromes than in primary psychiatric disorders such as schizophrenia.

Delusions: Delusions are common and often lead to misdiagnoses of a primary psychotic disorder. Delusions in delirium are usually paranoid and bizarre but are not typically fixed or well developed. Delusions may be a form of confabulation, as the patient tries to make sense of internal and external stimuli in the face of distractibility, disorganization of thought, and perceptual disturbances.

Language disturbances: Slow, slurred speech, paraphasia, dysgraphia, word-finding difficulty, and reduced comprehension may be present. Expressive or receptive aphasia may develop in severe or prolonged delirium.

Psychomotor disturbances: Behavior may vary from absence of voluntary movement to restlessness with purposeless or inappropriate motor activity. Patients may injure themselves or others as a result of clumsiness, agitation, or purposeless aggression.

Sleep disturbances: These include daytime drowsiness with frequent napping, nighttime insomnia, and fragmented sleep. Symptoms of delirium may worsen at night ("sundowning"). Dreamlike experiences may occur when awake.

Disturbances in affect: Affect may be constricted, labile, or flattened. These emotional states may also be responses to the cognitive and perceptual disturbances that impair the patient's appreciation of reality.

(e.g., tremors, elevated blood pressure, and rapid heart rate in alcohol withdrawal; fever in infection; pupillary signs in intoxication).

Delirium often develops in hospitalized patients who are seriously ill or recovering from surgery. The medical or surgical team may mistakenly diagnose a primary psychiatric disorder, based on the presence of hallucinations, paranoia, agitation, or uncooperativeness, without considering the context of symptoms or their acute course.

Causes of Delirium

What causes delirium?

Box 45.2. Causes of delirium

1. **Drugs**
   - Sedatives
   - Opioids
   - Other drugs with anticholinergic activity (drugs for Parkinson's disease; antihistamines; tricyclic antidepressants; some drugs for nausea)
   - Alcohol intoxication/withdrawal
   - Illicit drug intoxication/withdrawal
   - Polypharmacy
   - Misc.: corticosteroids, fluoroquinolones, dopamine agonists, muscle relaxants, some cancer chemotherapy, anti-retrovirals

2. **Metabolic/electrolyte abnormalities**
   - Hypoglycemia/Hyperglycemia
   - Hypoxia
   - Hypercapnia
   - Hypernatremia/Hyponatremia
   - Hypercalcemia/Hypocalcemia
   - Acid-base disturbances
   - Fever/Hypothermia

3. **Endocrine disorders**
   - Hypothyroidism/Hyperthyroidism
   - Cushing's syndrome
   - Adrenal insufficiency

4. **Nutritional deficiencies**
   - Wernicke's encephalopathy (vitamin B_1 deficiency)
   - Vitamin B_{12} deficiency

5. **Infections**
   - CNS infections – meningitis, encephalitis, AIDS, neurosyphilis, Lyme disease
   - Any infectious process (e.g., UTI, pneumonia)

6. **Systemic inflammatory disorders/vascular disorders**
   - Systemic lupus erythematosus
   - Paraneoplastic syndromes
   - Disseminated intravascular coagulation
   - Thrombotic thrombocytopenic purpura

7. **Organ system failure**
   - Uremia
   - Hepatic encephalopathy
   - Hypoperfusion (e.g., shock, congestive heart failure)

8. **Primary neurological disease**
   - Head trauma
   - Elevated intracranial pressure
   - CNS neoplasms
   - Seizures – ictal, postictal, and interictal states
   - Vertebrobasilar stroke
   - Right (nondominant) parietal lobe infarct

9. **Severe stress**
   - Surgery
   - Prolonged sleep deprivation
   - Prolonged immobility, physical restraints
   - Severe pain

Note. CNS = central nervous system; UTI = urinary tract infection.

Delirium results from the global disruption of neuronal circuits that sustain consciousness, higher-level cognitive functions, and normal regulation of vital functions: temperature, circulation, and respiration. It may be difficult to identify a single cause, since serious medical conditions, temporary metabolic derangements, and the effects of medical treatment or street drugs often coexist in vulnerable populations (see Box 45.2).

These diverse etiologies all may disrupt neuronal activity. Intervention is urgent; delirium may indicate a process that, unchecked, will result in permanent brain injury or even death. Thus, in various populations, especially elderly patients in institutional settings, delirium is associated with increased risk of death.

As illustrated in the case above, prompt, effective treatment of the underlying condition, when possible, may reverse delirium completely. Full resolution may not occur in people who have other underlying neurological impairments (e.g., in delirium secondary to an acute infection in a person who has previously had a stroke).

The mature human brain has multiple overlapping functions and dense connections that make it resilient to physical stressors. Pediatric and geriatric patients often lack this cognitive reserve, making them more susceptible to delirium. It also takes longer for their delirium to clear. Other major risk factors that reduce cognitive reserve include pre-existing medical conditions and functional impairments (see Box 45.3). Patients in hospitals and nursing homes are especially vulnerable.

Box 45.3. Risk factors for delirium

- Young or old age
- Preexisting cognitive impairment (dementia or intellectual disability)
- Preexisting medical conditions (especially neurological conditions such as head injury, stroke, epilepsy)
- Baseline poor health or disability
- Environmental conditions: sensory deprivation (including impaired vision or hearing), meaningless stimulation, overstimulation
- Other: fecal impaction, bladder catheterization, invasive radiological studies

---

What brain dysfunctions produce delirium?

Delirium is the consequence of alterations in neurotransmitter and chemical signaling. Although the syndrome typically indicates global impairment, research using functional neuroimaging, brain lesion studies, and performance on neuropsychological tests has clarified the relation between symptoms and specific brain regions (see Box 45.4).

Box 45.4. Neuroanatomical correlates of the clinical features of delirium

Frontal lobe and prefrontal cortex: Inattention, thought disorganization, delusions, perceptual disturbances, disorientation and memory deficits, language impairments, psychomotor disturbances

Basal ganglia, thalamus, and hippocampus: Inattention, thought disorganization, delusions, perceptual disturbances, disorientation and memory deficits, disturbances in affect, psychomotor disturbances, sleep disturbances

Cingulate gyrus: Psychomotor disturbances, language impairments

Temporal lobe: Delusions, perceptual disturbances, memory deficits

Parietal lobe: Inattention, delusions, perceptual disturbances, disorientation

Occipital lobe: Perceptual disturbances

Brainstem: Inattention, altered level of consciousness, sleep disturbances

---

Several neurotransmitter systems function abnormally in delirium (see Box 45.5). Neurons that synthesize and release monoamine neurotransmitters cluster mainly in brainstem and other subcortical nuclei; their axons terminate in dispersed cortical and subcortical areas, where receptors that respond to particular neurotransmitters regulate their excitatory or inhibitory effects. This interaction is reciprocal; subcortical input influences cortical responses and vice versa. Cortical neurons also directly regulate one another by synthesizing, releasing, and responding to gamma-amino-butyric acid (GABA; generally inhibitory) and glutamate (generally excitatory). The coordinated activity of particular networks of neurons is necessary for complex functions such as cognition, emotion, personality, language, perception, and behavior. In addition, chemical factors originating outside the brain, such as cytokines and hormones, as well as medications and substances of abuse that cross the blood–brain barrier, affect the activity of these networks.

Box 45.5. Neurochemical alterations in delirium

- Acetylcholine deficiency
- Dopamine excess
- Serotonin excess or deficiency
- Norepinephrine excess
- Histamine excess or deficiency
- GABA excess or deficiency
- Glutamate excess or deficiency
- Glucorticoid excess
- Cytokine excess (IL-1, IL-6, TNF-alpha)

The end result of all of these potential derangements is diffuse *hyperpolarization* of neurons that makes them less likely to generate action potentials. Patient behavior may seem hyperactive, but neuronal hypoactivity typically appears on an EEG as *diffuse slowing* of the dominant rhythms, generalized delta waves, and loss of reactivity of the EEG to eye opening and closing. The EEG is the only objective test with *specific* findings in delirium. The degree of slowing correlates well with the degree of cognitive impairment.

Managing Delirium

| How is delirium managed? |

Optimal management of delirium involves four components: (1) treatment of the underlying cause, (2) modification of risk factors, (3) environmental interventions, and (4) pharmacological management of symptoms (see Box 45.6). Early intervention is critical to successful outcome. In addition, management must be flexible, as symptoms fluctuate in quality and severity.

Box 45.6. Management of delirium

1. **Treatment of underlying cause:** Specific interventions include antibiotics for infection, discontinuation of medication, administration of oxygen, and correction of metabolic/electrolyte abnormalities.
2. **Modification of risk factors:** Avoiding medications that might cause delirium; improved management of pain and discomfort, and correction of sensory deficits. Ideally, these risk factors should be addressed preemptively rather than reactively.
3. **Environmental interventions:** Controlling external stimuli to promote relaxation and uninterrupted sleep; using clocks and calendars to help orientation; utilizing familiar persons as caregivers; optimizing temperature and lighting, and encouraging mobility and activity. Physical restraint may be necessary if the patient poses a risk to self or others, but restraints may worsen delirium. Their use exposes patients to other complications.
4. **Pharmacological management:** Medications are primarily used to control acute agitation but may have value in scheduled dosing to manage thought disturbances, inattention, paranoid delusions, mood lability, and insomnia. The medications most often used are low doses of the high potency, typical antipsychotics (e.g., haloperidol) preferred for their limited anticholinergic effects. Atypical antipsychotics and nonbenzodiazepine hypnotic agents (e.g., trazodone) are also commonly used. Benzodiazepines should not be used alone except in alcohol or benzodiazepine withdrawal, as they may worsen delirium from other causes. In all cases, but especially in older patients, dosing should begin low and be titrated upward slowly.

Secondary Syndromes

A 23-year-old military veteran was brought to his primary care physician by his wife. Following rehabilitation for a concussive head injury, he has had significant changes in his personality. Although physically unimpaired, he has stopped showing interest in any activity, often sitting for prolonged periods staring at the television. His wife describes him as impulsive, with poor table manners and socially inappropriate behavior, and subject to marked mood swings with little to no provocation. An MRI of the patient's brain reveals white matter loss in the frontal lobe with old microhemorrhages.

| What are secondary syndromes? |

Secondary syndromes are presentations that resemble typical psychiatric conditions or symptoms (e.g., depression, anxiety, panic, mania, psychosis) but which are caused by an identifiable medical condition (Box 45.7). Clinicians may improperly institute symptomatic treatment while overlooking potentially treatable or reversible causes. This error can be avoided by including a detailed medical history during psychiatric assessment and by recognizing the typical psychiatric symptoms that may develop in the course of a systemic condition. Features that are not typical for the identified psychiatric disorder, such as presentation at an unusual age, also may suggest a medical etiology. Clinicians should have a low threshold of suspicion for ordering laboratory studies and neuroimaging or other diagnostic techniques. A thorough review of medications that could be causing or contributing to a patient's psychiatric symptoms is essential.

By definition, the symptoms related to the impact of a medical illness on a patient's life (e.g., depression in a patient with a painful condition who can no longer work) are diagnosed as *adjustment disorders*, not secondary syndromes. Discreet psychiatric syndromes associated with alcohol or other substance use have their own domain in DSM-5 – namely, *depression secondary to alcohol use* or *psychosis secondary to hallucinogen use*. History and urine toxicology screening will identify most of these conditions.

Many of the causes of delirium (Box 45.7) may also produce other psychiatric syndromes.

Box 45.7. Some conditions associated with secondary psychiatric syndromes

Depression	Hypothyroidism Hypercalcemia Pneumonia Mononucleosis Atherosclerotic cardiovascular or cerebrovascular disease Chronic anemia Syphilis Vitamin D deficiency B_{12}/folate deficiency Lyme disease Traumatic brain injury (CTE) Sleep disorders (especially sleep apnea) Hypercortisolemia Hypocortisolemia (adrenal failure) Testosterone deficiency SLE, other autoimmune disorders Uremia Hepatic encephalopathy Medication reaction	**Mania**	Hypercortisolemia Brain injury (CTE) Vasculitis Limbic encephalitis
		Anxiety	Asthma Hyperthyroidism Hypoglycemia Hypocalcemia/hypomagnesemia Pulmonary embolism Arrhythmias Anemia Hypotension Severe allergic reaction Pheochromocytoma Carcinoid Temporal lobe epilepsy (partial complex seizure disorder) Syphilis Encephalitis COPD
Psychosis	Epilepsy (Partial complex seizure disorder: late complication) Hypothyroidism ("myxedema madness") Hyperthyroidism Hypocalcemia Hypercortisolemia Limbic encephalitis	**OCD**	Heavy metals (lead) PANDAS Encephalitis Parkinson's disease

Note. COPD = chronic obstructive pulmonary disease; CTE = chronic traumatic encephalopathy; OCD = obsessive-compulsive disorder; PANDAS = pediatric autoimmune neurological disorders associated with streptococcal infections; SLE = systemic lupus erythematosus.

Like delirium, the secondary syndromes are most often associated with systemic processes (metabolic abnormalities, infections, diffuse vascular diseases, endocrinopathies) rather than diseases of particular organs. Unlike delirium, secondary syndromes do not follow a typical waxing and waning course. They generally involve selective rather than global brain dysfunction. Cognitive impairment, when present, is usually subtler than that seen in delirium. Secondary syndromes do not produce diffuse background slowing on EEG. Acute onset and rapid remission following treatment are more typical of delirium.

It is obviously impossible to consider every possible medical etiology when evaluating a psychiatric disorder. A careful history will identify or rule out the need to further evaluate someone for the sequelae of a head injury or a previously diagnosed medical condition. Noninvasive, widely available blood tests screen for metabolic and endocrine disorders, most vitamin deficiencies, autoimmune disorders, HIV, and syphilis. Searching for relatively common conditions like hyperthyroidism that may appear at any age, including the ages of risk for a primary psychiatric disorder, is cost effective. For example, postpartum thyroid disorders, in particular, are not uncommon and are often overlooked as a cause of postpartum mood syndromes. Judgment is required when deciding whether to screen more thoroughly for conditions that are extremely rare (e.g., pheochromocytoma), or difficult to assess (limbic encephalitis, partial epilepsy, multiple sclerosis).

Once a secondary syndrome has been identified, psychotropic medication may still be needed and helpful. Concurrent treatment of the underlying medical condition, where possible, may arrest progression, facilitate recovery, and foster future well-being.

3. Secondary syndromes may usually be distinguished from delirium by
   A. absence of altered consciousness
   B. disorganized thought
   C. disturbances in affect
   D. hallucinations
   E. paranoid delusions

Answer Key on p. 466

Recommended Readings

Burns, A., Gallagley, A., & Byrne, J. (2004). Delirium. *Journal of Neurology, Neurosurgery, and Psychiatry, 75,* 362–367. http://doi.org/10.1136/jnnp.2003.023366

Kalish, V. B., Gillham, J. E., & Unwin, B. K. (2014). Delirium in older persons: Evaluation and management. *American Family Physician, 90,* 150–158. PMID: 25077720

Maldonado, J. (2008). Pathoetiological model of delirium: A comprehensive understanding of the neurobiology of delirium and an evidence-based approach to prevention and treatment. *Critical Care Clinics, 24,* 789–856. http://doi.org/10.1016/j.ccc.2008.06.004

Review Questions

1. Which of these clinical features does **NOT** suggest the diagnosis of delirium?
   A. Altered level of consciousness
   B. Distractibility
   C. Fluctuating course
   D. Identifiable physical cause
   E. Insidious onset

2. The EEG in delirious patients will show which of the following?
   A. Diffuse slowing of dominant rhythm
   B. Focal increase in delta wave activity
   C. High-frequency wave patterns
   D. Increased reactivity to eye opening and closing
   E. Increased sleep spindles

46 Neurocognitive Disorders: Dementia

Michael Peroski, DO, and Julia B. Frank, MD

- Is dementia one syndrome or many?
- What role does gene–environment interaction play in dementia?
- What are the consequences of dementia for the individual and society?
- What treatments affect the course and outcome of dementia?
- Is dementia preventable?

What Is Dementia?

Is dementia one syndrome or many?

Dementia is a syndrome of general loss of cognitive functions and significant functional deterioration, out of proportion to changes expected with normal aging. Typically, dementias evolve over time. In the first, preclinical stage, neurons are damaged but symptoms are undetectable. In the second stage, *mild cognitive impairment* (MCI), patients show deficits in one or more cognitive domains but are still able to conduct their activities of daily living (ADLs) and can function independently. In the third stage, dementia or *major cognitive impairment*, patients can no longer complete ADLs and require some assistance up to and including total care by others. Persons with dementia may also experience delusions and hallucinations. People with MCI do not inevitably develop dementia.

In contrast to dementia, the cognitive abilities of those with *developmental intellectual disorders* lag behind or never reach expected levels. The actual deficits found in the two groups – slowing of thought; poor memory and concentration; deterioration of personality; and diminished ability to learn, manipulate information, or perform basic tasks of self-care – overlap.

In its fifth edition, the *Diagnostic and Statistical Manual of Mental Disorders* (DSM-5) places the old term *dementia* within the category of *major neurocognitive disorders. Mild cognitive impairment* is now formally termed *mild neurocognitive disorder*. Both major and mild disorders may be further specified as possibly due to a particular process, such as *major neurocognitive disorder due to Alzheimer's disease*. The World Health Organization's *International Statistical Classification of Diseases and Related Health Problems, 10th edition* (ICD-10) includes the term *dementia* with a variety of specifiers. For example, ICD-10 classifies Alzheimer's disease as "with behavioral disturbance and/or depressed mood."

Causes of Dementia

Dementia may result from genetic processes that are expressed directly in neurological tissue (primary degenerative, familial dementias; see Table 46.1), from progressive deterioration of the blood supply to the brain (vascular dementia), or from metabolic, infectious, toxic, traumatic, autoimmune, or endocrine insults to the brain. Many cases reflect mixed etiology – that is, vascular or secondary processes may trigger the expression of genetically regulated cell damage and death.

Table 46.1. Varieties of dementia

Variety	Known Genetic Factors	Distribution of Lesions	Pathology/ Proteins	Symptoms	Comments
Dementia of the Alzheimer's type (DAT)	APOEe4 genes, chromosome 19; Also chromosomes 1, 4, and 21	Cortical radiations of cholinergic neurons, especially hippocampus, parietal, and occipital lobes	Beta amyloid, tau proteins, granulovacuolar degeneration, neurofibrillary tangles; presenilin 1 and 2 (amyloid precursor proteins)	**Early:** short-term memory loss, apraxia, progressive confusion, inability to sequence, learn, recognize people **Later:** personality changes, depression, paranoia, visual hallucinations	Most prevalent Incidence increases with age
Vascular dementia ("multi-infarct dementia")	RAS, Notch 3, TRIM 45, TRIM 67	Diffuse blockages of small vessels	Small infarcts APOE (protein)	Variable, stepwise deterioration	Often coexists with DAT Second most prevalent Related to other cardiovascular risk factors (smoking, HTN, DM)
Huntington's disease (HD)	36–250 repeats of CAG on chromosome 4	Destruction of caudate nucleus, radiations of caudate fibers	Increased Huntingtin protein	Paranoia, impulsive dyscontrol, memory loss, psychosis, chorea	CAG repeats: < 35 unaffected; 36–40 ± affected; > 40 affected
Parkinson's disease (PD)	Most cases idiopathic or sporadic SNCA, LRRK 2, PARK 2, PARK 7, PINC1	Cortical radiations of dopamine neurons originating in basal ganglia	Lewy bodies (alpha synuclein) Changes due to cholinergic deterioration	Tremor, rigidity, memory loss, cogwheeling, paranoia, apathy, aggression, slow movement (bradykinesia), expressionless face (masked facies), changes in speech, small handwriting (micrographia)	Dementia occurs late in some PD
Lewy body dementia	Rarely variant of GBA gene	Similar to PD but spares temporal areas	Lewy bodies (alpha synuclein)	Severe motor symptoms, visual hallucinations early, memory loss, personality change	Much rarer than DAT but second most common *primary* degenerative dementia

Table 46.1. (continued)

Variety	Known Genetic Factors	Distribution of Lesions	Pathology/ Proteins	Symptoms	Comments
Pick's disease (primary frontotemporal dementia)		Frontal and temporal lobe atrophy		Impulsive/ disinhibited or anergic/ apathetic, poor hygiene, loss of social skills, aphasia, no insight; memory may be spared	Subclassified with or without aphasia Affects language centers of the frontal and temporal lobes
Dementia secondary to other diseases/ deficiencies/ injury (see Table 46.2)		Mixed, fronto-temporal symptoms may predominate early		Memory loss, personality change, often motor abnormalities, depression Specific symptoms depend on the area of the brain affected	Partly preventable Progression varies with underlying condition

Note. DM = diabetes mellitus; HTN = hypertension.

At age 52, Dr. E. could not remember details of patients she had just examined. Neuropsychological tests showed severe loss of short-term memory and inability to manipulate information. Initially, aware of these changes, she retired. Within a year, she no longer recognized her impairments. Her affect became shallow and labile, and she began to get lost, even at home. Over the next 5 years, she became unable to dress or feed herself, spoke only in fragments, and slept erratically throughout the 24-hr day. She suffered from visual hallucinations, sat for hours or wandered aimlessly, and developed incontinence. She died of aspiration pneumonia, 7 years after the onset of symptoms.

Dr. E. suffered from *dementia of the Alzheimer's type* (DAT) or **Alzheimer's disease**, a primary degenerative dementia first described by Alois Alzheimer in 1906. Alzheimer and other German pathologists correlated cognitive and behavioral deterioration with lesions of cortical tissue: plaques made of beta amyloid, neurofibrillary tangles later found to include tau proteins, and granulovacuolar degeneration. Such work proved

that disorders of mentation stemmed from damage to the brain.

Early research classified dementia based on pathological changes. Because many patients are never autopsied, current diagnosis relies on the imprecise methods of bedside classification. The observable differences between, for example, DAT and Lewy body dementia are often too subtle to be recognized during life.

A more useful classification categorizes dementias based on clinical course, neuropathology, or etiology. Parkinson's disease (PD), Huntington's disease (HD), Pick's disease, and DAT are primary degenerative neurological conditions of variable etiologies, recognized in part by a pattern of symptoms and in part by pathological lesions. HD is the expression of an autosomal dominant genetic lesion (see Table 46.1). DAT and dementia in PD result from the interaction of genetic risk factors and known and unknown environmental conditions. Creutzfeldt-Jakob disease (CJD), a dementia that also follows a relentless degenerative course, is caused by a prion, a protein with no genetic material.

Table 46.2. Examples of dementias of known etiology

Etiology	Pathology	Symptoms and Progression
Primary HIV infection of CNS or AIDS-related infections	Damage may be focal or diffuse	Typically prominent frontal symptoms: personality change, loss of fine motor skills, cognitive slowing, attentional impairment May improve with treatment of underlying infection
Multiple sclerosis	Characteristic scattered lesions throughout the brain	Symptoms worsen during flares May be partially reversed or arrested by treatment
Autoimmune disorders (lupus)	Effects of vasculitis	Rapidly progressive in uncontrolled disease (seizures) Can improve with corticosteroid treatment
Alcohol related	Diffuse toxic damage, sometimes prominent cerebellar damage	Permanent but may not progress if drinking stopped
Thiamine deficiency (vitamin B₁): related to alcoholism or malnutrition	Selective deterioration of mammillary bodies	Early acute stage, "Wernicke encephalopathy," classically presents with triad of ophthalmoplegia, ataxia, and confusion Reversible with treatment Later "Korsakoff psychosis" irreversible, severe loss of short-term memory Both classically include confabulation
Following closed head injury	Diffuse axonal injury, cerebral contusions, and scarring Acceleration of DAT type changes Chronic traumatic encephalopathy	Often frontal and temporal damage in cortical areas near bone Personality change and diminished executive functions Younger people may recover considerable function Depression, mania, or psychosis may occur
Hypothyroidism		Sluggishness, loss of motivation, slowed thought Improves with thyroid hormone replacement
B₁₂/Folate deficiency (intrinsic or secondary to alcoholism)	Reduced brain volume, alteration in the production of myelin and neurotransmitters	Anemia, gait disturbance, sensory loss, weakness, hypotension Possibly reversible if not prolonged
Normal pressure hydrocephalus	Compression of cortical tissue surrounding cerebral ventricles	Prominent gait disturbances and urinary incontinence, personality changes May remit with early diagnosis, insertion of shunt

Note. CNS = central nervous system; DAT = dementia of the Alzheimer's type.

Vascular dementia differs clinically from primary degenerative dementia by classically following a stepwise, rather than steady, downhill course. The degenerative changes in vascular dementia follow the distribution of the small arteries and arterioles that are blocked. Vascular dementia is often a late life complication of diabetes, hypertension, dyslipidemia, or other cerebrovascular risk factors.

Dementias of other etiology produce different patterns of tissue damage, different patterns of symptoms, and different prognoses (see Table 46.2).

Pathogenesis of Dementia

Clinically, the distribution of pathological changes in dementia corresponds broadly to two distinct patterns of symptoms and behaviors. The initial lesions of DAT appear in the hippocampus and *posterior brain*. Other dementias (classified variably as *subcortical dementia*, *frontotemporal dementia* [FTD], or simply *non-DAT*) first damage the prefrontal and temporal cortices, the basal ganglia, and associated limbic areas. Such distinctions are most meaningful early on. In later stages, severe dysfunction and widespread destruction result in global impairment.

The posterior brain is particularly specialized for receiving and initially processing stimuli and associating them with memory. It has been termed the *perceptual integrating brain*, in contrast to the *anterior* or *action brain*. The areas of the action brain are specialized for inhibiting or moderating emotion and action, conscious cognitive processing, expressive language, social skills, and executive functions (e.g., sequencing, holding information in a buffer zone so that it can be manipulated, abstraction, deciding between alternatives).

The areas of the perceptual integrating brain are linked by a neuronal network whose primary neurotransmitter is *acetylcholine* (AcH). These neurons originate in the nucleus basalis of Meynert. DAT, in particular, results from a selective, possibly genetically programmed, deterioration of this network. The plaques and neurofibrillary tangles of DAT cluster in the limbic and cortical areas where these cholinergic axons terminate.

The pathological changes of FTDs appear in the frontal and temporal areas that receive both cholinergic input and input from adrenergic neurons in the brainstem and from dopaminergic neurons in the basal ganglia, including the caudate (HD) and the substantia nigra (PD).

While it is conceptually useful to describe different dementias by a typical course and set of symptoms, many cases show mixed features. For example, patients with DAT can have parkinsonian features and may show the histopathological findings of both PD and DAT at autopsy.

> What role does gene–environment interaction play in dementia?

> The folksinger, Woody Guthrie, became impulsive, paranoid, and demented in his late 40s. His mother and several of his children had similar symptoms and died young. During his lifetime, his condition was recognized as Huntington's disease, a dementia and movement disorder that follows a clear pattern of autosomal dominant inheritance.

The identification of **familial forms of dementia** has led to studies in neurogenetics. For example, variants exist in the gene on chromosome 19 that codes for apolipoprotein E (APOE), a substance that accumulates in amyloid plaques. The inheritance of two alleles coding for APOE4 (APOE4/4) is associated with widespread formation of plaques (but not neurofibrillary tangles) by age 70. The brains of those with APOE2/3 show diffuse plaques only in extreme old age (> 90 years), if at all. Those with one APOE4 allele show intermediate levels of plaque formation. The presence of the APOE4 gene is, thus, a risk or susceptibility factor for the early onset of DAT. Mutations or abnormalities of chromosomes 1, 14 and 21 (including *trisomy 21*, the genetic lesion of *Down syndrome*) are associated with other abnormal proteins (presenilin 1 and 2, also called amyloid precursor proteins) that contribute to the onset and course of DAT. In people with these rare genetic variants, DAT may be an autosomal dominant condition that appears at an early age.

Huntington's disease follows the pattern of autosomal dominant inheritance. A gene on chromosome 4 codes for the protein huntingtin. This gene has an abnormally high number (> 35) of repeats of the sequence CAG. Although the normal functions of huntingtin are unknown, in HD, the presence of the abnormal protein correlates with destruction of the caudate nucleus of the basal ganglia. This produces a characteristic "butterfly pattern" visible on computed tomography (CT) or magnetic resonance imaging (MRI) scans. As the caudate deteriorates, patients develop chorea, severe dysregulation of emotion, psychosis, and significant losses of cognitive function beginning in middle age.

Among the dementias, only HD results entirely from known genetic factors. The pathogenesis of most other dementias relates to the *allostatic load* of accumulated risk factors, or the piling up of multiple minor or moderate central nervous system (CNS) insults such as head injury, vascular blockage, nutritional deficits, infections, or autoimmune processes. Factors such as the presence of APOE4 genes may determine an individual's capacity to compensate for or repair damage, accounting for the variable time of onset and initial distribution of lesions.

Clinical Recognition of Dementia

A 75-year-old woman is brought to her physician's office after she left a pot on the stove, and then locked herself out of the house because she could not remember where she kept her extra key. Her daughter says that her mother has become gradually more forgetful over the past 2 years, although she covers up her lapses by asking questions, often repeatedly.

A 40-year-old man infected with HIV takes antiretroviral medication erratically. He shows personality changes, with irritability and apathy replacing a normally cheerful, curious, and outgoing disposition. He has considerable loss of short-term memory and difficulty manipulating information as measured by serial subtractions, but no disorientation or aphasia. His Mini–Mental State Examination score is 24. His partner reports other impairments, including sleeping at odd hours, loss of balance, paranoia, and weight loss.

People with dementia need medical, neurological, and behavioral assessment. Repeated mental status examinations document baseline cognitive deficits and their progression over time. These examinations can include the Folstein Mini–Mental State Examination (MMSE), Montreal Cognitive Assessment (MoCA), HIV Dementia Scale, Frontal Assessment Battery (FAB), or any number of other specific examinations of cognitive domains (see Chapter 39: The Psychiatric Evaluation). Concurrent input from caregivers using measures like the Dementia Severity Rating Scale is essential to identify the functional deficits that may benefit from rehabilitative or supportive care. Neuropsychological testing is more extensive and precise and may uncover preserved functions that can be strengthened by treatment (see Appendix: Psychological Testing). Evaluators should repeatedly ask about or measure behavioral deficits and psychopathological symptoms (e.g., extreme or labile moods, hallucinations, paranoia) as these treatable sources of disability contribute heavily to caregiver burden. General medical assessment and treatment are essential. Neuroimaging, cerebrospinal fluid (CSF) examination, or other invasive testing may confirm the presence of particular conditions (infections, HD, or multiple sclerosis). Genetic studies may also be important to family members.

> What are the consequences of dementia for the individual and society?

Incidence of DAT rises with age, with 20% prevalence in people age 80. The rate doubles roughly every 5 years. Up to 50% of people > 85 may have some degree of dementia. By 2050, if current trends continue, 3.8 million people in the US and 115.4 million people globally will have dementia. The cost of dementia (reflecting both care and the lost productivity of patients and caregivers) exceeds US $100 billion annually in the US. In 2010, the worldwide cost of dementia care was US $604 billion dollars, or 1% of the world's GDP. If interventions could delay the onset of DAT by 5 years, in 50 years, 4 million fewer patients would develop DAT in the US alone.

Widespread HIV infection, increased survival from closed head injury, epidemic alcohol abuse, diabetes, and atherosclerotic cardiovascular disease are modifiable contributors to the incidence and prevalence of dementia, including in younger people.

Treatment of Dementia

> **What treatments affect the course and outcome of dementia?**

Some dementias (e.g., those resulting from CNS HIV infection) may be stopped or reversed by treating the underlying cause.

The lesions of DAT cluster in areas of the brain where AcH is most common. The medications used to treat DAT include donepezil, rivastigmine, galantamine, and tacrine, which inhibit acetylcholinesterase and thereby increase AcH, and memantine, an N-methyl D-aspartate (NMDA) antagonist. These agents have only mild effects in DAT and have not been shown to slow the progression from MCI to DAT. Many other agents are under investigation.

Drugs for PD either increase dopamine directly or indirectly through inhibiting its metabolism. These agents include levodopa (frequently combined with carbidopa to get more L-DOPA across the blood–brain barrier); dopamine agonists such as bromocriptine, pramipexole, and ropinirole; and monoamine oxidase B inhibitors such as selegiline and rasagiline.

While there is no treatment per se for HD, tetrabenazine has been approved by the US Food and Drug Administration (FDA) to treat HD chorea.

Older patients who are depressed often have prominent cognitive impairments ("pseudodementia" or *dementia syndrome of depression*) that may improve with treatment of depression (including antidepressants and electroconvulsive therapy). Even if some cognitive impairment persists, relieving depression improves function and reduces caregiver burden.

Psychotic symptoms or uncontrolled aggressive behavior in demented patients may respond to low doses of antipsychotic medication. However, the use of antipsychotic drugs in dementia may increase mortality. Behavioral and psychosocial interventions are often more effective in mild to moderate cases of agitation.

Currently available medications do not target the various abnormal proteins that accumulate in the brain of people with dementia. The multicenter Anti-Amyloid Treatment in Asymptomatic Alzheimer's Disease (A4) trial is currently testing antiamyloid treatments in patients with mild cognitive impairment.

Supportive medical, behavioral, and family intervention may improve the lives of people with dementia. Treatment of concurrent infections, other diseases, and good nutrition help maintain cognitive function. Providing a safe and adequately, but not overwhelmingly, stimulating environment preserves patient autonomy, at least for a time. Encouraging whole families to participate in the maintenance of a person with dementia is crucial because individuals, especially elderly spouses, who shoulder the entire burden of dementia care often develop depression and uncontrolled illnesses. Offering prepared meals and day treatment helps keep patients with dementia in community settings. Anything that delays the point at which patients require nursing home care improves quality of life and reduces financial hardship. However, complete care in often necessary in the last year or so of life. Health care professionals must help families recognize when they have arrived at that difficult point.

> **Is dementia preventable?**

The prevention of dementia is a crucial public health goal. The tissue changes of dementia occur late and typically represent irreversible damage. Current efforts to prevent head injury and aggressively treat hypertension, diabetes, dyslipidemia, endocrinopathies, vitamin deficiencies, autoimmune diseases, alcoholism, and other chronic conditions are important strategies for preventing dementia.

The famous Minnesota Nun Study (1986) suggests another, intriguing possibility. In this study, the verbal abilities revealed in documents written by young women were correlated with their later cognitive capacities and, ultimately, brain findings at autopsy. The acquisition of sophisticated language skills early in life and higher levels of education moderated the symptoms of dementia, even in subjects with clear neuropathological changes of DAT. This suggests that early stimulation may create cognitive reserve that buffers the effect of later degenerative processes.

Recommended Readings

Albert, M. S., DeKosky, S. T., Dickson, D., Dubois, B., Feldman, H. H., Fox, N. C., ... Phelps, C. H. (2011). The
diagnosis of mild cognitive impairment due to Alzheimer
disease: Recommendations from the National Institute
on Aging – Alzheimer's Association workgroups on
diagnostic guidelines for Alzheimer disease. *Alzheimer's
Dementia*, 7, 270–279.

Mace, N. L., & Rabins, P. V. (2011). *The 36 hour day: A family guide to caring for persons with Alzheimer disease,
related dementing illnesses, and memory loss in later life*
(5th ed.). Baltimore, MD: Johns Hopkins Press Health
Book.

Petersen, R. C. (2011). Clinical practice: Mild cognitive
impairment. *New England Journal of Medicine*, *364*,
2227–2234. http://doi.org/10.1056/NEJMcp0910237

Thies, W., & Bleiler, L. (2011). Alzheimer's disease facts
and figures. *Alzheimer's Dementia*, *7*, 208–244. http://
doi.org/10.1016/j.jalz.2011.02.004

Review Questions

1. A woman diagnosed with hypertension when she was 64 became anxious and forgetful around age 75. At age 77, her mini–mental status score was 18. Retest at age 78 was unchanged, but at 79, she developed aphasia, with a drop in score to 12. Her caregiver confirmed that loss of function was erratic (e.g., she would be stable, then suddenly lose a capacity such as knowing where she kept things or how to put on clothes). After her death at age 80, an autopsy showed
   A. diffuse lesions containing presenilin and huntingtin
   B. enlargement of the fourth ventricles and diffuse cortical atrophy
   C. Lewy bodies clustering primarily in the frontal and temporal lobes
   D. plaques, granulovacuolar changes, and neurofibrillary tangles
   E. signs of infarction of medium and small blood vessels, with lesions of different ages

2. A 49-year-old man with trisomy 21 (Down syndrome) and an IQ of 65 lives in a group home and works assembling packages in a sheltered workshop. Over the course of a year, he loses the ability to work, becomes with-

drawn and uncooperative, and speaks much less than before. This deterioration should be considered
   A. delirium of unknown etiology
   B. dementia, since he has lost previously acquired capacities
   C. expected neurodevelopmental degeneration
   D. organic personality syndrome
   E. psychosis secondary to trisomy 21

Answer Key on p. 466

47

Stress Disorders, Bereavement, and Dissociative Disorders

Julia B. Frank, MD

- What is traumatic stress, and how is it relevant to psychiatric disorders?
- What is demoralization, and how does it relate to trauma and adjustment disorders?
- What does bereavement illustrate about stress reactions and their treatment?
- What bio-behavioral mechanisms underlie PTSD?
- How are stressor-related disorders treated? What is trauma-informed care?
- What are dissociative disorders, and how are they treated?

Traumatic Stress

> Once raped in a dark room, a 30-year-old woman experiences nightmares and breaks into a sweat whenever it is dark, feeling constantly threatened, jumpy, and unable to concentrate. She avoids talking about the rape, watching related shows on TV, or any other reminders. In not discussing her experience, her belief that she was somehow responsible and doomed to another attack goes uncorrected, and she remains in a constant state of high arousal.

> What is traumatic stress, and how is it relevant to psychiatric disorders?

Stress of every kind disrupts normal physical and psychological homeostasis, triggering adaptive biological and psychological reactions to restore equilibrium (see Chapter 7: Stress, Adaptation, and Stress Disorders). Stress that overwhelms a person's ability to adapt (e.g., severe or chronic stress) may result in a variety of illnesses, including mental illnesses such as *adjustment disorders, acute stress disorder,* and **posttraumatic stress disorder** (PTSD). Two childhood disorders, *reactive attachment disorder* and *disinhibited social engagement disorder,* are included in this domain (see Table 47.1)

Adjustment Disorders

Following a mild to moderate stressor, or repetitive (chronic) stressors, people may develop **adjustment disorders**. Adjustment disorder may be diagnosed when a person develops symptoms after trauma or stress, such as a divorce or a serious illness. The symptoms of adjustment disorders must be beyond what is typical following similar stressors, and cause significant distress or impairment, or both. **Acute adjustment disorders** last less than 6 months. **Chronic adjustment disorders** persist longer.

> A 50-year-old woman cannot stop thinking about the death of her ailing cat 3 months ago, a loss that coincided with the finalization of her divorce. She has withdrawn from friends because condolences irritate her, and she has sudden crying spells at work. She can cheer up when she is busy, and her sleep is only disrupted by awakenings when she thinks she hears a cat crying.

Adjustment disorders are qualified as *with depressed mood, with anxiety, with mixed anxiety and depressed mood, with disturbance of conduct,* or *with mixed disturbance of emotions and conduct disorders.* The diagnosis excludes normal bereavement reactions (see section "Bereavement" below).

Table 47.1. Conditions in which trauma or other stressors play a causal or exacerbating role

Condition	Research Indicating Role of Stress	Phenomenology	Implications
Somatic symptom disorders	"Multiple unexplained symptoms" identified in veterans and those closely affected by 9/11, other population based traumas; high rates of early trauma associated with some functional conditions (IBS, pelvic pain)	Uncontrolled stress responses magnify pain, disrupt autonomic activity	High demand for medical services after population trauma. Need for trauma-informed care in many medical settings
Borderline personality disorder	High rates of sexual, emotional abuse in childhood/adolescence	Self-protective dissociation during trauma becomes a consistent reaction Leads to difficulty modulating emotions, especially rage, self-loathing Hypersensitivity to subtle triggers Inconsistent perceptions of others Self- mutilation may be effort to break through dissociative numbness	Hospitalization for self-injury; symptoms also triggered by restrictions of hospital care Effective therapy focuses on current thoughts and behavior, but role of trauma is accepted and explored in psychotherapy after behavioral stabilization (see Chapter 40: Principles of Psychotherapy)
Generalized anxiety disorder	Identified in cohort studies after population-based trauma, relates in part to ongoing stresses in the posttraumatic environment	Generalized arousal, lack of sleep, uncontrollable worry about many situations	Worsens chronic illnesses (especially ASCVD, diabetes); many turn to medical providers as source of safety
Major depressive disorder	Identified in cohort studies after population-based trauma, relates in part to ongoing stresses in the post traumatic environment	Lack of sleep, feelings of helplessness, guilt, hopelessness, lack of outlets for positive activity	Meaning of stress may affect focus of psychotherapy
Reactive attachment disorder	(Childhood disorder) First identified in infants and young children in institutional settings, including prolonged hospitalization for medical conditions	Despairing response to loss or prolonged separation from primary caregiver; profound social withdrawal, listlessness	May affect survival, future relationships, capacity for emotional regulation Institutional routines should provide consistent care, include parents
Disinhibited social engagement disorder	(Childhood disorder) Related to multiple care givers in the absence of a stable attachment figure	Child does not discriminate familiar and unfamiliar people, goes with anyone	Affects future relationships and capacity for emotional regulation

Note. ASCVD = atherosclerotic cardiovascular disease; IBS= irritable bowel syndrome.

Demoralization

What is demoralization, and how does it relate to trauma and adjustment disorders?

The psychological state of **demoralization** is a response to events that are perceived as threatening and uncontrollable (e.g., threatening economic, marital, or medical conditions). Demoralized individuals feel incompetent and distressed, although they may or may not have symptoms of a defined mental disorder. Demoralization may remit when the threatening circumstances change, as when a cancer goes into remission. Psychotherapy that increases hope and encourages mastery may exert many of its effects by addressing demoralization.

Although not part of the diagnostic criteria, symptoms such as headaches, other pains, or gastrointestinal dysfunction are common in stress-related disorders and states of demoralization. Individuals who seek help for physical distress may not disclose the precipitating event, or even be aware of it unless asked. Stress, both recent and from early life, may contribute to the pathogenesis or course of a psychiatric disorder not directly related to the stressor.

Bereavement

What does bereavement illustrate about stress reactions and their treatment?

Loss or the end of an emotionally important relationship is an especially stressful event that can result in the disruption of physical, psychological, and behavioral adaptation. People experience **grief** or **bereavement** in response to death and other losses (e.g., divorce, loss of job or pet). Symptoms after a significant loss, even when severe, do not necessarily constitute a mental disorder.

According to **attachment theory** some mammals and most primates and human children react to disrupted attachment, with fluctuating arousal, protest, agitation, withdrawal, sometimes aggression, and eventual reorganization of behavior.

Grief in adults includes preoccupation with the loss, searching, sadness, guilt, anger, despair, anxiety, and a desire for consolation from others coupled with the need for time alone. Other symptoms include difficulty concentrating, anorexia, restlessness, and poor sleep. Fleeting experiences of hearing or seeing a lost person are not uncommon. Grief may exacerbate trait vulnerabilities, such as tendencies to internalize or externalize distress, poor self-esteem, and negative expectations of the future. It may also precipitate an existential crisis or spiritual alienation.

As with stress, it is the meaning or significance of the loss in a particular social context, rather than the loss itself, that determines the person's response. Age, gender, and culture influence the experience and expression of grief. Losses due to suicide, violence, accident, or disaster typically trigger severe reactions. Anxiety over the material consequences of a loss can exacerbate distress. Signs of *complicated grief* include increased substance use, intense guilt, prolonged anhedonia, inability to find meaning in life, and suicidal ideation, qualities that may warrant a psychiatric diagnosis and treatment.

Mourning rituals (e.g., funerals, a defined period of withdrawal from social activities, memorial gatherings) are important for restoring meaning and helping the bereaved to structure their experience and reconnect with others. People experiencing hidden or shameful losses, or losses other than death, may not receive such help. Much mental health care, especially group therapies and the routines of inpatient settings, have a beneficial, ritualistic aspect. Seeing a medical provider and having a physical exam may serve similar purposes, especially for those who are grieving or shaken by trauma.

Grief is a central concern of the emerging specialty of **palliative care** (see Chapter 33: Palliative Care), which addresses both *anticipatory grief* and *grief following a loss*. Although nurses, social workers, and clergy may provide specialized counseling, all practitioners should know how to help families and patients by expressing sympathy while explaining and predicting the eventual resolution of grief, based on knowledge of its natural history.

Posttraumatic Stress Disorder

In current diagnoses, *traumatic stress* is defined as experiences that threaten the life or the bodily or psychological integrity of a person. It is often, although not always, sudden or unexpected and may be associated with intense sensory stimulation such as gruesome images, aversive smells, or very loud noises.

Causes of PTSD

Providers have historically attributed posttraumatic symptoms to invisible physical injuries. In the 19th century, posttraumatic nervousness and pain were attributed to "railway spine," thought to be due to occult damage to the spinal cord and brain from train travel or accidents. In the US Civil War, doctors diagnosed "soldier's heart." In World War I, postcombat nervousness, confusion, irritability, nightmares, apathy, and extreme startle responses were attributed to "shell shock," or prolonged exposure to active warfare. In World War II and the Korean Conflict, these symptoms were relabeled as "battle" or "combat fatigue." By the late 1980s, following the Vietnam, Gulf, and Afghanistan wars, PTSD became an accepted diagnosis describing the psychological sequelae of prolonged exposure to severe combat conditions (see Box 47.1).

The search for occult physical causes continues, focused on exposure to chemical agents (Agent Orange in Vietnam, nerve gas in the Gulf War) and, most recently, in attention to traumatic brain injury (TBI), or concussive brain damage resulting from proximity to explosions. Exposures and explosions have real physical sequelae, but the boundary between the effects of physical and psychological trauma is not always clear cut.

Aside from combat, typical traumatic stresses in contemporary America include accidents, natural and manmade disasters, and victimization by violence (including intimate partner violence and rape). People with limited control over their lives, including the young, old, and people who face discrimination or have limited resources, experience higher rates of trauma and more barriers to recovery.

Exposure to traumatic stress can exacerbate medical and psychiatric conditions. Compared

---

Box 47.1. Criteria for the diagnosis of PTSD

Criterion A: (required)
Exposure to life-threatening events, serious injury, or sexual violence that is directly experienced, witnessed, or affecting a close friend or relative

Repeated exposure to the aftermath of trauma (e.g., by first responders or police) qualifies, but exposure through media does not

Cluster B: Intrusion (one required)
Recurrent, unwanted memories or thoughts related to the trauma (forced recollection); nightmares or distressing dreams; brief reliving of events (flashbacks, may be momentary); psychological distress in response to cues; in children, repetitive play with traumatic themes

Cluster C: Avoidance (one required)
Efforts to avoid memories or cues related to trauma; behavioral avoidance of trauma related places, people, objects

Cluster D: Persistent negative alterations in cognition or mood (two required)
Inability to remember parts of the trauma (dissociative amnesia); exaggerated (generalized) negative beliefs about self/others; distorted cognitions about causes of the trauma (self blame); negative emotions (horror, anger, guilt, shame); loss of interest in activities; feelings of detachment/estrangement from others; inability to experience positive emotions

Cluster E: Recurrent arousal (two or more)
Angry outbursts; reckless or self destructive behavior; sleep problems; exaggerated startling; vigilance towards possible threats or repetition of the trauma; impaired concentration

Dissociative symptoms specifier
Depersonalization (estrangement, feeling in a dream, of being outside oneself, distorted sense of time); derealization (external world seems unreal, distant, distorted)

Delayed expression specifier
Full blown symptoms do not begin until at least 6 months after trauma; some symptoms may be present earlier

---

Note. For DSM-5 criteria see American Psychiatric Association. (2013). *Diagnostic and statistical manual of mental disorders* (5th ed.). Arlington, VA: Author.

with psychiatric outpatients, hospitalized psychiatric patients have much higher rates of both childhood adversity and recent trauma. This suggests that the experience of trauma contributes to the suicidality, alienation, and aggressiveness that require the most intensive and restrictive treatments, independent of diagnosis.

The most pathogenic events are those attributed to human error or malevolence, and those that disrupt critical life structures. While the severity of a trauma is predictive of PTSD, the impact of the stressor depends on the survivor's *appraisal* of its meaning. Good general health, adequate social resources, and the psychological qualities of sociability, humor, flexibility of thought, perseverance, emotional self-awareness, and an internal locus of control contribute to individual resilience.

Ameliorating/Aggravating Factors in PTSD

Posttraumatic conditions are also crucial. Reconnecting with important others and reestablishing usual activities and routines may quickly restore a sense of coherence and meaning, reducing or preventing PTSD. People who are isolated, or who cannot return to normal life (e.g., survivors of natural disasters, refugees) are at high risk for ongoing symptoms and dysfunction. Conversely, being part of a strong social network, having a structured daily routine, and healthy spirituality are factors that predict *resilience* in the face of stress or trauma.

A past personal history of trauma increases vulnerability, possibly by inducing persistent epigenetic changes in stress reactive bodily systems, along with influencing the person's *locus of control* and self-concept. Understanding the role of modifiable environmental factors and sources of resilience helps guide intervention in the immediate post traumatic period. Even in an emergency room or other medical setting, treating the traumatized person with respect, providing well-targeted reassurance, and facilitating contact with family, reduces anxiety and may have preventive value.

In the diagnostic criteria, all symptoms must occur after the trauma, and the syndrome must cause impairment or distress. Substance-related symptoms (for example, impaired memory because of intoxication) are excluded.

Acute stress disorder is diagnosed if nine of the symptoms listed in Box 47.1 begin within 3 days of an event and persist up to 1 month, after which the diagnosis changes to PTSD.

What bio-behavioral mechanisms underlie PTSD?

Studies of animals subjected to conditioned fear, and of humans exposed to trauma, have explored the neurobiology of PTSD, opening the way to pharmacological treatments and select forms of psychotherapy. In particular, sudden, life-threatening stress may activate a reflexive response pathway that involves the amygdala and adrenergic nervous system, bypassing the hippocampal and cortical processing involved in a measured, modulated response. Prolonged, increased adrenergic activity in response both to the trauma and to recurrent memory of the trauma manifests itself in persistently increased arousal (symptom cluster D). Imaging and microscopic studies have correlated enlargement and changes in the cytoarchitecture of the amygdala with signs of enduring post traumatic arousal.

The adrenergically mediated fight-or-flight response (see Chapter 7: Stress, Adaptation and Stress Disorders) simultaneously facilitates self-protective behaviors and triggers a slower response of the hypothalamic-pituitary-adreno-cortical (HPA) axis to increase the production of corticosteroids from the adrenal glands. Increased glucocorticoids and possibly mineralocorticoids maintain blood pressure, reduce inflammation, and otherwise support the body's adaptation to stress. Glucocorticoids have both genomic effects and direct effects on brain cytoarchitecture. Other mediators such as brain-derived neurotrophic factor (BDNF) and oxytocin may be activated, possibly mediating neural plasticity in response to stress.

In the usual stress response, glucocorticoid suppresses or terminates the acute adrenergic response, but in PTSD, either the initial release of cortisol is insufficient, or glucocorticoid receptors (GR) function differently, partly due to epigenetic effects. People with PTSD may show low levels of urinary cortisol and high levels of norepinephrine metabolites. A large-scale study of veterans exposed to trauma has identified polymorphism of the FKBP5 gene (which affects GRs) to be a predictor of risk for PTSD after exposure to trauma. High levels of cortisol following trauma also contribute to (reversible) shrinkage of the hippocampus, a well-validated finding in PTSD research. High cortisol levels also correlate with changes in the cytoarchitecture of the orbitofrontal cortex, which processes stimuli from many areas.

Treatment of PTSD

> How are stressor-related disorders treated? What is trauma-informed care?

In favorable circumstances, most people exposed to trauma or other degrees of stress recover without treatment. For those who do not, psychotherapy, with or without medication, is the mainstay of treatment.

A strong alliance between therapist and patient directly addresses the isolation that survivors of trauma feel. Group therapy, in some settings, also may have a powerful restorative affect. Most therapies involve allowing or encouraging (but not forcing) patients to tell their stories, sometimes repeatedly. Unprocessed experience is relived as though it were still happening; repeated processing helps restore the patterns of normal memory, reconnects the experience to its original temporal context, differentiates it from the present, and confronts the avoidance that prevents corrective learning. Therapy also may involve specific techniques to reduce arousal, including breathing, mindfulness, and vigorous exercise. These interventions may reduce the anatomical changes associated with trauma. While they do not necessarily remove all symptoms, they provide the individual with a greater sense of control.

Fluoxetine and other antidepressants have been shown to reduce the intrusive and arousal symptoms of PTSD. Alpha-adrenergic blocking agents may selectively relieve nightmares. The restoration of normal sleep greatly facilitates healing from trauma. Benzodiazepines, although commonly prescribed, are generally not helpful.

Understanding the broad, but often hidden, impact of prior trauma supports the implementation of *trauma-informed care* in medical and psychiatric institutions. The term covers systematic efforts to reduce the aversive, disempowering,

or disheartening aspects of being a patient. Like other forms of *patient-centered care*, this approach should be congruent with the patient's cultural background and expectations. It typically involves offering patients choices, placing their needs over the needs of the setting, doing everything possible to minimize isolation and disability, and responding sensitively and empathically to the sometimes disruptive, idiosyncratic reactions patients have to their illness or treatment.

A related method is *psychological first aid,* a program developed by the military to help responders address the immediate needs of people involved in events such as a fire, mass shooting, plane crash, or natural disaster. Psychological first aid builds on the understanding of resilience. It involves ensuring that people are out of immediate danger, allowing but not forcing them to speak of their experience, reconnecting them with others, and expecting and predicting that most will recover, while providing information about help for those who do not.

Dissociative Disorders

> What are dissociative disorders, and how are they treated?

Dissociation is the disruption, loss, or absence of the usual integration of memory, consciousness, and personal identity. *Normal* dissociation commonly occurs, for example, when a person is absorbed in a book and unaware of the surrounding environment. Dissociation also occurs during periods of fatigue and monotony such as driving a long stretch of highway without remembering doing so. **Hypnosis** is essentially dissociation induced by intense concentration.

Dissociation can be a protective response to trauma or intense and recurrent *stress*. It allows the individual to ignore pain or anxiety and cope with the emergent situation. *Pathological dissociation* is dissociation that occurs repeatedly and out of context, resulting in impaired functioning especially in close personal relationships and stressful environments. Pathological dissociation is generally experienced as occurring randomly or "out of the blue," although it may be triggered by

Table 47.2. Dissociative phenomena and related disorders

Dissociative Disorders	Description	Example	Comment
Dissociative amnesia	Inability to remember stressful personal events or period of time May be subtly confused or in no distress	Woman wakes in a hotel room wearing unfamiliar clothes; does not recall travel there; remembers her name, age, profession, but not violent confrontation with her partner Veteran cannot recall witnessing death of friend, training together, last months of deployment	Often occurs after a traumatic event Can last hours to months or years F > M ratio 3:1
Depersonalization/ Derealization disorder	Detached from one's own body and emotions; detached from one's surroundings; feels robotic; describing someone else or separate from the environment (like watching a movie)	After receiving a kidney transplant, a man feels no spontaneous joy or interest, and feels like he's watching himself from a distance Sleep deprived intern feels as if working behind glass curtain in two dimensional space; puzzled by familiar equipment, but uses correctly	Persistent or intermittent No memory loss May occur in reaction to medical procedures or states of severe anxiety Person typically has insight into condition
Dissociative identity disorder (formerly multiple personality disorder)	Person has two or more identities, each typically expresses a particular affect Person is aware of being divided, but may not know all the states or that they operate independently	A woman in psychotherapy varies between giddy, cheerful, miserable, childlike, sullen, angry, and terrified Emotional states shift abruptly; refers to self in third person and is unaware of inconsistency	Different states called "alters" Person unable to integrate unacceptable emotions tied to memories not normally available Alters may claim their own personal histories, identities, and names Associated with early trauma such as abuse Switching among alters occurs during stress May meet criteria for *borderline personality disorder*

cues related to prior trauma of which the patient is unaware.

A woman involved in a multicar accident stands beside her car directing traffic until the police arrive. Only then does she realize she has a broken arm. At the time, she had felt herself standing outside her body, watching the scene from a distance.

Dissociative disorders have been reported worldwide. They are frequently manifested as dissociative trance or possession disorders that reflect culturally specific explanatory models. Dissociation can occur as part of serious psychiatric disorders, including *schizophrenia*. Rarely, dissociation signifies a neurological disorder (e.g., *partial complex seizures*).

Risk Factors for Dissociation

A history of severe family dysfunction and poor premorbid emotional, social, or occupational functioning predisposes people to pathological dissociation. Repeated dissociation beginning early in life (e.g., after abuse) affects the child's ability to form realistic perceptions of other people. This primes catastrophic responses to hints of separation or disconnection. The person may develop a tendency to see others as all good or all bad, even holding contradictory views of a single person.

Susan, a 32-year-old woman, seeks treatment for chronic depression, anxiety, and thoughts of suicide. She reports having been sexually and physically abused as a child and being raped during adulthood. She complains of "spacing out" and experiences minutes to hours of amnesia, after which she may find herself walking unfamiliar streets or wearing clothing in a style different from her own. She reports hearing angry voices inside her head. One day, she tells her therapist to call her Kim. "Kim" says Susan knows nothing about her, mocks Susan's timidity, and is irritable and aggressive, especially when discussing fears. Later in the session, Susan returns. She has no memory of Kim, but is aware of a time gap in the session.

In dissociated states, especially *dissociative identity disorder* and *dissociative amnesia* or *fugue* people may act in ways that violate their own and other's sense of social appropriateness and morality. The person can carry out complex behaviors, but may not remember, or feels unable to remember, doing them. For this reason, people who dissociate are sometimes suspected of malingering or falsifying their history to avoid punishment or responsibility.

The phenomenon of dissociation raises questions about the validity of all memories. Researchers have shown that memory of an event can change in response to questioning by authority figures. Thus, therapists who assume that all dissociation results from unremembered victimization may inadvertently foster the development of false memories. This has led researchers to question whether *dissociative identity disorder* occurs spontaneously, or is a "way of explaining" contradictory aspects of one's personality.

An unproven memory can disrupt whole lives, especially if a person tries to get confirmation – or seek legal justice – against someone remembered, long after the fact, as a perpetrator of abuse. Family informants and hospital and legal records should be carefully researched to objectively verify the reports of patients with dissociation who claim early *victimization*.

Bio-Behavioral Mechanisms of Dissociation

The mechanisms underlying dissociation are not fully understood. Some psychotropic drugs, particularly ketamine, phencyclidine (PCP), and LSD can induce dissociative states. Neurochemically, this suggests that dissociation relates to disruptions of the subcortical and cortical networks that express monoamine neurotransmitters (dopamine, serotonin, norepinephrine, and acetylcholine) and endogenous opioids. Dissociation may also involve imbalances of gamma-amino-butyric acid (GABA) and glutamate in the cortex.

Treatment for Dissociative Disorders

Although treatment for depression or anxiety sometimes relieves moods that induce dissociative states, no psychotropic drug to prevent dissociation is currently available. Someone suffering fugue or amnesia typically can benefit from reassurance and an exploration of possible triggering events. **Psychodynamic psychotherapy**, which explores emotional memories of triggering events and their meaning, may be effective. **Hypnosis** to induce dissociation therapeutically is potentially helpful in facilitating intervention while the person is in the dissociated state. However, it can also be harmful, because people under hypnosis are suggestible and may generate "memories" or states in response to the therapist's inquiries and assumptions. **Mindfulness**, a technique used in **dialectical behavior therapy**, has been shown to facilitate awareness of one's own bodily state and more realistic perceptions of others.

Recommended Readings

Bell, V., Oakley, D. A., Halligan, P. W., & Deeley, Q. (2011). Dissociation in hysteria and hypnosis: Evidence from cognitive neuroscience. *Journal of Neurology, Neurosurgery, and Psychiatry*, 82, 332–339. http://doi.org/10.1136/jnnp.2009.199158

Herman, J. (1992). *Trauma and recovery: The aftermath of violence from domestic abuse to political terror*. New York, NY: Basic Books.

Jamison, K. R. (2009). *Nothing was the same*: A memoir. New York, NY: Knopf.

Watkins, L. E., Han, S., Harpaz-Rotem, I., Mota, N. P., Southwick, S. M., Krystal, J. H., ... Pietrzak, R. H. (2016). FKBP5 polymorphisms, childhood abuse and PTSD symptoms: Results from the National Health and Resilience in Veterans Study. *Psychoneuroendocrinology*, 69, 98–105.

Review Questions

1. Five months ago, a 62-year-old man lost his wife of 30 years to cancer. He cannot clean out her closet. He has lost 15 pounds and oscillates between bouts of restlessness and lethargy. Initially, he could sleep for only 4 to 5 hr at night, but this seems to be improving. He spends a lot of time with his adult children. The appropriate professional advice would be:

   A. "Feel free to ask me questions about your wife's illness and treatment."
   B. "I am sorry for your loss, but I feel confident that over time, you will learn to live with it."
   C. "I wonder if you can't get over this because you have unresolved guilt about this relationship."
   D. "It's time to bite the bullet, give away your wife's things, and start to rebuild your life."
   E. "You should be over the acute mourning by now. You seem to be getting depressed."

2. A soldier feels numb and sad after his second overseas deployment is extended. He believes the leadership of his unit is unresponsive to his need to get back to his family. He cannot imagine feeling better when the deployment ends because he considers himself unemployable outside the military. This soldier is likely to respond best to
   A. antidepressant therapy
   B. leave for recreation and relaxation
   C. more contact with his family
   D. motivational talks from his commanding officer
   E. psychotherapy

3. Among the following, the most appropriate description of this soldier's condition is
   A. adjustment disorder with mixed emotional features
   B. demoralization
   C. depressive disorder, not otherwise specified (NOS)
   D. inability to adjust to military life
   E. malingering

Answer Key on p. 466

48 Obsessive-Compulsive and Related Disorders

Julia B. Frank, MD

- What features are shared by the conditions in the category of obsessive-compulsive and related disorders?
- How does the neurobiology of these disorders relate to current treatment approaches?

Characteristics of Obsessive-Compulsive and Related Disorders

What features are shared by the conditions in the category of obsessive-compulsive and related disorders?

As the name implies, *obsessive-compulsive and related disorders* involve intrusive, repetitive, or stereotypic thoughts (**obsessions**) and an irresistible need to perform some mental action or behavior (**compulsion**). **Obsessive-compulsive disorder** (OCD) usually includes both elements, with the compulsions serving to relieve the negative affect (anxiety, guilt, or shame) associated with the obsession (Table 48.1). *Trichotillomania* and *excoriation disorder* connote compulsive hair pulling or skin picking that may be or become mindless, occurring without conscious motivation. *Body dysmorphic disorder* describes a preoccupation with an imagined, usually visible physical defect or quality that may induce compulsive examination or checking behavior, often with the less stereotypic response of social avoidance.

A 6-year-old boy cannot go to sleep until he says his prayers exactly right, 5 times in a row. After even one error, he starts over from the beginning. He struggles in school because small errors such as coloring outside the lines induce fits of crying and agitation.

A dermatologist treating a 35-year-old woman notes that she has bald patches on her scalp and broken hair shafts,

and lacks eyelashes. When asked, she admits to pulling out hair as a "nervous habit," although she is concerned about the resulting disfigurement.

A 39-year-old man asks his primary care provider for steroid cream because of severe chafing on his hands. He says that he has always washed his hands frequently, up to 30 times per day, but recently he has started to use diluted bleach, because he just doesn't feel clean otherwise.

An unmarried 40-year-old man avoids interacting with his nieces and nephews because of intrusive thoughts that he might inadvertently touch them in a sexual way.

Fragmentary obsessions and compulsions are a normal part of human life with analogs in other species. It is developmentally normal for a toddler to insist on following certain routines, especially those related to toileting or to going to sleep. Many people ruminate about their past behavior, or obsessively seek to undo losses or failures. We perform many actions of daily life in stereotypic fashion and are unsettled when these patterns are interrupted.

Diagnostic Criteria

The symptoms of OCD and related disorders differ in quality and kind. In most cases, the obsessive thoughts are "ego dystonic," experienced as disruptive of a sense of self or the continuity of normal thought. They may be senseless, as when

Table 48.1. DSM-5 obsessive-compulsive and related disorders

Disorder	Prevalence and Gender Ratio	Treatment and Outcome	Notes
OCD	2–4% lifetime prevalence Usual onset before age 30 Prepubertal onset more common in males Female onset peaks in postpartum period	SSRIs, clomipramine: 40–60% respond SNRIs also used Exposure and response prevention (ERP) ~80% response Deep brain stimulation of ventral striatum (FDA approved)	As common as schizophrenia Children may lack insight
Trichotillomania (hair pulling)	0.8% prevalence F > M Onset around puberty	Habit reversal therapy Mixed results for SSRIs, antipsychotics, naltrexone and N-acetylcysteine	Seen by dermatologists
Excoriation disorder (skin picking)	2–5% prevalence F > M	Habit reversal therapy	Few seek psychiatric treatment Seen by dermatologists
Body dysmorphic disorder (obsessive preoccupation with flaw in appearance) "Muscle dysmorphia" in men (preoccupation with musculature)	1–3% general population Higher prevalence in those with other OC-related disorders and anorexia nervosa Adolescent/early adult onset F:M 1:1	ERP first line SSRIs, clomipramine: 60–80% improvement Delusional form may respond to antipsychotics	Insight varies, may be delusional Associated with being unmarried/unemployed, suicidal ideation or attempts May seek plastic surgery
Hoarding disorder	2–6% prevalence? M > F	Treatments less effective than for OCD	Insight varies; may include delusions; usually comorbid with mood or anxiety disorders

Adapted from Black, D. W., & Andreasen, N. (2014). Obsessive compulsive disorders. In D. W. Black & N. C. Andreasen, *Introductory textbook of psychiatry* (6th ed., pp. 219–238), Washington, DC: APPI. F > M = ratio of females to males (greater than); OCD = obsessive-compulsive disorder; SNRIs = serotonin and norepinephrine reuptake inhibitors; SSRIs = selective serotonin reuptake inhibitors.

someone feels the need to count the words in a sentence, rather than read them. Symptomatic compulsive behaviors are highly inflexible and resistant to change. The associated anxiety, guilt, and shame may cause great distress. By definition, to consider the diagnosis, the symptoms must impair daily functioning, impeding learning, work, or relationships.

The typical obsessions or negative thoughts of OCD relate to rudimentary social capacities, sug-gesting that they originate in subcortical areas of the brain that also generate emotions and elementary social behavior. The activity of these centers is represented in the cortex by consciously experienced repetitive words, thoughts, or images. Box 48.1 lists the common obsessions in roughly descending order of frequency, along with typical compulsions.

Certain drugs, especially amphetamines and related compounds, may trigger obsessive-

Box 48.1. Characteristic obsessions and compulsions in obsessive-compulsive disorder

Fear of contamination
Washing, cleaning

Pathological doubt
Unwarranted, repetitive doubts about something one has said or done

Fear of harm
Checking locks, doors, windows, appliances

Fear of offending or harming others, including deities; may include thoughts about having done something inappropriate such as blaspheming, conveying some unintended sexual signal, or having injured someone
Washing, checking for odors, praying, apologizing or performing inner or behavioral rituals to expiate the offensive thoughts

Discomfort with asymmetry or unevenness
Reordering or rearranging

Somatically focused obsession (see body dysmorphic disorder)
Checking mirrors; self-monitoring; seeking medical remedies

Fear of losing or being without a necessary or meaningful object (see hoarding disorder)
Hoarding useless or meaningless materials

compulsive (OC) symptoms. OC symptoms may develop after head injury or in conditions that affect the basal ganglia (e.g., Parkinson's disease and Huntington's disease). In children, OC symptoms should prompt assessment for Tourette's disorder, pediatric acute neurological syndrome (PANDAS), and autism spectrum disorders. OC symptoms and behaviors may appear during the prodrome of a psychotic episode or during an episode of severe major depression.

In light of these associations, any patient with OC symptoms should receive a thorough psychiatric and physical assessment, looking for symptoms of other conditions, family history, characteristic motor finding (tics and other stereotypic movements), and urine toxicology. Exposure to heavy metals, especially lead, should be considered in high-risk populations (industrial workers, children who live in old houses or who drink contaminated

water), as heavy metals tend to accumulate in the basal ganglia, which are involved in tics and stereotypic motor activity.

Differentiating OCD from the many other psychiatric disorders that involve compulsive, maladaptive behavior can be challenging. The compulsions of OC disorders tend to be internalizing or self-directed, temporarily relieving internal distress. The disorders of impulse control (fire setting, kleptomania, pathological gambling) are other-directed or more driven, at least initially, by the pursuit of reward (see Chapter 49: Disruptive, Impulse-Control and Conduct Disorders). Substance use disorders, similarly, are usually reward driven; however, they may evolve into efforts to avoid the distress of withdrawal and abstinence.

The obsessions of **obsessive-compulsive personality disorder** (OCPD) usually represent exaggerated but normal concerns with order and adherence to rules. Even though they may be somewhat rigid in their beliefs and behaviors, people with OCPD do not engage in rituals. The characteristic preoccupations of anxiety disorders typically relate to normal fears about health, real dangers, or repetition of past trauma.

Neurobiological Mechanisms

> How does the neurobiology of these disorders relate to current treatment approaches?

Functional neuroimaging in humans has revealed hyperactivity of the cortical-striatal-thalamic-cortical (CSTC or CST) circuit in OCD ("hyperfrontality"). This contrasts with the activation of related but not identical fear networks in anxiety disorders. Current research has illuminated the functions of this bundle of neural pathways, some of which are involved in reward, learning, and habit formation in humans and other animals.

OCD has a significant genetic component, with an up to 85% concordance in identical twins, compared with a 50% concordance in fraternal twins, and observed familial transmission. Studies in mice genetically engineered to selectively eliminate parts of the CSTC network are beginning to uncover specific genes that may be involved (Box 48.2).

Box 48.2. Functions of elements of the CSTC

OMPFC or OMC
Area of the medial frontal cortex that monitors and filters perceptions before they reach conscious awareness

Striatum
Ventral areas of the basal ganglia; generates the experience of reward; involved in motivation and the emotional valence of a perception or experience
Connected to nucleus accumbens

Thalamus
Relays internal and external perceptions to the OMPFC

Other nuclei and structures of the basal ganglia
Stereotypic motor behavior, including grooming in animals

Note. CSTC = cortical-striatal-thalamic-cortical circuit; OMC = orbitomedial cortex; OMPFC = orbitomedialprefrontal cortex.

Reciprocal activity defines the CSTC circuit: Subcortical activity may trigger conscious or cortical experience, and conscious thoughts may modulate or trigger the subcortical circuitry. *Learning theory* describes the effects of this reciprocity in intact animals. Behaviors in direct pursuit of reward are positively reinforced, while those that avoid or relieve distress are maintained by negative reinforcement. The compulsions of OCD relieve or take away the negative experience of the obsessive thoughts; this relief of distress increases the likelihood that the compulsive behavior will recur.

Treatment Options

Phenomenologically, obsessions may trigger compulsions, or compulsions may generate thoughts that give meaning to obsessions after the fact. When the obsessions of OCD are modified by psychotherapeutic techniques that teach people how to ignore or interrupt them, or to control the behavioral responses they generate, the neuroimaging findings may normalize.

These pathways of the CSTC express neurotransmitters, especially the monoamines affected by drugs that enhance the activity of serotonin and the norepinephrine and dopamine that serotonin regulates. The selective serotonin reuptake inhibitor (SSRI) fluvoxamine has been approved by the US Food and Drug Administration (FDA) for the treatment of OCD, but any SSRI at high doses for long periods of time may be effective. Dopamine antagonists are sometimes helpful. SSRIs also may benefit patients with trichotillomania and body dysmorphic disorder. Clomipramine, a modified tricyclic antidepressant with marked serotonin-regulating activity, may be effective when SSRIs are not; however, intense anticholinergic side effects limit its use.

The cortical elements of the CSTC circuit express and respond to glutamate. These findings underlie recent research into the possible benefits of glutamatergic drugs (memantine, riluzole) for patients refractory to treatment. Evidence also supports the efficacy of direct modification of the CSTC circuit through deep brain stimulation or, in very severe cases, surgical interruption of critical pathways.

Psychotherapy that builds on the principles of behavioral learning has equal or greater efficacy than medication for OCD. The strongest evidence supports educating the patient about the disorder, helping the person recognize and record symptoms to make them more conscious and open to reflection, and implementing exposure and response prevention. This technique might involve urging a person with obsessions about contamination to dirty their hands on purpose, and then experience the associated distress but not wash until the distress spontaneously subsides, which may take hours. A person who has obsessive, irrational fears about offending others might be encouraged first to imagine various social encounters, then urged to interact in brief and then longer periods in different contexts. Patients use therapy to reflect at each step on the associated distress and how long it takes to abate, developing insight into their distorted estimation of consequences and incorrect predictions. Importantly, therapy persuades patients to undertake exposure rather than forcing it upon them. When this technique is successful, the obsessive thoughts gradually become less frequent and compelling, and the compulsions subside.

Recommended Readings

Grant, J. E. (2014). Obsessive compulsive disorder. *New England Journal of Medicine, 371*, 646–653. http://doi.org/10.1056/NEJMcp1402176

Kwon, J. S., Jang, J. H., Choi, J.-S., & Kang, D.-H. (2014). Review: Neuroimaging in obsessive compulsive disorder. *Expert Review of Neurotherapeutics, 9*, 255–269. http://doi.org/10.1586/14737175.9.2.255

Rapoport, J. L. (1991). *The boy who couldn't stop washing: The experience and treatment of obsessive compulsive disorder.* New York, NY: Penguin Putnam.

Review Questions

1. The mother of a 3-month-old girl is horrified by gruesome images of dropping her daughter and killing her. She has no conscious desire to hurt the child, and she says prayers in her head over and over to free herself from the thought. The pathogenesis of her symptoms relates to
   A. imbalance of glutamate and GABA in cortical synapses
   B. masked depression with postpartum onset
   C. sleep deprivation
   D. the effect on serotonin activity of the normal postpartum fall in estrogen
   E. unacknowledged ambivalence about being a mother

2. A 23-year-old woman avoids social activity and pursues only online work because she believes that the asymmetry of her eyebrows makes her look hideous. She checks her reflection in the mirror multiple times daily and has consulted a dermatologist about having her eyebrows removed and replaced with tattoos. She might benefit from
   A. habit reversal therapy
   B. having the tattoo procedure she has requested
   C. high doses of an SSRI over a period of 3 months
   D. supportive psychotherapy
   E. treatment with a dopamine agonist drug

Answer Key on p. 466

49 Disruptive, Impulse-Control, and Conduct Disorders

Mariel R. Herbert, MD, and Julia B. Frank, MD

- How do internalizing and externalizing tendencies relate to psychopathology?
- What are the disruptive, impulse-control, and conduct disorders?

A ninth-grade girl and a ninth-grade boy both try out for the school play but do not get cast. The girl decides she was at fault for not speaking loudly enough and because she is too fat. The boy blames the director for showing favoritism and puts a threatening anonymous note in her mailbox.

Factors Affecting Development of Impulse Control

The development of a categorical system for diagnosing psychopathology has paradoxically facilitated the study of transdiagnostic factors (i.e., elements or processes that cut across existing diagnostic boundaries). Patterns of extensive *comorbidity* highlight the overlap between anxiety and depression (as symptoms or diagnosed disorders) and among disorders related to impulse control (attention deficit disorder, substance misuse, antisocial behavior). These clusters point to similarities in biological organization or social learning underlying diverse diagnostic categories.

Internalizing and Externalizing Tendencies

How do internalizing and externalizing tendencies relate to psychopathology?

Distinctions between **internalizing** and **externalizing** qualities (locus of control), and between **positive** and **negative affectivity** have particular utility for organizing psychopathology in ways that go beyond prevailing categorical systems. *Internalizing* connotes the tendency to experience distress as coming from within. It has been further divided into *anxious misery* and *fearfulness.* *Externalizing* connotes impulsivity and limited constraint (determination to control a behavior), in response to environmental cues or internal emotional states (see Chapter 2: Predisposition).

In the course of typical development, capacities for emotional and behavioral self-control evolve in response to the physical maturation of inhibitory neurological pathways and to the imposition of social norms by parents and others in authority. Impulse control normally increases steadily throughout childhood. It may diminish briefly early in adolescence, when pubertal hormones strengthen the intensity of earlier impulses, but should reassert itself by the later teenage years (see Chapter 14: The School Years). Much dysfunctional impulsive behavior relates to externalizing factors associated with negative emotionality. Individuals with these qualities may violate the rights of others and fail to conform to normal social rules and expectations.

Internalizing problems primarily affect individuals, engendering suffering and a desire for relief. Externalizing problems, though originating within the individual, have consequences for others. Including both internalizing and externalizing problems within the overall domain of psychopathology has the unfortunate effect of increasing the negative stigma against all mental illness. Society views internal distress like other medical symptoms, but may criminalize behavior that affects others. However, understanding the processes that produce externalizing disorders offers hope that at least some forms of destructive social behavior can be prevented or changed by treatment. Appropriate interventions may help individuals acquire self-control, develop more prosocial emotions, and avoid the consequences, for themselves and others, of their difficulty inhibiting impulses, especially disruptive or destructive ones.

Disruptive, Impulse-Control, and Conduct Disorders

> What are the disruptive, impulse-control, and conduct disorders?

Many disorders, especially attention-deficit/hyperactivity disorder (ADHD), addictions, and mania, include elements of externalization. When these qualities appear in more discrete form – that is, in people who do not meet criteria for another disorder – the *Diagnostic and Statistical Manual of Mental Disorders, 5th edition* (DSM-5) provides the domain of **disruptive, impulse-control and conduct disorders**. Internalizing elements, especially guilt about problem behavior, do not preclude the diagnoses in this domain.

The *disruptive, impulse-control, and conduct disorders* category comprises six disorders, as well as *other specified* and *unspecified* disorders:

- Oppositional defiant disorder,
- Intermittent explosive disorder,
- Conduct disorder (pre-adult antisociality),
- Antisocial personality disorder (see Chapter 51: Personality Disorders),
- Pyromania, and
- Kleptomania.

To determine if an individual's symptoms constitute a disorder, the clinician must consider frequency, pervasiveness across situations, and impairment relative to age, gender, and cultural norms. A diagnosis cannot be made if the symptoms are better explained by another psychiatric disorder or social or biological cause (e.g., onset occurring after head injury).

Pathological gambling is covered in this chapter as a disorder of impulse control, although the DSM-5 classifies it within the domain of addictions, underscoring the complexity of classifying behaviors with multiple determinants.

Impulse, Temptation, or Drive to Act in a Manner Harmful to Self or Others

Before acting on some impulse, persons with impulse-control disorders typically feel increased tension or arousal, even though the behavior may seem sudden or unpredictable. The person, who is aware of prodromal arousal, may try to resist or may anticipate negative consequences. After acting impulsively, the person typically feels pleasure or release, thus reinforcing the impulse and the resultant behavior. Guilt and regret may occur later, particularly when consequences of the behavior get the individual into trouble. When the impulsive acts include criminal behavior, the assignment of responsibility and assessment of the person's capacity for self-control may fall to the courts. Forensic mental health clinicians specialize in such assessments.

Oppositional Defiant Disorder

Oppositional defiant disorder (ODD) denotes a pattern of angry or irritable mood, argumentative or defiant behavior, sometimes involving vindictiveness over 6 or more months. Onset is usually during the preschool years. A child may exhibit the behavioral characteristics without change in mood, or only have problems when interacting with siblings or adults close to them, particularly if the home environment is traumatic or neglectful. Individuals with ODD may not view themselves as angry, but generally have baseline high emotional reactivity and poor frustration tolerance. Co-occurring disorders include ADHD and conduct disorder (see below). The disorder rarely persists in pure form into adulthood. The associated negative affectivity more often evolves into adult depression or anxiety disorder (see Chapter 43: Depressive and Bipolar Disorders).

Effective treatment of ODD includes early school-based intervention, behavioral therapy, and skills training for the child and parents.

Intermittent Explosive Disorder

Persons with **intermittent explosive disorder** (IED) experience multiple episodes of sudden rage in which they assault others or destroy property. Their anger is disproportionate to the triggering event. They do not show undue aggressiveness or impulsivity between episodes and they often express remorse afterwards.

IED commonly begins during the second or third decade but may persist into adulthood. First-degree relatives are at increased risk for the disorder, implying a role for genetic factors. Children and adolescents with IED may be hyperactive, with aura-like experiences, hypersensitivity to photic and auditory stimulation, and postictal-like changes in sensorium (e.g., memory loss). *Predisposing factors* include perinatal trauma, head trauma, encephalitis, and hyperactivity. Early adversity (e.g., exposure to child abuse, threats to life) is an important predisposing factor.

The most effective treatment is a combination of psychotherapy and medication. Selective serotonin reuptake inhibitors (e.g., fluoxetine, paroxetine, sertraline) may be effective. Anticonvulsants, antipsychotics, propranolol, and lithium have been used with mixed results.

Conduct Disorder

Conduct disorder involves persistent violation of the rights of others and/or rule breaking, along with aggression, property destruction, deceitfulness, theft, and truancy. Such behaviors typically begin before age 13. Deficits in prosocial emotions (empathy and guilt) may be specified as part of the diagnosis. ODD in childhood may presage conduct disorder that is not recognized until adolescence. The diagnosis of adult antisocial personality disorder requires the presence of aspects of conduct disorder before age 15.

Lower heart rate and skin conductance, neurological abnormalities (e.g., in the prefrontal cortex and amygdala), and reduced reactivity of basal cortisol have been found in both ODD and conduct disorder, but these are not equivalent conditions. Children with pure ODD are more likely to develop anxiety or depression rather than antisocial personality disorder as adults. Developmental

and social factors may influence how core physiological qualities are expressed in behavior over time.

Effective treatment of conduct disorder involves intensive, long-term, multisystem therapy, similar to that for ODD. Patients with either disorder are at risk for serious consequences, including involvement with the criminal justice system.

Pyromania

Repetitive, deliberate fire setting that relieves tension or arousal, and attraction to fires and firefighting equipment characterize **pyromania**. Affected individuals may make elaborate preparations prior to setting a fire. This disorder often begins in childhood. Its consequences worsen over time. Pyromania is associated with intellectual disability, alcohol use disorder, and behaviors such as truancy or harming animals. Pyromania should not be diagnosed if sociopolitical beliefs or desire for personal gain motivate the fire setting, or if the behavior is a symptom of another psychiatric disorder (e.g., a response to command auditory hallucinations). Children are likely to respond to nonpunitive behavioral therapy. Due to its potentially devastating consequences, pyromania must be treated as soon as it is diagnosed. An affected child may make a full recovery.

Kleptomania

Persons with **kleptomania** cannot resist the impulse to steal unnecessary items, which are then returned, given away, or hidden. For affected persons, the act of stealing is an end in itself. They do not plan, but they do avoid situations in which the danger of being caught is obvious. When caught, they experience humiliation. Stealing episodes may occur dozens of times per month. Kleptomania waxes and wanes, tends to be chronic, and recurs during periods of stress. Neurological disease, intellectual disability, faulty monoamine metabolism, and focal neurological signs have been associated with kleptomania. Fewer than 5% of shoplifters have kleptomania. The disorder is more common in females. Behavior modification can be effective even for those with low motivation. Selective serotonin reuptake inhibitors may be beneficial.

Gambling Disorder

Formerly termed *pathological gambling,* **gambling disorder** includes preoccupation with gambling, increasing stakes to achieve excitement, gambling to escape problems and recoup losses, lying to hide the magnitude of the problem, supporting gambling through illegal but usually nonviolent means (e.g., embezzlement and fraud), and relying on others to pay gambling debts.

> Pathological gambling is estimated to affect up to 1.6% of the adult population worldwide, with men affected more often than women. Although it may begin at any age, adolescent onset is more common in men, and onset in middle age more common in women. Sons of affected fathers and daughters of affected mothers are at risk for the disorder. In the US, affected women are likely to be married to alcoholic, generally absent men.

Gambling disorder may coexist with mood and anxiety disorders. Impulsivity and deficient capacity to assess risk, in particular, may be signs of mania. *Predisposing factors* include childhood attention deficit disorder, loss or absence of a parent before age 15, inappropriately harsh or lax parental discipline, parental modeling with exposure to gambling during childhood or adolescence, lack of family emphasis on financial planning, and excessive emphasis on material goods.

Societal standards about gambling are changing. State governments now sponsor lotteries, once considered immoral, and once illegal forms of betting have become popular means of generating tax revenue. The Internet has greatly expanded opportunities for gambling. This development is too recent to allow for solid research into the relationship between Internet gambling, other Internet addictions, and gambling disorder. DSM-5 includes a category, *Internet gaming disorder,* as a condition for further study. Gambling behavior merits a diagnosis only when the person becomes preoccupied with the activity and does not stop despite mounting adverse social consequences.

Impaired metabolism of catecholamines (especially norepinephrine) has been associated with the development of pathological gambling. The reinforcing effects of self-stimulation and tension reduction (relief) serve to maintain and increase the behavior. The most effective treatment is the 12-step peer group support offered by **Gamblers Anonymous** (GA).

Recommended Readings

Carragher, N., Krueger, R. F., Eaton, N. R., & Slade, T. (2015). Disorders without borders: Current and future directions in the metastructure of mental disorders. *Social Psychiatry and Psychiatric Epidemiology, 50,* 339–350. http://doi.org/10.1007/s00127-014-1004-z

Hollander, E., & Stein, D. J. (Eds.). (2006). *Clinical handbook of impulse-control disorders.* Washington, DC: American Psychiatric Press.

Odlaug, B. L. (2013). Personality disorders and dimensions in pathological gambling. *Current Opinion in Psychiatry, 26,* 107–112. PMID: 23041794. http://doi.org/10.1097/YCO.0b013e32835997df

Review Questions

1. A department store security guard tells a 45-year-old woman to empty her handbag and finds three bottles of nail polish, a pair of reading glasses she does not need, and some costume jewelry. She claims tearfully that she picked them up by mistake and would be happy to return them. This scenario is consistent with
   A. antisocial personality disorder
   B. conduct disorder
   C. internalizing adult behavior
   D. kleptomania
   E. other specified impulse-control disorder

2. Which of the following disorders is **NOT** associated with a build up of tension, followed by an impulsive act that brings pleasurable relief?
   A. Accessing a pornographic website
   B. Deciding to enter a casino, despite major previous losses

C. Extorting lunch money from a
   younger student
D. Kleptomania
E. Pyromania

Answer Key on p. 466

50 Somatic Symptom and Related Disorders

Julia B. Frank, MD, and Stephanie H. Cho, MD

- What are somatic symptom disorder and other disorders in the somatic symptom domain?
- What are the mechanisms of symptom generation and anxious focus?
- How does understanding mind–body interaction guide treatment?

Stress and Somatic Symptoms

Mrs. F. is a 34-year-old, recently married, professional woman who is seeking evaluation of persistent, diffuse lower abdominal pain that she attributes to self-diagnosed "polycystic ovaries." She worries this means she is infertile. She expects to be sent for an ultrasound and multiple blood tests and to receive a definitive answer about her fertility. When asked, she acknowledges ambivalence about getting pregnant, although she has always thought she wanted to be a mother. Her ultrasound shows normal ovaries. She responds, not with relief, but with further questions about rarer disorders.

Many people consult medical providers describing symptoms more severe than those expected from an existing illness. Others may describe symptoms for which medical evaluation finds no adequate cause. Often these are transient states that respond to simple reassurance. Some patients, however, are preoccupied with concern about illness that undermines their ability to handle the demands of ordinary life. Such people may request repeated evaluations or unsuccessful treatments. They may strongly wish for effective medical attention yet profoundly mistrust medical professionals, whom they feel fail to understand and help them. Obsessive Internet browsing for explanations and support, which tends to magnify rather than reduce their concerns, is not uncommon.

Psychiatric diagnosis places such patients in the domain of *somatic symptom disorders*. This term connotes conditions ranging from exces-

sive distress over one or more bodily symptoms not fully explained by the person's physical state (*somatic symptom disorder,* formerly *somatization disorder*), to the unwarranted conviction that one has a serious disease (*illness anxiety disorder,* formerly *hypochondriasis*), to a cryptic neurological symptom that seems related to stressors that the person cannot consciously acknowledge or resolve (*neurologic symptom disorder* or conversion disorder), and several other conditions listed in Table 50.1.

Patients with any of the somatic symptom disorders are often judged harshly by both laypeople and professionals, who suspect them of feigning illness or trying to escape from responsibility. When pain is one of the presenting symptoms, inappropriate prescription of opiates and medically induced drug dependence is a real risk. Patients with cryptic, distressing symptoms may also suffer complications from unnecessary surgery or invasive diagnostic tests.

Until recently, the prevailing **explanatory model** for excessive illness concerns postulated that people were "somaticizing," defined as expressing disavowed emotion or unconscious conflict in physical symptoms, often rewarded or reinforced by receiving medical attention. Contemporary understanding of somatization has expanded to encompass the range of normal variation in how people experience bodily sensations, the role of traumatic or stressful experiences in shaping people's interpretations of bodily experience, and the physical effects of acute, persistent, or traumatic stress. Patients may or may not be fully aware of the involved stressors. They often lack insight into their psychological tendency to magnify distress and underestimate their ability to cope. Anxious focus on bodily sensations may trigger further symptoms that are stressors in themselves.

The bidirectional relationship between stress and symptoms involves both conscious patterns of thought and the activity of nonconscious, autonomic neurological, and neuroendocrine pathways. The usual task of medical evaluation, which is correlating the experience and expression of symptoms with lesions of bodily organs, becomes elusive and sometimes impossible.

> **What are somatic symptom disorder and other disorders in the somatic symptom domain?**

In the mid-20th century, Franz Alexander proposed a category of **psychosomatic disorders**, specifically "colitis," "arthritis," asthma, ulcers, neurodermatitis, hypertension, and anorexia, in which

psychological factors played a major *etiological* role. Subsequent advances in medical science disproved the role of psychological factors as the sole or primary etiology of many bodily conditions. For example, gastric ulcers are now attributed to infection with *Helicobacter pylori*; ulcerative colitis (*inflammatory bowel disease* or IBD) is understood as primarily a genetic disorder. However, recent epidemiological studies and new technologies illuminating the mind–body interface have shown that perceived stress may be one etiological factor among many, particularly in functional syndromes like *irritable bowel syndrome* (IBS) in which symptoms mimic those of IBD, but the tissues of the gastrointestinal system are grossly intact. Chronic fatigue syndrome and fibromyalgia mimic the symptoms of diseases like lupus erythematosus or rheumatoid arthritis, but do not involve the same tissue damage and do not progress as these conditions may. Similarly, asthma may be triggered by many factors, ranging from environmental allergens to psychological stress.

Table 50.1. Diagnostic categories for somatic symptom and related disorders

Disorder	Defining Criteria	Epidemiology, Comorbidity, Associated Findings	Comment
Somatic symptom disorder	Excessive distress resulting from one or more somatic symptoms	Symptoms may or may not have identifiable cause F > M 5–7% of general population In children, often a single, prominent symptom	Recommended treatment: avoid unnecessary testing, offer routine visits to show concern and availability Treat recognized functional syndromes (IBS, migraine headaches, fibromyalgia) May respond to CBT to deflect attention and encourage exercise; partial response to some psychotropic medications (antidepressants)
Illness anxiety disorder	Persistent preoccupation with having or acquiring a serious illness, with mild or absent symptoms	May lead to aggressive testing, iatrogenic injury, increased anxiety M = F 2–5% of patients seen in primary care Transiently seen in medical professionals in training ("second year syndrome," responsive to reassurance) Chronic or recurrent	Providers often frustrated and dismissive, increasing patients' anxiety and resentment May respond to CBT, other psychotherapy

Table 50.1. (continued)

Disorder	Defining Criteria	Epidemiology, Comorbidity, Associated Findings	Comment
Conversion disorder (or functional neurological symptom disorder)	Alteration or loss of physical functioning incompatible with clinical findings (e.g., focal paralysis, nonepileptic seizures)	F > M 5% of referrals to neurology clinics Onset may be associated with stress or trauma Dissociative symptoms common at onset or during episodes	Symptoms assumed to be unconsciously generated May remit with hypnosis or psychotherapy May require physical therapy or other ritual of care Can become chronic
Factitious disorder (imposed on self or imposed on others)	Purposeful self-infliction of signs of illness or injury to elicit medical attention and care Inflicted injury may be serious, require treatment	1% of general hospital inpatients Often report history of child abuse or neglect Typical patient familiar with health care, may be a health care professional Popularly known as "Munchausen syndrome"	Desire for care assumed to be unconsciously motivated May respond to empathic interview targeting stresses May be imposed on dependent child or older patient ("by proxy")
Malingering	Purposeful self-injury, infliction or feigning of illness to escape punishment or achieve financial or other compensation	Common among prisoners and soldiers Otherwise associated with antisocial personality disorder	Aberrant illness behavior, NOT a mental illness
Unspecified somatic symptom and related disorders	Somatic symptom(s) with associated distress that does not meet full criteria for somatic symptom disorder	Lasting < 6 months or otherwise not meeting diagnostic criteria for related disorders	
Psychological factors affecting other medical conditions	Other medical condition is adversely affected by at least one psychological or behavioral factor	Particularly important in chronic illness, chronic pain; affects treatment adherence	Increases risk of suffering, disability and even death from the medical condition May respond to psychotherapy

Note. CBT = cognitive behavioral therapy; F > M = female to male ratio (greater than); IBS = irritable bowel syndrome. For DSM-5 criteria see American Psychiatric Association. (2013). *Diagnostic and statistical manual of mental disorders* (5th ed.). Arlington, VA: Author.

Diagnostic Criteria for Somatic Symptom and Related Disorders

The *Diagnostic and Statistical Manual of Mental Disorders, 5th edition* (DSM-5) diagnostic categories for **somatic symptom and related disorders** are based on *patterns of symptoms* and the association of some behavioral patterns with particular motivational factors (see Table 50.1). Older criteria specified that the symptoms should be "medically unexplained." This criterion encouraged practitioners to declare symptoms as "psychiatric" simply because a medical etiology could not be found, or a medical treatment proved ineffective. Such assessment alienated and stigmatized patients without explaining their troublesome experience or opening avenues for treatment.

The present definition of somatic symptom disorders denotes intense concern about *prominent somatic symptoms or illness associated with disproportionately severe distress and impairment.* It encompasses both symptoms without discernible cause and those that occur in the presence of a recognized disease (which may or may not have associated physical findings) that engender a level of distress and disability beyond the expected response to a particular condition.

While these diagnostic categories are relatively reliable, they do little to guide treatment. Furthermore, patients who meet criteria for a somatic symptom disorder may have recognized, criterion-based medical syndromes (IBS, migraine or tension headaches, cystitis, fibromyalgia, or chronic fatigue syndrome) or chronic diseases with diffuse findings (e.g., lupus erythematosus, multiple sclerosis) and be treated primarily in nonpsychiatric settings. Dividing patients between different specialties impedes treatment. In fact, a strong medical provider–patient relationship and psychotherapy together benefit sufferers from many of these conditions. Symptomatic medical treatment or psychotropic medication may also be of some benefit.

The Mind–Body Interface

> What are the mechanisms of symptom generation and anxious focus?

The relationship between mental and physical states, also called the **mind–body interface**, is bidirectional and complex. Stress both causes and results from pain or other dysfunction.

The factors that underlie the perception of, and response to, bodily symptoms include (1) the activity of neural structures that process and respond to somatosensory information, (2) stress responsive elements of the autonomic nervous system (ANS) and the neuroendocrine system, (3) activity of the enteric nervous system, and (4) psychological tendencies to perceive things as ominous and overwhelming. Psychological factors may reflect responses to chronic or severe stress or the effects of environments in which illness behavior is learned and reinforced.

Neural Structures That Process and Respond to Somatosensory Information

The brain receives continuous input from the body. Stimuli applied to the skin and those that trigger pain are relayed along well-delineated pathways to the somatosensory reception area caudal to the motor strip of the frontal cortex, where they are consciously registered and localized to their site of origin. The pathways that carry input arising in internal organs are less easily identified. Clusters of cells (nuclei) in the brainstem and elsewhere monitor factors such as pH, blood levels of oxygen and carbon dioxide, and blood pressure, and respond automatically to maintain homeostasis. For example, we are not typically aware of our blood pressure, heart rate, or routine peristalsis. Stimuli such as the urge to move one's bowels or to urinate or to catch one's breath, and noxious stimuli like pain and nausea do, however, reach consciousness.

Localized and diffuse information from the body is filtered through the *anterior cingulate gyrus* and the *orbitomedial or medial prefrontal cortex*, which provide context, associating stimuli with memories and other sensations and assigning emotional value as neutral, aversive, or rewarding. A process of *central sensitization* may occur, in which stimuli are magnified rather than suppressed. Sensitizing factors include genetic sensitivity of receptors or pathways, repetitive stimulation that affects the threshold of perception (conditioning), and learned responses to discomfort.

The existence of a complex, common pathway for processing noxious stimuli from multiple sources helps explain why people with somatic symptom disorder typically have a host of symptoms, not just one or two.

The interpretation and emotional valence of symptoms may prompt voluntary action, including the search for explanations and efforts to avoid further exposure. People consult friends, family, books, the Internet, and medical providers. They may withdraw from many activities as well as social engagement, leading eventually to significant disability or impairment.

Autonomic and Neuroendocrine Responses to Stress

The regulation of vital processes involves multiple redundant systems. Important regulatory neural pathways originate in nuclei of the hypothalamus, a structure that mediates interactions between the central nervous system and the rest of the body. Hypothalamic nuclei determine the function of the ANS, which coordinates both stress responses and maintenance functions through continuous adjustment of the balance between norepinephrine and acetylcholine, two generally opposing neurotransmitters (see Chapter 7: Stress, Adaptation, and Stress Disorders).

The neurons that release norepinephrine make up the *sympathetic* ANS. Sympathetic activity leads to increases in heart rate, blood pressure, respiration, and muscle tension, while slowing the gut and inhibiting some aspects of reproductive organ function. A sudden increase in norepinephrine activity underlies the **stress** or **fight-or-flight response**. It allows the individual to respond quickly to immediate threats by running away or by aggressive action.

Neurons that release acetylcholine make up the *parasympathetic* ANS. They induce the opposite, **relaxation response**, which includes slowing heart rate, lowering blood pressure, increasing gut motility for digestion, and regulating sleep and circadian rhythms.

Autonomic functions are not entirely automatic; the perception of threat, which may come from exposure to previous stress or trauma, may shift or disrupt the balance between sympathetic and parasympathetic activity, generating pain, bowel dys-

function, sexual dysfunctions, dizziness, or fatigue. In some cases, the symptoms fit the pattern of the vegetative signs associated with known psychiatric disorders (e.g., the insomnia or fatigue of major depression, or the rapid heart rate, shallow breathing, and dizziness of an anxiety disorder).

The hypothalamic-pituitary-adrenocortical (HPA) axis is another, slower acting stress response system that complements the acute responses of the ANS. HPA accommodation to stress involves the release of corticosteroids from the adrenal glands, which moderates immune responses, the activity of thyroid hormones that regulate metabolism, and reproductive hormone activity that influences both neurodevelopment and sexual behavior. Stress-influenced immune or autoimmune activity, metabolism, and sexual dysfunction may generate symptoms that cannot be linked to lesions of single organ systems.

The early characterization of somatization as *hysteria* (etymologically, the effects of a "wandering" uterus) was based on the observation that most forms of somatization are 2 to 10 times more common in adult women than in adult men. Female reproductive hormones affect the activity of serotonin and other neurotransmitters. Estrogen and serotonin covary in the nervous system, and cryptic somatic symptoms are especially prevalent in women during the reproductive years, when hormone levels fluctuate. For complex reasons, symptoms that vary across the menstrual cycle can be severe. Severe pain in particular may be attributable to endometriosis, yet some women with widespread lesions have very mild symptoms, while others with less tissue involvement may be deeply affected. Women are also more vulnerable to certain sensitizing or precipitating stressful experiences, including childhood or adolescent sexual abuse, interpersonal violence, low socioeconomic status, and lack of perceived control over threatening or aversive circumstances.

This list of the mechanisms by which people experience physical symptoms and feelings of illness provides only a few illustrations. For example, the gastrointestinal system is lined with regulatory neurons (the enteric nervous system) that respond to many different environmental factors, ranging from chemicals in food to various types of stress.

Other factors that produce symptoms include neurochemicals called cytokines, which engender the feeling of being ill that accompanies many infections. Neurochemicals that influence cellular function, especially those regulating cell damage and cell repair, also may be found to be mediators of somatic symptoms. The process of dissociation, which can be a manifestation of epilepsy or a response to severe or repeated threats, especially early trauma, also influences somatosensory processing and even motor function, contributing to the expression of cryptic symptoms (e.g. conversion disorder, somatic symptoms in the course of posttraumatic stress disorder or dissociative disorders).

Exposure to Chronic or Severe Stress or Environments in Which Illness Behavior Is Learned and Reinforced

Conscious preoccupation with bodily function is a common thread underlying disorders in the somatic symptom domain. The most basic psychological process involved in the awareness of bodily stimuli is directed attention, a partly automatic response to threat facilitated by the activity of the **amygdala**. With effort, attentional focus can sometimes be brought under conscious control.

Cultural factors also shape the interpretation of bodily experience. For example, some cultures view sexual arousal during dreams as sinful. In contemporary society, concern about the hidden dangers of chemicals and pollutants prompts some people to attribute various symptoms to allergy or chemical sensitivities that are difficult to prove. In many cultures, focus on a physical symptom is a legitimate way of avoiding inner or interpersonal conflict. Past psychological trauma also plays a role in symptom generation. For example, particularly high rates of past sexual abuse have been found in women seeking treatment for IBS.

Familial experience, especially during development, shapes the meaning of perceived symptoms. Individuals who experienced serious illness in themselves or a close family member during childhood are more inclined to interpret sensations as ominous and a reason to seek help or adopt the *sick role*. A person who experiences dizziness on standing but expects this as the result of taking antihypertensive medication will accept the problem without distress. Someone whose mother died of a stroke may react to dizziness by going to the emergency department, where they will be viewed askance as someone who is "somaticizing."

Poverty, deprivation, and social isolation may trigger physiological stress responses and make people more anxious about signs of illness, since disability may threaten their basic survival. At the same time, health care may be one of the few avenues of help available to people in adverse social situations.

Therapeutic Approaches

> How does understanding mind–body interaction guide treatment?

A medical system governed by technology, standardization, and efficiency discourages professionals from taking the time to understand the developmental, personal, and sociocultural contexts of illness. Providers fear patients will resent questions about psychological stress, perceiving them as dismissive. Medical journals and popular media abound with stories of common complaints that turn out to be something unusual. Time spent uncovering and resolving emotional problems that account for much of patients' somatic distress rarely receives media attention. Patients expect extensive testing; providers order tests to avoid missing subtle or serious disease. Such activity accounts for billions of health care dollars. The first step in treatment is to do no harm: avoiding unnecessary interventions and withholding harsh judgment, recognizing that the mismatch between people with cryptic symptoms and medical care is not the simple result of personal psychopathology.

Beyond avoiding harm, affirmative treatment may ameliorate some of the somatic symptom disorders, particularly those that have not become longstanding and pervasive. **Cognitive behavioral therapy** (CBT) focuses on (1) educating people about the functioning of the body's stress response, (2) explaining that the symptoms patients experience are based in stress responses meant to protect the body against various dangers, (3) helping patients accept that they are misinterpreting bodily sensations as ominous, (4) acknowledging stressor events as contributory causes of distress and illness exacerbation, and (5) suggesting that focusing on resolving or managing the stress will improve the problem. CBT teaches people to distract themselves or ignore symptoms and focus on improving function. Encouraging vigorous aerobic exercise has particular benefit in stabilizing the activity of the ANS and the symptoms related to autonomic dysfunction.

Psychodynamic psychotherapy benefits people with uncontrolled stress responses by providing an accepting and encouraging environment for people to express, reflect upon, and reinterpret their bodily experiences and coping strategies. Psychodynamic therapists should avoid alienating somatically distressed patients by implying that they are unconsciously producing symptoms to achieve some hidden goal or that nothing is physically wrong. So-called *acceptance and commitment therapy* avoids these pitfalls.

Symptoms that do not correspond to normal structural neurological organization (functional neurological or conversion symptoms; see Table 50.1) may respond to the exploration of underlying conflict when the person is in a deeply relaxed state such as **hypnosis**. Children are especially responsive to this technique. Participation in medical rituals that validate the symptom and offer a path toward rehabilitation, such as physical therapy, may be needed, especially for prolonged impairment that has led to disuse atrophy. Meditation and other *integrative medicine* interventions may help patients temporarily focus away from their symptoms or engender **relaxation** (increased parasympathetic tone) that relieves stress and tension, even if the techniques do not directly address precipitating or perpetuating psychosocial factors. Similar mechanisms may account for the "healing" that occurs through religious rituals.

Antidepressant medication may relieve some functional symptoms either directly or by improving associated negative mood. Tricyclic antidepressants and dual-acting agents, in low doses, may moderate central sensitization or other processes that exacerbate pain. Once symptoms are controlled, the person may view other stressors as less severe or overwhelming. Inadequate sleep also contributes to symptom formation. Although many sedatives have unwanted side effects, and should be used sparingly or avoided completely, sedating antidepressants or behavioral interventions like **sleep hygiene** may be helpful.

Which interventions to offer which patient is less a function of diagnosis than of the patient's willingness and ability to trust the medical provider or therapist enough to accept that troubling symptoms are not simply what they seem to be. A consistent, concerned, and medically conservative approach recognizes the patterns and circumstances that suggest somatization and avoids unnecessary tests or overzealous treatments that reinforce patients' catastrophic thinking. At the same time, providers must be willing to change their view of a patient and pursue other diagnostic possibilities if new symptoms arise or if efforts to manage somatization do not have the expected effect.

Recommended Readings

Allen, L. A., & Woolfolk, R. L. (2010). Cognitive behavioral therapy for somatoform disorders. *Psychiatric Clinics of North America*, *33*, 579–593. http://doi.org/10.1016/j.psc.2010.04.014

Harding, K. J. K., & Fallon, B. A. (2014). Somatic symptoms and related disorders. In J. L. Cutler (Ed.), *Psychiatry* (3rd ed., pp. 323–350). New York, NY: Oxford University Press. http://doi.org/10.1093/med/9780199326075.003.0010

Warnock, J. K., & Clayton, A. H. (2003). Chronic episodic disorders in women. *Psychiatric Clinics of North America*, *26*, 725–740. http://doi.org/10.1016/S0193-953X(03)00042-X

Review Questions

1. Mr. W. is a 45-year-old man whose father died young of a heart attack. After going to the emergency department for severe epigastric pain that was eventually attributed to reflux, he becomes convinced he suffers from heart disease and that the diagnosis was missed. He continues to feel chest discomfort and visits several cardiologists, requesting a stress test, a 24-hr EKG, and blood tests. His presentation is most consistent with which of the following diagnoses?
   A. Conversion disorder
   B. Factitious disorder
   C. Illness anxiety disorder

D. Psychological factors affecting other medical conditions

E. Somatic symptom disorder

2. Mr. W. is referred for cognitive behavioral therapy. The rationale for this referral is that
   A. he is expressing distress over some unconscious, upsetting problem that the therapist can explore
   B. his insurance company will reject further claims for further tests or consultations
   C. it is inappropriate to use medical resources for someone who clearly has no serious organic disease
   D. sending him to therapy tactfully communicates that he does not have a real medical problem
   E. therapy may help him change his focus and correct his interpretation of his symptoms

3. A veteran returns from overseas deployment and is convinced that he was exposed to chemical weapons, although the army denies that any chemical weapons were used in the area where he served. He is preoccupied with nausea, fatigue, and headaches to the extent that he cannot work. His wife encourages him to see doctors and get a diagnosis for his symptoms. His care should involve
   A. annual endoscopies, with biopsies, in search of signs of tissue damage
   B. discussion of his military experiences and exploring why he believes he was poisoned
   C. referral to a veterans advocacy organization
   D. refusal of further services on the grounds that he is malingering
   E. treatment with antibiotics to eradicate occult *Helicobacter* infection

Answer Key on p. 466

51 Personality Disorders

Mariel R. Herbert, MD, and Julia B. Frank, MD

- How does DSM-5 define and cluster personality disorders?
- What are some limitations of the categorical approach to diagnosing personality?
- What is the dimensional approach to personality?
- What does research reveal about the formation of personality and the possibility of preventive intervention?
- How are personality disorders treated?

What Are Personality Disorders?

Warren, a 44-year-old, married college graduate trained in tech support, consults a psychotherapist after losing his job. When interacting with new people, he fears he will say or do something embarrassing. His wife would like them to socialize more, but he believes others see him as "weird." He never applied for promotion in the firm where he worked for 15 years; interviewing for a new job seems overwhelming. He has mild insomnia, but otherwise has symptoms only when in a new social situation or preparing for one. Warren reports he has been anxious since age 14. After his parents divorced, he moved often and was bullied in several of the high schools he attended. Then, as now, he had only one or two friends.

How does DSM-5 define and cluster personality disorders?

The core features of a **personality disorder**, as described in the *Diagnostic and Statistical Manual of Mental Disorders, 5th edition* (DSM-5), are longstanding, pervasive maladaptive patterns of thought, emotion, and behavior that do not correspond to a particular psychiatric syndrome and are not transient manifestations of another medical or psychiatric condition or substance use. DSM-5 categorizes 10 discreet personality disor-

ders. Criteria for these disorders cover observable problem behaviors, disordered emotional regulation, and dysfunctional cognitive schemas, often leading to disturbed relations with others and difficulty fulfilling culturally assigned roles and expectations. Certain problem behaviors associated with personality disorders, such as uncontrolled gambling, may be diagnosed as separate disorders in their own right.

Categories of Personality Disorders

Many of the criteria that define the categorical personality disorders are *ego syntonic* – that is, they seem normal and realistic to the person and are consistent with the person's self-image or ego ideal. Also, by definition, some elements of a personality disorder must have appeared at least by adolescence, even though a personality disorder diagnosis should not be applied until after age 18, when patterns of behavior become more stable (Table 51.1).

Limitations of Using Diagnostic Categories

One trick for remembering these disorders is to identify them with familiar fictional characters. For example, villains like Hannibal Lecter (in the

Table 51.1. Personality disorders

Disorder (Cluster)	Brief Description
Paranoid (A)	Views others as untrustworthy, exploitative; sees self as victim; responds with behavior aimed at stymying the malevolent intentions of others
Schizoid (A)	Aloof, prefers to be alone and does not enjoy interpersonal encounters; difficulty reaching intimacy with others; limited range of emotion
Schizotypal (A)	Eccentric, often odd or subtly disorganized speech and behavior; not delusional but may believe self to have special abilities; uncomfortable in close relationships
Histrionic (B)	Excessive emotionality that disrupts healthy relationships
Antisocial (B)	Exploits others; manipulative and irresponsible; difficulty maintaining relationships and adhering to societal standards; may participate in criminal activity
Borderline (B)	Shifting affects and self-image; prominent anger with fear of abandonment; "pushes and pulls" others simultaneously; impulsive; self-destructive
Narcissistic (B)	Grandiose; generally disdainful of, and needing admiration from, others
Obsessive-compulsive (C)	Perfectionistic, orderly, controlled; driven by logic rather than emotion
Avoidant (C)	Inhibited and sensitive; wants relationships but fears rejection and humiliation
Dependent (C)	Relies on others to make decisions; fears loss of emotional support, may stay in unhealthy relationships

For DSM-5 criteria see American Psychiatric Association. (2013). *Diagnostic and statistical manual of mental disorders* (5th ed.). Arlington, VA: Author.

movie *The Silence of the Lambs*) are typically narcissistic and antisocial. Luna Lovegood from the Harry Potter series of books and movies exemplifies schizotypal personality. Winnie the Pooh's friend Piglet is dependent and avoidant. Leo Bloom in the movie *The Producers* is histrionic.

> What are some limitations of the categorical approach to diagnosing personality?

While the diagnostic categories listed in Table 51.1 and their fictional counterparts suggest distinct disorders, in real life the categories overlap. Different observers may diagnose different personalities in the same person, or the same person may show elements of different disorders over time, making the definitions of the disorders unreliable. For example, people with avoidant, borderline, or dependent personality disorders all suffer from anxiety, and all both crave and retreat from close relationships. Depending on which quality seems most evident at the moment, an individual's diagnosis may change from one time of presentation to another.

To make them more flexible and reliable, personality disorder diagnoses have been grouped into clusters: A (odd, eccentric), B (dramatic, emotional, erratic), or C (anxious, fearful), or "Mad," "Bad," or "Sad" (as shown in Table 51.2). Problems of validity remain as the disorders as defined are based on descriptive characteristics, not etiological similarities. Longitudinal follow-up and genetic studies that link some personality disorders to major syndromes do support the validity of schizotypal, antisocial, and avoidant personality disorders. However, the validity of the other personality disorders is less clear.

Gender, either as a biological characteristic or a collection of social expectations, shapes the qualities and behaviors that constitute personality disorders, particularly patterns of relationships and emotional expressiveness. Male patients are more likely to be diagnosed with antisocial or obsessive-compulsive personality disorder, and females as histrionic, dependent, or borderline.

Critics also note that personality disorder diagnoses may medicalize cultural differences. Cultures with strict gender boundaries and spheres of influence tend to value the qualities of dependent personality in women, and to punish deviation from this norm. Qualities such as aggressive competitiveness and freedom from close ties may be admired in Eurowestern societies, but signify dysfunction in cultures in which family or group membership constitutes the core of identity and personality.

The elements that make up personality disorders may also be transient manifestations of syndromic psychiatric disorders (see Table 51.2). The illness of depression exaggerates the tendency to feel indecisive and helpless, core aspects of dependent personality. Mania is associated with exaggerated self-esteem, disregard for the feelings of others, and other qualities associated with narcissistic personality disorder. Addictions often drive antisocial behavior.

Of note, the diagnostic criteria exclude dysfunctions related to acute psychiatric conditions or the effects of substance use. When significant distress and impairment are apparent, but the full criteria for a specific personality disorder are not met, or when the qualities of several personality disorders coexist, the appropriate diagnoses are *other specified* or *other unspecified* personality disorder.

The diagnostic criteria specifying duration and pervasiveness across settings direct attention away from personality problems that are specific to a particular context or of recent onset. By the time a person's difficulties fully meet the criteria needed for diagnosis, they may not be changeable. This self-fulfilling prophecy of treatment refractoriness discourages practitioners from recognizing and trying to intervene with milder or more malleable personality problems.

The Dimensional Approach to Understanding Personality

What is the dimensional approach to personality?

After extensive debate, the DSM-5 committees retained the categorical system to maintain conti-

Table 51.2. The clustered classification of personality disorders

Types of Personality Disorder	Traits	Label	Associated Syndromes
Cluster A (odd-eccentric) "Mad"	Suspicious, mistrustful Alienated, odd Detached, uninterested in relationships	Paranoid Schizotypal Schizoid	Delusional disorder Schizophrenia Autism spectrum
Cluster B (dramatic- emotional) "Bad"	Amoral, destructive Unstable moods and relationships Dramatic, flamboyant Inflated self-image	Antisocial Borderline Histrionic Narcissistic	Disorders of impulse control, substance abuse PTSD Mania
Cluster C (anxious-fearful) "Sad"	Excessive anxiety Over-reliance on others Perfectionistic, inflexible	Avoidant Dependent Obsessive Compulsive	Social phobia Depression

Note. PTSD = posttraumatic stress disorder. For DSM-5 criteria see American Psychiatric Association. (2013). *Diagnostic and statistical manual of mental disorders* (5th ed.). Arlington, VA: Author.

nuity with earlier practice and the existing psychiatric literature. Psychologists have developed an alternative, *dimensional* approach that combines the study of impaired personality *function* and pathological *traits*. DSM-5 Section III acknowledges this alternative by providing a hybrid dimensional-categorical model for diagnosis that is of particular value in nonmedical, behavioral health settings (e.g., counseling centers, academic departments of psychology).

Personality functioning denotes how a person experiences self (identity and self-direction) and others (empathy and intimacy). A person functioning at a healthy, adaptive level has a complex psychological world with a generally positive self-concept and sense of self-agency, an appropriately regulated emotional life, and the capacity for reciprocal, fulfilling interpersonal relationships. Levels of impairment can be assessed for each specific area.

A **personality trait** is an enduring characteristic that the person expresses over time, in multiple contexts (see Chapter 2: Predisposition). Although the range of identifiable traits covers all the words we use to describe ourselves and others, clinical research has focused on five core traits that exist on continua between opposite poles. The **five factor model** (FFM) sorts people by degrees of social interest (extraversion vs. introversion), negative affectivity ("neuroticism" vs. detachment), agreeableness vs. disagreeableness (antagonism), conscientiousness vs. carelessness (disinhibition), and openness vs. closed-mindedness (psychoticism). According to this model, everyone's personality encompasses elements or *facets* of these traits. People with personality *disorders* have traits that are unduly persistent, inflexible, or expressed in inappropriate contexts. A commonly used questionnaire, the Personality Psychopathology 5 (PSY 5), trans-

Table 51.3. Personality traits and facets and associated disorders: five factor model

Trait (read down)	Extraversion	Neuroticism (negative affectivity)	Openness (psychoticism)	Conscientiousness	Agreeableness
Extreme	Attention seeking Excitement seeking **(Narcissistic, Histrionic)**	Ashamed Moody Insecure Labile **(Borderline, Avoidant, Dependent, Histrionic, Paranoid)**	Magical thinking Eccentric Perceptual distortions **(Schizotypal)**	Perfectionistic Detail-minded Intolerant **(Obsessive-compulsive)**	Gullible Selfless Submissive **(Dependent)**
Mid-range (normal personality)	Sociable Friendly Balanced interactions	Stable, appropriate emotions Able to assess risk	Curious Intellectual Creative Lucid, realistic	Punctual Reliable Concerned for others	Tolerant Warm Kind, trusting Empathic
Extreme	Withdrawn Anhedonic **(Schizoid, Paranoid)**	Fearless Shameless **(Antisocial, Narcissistic)**	Inflexible Closed-minded **(Obsessive-Compulsive, Borderline)**	Distractible Irresponsible Rash **(Histrionic, Antisocial)**	Deceitful Manipulative Callous **(Antisocial, Borderline, Narcissistic)**
Trait (read up)	Introversion	Detachment	Closed-mindedness	Disinhibition	Antagonism

lates this approach into standards for assessing personality dysfunctions.

Research supporting the dimensional-categorical approach has involved extensive clinical interviews and validated measures such as the Adult Trait Questionnaire (ATQ), the Minnesota Multiphasic Personality Inventory (MMPI), and the Myers-Briggs Type Indicator. People characterized themselves on these scales in terms of typical thoughts, emotional responses, and behaviors. Factor analyses then identified domains related to, but not duplicating or confirming, the current DSM-5 personality disorders (Table 51.3). Clinicians using this method characterize patients as having *personality disorder – trait specified* (PD-TS), by specifying the abnormal traits measured. Though this method provides a more nuanced picture of personality than a purely categorical assessment, it requires skills taught more often in psychotherapy and psychology training programs than in psychiatry and medicine.

Because individual traits are not necessarily linked, this classification allows for the characterization of a broad variety of personality qualities and dysfunctions. Someone who is extremely extraverted and antagonistic might be a gang leader, diagnosable as both antisocial and narcissistic; someone who is extraverted but agreeable and conscientious might be a successful politician, although still narcissistic to a certain degree.

Trait-based personality assessment has been used extensively in organizational psychology and may contribute to the design of high-functioning teams, including clinical care teams.

Factors Influencing the Development of Personality

What does research reveal about the formation of personality and the possibility of preventive intervention?

All approaches to personality disorders agree that the *temperament* and traits underlying personality originate in genetic endowment and variation. Genetic qualities appear early in development, then are modified by experiences during formative periods. Twin studies have shown that traits such as social avoidance, oppositionality, and affective lability are more than twice as common in monozygotic than dizygotic twins. Nonhuman primate studies have identified differences in thresholds and persistence of arousal in the neonatal period, when genetic influence is most apparent.

Studies in animals and humans link specific genes to patterns of behavior. Aggressiveness, in particular, reflects variation in the inheritance and expression of a promoter gene region that determines the function of the *serotonin transporter receptor protein* (5-HTT). Comparisons between individuals with two long, one long, and one short (polymorphism), or two short alleles of this gene find that male infants with two long alleles are highly resistant to developing antisocial behaviors, while those with two short alleles show such behaviors significantly more often than those with polymorphism. These data are consistent with the finding that aggressive individuals and those who attempt or complete violent suicide have low levels of the serotonin metabolite 5-HIAA in their spinal fluid. Clinically, this finding has allowed for the identification of male infants at particularly high risk for developing conduct disorder and antisocial personality disorder.

The temperaments recognized in infants (flexible, difficult, slow to warm up) may not persist into childhood and adulthood, but adults do have general dispositions toward adaptability, sensitivity, and capacity for self-regulation as elements of personality. Adverse experiences during development, especially trauma, neglect, and unpredictability, may exaggerate a particular trait to the point that an adult displays a personality disorder. This process may involve social learning (the adoption of beliefs and behaviors) or the influence of stress-induced hormonal and neurochemical responses (epigenetic factors) on the expression or suppression of genes. Variation in the activity of monoamine oxidase A (MAOA) has been associated with childhood trauma and antisocial behavior in males (see Chapter 7: Stress, Adaptation, and Stress Disorders).

Factors that foster successful adaptation and buffer stress responses (e.g., a stable nurturing home life or a strong adolescent peer group) may conversely reduce the risk of developing a disorder. For example, early intervention to improve parental behavior and limit stress has been found to reduce the development of avoidant and antisocial personality disorders in genetically at-risk children. Such research demonstrates the clinical relevance of studies that show how environmental factors, especially the quality of very early **attachments**, modify gene activity and the formation of neuronal networks during development. (see Chapter 4: Brain Networks in Health and Illness)

Understanding the role of stress in personality formation highlights the relevance of personality to critical elements of medical care, especially patients' willingness to trust providers and capacity to adhere to treatment. Being ill and interacting with the medical system are inherently stressful for many people, and stress can exaggerate maladaptive traits and qualities. A dependent person may alienate a provider with constant requests for more care or reassurance, prompting the provider to order unnecessary tests or treatments. A narcissistic person may become litigious if left with a deformity or disability that contradicts their sense of perfection and specialness. Someone who is prone to impulsiveness or disorganization may have great difficulty adhering to the complicated management of a chronic illness. Learning to recognize and respond to personality-based stress responses is an important clinical skill, as is self-awareness in the provider.

Treating Personality Disorders

How are personality disorders treated?

Contemporary treatments recognize that personality disorders differ from other psychiatric syndromes more in degree than in kind. Effective treatments strategically target particular symptoms or traits, rather than the pervasive, longstanding patterns of behavior subsumed in the construct of the personality disorder.

People whose disorders involve intense anxiety (avoidant, dependent, borderline) or impulsiveness (borderline) may benefit from treatment with serotonergic antidepressants (selective serotonin reuptake inhibitors [SSRIs] or serotonin

and norepinephrine reuptake inhibitors [SNRIs]). Elements of schizotypal and paranoid personality disorders may respond to antipsychotic drugs. Clinical experience and careful consideration of risks and benefits are essential. No psychotropic drug has specific US Food and Drug Administration (FDA) indications for use in personality disorders.

Effective psychotherapeutic interventions for persons with personality disorders address both current manifestations and the developmental trauma, neglect, or abuse that have exacerbated a patient's underlying tendencies. These treatments rely on a mixture of *supportive, psychodynamic, interpersonal,* and *cognitive behavior* approaches. Therapists help patients recognize the impact of stress and disordered attachments, including victimization (trauma), on their current thinking and behavior. Treatments enhance patients' self-awareness, cognitive flexibility, and capacity for self-control.

Evidence-based studies of outcome particularly support **dialectical behavior therapy** (DBT), a method initially developed for people with recurrent suicidal behaviors, many of whom have been diagnosed as borderline. DBT involves psychoeducation, skills modules, confronting distorted cognitions, and stabilizing self-destructive behavior before exploring its roots. The psychodynamic elements of this treatment include fostering patients' awareness of their own bodily reactions (*mindfulness*) and more accurate interpretations of other people's motivations and behavior (*mentalization*). Peer groups that offer both support and confrontation can be particularly useful for patients in DBT.

Transference-focused psychotherapy (TFP) is another evidence-based, structured treatment in which psychodynamic elements predominate. TFP considers the therapy relationship as a laboratory that brings out multiple maladaptive elements of personality disorder, especially borderline personality disorder. The patient and therapist reflect on these elements together, and, in the process, understand and change the patient's internalized, conflicting views of self and others, which fosters more stable self-representation and balanced interpersonal relationships.

Recommended Readings

Bastiaansen, L., Hopwood, C. J., Van den Broeck, J., Rossi, G., Schotte, C., & De Fruyt, F. (2015). The twofold diagnosis of personality disorder: How do personality dysfunction and pathological traits increment each other at successive levels of the trait hierarchy? *Journal of Personality Disorders, 7*(3), 280–292.

Byrd, A. L., & Manuck, S. B. (2014). MAOA, childhood maltreatment, and antisocial behavior: Meta-analysis of a gene-environment interaction. *Biological Psychiatry, 75*(1), 9–17. http://doi.org/10.1016/j.biopsych.2013.05.004

Gabbard, G. O. (2005). Mind, brain, and personality disorders. *American Journal of Psychiatry, 162*, 648–655. http://doi.org/10.1176/appi.ajp.162.4.648

Gunderson, J. G. (2011). Clinical practice: Borderline personality disorder. *New England Journal of Medicine, 364*(21), 2037–2042. http://doi.org/10.1056/NEJMcp1007358

Harkness, A. R., McNulty, J. L., & Ben-Porath, Y. S. (1995). The Personality Psychopathology Five (PSY-5): Constructs and MMPI-2 scales. *Psychological Assessment, 7*(1), 104–114. http://doi.org/10.1037/1040-3590.7.1.104

Samuel, D. B., & Widiger, T. A. (2008). A meta-analytic review of the relationships between the five-factor model and DSM-IV-TR personality disorders: A facet level analysis. *Clinical Psychology Review, 28*(8), 1326–1342. http://doi.org/10.1016/j.cpr.2008.07.002

1. L. J. is a 42-year-old woman brought to the emergency department following her third suicide attempt. She has been divorced twice. Her husband of 6 months describes her as excessively demanding, angry, and reckless. She has bouts of heavy drinking that she says are provoked by the fear he is going to leave her.

2. R. S., a 27-year-old graduate teaching assistant (TA), was recently placed on administrative leave after breaking into a professor's office to read his TA evaluations. R. S. suspected the professor of substituting the evaluations of another graduate student, who was being investigated for theft, as a way of ruining R. S.'s career.

3. Dr. M., a general practitioner, finds it difficult to care for Mrs. L., a 50-year-old woman with stable, treated hypertension and recurrent tension headaches. She frequently requests appointments to get Dr. M.'s advice about nonurgent matters, such as whether she should try estrogen replacement when she is in menopause, or whether moving to a new house might be too stressful for her. Often these requests come just before Dr. M. is due to leave on vacation.

Answer Key on p. 466

Review Questions

Directions: The items below consist of lettered headings followed by numbered descriptions. For each numbered description, choose the *one* lettered heading to which it is *most* closely associated. Each lettered heading may be used *once, more than once,* or *not at all.*

Match the case scenario with the personality disorder with which it is most consistent.
    A. Antisocial
    B. Borderline
    C. Histrionic
    D. Dependent
    E. Paranoid

52 Pharmacological Interventions for Psychiatric Disorders

Mariel R. Herbert, MD, and Julia B. Frank, MD

- Who prescribes or takes psychotropic medications?
- What are the main classes of psychotropic medication?
- How effective are antidepressants?
- What ethical issues arise with psychopharmacological treatment?

Psychotropic Medications

Who prescribes or takes psychotropic medications?

Psychotropic medications target the *mind* by influencing activities of the central nervous system (CNS). These substances may affect the cortical regions involved in conscious thought, experienced emotion, and willed behaviors, as well as limbic and brainstem centers that generate emotion and regulate such functions as sleep, appetite, autonomic activity, and capacity for pleasure (see Chapter 3: The Nervous System, and Chapter 4: Brain Networks in Health and Illness).

To market a drug in the US, pharmaceutical companies must demonstrate safety in animals followed by **double-blind placebo-controlled** studies in human populations with carefully delineated problems. Subjects are randomized to receive either an active drug or an inactive placebo. Neither subject nor researcher knows ("double blind") which substance is being taken until the data are analyzed. The role of the US Food and Drug Administration (FDA) is to determine that a drug is safe and efficacious before allowing it to be sold.

Any practitioner with prescribing authority may use approved medications outside of their FDA indications ("off-label use"). Nonpsychiatric physicians, physician assistants, dentists, and advanced practice nurses write 80% of all psychotropic medication prescriptions. Off-label use typically targets symptoms such as insomnia, fatigue,

pain, or anxious arousal, rather than defined disorders. Patients who do have the disorders for which the drug was developed often have complicating conditions that exclude them from FDA trials.

Prescribing authority requires extensive education in the chemical properties of medications, including their mechanisms of action, absorption, distribution, metabolism, half-life, excretion, toxicity, and positive and adverse effects throughout the body. Prescribers must also stay abreast of research findings not included in FDA approvals, and of systematic evaluations of clinical experience. These matters lie beyond the scope of this chapter, which broadly covers a selection of commonly used psychotropic medications, including some off-label uses. We focus especially on the aspects of medications that may affect patient acceptance. Whether the information relates to FDA-indicated or off-label use, *none of the material in this chapter should be taken as advice to prescribe a particular drug for a particular patient or condition.*

What are the main classes of psychotropic medication?

Most contemporary psychopharmacology is **empirical** (i.e., based on investigations that verify and refine what may be serendipitous discoveries). In the late 1940s, the observation that the adjunct anesthetic chlorpromazine relieved hallucinations led to trials supporting its use in schizophrenia.

A drug for tuberculosis, iproniazid, improved patients' moods, revolutionizing the understanding and treatment of depression. Empirically discovered drugs have become chemical probes fostering research into the role of neurotransmitters such as dopamine (DA) and serotonin (5-HT) in various mental functions (see Chapter 3: The Nervous System). Genetic studies and functional neuroimaging extend this knowledge, providing complex, although still incomplete, understanding of how psychiatric symptoms and disorders relate to brain activity.

Psychotropic medications are classified by (1) their **chemical structure** (e.g., tricyclics, phenothiazines, opiates), (2) the **conditions they target** (e.g., antidepressants, antipsychotics, anxiolytics, mood stabilizers, sedative hypnotics, stimulants), or (3) some element of their **mechanism of action** (e.g., selective serotonin reuptake inhibitors, dopaminergics). Although clinically useful, classifying drugs by a target condition can be misleading, because drugs that affect one condition may also modify others. Antidepressants, for example, both relieve and exacerbate anxiety. Each clinical grouping includes drugs from different chemical classes, with different mechanisms of action. Some drugs fall into several classes.

Antidepressants

The 26 antidepressants that were FDA approved as of the summer of 2016 fall into seven classes. The choice for a particular patient depends on the person's target symptoms, coexisting medical conditions, allergies, and tolerance for side effects (see Table 52.1). Most antidepressants affect the balance of 5-HT, norepinephrine (NE), and dopamine (DA) in neural synapses. They also modify the expression of genes governing receptor function in the CNS. These mechanisms take time; all antidepressants are characterized by *response latency*, a period of 2 to 8 weeks before the response to the drug can be differentiated from a placebo response or to demonstrate a clear nonresponse. Unfortunately, undesirable effects may appear earlier. Any drug must be given in adequate dose and for sufficient time before deciding to change the treatment. Patients may require support for continuing to take a medication when it does not seem to be working.

Patients who respond to an antidepressant should continue on it for at least 4 to 6 months. Premature discontinuation may precipitate a relapse of depression. Abruptly stopping some antidepressant agents without an appropriate taper

---

Table 52.1. Antidepressant medications: common and serious side effects by class

Class and Examples of Medications	Common Side Effects	Serious Side Effects	Special Concerns
Tricyclic (TCA) desipramine nortriptyline (TCAs with the mildest anticholinergic effects)	Blurred vision Dry mouth Orthostatic hypotension Sedation Sexual dysfunction Weight gain	Cardiac conduction defects Seizure provocation (lowered seizure threshold) Worsen glaucoma/ urinary retention Drug–drug interactions	Dangerous or lethal in overdose Older patients more sensitive to anticholinergic side effects
Selective serotonin reuptake inhibitor (SSRI) citalopram escitalopram fluoxetine paroxetine sertraline	Nausea Diarrhea Sedation or insomnia Sexual dysfunction Headache Weight gain (long-term use)	Drug–drug interactions Agitation Increase in suicidal ideation or behavior in people aged < 25	Withdrawal syndromes except with long half-life SSRI (fluoxetine – may stop without tapering) Common and mild side effects may resolve within a few weeks

Table 52.1. (continued)

Serotonin and norepinephrine reuptake inhibitor (SNRI) venlafaxine desvenlafaxine duloxetine levomilnacipran	Similar to SSRI profile Constipation, dry mouth (especially venlafaxine)	May cause sustained BP elevation (venlafaxine) Hepatic toxicity (duloxetine)	Withdrawal syndrome Used for depression +chronic pain or stress incontinence (duloxetine especially) Levomilnacipran is new, possibly more effect on NE; clinical implications of difference not clear
Dopamine and norepinephrine reuptake inhibitor (DNRI) bupropion	Insomnia Anxiety Agitation	Seizure risk escalates when exceed recommended single or maximum dose Psychosis in older patients and those with risk factors like schizophrenia	Seizure risk in overdose Relatively contraindicated in eating disorders, seizure disorders, and/ or in patients on agents that may lower the seizure threshold – e.g., tramadol Useful for tobacco cessation and depression
Norepinephrine and specific serotonin antidepressant (NaSSA) mirtazapine	Sedation Weight gain Increased appetite		Sedation or weight gain lead to discontinuation in ~10% of exposures
Monoamine oxidase inhibitor (MAOI) phenelzine tranylcypromine selegiline transdermal patch	Sedation or insomnia Weight gain Orthostatic hypotension	Dangerous hypertension with tyramine ingestion Drug–drug interactions require dietary restrictions and careful patient education	Selegiline transdermal does not require dietary restrictions at low doses (6 mg)
Multimodal antidepressants (block reuptake and modulate other receptor activity, may target multiple neurotransmitters) (sometimes called serotonin antagonist and reuptake inhibitor [SARI]) trazodone vortioxetine vilazodone	Sedation at lower doses Similar to SSRIs	Priapism with trazodone	Vortioxetine and vilazodone are new, expensive, not available as generics. Not in use long enough to identify rare toxicities or effects in special populations

Note. BP = blood pressure; NE = norepinephrine.

may result in a distressing discontinuation syndrome. Patients who need to take antidepressants indefinitely need to consider other adverse effects and long-term consequences (e.g., nonrestful sleep, weight gain).

Antidepressants may induce agitation or frank mania, particularly in patients who have, or are genetically at risk for, bipolar disorder. Antidepressants have been implicated in increasing suicidal ideation in adolescents. Although the FDA warns against using any antidepressant in people less than 25 years old, withholding them has reduced the recognition and treatment of depression in this population.

The most commonly prescribed antidepressants are the **selective serotonin reuptake inhibitors** (SSRIs). Reuptake terminates the synaptic activity of neurotransmitters. Blocking reuptake increases the availability of 5-HT, a regulator of NE and DA activity. The major advantage of SSRIs is their wide *therapeutic index*, the difference between a usual effective dose and a dangerous one. SSRIs used alone are almost never lethal in overdose. Their main adverse effects are headache, loss of sexual interest, anorgasmia or delayed orgasm, and gastrointestinal distress. SSRIs can worsen anxiety, especially in the early weeks of use.

Combining an SSRI with other drugs that potentiate serotonin may precipitate the *serotonin syndrome*: nausea, diarrhea, headache, confusion, rapid heart rate, increased blood pressure, dilated pupils, sweating, and, in the most severe instances, seizures, coma, and death.

The next most commonly prescribed antidepressants are dual-acting agents, sometimes called **serotonin and norepinephrine reuptake inhibitors** (SNRIs). These medications block the reuptake of both 5-HT and NE. Common side effects include those of the SSRIs, plus constipation and dry mouth. Dual acting agents may be effective for people who do not respond to SSRIs. They have also been shown to be effective in treating pain and cryptic somatic symptoms.

Both the SSRIs and SNRIs were developed to improve on safety and tolerability of the older **tricyclic antidepressants** (TCAs), which block the synaptic reuptake of many monoamine neurotransmitters. The oldest TCAs and dual-acting agents also have *anticholinergic side effects*, specifically, dry mouth, constipation, sedation, low

blood pressure, rapid heartbeat, urinary retention, and worsening of glaucoma or dementia symptoms, in varying degrees. Tricyclics have a narrower therapeutic index than SSRIs and can be lethal in overdose. However, they may be beneficial when others fail. In low doses, they may also benefit people with pain and functional somatic symptoms, including migraine headaches.

Table 52.1 lists commonly prescribed antidepressants, differentiated by side effects and toxicity. All have similar efficacy, although individual patients may respond to one and not another. Special concerns for all of them include varying degrees of agitation, anxiety, or suicidal thought; worsening of bipolar disorder; and the warning against unmonitored use in young people.

How effective are antidepressants?

The answer to this critical question depends on the conditions under which these medications are used, for whom, and for how long. The **Sequenced Treatment Alternatives to Relieve Depression (STAR*D)** study was a 7-year, multisite investigation of the treatment of depression in 4,000+ primary care patients, of whom 3,000+ qualified for treatment. While initial response to an SSRI was disappointing (27% of the 4,000 screened showed a response, who made up about half of those actually treated), the overall response rate after patients underwent various additional or alternate treatments was 55% to 67%. These results have incited controversy, as they did not cover all available therapies, and patients were not selected for likelihood of responding to medication. The study did, however, mirror the real conditions of practice and provides a benchmark against which to measure future developments.

Trials like STAR*D highlight the importance of *measurement-based care*, or the recording of symptoms over time with reliable and valid psychometric instruments. Patients have difficulty accurately remembering symptoms after more than a few weeks. A bedside depression rating scale (e.g., the self-reported *Patient Health Questionnaire* [PHQ-9]), the (proprietary) *Beck Depression Inventory II,* or the clinician-rated *Hamilton Depression Scale*) may define the level of antidepressant response, and inform medication management decisions. Even when not using these measures, clinicians should consistently record information across all relevant symptom domains (e.g., low mood, suicidal thoughts, crying spells, anxiety, irritability, agitation; decreased concentration, energy, motivation, or pleasure; thoughts of guilt, helplessness, and hopelessness) (see Chapter 39: The Psychiatric Evaluation).

The goal of treatment is complete remission of depressive symptoms. Trials of different drugs may be needed to identify the most effective, best-tolerated medication(s) for a given patient. Some patients who do not respond to one antidepressant may respond to another from the same or a different class. Augmenting the antidepressant with another kind of medication entirely can be useful in some *treatment refractory* cases.

Effective, physical treatments for depression outside of medication include phototherapy (bright light), electroconvulsive therapy (ECT), transcranial magnetic stimulation (TMS), and *botulinum toxin* injections into muscles of the forehead.

Antipsychotic Medications

Nearly all antipsychotic medications derive from the observed antipsychotic activity of the phenothiazine **chlorpromazine**. Chlorpromazine broadly blocks the activity of CNS DA. Blocking DA in the mesolimbic pathway reduces *positive psychotic symptoms*, but blocking other pathways produces many undesirable effects, including sedation, motor dysfunction ("drug-induced parkinsonism" or **extrapyramidal side effects [EPSE]**), and elevated levels of prolactin, the hormone that promotes lactation after childbirth. Despite these drawbacks, the antipsychotic drugs as a class have a wide therapeutic index and are not lethal in overdose. A rare and dangerous complication, the **neuroleptic malignant syndrome** (NMS) of severely elevated temperature, muscle rigidity, and autonomic dysfunctions occurs in 0.2% of patients taking usual doses of typical and atypical antipsychotics. Untreated NMS may be fatal.

Several waves of innovation have refined **dopamine-blocking drugs** to target critical receptors selectively and reduce undesired effects. Butyrophenones (haloperidol) are less sedating but cause more severe EPSE than the phenothiazines. Their use often requires cotreatment with anticholinergic, anti-Parkinson's drugs.

A major breakthrough occurred with the advent of drugs that act primarily as **mesolimbic 5-HT2 blocking agents**, secondarily reducing mesolimbic DA activity, but sparing other pathways. Risperidone was the first so-called **atypical** or **second-generation antipsychotic**. Different drugs (see Table 52.2) cause variable levels of EPSE, weight gain (leading to hyperlipidemia and diabetes), sedation, and elevated prolactin (causing breast growth and lactation in men, and lactation and reduced fertility in women). Medication-induced weight gain contributes to the excessive nonpsychiatric mortality in patients in long-term treatment. Baseline and periodic monitoring of body mass index, hemoglobin A1c, fasting plasma glucose, and fasting lipids is recommended.

Most antipsychotic drugs prolong the QTc interval, a cardiac effect measured on EKG. Combining these medications with others with similar effects (e.g., sulfamethoxazole, trimethoprim) may increase patients' risk of developing a potentially fatal cardiac arrhythmia (*torsade de pointes*). Serial EKGs in hospitalized patients and baseline EKG measurement in outpatients should be obtained to screen for QTc interval prolongation.

While the tolerability of these drugs varies, only one, clozapine, is proven to sometimes relieve schizophrenic symptoms refractory to other drugs. It has intense anticholinergic effects and requires special monitoring for suppression of white blood cells (agranulocytosis), leading to susceptibility to fatal infections. Prescribing clozapine is subject to special FDA regulations and requires specific training.

Patients' adherence to antipsychotic medication is often erratic, which has led to the development of medications that can be given by injection every two weeks or monthly (depot medication). Since antipsychotic therapy may need to continue indefinitely, cost is a major concern, both for patients and for public and private insurance providers. Older medications are generally cheaper than newer medications, but restricting access to the newer, more tolerable drugs may significantly impair adherence and outcome.

Antipsychotic medications are also used to control agitation in hospitalized psychiatric patients. They should be used with great caution

Table 52.2. Selected antipsychotic drugs: adverse effects and special considerations

Typical Antipsychotic	Common Adverse Effects	Serious or Toxic Adverse Effects	Special Considerations
Chlorpromazine (CPZ)	++EPSE +++ACH +++Sedation	Hypotension Jaundice Weight gain	Other drugs dosed in "CPZ equivalents" Threshold of efficacy equivalent to ~ 400 mg
Thioridazine	+ EPSE ++++ACH Retrograde ejaculation +++Sedation	Hypotension Jaundice Weight gain	Pigmentary retinopathy at doses > 800 mg/day
Clozapine	0 EPSE +++++ACH +++Sedation	Agranulocytosis Jaundice Orthostatic hypotension and tachycardia (early in treatment) Weight gain	Monitor blood counts (required, national registry) *Reduces suicide rate in schizophrenia* *Used for refractory psychotic disorders and for prominent or persistent negative symptoms*
Perphenazine	++++EPSE ++ACH ++Sedation	Weight gain? Tardive dyskinesia	
Fluphenazine	++++ EPSE ++ACH +Sedation	Weight gain? Tardive dyskinesia	Depot formulation: IM injection every 2 weeks, enhances adherence
Haloperidol	+++++EPSE +ACH +Sedation	Angina in cardiac patients Sudden cardiac death Weight gain Tardive dyskinesia	Depot formulation: IM every 2 weeks Contraindicated in Parkinson's disease Caution in severe cardiovascular disease Commonly used for agitation and aggression in the hospital or emergency setting
Atypical Antipsychotic			
Olanzapine	+EPSE +ACH ++Sedation	Weight gain++ Dysphagia Asthenia Postural hypotension Joint pain	Can be used for agitation and aggression without adding an anticholinergic for EPSE prevention Contraindicated in any unstable medical condition
Risperidone (paliperidone, iloperidone)	+EPSE (at high doses) +ACH +Sedation	Weight gain	Depot formulation: IM every 2 weeks; expensive At doses > 6 mg/day: more EPSE FDA approved for irritability (associated with autism) in children as young as 5 years

Table 52.2. (continued)

Quetiapine	+ EPSE +ACH +++Sedation	Weight gain	Does not raise prolactin levels May be monotherapy for bipolar depression (not first-line agent)
Ziprasidone	+EPSE +ACH +Sedation	Dizziness and orthostatic hypotension (dose-related)	Does not typically cause weight gain Possible increase in risk of arrhythmia due to prolongation of QTc interval
Aripiprazole	+EPSE +ACH +Sedation	Sometimes weight gain, often not Restlessness	Depot formulation: IM every 4 weeks (expensive) May be used to augment SSRIs for refractory depression Has not been shown to significantly affect QTc interval
Asenapine	+EPSE + ACH +Sedation	Weight gain	Sublingual formulation
Lurasidone	+EPSE +ACH +Sedation		No warning for QTc prolongation Possibly weight neutral

Note. + = infrequent, mild; ++ = occasional; +++ = frequent, moderate; ++++ = common, moderate to severe; +++++ = common and severe. ACH = anticholinergic side effects; EPSE = extrapyramidal side effects ; IM = intramuscular; SSRIs = selective serotonin reuptake inhibitors. Adapted from Zeier, K., Connell, R., Resch, W., & Thomas, C. J. (2013). Recommendations for lab monitoring of atypical antipsychotics. *Current Psychiatry, 12*(9), 51–54.

for psychotic symptoms or agitation in patients with delirium or dementia, after other measures have failed, because they may increase mortality in elderly demented patients.

Medication in Bipolar Disorder ("Mood Stabilizers")

Bipolar disorder, which by definition involves recurring states of mania or hypomania and depression, is challenging to treat. Medications that relieve acute depression may induce mania or increase cycling, and medications that modify cycling may have limited efficacy in acute episodes of mania or depression. Atypical antipsychotics, covered above, are often used.

Medications specifically targeting mood cycling are lithium carbonate and various **antiepileptic drugs** (AEDs), sometimes called *mood stabilizers*.

Lithium is a naturally occurring ion. Some 19th-century neurologists and doctors at mineral spas recognized its calming properties. In the 1960s, an Australian psychiatrist, John Cade, demonstrated its efficacy in ending manic episodes. Subsequent work found that it prevents and relieves mania and sometimes depression. It is the only drug that clearly reduces the suicide rate in bipolar disorder. Lithium's mechanism of action is not fully understood. Despite its efficacy, its very low therapeutic index and its side effects (tremor, thirst, frequent urination, weight gain) make it difficult to use. Safe use requires close patient follow-up.

Researchers seeking a safer mood stabilizer noted that bipolar episodes resemble epileptic events: Subthreshold symptoms may accumulate until a full-blown mood episode occurs. Subsequent episodes occur at lower and lower thresholds. This *"kindling hypothesis"* supported successful trials of AEDs in bipolar patients. Various forms of valproic acid and carbamazepine and its metabolite oxcarbazepine relieve and prevent mania and possibly prevent depression. AEDs have a markedly wider therapeutic index than lithium.

A unique AED, lamotrigine, relieves and may prevent bipolar depression. It has a potentially fatal toxicity manifested by a skin rash indicating underlying vasculitis (Stevens-Johnson syndrome [SJS]). Increasing the dose very slowly (over the course of months) to a therapeutic level reduces the risk of SJS, but limits its use in acute episodes. It is well tolerated as a maintenance (preventive) therapy, as it has few side effects.

Valproic acid and carbamazepine have more side effects than lamotrigine, and both also have potentially fatal, rare toxicities (i.e., hemorrhagic pancreatitis and bone marrow failure or agranulocytosis, respectively). These complications are not related to rate of introduction, so the drugs can be used in situations requiring immediate effect.

Patients taking AEDs need laboratory monitoring; therapeutic effects are dose related, and complications can be identified in serum chemistries and blood counts. AEDs also may interact with other drugs, affecting blood levels and possible toxicity.

Anxiolytics, Sedatives, and Stimulants

Antidepressants and antipsychotics reduce chronic anxiety associated with their target disorders. The response latency of these drugs makes them less useful for acute anxiety although, when taken over time, the SSRIs and dual-acting agents prevent panic attacks.

Sedatives have been known to medicine since antiquity. Early antianxiety drugs (barbiturates) modulated the *brainstem* areas involved in general arousal and alertness. High doses induced lethal respiratory suppression. Newer anxiolytics target mainly *cortical* areas, in which the neurotransmit-

ter **gamma amino butyric acid (GABA)** balances the activity of the excitatory neurotransmitter **glutamate**. The brain has endogenous benzodiazepine receptors that regulate the expression of GABA. The benzodiazepines, affecting mainly the cortex, are far safer in overdose than the older sedatives.

Benzodiazepines quickly relieve anxiety, which makes them susceptible to abuse and subject to withdrawal effects (similar to alcohol withdrawal), especially if stopped abruptly. Judicious use during periods of high stress or while waiting for another drug to take effect does not generally lead to addiction. Benzodiazepines with a slower onset of action (e.g., clonazepam) tend to be less reinforcing and less likely to be abused.

Modified benzodiazepines (e.g., flurazepam) given to improve sleep have similar advantages and disadvantages. They work initially, but patients may develop *tolerance,* requiring higher doses to get the same effects. Discontinuing sedatives after regular use typically leads to recurrent sleep problems. Newer agents (e.g., zolpidem) preserve normal *sleep architecture* and so are less likely to induce tolerance, and their discontinuation is smoother. For both anxiety and sleep, the early implementation of cognitive behavior strategies may help patients minimize their use of medication with its associated risks (see Chapter 6: Chronobiology and Sleep Disorders).

Stimulants (e.g., methylphenidate, dextroamphetamine) improve concentration and attention in people with *attention-deficit/hyperactivity disorder* (ADHD). Although distantly related chemically to the highly addictive drug cocaine, stimulants prescribed for appropriately diagnosed children improve their general adaptation. In addition, treated children are actually less likely than their untreated peers to abuse drugs in adolescence or adulthood. Stimulants that are less rapidly absorbed, longer acting, or made from precursors are less likely to be abused. For adults with ADHD, other nonstimulant agents (e.g., atomoxetine, guanfacine) may be considered, but they seem somewhat less effective than stimulants.

Drugs for Other Conditions

Novel therapies are in development for challenging clinical and public health problems, especially dementia and addiction. Drugs that increase acetylcholine activity have some value in treating dementia. Alcoholics may benefit from *disulfiram*, which induces nausea and vomiting in response to alcohol; *naltrexone*, which reduces craving and the tendency to binge drink; and *acamprosate*, which also reduces craving. Psychotropic drugs promote **harm reduction** in *opiate addiction*, where substitution therapies like *methadone* (a long-acting opiate agonist) and *buprenorphine* (a mixed agonist/antagonist) are demonstrably superior to abstinence strategies in reducing relapse, criminal behavior, and functional impairment (see Chapter 24: Substance-Related and Addictive Disorders).

Beyond target symptoms and the qualities of a medication, patient preference, setting, available expertise and resources, and contraindications to particular medications govern the selection of treatment. The best predictor of any patient's response to a given medication is their prior response or nonresponse.

Ethical Issues in Pharmacological Treatment

> What ethical issues arise with psychopharmacological treatment?

Psychotropic medications clearly benefit patients with severe and persistent psychiatric disorders. However, their use raises questions about the meaning of personal experience, patient autonomy, and the boundaries of normal and disordered functioning.

Symptoms have meaning in people's lives. When offered medicine to relieve nightmares and reduce intrusive recollection, veterans with combat trauma (i.e., posttraumatic stress disorder) have accused doctors of "drugging the vet to make him forget." They questioned whether the goal of treatment was to relieve their suffering or to absolve society of the responsibility for causing it.

Using medication to change a person's thoughts or perceptions can be viewed as *undermining autonomy* as a form of social control, even when intended for the good of the person (ethical

principle of *beneficence*). Eliciting informed consent preserves autonomy, but some psychiatric disorders compromise patients' cognitive capacities and judgment, precluding genuinely informed consent. Many states provide special legal procedures regulating who can be treated without consent, especially in the face of imminent harm to self or others. Using psychotropic drugs in minors, who lack legal capacity to consent, also poses ethical and clinical concerns. While the problem of medication overuse in young people has received widespread attention, withholding effective therapies because of a patient's age is also inappropriate.

Patients sometimes fear becoming addicted to psychotropic medication. Drugs that enhance the mesolimbic DA pathway, stimulate opioid receptors, or modify arousal (stimulants or sedatives) are the medications most often abused. An animal's preference for a drug over food or water or the development of a street market also indicates a drug's abuse potential. Antidepressants, antipsychotics, and mood stabilizers are rarely abused. Sedatives and opiates may be. It is important to discuss with patients how certain medications are or are not addicting when used appropriately.

Recommended Readings

Hoop, J. G., & Spellecy, R. (2009). Philosophical and ethical issues at the forefront of neuroscience and genetics: An overview for psychiatrists. *Psychiatric Clinics of North America, 32*, 437–449. http://doi.org/10.1016/j.psc.2009.03.004

Preston, J., & Johnson, J. (2014). *Clinical psychopharmacology made ridiculously simple* (8th ed.). Miami, FL: Medmaster.

Additional Resources

National Institute of Mental Health. (2016). *Mental health medications.* Washington, DC: US Department of Health and Human Services. Available at http://www.nimh.nih.gov/health/topics/mental-health-medications/mental-health-medications.shtml

National Institute of Mental Health. (2006). *Questions and answers about the NIMH Sequenced Treatment Alternatives to Relieve Depression (STAR*D) study – All medi-

cation levels, Nov 2006. Washington, DC: US Department of Health and Human Services. Available at https://www.nimh.nih.gov/funding/clinical-research/practical/stard/index.shtml

Review Questions

1. A 34-year-old woman taking depot haloperidol for schizophrenia wishes to become pregnant but is not conceiving with unprotected intercourse. She should be switched to
   A. clozapine
   B. oral haloperidol
   C. quetiapine
   D. risperidone
   E. ziprasidone

2. A 28-year-old man being started on an SSRI for depression should be warned about
   A. anticholinergic side effects
   B. gynecomastia (breast growth)
   C. possible cardiac arrhythmias
   D. sexual dysfunction
   E. Stevens-Johnson syndrome

3. A couple fears that putting their child with diagnosed ADHD on stimulant medication will result in drug addiction. They can be told that
   A. adolescents with ADHD who receive stimulants are less likely than their untreated peers to become addicted to illegal drugs
   B. nonstimulant drugs are equally effective for ADHD in children
   C. stimulants and addictive drugs are not related
   D. the child should decide whether or not to take medication
   E. the medication will be stopped before her child reaches the age of risk for addiction

Answer Key on p. 466

Appendix: Psychological Testing

Rory P. Houghtalen, MD

- How do psychological tests complement other methods of medical or psychiatric assessment?
- What are some commonly administered psychological tests?

Psychological tests are standardized methods of characterizing cognition. emotion, and behavior in both normal and clinical populations. Used properly, they may clarify diagnosis, inform treatment planning, and measure change over time.

Psychological tests are designed to measure what they purport to measure (**validity**) and to do so consistently (**reliability**). They should meet rigorous psychometric standards of **specificity**, **sensitivity** and **standard measurements of error**. The statistical methods of test interpretation provide *objective* measurement of psychological function, although the data to which these standards are applied may include reports of test takers' subjective experience. The validity and reliability of test results also depend on subjects' motivation and effort.

As any student who has taken a standardized test knows, factors affecting effort range from the expectations of the examiner and the subject, to the general health of the subject, and even to whether the test taker is hungry or tired. Standardized conditions for test administration and, in some tests (e.g., the Minnesota Multiphasic Personality Inventory [MMPI]), various internal measures of validity reduce the impact of these confounders. When present, internal measures may identify subjects attempting to suppress, exaggerate, or malinger deficits.

Common bedside measures, particularly the Patient Health Questionnaire 9 (PHQ-9), the Montreal Cognitive Assessment (MoCA), or the Mini–Mental State Examination (MMSE; see Chapter 39: The Psychiatric Evaluation) are composed of elements of more complex tests. The scores on the shorter tests roughly correlate with those of the tests from which they were derived. For example, the cognitive probes of the mental status exam (measuring concentration and attention by serial subtractions or digit span) come from the well-validated Wechsler intelligence scales (IQ tests). Bedside tests may be used with minimal training. More complex psychological tests generally require licensed psychologists with specialized training to administer, interpret, and analyze them properly.

How do psychological tests complement other methods of medical or psychiatric assessment?

In general medicine, neuropsychological tests may clarify the nature and extent of problems to improve the habilitation and rehabilitation of people with brain-based conditions (e.g., strokes, head injuries, dementing conditions, or developmental disorders). It is always important, however, to consider the goals of testing before requesting a battery of assessments that can be time consuming, expensive, and add little to the diagnosis or treatment.

Testing also can contribute to forensic assessments such as evaluating a person's capacity to make financial or health care decisions. Other forensic applications include appraisal of criminal responsibility, competency to stand trial, and claims of psychological injury.

Applied to psychopathology, providers may request psychological or neuropsychological testing to define or refine a *diagnosis*, confirm suspected deficits or problems, or quantify the nature and extent of a problem.

A 20-year-old man seeks assessment for problems getting along with others. He is emotionally constricted, has outbursts that resemble tantrums, and has been unable to finish high school. The provider refers the man for psychological testing to try to differentiate intellectual deficits from personality disorder or prodromal psychosis. The testing professional takes a thorough history, reviews the man's school records, and decides to administer an IQ test, some subtests of the Halstead Reitan Battery, and a Minnesota Multiphasic Personality Inventory. The report to the provider identifies previously unrecognized problems of comprehension and processing speed, along with personality traits of low self-esteem and poor frustration tolerance, but finds no evidence of psychosis.

Normed tests may also establish a *baseline* that permits measurement of change over time. For example, many school districts now require cognitive screening before participation in contact sports. Testing is repeated after a concussion to establish postinjury findings and degree of recovery, and to determine if and when return to play is safe. Measurement of change is also a bedrock element of human behavioral science research, especially the evaluation of therapeutic outcomes.

What are some commonly administered psychological tests?

Table A1 provides examples of and facts about some commonly used psychological tests.

Table A1. A sample of commonly used psychological tests

Test	General Description	Common Uses
Intelligence or ability tests Wechsler intelligence scales Stanford-Binet test Kaufman scales	Standardized tasks of cognitive abilities that represent the construct of intelligence Scales yield an intelligence quotient (IQ), and index scores of major cognitive domains (e.g., verbal, visual, quantitative, sequential reasoning) IQ and index scores compare the subject's function with that of others of similar age and demographics	Diagnosis and classification of intellectual disability, other developmental disorders and acquired cognitive disorders, such as brain injury Determination of general cognitive ability to guide treatment planning and disposition Academic placement and vocational planning
Achievement tests Wide Range Achievement Test Woodcock Johnson Wechsler Individual Achievement Test	Tests of academically-based skills and knowledge (e.g., reading, spelling, mathematics, written expression) Scores are typically reported as grade levels and age percentiles	Diagnosis of learning disability Academic placement and vocational planning

Table A1. (continued)		
Neuropsychological tests Halstead Reitan Battery Wechsler Memory Scale Boston Naming Test Rey Complex Figure Test Dementia Rating Scale Verbal learning tests	The list to the left includes examples of standardized tests of memory, language, attention, concentration, visual-spatial abilities, sensory/motor integrity, and frontal-executive functions Administered as a fixed battery or tailored to assessment purpose Scores reported as age percentiles, index scores, or impairment index	Assessment of cognitive dysfunction due to acquired brain damage or disease for diagnosis or treatment planning Assessment of developmental cognitive disorders for academic and vocational planning
Tests of personality and psychopathology Minnesota Multiphasic Personality Inventory Millon Clinical Multiaxial Inventory	Assess response style, emotional states, attitudes, behavioral traits/tendencies, interpersonal function, motivation, and presence and severity of psychopathology Standardized statements that require true–false response options Imbedded scales allow assessment if self-report is bias (e.g., social desirability, symptom exaggeration, defensiveness)	Assessment of personality characteristics and presence or severity of psychopathology Screening for psychopathology that may not be openly reported on interview Assessment of symptom exaggeration and feigning
Projective tests of personality and psychopathology Rorschach test Thematic apperception test Projective drawings Sentence completion	Use of ambiguous test stimuli to assess unconscious motives, feelings or response tendencies Based on the *projective hypothesis* that response to an ambiguous stimulus is a projection of the subject's perceptual style, feelings, thoughts, attitudes, desires, experiences, and problem-solving skills Subjectivity in interpretation limits reliability and validity and utility in some settings (e.g., forensics)	Diagnosis of psychopathology Assessment of emotional needs, reality testing, thought organization, and attitudes regarding interpersonal relationships

Answer Key to Review Questions

Chapter 1
1. A
2. A
3. D

Chapter 2
1. D
2. E
3. C
4. C
5. D
6. B

Chapter 3
1. E
2. C
3. B
4. D

Chapter 4
1. C
2. C
3. D

Chapter 5
1. C
2. B
3. D

Chapter 6
1. A
2. D
3. B
4. A

Chapter 7
1. E
2. B
3. D
4. D

Chapter 8
1. B
2. A
3. D
4. C

Chapter 9
1. B
2. B
3. B
4. A
5. C

Chapter 10
1. D
2. B
3. C
4. B

Chapter 11
1. D
2. C
3. A
4. E
5. E
6. A
7. E
8. C
9. D
10. C
11. E

Chapter 12
1. E
2. A
3. C

Chapter 13
1. D
2. D
3. C
4. A

Chapter 14
1. A
2. E
3. B
4. B

Chapter 15
1. C
2. D
3. A

Chapter 16
1. E
2. E
3. B
4. A
5. A

Chapter 17
1. E
2. E
3. D
4. D
5. B

Chapter 18
1. C
2. E

Chapter 19
1. E
2. A

Chapter 20
1. B
2. E
3. D

Chapter 21
1. A
2. E
3. A

Chapter 22
1. E
2. C
3. E
4. C

Chapter 23
1. C
2. D
3. D
4. C

Chapter 24
1. C
2. C
3. C

Chapter 25
1. E
2. E
3. E

Chapter 26
1. B
2. C
3. E
4. A

Chapter 27
1. D
2. E
3. D

Chapter 28
1. False
2. False
3. True

Chapter 29
1. E
2. E
3. E

Chapter 30
1. D
2. D
3. D

Chapter 31
1. A
2. C
3. E
4. D

Chapter 32
1. A
2. C
3. A

Chapter 33
1. E
2. E
3. E

Chapter 34
1. D
2. C
3. B
4. C

Chapter 35
1. A
2. C
3. C
4. B
5. C
6. B

Chapter 36
1. E
2. D
3. E
4. A
5. C

Chapter 37
1. E
2. D
3. D
4. E

Chapter 38
1. E
2. D
3. B

Chapter 39
1. E
2. A
3. B

Chapter 40
1. B
2. B
3. D

Chapter 41
1. C
2. B
3. A
4. B

Chapter 42
1. D
2. A
3. B
4. D

Chapter 43
1. B
2. C
3. E

Chapter 44
1. A
2. B
3. B

Chapter 45
1. E
2. A
3. A

Chapter 46
1. E
2. B

Chapter 47
1. B
2. E
3. B

Chapter 48
1. D
2. C

Chapter 49
1. D
2. C

Chapter 50
1. C
2. E
3. B

Chapter 51
1. B
2. E
3. D

Chapter 52
1. C
2. D
3. A

Practice Exam

Martha A. Bird, MD, Olle Jane Z. Sahler, MD, Julia B. Frank, MD, and Christine E. Tran-Boynes, DO

Questions

Most of the following questions about aspects of behavioral science are presented in the formats used by the US Medical Licensing Examination (USMLE). The answers are accompanied by in-depth explanations. Although some of the topics covered here reinforce information in the text, some questions are included to introduce additional topics and new information.

1. A homosexual couple wants to marry and adopt a child. They are told that compared with heterosexual couples, they are more likely to
   A. experience increased conflict
   B. face greater societal prejudice
   C. have poorer emotional health
   D. show poorer parenting skills
   E. raise gay or lesbian children

2. You have been asked to create a template for patient education to be used by all of the clinicians in your managed care group practice. When planning for patient education, it is most important to remember that
   A. more disease information provided at the time of diagnosis leads to better adherence
   B. patients perceived as intelligent by the clinician typically remember significantly more information
   C. patients' level of education correlates positively with adherence
   D. patients' perception of the time spent giving information correlates positively with adherence
   E. patients' recall of instructions improves following warnings about the consequences of nonadherence

3. A doctor in the process of remarrying after divorce consults a colleague in mental health for current information about stepfamilies and learns that stepfamilies
   A. are becoming less prevalent
   B. are becoming the most common family form
   C. have fewer financial problems overall
   D. have more pathology than other family forms
   E. rarely end in divorce if young stepchildren are involved

4. A college freshman comes to the student health department suffering from sadness, sleep problems, and difficulty focusing on schoolwork. Her family did not want her to go away to school, but a large scholarship proved impossible to turn down. She says her mother is unhappy with her being so far away. She describes her family as very close, saying she and her mother "share everything." She misses being an integral part of every family activity. This student's family exemplifies which of the following family processes?
   A. Cohesion
   B. Enmeshment
   C. Infantilization
   D. Scapegoating
   E. Splitting

5. A 35-year-old man with chronic schizophrenia is brought to the emergency department by his parents because of nonadherence to medication and increased symptoms. When interviewed by the social worker, the parents do not seem to understand his illness. His mother says she is aggravated by his "laziness," and his father says he just doesn't seem to be trying to do anything. Both sound angry as they talk about him. This pattern of family response has been called
   A. exploitation for secondary gain
   B. help seeking, help rejecting
   C. high expressed emotion
   D. parentification of an adult child
   E. triangulation

6. A 55-year-old man drinks a 6-pack of beer every night and at least two 6-packs plus whiskey on Saturdays and Sundays. He brags about his "strong head for liquor." He denies any serious health or legal consequences related to drinking. He says that he plans to teach his 15-year-old son to drink responsibly. "If he does like I do, he should be fine, don't you think?" he asks. What advice should be given to this man about educating his son in the use of alcohol?
   A. If he wants the boy to try alcohol, it should be at a meal with adults who do not condone drunkenness

B. Teach his son to avoid daily drinking, to prevent him from developing an alcohol problem

C. The boy will be fine if he drinks only beer or wine and avoids hard liquor until he is at least 18

D. The safe limit of alcohol use for an adolescent is one beer or 4 ounces of wine in a 24-hr period

E. The son is at low risk for alcoholism because high tolerance is genetic

7. Case studies of physicians who seek care for problems in their intimate relationships suggest that distress is most commonly the result of

A. financial problems stemming from the high cost of medical education

B. one partner being a physician and the other not

C. personality characteristics that affect communication or the capacity for intimacy

D. the time demands of the physician's specialty

E. the stress carried over from medical school and residency training

8. The empathetic way to present a patient or family with the option of agreeing to be treated under a "do not resuscitate" order is to

A. check in the chart for a previous advance directive and avoid raising the issue if the patient's wishes are already known

B. emphasize that the patient will not be abandoned and that all treatment, including palliative care, will be provided

C. explain that "do not resuscitate" only means refusal of external chest massage, assisted respiration, or electrical defibrillation

D. explain that resuscitation does not generally improve or prolong the lives of patients with multisystem disease

E. let the patient and family talk together privately and then accept the decision they reach, without question

9. Mr. G. has just been diagnosed with diabetes. His care provider recommends changes in diet and once-a-day insulin injections, but is concerned that Mr. G. will not remember the instructions he has been given. In this, and similar situations, patient recall of medical instructions is maximized when the

A. most important information is given at the beginning of an interaction

B. patient is allowed to fill in the specific details to adapt the instructions to their own situation

C. patient is discouraged from interrupting by asking questions

D. provider presents extensive information

E. provider's instructions are all given completely in a single session

10. A 47-year-old male machine-tool operator drinks two six-packs of beer daily. He reports that he has recently become concerned that he might have an alcohol problem. He has not talked to anyone about it for fear that people will think that he is "being a wimp." According to the stages of change model, he is most likely in which stage of change?

A. Action
B. Contemplation
C. Maintenance
D. Precontemplation
E. Preparation

11. Dr. J., a male university professor, is in the hospital after being diagnosed with colon cancer. During a visit by his care provider, they discussed only nonmedical topics such as fishing and the trials and tribulations of watching children grow up. Of the following, this interaction illustrates what type of awareness context?

A. Closed awareness
B. Delayed affectation
C. Mutual pretense
D. Open awareness
E. Suspicion awareness

12. A 35-year-old male patient calls his primary care provider to be examined regarding "problems with my stomach." He reports a week of nausea accompanied by some dizziness, but no problems eating or defecating. On physical exam, he reports substantial abdominal tenderness, not localized to any particular quadrant. The medical record documents a history of a broad range of medical complaints for which no underlying cause can be determined. At this point, the examiner's best course of action would be to

A. ask the patient for permission to speak to a family member

B. ask the patient to say more about his symptoms

C. gather a complete substance abuse history from the patient

D. tell the patient that he is fine and will feel better after a few days of rest

E. tell the patient that he may be a hypochondriac

13. In her qualitative research, Elisabeth Kübler-Ross developed a much-used model for understanding patients' reactions to death and dying. She observed that patients expressed denial, anger, bargaining, depression, and acceptance. Clinicians applying this model should be aware that

A. it adequately describes the experience of dying for the average person

B. patients must reach the final stage of acceptance before death can occur

C. the stages of experiencing dying occur only in patients with a lingering death trajectory

D. the stages of the model are valid, but most patients do not experience most of them

E. while the emotional states described are real, they do not represent distinct sequential stages

14. Patient adherence with treatment is facilitated by the formation of a partnership between clinician and patient. The notion of *self-monitoring* has been used to facilitate patients' active involvement in their care. Clinicians who try to teach patients to monitor themselves should be aware that

A. patients should monitor behavior such as dietary intake rather than outcomes such as weight loss

B. recording behaviors daily or weekly is more effective than recording throughout the day

C. self-monitoring alone cannot increase adherence with treatment

D. self-monitoring does not improve patients' awareness of their adherence

E. self-monitoring works best when the patient is assertive

15. As a clinical supervisor, you have reviewed the histories obtained by first-year trainees, finding that many of the histories lack items covering sexual preferences or behaviors. In discussing the results of this review, you should realize that failure to obtain adequate sexual histories from patients occurs most often because

A. even experienced clinicians are uncomfortable discussing sex

B. most patients have no sexual issues

C. patients are embarrassed about talking about sexual topics

D. patients believe that sexual issues are private and should not be discussed

E. patients' strong religious or moral qualms about sex interfere with discussing the topic

16. A 33-year-old male married patient enjoys dressing in women's clothes. The patient states that this cross-dressing enhances sexual pleasure and that his wife cooperates with him by buying him outfits. This type of sexual behavior is most correctly described as

A. gender dysphoria

B. homosexuality

C. transsexualism

D. transvestic behavior

E. transvestic disorder

17. In meeting with a patient who has a terminal illness, a nursing student is asked: "Why is this

happening to me? I've always tried to be a good person." This statement indicates that the patient is most likely in which one of the following stages of coping with dying as described by Kübler-Ross?

A. Anger

B. Bargaining

C. Confusion

D. Denial

E. Depression

18. A young heterosexual couple has been having sexual difficulties ever since they were married about a year ago. The couple did not engage in premarital sexual intercourse because of religious principles. The husband complains of frequent erectile dysfunction, and the wife has not experienced orgasm on many occasions. When approaching this problem, the clinician should first evaluate for the presence of

A. anatomic structural disparity

B. autonomic nervous system abnormalities

C. endocrine disorders

D. performance anxiety

E. significant psychopathology in one or both partners

19. A 34-year-old man confides to his care provider that, although he has good friends and a close family, over the past year, he has become increasingly reluctant to attend holiday or business-related get-togethers. He states that he feels awkward and clumsy and thinks people may be laughing at him behind his back. He is especially afraid that he will say the wrong thing, or spill his drink on someone. He seems agitated as he describes his concerns. Based on this patient's statements and presentation, the best provisional diagnosis would be

A. agoraphobia

B. generalized anxiety disorder

C. histrionic personality disorder

D. narcissistic personality disorder

E. social anxiety disorder

20. Many families have a member who is considered the "health expert." This person often makes an initial health assessment and treatment plan and then decides whether a medical provider should be consulted. Although this role differs from family to family, this individual is most frequently the

A. best educated

B. oldest female

C. oldest female child

D. oldest male

E. oldest male child

21. Mr. S. admits to consuming three to four beers each evening to help him "settle down after a hard day of work." Using the CAGE questionnaire, you discover that: (1) he sometimes feels that he needs to reduce his drinking; (2) he feels bad some mornings after drinking the night before; (3) he becomes irritated when his wife "bugs him" about drinking every evening; and (4) he sometimes drinks in the morning. He says that he never gets "drunk." Based on this presentation, you should conclude that
   A. he is displaying a culturally normal pattern of alcohol use
   B. he is lying about never getting "drunk"
   C. he most likely has a moderate to severe alcohol use disorder
   D. he should be referred to an inpatient alcohol treatment center
   E. laboratory studies are needed to confirm the diagnosis of an alcohol use disorder

22. A 28-year-old woman is concerned because she is no longer interested in sex, with her husband or anyone else. Questioning reveals that she never has an orgasm during intercourse with her husband. She reports no symptoms of acute or chronic illness. When taking this patient's history, which one of the following questions would be most helpful in selecting a treatment approach?
   A. Are you satisfied with your sex life?
   B. Do you have an orgasm with manual or other clitoral stimulation?
   C. Does your husband have difficulty achieving or maintaining an erection?
   D. What do you think your problem is?
   E. What is the approximate frequency of your sexual activity?

23. You are caring for a husband and wife, both in their mid-40s, who have seen you separately and together. Both work outside the home, and their two children are in high school. The wife recently saw you for a vaginal discharge. You have just received the results of testing for chlamydia and gonorrhea, but you have not yet talked with her about them. Her husband calls and leaves you the message that he is calling on behalf of his wife and would like the results of her tests. The best way of dealing with this would be to
   A. call the husband back and give him the results
   B. call the wife and tell her about her husband's inquiry
   C. e-mail the results to the wife, with a copy to her husband
   D. tell the husband he should come in to discuss the results privately

   E. tell the husband you cannot share information without his wife's permission

24. A 50-year-old male accountant develops diabetes mellitus that is not adequately controlled with diet and oral hypoglycemic agents. A diabetes specialist meets with him to discuss initiating insulin therapy. Saying that insulin is "poison," the patient declines the treatment. However, he does not explain that his mother had to have her leg amputated 1 year after beginning insulin. When reflecting on this situation, which of the following is most correct?
   A. A family system problem is interfering with the treatment plan
   B. The patient and provider have differing beliefs about insulin
   C. The patient's passivity makes the probability of adherence poor
   D. The specialist might convince the patient to use insulin by explaining treatment in more detail
   E. The specialist should tell the patient he is being irrational

25. A 10-year-old child is referred for assessment of difficulties in school. The child's developmental status would be best assessed by a focus on which five domains?
   A. Biological, environmental, physical, language, and physiological
   B. Gross motor, fine motor, neurosensory, behavioral, and visual
   C. Math, reading, spelling, the creative arts, and handwriting
   D. Physical, neurological maturational, cognitive, speech/language, and psychosocial
   E. Sensory, gastrointestinal, physical, sexual, and psychological

26. A boy is observed bringing his hands to midline and is able to roll prone to supine. He laughs and giggles in response to voices. The record of his care shows that his weight has doubled since birth. Assuming that the boy shows normal patterns of development, what is his likely age?
   A. 1 month
   B. 3 months
   C. 5 months
   D. 7 months
   E. 9 months

27. You must tell your 68-year-old patient that he has metastatic prostate cancer. After you have made the patient feel as comfortable as possible and ensured that you will not be interrupted, you begin speaking with him. In this conversation, you learn

that the patient knows very little about his condition. The best next step would be to
A. check that you are communicating on the same level
B. discover how much information he would like to have
C. discuss what support systems he has
D. establish physical contact by patting his hand
E. give him information in small non-"medspeak" chunks

28. A hospital is considering building a new clinic in another part of the city. Its administration has been asked to develop a description of the residents in the service area. Among the following, what information about this service area would be most helpful in determining health care needs?
A. A broad description such as "working poor"
B. Culture of the potential patient population
C. Detailed information about the primary and secondary groups
D. Socioeconomic status
E. Statistics on race and household income

29. During the first months of life, a child's experience of the world is focused on sensations and movement, and learning how action and experience correspond. The child has not yet attained the realization of object permanence. Attachment to the primary caretaker is the dominant social dynamic. The developmental psychologist Piaget refers to this stage of life as the
A. action vs. inaction stage
B. exploratory stage
C. oral stage
D. sensorimotor stage
E. trust vs. mistrust stage

30. Mr. D. has been nonadherent with his treatment regime. The clinician providing care decides to make use of the goal-setting technique to increase adherence in the future. Published guidelines and clinical experience in the use of *goal setting* to increase patient adherence suggest that the technique will be most effective when
A. goals are defined by the care provider to insure appropriate priorities
B. goals are graduated to maximize success experiences
C. goals are maintained consistently, without alteration
D. goals are sufficiently broad to allow the patient leeway in meeting them
E. patients seek to "shoot for the moon" and achieve maximal results

31. Mr. J. has a documented history of heavy drinking and symptoms consistent with a significant alcohol use disorder or alcoholism. Yet, he actively denies any drinking problem and distorts the amount, frequency, and consequences of his drinking. Using the stages of change model, the clinician's next best action would be to
A. enlist his wife or significant other to convince the patient to stop drinking
B. comment that it sounds like he does not see a problem with his drinking
C. recommend an inpatient treatment program
D. schedule a return appointment but make no comment at this point
E. send the patient to a local Alcoholics Anonymous (AA) meeting

32. A baby girl is presented with a toy ball. After she plays with it for a moment, the ball is taken away and hidden. Even though it is completely out of sight, she searches for the ball. Attainment of this degree of object permanence suggests that the child's age is closest to
A. 2 months
B. 4 months
C. 6 months
D. 8 months
E. 10 months

33. A 75year-old man presents with a 1-month history of difficulty sleeping, loss of interest in his usual activities, feeling worthless, difficulty concentrating, and thoughts of suicide. Three months ago, he suffered a stroke. He has largely recovered, except for some gait disturbance and problems using his left hand, which appear to be permanent impairments. He has lost 4 lb (1.8 kg) in the last 2 months. Based on this information, it is most reasonable to conclude that
A. a careful history and physical is indicated to detect a probable occult malignancy
B. he is disappointed in not making a full recovery and requires brief counseling
C. he should be enrolled in a "stroke survivors" group to boost his spirits
D. he should be screened for a substance use disorder
E. he may benefit from treatment with antidepressant medication

34. When examining an infant for primitive reflexes such as the Moro, asymmetrical tonic neck, rooting, and palmar grasp, none is found to be present. This indicates the infant is older than
A. 1–2 months
B. 3–4 months

C. 5–6 months
D. 7–8 months
E. 9–10 months

35. You inform a 40-year-old man that his 72-year-old father has developed liver metastases from his colon cancer that was resected a year ago. The man's face becomes bright red, and he angrily replies, "The surgeon said it was all removed. I'm going to sue that goon." Which of the following would be your best response at this point?
   A. "I'm sorry, but it's not the surgeon's fault that your father's cancer recurred."
   B. "What do you know about the typical course of colon cancer?"
   C. Sit quietly for a few minutes and then terminate the interview.
   D. "You are too angry at the surgeon for apparently misleading you."
   E. "You must be very upset that your father is ill from his cancer again."

36. A 55-year-old man reports to his primary care provider that he has been suffering from periodic erectile dysfunction with his wife. The provider should tell him that the most common cause of erectile dysfunction in middle-aged men is
   A. abnormalities of the urinary tract
   B. excess intake of alcohol
   C. marital infidelity
   D. onset of diabetes mellitus
   E. physiological decline that accompanies aging

37. A terminally ill woman with heart disease says, "It's the doctor's fault that I got sick. She didn't take my blood pressure, and she never told me to watch my diet!" This behavior is most consistent with which of the following stages of coping with dying?
   A. Anger
   B. Denial
   C. Depression
   D. Fear
   E. Guilt

38. Mrs. H. lost her husband of 50 years 6 months ago. Since that time, she has stayed by herself, refused visitors, and cries frequently. Her daughter wonders if – by now – it is time for her mother to be acting like her usual self. It would be appropriate to tell the daughter that normal coping with death often includes
   A. feeling depressed for several months afterward
   B. feelings of hopelessness lasting 2 or more years
   C. profound guilt feelings lasting 6 months or more

D. sleep disturbances lasting 8 months after the death
E. threats of suicide during the first several months of bereavement

Items 39 and 40

During a routine physical exam, a middle-aged man reports recent stress in his marriage. He states that he and his wife rarely try to have sex, and the last time they tried, he was unable to maintain an erection. When questioned, he indicates that he commonly has morning erections. The medical record indicates no chronic illnesses, and the patient is not currently taking any medications.

39. At this point, the clinician providing care should
   A. order a nocturnal penile tumescence study
   B. recommend that his wife come in for a private session
   C. request a joint visit with the patient and his wife
   D. smile gently and tell him that this is bound to happen once in a while
   E. suggest trying a different position during intercourse

40. At a follow-up visit 1 month later, the patient reports trying intercourse once more but without success. At this point, the most appropriate intervention would be to
   A. indicate that this is a normal change with aging and encourage him to accept it
   B. recommend a penile implant
   C. recommend attempting intercourse with a different partner, if his wife agrees
   D. refer for joint sex therapy with use of sensate focus
   E. suggest the use of the squeeze technique

41. Dr. J. told the office staff that the Chinese patients in the practice have problems with English, believe in herbal medicine, and view women as inferior. Dr. J.'s description of Chinese patients is an example of
   A. bias
   B. bigotry
   C. intolerance
   D. stereotyping
   E. stigmatizing

42. When designing a program to assist "impaired" medical students, the organizers should remember that, compared with others in the population of the same age, medical students are most likely to abuse

A. alcohol
B. barbiturates
C. cocaine
D. heroin
E. tobacco

43. Part of being a competent clinician depends on not only knowing the right thing to say in a given situation, but also knowing when not to say anything. In which of the following difficult situations would a clinician's silence be most appropriate?
A. A home visit is made to discuss changes in a cancer patient's pain medicine
B. A man is concerned about difficulties maintaining an erection
C. A recently diagnosed terminally ill patient is in the hospital
D. A woman is anxious about her inability to experience orgasm
E. Alcohol abuse is suspected in a patient being seen in the office

44. A 40-year-old patient whom you are seeing for an ear infection smokes a pack of cigarettes a day. After discussing her ear infection, you tell her that smoking greatly increases her risk for heart disease. She responds, "Yes, I know. I'd really love to quit. I'm planning to do it sometime." You ask her when. She replies "Oh, once I lose some weight, I think I'll try." This patient most likely would be classified as being in which *stage of change*?
A. Contemplation
B. Maintenance
C. Precontemplation
D. Preparation
E. Procrastination

45. You are nearing the end of training and are looking at practice opportunities. You realize that there are numerous factors that will influence your decision regarding the practice you choose. Some are considered *intangible*. One of the intangible aspects to consider is the
A. accountant who conducts annual audits of the practice income
B. age and gender mix of the patients
C. daily rituals of the office staff and clinical providers
D. design and age of the practice building
E. framed mission statement hanging in the waiting room

46. A new department is forming within an academic medical center. You have been asked to chair this new department and have been given the necessary resources to build a premier section for your specialty. From your medical school studies about organizations, you remember that the most important task in managing professional people is
A. dealing with reduced effectiveness
B. evaluating performance
C. hiring them
D. managing information
E. motivating them

47. Sally is just beginning to pull herself into an upright position by using the railings on her crib. Before she can learn to walk, she, like any toddler, must first
A. develop leg muscles by crawling
B. develop sophisticated balance skills
C. master object permanence
D. master the mechanics of weight shifting
E. overcome separation anxiety

48. Human behavior reflects the interaction of heredity and learned behaviors. A key finding from research focused on this interplay tells us that
A. genetic and environmental influences interact across generations but not across individual developmental stages
B. genetic influences are easily distinguished from learned environmental adaptations
C. learned adaptive responses that contribute to survival are passed on to successive generations
D. learning influences individual development, but there is no evidence of an evolutionary effect
E. the capacity to learn, but not what was learned, is passed on genetically

49. The Minnesota Multiphasic Personality Inventory-2 (MMPI-2) is a sophisticated test with a built-in check to determine whether a person's responses are genuine or merely an attempt to "look good." The validity scale on the MMPI-2 that is used to assess the test taker's need to present themselves in a favorable or socially desirable light is the
A. F or infrequency scale
B. K or correction scale
C. L or lie scale
D. Pt or psychasthenia scale
E. SE or self-esteem scale

50. The notion that removing or avoiding an aversive stimulus can lead to behavioral change is most helpful in explaining
A. avoidance–avoidance conflict
B. cognitive dissonance
C. intrinsic motivation
D. secondary reinforcement
E. the opponent-process hypothesis

51. You are talking with a 64-year-old man in the hospital. He has just been diagnosed with lung cancer. He has metastases to his lumbar spine causing back pain. He has no evidence of neurological problems. When you ask him if he would like to know the biopsy results, he replies that he trusts you to care for him and that he would rather not hear the results. Which of the following is your best response at this time?

A. "Even though you don't want to hear, we need to talk now so we can discuss treatment."
B. "I understand. There's really no reason why you should have to know."
C. "I'll order some pain medication and come back tomorrow to see if you'd like to talk then."
D. "Is there anyone in your family I can talk to?"
E. "You must think I'm going to tell you bad news, and you don't want to hear it."

52. A monkey has learned that if he lifts his foot when a bell is sounded, he can avoid a painful electric shock. What biological mechanism most likely makes this simple learning paradigm possible?

A. Protein kinase delays the action potential of the neuron by blocking neurotransmitter release
B. Sequential stimulation of two adjacent neurons enhances the efficiency of their connecting synapse
C. The cerebellum reduces motor reactivity under the influence of serotonin activity
D. The hippocampus sends simultaneous sensory signals to relevant cortical storage areas
E. The orbito-medial frontal cortex matches sensory input with the desired behavior

53. A 20-month-old-boy is playing while his mother watches. He moves a toy truck along the floor and then hands it to his mother. When communicating with this child, the clinician should remember that, at this stage of development, a child's capacity for cognition is based on

A. formulation of internal mental symbols
B. movement and sensations
C. performance of actions to achieve outcomes
D. representation of reality through the use of words
E. what they see before them

54. Mr. and Mrs. P. and their three children live in St. Louis. They receive food stamps and are considered of low socioeconomic status (SES). Mrs. P. has hypertension, and her husband has diabetes; both have frequent problems with respiratory infections. Which of the following statements

characterizes the relationship between their SES and their health status?

A. Adverse health behaviors such as smoking and not exercising are more predictive than SES of health status
B. In "classless" societies such as the US, health status is fairly even across SES levels
C. Inability to afford health insurance results in adverse effects on health
D. SES affects health by limiting access to basics such as food, shelter, and clean water
E. SES is the factor that most strongly predicts experiencing poor health

55. A 48-year-old homeless man appears at a free clinic complaining of gastrointestinal (GI) distress and headache. He states that he has been living under the bridge of a local highway for the past 3 months. He has lost contact with his spouse and two children. When examining this individual, the clinician should keep in mind that the most frequent health problems of the homeless are

A. HIV and AIDS-related problems
B. mental illness and substance abuse–related problems
C. skin problems
D. upper respiratory infections
E. venereal diseases

56. A 45-year-old man is brought to a clinician by his wife who complains, "He has always had his little quirks, but things are getting out of hand." She explains that her husband refuses to leave the house and has become increasingly terrified when forced to do so. Examination of the patient shows him to be in a highly anxious state characterized by sweating palms, shallow breathing, and a rapid pulse. He sits slouched over, avoids eye contact, and scans the room around him as if waiting for something to happen. Based on these findings, the clinician is most likely to diagnose

A. agoraphobia
B. delusional disorder
C. dysthymia
D. paranoid personality disorder
E. social phobia

57. A 19-year-old man is brought to the local emergency room in a delirious state. The patient is calm, but communication with him is difficult. He is nonresponsive to questions regarding time and place. Further examination is disrupted when the patient begins to have seizures. This patient is most likely withdrawing from

A. amphetamines
B. benzodiazepines

C. hallucinogens

D. heroin

E. phencyclidine

58. A 35-year-old man seeks treatment from a psychiatrist at the insistence of his wife because he demands that she wear high-heeled shoes every time they have sex. At first, she complied with his request, but now she feels that his behavior is negatively affecting their relationship. He admits that he cannot achieve erection and orgasm when she does not wear her high-heeled shoes. He frequently masturbates while thinking about her shoes. Which of the following best describes this man's condition?

A. Fetishism

B. Fetishistic disorder

C. Masochism

D. Sadism

E. Transvestism

Items 59 and 60

A 44-year-old woman is referred for evaluation by her employer because she has been increasingly difficult to deal with over the past month. While being evaluated, the woman is understandable but extremely talkative. In her conversation, she jumps from one topic to another. She reports that she recently embarked on a "great shopping spree" because she "deserves nothing but the best." After work she volunteers at four different community programs and says she is looking for additional activities to occupy her time. When asked how she finds the time for all of this, she reports that she needs only 3 hr of sleep per night.

59. Based on this information, the most likely diagnosis for this woman is

A. bipolar disorder

B. hypothyroidism

C. narcissistic personality disorder

D. obsessive-compulsive disorder

E. vascular dementia

60. Long-term treatment of this woman would most likely include

A. chlorpromazine

B. clonazepam

C. diazepam

D. fluoxetine

E. lithium carbonate

Items 61 and 62

A mother brings her 5-year-old daughter to the pediatrician's office complaining that the child has recently developed enuresis after being fully toilet trained for almost 3 years. The girl seems shy at first when talking to the clinician, but soon begins to make eye contact and answer questions. The clinician discovers that the child has recently begun to attend kindergarten and that her mother gave birth to a baby boy in the past month.

61. The girl's enuresis is most likely the result of which of the following defense mechanisms?

A. Projection

B. Reaction formation

C. Regression

D. Sublimation

E. Undoing

62. The first intervention the clinician should try is to

A. advise the mother about helping the child cope with life transitions

B. observe and follow up in anticipation of spontaneous recovery

C. prescribe a course of imipramine

D. suggest that the child change to a different kindergarten class

E. talk with the child about why enuresis is a bad thing

63. An evaluating professional asks Jennifer, a 2-year-old girl dressed in overalls and a baseball cap, whether she is a boy or a girl. The child seems confused by the question and looks at her mother while saying nothing. When given a set of toys to play with, the child selects a truck and proceeds to roll it around the room. This type of behavior suggests that the girl most likely

A. has no siblings at home

B. is at risk for developing a gender identity disorder later in life

C. is showing developmental age and gender appropriate behavior

D. will grow up to be relatively shy

E. will grow up to have a sexual preference for women

Items 64 and 65

A 25-year-old woman with a history of depression and substance abuse is referred for additional evaluation following a suicide attempt. During the interview, the woman reports that the suicide attempt occurred in response to her boyfriend of 3 months breaking up with her. She describes herself as feeling "empty" and says that the ex-boyfriend "was everything to me." Without him, she says she is "not sure who I am or why I'm here." She begins crying, saying that "everyone always abandons me." When asked what she is going to do now, the patient becomes suddenly very angry and says, "You can't wait to get rid of me either."

64. Based on this initial interview, you suspect this patient may have a personality disorder in addition to depression and substance abuse. The most likely type is
A. borderline
B. histrionic
C. narcissistic
D. paranoid
E. schizoid

65. The most effective primary treatment for the personality disorder described here would be
A. a 6-month course of alprazolam
B. behavior modification
C. family therapy
D. group psychotherapy
E. individual cognitive behavior therapy

66. Mr. W. presents to the emergency department complaining of trouble breathing. He is disheveled and malodorous. He has no permanent residence and typically sleeps under an overpass. A member of the team comments, "If people like this would just get a job and take care of themselves, they wouldn't be in this shape." This comment is an example of
A. anchoring
B. availability bias
C. confirmation bias
D. fundamental attribution error
E. stigmatization

67. Ms. H. comes from a family that has been poor for several generations. She recently left an abusive relationship, and she and her children now live in a shelter. When her primary care clinician asks her about returning to school or enrolling in a training program, she states, "I don't think that would help.... Nothing ever works out." This comment is most reflective of

A. denial
B. histrionic personality disorder
C. learned helplessness
D. obstinacy
E. regression

68. A 40-year-old man consults a therapist out of concern about his persistent fantasies of watching strangers have sex. Recently, he has begun watching his female neighbor disrobe. He states that his neighbor is not aware of him watching her. He watches pornography all day and, as a result, rarely leaves the house. Two weeks ago, he was fired from his job as a house painter due to his absenteeism. What is the most likely diagnosis?
A. Exhibitionism
B. Fetishism
C. Frotteuristic disorder
D. Voyeurism
E. Voyeuristic disorder

69. A 55-year-old man diagnosed with schizophrenia at age 18 is asked to complete the Wisconsin Card Sort Test (WCST), a task that requires categorization and problem-solving abilities. Examination of the functioning of this patient's brain by means of a PET scan during the card-sorting task would most likely show that, when compared with individuals that do not have schizophrenia, the patient has decreased activity in the
A. cerebellum
B. frontal lobes
C. occipital lobes
D. parietal lobes
E. temporal lobes

70. Behavior, belief, expression, and even cognition vary across human cultures. When trying to gauge the impact of culture on day-to-day medical practice, the practitioner should remember that a person's culture may
A. be an unchanging and unchangeable aspect of human functioning
B. be important to the patient but should not affect the practitioner's recommendations
C. cause patients to reject care recommended by practitioners from other cultures
D. have minimal impact on most clinical encounters
E. influence health, illness, and therapy

71. An overview of US census data over the past 50 years reveals some strong and continuing secular demographic trends. In particular, these data show that the near future will be characterized by

A. a decrease in the number of Hispanics
B. a lower average age for the White population
C. a steady increase in the size of ethnic minority populations
D. less concern about culture as a factor in health care delivery
E. zero population growth by the year 2040

72. Mrs. L., an 82-year-old African American woman, complains to her primary care provider that she has "high blood." Anthropological research has identified and characterized "high blood" as a folk illness. At times, Mrs. L. says she can feel her blood rising up to her head. She reports that when she drinks vinegar in flavored water, she can feel her blood return to normal. Her provider tells her that she has hypertension and recommends a low salt diet. When treating Mrs. L., the provider should remember that
A. as a folk illness, high blood has no defined etiology, pathophysiology, or treatment
B. *high blood* and *hypertension* are different names for the same thing
C. high blood and hypertension are examples of how interpretations of body symptoms are culturally influenced
D. providers need to eradicate folk illness beliefs that contradict conventional medical beliefs
E. providers should guide patients away from incorrect understanding of their conditions

73. Yesterday, you explained to a woman from Pakistan that the diarrhea her child was experiencing needed to be treated with antibiotics and fluids. Today, you learn that the child is not being given the medication or fluids as recommended. At this point, the most appropriate reaction on your part would be to
A. chastise the mother for endangering her child's well-being by not following your directions
B. explore the possibility that the mother believes your recommendations will make the child worse
C. hospitalize the child whether or not the mother agrees
D. notify Child Protective Services that the child is not being well cared for
E. refer the mother to the nurse responsible for patient education

74. A patient reports that he has been taking buffered aspirin and doing strengthening exercises to alleviate back pain. The patient further reports that this approach worked for a good friend who was having a similar problem. This patient got his medical advice from which sector of healers?

A. Folk
B. Paraprofessional
C. Pharmaceutical
D. Popular
E. Professional

75. The mother of a 5-year-old child lingers for an hour in the hallway after bringing her son to kindergarten. During this time, the boy appears happy, but pays little attention to the teacher or the other children. Eventually, the teacher convinces the mother to bring her son to the classroom, reassure him, and then leave. After several days of crying and being fearful after his mother leaves, the boy becomes calmer, stops crying, and displays less fear. This change in the boy's behavior is most likely the result of
A. extinction
B. intermittent reinforcement
C. maturation
D. shaping
E. sublimation

76. A woman graduated from a combined medicine–pediatrics residency 5 years ago and began practice as the only physician in a rural county of her home state. In this role, she provides care to anyone who comes to her office, whether they are patients formally enrolled in her practice or not. Many of her patients are unable to pay their medical bills, but she continues to see them whenever they need her services. One of her regular patients, a community leader who always pays his bills on time, complained to her that he felt it was inappropriate for him to have to wait while she is caring for "deadbeats" who happened to show up at her office. The doctor explained that because she is the only one in the area, it is her obligation to ensure that medical services are available to all sick people in the county. This explanation is based on the ethical principle of
A. beneficence
B. fidelity
C. honesty
D. justice
E. nonmaleficence

77. One of the core functions of clinicians is to confirm a patient's assignment to the sick role. In any given community, the function of the "sick role" is to
A. allow estimates of the prevalence of various diseases
B. force the individual to seek medical care
C. legitimize withdrawal from regular activities and requests for assistance

D. permit collection of epidemiological data on disease incidence

E. require hospitalization

78. Cultural background and ethnic identity are key elements in patients' medical decisions. Strong identification with a particular ethnic group is most likely to influence their

A. choice of healers

B. desire for good health

C. response to physiological effects of illness

D. type of health insurance

E. willingness to work

79. A 60-year-old man is referred to a psychiatrist as part of a work-up for sex reassignment surgery. He denies depression, but he states he is a "female stuck in a man's body." He has identified as female since the age of 5 and began dressing in women's clothing when he was 15. His only sexual experiences have been with men, and he is currently in a 4-year relationship with a male partner. However, he views himself as a "straight woman" and has never identified as a gay man. What is the most likely diagnosis?

A. Body dysmorphic disorder

B. Delusional disorder

C. Fetishism

D. Gender dysphoria

E. Transvestism

80. A colleague asks your advice about improving his capacity to work with patients from different ethnic and cultural backgrounds. He lists different options he is considering. Of all the options he presents, you tell him that the one *least* likely to result in improved multicultural patient-centered care is

A. adapting his style of communication to fit patients' preferred styles

B. being aware of personal biases and prejudices

C. being his own genuine self, knowing that patients will understand what he means

D. learning about himself as a cultural being

E. learning culturally appropriate patient-centered communication skills

81. Nonverbal gestures communicate different messages depending on ethnic background. Misconceptions about what is communicated can lead to difficulties in the patient–provider relationship. Among the following, which generality about how nonverbal gestures are interpreted is correct?

A. American Indians: pausing less than a few seconds for a reply to a question conveys lack of interest

B. Arabs: offering things with the right hand is revolting

C. Asians: looking away is experienced as disrespectful

D. Asians: speaking loudly is experienced as an expression of eagerness to be understood

E. Europeans: making direct eye contact is experienced as invasive

82. During a well-child visit, a mother expresses concern about her 4-year-old daughter's weight, which has risen over the past year from the 83rd to the 85th percentile for her age. The mother reports that a nutritionist advised her to limit the child's daily intake to about 1,200 kcal. She has been keeping a journal of everything her daughter eats. Reviewing the journal you notice that, although the child's intake does appear to be about 1,200 kcal/day, much of the child's diet consists of fast food meals, peanut butter and jelly sandwiches, and high-fat dairy products. Which of the following statements is NOT a potential explanation for why the child has continued to gain too much weight?

A. Even if the child is not exceeding the recommended daily calorie intake for her age, the high fat content of her diet may still cause her to gain weight excessively

B. The dietitian's recommendation was incorrect because a 4-year-old child should not consume more than 900 kcal/day

C. The mother has been inaccurate in her estimations of portion sizes, and her daughter has actually been consuming more than 1,200 kcal daily

D. The mother has not always read the nutrition facts labels for the foods she has given her daughter and so has often been inaccurate in estimating caloric content

E. The mother is likely unaware of food the child is consuming when she is at daycare or someone else's house

83. A 25-year-old woman is brought to the emergency room by her husband because she has been sleeping only 1 hour a night for 2 weeks. She states, "I don't need to be here. I am on top of the world! I am starting 10 different businesses, and they will all be successful!" When the interviewer attempts to ask further questions, she has trouble answering and instead, jumps from one topic to another. She speaks so fast that it is hard to understand her. Her husband reports that she has maxed out their credit cards. Her urine drug screen is negative. Which of the following is the treatment of choice for this woman?

A. Buspirone

B. Lithium

C. Lorazepam
D. Sertraline
E. Zolpidem

84. At a routine annual checkup, an X-ray shows that Mr. E., a 75-year-old longstanding patient, has metastatic lung cancer. He has had no symptoms, except for mild fatigue. The evaluating clinician is struggling with whether to inform Mr. E. of his condition now or wait until he begins to deteriorate. The best course of action would be to
A. encourage Mr. E. to obtain life insurance before breaking the bad news
B. immediately inform him of his condition
C. tell his relatives, but not the patient
D. tell the patient that he has a "tumor", but say it can be easily treated
E. wait until he becomes significantly symptomatic before informing him

85. Recently, providers in your clinic have been seeing patients from an immigrant community, who are presenting with a pattern of symptoms that does not fit any familiar diagnostic pattern. Physical examination findings and test results are normal. You and your colleagues should
A. ask the state health department to quarantine the entire community
B. assume that all patients from the community will present with the same syndrome
C. conclude that these individuals are trying to "work the system" to get pharmaceuticals to sell on the street
D. consider that they may be suffering from a culturally specific syndrome, perhaps related to the stress of immigration
E. tell the patients that they are not ill and should return home and resume all regular activities

86. One way of assessing families is to examine the family's structure or the way that it is organized. An outline of these structural components makes it easier to understand how family dynamics are likely to have an effect on the patient and the patient's care. Which of the following describes a structural element of family life?
A. Boundaries
B. Communication style
C. Family secret
D. Parentification
E. Scapegoating

87. Although various patterns of family organization exist, certain patterns are so common that they have been given defined labels. Consider a patient whom a colleague tells you comes from a "disengaged" family system. This assessment implies that
A. boundaries around individuals within the system are closed
B. boundaries around the family system are closed
C. boundaries between the father and other family members are closed
D. emotional processes resonate quickly throughout the family system
E. interpersonal boundaries within the family system are diffuse

88. A 52-year-old woman with metastatic breast carcinoma has been managed at her local community hospital since diagnosis. Her care team has consulted with a renowned regional tertiary care center regarding all aspects of her care and has followed the consultants' recommendations meticulously. However, as the patient's condition gradually deteriorates, she requests transfer to the regional medical center. Although her treatment regimen does not change, shortly after arriving at the medical center the patient states she "feels better" and is glad to be under the care of "the famous specialists" at the center. This improvement likely reflects
A. changes in nutritional supplements
B. natural history of the disease
C. nonspecific therapeutic effects
D. placebo effect
E. specific effects of treatment

89. The training of medical professionals involves socialization as well as the acquisition of medical knowledge. The acquisition of competence as part of this socialization process is best described as
A. being able to judge whether a patient is able to act in their own best interests
B. combining technical expertise and effective human relations skills to be a "total" clinician
C. having the human relational skills required to perform well as a clinician
D. having the mental capability to be responsible for one's own behavior
E. having the technical expertise to perform well as a clinician

90. Preventive intervention is critical for good health outcomes at any age. Of all of the areas that can be targeted for preventive education among adolescents, the one that would lead to the greatest reduction in the incidence of death for this age group is
A. homicide
B. motor vehicle accidents

C. physical abuse
D. sexually transmitted disease
E. suicide

91. A mother brings her 10-year-old son to see a clinician, complaining that he has been "walking in his sleep." She reports that he walks up and down the stairs 2 or 3 times and then, after letting out a low moan, returns to bed and is quiet again. She asks what his actions mean and, specifically, what he is dreaming about while he is climbing the stairs. The clinician's most appropriate response would be that the
A. best thing to do is wake him up and tell him to go back to bed
B. boy is probably not dreaming while he is walking in his sleep
C. boy is searching for something that he lost
D. boy will stop walking in his sleep if he goes to bed later
E. stairs may be a symbol of the boy's drive to succeed in life

92. Within families, certain individuals may assume or be given particular tasks or responsibilities, often based on age, gender, and family position. The typical constellation of family roles often reflects cultural expectations. A father who takes the role of primary caregiver to an infant is stepping outside which role found to be assumed by fathers in the traditional nuclear family?
A. Competitive
B. Functional
C. Instrumental
D. Socioemotional
E. Symmetrical

93. A 28-year-old man initially came to psychiatric treatment at age 22 because of hearing voices that told him to hurt himself. At the time, he believed that agents of the US government were following him, and he became socially withdrawn. Although medication has relieved his hallucinations and delusions, he now displays uncontrollable twitching and writhing movements of his lips, tongue, and arms. Which medication is most likely causing his condition?
A. Benztropine
B. Diphenhydramine
C. Haloperidol
D. Lorazepam
E. Sertraline

94. For the past year, a 27-year-old woman has told anyone who will listen that Justin Bieber is in love with her. She explains that he has asked her to marry him through the lyrics of his songs. She is also convinced that he spoke directly to her during one of his concerts on television. For the past 2 weeks, she has been sleeping for only an hour at night yet denies being tired. Her family and friends have expressed concern because she has been speaking so rapidly that they have difficulty understanding her. The day before she was brought for treatment, she put several thousand dollars of debt on a credit card "in preparation for my wedding to Justin Bieber." What is the most likely diagnosis?
A. Bipolar disorder with psychosis
B. Brief psychotic disorder
C. Schizoaffective disorder
D. Schizophrenia
E. Schizophreniform disorder

95. Parents blame their 15-year-old daughter for most of the problems in the family. She creates emotional tension at home and is acting out at school. What term best describes her role in this family system?
A. Disengaged
B. Emotionally cutoff
C. Enmeshed
D. Parentified
E. Scapegoated

96. A 27-year-old woman reports that she often feels the urge to smoke after having sex or after eating. Which theory of motivation best helps to explain why she feels this impulse?
A. Arousal
B. Drive
C. Expectancy
D. Humanistic
E. Sociocultural

97. Various factors influence patient adherence to medical prescriptions, including the patient's motivation. The expectancy theory of motivation would attribute a patient's adherence to a medical treatment regimen to the patient's
A. belief system
B. cultural system
C. family history
D. homeostasis level
E. reinforcement experience

98. Dual-physician marriages are becoming increasingly common as more women enter the practice of medicine. These marriages face unique challenges. Surveys of two-physician marriages have found that
A. dual-physician marriages have a higher than average divorce rate

B. female spouses are more likely to consider family obligations when selecting practices

C. males and females have similar earning potential

D marital partners choose practice sites regardless of spouse preference

E. marital partners take equal lengths of time in training

99. A 16-year-old boy who describes himself as gay comes for a physical exam so he can play tennis at school. He seems subdued in the office, and the examiner asks how he is doing. He describes feeling socially isolated and says that he switched to tennis because he felt bullied and teased when he played team sports like basketball and soccer. His grades have dropped from As and Bs to Bs and Cs over the past year. He denies drinking or the use of street drugs, but he admits to feeling apathetic and sad. On questioning, he says that, at times, he feels life is not worth living, and he has had some suicidal thoughts, especially since he has come out to his parents. They seem unperturbed, but a few close friends have turned away from him saying they "can't deal with it." As someone who defines himself as homosexual, is he at higher or lower risk of suicide than heterosexual peers with this level of symptoms?

A. Higher, due to self-hatred for his sexual orientation

B. Higher, due to the prejudice and discomfort he elicits in his peers

C. Lower, as he is less likely to consider violent means of suicide than heterosexual peers

D. Lower, because his openness suggests greater psychological maturity

E. Lower, since, as a homosexual male, his suicide risk is closer to that of a female

100. In the traditional nuclear family in the US, the wife is usually the main caretaker and nurturer in the family. What term best describes the functional role fulfilled by this traditional wife?

A. Child-focused

B. Enmeshed

C. Instrumental

D. Parentified

E. Socioemotional

101. An 8-year-old child has been bedridden for the past week with an unidentified infection. The parents are anxious about the state of the child's health. During times of illness such as this, this child is most likely to have difficulty coping with

A. dependency on others

B. limitation of activity

C. loss of affection from parents

D. removal from friends

E. unexplained nature of events

102. A 27-year-old woman has been bedridden with the latest strain of influenza for the past 3 days. When visited by her family clinician, she is most likely to complain about feelings of

A. anger

B. blame

C. guilt

D. helplessness

E. hopelessness

103. His clinician has told Mr. P. that he has an elevated prostate-specific antigen (PSA) level but that before a definitive diagnosis can be made, the test must be repeated in a month. During this interval, Mr. P. becomes impatient. The most effective coping strategy for this and other medical problems requiring patience is

A. confronting the doctor

B. identifying the issues

C. practicing relaxation exercises

D. seeking information

E. venting frustration on others

104. Different types of learning have been identified and isolated in laboratory experiments. This allows research to be performed on the specific physiological substrates associated with particular types of learning. One type of learning has been called *implicit learning*. Implicit learning

A. involves the association of sensory stimuli with sequential motor system responses

B. is made possible by complex association mechanisms among diverse stimuli

C. occurs over a wide span of time

D. requires structures in the cortex for long-term information storage

E. requires the conscious participation of the individual

105. Mr. S. is 25 years old, 6 feet tall, and lives in a low-income neighborhood. He often grabs a quick meal at one of the several fast-food restaurants or convenience stores he passes on the 1-hr drive to and from his accounting job in the city. Six months ago, Mr. S.'s company implemented a workplace wellness program that includes healthy cafeteria meals and free access to a convenient gym, where he has been working out at lunchtime about twice a week. Mr. S. was raised in a traditional household (he still gathers with his family for a large dinner every Sunday). Both of his parents and two of his four brothers are obese. Over his past few yearly checkups, Mr. S.'s body mass index (BMI)

has increased from 22.5 to 23.7 to 24.8. What can be said about Mr. S.'s risk for obesity?

A. Elements of his built and social environment may both aid and constrain his ability to maintain a healthy weight

B. His upbringing and family history of obesity will make it nearly impossible for him to avoid becoming obese himself

C. It is normal and healthy for a man's BMI to increase steadily during his early 20s, and since he is still considered "normal weight," he should not be concerned

D. The built environment surrounding him only promotes unhealthy choices and increases his risk of obesity

E. The increase in his BMI is not cause for concern, because it is probably due to an increase in muscle mass from lifting weights at the company gym

106. A 55-year-old woman with lymphoma is struggling with the effects of chemotherapy. She decides to pursue hypnosis and is told that this should help with many of her symptoms, but not

A. alopecia due to chemotherapy

B. management of chronic pain

C. reducing the frequency of flare ups of genital herpes

D. relief of gastrointestinal symptoms

E. smoking cessation

107. While recovering from surgery to treat her breast cancer, a woman is encouraged to attend a support group for breast cancer survivors. She seems uneasy about attending. She may be told that an illness-specific patient support group may help her

A. actively solve problems

B. forget about the illness

C. laugh at adversity

D. learn to accept negative outcomes

E. see that others are worse off

108. Mr. H. has just been diagnosed with an inoperable brain tumor. Although his prognosis is poor, he continues to be cheerful and to talk amicably with all who visit him. When faced with a patient who appears cheerful in the face of a poor prognosis, the clinician should

A. continue to remind the patient of his grave prognosis

B. gently point out to the patient that he is in denial

C. refuse to care for the patient until he accepts his prognosis

D. speak with his family about his condition

E. understand that the patient may need more time to adjust

109. Ms. G., a new patient, tells you that psychological feeling and physical health have nothing to do with each other. A patient, such as this, who believes that mind and body are separate, would be *least* likely to respond to which of the following treatments for pain?

A. Analgesics

B. Antidepressants

C. Relaxation training

D. Surgery

E. Trigger point injections

110. Care that is provided in a way that is compatible with a patient's belief system is termed

A. acceptable

B. accessible

C. adequate

D. appropriate

E. available

111. A 20-year-old man is brought into the emergency department by his friends after he collapsed at an all-night dance club after dancing for several hours. His friends suspect that he ingested some substance of abuse (drugs or alcohol) when he first arrived at the club. Initially, he had been acting extremely happy, said he "now understood" a friend's perspective on a number of topics about which they had previously disagreed, and was noticeably energized. Although typically reserved, he was hugging multiple others as he danced. He later was noted to be grinding his teeth and complaining about being intensely hot. At time of presentation, he was tachycardic with borderline hypertension. He was also extremely anxious. If he had ingested something, which of the following drugs of abuse is most likely?

A. Alcohol

B. Hydrocodone

C. Lorazepam

D. Marijuana

E. MDMA/ecstasy

112. A 74-year-old man who lives alone makes an appointment with a primary care provider because he has a moderately severe cold. Many patients who seek help for a minor, self-limited problem are really seeking

A. a particular diagnosis

B. a prescription

C. an excuse to avoid work

D. help with a psychological problem

E. reassurance

113. How and by whom health care decisions are made affects adherence with recommended treat-

ment. Although individual variations exist, in Asia, Mexico, and the Middle East, the dominant cultural model puts the burden of health decisions on the
A. community
B. family
C. patient
D. provider
E. religious leader

114. Some stressful life events are associated with a negative impact on health, while others are not. The impact a stressful event will have on a given person's health is most dependent on
A. the magnitude of the event
B. the number of people involved
C. the subjective experience of stress associated with the event
D. the type of change involved
E. whether the event is positive or negative

115. Decisions about end-of-life care are some of the most difficult that patients and their families have to make. When discussing the options, the clinician should tell them that, compared with death in a hospice, death in a hospital is likely to be more
A. conducive to family visits
B. dependent on technology
C. focused on the timing of death
D. palliative in nature
E. respectful of religious practices

116. Three weeks after the death of her husband, a distressed widow visits her primary care clinician. She tells him that 2 days ago she was sure that she saw her husband alive, strolling along the opposite side of the street. "I called to him," she says, "but he didn't turn around." The clinician should tell her that
A. a brief course of antidepressant medication is indicated
B. she is defending against her spouse's death
C. she needs to be hospitalized
D. she was having an hallucination
E. such experiences are common in grieving people

117. Coping with the death of a loved one is always difficult, but some deaths seem to be harder to deal with than others. The cause of death that seems to make grieving most difficult is death that involves
A. an automobile accident
B. cancer
C. heart attack
D. HIV/AIDS
E. suicide

118. Informed consent is the basic principle that underlies medical decision making in the US. No medical decision should be made without it. Informed consent is best understood as the requirement that
A. everyone participating must concur before a medical procedure is performed
B. the patient has all necessary information before deciding to undergo medical treatment
C. the patient's family be advised before medical procedures are undertaken
D. the patient's primary care clinician be informed before a subspecialist performs a procedure
E. the provider be well-informed before consenting to perform a procedure

119. An 80-year-old man lost his wife of 55 years after a long illness. Epidemiologically, following such a death, the surviving spouse is at highest risk of death themselves for a period of
A. 3 months
B. 6 months
C. 12 months
D. 24 months
E. no set time period

120. During the course of a new patient visit, a 24-year-old, single woman confesses to using amyl nitrate about once a week. Her most likely reason for this behavior is to
A. calm down after work
B. ease her through a "bad trip"
C. enhance sexual experience
D. give her more energy
E. help her sleep

121. A dentist notes that Mr. J.'s teeth are worn and ground down. The patient reports that his wife has told him that he grinds his teeth in his sleep. "It really keeps her awake," he says. This teeth grinding most likely occurs during what stage of sleep?
A. Stage 1
B. Stage 2
C. Stage 3
D. Stage 4
E. REM Stage

122. You are an ophthalmologist. An elderly Chinese-Vietnamese man comes in accompanied by his daughter-in-law. In response to open-ended questions, the daughter-in-law explains that her father-in-law's vision in his right eye has slowly become worse, making him almost blind, as he lost the vision in his left eye after an injury about 20 years ago. Now his vision is so bad that he is a danger to himself and others. For example, he recently lit the gas stove while there was a newspaper

nearby that caught fire. The family has tried traditional Chinese and Vietnamese treatments with no improvement, and now the family wishes to obtain your opinion. You find a moderately dense cataract in the right eye and a dense corneal opacity in the left eye. You surmise that the man might be afraid of surgery to repair the defects, so you take his hand, look caringly at him, lean forward, raise your voice a little so that he can hear better, and say "Grandfather, you are going blind, but I can help you. We can operate on your eyes. We can use a plastic piece to replace the old lens on the right eye. And we can use part of another person's eye to replace part of your left eye that was damaged years ago. If you do not let us operate, however, you will go completely blind. If you sign this consent form, we can schedule the first operation next week." The daughter-in-law does not interpret for him, but says, "Thank you, doctor. I will tell my husband about your recommendations." Without looking at you, she leads her father-in-law away, but they never return. Looking back over this exchange, you decide that the *least* likely reason for this outcome is that you

A. called him grandfather
B. did not ask them about their reactions to the operations
C. did not ask who would make the decision and sign the consent form
D. looked directly at him for a prolonged period of time
E. said he would go blind if he did not have the operations

123. H. G. is a 21-year-old man referred for psychological evaluation by the local court system after being arrested for a series of burglaries. During his arrest, he severely injured one of the arresting police officers. When interviewed, he is very pleasant, even charming. He answers all questions while smiling and making good eye contact with the examiner. When questioned about injuring the police officer, he continues to smile and expresses no remorse. Past history reveals that he was placed in juvenile detention for a year at age 14 after being found guilty of vandalism and burglary. Based on this initial presentation, the clinician provisionally diagnoses which personality disorder?

A. Antisocial
B. Borderline
C. Histrionic
D. Paranoid
E. Schizotypal

124. A medical student is assigned to explain to a patient that he has a terminal condition. The stu-

dent researches the details and latest prognostic data about the patient's disease. In the morning, she makes a full and detailed presentation to the patient, citing the latest medical information, including an in-depth explanation of the underlying biochemical mechanism of the illness. After the presentation, the patient confides to a nurse on the ward that he "really didn't get" most of what the student presented. The most likely defense mechanism being used by the student in this instance is

A. denial
B. intellectualization
C. isolation of affect
D. reaction formation
E. sublimation

125. Stressful life events can affect people's physical as well as psychological health. As measured by the Holmes and Rahe Social Readjustment Rating Scale, which of the following life events is associated with the greatest stress?

A. Death of a spouse
B. Divorce
C. Incarceration for more than 1 year
D. Loss of a job
E. Surviving an automobile accident

126. Neuronal development progresses through a series of defined stages as the child ages. Neuronal migration, which provides the substrate for brain development, is generally completed by

A. birth
B. 2 months of age
C. 4 months of age
D. 6 months of age
E. 12 months of age

127. A 66-year-old woman is admitted to the hospital for total knee replacement surgery. On post-op day 3, she experiences auditory and visual hallucinations. On physical examination, she is visibly tremulous and diaphoretic. She is oriented to name but not to place or date, and is very agitated. Which of the following would be the treatment choice?

A. Acamprosate
B. Antipsychotic
C. Benzodiazepine
D. Lithium
E. Selective serotonin reuptake inhibitor

128. A patient is having difficulty sleeping. His clinician advises him to listen to a relaxation tape every evening for half an hour prior to going to sleep. Eventually, the patient reports that he falls asleep almost at once as soon as he hears the voice on the tape, even without going through the relaxation

routine. This phenomenon is most likely due to the operation of

A. biofeedback
B. classical conditioning
C. inhibition
D. intermittent reinforcement
E. modeling

129. An overweight, middle-aged woman of average height and in good general health requests advice about diet and weight loss. She says that she has dieted repeatedly throughout her life, and now she cannot lose weight even if she eats only 1,400 kcal/day. She is cold, constipated, and lethargic. She denies binging or purging, and she still has normal menstrual cycles. Her thyroid function tests are normal. The next step should be to

A. order a basal metabolic rate test to investigate if she is hypometabolic
B. send her to Overeaters Anonymous for psychological support
C. suggest she try a very-low-calorie diet, or even a liquid fast, to restart the process of weight loss
D. suggest that people often underestimate dietary intake
E. try to motivate her to lose weight by emphasizing the health risks of obesity

130. Mr. W. has been diagnosed with chronic generalized anxiety disorder (GAD). The benzodiazepine medication commonly prescribed for this condition is believed to be effective because it

A. decreases norepinephrine in the locus ceruleus
B. increases acetylcholine activity in the temporal cortex
C. increases GABA activity diffusely throughout the brain
D. reduces available dopamine in the medial forebrain bundle
E. reduces post synaptic serotonin activity

131. Animal models are often used to predict the action of new pharmacological agents in humans. A dog in a research laboratory is injected with a drug that imitates the effects of glutamate. Over the next hour, what behavior is the dog likely to exhibit?

A. Hiccups
B. Hypersomnolence
C. Manic-like hyperactivity
D. Seizures
E. Unusual quiescence

132. Monitoring the action of dopamine in which neuronal area provides the strongest evidence for the involvement of dopamine in the initiation of movement?

A. Locus ceruleus
B. Mesolimbic-mesocortical tract
C. Nigrostriatal tract
D. Raphe nuclei
E. Tuberoinfundibular tract

133. A researcher wishes to correlate a behavior with serotonin (5-HT) activity. This would require measuring the serotonin metabolite 5-hydroxyindoleacetic acid (5-HIAA) levels in a subject's

A. blood
B. cerebrospinal fluid
C. sweat
D. tears
E. urine

134. Waking up from a bout of REM sleep, a man being studied in a sleep laboratory reports dreaming about brightly colored balloons flying over a field. The words and images that provide the raw material for such mental representations originate in the

A. amygdala
B. basal ganglia
C. cerebellum
D. hippocampus
E. reticular activating system

135. Following an automobile accident, Mr. S. presents with monotone speech devoid of emotional inflection. He evidences no difficulty understanding what is said to him. A CAT scan of the head is ordered. The results are most likely to show a lesion in

A. Broca's area on the left side
B. Broca's area on the right side
C. Exner's area on both the right and the left sides
D. Wernicke's area on the left side
E. Wernicke's area on the right side

136. Animal models provide a method for understanding the functional importance of the neurological system. A rat that is receiving electrical stimulation of the orbito-fronto-cerebral region will most likely display

A. excessive aggression
B. excessive fluid intake
C. hypersexuality
D. manic-like hyperactivity
E. refusal of food despite being hungry

137. A stockbroker spends his days closely monitoring the financial markets and buying and selling according to his observations of market activity. His profit and loss record is mixed. He complains that he is preoccupied with trading and cannot stop following the markets even when he is on

vacation. The mechanism that most likely under-lies his excessive attention to the financial markets is
A. continuous operant reinforcement
B. fixed interval operant reinforcement
C. habituation
D. stimulus generalization
E. variable ratio operant reinforcement

138. Following a fall down the stairs, Mrs. F., a 77-year-old widow, is nonresponsive to stimulation on the left side of her body. When asked to reproduce a presented figure, she is able to draw the right-hand side exactly, but neglects the left-hand side of the figure entirely. Based on this initial evaluation, further physiological examination of the patient is most likely to show a lesion in the
A. dominant parietal lobe
B. dominant temporal lobe
C. nondominant parietal lobe
D. nondominant temporal lobe
E. orbito-medial frontal cortex

139. A 21-year-old female college student presents to the student mental health center with anxiety. Yesterday, when giving an oral presentation, her voice trembled and her hands shook. She was so embarrassed that she refused to return to class. She describes herself as "very self-critical." She wants to have a boyfriend, but she believes that she will be rejected because "I'm not pretty enough." She has one friend with whom she goes out to dinner once a week. However, she avoids going to parties because she thinks that people will not like her. What is the most likely diagnosis?
A. Antisocial personality disorder
B. Avoidant personality disorder
C. Dependent personality disorder
D. Paranoid personality disorder
E. Schizoid personality disorder

140. Over a 24-hr period, you are tracking the cardiac functioning of Mr. B., a 45-year-old office worker who currently does not engage in regular exercise. Assuming that Mr. B. evidences normal biological rhythms, you would expect to find his highest cardiac contraction rates
A. just after awaking in the morning
B. in the middle of the morning
C. in the afternoon
D. just before going to bed at night
E. during REM sleep

141. Although used interchangeably by many people in day-to-day life, the concepts of illness and disease refer to different aspects of a person's perception

of health. In contrast to *illness,* the term *disease* refers to
A. acquired health problems rather than inherited health characteristics
B. chronic rather than acute medical problems
C. health from an epidemiological rather than a medical perspective
D. objective pathology rather than subjective experience
E. the impact of poor health on social functioning

142. A 21-year-old college student is diagnosed with diabetes following a major episode of ketoacidosis requiring hospitalization. He is currently at home recovering and learning how to manage his blood sugar levels. As generally accepted, the concept of the sick role
A. applies only to those with long-term chronic conditions
B. defines the obligations of medical professionals to care for those who are ill
C. places responsibility for having the patient get well on the medical professional
D. relieves the individual from usual responsibilities during an illness
E. specifies a set amount of time to be devoted to illness recovery

143. Mrs. W. receives a letter from her health maintenance organization (HMO) informing her that she had abnormal cells on the Papanicolaou test (Pap smear) taken during her last visit. The letter instructs her to schedule a follow-up appointment. At a visit 2 weeks later, she talks about a pain in her back but does not mention or seem to remember receiving the letter about her Pap smear. The defense mechanism that most likely accounts for Mrs. W.'s inability to remember the letter is
A. denial
B. intellectualization
C. rationalization
D. somatization
E. undoing

144. Mr. J., a patient with a long history of hypertension and cardiac problems, confides to his primary care provider that he is "feeling depressed" about the recent loss of his job. The provider's best response would be to
A. call his wife to ask how he has been at home
B. probe for the presence of other depressive symptoms
C. refer Mr. J. to a local psychiatrist for evaluation
D. tell him that his mood will pass in a couple of weeks
E. write Mr. J. a prescription for an antidepressant

145. On the first day of kindergarten, the mother of a 5-year-old boy tells him that she will not leave right away when dropping him off at school. However, over the next few days, she finds that each day he insists that she stay a little longer and begins to cry when she starts to leave. This morning she reluctantly stayed with him for more than an hour. This change in the mother's behavior can be best explained as an example of
   A. extinction
   B. fading
   C. negative reinforcement
   D. positive reinforcement
   E. secondary reinforcement

146. Ms. S., a 62-year-old Afro-Cuban woman, has to make some choices about her treatment for a breast mass. She arrived in the US 4 months ago and qualified for the special benefits accorded to refugees from Cuba, including a US government–sponsored program to promote refugee health. She found a lump in her breast that proved to be an adenocarcinoma. In the last 2 months, the patient has missed several appointments with the surgeon to discuss various treatment approaches, including mastectomy, radiation therapy, and chemotherapy. Rather, she has sought assistance from healers who have been treating her with herbal medicines and performing Santería rituals. Her youngest son (who has been in the US for 20 years and is a Christian) has taken her to the healers and has paid for her treatments. Which of the following is the *least* likely reason for Ms. S. to consult traditional Santería healers rather than allopathic providers?
   A. Cultural factors, such as interpretation of signs and symptoms, and beliefs about disease
   B. Economic factors, such as the cost of medical treatment
   C. Historical factors, such as familiarity with the healer and the success or failure of treatments
   D. Social factors, such as the patient's and healers' social classes, ethnic identities, and language abilities
   E. Structural factors, such as distance to the healer and available transportation

147. According to Kleinman's categorization, an example of a healer from the popular sector would be a
   A. chiropractor
   B. medical professional
   C. nurse midwife
   D. parent
   E. psychic palm reader

148. P. is angry with his professor for being late to an appointment. When the professor does appear, P. tells him how angry he was with a dentist he saw earlier in the day who made him wait for more than 30 min for no apparent reason. P. is most likely using the defense mechanism of
   A. conversion
   B. displacement
   C. projection
   D. reaction formation
   E. repression

149. Physical examination shows J. D. to have normal body strength, responses to sensation, speech, and comprehension. When engaged in conversation, he communicates clearly. However, when asked to tie his shoelaces, he is unable to do so. This type of dysfunction is most commonly called
   A. agnosia
   B. anosognosia
   C. aphasia
   D. apraxia
   E. aprosody

150. A 45-year-old man who exercises regularly and watches his diet admits to smoking a pack of cigarettes a day. He says that he has tried to quit repeatedly over the years. During his longest period of abstinence (3 months) he gained 15 lb (6.8 kg). His father, an obese nonsmoker, died of a heart attack at age 60. The patient believes that, for him, the risks of smoking are lower than the risks of obesity. The person counseling him should
   A. accept this assessment and focus on other aspects of his life that may affect cardiovascular risk
   B. confront the rationalization of his addiction and suggest a 12-step program to help him quit
   C. explore his feelings about the loss of his father as contributing to his smoking, and suggest psychotherapy
   D. explain the relative risks of smoking and obesity on heart health and suggest he quit and accept weight gain
   E. recommend nicotine replacement or bupropion to reduce potential weight gain

151. When introduced to someone at a party, Ms. S., a middle-aged woman and heavy drinker, is able to converse in a normal manner. However, as the conversation progresses, it becomes evident that she is making up things to cover her inability to remember past events. She is also unable to remember the name of the person she had been talking to, when questioned later in the evening. A deficiency of which of the following substances most likely accounts for this pattern of behaviors?

A. Copper
B. Niacin
C. Potassium
D. Thiamine
E. Zinc

152. A 45-year-old man is placed on a narcotic-based pain medication following abdominal surgery. The medication is prescribed on a time-contingent basis. He is told that he can only take one pill every 6 hr regardless of how much pain he feels. This type of prescription is an example of a reinforcement schedule generally referred to as
A. continuous
B. fixed interval
C. fixed ratio
D. noncontingent
E. variable ratio

153. Which of the following is a top-down list of factors that could affect dietary intake based on the hierarchy of the social ecological model of health behavior?
A. Cost of fruits and vegetables at the local farmers' market, dieting practices of friends, number of fast-food restaurants in the neighborhood, personal preference for sweet and salty foods
B. Genetics, international trade agreements, lack of grocery stores in the community, traditional ethnic dietary practices
C. Local farming practices, social pressure to consume fast food, genetics, US food imports
D. Parents' diets, personal dislike of most vegetables, number of grocery stores in the community, junk-food television advertisements
E. USDA subsidies to cattle farmers, quality of produce in local grocery stores, frequency of fast food consumption by coworkers, personal food preferences

154. J. F., a 43-year-old office worker, has smoked two packs of cigarettes a day for the past 25 years. He tells his clinician that he eats a lot of "junk food" and gets little exercise. The behavior that is most likely to significantly reduce J. F.'s risk of heart disease is
A. modifying his diet to exclude high-fat foods
B. signing up for Weight Watchers
C. starting a rigorous weight-lifting program
D. stopping smoking
E. taking a cholesterol-lowering medication

155. H. Y., a 47-year-old woman, presents to her primary care provider feeling "a little out of sorts." In spite of feeling under the weather, she has made no changes in her daily routine as a legal secretary and mother. In fact, she only came to the office to have a rash evaluated so as not to expose her family and coworkers. Physical examination reveals a rash accompanied by a low-grade fever. A diagnosis of rubella is confirmed. Based on this presentation, H. Y. has
A. disability, without sick role
B. disease, but not illness
C. illness, but not disease
D. infection, but not disease
E. sickness, but not disability

156. Calvin, a 2-year-old boy, is brought in for evaluation of an earache. One week before, a nurse had given Calvin an immunization shot that elicited a great deal of crying. In the exam room, Calvin is playing happily with his stuffed tiger and interacting calmly with his mother. As the nurse enters, he begins to cry and tries to leave. Calvin's reaction to the nurse is most likely the result of
A. classical conditioning
B. fading
C. negative reinforcement
D. positive reinforcement
E. shaping

157. A 3-year-old boy has recently begun to have major temper tantrums each morning when it is time to go to childcare. This causes considerable frustration for his mother who is then late for work. These temper tantrums are new. Previously, the boy had gone to childcare without incident. At her wit's end, the mother calls the pediatric office and asks for advice. She receives a recommendation to use a "sticker chart": The boy will get a sticker for each of three identified behaviors (eating breakfast, getting into the car, and walking into the childcare building). At the end of the day, the boy will be given a small treat if he has collected three stickers for that day. This strategy is an example of the use of
A. biofeedback
B. desensitization
C. flooding
D. shaping
E. token economy

158. You observe an emotional outburst from a patient who is upset for an unknown reason. A functional brain scan of this patient would show that, during this emotional behavior, the part of the brain that is likely to be the most active is the
A. cerebellum
B. limbic system
C. neocortex
D. pineal body
E. reticular activating system

159. A clinician and spouse were invited to an early dinner party. However, office and hospital laboratory results had to be reviewed before the clinician was able to leave work that night. As a result, the couple missed the party. This vignette exemplifies the ethical principle of
A. beneficence
B. fidelity
C. honesty
D. justice
E. trust

160. A primary care provider has practiced in a rural area of Minnesota for over 30 years. In general, the provider's relationships with patients can be considered paternalistic, a style learned from an older provider who founded and ran the practice until he died 20 years ago. One of the core characteristics of a paternalistic clinician is
A. mutual exchange of information between clinician and patient
B. patient passivity during encounters with clinicians
C. respect for patient autonomy
D. sharing of medical decision making by clinicians and patients
E. valuing patients' moral integrity

161. A 4-year-old Cambodian child has a temperature of 39 °C and linear bruises on the chest, back, and upper arms. Her grandmother brought her into the clinic because the child's parents are working. The clinic's Cambodian interpreter is not a native speaker of Cambodian and does not know what may have caused the bruises. What is the most likely explanation?
A. Child abuse
B. Coagulopathy
C. Mongolian spots
D. Sepsis
E. Traditional healing practice

162. In the US, an effective clinician–patient relationship is central to delivery of comprehensive health care services. Both patient satisfaction and positive care outcomes have been tied to the quality of this relationship. One of the central characteristics of a good clinician–patient relationship is
A. acknowledging differences in understanding of health-related issues
B. clinician dominance in the relationship
C. passive patient behavior when receiving medical services
D. patients' inability to make informed medical decisions
E. the clinician's superior moral integrity

163. The concept of explanatory models is useful in helping to understand differences among the perspectives of patients, family members, and healers. Over the years, clinical experience has shown that almost all explanatory models
A. do not change once they are formed
B. eventually come to be shared among patients, family members, and healers
C. include the five concepts of pathophysiology, natural history, preferred treatment, etiology, and ethnic identity
D. include the three concepts of etiology, treatment, and ethnic identity
E. lead to fewer conflicts when shared between patient and provider

164. Differentiating between normal grief and a psychiatric disorder is difficult because many of the defining diagnostic criteria are shared. Difficulty sleeping, anhedonia, appetite disturbance, and loss of energy are present in both grief and
A. anxiety
B. depression
C. panic disorder
D. personality disorder
E. psychosis

165. As part of answering questions on a mental status examination, a patient with schizophrenia describes the voices he hears as coming from the plumbing. Commonly called lack of insight, this answer more precisely illustrates
A. deficient short-term memory
B. dissociation
C. disturbed source identification
D. impaired concentration
E. poor judgment

166. Rates of deaths by suicide are substantially higher for older persons than for the rest of the population. Clinical experience suggests that older persons are more likely to complete suicide because they are
A. less likely to communicate their intentions
B. more experienced because they are older
C. more likely to become clinically depressed
D. more likely to choose overdose as the means
E. more likely to live in poverty

167. S. and E. met several years ago in college and married recently. They seem somewhat apprehensive and seek advice about what they should expect in their interactions with their families during this time early in their marriage. They should be advised that most American couples experience
A. being emotionally cutoff from their families of origin

B. disengagement from parents

C. enmeshment with parents

D. the formation of a family subsystem with relatively closed boundaries around it

E. the formation of a family subsystem with relatively open boundaries around it

168. According to a report published by the University of Chicago on sexual behavior in the US,

A. marital status is an important predictor of sexual activity among older men, but not women

B. sexual activity for both genders is most frequent in the 20s and declines with age

C. sexual activity over a lifetime correlates positively with socioeconomic status

D. people feel little interest in or desire for sexual activity after the age of 60

E. women do not reach their sexual peak until their mid-50s

169. Although divorce patterns have fluctuated over the past 30 years, a number of age-related trends have been relatively stable. An examination of these trends shows that

A. a couple marrying before age 21 has a lower risk of divorce than a couple marrying after 30

B. adults who divorce after age 50 are unlikely to remarry

C. adults who remarry later in life have less stable marriages than those who remarry as young adults

D. divorce is most common between the ages of 30 and 45

E. less than 10% of divorced adults remarry within 5 years after divorce

170. A prison psychiatrist evaluates a 28-year-old man incarcerated for murder. He has a history of multiple arrests as an adult and as a juvenile. During his childhood, he was in special education classes and was expelled during his sophomore year of high school for gun possession. The psychiatrist gives him the diagnosis of antisocial personality disorder. Which psychiatric disorder likely preceded the antisocial personality disorder diagnosis he now receives?

A. Alcohol use disorder

B. Conduct disorder

C. Gambling disorder

D. Major depressive disorder

E. Oppositional defiant disorder

171. Mrs. K. is a 60-year-old woman with a history of diabetes and hypertension. Her son reports that, over the past month, she has become disoriented and confused: "One day she seems better, and then suddenly she seems worse." Her Montreal Cognitive Assessment (MoCA) score is 22 out of 30. Physical examination reveals muscle weakness on the left side of her body. Based on this preliminary examination, the most likely diagnosis for Mrs. K. is

A. Alzheimer's dementia

B. Creutzfeldt-Jakob disease

C. Huntington's disease

D. Pick's disease

E. Vascular dementia

172. Before clinicians can be empathetic with patients, they must first be clear what empathy means. Which of the following examples identifies an important behavioral manifestation of empathy?

A. Appearing relaxed and taking extra time

B. Minimizing nonverbal distractions

C. Remaining calm despite a patient's anxiety

D. Speaking in language that is similar to the patient's

E. Taking notes during a clinical interview

173. A family clinician is counseling a patient concerning weight loss strategies to help relieve pressure and pain in his arthritic knees. The patient becomes irate, stating that he feels criticized and put down. The clinician reacts with amazement to what seems appropriate patient education. The patient's reaction is most likely the result of

A. a personality disorder

B. countertransference by the clinician

C. denial on the part of the patient

D. inadequate expression of empathy by the clinician

E. transference by the patient

174. An 83-year-old patient requires hospitalization for an interaction between several prescribed medications. This illustrates the increasingly common problem of an iatrogenic condition or disease. *Iatrogenesis* is defined as

A. a hypnotic suggestion made by a medical professional to increase patient compliance

B. a negative patient reaction to the demeanor of a medical professional

C. an unrecognized premorbid condition uncovered during treatment for another problem

D. malingering or presenting false information to a care provider

E . problems or complications brought on by medical treatment

175. A task of adolescence is separation from parents. Some adolescents find this process easier than others do. Which of the following types of family

system has the most difficulty adapting to the stage of adolescent separation?

A. Disengaged
B. Enmeshed
C. Extended
D. Multigenerational
E. Overprotective

176. A medical student was spending a month in a private medical practice in rural North Carolina. The head of the practice had been in solo practice for 20 years and was on call whenever he was in town. He had a loving and supportive relationship with his wife and family, all of whom agreed with, and were committed to, traditional principles of professional behavior. The doctor and his wife were planning on a quiet dinner to celebrate their 25th wedding anniversary when he was called to the hospital for a difficult obstetrical delivery. He missed the dinner, and the medical student was amazed that his wife did not become angry because their plans for the evening were upset. Based on the information above, her most likely answer to the question of why she wasn't angry was

A. "He'll make it up to me next year."
B. "Patients come first when care is really needed."
C. "People would talk if he didn't go to take care of a patient."
D. "The kids are more fun to be with anyway."
E. "When you've been married this long, you know your husband's job comes first."

177. A 24-year-old, cohabitating woman has come to the emergency room (ER) four times in 6 months, seeking treatment for severe headaches. An MRI of the brain done at the second visit was normal. The headaches are preceded by visual distortions and accompanied by nausea. They tend to occur premenstrually or after a stressful week. On questioning, she has chronic pelvic pain but a work-up for endometriosis was negative a year ago. She also has cramping abdominal pain, bloating, and gas that, at times, keep her from going to work. She does not have a primary care provider. The astute ER clinician suspects this patient

A. has a history of maltreatment or abuse by an intimate partner
B. has conversion disorder
C. has panic disorder
D. is malingering and has an undiagnosed opiate addiction
E. suffers from illness anxiety disorder

178. A clinician earns a reputation for allowing patients sufficient opportunities to discuss all aspects of their medical care. Patients say the clinician respects their opinions and frequently negotiates management plans with them, deferring to their rights to determine what should be done for their body. The principle that best describes this behavior is

A. beneficence
B. justice
C. moral virtue
D. nonmaleficence
E. respect for autonomy

179. Expectations regarding the role of clinicians in society are based on knowledge of traditional ethical principles and behaviors. Clinician adherence to the majority of these principles and behaviors requires specific actions. Adherence to which of the following principles requires no action by the clinician?

A. Beneficence
B. Justice
C. Moral virtue
D. Nonmaleficence
E. Respect for autonomy

180. Miss M., a 93-year-old woman with invasive esophageal carcinoma, has been in a nursing home for 6 months. Her single sibling, a sister, visits her periodically. Since admission, Miss M. has lost 40% of her body weight. She suffered several episodes of bleeding from her esophagus that required multiple transfusions. She is considered terminally ill with only a short time to live regardless of medical treatment. She has been mentally alert at all times, and competent to make decisions. She has decided to forgo additional transfusions and to die comfortably at the nursing home. In planning for this course of action her care providers should consider

A. her insurance coverage
B. her relationship with her care providers
C. her relationship with the nursing home director
D. her sister's feelings about the decision
E. regulations regarding blood transfusions

181. An 18-year-old high school senior is being seen because of anxiety. She spends 2 hr in the shower each morning because she is afraid of germs. Afterwards, she spends another hour aligning the towels and mats in the bathroom. Before she leaves the bathroom, she has to tap the doorknob "exactly 100 times, or else I get nervous." Prior to driving to school, she has to clean the steering wheel of her car 5 times with a bleach wipe. Due to her behavior, she has frequently been late to school, and she is in danger of failing two

classes. Which of the following diagnoses is most likely?

A. Generalized anxiety disorder
B. Illness anxiety disorder
C. Obsessive-compulsive disorder
D. Obsessive-compulsive personality disorder
E. Obsessive-compulsive personality traits

182. Research on the effects of the growing number of women entering medical practice has demonstrated a number of differences between the practice patterns of male and female doctors. This research has shown that female physicians

A. are poorer at child rearing than mothers in comparable professions
B. as surgeons, are less aggressive about performing invasive procedures
C. as surgeons, have lower technical skills than male surgeons
D. have incomes equal to those of male physicians
E. show greater confidence in their interpersonal skills

183. Many life decisions, including career choice, can be the result of transference. An example of transference in career decision making might be choosing a career in health care

A. after experiencing a significant childhood illness
B. based on a role model outside the family
C. because a family member has a history of substance abuse
D. because a parent is a health care provider
E. because of admiring a genial medical character on television

184. When surveyed and asked to self-describe their personality, what proportion of physicians label themselves as "compulsive?"

A. 20%
B. 40%
C. 60%
D. 80%
E. 95%

185. In the Martin family, each time a family member has a problem, everyone else is affected by it. There is little individual autonomy in the family, and much emotional intensity. When describing this family, the most appropriate term would be

A. child-focused
B. disengaged
C. enmeshed
D. parentified
E. triangulated

186. A mother brings in her 14-year-old daughter with concern that the girl "just doesn't seem to have much interest in anything." Examination shows the girl to be 5-foot-5-inch tall with a weight of 95 lb (43 kg). Despite her low weight, she reports feeling "fat" and is very afraid of gaining weight. Enlargement of the parotid gland and halitosis are noted. Upon questioning, the girl confesses to binge eating and purging by vomiting, which she has carefully hidden from her parents. She reports feeling sad much of the time, and says she just does not fit in with others her own age. Continued physical examination of this girl is most likely to show which of the following additional signs?

A. A deep, red rash on the upper back
B. Elevated heart rate
C. Fine hair on the back and arms
D. Loss of tendon reflexes in the knees
E. Sensitivity to light

187. An emergency department clinician is looking for a psychological assessment tool that will screen emergency room patients for suicide risk. Several tools exist, but the clinician wants to determine if they are appropriate for this particular purpose. When reviewing these tools, the clinician should pay special attention to information about the

A. administration
B. bias
C. consistency
D. reliability
E. validity

188. When applying for a position as a bank teller, J. was surprised when he was asked to complete the Minnesota Multiphasic Personality Inventory (MMPI). He had recently learned about the test in graduate school and knew it was very useful with certain patient populations. However, he had serious doubts about its usefulness in selecting employees. J.'s doubts about the MMPI's use for employee selection reflect concerns about

A. bias
B. convergence
C. precision
D. reliability
E. validity

189. Universities and medical schools often use applicants' scores on tests such as the MCAT, GRE, and SAT as part of their admission decisions. These schools hope that these tests will help them determine which applicants will be successful in their programs. To be useful in this capacity, these tests must have strong

A. construct validity
B. content validity
C. criterion-related validity
D. face validity
E. predictive validity

190. Which of the following menu selections is the healthiest choice with regard to total calories, fat, and saturated fat?
  A. Chili's: Cobb Salad – bed of lettuce topped with grilled chicken, applewood-smoked bacon, avocado, cheese, red bell peppers, egg, and avocado ranch dressing – with a cup of sweet corn soup
  B. Outback Steakhouse: Half a rack of baby back ribs – smoked, grilled and brushed with a tangy barbecue sauce served with Aussie Cheese Fries
  C. Red Lobster: Walt's Favorite Shrimp – hand-breaded, butterflied shrimp, fried to a golden brown – and a side Caesar salad
  D. Subway: 12-inch sub – hearty Italian bread with Black Forest ham, Swiss cheese, and ranch dressing – and a bowl of vegetable beef soup
  E. Wendy's: Homestyle Chicken Fillet Sandwich – specially seasoned, lightly breaded, and topped with mayonnaise – and a small order of fries

191. By definition, a woman is menopausal if she
  A. has frequent hot flashes, disturbed sleep, and irregular menses
  B. has not menstruated in the past 3 months
  C. has not menstruated in the past year
  D. has noted a significant change in her premenstrual symptoms
  E. is over 45, has unprotected sex, and has not conceived over the past year

192. A 50-year-old man with a history of schizophrenia reports to his provider that he has been feeling "uncomfortable" lately. When questioned more closely, the patient reports dry mouth, constipation, and infrequent urination; occasionally, he has blurry vision and confusion. These symptoms are typical medication side effects related to antagonism of which of the following receptors?
  A. Dopamine
  B. Histamine
  C. Muscarinic
  D. Norepinephrine
  E. Prolactin

193. Which of the following activities is the best choice for a healthy new mother who is trying to lose weight gained during pregnancy and has only half an hour each day to exercise at the local gym?

A. Alternating between 5-min intervals of walking briskly and running at a moderate pace on a treadmill
B. Riding a stationary bike at a constant pace with moderate effort
C. Swimming laps at a moderate pace
D. Using the rowing machine at a constant pace with moderate effort
E. Whatever activity she thinks she is likely to do consistently

194. IQ scores are *norm referenced*. This means that each individual's test score is compared with a normative range to derive the actual IQ. When looking at the distribution of IQ scores represented on the normal curve, approximately 68% of people score
  A. > 130
  B. > 100
  C. 85–115
  D. < 100
  E. < 70

195. J. G. is a 19-year-old college student referred by his dean for evaluation by a counselor. The dean acted after hearing from students that J. G. was "impossible to live with" and was disrupting classes. At the initial interview, J. G. is dressed in mismatched clothing and seems anxious and suspicious. He giggles under his breath, and then laughs for no apparent reason. As the session progresses, J. G. confesses that he can hear what the evaluator is thinking. His speech is coherent, but characterized by odd choices of words that seem to hold some hidden private meaning for him. He reports no close friends other than his brother whom he sees once a month. Among the following types of personality disorder, which is the most likely diagnosis for this patient?
  A. Antisocial personality disorder
  B. Borderline personality disorder
  C. Narcissistic personality disorder
  D. Schizoid personality disorder
  E. Schizotypal personality disorder

196. Daniel, a 6-year-old boy, is brought by his mother to see his pediatric provider. His mother reports that during sleep, Daniel sits up in bed and screams for about a minute, and then lies back down to sleep again. In the morning he seems to have no recollection of these episodes. The evaluator should advise the mother that Daniel is most likely experiencing
  A. acute adjustment reaction
  B. bruxism
  C. hypnogogic hallucinations

D. night terrors

E. nightmares

197. A 55-year-old man with a history of hypertension is admitted to the hospital for removal of his gall bladder. He reports feeling anxious about his pending operation. The surgeon should keep in mind that the patient is most likely to recover sooner and request less pain medication if he

A. has complete information about the surgical procedure and recovery

B. has confidence in his surgeon's technical skill

C. is given postoperative pain medication on demand

D. is pleased with his nursing care

E. likes his surgeon personally

198. The second year of life, sometimes called the "terrible twos," can be a trying time for parents and older siblings. The change in outlook on the world typical of this developmental stage is characterized by ability to

A. adhere to rule-based play

B. create plans

C. distinguish unique facial features

D. imagine alternatives

E. recognize adult standards

199. During an assessment, a patient is asked to look at a picture and make up a story about it. The patient tells a story about two lovers who are fighting, but then make up. The patient is most likely being psychologically assessed with the

A. Bender Visual Motor Gestalt Test

B. Benton Visual Retention Test

C. Minnesota Multiphasic Personality Inventory

D. Peabody Picture Vocabulary Test

E. Thematic Apperception Test

200. The concept of homeostasis helps to explain long-term physiological reactions to stressful events and how these reactions mediate strategies for coping with stress. In this context, the notion of homeostasis refers to

A. average physical reaction time to unexpected stimuli

B. balancing interpersonal with psychological needs

C. the ability of the body to metabolize food and convert it to energy

D. the capacity to balance the sex drive and the aggression drive

E. the tendency for the body to maintain a particular state

201. Type A behavior, which describes impatience, competitiveness, and aggression, is associated with increased chances of disability and disease. This pattern is seen in people who

A. are exposed to more stressful environments

B. have greater ability to withstand stress

C. have greater competence in problem solving

D. have strong psychological need for control over situations

E. withdraw socially when faced with stressful events

202. A 10-year-old patient has been having academic difficulties at school. A psychologist suggests administrating a brief screening test that provides a rough estimate of neurological and developmental functioning. The test most likely suggested by the psychologist is the

A. Bender Visual-Motor Gestalt Test

B. Draw-A-Person test

C. Luria-Nebraska Neuropsychological Battery

D. Rorschach Test

E. Wechsler Memory Scale

203. When individuals are forced to impose meaning on an ambiguous stimulus, it is assumed that their responses will reflect their true conscious and unconscious feelings, thoughts, attitudes, desires, experiences, and needs. This assumption is an example of

A. reaction formation

B. subjective press

C. the Gestalt laws of perception

D. the law of effect

E. the projective hypothesis

204. A 16-year-old girl is being evaluated for a possible eating disorder. She has lost 10 lb (4.5 kg) in 3 months, but denies dieting or any intention of losing weight: "It just happened." Of the following combinations of symptoms, signs, and lab findings, which would raise suspicion about a medical condition underlying the weight loss?

A. Amenorrhea, alopecia, low gonadotropins

B. Anorexia, carotenemia, neutropenia

C. Constipation, hypothermia, mildly elevated liver enzymes

D. Early satiety, bradycardia, low blood sugar

E. Fatigue, hyperpigmentation of the skin, hyperkalemia

205. Different behavior patterns characterize different developmental stages. Children in Piaget's preoperational stage of development are most likely to

A. be able to put together simple picture puzzles

B. be able to use symbols to represent reality

C. explore their environment by physical manipulation of objects

D. have sophisticated mental processes

E. need the presence of an event to think about it

206. An 18-year-old patient married in order to leave her parental home. Since her marriage, she has had no contact with her parents. What label best describes the dynamic between this woman and her parents?
    A. Emotionally cutoff
    B. Enmeshed
    C. Parentified
    D. Scapegoated
    E. Triangulated

207. A clinician is interested in assessing the trait of obsessiveness. To obtain information about how much of this or any other trait or attribute a person possesses, the clinician should be most concerned with
    A. construct validity
    B. content validity
    C. criterion-related validity
    D. face validity
    E. predictive validity

208. Dr. S. was considering giving the Benton Visual Retention Test to an 8-year-old patient who recently received a severe blow to the head in an accident. This test has an interrater reliability coefficient of .95. This implies that Dr. S. should
    A. abandon the test, since its reliability is extremely low
    B. consider this test, since its reliability is very strong
    C. continue to investigate the test, since its reliability is moderate
    D. give the test on two separate occasions to confirm the results
    E. look for a test with a reliability coefficient over 1.00

209. A 16-year-old girl you have been seeing for obesity for the last year comes in for a follow-up appointment. She proudly reports that, since you last met 3 months ago, she has gotten rid of all the potato chips (her "biggest vice") in the house and now has cut up fruit in the refrigerator to eat for snacks. She has also stopped drinking sugared soft drinks. According to the stages of change model, she is most likely in which stage of change?
    A. Precontemplation
    B. Contemplation
    C. Preparation
    D. Action
    E. Maintenance

210. When there is public disclosure of financial records and quality standards, we refer to this kind of medical care as
    A. acceptable
    B. accountable
    C. adequate
    D. appropriate
    E. available

211. Mr. R., a patient with hypertension, stops taking a new medication he had asked for after he saw an ad for it on TV. When questioned about this nonadherence, he is evasive and avoids eye contact with the prescriber. Which intervention is most likely to help him resume his treatment?
    A. Changing to a drug covered by his insurance plan
    B. Explaining the health hazards of elevated blood pressure
    C. Explaining the side effects of the medication
    D. Increasing his medication to 3 times a day rather than twice
    E. Urging him to attend a hypertension support group

Items 212–214

A 32-year-old woman has a history of being treated for a psychiatric illness with a long-term medication. She is also on an oral contraceptive. Not realizing the psychotropic medication could decrease the level of her oral contraceptive, she has not been using any other form of contraception. She subsequently becomes pregnant. Her infant is born with spina bifida.

212. Which psychotropic medication was this patient most likely taking?
    A. Carbamazepine
    B. Lamotrigine
    C. Lithium
    D. Risperidone
    E. Valproic acid

213. If all of the possible medications this patient could have taken for her illness are mainstays of treatment for this illness, which of the following is the most likely psychiatric condition for which she is being treated?
    A. Bipolar I disorder
    B. Major depression, recurrent
    C. Persistent depressive disorder
    D. Posttraumatic stress disorder
    E. Schizophrenia

214. Which of the following medications has been found to be "antisuicidal" (that is, reduces the risk of suicide attempts and death by suicide) in patients with this disorder?
    A. Carbamazepine
    B. Lamotrigine
    C. Lithium
    D. Risperidone
    E. Valproic acid

215. The Yerkes-Dodson law and its accompanying curve relate the effects of stress on learning and performance. Per the Yerkes-Dodson curve looking at optimal and problematic effects of stress, which of the following is true?
    A. Low stress environments are the most conducive to learning new tasks
    B. Moderate stress interferes more than high stress with learning new tasks
    C. Performance of all tasks declines in high stress situations
    D. Performance of well-practiced material is less likely to decline under high stress conditions
    E. Stress plays a negligible role in learning and performance

216. P. W. is a 37-year-old man with schizophrenia. While being interviewed, he states, "My landlord brought little pigs house. Driving. Okay. Hope they get. It seems like little Todd. Yes." Which thought process problem does this dialog best illustrate?
    A. Circumstantiality
    B. Clang associations
    C. Neologisms
    D. Tangentiality
    E. Word salad

217. Ms. C., a 40-year-old woman with schizophrenia, tells you she has been watching the news. She reports that the broadcasters have been talking about HIV and specifically about her being HIV positive. She is certain the news people know of her HIV status and that now everyone will know. Thought content such as this is best explained by which of the following?
    A. Depersonalization
    B. Hallucinations
    C. Ideas of reference
    D. Obsessions
    E. Ruminations

Items 218 and 219

A trainee is asked to assess the heart rate of a panel of 10 cardiac patients. The resting heart rates of these patients are 70, 68, 84, 76, 88, 66, 56, 70, 80, and 60 beats per minute.

218. Based on these measurements, what is the modal heart rate for this set of data?
    A. 56
    B. 66
    C. 70
    D. 80
    E. 88

219. What is the median heart rate for this set of patients?
    A. 56
    B. 66
    C. 70
    D. 80
    E. 88

220. A 17-year-old male high school football star is injured in an automobile accident. His injury is not life threatening, but will keep him bedridden for several months. He is likely to have the hardest time coping with
    A. his dependency on others
    B. his limited activity
    C. his social isolation
    D. the pain of his injury
    E. the unexplained nature of events

221. A 15-year-old girl who was formerly a very good student with many friends and interests has become moody at home. She is irritable with her parents, and she constantly reacts to small frustrations with tears. She is often up late and then has trouble getting up in the morning. She varies between lack of appetite and a tendency to eat lots of carbohydrates, especially chocolate. At times, she seems unusually animated around her friends, but then will refuse invitations to socialize, saying she is too tired, too fat, or that all her friends are "boring." Her grades have dropped over the past 6 months. Last week, her mother overheard her say to a friend on the phone that she seriously wishes she were dead. This presentation is most consistent with
    A. attention-deficit/hyperactivity disorder
    B. body dysmorphic disorder
    C. borderline personality disorder
    D. major depression
    E. normal puberty

222. In recent years, the popular media have frequently discussed intelligence and its assessment. After reading some of these accounts, one of your patients comes to you, and knowing that her child is about to be given an IQ test at school, asks you what the facts are. Which of the following statements about intelligence would you make, based on the current state of knowledge?
    A. Intelligence tests are based on one agreed-upon definition of intelligence
    B. IQ and intelligence are the same thing
    C. Most differences in IQ scores are primarily due to environmental factors
    D. Race predicts what IQ score a particular individual will obtain
    E. Tests of intelligence generally attempt to measure ability, not achievement

223. The rising interest in preventive medicine in the US partly reflects broader changes in the health care delivery system. Health care providers being compensated under which type of payment system are most likely to support a new program aimed at the primary prevention of disease?
    A. HMO
    B. Indemnity insurance
    C. Medicaid
    D. Medicare
    E. PPO

224. Data examining the current trends for AIDS-related deaths in one of the Midwestern states show a dramatic decrease in AIDS-related mortality, but little change in the incidence of AIDS. Given this information, we should also expect to find
    A. a decrease in AIDS-related medical care
    B. a decrease in survival rate following diagnosis
    C. an increase in AIDS prevalence
    D. an increase in HIV infections among family members
    E. an increase in the number of people practicing safe sex

225. During assessment, a patient was administered the WAIS, MMPI, the Tactile Performance Test, the Speech Sounds Test, and the Categories Test. The patient is probably being evaluated for brain dysfunction with the
    A. Bender Visual-Motor Gestalt Test
    B. California Personality Inventory
    C. Halstead-Reitan Neuropsychological Test Battery
    D. Luria-Nebraska Neuropsychological Battery
    E. Thematic Apperception Test

226. For the past 6 months, a 36-year-old man reports suffering from butterflies in the stomach, sweaty palms, vague apprehension, poor concentration, and difficulty falling asleep. He reports that nothing makes him feel better except taking long walks along the lakefront by himself or singing a special song to himself. His relationships with others have deteriorated, and he fears being fired from his job. Based on this presentation, the most likely diagnosis for this man would be
    A. agoraphobia
    B. generalized anxiety disorder
    C. panic disorder
    D. obsessive-compulsive disorder
    E. social phobia

227. A student, apprehensive about an upcoming anatomy exam, is observed sitting in the exam room opening and closing both fists while breathing deeply. The student is probably trying to control anxiety by means of
    A. biofeedback
    B. meditation
    C. progressive relaxation
    D. self-hypnosis
    E. the stress response

228. A 13-year-old girl began pubertal development at 9 and had her first menstrual period at 10 years 6 months. She is at the 90th percentile for height. An older brother, who teased her about gaining weight, is now at college. Her mother and father are in the process of an acrimonious divorce. Her father is on a cholesterol-lowering diet. She is interested in going out for the school cross-country team and has started dieting to get in shape for the season. Which of the following is the most important risk factor for her to develop an eating disorder?
    A. Brother teasing her about her weight
    B. Dieting to get in shape for the cross-country team
    C. Early pubertal development
    D. Father being on a diet
    E. Parental separation and conflict

229. On a cold day in January, a 40-year-old, well-nourished man arrives at the emergency room wearing running shorts, a tank top, and very expensive running shoes. He was picked up running along a controlled access highway. He says he has started training for a marathon and needed a long unbroken course to run on. His demeanor is haughty, alternating between amused condescension and irritable impatience. His speech is rapid, and he is difficult to interrupt. As the examiner

challenges his story, the details keep shifting. He is convinced he will win the marathon in the spring, even though this is his first training run. Since recently losing his job, he feels he will have more than adequate time to pursue his athletic goals. He is oriented to person, place, and time. He can recall three of three objects at 0 and 5 min. He interprets the proverb "Do not judge a man until you have walked a mile in his shoes" as meaning, "The way to win a race is to be sure you know what the other guy has on his feet." This description is most consistent with

A. delusional disorder
B. histrionic personality disorder
C. mania
D. masked depression
E. narcissistic personality disorder

230. Thinking can be usefully separated into a number of different processes, each appropriate to different types of problems and situations. The situation in which a clinician, while examining a set of patients, categorizes a number of symptoms as sharing some features in common, is best regarded as an example of

A. concept formation
B. convergent thinking
C. hypothesis testing
D. insightful thinking
E. stimulus discrimination

231. A person's experience of reality is not simply absorbed from the environment, but constructed by means of mental representations. Language plays a key role in this process. Language shapes the individual's perception of reality by

A. assigning meaning to sounds
B. defining how experiences are described and what is remembered
C. limiting what the individual senses
D. modifying the meaning of words through vocal intonation
E. restricting perception to only what can be put into words

232. After he is discharged, Mr. G. reports that one of the nurses on the inpatient unit attempted to poison him. Although an investigation shows this allegation to be groundless, Mr. G. continues to insist that it is true. An examination of Mr. G. is most likely to find that he is experiencing

A. a delusional episode
B. an hallucination
C. an illusion
D. confabulation
E. sensory distortion

233. Intelligence is one of the variables most predictive of human development and behavior. Over the past several years, there has been considerable debate about what intelligence is and how it functions. Based on a growing body of work, we can now say with confidence that

A. intelligence is determined by heredity and is uninfluenced by experience
B. intelligence is generally defined in terms of verbal ability and problem-solving skills
C. measures of intelligence are usually based on divergent thinking
D. rapid processing of information is a universal characteristic of high intelligence
E. significant differences in intelligence exist among races

234. Choose the answer that ranks the signs of thought disorder from least to most severe.

A. Circumstantiality, loose associations, flight of ideas, tangentiality
B. Circumstantiality, tangentiality, flight of ideas, loose associations
C. Flight of ideas, circumstantiality, loose associations, tangentiality
D. Loose associations, tangentiality, circumstantiality, flight of ideas
E. Tangentiality, loose associations, circumstantiality, flight of ideas

235. After hearing the description of a patient's illness, a clinician repeats the essential symptoms to him and reflects back the patient's reaction to those symptoms. The clinician receives confirmation from the patient that they understand the patient's description. In this example, the clinician has demonstrated

A. accurate empathy
B. clinical judgment
C. concept formation
D. divergent thinking
E. paralinguistic communication

236. A woman decides she will give herself permission to buy a new dress after she loses 10 lb (4.5 kg). This procedure, in which the person plans rewarding consequences for attaining set goals, is best referred to as the technique of

A. cognitive rehearsal
B. cognitive restructuring
C. problem solving
D. self-control contracting
E. skills training

237. A student is afraid of failing an upcoming examination, making self-statements like "I don't know

what to do" or "I'm so stupid and there's nothing I can do." The student is encouraged to remember how much they study and to believe that "Hard work leads to good results." This technique, in which the student is encouraged to replace maladaptive cognitions with adaptive cognitions, is generally referred to as

A. cognitive rehearsal
B. cognitive restructuring
C. problem solving
D. self-control contracting
E. skills training

238. You have been asked by a local community agency to address a group of young adults about common developmental issues for people their age. As you prepare your remarks, you should remember that, as a group, the young adults you are addressing most likely

A. are striving to develop stable intergenerational relationships by seeking independence
B. are working at being part of the adult culture
C. generally disregard advice from older persons
D. have dreams and aspirations that are mostly developed from the wishes of the family of origin
E. occupy the majority of their time pursuing leisure activities and avoiding commitments

239. Without the hippocampus, learning that is based on retention of long-term memories is impossible. What is the functional process by which the hippocampus and the associated structures of the limbic system facilitate this type of learning?

A. They connect various cortical storage sites to form combined memories
B. They directly stimulate the release of neurohormones from the adrenal gland
C. They forward all incoming sensory information to the neocortex for permanent storage
D. They guide the learning of motor skills in the brainstem
E. They promote synaptic depolarization to facilitate neuronal transmission

240. Mr. I., a 35-year-old man, presents with a history of anxiety attacks that include palpitations, tingling of the extremities, feeling dizzy and faint, difficulty breathing, and a belief that he is going to go crazy or die. When attempting to determine if he has actual panic disorder vs. another mental health disorder with panic attacks, which of the following is the most important differentiating factor for a diagnosis of panic disorder?

A. Determining if he has anxiety at times other than during attacks

B. Determining if the attacks have led to actual episodes of fainting
C. Determining if the attacks were associated with a stressor
D. Determining if the attacks were associated with low blood sugar
E. Determining the duration of the attacks

241. For most young adults, what event is most likely to be accompanied by self-awareness of a transition into full-fledged adulthood?

A. Becoming a parent
B. Death of a parent
C. Getting married
D. Graduation from college
E. Starting a first job

242. A white rat is placed in a cage that contains a lever and a chute through which food can be dispensed. The rat presses the lever and receives a food pellet. After receiving the food, the rat again presses the lever. This type of learning is most influenced by

A. emotionally intense responses
B. genetically programmed reflexes
C. simultaneously occurring stimuli
D. specific stimulus cues at critical periods
E. the consequences of behavior

243. A clinician suspects that a newly referred 85-year-old woman patient may be in the early stages of dementia. The most direct way to identify dementia in its early stages is to

A. administer the Mini–Mental State Examination
B. administer the Wechsler Adult Intelligence Scale
C. ask a family member to describe the patient's recent behavior
D. do a computed tomography scan
E. observe the patient's behavior with peers over a 2-day period

244. A visiting nurse has been delegated to assess an elderly client's capacity to complete activities of daily living (ADLs) in order to determine the level of medical assistance needed. By convention, the ADLs of a typical geriatric assessment are

A. ambulating, climbing stairs, and sitting
B. driving, using the phone, and watching tv
C. eating, bathing, and going to the toilet
D. shopping, cooking, and dressing
E. using the phone, driving, and cooking

245. When a behavior, symptom, or learned association ceases to be reinforced, it tends to weaken or decrease in frequency. This phenomenon is best described as

A. free operant behavior
B. negative reinforcement
C. positive reinforcement
D. response extinction
E. stimulus generalization

246. A 2-year-old girl is afraid of cats. To change this, she is put in a room with her favorite music playing while a friendly cat is gradually brought toward her. Finally, she is encouraged to pet the cat. This example illustrates which of the following principles of learning?
A. Aversive conditioning
B. Critical period learning
C. Negative reinforcement
D. Positive reinforcement
E. Response extinction

247. A man learns to control his blood pressure by means of trial-and-error practice while watching a gauge that gives him feedback about the fluctuations in his blood pressure. The effectiveness of this technique is based on the operant principle that
A. a high-frequency reinforcer will reward a low-frequency target behavior
B. behavior is controlled by selectively manipulating the consequences
C. consequences are controlled by controlling the stimuli
D. information about the consequences of behavior is reinforcing
E. motor performance is more easily reinforced than other forms of responses

248. A mother is trying to decide about play activities for her son's eighth birthday party. When making these arrangements, she should remember that children at this age will prefer
A. the company of anyone of the same age who likes the same activities
B. playing in mixed-gender groups
C. simple fantasy games
D. structured games and sports
E. watching, rather than participating in sports

249. A 10-year-old boy was recently diagnosed with insulin-dependent diabetes mellitus. When counseling the child and his parents, the provider must stress that the child should be
A. encouraged to continue with school activities such as team sports and physical education
B. encouraged to explain to teachers and peers why his activities will be limited
C. exempted from family chores to attend to managing his illness

D. expected to be absent from school periodically as a consequence of his illness
E. expected to have difficulty relating to peers as he gets older

250. Social learning theory has expanded our understanding of how people learn and change their behavior beyond simple, animal-based models. The operation of social learning is most easy to recognize because it is
A. dependent on the reinforcement value of relationships
B. distinct from classical and operant learning
C. the least dependent on evaluative feedback
D. the least influenced by environmental conditions
E. unrelated to the individual's survival

251. Because of its ability to mount a prolonged response to sustained and intense stressors, which of the following systems potentially exerts the most detrimental effects on the body under conditions of chronic stress?
A. Autonomic nervous
B. Endocrine
C. Immune
D. Limbic
E. Musculoskeletal

252. A person feels physiologically aroused. The emotional label (e.g., grief, anger, joy) that is given to this felt state typically depends upon
A. gender differences within a culture
B. sociocultural display rules
C. the context in which arousal occurs
D. the heredity of the individual
E. the intensity and quality of the arousal

253. A girl is born prematurely at 28 weeks gestational age. Based on current clinical experience, the best estimate of this girl's chance of surviving until her first birthday is closest to
A. 25%
B. 33%
C. 50%
D. 75%
E. 90%

254. Low birth weight is associated with a number of physical and developmental problems. What is the approximate percentage of infants weighing 1,000 g or less at birth who survive and subsequently have major disability?
A. 15%
B. 25%

C. 33%

D. 50%

E. 66%

255. In an effort to control costs, a hospital reduces the nursing staff by 20%. The decision about whom to terminate is based on seniority within the nursing hierarchy. Initially, the hospital enjoyed considerable savings. However, over the next several months, the number of hospital admissions decreased by almost 30%. A subsequent analysis found that the bulk of nurses terminated came from the ranks of "admitting nurses," who were responsible for timely and efficient processing of new patients. As a result, there was an unintended reduction in patient flow that was compounded by less patient satisfaction. Because patients chose to go elsewhere for care, the hospital found itself in worse financial condition than before the decision to reduce the number of nurses. The notion of *unintended consequences* and the observation that changes in one part of the system will have consequences for other parts of the system is best captured within which of the following theoretical perspectives?

A. Conflict theory – adaptation

B. Formal – implicit theory

C. Goal attainment – structural functional analysis

D. Symbolic interaction – latent pattern maintenance

E. Utilitarianism – integration

256. A 12-year-old patient shows some depressive symptoms. She is responsible for taking care of the household and caring for her younger siblings after school until her parents return from work. What term best describes her role in this family system?

A. Child-focused

B. Enmeshed

C. Instrumental

D. Parentified

E. Triangulated

257. Many of the conflicts we feel in our day-to-day lives are explainable within the framework of behavioral psychology. For example, food that someone finds particularly tasty but that also may cause undesirable weight gain or cavities is an example of which type of conflict?

A. Approach-approach

B. Approach-avoidance

C. Avoidance-approach

D. Avoidance-avoidance

E. Oedipal

258. A patient reports that there is emotional distance and many independent activities among members of the family. Even traumatic events involving family members evoke little response. What family dynamic best describes this family system?

A. Disengaged

B. Enmeshed

C. Parentified

D. Scapegoated

E. Triangulated

259. The parents of a 1-year-old child ask their pediatric care provider about potential risks to their child's health. They should be told that the most significant health risk to children during the second year of life is

A. environmental poisons

B. failure to thrive

C. hearing loss

D. infection

E. injury

260. Different people see the world differently. Even people undergoing identical experiences may recall and respond to them differently. These individual differences in the manner in which experiences are perceived, processed, and assigned meaning are called

A. cognitive styles

B. defense mechanisms

C. delusional thoughts

D. schemas

E. sensations

261. Defense mechanisms can be thought of as cognitive processes, as well as affective controls. The reconceptualization of an event or memory in sufficiently abstract terms to change the emotional quality of its meaning describes the defense mechanism of

A. denial

B. intellectualization

C. projection

D. repression

E. sublimation

262. During the first month after the birth of his son, Mr. H. woke up every night when the child cried. However, after the first month, he no longer awoke, although his wife continued to do so. This change in behavior by Mr. H. is most likely explained by the principle of

A. accumulated fatigue

B. adjustment reaction

C. habituation

D. just noticeable difference
E. threshold detection

263. Changes in disease patterns over time provide information about their contributing causes. Over the past 10 years, demographic and epidemiological data regarding suicide worldwide have shown that suicide rates are
A. generally constant over time
B. higher for Hispanics who immigrated to the US than those remaining in their country of origin
C. lower for people in their teens and early 20s
D. lowest among white men in the US
E. lowest in industrialized nations

264. A 22-year-old man with schizophrenia is hearing voices telling him to kill himself. In the emergency room, a urine toxicology screen is positive for cocaine, and you smell ethanol on his breath. Appropriate management would include
A. confrontation regarding the severity of his substance abuse problem
B. discharge to home, once sober, with follow-up in 1 week
C. psychiatric hospitalization with one-to-one monitoring
D. referral to Alcoholics Anonymous or Narcotics Anonymous
E. referral to outpatient psychotherapy

265. A first-year resident assumes the care of a woman who has had diabetes mellitus for many years. The patient was previously under the care of a recently retired faculty member noted for his authoritarian manner. She is notorious among office staff for her lack of adherence to prescribed treatment regimens. When seeing the patient in the office for the first time, the resident notes that her diabetes is out of control despite multiple office visits, dietary counseling, large insulin doses, and a prescribed exercise regimen. To improve the patient's adherence to treatment recommendations, the first step the resident should take is to
A. explain the negative health consequences of noncompliance with recommendations
B. inform her that diabetes is incurable and improvement unlikely without good treatment
C. question the patient about her failure to follow treatment recommendations
D. show concern and ask what assistance she would like to help her manage the diabetes
E. tell the patient how she can best control her diet

266. A 70-year-old woman has been diagnosed with Alzheimer's dementia. Because she had to leave school early to support her family, she never graduated from high school. She has made her living for more than 50 years by cleaning office buildings. When questioned, she has little insight into her memory deficits. During the past year, she has been well cared for by her daughter while enrolled in a protocol for a new experimental treatment. Unfortunately, the results of the trial have been poor. Now her daughter is concerned that her mother might be suicidal. Which feature of this patient's history would be most likely to place her at risk for death by suicide?
A. A family member is a caregiver
B. Enrollment in an experimental drug protocol with poor results
C. Lower socioeconomic status
D. Minimal schooling
E. No insight about her memory deficits

267. While flying to visit a relative for a holiday, you find yourself sitting next to a well-dressed woman in her late 20s. You make polite conversation with her at first, but then turn your attention to a book that you brought with you to read. Your reading is interrupted 15 min later when the woman begins to shake, hyperventilate, and sweat profusely. She is wild-eyed and her face is contorted in fear. Between great, gasping gulps of air she says that she is having a panic attack. At this point, what is the action you should take?
A. Ask her how frequently she has attacks
B. Give her a hard candy to suck on
C. Have her breathe into an airsickness bag
D. Hold her hand and tell her to calm down
E. Try to distract her by telling her a story

268. A first-time mother seeks professional advice as to how to care for her infant. She has been reading about sudden infant death syndrome (SIDS) and has been following the current medical recommendations for prevention. She asks if following these recommendations will alter her child's development in any way. She can be told that her child may show
A. accelerated auditory discrimination
B. delays in developing a social smile
C. delays in learning to crawl
D. delays in speech acquisition
E. increased thumb-sucking behavior

269. When diagnosing major depressive disorder, the mnemonic SIG E CAPS can be used. Which of the following correctly identifies the meaning of a letter in this mnemonic?

A. *A* for Anhedonia
B. *E* for Energy
C. *E* for Enthusiasm
D. *I* for Involutional melancholia
E. *P* for Paralysis

270. Theories improve our understanding of how the world works by providing models for the mechanisms of behavior. Which of the following theories of motivation is most closely associated with instinctual theory?
A. Arousal
B. Cognitive
C. Drive
D. Expectancy
E. Sociocultural

271. S. G. is a 16-year-old girl who recently announced to her friends and family that she is gay. She was raised in a single-parent family and has a history of being close to her mother but having intense conflicts with homophobic peers. She has no psychiatric history and denies any psychiatric symptoms currently. She does have ADHD that is managed well with medication. During questioning, she reports that her mother keeps a handgun in a locked gun safe in the house "for protection." Given this history, the strongest risk factor for suicide attempts by S. G. would be
A. being close to her mother
B. being lesbian
C. having a handgun in the household
D. having ADHD
E. peer victimization for being lesbian

272. The timing of puberty has a number of identifiable social, psychological, and behavioral consequences for adolescent boys. A survey of adolescents in the US has found that one of the more common behavioral correlates of late puberty in boys is
A. conduct disorders and delinquency
B. immature behavior and lower self-esteem
C. improved academic competitiveness
D. improved athletic competitiveness
E. improved musical abilities

273. A 21-year-old college senior living in a sorority eats very little at communal meals, but binges at night on ice cream and cookies. She then purges by vomiting. This behavior has gone on for 6 months, several times per week. What would be the most effective medication to prescribe for her condition?
A. Antiemetic
B. Antipsychotic
C. Appetite suppressant

D. Benzodiazepine
E. Selective serotonin reuptake inhibitor

274. The parents of a 14-year-old girl with restrictive anorexia nervosa are interested in learning about the Maudsley method. Of the following, which describes a core feature of family-based therapy?
A. After weight restoration, parents must continue to monitor caloric intake to maintain recovery
B. In early treatment, the focus is on behavior change and not underlying psychiatric pathology
C. To begin recovery, it is essential to first determine what family issues caused the eating disorder
D. To establish their authority, parents must make their child eat
E. To support the development of autonomy, parents need to encourage their child to choose what to eat

275. A 27-year-old woman comes in for a routine checkup. Examination reveals nothing out of the ordinary except for some general nervousness. Finally, she reports that she is "beginning to feel old," and asks what she should expect at her age. She may told that
A. brain cell development peaks by 30 years of age
B. her brain cells continue to grow in complexity until the late 40s
C. she has passed the time of peak intellectual achievement
D. she should cut back on athletic activity to avoid injury
E. the human body is in its peak physical condition from 20 to 30 years of age

276. A clinician administering a Mini–Mental State Examination (MMSE), asks an 80-year-old man to name objects, repeat a sentence, and follow a verbal command. These questions all test for different types of
A. agnosia
B. amnesia
C. aphasia
D. apraxia
E. executive function

277. Compared with her siblings, Katya seems to be more focused on high achievement. The *achievement need* of some people helps to explain the life choices that they make in their adult years. Achievement need can be best understood as
A. a desire to enhance cognitive development
B. an outgrowth of Type A behavior patterns

C. similar to innate cognitive ability

D. the core motive fostering the desire to have children

E. the desire for control over others

278. Mark is 20 years old. As a person moving from adolescence to adulthood, he is likely to experience

A. a decline in task-oriented behavior

B. decreased capacity to consider the consequences of impulsive action

C. increased capacity for interpersonal relationships

D. increased difficulty with complex decision making

E. increased focus on maintaining an independent self-identity

279. Seeking to undertake a business initiative, an entrepreneur decides to develop a health and outing club that caters only to single adults. He has to decide how to market his idea to the appropriate population. In doing so he relies on studies examining the lives of these singles which show that

A. approximately 20% of young adults choose long-term singlehood

B. more than half of nonmarried individuals are homosexual

C. most periods of singlehood last longer than 5 years

D. singlehood has disadvantages for career opportunities

E. the proportions of sexually active single men and women are nearly equal

280. A well-educated, 75-year-old woman is brought in by her family because of change in mental status. She has been treated in the past for depression, but has not been on medication for 5 years. She lives in an assisted living facility, where staff have noticed that she has rarely come to meals over the past 3 months. She seems sluggish and apathetic. On questioning, she describes feeling worthless and as though life has become meaningless. She formerly had many friends and enjoyed going on outings organized by the facility. When asked to answer questions on the mental status exam, she seems hesitant and self-doubting, saying, "That's too hard" or "I am sure I won't be able to do that." She has to be prodded to finish tasks such as serial subtraction. Despite these findings, her final score is 28, well within the normal range for her age. This presentation suggests

A. delirium

B. generalized anxiety disorder

C. pseudodementia

D. senile dementia of the Alzheimer's type

E. subcortical dementia

281. After several years of general clinical practice, you notice that, although individual variation exits, relationships of young adults with their parents share a number of common features. The most common relationship pattern in this age group is

A. establishing a collegial relationship with parents typically begins during young adulthood

B. most young adults resist financial help from their parents because they want to establish independence quickly

C. most young adults seek to pattern their "sense of self" after that of their parents

D. the process of raising questions about family of origin rarely begins before the age of 30

E. young adults maintain relationships with parents similar to those set in place during childhood

282. Practicing in a relatively homogenous area, with a high proportion of members of a single ethnic group, a primary care clinician seeks insight into the group's system of beliefs and practices regarding health and disease. In trying to understand the underpinnings of those beliefs, the practitioner reviews medical anthropological research that shows health beliefs are most closely associated with cultural beliefs about the

A. natural world, such as ideas about germs, stars, and the sun

B. social world, such as ideas about family members' relationships

C. supernatural world, such as concepts of spirits, death, and afterlife

D. natural and supernatural worlds

E. natural, supernatural, and social worlds

283. A basketball player is trained to repeatedly visualize attempting and making a free throw in a game, with the fans yelling and the opposing players trying to be distracting. The technique the athlete is using to visualize behaviors is an example of

A. cognitive rehearsal

B. cognitive restructuring

C. problem solving

D. self-control contracting

E. skills training

284. The excitatory amino acid glutamate functions as a neurotransmitter in major neural pathways of the hippocampus. Upon neuronal excitation, glutamate binds with two types of protein receptors, NMDA and non-NMDA, on the cell membrane of

the postsynaptic neuron. How do NMDA and non-NMDA activation contribute to learning?

A. Because stimuli activating NMDA receptors are weaker than those activating non-NMDA receptors, the NMDA response becomes conditioned to non-NMDA stimuli

B. Combined NMDA and non-NMDA activation blocks depolarization of the synapse

C. Combined NMDA and non-NMDA activation releases magnesium in the cell body, facilitating transmission at the synapse

D. Convergence of NMDA and non-NMDA receptor activation slows, prolongs, and increases the efficiency of the synapse, facilitating complex sensory learning

E. Glutamate activation neutralizes the antagonistic actions of NMDA and non-NMDA, permitting the neuron to fire

285. Mikail, a 15-year-old boy, has grown through three shoe sizes in a year, and feels clumsy and awkward. He is anxious to know what to expect about his further growth. Which of the following combinations of changes in height and weight is most commonly seen during puberty?

	Height	Weight
A.	+ 50%	+ 50%
B.	+ 25%	+ 50%
C.	+ 25%	+ 25%
D.	+ 10%	+ 25%
E.	+ 10%	+ 10%

286. Anika, a 13-year-old girl, does a research project that shows that the average height of the girls in three classes in her grade exceed that of the boys. What explains the finding that during early adolescence, females are generally taller than males of the same age??

A. Boys expend more energy in physical activity and so require more time to grow

B. Boys receive more familial attention than girls do

C. Boys show compensating advances in mental capacity compared with girls of this age

D. Earlier height gain in girls reflects the body's adaptation to reproductive functioning

E. Girls are better nourished at the onset of puberty

287. An experienced fifth-grade teacher in the US notes that, over the years, more and more of the students seem to be entering puberty by the late elementary grades, some as early as age 8 to 10. Current thinking suggests this trend is an outgrowth of

A. changes in the average age at first marriage

B. decreases in chronic diseases of childhood

C. global warming

D. improved health and nutrition

E. social needs for earlier reproductive maturity and childbearing

288. A 54-year-old woman complains of pain in her lower back. During the subsequent history taking and physical examination, what variable will best tell the clinician whether the patient's pain is acute or chronic?

A. Cause

B. Duration

C. Family history

D. Intensity

E. Site

289. The father of a 15-year-old boy is concerned about his son's development. His voice has not begun to change, he has only traces of body hair and acne, and he has not had an obvious growth spurt. A clinical endocrinologist should assess the function of which two structures that interact with the gonads to regulate the progress of puberty in adolescence?

A. Hypothalamus and the adrenal gland

B. Hypothalamus and the pituitary gland

C. Hypothalamus and the thyroid gland

D. Pituitary gland and the adrenal gland

E. Pituitary gland and the thyroid gland

290. During a pediatric visit, a 10-year-old boy with diabetes is listening to an explanation of his condition. His instructor makes every effort to keep the explanations as simple as possible. Children this age need simple explanations during a health care visit because they

A. are at the stage of concrete operations

B. are highly distractible and do not listen well

C. do not trust authority figures of any sort

D. have not achieved a high enough level of education

E. have not attained their full level of intelligence

291. A set of middle-aged parents asks what they should expect regarding their son as he moves through adolescence. Research examining the actual events that accompany this period strongly suggests that, for most adolescents,

A. boys adjust to pubertal change more easily than girls

B. development is necessarily filled with turmoil

C. developmental struggles are rare to nonexistent

D. developmental struggles are relatively minor

E. struggling with their transition to adulthood is psychologically traumatic

292. A 15-year-old girl is seeing her primary care provider for a checkup. At the end of the examination, she asks, with some embarrassment, for advice on a problem that she is having. When counseling a girl this age, the provider should remember that this developmental period is typically characterized by
A. a strong focus on one-on-one intimate relationships
B. adjusting to the changes of puberty
C. desire to stand out among one's peers
D. goal formation related to career
E. intense concern about social and peer relationships

293. Research studies designed to test the effectiveness of newly developed oral medications typically have two groups of study subjects: those who receive the drug being studied and those who receive an inert pill which looks identical to the study drug. This study design intends to eliminate which of the following factors that might contribute to a drug's efficacy?
A. Investigator bias
B. Natural course of the disease
C. Nonspecific treatment effects
D. Placebo effect
E. Specific treatment effects

294. The three leading causes of death among adolescents and young adults in the US in 2015 were
A. accidents, suicide, and drug overdoses
B accidents, suicide, and homicide
C. cancer, accidents, and suicide
D. cancer, congenital heart disease, and accidents
E. suicide, accidents, and drug overdoses

295. Interventions properly selected and performed by trained professionals are referred to as
A. acceptable
B. accessible
C. adequate
D. appropriate
E. available

296. Two soldiers are hospitalized after a motor vehicle accident in which a third soldier was killed. Both are being treated for compound fractures of one leg and the opposite arm. The soldier who was driving the vehicle and feels responsible for the accident asks for pain medicine more often and wants higher doses than the soldier who was the passenger. This situation illustrates that the degree of pain people experience from particular conditions is strongly influenced by the
A. availability of narcotics
B. location and extent of tissue damage
C. meaning of the pain
D. prior level of fitness
E. time of day

297. A baby with the adrenogenital syndrome is genetically female but has ambiguous genitalia at birth. At the age of 3, this child wears overalls and plays with trucks, but states categorically, "I'm a girl, silly." The stable conceptualization of being either a male or a female despite superficial features such as dress or mannerism is most often referred to as
A. gender identity
B. parental identification
C. sex role schema
D. sex role stereotype
E. sexual orientation

298. Health care providers contribute to both increased longevity and better quality of life. Over the past century, life expectancy in the US has risen steadily. This increase in life expectancy at birth is largely due to
A. better nutrition with an emphasis on lower fat diets
B. higher levels of income and better health insurance
C. improved health and health care in older adults
D. reduced smoking among adults
E. reductions in infant mortality rates

299. A clinician suspects that a patient may have been a victim of childhood sexual abuse and requests that certain psychological tests be administered. However, the clinician does not tell the subject or the test administrator the purpose of the screening, to guard against
A. a placebo effect
B. bias
C. destroying the reliability of the test results
D. influencing the construct validity of the test
E. stigmatizing the patient

300. A student is preparing to take a 3-hr multiple-choice exam. This will be a timed test. To do his best under this time pressure, the student should remember that
A. arousal is unrelated to performance
B. arousal levels that vary as the task proceeds are associated with optimal performance
C. high levels of arousal are best for optimal performance

D. low levels of arousal are best for optimal performance

E. moderate levels of arousal are best for optimal performance

301. Piaget used a number of simple tasks to demonstrate children's capacities at different stages of development. In the so-called three mountain experiment, a 4-year-old girl is shown a plastic model of three mountains (snow on one, a red cross on another, and a hut on the third one). A doll is seated opposite the child thus viewing the mountains from a different side. The child is shown photos of the mountains taken from different sides and asked to indicate which showed the doll's view. The girl selects the one showing the same view the girl sees. This experiment was used to demonstrate the concept of

A. centration
B. conservation
C. egocentrism
D. magical thinking
E. object permanence

302. A 5-year-old child claims that a stuffed animal is feeling sad and offers it a cookie to cheer it up. This process is usually called

A. animism
B. artificialism
C. autism
D. magical thinking
E. symbolization

303. Children develop both language and conceptual abilities before they enter school. For example, a typical 6-year-old child already has a vocabulary of about how many words?

A. 1,000
B. 5,000
C. 10,000
D. 25,000
E. 50,000

304. According to Erikson's theory of social development, the developmental dialectic that pushes a 5-year-old boy in two directions would be

A. autonomy vs. shame
B. identity vs. role diffusion
C. industry vs. inferiority
D. initiative vs. guilt
E. trust vs. mistrust

305. The notion of a teenage subculture is a relatively new phenomenon. Historically, the transition between childhood and adulthood was seen as occurring without this intermediate stage. The modern creation of a subculture is most likely due to

A. increased use of computer technology
B. increased use of illegal drugs
C. media influences such as MTV
D. pressure to move into adult roles too quickly
E. society's moratorium on growing up

306. A 90-year-old woman is admitted to the hospital for treatment of a urinary tract infection. She is prescribed a common sleep medication at half the dose used for the 50-year-old patient in the next bed. Lower medication doses are generally required for a comparable therapeutic effect in older patients because of

A. age-related cardiovascular disease
B. drug interactions due to polypharmacy
C. lower tolerance of side effects
D. poorer absorption of oral medications
E. slower rate of metabolism

307. A 74-year-old woman presents with memory deficits, decreased ability to dress herself, and forgetting to turn off the stove when finished cooking. Her family reports that deficits have appeared gradually over the past several years. When approached by her son, she fails to recognize him and asks for an introduction. She is able to converse about events from the distant past, but cannot recall how or why she was brought to see the clinician. On neurological examination, she has no evidence of any focal neurological signs. Without any further information being given, the clinician should assume that these symptoms are most likely the consequence of

A. Alzheimer's disease
B. brain tumor
C. cerebrovascular accident
D. iatrogenic effect of medication
E. normal senile changes

308. Reinforcement is the key event in operant conditioning. The effect of reinforcement is well known, but less is known about what makes something a reinforcer. For example, the Premack principle tells us that

A. a high-frequency behavior or reward can be used as a reinforcer for a low-frequency target behavior

B. a low-frequency behavior can be used to punish an undesired high-frequency behavior

C. a low-frequency behavior, because of its higher value, can be used to reward a desired target behavior

D. a moderate-frequency behavior will have a more pronounced effect than either a high- or low-frequency behavior
E. if an individual seeks out and engages in an activity, it is because it is desirable and, therefore, a reinforcer

309. Having just read Erikson and his stages of development, a 64-year-old woman decides that she is in the stage of *ego integrity vs. despair*. The next time she attends a party, she asks a guest who is a health care professional what this means and is told that the challenge of this stage of life is
A. adjusting to impending death and dying
B. balancing life's accomplishments and failures
C. coping with depression and loss
D. growing older with dignity
E. reviewing one's family life

310. Human development passes through a number of different stages across the lifespan. "Successful" development is most closely linked to
A. avoiding personal loss
B. economic status
C. educational attainment
D. maintaining good physical health
E. successful negotiation of transitions

311. The staff of an outpatient clinic in an ethnically diverse area have evaluated patients presenting with *crises de foie, mal de ojo, ataques de nervios*, and *bulimia nervosa*. All of these disorders are
A. conditions based on superstitious beliefs
B. culture-bound syndromes that describe a type of soul loss
C. ethnically recognized chronic diseases
D. illustrations of how people interpret bodily signs and symptoms in culturally specific ways
E. reflections of patients' lack of education

312. Puberty is marked by a number of predictable physical and social changes. The hormonal changes that are most closely linked to puberty
A. are seldom observed during the middle childhood years
B. do not relate to increased subcutaneous fat during middle childhood
C. include increases in adrenal steroids, beginning as early as age 7
D. involve estrogen increases in girls only
E. occur at about the same age for 90% of children

313. The social and psychological changes that characterize middle childhood are made possible by accompanying physical changes. Among these changes is a pattern of neurological development characterized by a significant increase in the
A. circumference of the head
B. complexity of synaptic connections
C. mechanism of neuronal processing
D. number of neurons
E. number of neurotransmitters

314. Observable behavioral changes are the dominant means of tracking development in middle childhood. These reflect predictable changes in neurological function. The electroencephalogram (EEG) provides a noninvasive method for measuring brain function in human subjects. EEG studies in middle childhood have shown than development in this period is characterized by
A. decreased function-specific activity
B. destabilization between the hemispheres
C. expression of adult sleep architecture
D. increased alpha wave activity
E. transition to primary delta wave activity

315. An 8-year-old boy has recently been diagnosed with ADHD. While examining the child, the clinician should check for what other features that are often associated with ADHD?
A. Deficits in executive functions
B. Enhanced ability in visual-spatial tracking
C. Good relationships with peers
D. Increased ability to process verbal directions
E. Increased susceptibility to childhood infectious diseases

316. Among the signs that a child has reached middle childhood are changes in the child's cognitive capacities. This cognitive development allows the child to
A. consider how another person will feel in the future
B. easily manipulate abstract concepts
C. evaluate and characterize the psychological attributes of other people
D. form a self-generated philosophy of life
E. predict behavior across differing social situations

317. A 10-year-old boy insists that everyone follow the rules when playing his favorite board game. This insistence most likely reflects his wish to
A. avoid embarrassment
B. avoid punishment
C. be a replacement for his parents
D. be seen as good
E. dominate others

318. There are several distinct forms of learning. Which of the following answers best describes the developmental order of forms of learning from most genetically influenced to most environmentally influenced?
    A. Classical, operant, imprinting, reflex, one-trial, social
    B. Classical, reflex, imprinting, one-trial, social, operant
    C. Imprinting, reflex, one-trial, social, classical, operant
    D. Reflex, imprinting, one-trial, classical, operant, social
    E. Social, operant, classical, one-trial, imprinting, reflex

319. Physical changes during the middle years of adulthood set the stage for the later developmental stage of old age. Experience with adults in this age group has shown that
    A. few people recognize changes in physical health before the age of 50
    B. physical changes are most closely tied to chronological age and maturation
    C. physical changes can be predicted from social and interpersonal factors
    D. the age at which facial wrinkles occur and hair turns gray is fairly constant
    E. the signs of aging appear in women earlier than they do in men

320. A couple in their late 40s asks their provider what changes they should expect with respect to their sexual functioning as they age. Based on recent research examining changes in sexual functioning for men and women, the provider should tell them that
    A. over age 60, a couple's sexual activity is inversely related to how many children they have
    B. the female menstrual cycle begins to change during the 30s and 40s
    C. the level of sexual desire for men is correlated with the level of sperm production
    D. there is a "male climacteric" that corresponds to the female "menopause"
    E. White women begin menopause earlier than women of color

321. A 28-year-old man has not gone to a social or athletic event in 3 years. In the past, he had friends and enjoyed sports. He works from home in computer data entry. He is preoccupied with the asymmetry of his eyebrows, and over time, he has plucked out both eyebrows completely, trying to equalize them. He now consults a dermatologist about a hair transplant to repair the damage. This presentation is consistent with
    A. body dysmorphic disorder
    B. delusional disorder
    C. factitious disorder
    D. malingering
    E. social phobia

322. At 10 p.m. you are checking your personal e-mail. You receive a message from a patient you saw earlier that day indicating that she thinks she is experiencing a minor side effect from her new medication. The most appropriate course of action is to
    A. answer the patient's e-mail quickly so as not to harm the provider–patient relationship
    B. establish that the e-mail link is secure
    C. offer to meet on Facebook to chat about the patient's concern in a conversational manner
    D. refuse to communicate with the patient, in order to abide by HIPAA regulations
    E. respond by e-mail being precise and avoiding jargon because information communicated in this manner may be unclear

323. Adherence to treatment refers to active participation by patients in choosing to remain faithful to recommended treatment plans. High levels of adherence are associated with better medical outcomes. Clinicians should remember that patient adherence to treatment is most likely to *decline* when
    A. patient and clinician negotiate the treatment plan
    B. patient and clinician openly share opinions about the problem
    C. the clinician controls medical decision making
    D. the clinician provides additional information about the condition
    E. the patient's knowledge about the disease increases

324. Although much of traditional research on human development has focused on children, increasing attention has been paid in recent years to patterns of development across the life cycle, including so-called middle-age. Research into patterns of relationships between middle-aged persons and their older parents have shown that
    A. although adult children ask their parents for financial support, they rarely ask for advice
    B. feelings of dependency on parents have been resolved prior to this age
    C. middle age is usually marked by increasing psychological distance from parents
    D. most adult children and their parents have positive feelings about each other
    E. relationships with siblings are more important than relationships with parents

325. Prematurity is a major risk factor for a number of developmental abnormalities. For the average woman of normal childbearing years who becomes pregnant, the chance of giving birth prematurely is closest to
   A. < 1%
   B. 5%
   C. 10%
   D. 15%
   E. 20%

326. You are observing the reactions of a husband and wife as they receive bad news regarding the health of their newborn child. Gender differences in emotional reaction have been documented across cultures. Thus, when confronted by a challenging situation, a man is more likely than a woman to
   A. be less emotional
   B. conceal his emotions
   C. show happiness in public
   D. show more anger
   E. use different language to describe emotion

327. Pregnant women who use substances, either legal or illegal, risk damaging the fetus in a variety of ways. Maternal use during pregnancy of which of the following substances is responsible for the greatest number of cases of mental retardation in infants?
   A. Alcohol
   B. Anticonvulsants
   C. Cocaine
   D. Opiates
   E. Tobacco

328. A 48-year-old man presents to his provider with complaints of clumsiness. Examination reveals a subtle, but apparent resting tremor accompanied by a *pill-rolling* gesture in his left hand. When walking, he moves slowly and shuffles his feet. A preliminary diagnosis of Parkinson's disease is made. Increased levels of which of the following neurotransmitters would best support this diagnosis?
   A. Acetylcholine
   B. Gamma-aminobutyric acid
   C. Norepinephrine
   D. Prolactin
   E. Serotonin

329. A 35-year-old woman is concerned that she has been gaining weight over the past few months. She reports that her appetite has increased for unknown reasons. At the biochemical level, this woman is probably experiencing increased serotonin activity at which receptors?

   A. 5-HT1
   B. 5-HT2
   C. 5-HT3
   D. 5-HT4
   E. All of the above

330. A patient admitted to the neurological ICU with a complete C5 transection is intubated, placed on a ventilator, and connected to electronic monitors. Every few hours, the staff roll the patient over to prevent bedsores. However, nursing staff become concerned when they observe that the patient has not slept for 2 days and seems to be increasingly agitated and distressed. Unable to communicate with the patient because of the intubation, the staff calls for a consultant who can read lips. The consultant discovers that the patient was forcing himself to stay wake because he thought the reason the nurses were turning him was: "If I fall asleep, I will die." It never occurred to the nursing staff that their actions might be so interpreted, and they quickly reassured the patient that this was not the case. The patient, now so informed, gratefully falls asleep. The difference in meanings held by the patient and nursing staff is best addressed within which of the following theoretical perspectives?
   A. Conflict theory – adaptation
   B. Formal – implicit theory
   C. Goal attainment – structural functional analysis
   D. Symbolic interaction – latent pattern maintenance
   E. Utilitarianism – integration

331. A patient was referred for outpatient psychotherapy after a recent emergency room visit that involved several psychological assessments. The therapist wants to readminister the tests to identify any significant change in the patient's condition. To be relatively certain that any changes in results reflect true changes in the patient's condition and not the change in environment, the therapist needs to be most concerned about the tests'
   A. adaptive capacity
   B. bias
   C. concurrent validity
   D. content validity
   E. reliability

332. During combat, a young soldier sees a live grenade on the ground next to his friend. He immediately covers it with his body and is killed in the explosion. According to Durkheim's theory of suicide, which type of suicide does this example illustrate?
   A. Altruistic
   B. Anomic

C. Egoistic

D. Fatalistic

E. Heroic

333. Diminished ability to carry out personal or professional responsibilities is referred to in the literature as "clinician impairment." Which of the following examples would reflect clinician impairment?

A. Completed rehabilitation for cocaine dependence 6 months ago

B. Compulsive gambling that only occurs on weekends

C. Difficulty keeping up with charting requirements, due to limited computer skills

D. HIV infection without current symptoms

E. Status post stroke with residual impairment of gait

334. A 30-year-old woman seeks care for what she describes as "multiple chemical sensitivity." Since the age of 15, she has complained of headaches, body aches, fatigue, skin rashes, shortness of breath, unstable heart rate, and cramping abdominal pain. She also has painful menstrual periods and pelvic pain at mid cycle. Work-ups for endometriosis, asthma, and allergy have been negative, except for mild seasonal rhinitis that responds to intranasal steroids. She seems to derive a sense of self-worth from her interesting medical condition, having not been able to finish college, work consistently, or establish a close, intimate relationship. This presentation is most consistent with

A. avoidant personality disorder

B. malingering

C. obsessive-compulsive disorder

D. panic disorder

E. somatic symptom disorder

335. Which of the following is required of health care providers?

A. Accepting Medicaid coverage

B. Accepting Medicare coverage

C. Certification

D. Charging the same rates to all patients, regardless of insurance status

E. Licensing

Answers

1. B. *face greater societal prejudice.* Gay and les-
    bian couples are gaining acceptance in our
    society, but at present, they continue to expe-
    rience prejudice and nonacceptance manifest-
    ed as a nonrational fear of same-sex unions, a
    form of homophobia. Same-sex couples may
    suffer social isolation, increasing their risk
    for substance abuse, depression, and even
    suicide.

2. D. *patients' perception of the time spent giving
    information correlates positively with adher-
    ence.* One of the most potent forces deter-
    mining patient adherence is the relationship
    between the provider and the patient. The
    probability of adherence is greatest if the
    exchange is positive. The fear-induced warn-
    ings mandated by ethics and law can distract
    patients from the details of the instructions.
    Too much information all at once can lead to
    information overload. Memory depends upon
    attention and emotion as well as intelligence.
    Education is not related to adherence. In fact,
    highly educated patients may be as nonadher-
    ent as poorly educated ones, but for different
    reasons. For example, less educated persons
    may not understand instructions, or may face
    practical barriers to adherence; more educated
    persons may understand but not believe or
    accept the information provided. The refusal
    of many affluent parents to allow their chil-
    dren to be immunized against measles and
    other early childhood diseases illustrates this
    point.

3. B. *are becoming the most common family form.*
    The roles, rules, relationships, and loyalties in
    stepfamilies or blended families may fluctu-
    ate. A family therapist may assist components
    of the family to make the adjustments neces-
    sary for successful transition to a blended
    structure. Therapy helps family members be
    patient and flexible while members acclimate
    to often dramatic change.

4. B. *Enmeshment.* Enmeshed families have
    few boundaries between family members.
    Emotions resonate quickly between mem-
    bers, so that emotional states are often shared.
    Enmeshment is an extreme form of cohe-
    sion. Infantilization describes the process of
    not assigning a family member age-appro-

priate roles or responsibilities. Scapegoating
involves identifying one person as the cause
of all of a family's frustrations or failures.
Splitting is seeing something or someone as
all good or bad, usually in response to whether
or not that person is, at that moment, fulfilling
a specific need. Splitting is considered a psychological defense mechanism, not a quality
of family life, although it may be expressed in
behavior toward various family members.

5. C. *high expressed emotion.* This is a well-defined
    variable in family research, connoting emo-
    tionally intense, negative views that a family
    member expresses about a member who is ill
    or impaired. High expressed emotion indicates
    the family's failure to grant a patient the sick
    role, resorting instead to blaming and accus-
    ing, to explain the patient's inability to live up
    to normal expectations. High expressed emo-
    tion predicts relapse in patients with schizo-
    phrenia living at home. It adversely affects the
    outcome of other chronic psychiatric disorders
    such as depression and medical conditions
    such as chronic renal failure. *Exploitation for
    secondary gain* involves families expropriat-
    ing patients' resources for their own use. This
    is a common problem, but not described in the
    question. *Help seeking and help rejecting* is a
    pattern of patient behavior related to personal-
    ity disorder and neuroticism. *Parentification*
    is a term used to describe the inappropri-
    ate caretaking roles that children or adoles-
    cents sometimes assume in troubled fami-
    lies. It may adversely affect the child, who
    must contend with pressure to meet expecta-
    tions not appropriate to their age. However,
    parentification is not related to the course of
    schizophrenia. *Triangulation,* a concept from
    structural family theory, involves two family
    members communicating through a third per-
    son, usually crossing generational boundaries.
    Triangulation is a conflict-ridden situation
    with negative implications. In this case, the
    parents have a single view of their son.

6. A. *If he wants the boy to try alcohol, it should
    be at a meal with adults who do not condone
    drunkenness.* Intermittent but otherwise unre-
    stricted alcohol use may be, or evolve into,
    binge drinking, which is no safer than chronic
    daily drinking. The safe limits for an adult male

(or female) are no more than 14 units/week or six 6-ounce glasses of wine, 6 pints of ale or larger, or fourteen 1-oz drinks of hard liquor. Although these should be spaced evenly over the week, it is also recommended that there be 2–3 days without alcohol per week. Since low potency alcohol-containing beverages are served in higher quantities than stronger ones, it is still possible to develop alcoholism from wine or beer at any age. High tolerance is a risk factor for alcoholism, not a protective one. Note: there is little research on the appropriate limits for drinking alcohol in adolescents. In the US, the legal drinking age is 21.

7. C. *personality characteristics that affect communication or the capacity for intimacy.* Certain elements of physician identity (e.g., a desire to be in control, entitlement, inhibition of emotional expression, or expectations that the physician will be nurturing regardless of their own needs) may affect close relationships. Financial problems are real but need not destroy close relationships. Couples in which both partners are doctors are not necessarily more or less stable than those in which one partner is a physician, and the other is not. Although medical education and training can be stressful, physicians in any specialty may have satisfying or troubled relationships. Stress over time demands is more often a symptom than a cause of relational problems. Physicians often overcommit themselves at work to avoid problems at home, albeit they may perceive the demands as externally imposed.

8. B. *emphasize that the patient will not be abandoned and that all treatment, including palliative care, will be provided.* People may hear the request for a do not resuscitate (DNR) order as a statement that the case is hopeless and the staff have no real intention of caring for the patient. In fact, patients and families often accept the possibility of death, as long as they know that care will be compassionate, attentive and appropriate. Advance directives must be revised at every stage of a patient's illness. A previous order either requesting or refusing resuscitation may not reflect the patient's current priorities or status. The statement that resuscitation does not prolong or improve life is true, but does not address the concerns of patients and families about abandonment and neglect. Giving a technical definition of the order similarly avoids addressing

the emotional aspects of the decision. Respect for privacy is important, but letting the family discuss the matter with no input from the health care provider is a form of abandonment.

9. A. *most important information is given at the beginning of an interaction.* The first topic raised becomes the primary focus of attention and allows the patient time to consider the issues and to ask whatever questions they wish. Giving extensive information or too many instructions at once may overload the patient. Without patient questions and feedback, the clinician does not know if information is understood. Although it is helpful to tailor information to the patient's personal needs and constraints, leaving it to the patient to fill in all the details of a recommendation may lead to erroneous conclusions.

10. B. *Contemplation.* The patient is contemplating whether he has a problem or not before deciding to act. He has moved beyond precontemplation but has not yet reached the level of preparing for action, taking specific action, or maintaining a plan of action.

11. C. *Mutual pretense.* Both patient and provider have tacitly agreed not to talk about the patient's disease. There is no indication of any level of awareness in the exchange described.

12. B. *ask the patient to say more about his symptoms* as a way to facilitate differential diagnosis and to increase rapport with the patient. The symptoms presented are consistent with hypochondriasis, factitious disorder, malingering, or some as yet unidentified gastrointestinal problem. Speaking with a family member implies mistrust of the patient's ability to represent himself honestly and is likely to leave him wondering why corroboration from others is necessary. The history as described contains no special indications for substance abuse. The patient is not "fine"; he is suffering. To simply send the patient home trivializes his symptoms, and abets the patient if the complaint is due to malingering. Telling the patient that he is a hypochondriac leaps to a diagnosis prematurely and is likely to anger him.

13. E. *while the emotional states described are real, they do not represent distinct sequential stages.* The emotional states described by Kübler-Ross are best understood as points along a

continuous process; some points (e.g., anger) may be re-experienced several times. There is no "average" experience of the dying process. The pattern highlighted by Kübler-Ross is a useful guide, but every individual's experience is different. Given enough time, most patients do finally accept death. Some, however, never appear to allow themselves to do so. Culture, religious beliefs, life experience, and life satisfaction all play a part in patients' reactions to death and dying.

14.   A.   *patients should monitor behavior such as dietary intake rather than outcomes such as weight loss.* Paying close attention to behavior is most effective; therefore, recording throughout the day will increase awareness. Self-monitoring is dependent on awareness of one's behavior, not on any specific personality trait (e.g., assertiveness).

15.   A.   *even experienced clinicians are uncomfortable discussing sex.* Clinicians may employ the psychological defense mechanism of projection in believing that discomfort about a particular topic resides solely in the patient, but this is not the case. Clinicians must not allow their own discomfort to interfere with discussing sexual issues. A number of important medical issues, including sexually transmitted disease prevention and general well-being, require such discussions.

16.   D.   *transvestic behavior* is said to occur when an individual experiences recurrent and intense sexual arousal from cross-dressing but does not experience significant distress as a result of the behavior. Transvestic disorder occurs when an individual experiences significant distress or impairment socially, on the job, or in other significant domains of functioning, as a result of cross-dressing. Note that transvestites are mostly heterosexual – that is, they typically prefer partners of the opposite sex. Male transvestites see themselves as male and therefore are not transsexuals or experiencing gender dysphoria.

17.   A.   *Anger.* The patient is angry at what is perceived as an unfair consequence. Bargaining involves searching for ways to avoid the feared consequence, such as pursuing untried treatments or pleading with a higher power. Denial is the refusal to accept the reality of the impending death. Depression would manifest itself as despair and a sense of hopelessness.

Confusion is not one of the traditional Kübler-Ross stages for dealing with death and dying.

18.   D.   *performance anxiety* is one of the more common reasons for both impotence and anorgasmia. Although not a "disorder" as such, this anxiety should be explored before looking into physical or psychological pathology. A simple counseling session with each partner in this couple may save time and expense. At the very least, it would uncover or rule out performance anxiety and justify more detailed examinations.

19.   E.   *social anxiety disorder.* The fear of others making fun of him, and the conviction that he will do something shameful or stupid in public are all consistent with a diagnosis of social phobia. Although social anxiety is a type of anxiety disorder, it is distinguished by the stimulus that triggers the anxiety. Agoraphobia is a fear of being in situations that might cause severe anxiety or where help might not be available, not specifically the fear of ridicule or humiliation. Generalized anxiety disorder involves more varied fears (e.g., fears of harm coming to others, fears of loss or illness, or fears of a bad outcome from some situation). Strong expression of distress is not by itself a sign of histrionic personality. Narcissistic personality disorder involves the desire to be noticed and admired, not the painful self-consciousness of social anxiety disorder. Personality disorders are lifelong, and so are ruled out by the recent onset.

20.   B.   *oldest female.* Although family dynamics and cultural patterns differ, in many if not most family systems, the nonphysician health expert is an older woman (think "grandmother"). Age confers the experience required for expertise, and women typically act as caretakers. Education is not a key qualification in this informal network.

21.   C.   *he most likely has a moderate to severe alcohol use disorder (formerly, alcohol abuse or dependence).* The CAGE questions ask if someone has ever (1) tried to Cut down alcohol intake but did not succeed, (2) been Annoyed about criticism concerning drinking, (3) felt Guilty about drinking behavior, and (4) needed an Eye-opener in the morning to relieve anxiety and shakiness. Mr. S. gave positive answers to all four of these questions. Although some recent research has

suggested that the CAGE questions may be less predictive when evaluating certain ethnic populations, and may have some different implications for women than for men, a full set of positive answers strongly suggests that an alcohol problem exists. The positive predictive value of the CAGE questions is high enough that even though the prevalence of alcoholism is only 10%, a person who gives even two positive answers has a > 50% chance of having a problem. Not all alcoholics get drunk; many so-called functional alcoholics show few outward signs of intoxication. Inpatient treatment is not indicated for patients who are able to function (e.g., hold a job) or who have not had a chance to respond to other interventions such as motivational enhancement, intensive outpatient treatment, and self-help through organizations such as Alcoholics Anonymous (AA). Alcohol problems are typically diagnosed based on observed or reported behavior, not on laboratory testing.

22. B. *Do you have an orgasm with manual or other clitoral stimulation?* This question helps to determine whether the woman is anorgasmic, or whether some other problem, such as depression, might account for her lack of sexual interest. A *yes* answer suggests that changes in sexual technique might improve her experience. Asking about satisfaction and frequency misses the point: The patient has already expressed dissatisfaction, and her presenting concern is the infrequency of sexual activity. If her husband were impotent, it is unlikely that she would complain about her own lack of interest. Asking her what the problem is labels her feelings as a problem. A more targeted question will yield more specific and useful information.

23. E. *tell the husband you cannot share the information without his wife's permission.* Confidentiality between a patient and provider is essential for a trusting professional relationship. The Health Insurance Portability and Accountability Act (HIPAA) made longstanding customs about privacy into a law governing all past, present, and future information created or received in the course of providing treatment, obtaining payment for services, or performing research. Patients generally receive a written statement that says some information may be shared for usual business purposes (e.g., to justify payment), but is otherwise available only to the patient or their

designee. Information will be released to others only with the patient's written permission. HIPAA gives patients a legal right to know, upon request, with whom protected health information has been shared and under what circumstances it will be shared in the future. With a few defined exceptions (e.g., mandatory reporting of child abuse), the clinician should be sure the patient understands that confidentiality will be diligently maintained except in circumstances indicating imminent deadly danger to the patient or to someone else. In these situations, a clinician must act in the patient's best interest and in the interests of others who may be in danger or at risk.

24. B. *The patient and provider have differing beliefs about insulin.* The provider understands the effects and uses of insulin and considers it a good treatment. The patient's experience prompts him to see it is as intrinsically dangerous. Such difference in belief makes any communication about treatment options difficult. The question vignette does not illustrate a family systems problem. Although the family might share the patient's beliefs, the issue is not obviously one of family dynamics (interactions between family members). Adherence would be poor, based not on passivity, but on the patient's active rejection of the treatment. A detailed explanation of insulin will not be effective if the patient rejects the idea in the first place. Beliefs that differ from professional opinion do not necessarily indicate irrationality. Instead, they may reflect, as in this case, reasoning based on different life experiences. In any case, an accusation of irrationality is pejorative. The clinician should try to uncover and understand the basis for the patient's refusal.

25. D. *Physical, neurological maturational, cognitive, speech/language, and psychosocial* development make up the cluster of domains usually assessed. Development is not a single entity, but proceeds along several parallel, interacting trajectories. In certain circumstances, any of the domains listed might be appropriate for evaluation. However, answer D provides a checklist of the classic five.

26. C. *5 months.* The physical behavior, level of responsiveness to external stimuli, and appearance of the ability to laugh, combined with rate of weight gain all indicate a child of approximately this age. Recognizing the parameters of normal behavior at each stage

of development is critical for advising parents and detecting developmentally linked pathology.

27. B. *discover how much information he would like to have.* Although patients have the right to know everything that the provider knows about their medical condition, they also need to have some control over the level of detail with which facts are presented. Discussing support systems before giving any information about the disease would be premature. Prior to communicating about the patient's condition and gauging his reaction, physical contact may be misunderstood. Before deciding how to talk to the patient (e.g., in small chunks or laying all of the information out at once), asking the patient what he thinks would be most helpful is critical. Every patient is different.

28. A. *A broad description such as "working poor"* (residents who are unable to meet basic needs despite having a job). For the purpose of describing health care needs, a broad but clearly defined term such as *working poor* is more useful than socioeconomic status (SES), which stratifies people based on a combination of education and income. Populations of similar SES may vary along other dimensions, including health, because some jobs that pay high salaries do not require many years of education, and some low-paying jobs do require advanced education. Part-time employees and retired workers (primary and secondary groups) further complicate any characterization of the population of potential patients based on SES. The area to be served by a new clinic could encompass people of more than one culture or could be predominately of one race or ethnic group with several levels of assimilation.

29. D. *sensorimotor stage.* This stage is the beginning of cognitive development, during which the rudiments of assimilation and accommodation first appear. Schemas at this stage are combinations of movements and sensations, not objects with a life of their own. Freud called this same developmental period the oral stage. Erikson termed it the age of trust vs. mistrust.

30. B. *goals are graduated to maximize success experiences.* No one likes failure. Success in reaching a goal can, by itself, reinforce desired behavior. Making goals incremental

makes each step more attainable and helps to keep the patient motivated. Goals that are too broad are ambiguous. Goals set by the provider without patient input may ignore difficulties of which the provider is unaware. Furthermore, they typically lack the level of "buy in" from the patient needed for success. "Shooting for the moon" may feel great if the moon is actually hit, but the chances of failure are too great, and the goal just looks unattainable (and is therefore nonmotivating) to the patient. Goals must be flexible so they can be altered as circumstances change.

31. B. *comment that it sounds like he does not see a problem with his drinking.* The patient has not yet accepted that he has a problem. He is, thus, in the precontemplation stage of change. "Resisting the righting reflex" (one of the four guiding principles of motivational interviewing) by the use of reflective listening (one of the four foundational clinical skills of motivational interviewing) is a way to let him know you really heard and understood him. Encouraging others to convince him to stop drinking would be a violation of confidentiality and is likely to lead to further arguments from him about why drinking is not a problem (further solidifying his resistance to change). Encouraging immediate corrective action (AA or inpatient treatment) would be premature, as he does not recognize that there is a problem and so would not follow that advice. Failure to mention the problem and simply scheduling a follow-up visit will not help the patient to move from denial (precontemplation) to willingness to think he might have a problem (contemplation). Whenever possible, it is best to match an intervention to the patient's stage of readiness to change.

32. D. *8 months.* The realization that objects out of sight continue to exist is a critical developmental milestone. On average, children gain this capacity shortly after 6 months of age. Note that we must infer this sense of object permanence or constancy from the child's searching behavior, as she is too young to provide verbal answers to verbal probing.

33. E. *he may benefit from treatment with antidepressant medication.* The patient's difficulty sleeping, loss of interest in usual activities, feelings of worthlessness, difficulty concentrating, thoughts of suicide, and weight loss converge to support a diagnosis of depression,

rather than occult malignancy or substance use disorder. When a full depressive syndrome is present, it is appropriate to treat it, whether a specific cause is or is not identified. A person who is acutely and seriously depressed is unlikely to respond to brief counseling or peer support until their capacity to respond to positive input is restored. Depression that follows a stroke typically responds well to adequate pharmacological intervention, especially when coupled with psychotherapy based on principles of rehabilitation and support. Not treating this patient's depression exposes him to unnecessary suffering.

34. C. *5–6 months.* Each of these reflexes, present at birth, are lost as the child matures. The Moro and rooting reflexes disappear at about 3–4 months of age, tonic neck at about 4–6 months, and palmar grasp at about 5–6 months. Thus, 5–6 months is the earliest age at which these reflexes would be expected to have disappeared. Note that Babinski and placing reflexes persist until about 1 year of age.

35. E. *"You must be very upset that your father is ill from his cancer again."* This statement focuses the conversation on the patient's reactions to his father's illness, not his reaction to the surgeon. Reflecting the patient's emotional state indicates that you have heard it, while still reframing it. Asking about what he knows about the typical course of colon cancer is missing the opportunity to be empathetic regarding the emotion the man is experiencing and will likely result in his becoming more upset. Defending the surgeon makes you seem to be siding with the surgeon and risks making you another target of the patient's anger. Sitting quietly leaves the patient wondering what you, the care provider, are thinking. Talking about his anger with the surgeon leads the patient away from the real source of his distress – namely, the return of his father's illness.

36. E. *physiological decline that accompanies aging.* The incidence of erectile dysfunction in men increases with age. However, many men continue to be sexually active all their lives. Men who continue sexual activity retain capacity. Older men who attempt sexual relations only sporadically may find that they have more functional difficulty. Although erectile dysfunction may be the result of a pathological condition, a simpler explanation is most likely.

37. A. *Anger* is the second of the five stages or emotional states of coping with death and dying as described by Kübler-Ross. Note that the patient blames someone else for her condition. Denial is a refusal to accept the reality of the impending death. Guilt, not one of Kübler-Ross's stages, is more likely to be felt by friends and relatives of the dying person, or anyone who feels that they should have done more. Depression means despair, a realization that the death is unavoidable, but not yet accepted. Not telling a patient what is happening is likely to produce fear. However, patients need to be told bad news in a way that they can tolerate. Coming to grips with news of impending death takes time. Kübler-Ross's five stages are denial, anger, bargaining, depression, and acceptance.

38. A. *feeling depressed for several months afterward.* This reaction is called grief and is considered normal for months to a year or even more following an important loss. People need to know that grief takes time to resolve. Normal grief waxes and wanes. The acute symptoms are typically self-limited, although they may recur in mild form when triggered by some event, such as an anniversary or another loss. Pharmacotherapy is rarely necessary unless the bereaved person seems frozen in prolonged grief, or is expressing despair and suicidal thoughts, as described in the incorrect answer choices. Rituals of mourning and focused psychotherapy, especially interpersonal therapy, can facilitate the resolution of grief.

39. C. *request a joint visit with the patient and his wife.* It is unclear whether the stress in the marriage is contributing to the lack of sexual activity, or whether the lack of sexual activity is contributing to the marital stress. A joint visit with both the patient and his wife would help to clarify this issue and provide additional information about the sexual expectations of both partners. A joint visit also allows the provider to observe how the couple interacts, something that is not possible when interviewing the spouse separately. Because the patient has erections in the morning, a nocturnal penile tumescence study is not necessary. Saying that this is bound to happen trivializes the patient's concern. A change in sexual position is unlikely to resolve the low level of sexual frequency or the patient's reported impotence.

40. D. *refer for joint sex therapy with use of sensate focus.* This level of dysfunction is not a normal part of aging. A middle-aged man should be able to continue to perform sexually for as long as he wishes to do so. Penile implant seems unnecessary given that the patient has spontaneous erections in the morning. Other partners are less likely to help the couple function sexually together than they are to cause them to abandon their relationship. The squeeze technique is used to treat premature ejaculation, which is not this patient's problem.

41. D. *stereotyping.* Dr. J. has stereotyped or generally applied a set of characteristics to a group of people. He has made generalizations based on some observations but failed to consider individual differences. Bias would indicate that Dr. J. is inclined to behave in a positive or negative manner toward Chinese patients. Bigotry and intolerance connote rejection and prejudice. The term *stigmatizing* implies he places a lower value on Chinese patients than on others. Although Dr. J. has generalized a few characteristics to a group of people, his statements do not clearly show bias, intolerance, bigotry, or stigma.

42. A. *alcohol* is the most frequently abused drug at all ages and in all occupational groups. Surveys of medical students suggest they are more likely to abuse alcohol than are their peers in other educational programs. Less than 20% of medical students smoke, and anonymous surveys show that even fewer use the other drugs listed as options. Most physicians who abuse other drugs also abuse alcohol. In considering use rather than abuse, it appears that caffeine is the drug used most often by medical students.

43. C. *A recently diagnosed terminally ill patient is in the hospital.* Silence in this setting allows patients time to collect their thoughts and to ask whatever questions they may have. Just being present can help to assuage the fears of abandonment felt by some terminally ill patients. Substance abuse always requires a response when identified; silence only allows the problem to get worse. During a home visit with a clear goal, silence does not address the task at hand. Silence in the face of questions about sexual inadequacy may be misinterpreted by the patient as embarrassment on the part of the questioner. Substance abuse always

requires a response when it is identified; silence only allows the problem to get worse.

44. C. *Precontemplation.* She is not yet thinking about change, but she is thinking about thinking about it. This may seem like just putting it off, a type of procrastination, but procrastination is not recognized as a formal part of the stages of change model. If she were in the stage of contemplation, she would be actively thinking about change. To be in the stage of preparation, she would be making arrangements to facilitate change. For maintenance, she would be acting to keep changes in place once they have begun.

45. C. *daily rituals of the office staff and clinical providers* are important components of day-to-day practice. Although intangible, these social norms and mores are real and influence workplace atmosphere. Buildings and framed mission statements are solid physical things. The types of patients in the practice and the accountant who audits the practice are identifiable, concrete individuals.

46. C. *hiring them.* Because professionals expect to be able to define their own goals and the methods for achieving them, hiring decisions are critical. Whether or not a person gains entrée into an organization is the core control mechanism for managing professional conduct. Exclusion is the ultimate professional sanction. Professionals are expected to be self-motivated, to aspire to effectiveness, to gather the information they need, and to evaluate their performance by comparing themselves with their peers.

47. D. *master the mechanics of weight shifting.* Crawling is not a necessary preparation for walking. In fact, not all children learn to crawl. Object permanence is a milestone in cognitive development, not a prerequisite for the physical milestone of walking. Balance is important and continues to develop as children mature, but compared with the balance skills required to stand on tiptoes or bend to pick up an object, walking requires very minimal mastery of balance. Separation anxiety is generally a stage of socioemotional growth resolved by age 2; it is unrelated to walking.

48. C. *learned adaptive responses that contribute to survival are passed on to successive generations.* Better learning leads to better evolution-

ary survival. What is learned in one generation seems to be more easily learned in the next, suggesting that the learning is passed on. Genetic and environmental influences interact in complex ways that are difficult to separate. The interaction between genetics and environment changes as the individual moves through various developmental stages. This interaction is highlighted by the notion of so-called critical periods of development (e.g., brain growth spurt).

49. C. *L or lie scale.* The lie scale identifies those who are purposefully trying to avoid answering the test questions honestly and are answering in ways that are socially desirable but rarely practiced. The *infrequency scale* measures the tendency to give statistically rare responses (unusual or atypical), and serves as a check on random responding. The *correction scale* is used to identify psychopathology in those who would otherwise have profiles within normal range and allows mathematical adjustment of MMPI-2 scores to increase true positives. The *psychasthenia scale* assesses the ability to resist specific actions or thoughts, regardless of their maladaptive nature (obsessive-compulsive thoughts and behaviors). A *self-esteem scale* is not part of the MMPI-2.

50. E. *the opponent-process hypothesis* explains how a behavior that begins as a habit to achieve pleasure (positive reinforcement) needs to be sustained to avoid the pain of withdrawal (negative reinforcement). This hypothesized process underlies substance abuse and addictive behaviors. Avoidance–avoidance conflicts occur when one has to choose between the lesser of two evils. Cognitive dissonance occurs when a person performs a behavior contrary to an existing attitude and changes the attitude to match the manifest behavior. Intrinsic motivation occurs when behavior is reinforcing in its own right. Secondary reinforcement refers to a stimulus that is not directly reinforcing, but that can be exchanged for something that is reinforcing (e.g., in a token economy).

51. C. *"I'll order some pain medication and come back tomorrow to see if you'd like to talk then."* The patient needs to feel some control in this situation. Although the patient has the right to know everything, he also has the right to say he does not want to hear. Note that this does not mean that the physician

will withhold information indefinitely, only that the patient will be given time to prepare to receive the information. Going to a family member jeopardizes confidentiality, unless the patient requests this route of communication. Telling the patient what you think he is thinking seems intrusive and may trigger an angry response.

52. B. *Sequential stimulation of two adjacent neurons enhances the efficiency of their connecting synapse.* Protein kinase, and the structures mentioned (the hippocampus, the orbito-medial frontal cortex, and the cerebellum) are all associated with higher order learning and memory functions.

53. A. *formulation of internal mental symbols* is a hallmark of toddlerhood. Movement and sensation and performance of actions to achieve outcomes are most prominent in the earlier sensorimotor stage of development, though they persist into later phases. Around age 20 months, transitional objects begin to appear. Having mastered object permanence, the child need no longer rely simply on what is before them. Although some language is present at this age, it is not yet the organizing framework for mental representations. Instead, the child's representations are based on experiences and relationships, not on linguistic concepts given by others.

54. E. *SES is the factor that most strongly predicts experiencing poor health*, probably because of the stress of limited personal control over life circumstances. Low-income families in the US usually have basics such as food and clean water. Nevertheless, in the US, as in other countries, those with the lowest income have the highest morbidity and mortality. Results from the Whitehall studies of British civil servants confirmed that access to health care did not eliminate the adverse effects of low SES on health. While health-damaging behaviors are more common in those of low SES, these predict a smaller proportion of health problems than does SES itself.

55. B. *mental illness and substance abuse–related problems.* By some estimates, as many as 50% of all homeless suffer from mental illnesses or substance-related problems, primarily alcoholism. Mental illness and addiction may be the cause of the homelessness, or a result of coping with the stresses of homelessness, or

both. (Housing first programs that provide stable housing before offering treatment for addictions and mental illness are based on this understanding of the causes and effects of homelessness. They have been very successful in getting clients into stable living situations.) Note that as a group, homeless individuals are more likely to suffer from all of the options listed, but mental illness and substance use are most common.

56. A. *agoraphobia.* The patient displays anxiety, which the history suggests is related primarily to leaving the safe confines of his home. Patients with social phobia are more likely to fear being shamed or doing something to embarrass themselves in public. Dysthymia connotes depressive symptoms lasting more than 2 years. The patient lacks the global mistrust of paranoid personality disorder and the identifiable delusion of delusional disorder.

57. B. *benzodiazepines.* Abrupt withdrawal can produce delirium and seizures. Withdrawal from amphetamines produces fatigue and hunger. Withdrawal from heroin results in flu-like symptoms including nausea, diarrhea, shivering, and cramps. Hallucinogens and phencyclidine have no specific withdrawal effects.

58. A. *Fetishism* is recurrent and intense sexual arousal from either the use of, or highly specific focus on, nonliving objects or nongenital body parts not traditionally viewed as sexual – in this case, high-heeled shoes. The focus is manifested by fantasies, urges, or behavior. Fetishistic *disorder* requires that the affected patient experiences clinically significant distress or impairment in social, occupational, or other important areas of functioning as a result of the fantasies, sexual urges, or behaviors. In the case of the man in the question, he is not experiencing distress as a result of having fetishism. However, there is a mismatch in sexual desire and sexual satisfaction between the husband and wife. In masochism, a person experiences sexual arousal by being humiliated, beaten, bound, or otherwise made to suffer as manifested by fantasies, urges, or behavior. In contrast, a sadist gains sexual arousal from the physical or psychological suffering of another individual. A transvestite is a person, typically male, who feels intense sexual arousal from dressing in clothing of the opposite sex.

59. A. *bipolar disorder.* This patient matches the DSM-5 criteria for bipolar disorder, current episode manic. The distinguishing features are grandiosity, talkativeness, flight of ideas, distractibility, excessive involvement in activities, and decreased need for sleep for at least 1 week. *Hyper*thyroidism is possible, but not *hypo*thyroidism, which would be associated with decreased activity, sluggishness, and an increased need for sleep. Narcissistic personality disorder is characterized by a life-long, pervasive pattern of seeing oneself as special and deserving of privilege (entitlement). A person with obsessive-compulsive disorder would have recurrent intrusive thoughts, sometimes paired with ritualistic behaviors. The patient does not display characteristics of dementia, and her age makes vascular dementia, in particular, unlikely.

60. E. *lithium carbonate*, the treatment of choice for long-term control of bipolar disorder. Note that lithium must be taken consistently and at close-to-toxic levels to be efficacious. Chlorpromazine is an antipsychotic, but due to its side effects, it is not recommended for the log-term treatment of this condition. Clonazepam and diazepam are antianxiety medications. Fluoxetine is one of the selective serotonin reuptake inhibitors (SSRIs), a common treatment for depression and obsessive-compulsive disorder.

61. C. *Regression,* returning to an earlier level of functioning. The girl has lost the capacity to control her bladder as she returns to the wished-for infant state. Regression is common in children when siblings are born into the household. Projection refers to experiencing one's own thoughts or emotions as coming from others in the external world. Reaction formation suggests a reversal, doing the opposite of what one really feels. Sublimation is diverting unacceptable drives into personally and socially acceptable channels. Undoing is a ritual reversal which "fixes" or repairs what is wrong, in the sense that obsessive-compulsive hand washing "fixes" the feeling of being dirty.

62. A. *advise the mother about helping the child cope with life transitions.* The regression response should abate as the girl learns other means of coping, feels valued in participating in her brother's care, and receives positive reinforcement for attending school. As this child had already been toilet trained for several years,

the condition she is experiencing is "secondary enuresis" (resumption of enuresis after 6 or more months of urinary continence). Underlying psychological processes should be suspected if this occurs during a period of stress. The likely source of the stress needs to be identified and help extended to assist her in coping with it more effectively. Simply waiting does not address the problem. Imipramine could be a proper pharmacological choice, but should not be given without an exploration of the child's life circumstances. Changing kindergarten classes is unlikely to resolve the issue: The source of the problem is separation from home, not problems with the school environment. The child already knows that enuresis is "bad" and is probably embarrassed by it. Merely talking to her about what is an unconscious response is unlikely to be effective and may worsen her psychological distress.

63. C. *is showing developmental age and gender appropriate behavior.* The clothing is her parent's, not her, choice. She would not be expected to be able to identify herself by gender until about age 3. The truck does not have any gender-specific meaning for her, but is merely an object that is fun to move. This behavior does not suggest either a gender identity problem or a tendency toward homosexuality. Her social behavior gives no clues as to her level of shyness later in life, or the presence or absence of siblings at home.

64. A. *borderline* best matches the following DSM-5 criteria: unstable mood and self-image, self-damaging or self-sabotaging impulsivity, unstable but intense interpersonal relationships, self-mutilation, and suicidal gestures. Some traits of histrionic personality, especially intense emotional expression and overestimation of the intimacy in relationships, overlap with those seen in borderline personality. Other histrionic qualities, such as the wish to be the center of attention, seductiveness, and suggestibility, are not described in this vignette. Narcissism is manifested by presenting oneself as grand and omnipotent. Paranoid personality connotes a life-long pattern of pervasive mistrust of other people and situations. Schizoid individuals just want to be left alone.

65. E. *individual cognitive behavioral therapy.* Treatments that combine mindfulness, social skills training, and cognitive reframing of emotional reactions have proven effective in modifying the thoughts, emotions, and behaviors of people diagnosed as borderline. Alprazolam is an anxiolytic not indicated for use in this condition because psychotherapy is the treatment of choice. Behavior modification targets specific behaviors; it is effective by itself for phobias and a useful part of treatment for autism and many other conditions, but it does not address the psychological and emotional qualities of this personality disorder. Family therapy might be a useful adjunct to individual therapy, but should not be the primary approach. Group therapy is more appropriate for treating posttraumatic stress disorder, substance abuse recovery, and providing coping support.

66. D. *fundamental attribution error* is a cognitive disposition that involves minimizing the role of external factors and ascribing the cause of an individual's behavior or situation to their character or personality. Anchoring is the tendency to focus on a preliminary conclusion and not explore alternatives. Availability bias is the tendency to use easily recalled information in forming judgments. Confirmation bias is the tendency to seek information to confirm rather than refute an hypothesis. Stigmatization is assigning negative qualities to a person based on perceived differences from the general population. All are cognitive dispositions that can lead to medical errors.

67. C. *learned helplessness* is an acquired response to adversity that leads individuals to believe that they do not have control over their experiences and are powerless to change them. Denial is a defense mechanism that involves a failure to acknowledge or accept information or the reality of an experience. Histrionic personality disorder is characterized by excessive emotionality and excessive needs for attention. Obstinacy is the trait of being stubborn or perversely adhering to an unreasonable opinion. Regression is a defense mechanism involving reversion to developmentally earlier means of managing stress.

68. E. *Voyeuristic disorder.* Voyeurism is intense and recurrent sexual arousal from observing an unsuspecting person who is naked, undressing, or engaged in sexual activity, as manifested by fantasies, urges, or behaviors. In voyeuristic disorder, the individual with voy-

eurism has acted on these sexual urges with a nonconsenting person, or the sexual urges or fantasies cause clinically significant distress or impairment in social, occupational, or other important areas of functioning. In the case of the individual described in this vignette, the voyeuristic behavior is a disorder because the individual has both acted on his fantasies with a nonconsenting person and lost his job as a result of absenteeism because of the voyeuristic behavior. Exhibitionism is defined as intense and recurrent sexual arousal from exposure of genitals to an unsuspecting person. Fetishism is recurrent and intense sexual arousal from either the use of or highly specific focus on nonliving objects or nongenital body parts not traditionally viewed as sexual. In frotteuristic disorder, a person has acted on sexual urges to touch or rub, especially the genitals, against a nonconsenting person, or the sexual urges or fantasies regarding doing to cause clinically significant distress or impairment in social, occupational, or other important areas of functioning.

69.	B.	*frontal lobes.* Reduction in frontal lobe metabolism during the WCST (so called "hypofrontality') is a common finding in schizophrenia. The WCST involves working memory and requires the individual to classify items (e.g., into animals or birds), and then to change the classification system based on rule changes in the task (e.g., into animals and birds that are herbivores or carnivores). The cerebellum regulates movement and influences certain types of memory. The occipital lobes primarily process visual information. Parietal lobe dysfunctions involve agraphia, acalculia, and constructional apraxias. The temporal lobes are involved in the production of schizophrenic symptoms, but are not the primary locus of the cognitive dysfunction measured by the WCST.

70.	E.	*influence health, illness, and therapy.* Culture has a significant impact on all human interactions, including beliefs about health and disease, expectations of others, and behavioral practices relevant to clinical encounters. It should be taken into consideration when diseases and possible therapies are being identified or evaluated. The role of the health care provider and the culture of medicine may supersede other culturally influenced beliefs or behaviors. Thus, culturally incongruent providers can be effective and acceptable in

many situations, as long as they remain sensitive to cultural differences. Although cultural qualities may be quite stable and transmitted down generations, they are learned, not genetic. Far from being unchangeable, they evolve over time and in response to environmental challenges, including the challenges of illness and dealing with the medical system.

71.	C.	*a steady increase in the size of ethnic minority populations.* The average age of the White population is increasing, not decreasing. The population is projected to grow over the coming decades, although at a slower rate than in the past. Expected demographic changes include an increase in all minority populations to the point that Whites will make up less than 50% of the total population in the mid-21st century. Because the US population is becoming increasingly ethnically diverse, culture will remain a highly significant factor in the delivery of health care.

72.	C.	*high blood and hypertension are examples of how interpretations of body symptoms are culturally influenced.* Folk illness or culture-bound syndromes are ailments that are explained by coherent, culturally specific concepts of etiology, pathophysiology, and treatment. Symptoms may express both models of biological function and symbolize mental or social distress (as when they are attributed to disturbing events or relational tensions). Folk illnesses and culture-bound syndromes are not a separate category of phenomena, nor are they manifestations of exotic belief systems. All people interpret signs and symptoms within a cultural framework. Biomedical concepts and folk illness concepts may be congruent or contradictory. In the case presented, the patient's signs and symptoms have the culturally divergent labels of hypertension and "high blood." Regardless of how a conventionally trained provider views an illness, labeling other people's beliefs as superstitious is degrading. Working with patients' views of their malady is most likely to result in development of an effective treatment plan.

73.	B.	*explore the possibility that the mother believes that your recommendations will make the child worse.* Chastising the mother, notifying Child Protective Services, and hospitalizing the child are incorrect strategies. They do not address the basic problem: failure to communicate across cultures. All of these approaches are likely to alienate the mother and make it less likely that she will be receptive to negotiating therapeutic plans for her child or any other family member in the future. Referring the mother for education may be appropriate at some time, but as an initial step, it simply passes off the patient to someone else without addressing the problem.

74. D. *Popular* sector. The term *folk* sector refers to secular or sacred healers who have authority throughout a community. The *professional* sector refers to health care providers who are licensed and sanctioned by the government. *Paraprofessionals* and *pharmaceutical healers* are not part of the usual categorization of healers (popular, folk, and professional) described by Arthur Kleinman.

75. A. *extinction.* The child's crying stops or is extinguished by the mother's consistent behavior in leaving him after brief reassurance. Intermittent reinforcement occurs when some, but not every, response is reinforced. Maturation suggests that behavior change results simply from a natural developmental process. Shaping is the process of shifting reinforcements to gradually eliminate all but the desired responses. Sublimation is a psychological defense mechanism in which unacceptable impulses are satisfied by channeling them into socially acceptable avenues

76. D. *justice.* Justice refers to the fair administration of medical services and most closely applies to this case presentation. In contrast, beneficence is acting in the best interests of patients, fidelity is faithfulness to one's duties and obligations as a professional, honesty is truthfulness in dealing with patients, and non-maleficence is not harming patients.

77. C. *legitimize withdrawal from regular activities and requests for assistance.* The *sick role* is a social construct characterized by Talcott Parsons. It includes several elements, including the requirement that others must agree that a person is sick before they are eligible for special treatment. The incorrect answers relate to medically defined conditions or situations, not the social role of illness.

78. A. *choice of healers.* This choice includes the ethnic background of the provider, how that provider is viewed within the patient's particular cultural community, and how the pro-

vider understands and responds to the patient's belief system. Desire for good health and physiological response are found across ethnic groups. Type of health insurance and willingness to work are not typically culturally linked.

79. D. *Gender dysphoria.* Formerly known as gender identity disorder, gender dysphoria is defined by persistent feelings of experiencing a marked incongruence between one's experienced and expressed gender and primary or secondary sex characteristics; a strong desire to be rid of one's primary or secondary sex characteristics because of a marked incongruence with one's experienced and expressed gender; a strong desire for the primary or secondary sex characteristics of the other gender; a strong desire to be, and be treated as, the other gender; a strong conviction that one has the typical feelings and reactions of the other gender; and clinically significant distress or impairment associated with these feelings and desires. Body dysmorphic disorder is characterized by obsessive focus on a perceived flaw in appearance that is not observable or appears slight to others; at some point in the disorder the person has performed repetitive behaviors or mental acts in response to the appearance concerns. Delusional disorder requires the presence of one or more delusions (fixed beliefs that are not amenable to change in light of conflicting evidence) with a duration of 1 month or longer in the absence of other characteristic symptoms of schizophrenia. With somatic type delusions, the central theme usually involves bodily functions or sensations. Fetishism is recurrent and intense sexual arousal from either the use of, or a highly specific focus on, nonliving objects or nongenital body parts not traditionally viewed as sexual. In transvestism, a person, typically male, feels pleasure from dressing in clothing of the opposite sex.

80. C. *being his own genuine self, knowing that patients will understand what he means.* Effective education and skill development require that we learn about ourselves as cultural beings, which includes being aware of our personal biases and prejudices. It is vital to recognize patients as cultural beings, learn patient-centered communication skills, and be aware of potential abuses of power. Effective communication often requires giving up elements of our preferred "genuine" selves in

exchange for adapting our approach to fit patients' preferred styles.

81. A. *American Indians: pausing less than a few seconds for a reply to a question conveys lack of interest.* For some Arab patients, giving things with the left hand is revolting because the left hand is symbolically dirty, while the right hand is symbolically clean. Other cultural groups, such as Asians, feel that direct eye contact is invasive and disrespectful; instead, intermittent eye-to-eye contact with periods of looking away communicates respect. Speaking loudly to Asians can be experienced as an expression of anger. Looking someone eye-to-eye to communicate interest is typical of the Eurowestern culture.

82. B. *The dietitian's recommendation was incorrect because a 4-year-old child should not consume more than 900 kcal/day.* This statement is false. According to the recommendations of the American Academy of Pediatrics, which are consistent with the USDA's Dietary Guidelines for Americans, the estimated daily intake necessary for a 4-year-old female is 1,200 kcal. This estimate is based on a child who is sedentary; up to an additional 400 kcal/day may be necessary for a child who is physically active. The remaining choices (A, C, D, and E) are all, in fact, potential explanations for this child's excessive weight gain. Although there is conflicting evidence for this, several research studies have shown a positive relationship between fat intake (total fat and percentage of calories from fat) and body mass index and body fat percentage among children, independent of total calorie intake. Error in parental reporting of children's intake is an inherent limitation of the study of children's diets. It is also possible for the child to be consuming more calories than the mother is aware of, especially when the child is not under her supervision. It is entirely possible, and even highly likely, that the mother's journal of her child's diet contains inaccuracies, either due to incorrectly recording portion sizes, not having proper nutrition facts, or any of a number of other reasons.

83. B. *Lithium.* This woman presents with mania, for which the treatment of choice is a mood stabilizer such as lithium. Lithium and valproic acid are considered first-line mood stabilizers. Buspirone is a unique serotonergic medication used to treat generalized anxiety. Lorazepam

is a benzodiazepine, and zolpidem is an hypnotic and used for anxiety. Either might help sedate her, but would not address the mania itself. Sertraline is a selective serotonin reuptake inhibitor (SSRI), and is used for depression and anxiety, especially panic. An antidepressant alone should not be used in patients with bipolar illness without a mood stabilizing agent like lithium, or an anticonvulsant such as Depakote (divalproex sodium) or carbamazepine, or a second-generation antipsychotic medication, due to the risk of precipitating mania.

84. B. *immediately inform him of his condition.* Studies have shown that terminally ill patients prefer to be told of their condition without delay. However, care providers may shy away from this discussion because it makes them feel uncomfortable. Being informed allows patients to make plans that can considerably benefit both patients and their survivors. Fears that knowledge will lead to patient decompensation and agony are largely unfounded. Mr. E. is the person responsible for telling relatives about his disease and only if he wants them to know. To encourage Mr. E. to buy life insurance before telling him about his disease is blatantly dishonest, toward both Mr. E. and the insurance company.

85. D. *consider that they may be suffering from a culturally specific syndrome, perhaps related to the stress of immigration.* Telling symptomatic patients that they are not sick fails to acknowledge that cultural and psychological factors may be playing a significant role in their problem. Making assumptions about working the system or malingering represents negative stereotyping of the community. Quarantine is a drastic, disruptive measure reserved only for transmissible infectious diseases.

86. A. *Boundaries.* The family structure consists of such organizing characteristics as boundaries, triangles, and subsystems. Communication style, parentification, scapegoating, and family secret are components of family processes or patterns of interaction, not structures.

87. A. *boundaries around individuals within the system are closed.* Disengaged families have less permeable boundaries between individuals than more interactive families. Thus, other family members are less likely to be aware of and influenced by individual stresses or joys.

The boundaries around the entire family system, however, vary and would not necessarily be closed. The term *disengaged* is more correctly applied to all the members rather than just the father. Answers D and E are descriptive of enmeshed families.

88. C. *nonspecific therapeutic effects.* The patient's treatment regimen at the medical center was identical to the regimen at her local hospital. Therefore, symptom changes due to nutritional supplements, placebo effects, and specific effects of treatment are unlikely. Although symptom severity may fluctuate because of the natural history of the disease, significant fluctuations in later stages of metastatic breast cancer are not typical. The probable cause for improvement in the patient's symptoms is the nonspecific therapeutic effect associated with being treated at an impressive and renowned, tertiary medical center. It is likely that this improvement is being mediated through a greater sense of hope, increased confidence in her health caregivers, and a diminished sense of anxiety. It closely resembles a placebo response, but that term is typically reserved for a person's response to an inactive treatment.

89. B. *combining technical expertise and effective human relations skills to be a "total" clinician.* All professional health care disciplines require mastery of both art and science. The art involves understanding human nature, how people perceive events, and what motivates their behavior. The science involves understanding physiological functioning, how to diagnose diseases or disorders, and the pathophysiology of a variety of conditions to make judgments about appropriate treatment. Applying the art of medical care to the science of medicine permits professionals to interpret signs and symptoms in a given individual and negotiate a treatment plan that has the best chance of success.

90. B. *motor vehicle accidents* account for approximately 50% of adolescent deaths. Successful educational interventions would include not driving while under the influence of alcohol or drugs, not driving late at night, not driving with several friends in the car, driving at safe speeds, and wearing a seat belt. Adolescents' sense of personal invulnerability ("It can't happen to me") makes them especially prone to recklessness and "death defying" behav-

ior. This attitude also makes them vulnerable to sexually transmitted diseases, homicide, suicide, and various forms of abuse. The incidence of mortality associated with these problems, however, pales in comparison with that from motor vehicle accidents.

91. B. *boy is probably not dreaming while he is walking in his sleep.* Sleepwalking (somnambulism) occurs in delta (Stage 4) sleep. Most dreams occur in REM sleep, a different stage of the sleep cycle. If awakened while sleepwalking, the boy will be groggy and have a difficult time waking up (deep delta sleep). There is no evidence that changing the time of going to sleep affects somnambulism. Assigning meaning to the somnambulism is strictly speculative, although talking with the boy will likely reveal he has some anxiety when he is awake.

92. C. *Instrumental.* In some approaches to family sociology, men are traditionally seen as performing more goal-directed, task-oriented roles, while women perform more socioemotional caretaking roles. In more recent times, familial roles have been in flux with a move toward more symmetry between gender roles. In some relationships, this change has been accompanied by increasing competitiveness between fathers and mothers who share breadwinning and child-rearing duties.

93. C. *Haloperidol.* Extrapyramidal symptoms, including tardive dyskinesia, are neurological symptoms caused by side effects of antipsychotic medications, including haloperidol. Tardive dyskinesia, as described in the vignette, involves involuntary movements of the tongue, lips, face, and hands. The trunk and extremities may also be involved. The movements are typically not subjectively distressing, but they are disfiguring and usually irreversible. Tardive dyskinesia is more likely to occur when higher doses of medication (especially first-generation antipsychotics) are used over a long period of time. However, it can occasionally occur as a result of treatment with second-generation antipsychotics as well. It is more common in women than in men. Other extrapyramidal symptoms include acute dystonias (e.g., brief, often painful muscle contractions). The treatment of acute dystonia usually involves an anticholinergic medication, such as benztropine, or an antihistamine like diphenhydramine. Lorazepam is an anti-

anxiety medication and does not cause tardive dyskinesia. Sertraline is a selective serotonin reuptake inhibitor (SSRI) that is used in the treatment of depression. SSRIs do not cause tardive dyskinesia, although they can cause dyskinesias that typically resolve with dose reduction or discontinuation.

94. C. *Schizoaffective disorder.* Schizoaffective disorder is characterized by the patient meeting the diagnostic criteria for schizophrenia plus major depression or mania. The total duration of illness must be 6 months or longer, and for at least 2 weeks during the lifetime of the illness, the patient must have schizophrenia symptoms without mood symptoms to meet the criteria. In this case, the woman has had delusions, auditory hallucinations, and ideas of reference for a year, with signs of mania (decreased need for sleep, elevated mood, rapid speech, and increase in risk-taking behavior) for only 2 weeks. A diagnosis of schizophrenia would include all but the affective symptoms this patient has experienced. The criteria for schizophreniform disorder specify psychotic symptoms (and other elements of schizophrenia) that last between 1 to 6 months. Bipolar disorder with psychosis is incorrect because the psychotic symptoms preceded and *occurred in the absence of mood symptoms.* In bipolar disorder with psychotic features, the psychotic features primarily occur during the mood episode. In brief psychotic disorder, symptoms last less than 1 month.

95. E. *Scapegoated.* Scapegoating (identifying an individual as the sole source of a problem), may dissipate tension or stress in a family, thus deflecting attention from other problems and reducing the probability that the family will enlist outside help. In the case presented, the girl and her difficulties at school have become the focus of parental attention and frustration so that they do not have to deal with other problems – for instance, a dysfunctional marital relationship. The term *scapegoat* is biblical in origin and refers to the archaic practice of symbolically placing the sins of a community on the head of a goat and driving the goat into the wilderness.

96. C. *Expectancy.* The woman has come to expect (learned) that something (smoking) and gratification are associated. Arousal theory focuses on the need for the organism to maintain an optimal, but personally comfortable, level of activation. Drive theory focuses on the motivational influences of survival instincts such as the need for food, water, air, or sex. Humanistic theory focuses on the desire for self-actualization and self-expression. Sociocultural theory points out that the impetus for many behaviors can be linked to the social and cultural milieu in which they occur.

97. E. *reinforcement experience.* Past experience with reinforcement determines what consequences are expected for present behaviors. The past is the best, although not always accurate, predictor of the future. Belief system refers to the patient's personal, culturally derived sense of how the world works. Cultural systems are the source for belief systems about how the world and disease states work. Family history is often a key indicator of susceptibility to particular diseases, but not of patient adherence. Homeostasis is a seeking of equilibrium both within the organism and between the organism and the environment.

98. B. *female spouses are more likely to consider family obligations when selecting practices.* While divorce rates in dual-physician marriages are lower than in the general population, women physicians often place a higher priority on family and childbearing responsibilities than men do. As a consequence, female physicians experience interruptions in training time, lower salaries, and part-time employment more frequently than their male counterparts.

99. B. *Higher, due to the prejudice and discomfort he elicits in his peers.* Homosexual men have higher rates of suicidal behavior, especially in adolescence, compared with heterosexual peers. This appears to be related to the stigma and discrimination that they face. Such discrimination disrupts the supportive peer relationships that are crucial to the well-being and self-esteem of teenagers. Although achieving the capacity for intimacy is thought to be a somewhat later developmental imperative, opportunities to imagine and experiment with sexual relations are also crucial to adolescent self-esteem and identity development. In the absence of peer support, homosexuality makes this developmental task more complex. Additionally, the boy may have few opportunities to meet appropriate partners and a dearth of positive role models. Internalized homophobia (self-hatred for

one's sexual orientation) is not necessarily a feature of homosexuality. When homophobia is found, it is typically related to the degree of nonacceptance and discrimination that the person has experienced in their social environment growing up. Nonviolence and female patterns of suicidal behavior are not particularly associated with homosexuality in men. Homosexuality is not clearly associated with cognitive maturity, and, in fact, awareness of sexual orientation often predates adolescence.

100. E. *Socioemotional.* In most cultures, women have been trained to take primary responsibility for raising and socializing children (i.e., teaching them how to behave acceptably within their community and larger society) and fostering the emotional qualities (e.g., good self-esteem) necessary for them to become contributing members of wider socioeconomic and political groups.

101. E. *unexplained nature of events.* Young children view illness and associated noxious treatments as punishment. Many studies have shown that when they are provided with simple explanations about why they are sick and why certain therapies are necessary, they become less anxious and more cooperative, even when painful procedures (venipuncture, intramuscular injections) must be performed. Disappointments about limitation of activity and removal from friends can be overcome by providing alternative distractions. People of any age usually enjoy the dependency on others allowed by being ill, if it is short term. Children who are sick fear separation from parents but usually do not fear loss of affection.

102. D. *helplessness.* Helplessness ("I'm such a wreck I just can't do anything for anybody, including myself") is often the most difficult emotion for a patient to tolerate. It is easier to actively experience anger ("I'm so mad that I have to be sick during the holidays!"), guilt ("I should have gotten a flu shot"), or blame someone ("My sister gave this to me when she visited last week") than to feel there is nothing one can do. Hopelessness would be an unusual reaction to a short-term, self-limited illness.

103. C. *practicing relaxation exercises.* Relaxation is the most effective coping strategy for a problem requiring patience. The other responses are more likely to create or increase frustra-

tion and anxiety for the patient, the physician, and others, none of whom can change the circumstances. Some patients use waiting time to seek information. In the absence of a diagnosis, this behavior can lead to erroneous conclusions and unnecessary worries.

104. A. *involves the association of sensory stimuli with sequential motor system responses.* Implicit learning is felt by some to be the most primitive type of learning, and to form the foundation for all other learning. Implicit learning can occur below the level of the person's awareness. Implicit learning is made up only of simple experienced associations, not higher level cognitive processes, and therefore does not require higher order cortical functioning. Finally, implicit learning occurs over a short span of time after the experience of a sensation, which is then followed by motor action.

105. A. *Elements of his built and social environment may both aid and constrain his ability to maintain a healthy weight.* Living in a low-income neighborhood, with high availability of cheap unhealthy food, long work hours and job stress, and cultural norms that encourage the consumption of certain foods – often in excess – can all contribute to Mr. S.'s adoption of obesity-promoting behaviors. On the other hand, working in an environment that is supportive of healthy lifestyle choices may influence him toward behaviors that will help him maintain a healthy weight. This illustrates a concept called *risk regulation*. Although poor dietary intake and lack of physical activity are the actual *risk factors* for obesity, risk regulators are those factors that either present opportunities for, or impose constraints on, those behaviors. Since Mr. S. is 6 feet tall, the increase is his BMI over 3 years indicates that he has gained about 8 lb (3.6 kg) each year, which is not necessarily normal or healthy. The weight gain is likely to continue into overweight (if not obesity) if he does not change something about his lifestyle. Since the company gym opened only 6 months ago, the increase in BMI cannot be a result of Mr. S.'s lunchtime workouts producing this degree of muscle mass. Additionally, the company's workplace wellness program indicates that not all parts of his built environment promote unhealthy behaviors. Despite his family history and having grown up in an environment that encouraged overconsumption, Mr. S. is not necessarily destined to become obese.

106. A. *alopecia due to chemotherapy.* Hypnosis, a form of therapeutic communication in which patients learn to focus their attention on one area and reduce their focus on others, has a long history of usefulness in medicine. The systems most susceptible to psychological factors such as imagery, focus, and suggestion are the autonomic nervous system, the endocrine system, and the immune system. The autonomic nervous system influences muscle tone, vital signs, and gastrointestinal function, making hypnosis helpful in irritable bowel syndrome, nausea, and chronic pain, especially headaches and pain involving muscle spasm. Effects on the immune system may account for the impact of hypnosis on the course of herpes outbreaks. Smoking cessation is improved by reduction in anxiety, refocusing away from discomfort, and imagining a positive outcome. Hypnosis may reduce pain, nausea, and anxiety in patients receiving chemotherapy, but it does not affect hair loss.

107. A. *actively solve problems.* Illness-specific groups allow members to use their own experience to help each other handle the practical challenges and negative emotions associated with chronic conditions. They support both *problem-focused coping* and *emotion-focused coping.* Group members are unlikely to forget their illness, the major topic they come to discuss. The group works together to maintain optimism, not to simply accept the worst. Learning that others are worse off provides small comfort because the patient may eventually deteriorate herself. Being in a group of peers relieves patients of the burden of maintaining a façade of cheerful bravery, often expected by others who do not have the disease.

108. E. *understand that the patient may need more time to adjust.* Denial may represent an important coping mechanism for the patient at this early stage of knowing about his diagnosis and prognosis. Stripping away the patient's coping mechanism at this moment can accentuate his discomfort. It would alienate the patient to force him to "see the truth" until he is ready to do so.

109. C. *Relaxation training.* A patient who feels that the mind and body are separate is more likely to accept any kind of physical treatment (surgery, injections or pills, even antidepressants, if they are explained as affecting the body) than an obviously mind-oriented therapy such as relaxation training.

110. A. *acceptable.* Care may be accessible and available, but will not be used if it is unacceptable to a given patient. Acceptability requires that the patient and provider communicate in the same language, that care is delivered with compassion, and that cultural beliefs and practices of the patient are respected. If the quantity of available care is commensurate with the need, but the care is unacceptable to the patient even if it is appropriate (culturally syntonic) within the patient's community, the care provided still cannot be considered adequate because a specific patient may prefer to receive culturally divergent care. Thus, good communication between the patient and the provider is essential to giving acceptable care.

111. D. *MDMA/ecstasy.* MDMA is a synthetic drug structurally similar to both amphetamine and mescaline. It is known for its mood-enhancing, hallucinogenic, and stimulant effects that lead to increases in positive mood, trust, and energy as well as heart rate and blood pressure. The increases in energy its users experience can lead to overexertion, tachycardia, hyperthermia, cardiovascular collapse, and death. Alcohol, hydrocodone (opiate), and lorazepam (benzodiazepine) intoxication would all have either no effect on, or actually lower, heart rate and blood pressure and be unlikely to lead to excessive energy. Marijuana intoxication is also not associated with excessive energy.

112. E. *reassurance.* Many patients (sometimes called "the worried well") see a physician seeking reassurance. Their needs can often be met with periodic, scheduled office visits to give them a chance to discuss their health concerns without having to manufacture an illness. If this does not seem to solve the problem as expected, it would be appropriate to probe for deeper psychological problems, which the patient may be reluctant to disclose or feel to be outside the purview of medical treatment. While some patients do seek prescriptions and work excuses, this is less common than needing simple reassurance about health status. Many patients with minor complaints are not particularly interested in a precise diagnosis for their problem.

113. B. *family.* In these family-centered cultures, the family is the primary decision-making body; lesser roles are played by the patient, the health care provider, and the community. In certain circumstances, a religious leader may

be consulted, but the family makes the decision. Providers should be aware that decisions about seeking care, who will be consulted, and adherence with treatment recommendations will reflect collective, extended family discussions requiring more time and repeated explanations to achieve consensus.

114. C. *the subjective experience of stress associated with the event* is the major determinant of the impact a stressor will have. Different people will assess the magnitude of an event differently. The effect of other variables – how many people are involved, the type of change that accompanies the event, and whether the event is positive or negative – all depend on the meaning of the event for the person involved.

115. B. *dependent on technology.* A hospital death is more likely to involve "high technology," whereas a hospice death strives to involve friends and family, emphasizes pain control and palliation, and focuses on the process of death as a natural occurrence rather than as something to be fought and avoided. Religious practices should be respected equally in both settings.

116. E. *such experiences are common in grieving people.* People who are grieving often report that they have seen the dead person or that they have heard the dead person speak to them. These experiences are usually comforting. These events are not episodes of psychosis requiring hospitalization or further formal psychological intervention. Persons experiencing normal grief are not depressed and do not need to be medicated.

117. E. *suicide.* Suicide is the most difficult death to grieve for because of the anger survivors feel toward the person who committed suicide for causing such pain. In addition, survivors may feel overwhelming guilt for not recognizing the depth of the person's despair or otherwise stopping the suicide. The other types of deaths do not involve the same feelings of abandonment or responsibility in the bereaved.

118. B. *the patient has all necessary information before deciding to undergo medical treatment.* Informed consent focuses on the right of the patient to decide about a plan of care, after being provided with all relevant information. Informed consent does not permit withholding any information and does not pertain to providing all information to one or more family members, unless the patient so wishes or is incompetent to make decisions and has appointed a surrogate decision maker.

119. A. *3 months.* The risk of death for the survivor after the death of a spouse is 30% to 90% within the first 3 months, then about 15% in the months thereafter. Death due to cardiac problems is especially likely. Suicide is also prominent among older spouses who were married for many years. The suicide may take the form of inanition, or a lack of desire to continue living, manifested by not eating or not taking essential medications. Such a death may not be recognized as suicide.

120. C. *enhance sexual experience.* The hypoxia from using amyl nitrate ("poppers") is reported to increase the intensity of sexual experience. The mechanism appears to be the same as in autoerotic asphyxiation, which is frequently achieved by masturbating while hanging.

121. B. *Stage 2.* Teeth grinding, or bruxism, occurs during Stage 2, the most common type of sleep. Bruxism is associated with anxiety while awake, which may not be recognized by the patient. When this anxiety is identified and resolved, the bruxism usually abates. Most other sleep disorders (somnambulism, night terrors, enuresis) are associated with Stage 4 sleep. The pathology of narcolepsy is linked to the mechanisms that produce REM sleep.

122. A. *called him grandfather.* You, as the provider, did some things well, such as calling the man by a family title respectful of his position (grandfather). Other positive steps were speaking in laypersons' terms and asking open-ended questions about their perceptions of the problem early in the interaction. The remainder of the comments described, however, could have caused problems. The nonverbal cues meant to improve communication could have the opposite effect. Direct eye contact can feel rude, like staring. Asians, in particular, may communicate respect through brief intermittent eye contact. To say he will go blind unless he does as advised may be interpreted as the provider putting a curse on him. Also, he was not asked how he would feel about receiving an organ transplant. To some individuals, regardless of culture, the idea of having the body part of someone

else implanted is frightening and emotionally disturbing. Certain religious groups (e.g., Jehovah's Witnesses) explicitly prohibit this practice (and many Asians in the US belong to Christian denominations). Lastly, the daughter-in-law's final comment implies that, in this family, the patient's adult son has decisional authority. He may want to sign any consent form as well.

123. A. *Antisocial*. Although the information given does not list all of the formal criteria for this diagnosis, the man's criminal background and lack of regret combined with his charming manner are suggestive of antisocial personality disorder (Cluster B). A person who has borderline personality disorder is characterized by unstable affect and relationships. Someone who is histrionic tends to be flamboyant. A person with paranoid personality disorder approaches the world and everyone in it with mistrust. People with schizotypal personality disorder are strange or eccentric and often avoided by others because of these eccentricities.

124. B. *intellectualization*. To deal with the personal distress and anxiety she feels, the student strips away the affect of this emotionally charged encounter and replaces it with academic content that is emotionally irrelevant to the patient. In other words, the student substitutes cognition for affect and empathy. Denial refers to refusing to accept some clear feature of external reality. Simply removing the expression of affect would be isolation. Reaction formation entails acting opposite to actual, but unconscious, feeling and desires. Sublimation refers to gratifying an unacceptable impulse by acting in a socially acceptable manner.

125. A. *Death of a spouse*. The Holmes and Rahe Social Readjustment Rating Scale (SRRS or SRS) lists events in the past year that may require or precipitate life changes. It has been used extensively in studies of the relative impact of different events on health, rating them from 100 (most severe) to 11 (least severe). Ratings for different events may be added together to generate a score that predicts the likelihood of a stress-induced illness in the next 2 years. Events that disrupt important relationships have the most negative effects. The loss of a spouse through death has the most negative predictive value, espe-

cially for men, for whom spouses are often the primary source of social support and comfort. Divorce, which has a middle level rating, is likely to produce high levels of anger, which can, under some circumstances, be mobilizing. Although an automobile accident can be very stressful, it may not disrupt social support to the same degree as death or divorce. Though incarceration or loss of a job do affect social status and material support, such stresses still engender less health risk than the loss of a relationship. (The SRS does not list a number of events that other research has shown may adversely affect subsequent relationships and overall health. The omissions include victimization by violence [especially rape], military combat experience, and the impact of disaster).

126. A. *birth*. Although neuronal migration is virtually complete in the full-term newborn, the formation of dendrites and axons continues into childhood as the brain adapts to the environment. The number of dendrites peaks around puberty; after that, synaptic connections that are not used regularly disappear through dendritic pruning. New connections can be made until the time of death. Thus, contrary to the popular saying, you *can* teach an old dog new tricks!

127. C. *Benzodiazepine*. This woman is either experiencing withdrawal from alcohol or a sedative, typically a benzodiazepine. This type of withdrawal from either substance can be life threatening. Depending on the half-life of the substance, withdrawal appears between 12 and 72 or more hours of abstinence. Benzodiazepines treat both alcohol and sedative withdrawal. Different withdrawal protocols suggest a several day course of frequent, tapering doses with additional doses as needed contingent on vital sign and withdrawal symptom monitoring. Acamprosate is a unique drug that reduces the desire to drink alcohol, but does not treat acute withdrawal. Although antipsychotics are frequently used for agitation and hallucinations, they do not relieve the dangerously increased arousal of sedative withdrawal. The anticonvulsant mood stabilizers are sometimes used in sedative or alcohol withdrawal, but lithium would be dangerous and ineffective. Selective serotonin reuptake inhibitors (SSRIs) are used for the treatment of depression.

128. B. *classical conditioning.* The voice on the tape is similar to the bell used by Pavlov to induce salivation in a dog. The voice has become so closely associated with relaxation and sleep that it produces the reaction by itself, without the full relaxation routine. Biofeedback is a self-regulation intervention typically relying on graphical representation of a physiological parameter (e.g., heart rate or skin conductance) linked to a particular behavior. Inhibition is the mechanism that stops undesirable behaviors from occurring. Intermittent reinforcement refers to providing a positive or negative consequence irregularly rather than each time the target behavior occurs. Modeling is demonstrating a behavior.

129. A. *order a basal metabolic rate test to investigate if she is hypometabolic.* Persistent dieting may induce hypothalamic changes that down regulate the entire HPA axis. In such cases, both TSH (a pituitary hormone) and thyroid hormones remain relatively balanced. Peripheral measurements of thyroid function will be normal, but the patient is still hypometabolic. The direct test for hypometabolism involves feeding the patient a standard carbohydrate load and measuring exhaled CO2. The symptoms of hypometabolism resemble hypothyroidism. Paradoxically, increasing caloric intake may stimulate metabolism and allow for further weight loss. Patients may have trouble honestly estimating their intake of food (as they do with alcohol). Rather than confront the patient, however gently, it would be better to have her keep a detailed food record for a few days. In reviewing it with her, she may recognize the problem herself, rather than experiencing the humiliation of having it pointed out to her. Very-low-calorie diets are indicated primarily for people who are obese and need to lose weight quickly for medical reasons. Such diets must include behavioral and psychological support for losses to persist over time. Overeaters Anonymous is mainly for people who binge or describe themselves as emotional overeaters. The patient is already motivated to lose weight, and discussing health risks will likely just increase her sense of frustration and helplessness.

130. C. *increases GABA activity diffusely throughout the brain.* Gamma-aminobutyric acid (GABA) is an inhibitory transmitter. GABA and its precursor, glutamate, are found in about 70% of all brain synapses. Benzodiazepines bind to GABA chloride receptors, making more GABA available post synaptically. The increased availability of GABA reduces synaptic firing, thus reducing the felt sensation labeled as anxiety. Increases in norepinephrine are associated with a reduction in depressive symptoms. Excess dopamine is, among other things, associated with schizophrenia. Other medications that relieve anxiety (SSRIs, buspirone) reduce anxiety by raising post synaptic serotonin activity. Drugs that block acetylcholine may also be used for anxiety.

131. D. *Seizures.* Excess glutamate has long been associated with seizures. Severe hiccups are sometimes treated with neuroleptic medications (which block dopamine and acetylcholine) to suppress spasms of the diaphragm, which produce the hiccups. Manic activity is associated with high levels of norepinephrine and serotonin activity. Benzodiazepines, barbiturates, or other agents that increase GABA induce quiescence; excessive amounts of these agents can lead to hypersomnolence or coma.

132. C. *Nigrostriatal tract.* Dopamine is expressed in at least four neurological tracts labeled mesolimbic, mesocortical, tuberoinfundibular, and nigrostriatal. The nigrostriatal tract governs control of voluntary movement. Blocking dopamine activity in the mesolimbic or mesocortical tracts accounts for the antipsychotic properties of neuroleptic medications. Dopamine in the tuberoinfundibular tract inhibits the secretion of prolactin from the anterior pituitary gland. The neurons originating in the locus ceruleus express norepinephrine (a precursor of dopamine). The raphe nuclei are the source of brain serotonin, which regulates dopamine activity in many areas.

133. B. *cerebrospinal fluid.* To measure the relation between serotonin (5-HT) and behavior requires measuring its activity in the central nervous system (CNS). Its major breakdown product (5-HIAA) is more chemically stable than 5-HT. Cerebrospinal fluid (CSF) exists in a compartment separated from the rest of the body by the blood–brain barrier. It provides direct information about the CNS not confounded by 5-HT or 5-HIAA from peripheral sources, especially platelets and the gastrointestinal system.

134. D. *hippocampus.* The memories and images of REM sleep appear to originate in the hippo-

campus. Electrical activity in the hippocampus during REM sleep mirrors electrical activity in the cortex during the waking hours. The pons, lying above the cerebellum, seems to be critical for the initiation of REM sleep, but not its content. The reticular activating system plays a critical role in sleeping and waking, but is not directly implicated in REM sleep. The amygdala intensifies some emotions but does not store image-based memory. The basal ganglia coordinate motor activity.

135. B. *Broca's area on the right side* (nondominant language area) is involved in the motor aspects of speech (pitch, loudness, rhythm), which give emotional expressiveness to speech (*prosody*). Thus, a lesion in this area leads to the inability to add any inflection to speech. Lesions of Broca's area on the left side (dominant language area) lead to very slow, sparse, idiosyncratic, nongrammatical speech (*dysfluent aphasia*). Wernicke's area lesions on the left side (dominant language area) are associated with *fluent aphasia*. In fluent aphasia, speech production is unimpaired, but the speech does not make sense or includes unnecessary or incorrect words, and the person has difficulty comprehending what is said. Wernicke's area on the right side (nondominant language area) is involved in the sensory aspects of speech prosody, so a lesion here would lead to the inability to comprehend prosody. A lesion in Exner's area is associated with agraphia or inability to write.

136. E. *refusal of food despite being hungry.* This region of the brain plays a critical role in regulating all drives, including that of eating. Excessive aggression may result from a variety of abnormalities including excessive norepinephrine and lesions of the temporal lobes. Excessive fluid intake suggests diabetes insipidus, which is caused by injury of the pituitary gland and consequent reduction in the secretion of antidiuretic hormone (ADH). Hypersexuality (and inappropriate mouthing of objects) results from removal of the amygdalae (the Klüver-Bucy syndrome). Manic-like hyperactivity is most likely to result from intoxication with amphetamines or cocaine, which affect dopamine in the mesolimbic pathway that includes the nucleus accumbens.

137. E. *variable ratio operant reinforcement.* Variable ratio reinforcement makes both learning and extinction more difficult. Thus, even if there has been no recent reward (money-making trade), the stockbroker believes that the next response (trade) may be the one that pays off. Because he does not know when the payoff is coming, the urge to trade again is overwhelming and irresistible. Note that for ratio schedules, the payoff is contingent not on the passage of time, but on the quantity of the person's actions. Variable ratio (random) operant reinforcement is the mechanism by which individuals become addicted to gambling. Winning occurs frequently enough to keep the person interested and hopeful. The randomness of winning makes it possible to believe that next time will be "the" time. Habituation refers to a developing insensitivity to repeated stimuli, as when a person no longer attends to police sirens after living in the city for a while.

138. C. *nondominant parietal lobe.* The constellation of clinical findings associated with a lesion in the nondominant parietal lobe includes neglect of the left side and constructional apraxia. The patient typically denies any problem. Lesions of the orbito-medial frontal cortex result in withdrawal, fearfulness, and explosive moods. Lesions of the dominant parietal lobe are accompanied by Gerstmann's syndrome (agraphia, acalculia, finger agnosia, and right-left disorientation). Temporal lobe lesions are characterized by general psychotic behavior if the lesion is on the dominant side, and dysphoria, irritability, and loss of visual or musical ability if on the nondominant side.

139. B. *Avoidant personality disorder.* The case described is most consistent with avoidant personality disorder, characterized by social inhibition, fear of rejection, and feelings of inadequacy, despite the desire for relationships with others. Avoidant personality disorder may coexist with social anxiety disorder, which may include the symptoms of performance anxiety as illustrated in the vignette. The criteria for both avoidant personality disorder and social anxiety disorder require that the person's symptoms affect behavior in domains beyond performance alone. Antisocial personality disorder is characterized by aggression, impulsive, destructive behaviors, and lack of empathy. Those with dependent personality disorder are submissive, feel the need to be taken care of, and rely on others to make decisions for them. Paranoid personality disorder involves pervasive distrust and suspicion. Schizoid personality disorder involves volun-

tary social detachment, thought to reflect lack of interest in involvement with others.

140. C. *in the afternoon.* The combination of normal activity levels and internal biochemistry makes this the time of highest cardiac contraction rates. Although heart rate would be greater during REM sleep relative to other stages of sleep, overall, the heart works hardest when a person is awake.

141. D. *objective pathology rather than subjective experience.* Illness is the subjective label, or a self-description. Disease is a physiological fact. Illness can exist without disease (e.g., premenstrual syndrome [PMS]), and disease can exist without illness (e.g., hypertension).

142. D. *relieves the individual from usual responsibilities during an illness.* The sick role incorporates two rights and two obligations. The two rights are to be excused from normal responsibilities and to not be blamed for the illness. Note that although patients' behavior may have contributed to their condition (e.g., smokers with lung cancer), they are treated, not blamed, for their condition. The two duties of the sick role are to seek help to get well and to take steps to get well. Note that the sick role is about social relationships and is distinct from the concepts of illness (subjective label) and disease (objective pathology).

143. A. *denial.* She does not address the Pap smear information at all, as if this particular feature of reality does not exist for her. Intellectualization would be replacing affective reaction by cognitive processing (such as excessive information seeking). Rationalization implies justification, or saying why an unacceptable action or thought is acceptable in this case. Somatization is having physical symptoms that are not tied to discernible organ pathology and may relate to unacknowledged stress. Undoing suggests ritualistic action to reverse or repair something that is not acceptable.

144. B. *probe for the presence of other depressive symptoms.* Depression commonly accompanies long-term cardiac conditions and must be identified and managed along with any other health problems. Some studies have suggested that as many as one in five cardiac patients suffers from some form of depression. The added psychological burden of losing a job, especially if the loss is associated with situations over which the patient has no control (e.g., downsizing), magnifies the possibility that the patient in the vignette is depressed. Referral to a psychiatrist is premature and may not be necessary. Having a single provider manage both the cardiac problems and depression places less burden on the patient and reduces the chance of missing negative synergies in the drugs that are prescribed. Giving medications, involving family members, or telling the patient not to worry before exploring the full extent of the symptoms are never good ideas. Always complete the evaluation before recommending an intervention.

145. C. *negative reinforcement.* By lingering, the mother avoids the negative consequence of her son's crying and displeasure. Thus, she increases lingering to avoid the onset of the negative stimulus. Extinction signifies a reduction in an identified response. Positive reinforcement would mean that the mother gets some benefit or pleasure, which continues the behavior. Fading is gradual removal of the stimulus to below the level of the person's awareness while the behavior continues. A secondary reinforcer is something that, by itself, is not desired, but it changes behavior because of what can be done with it (e.g., in a token economy).

146. B. *Economic factors, such as cost of medical treatment.* Economic factors are probably least significant because the patient's care is covered by government refugee assistance funds. Structural factors may play a role, as she may not know how to drive and may be confused by the public transportation system, but her family has apparently helped her overcome these factors when she visits the healers. Cultural and social factors are probably playing the largest roles. The patient's interpretation of her breast lump, her experience of her bodily symptoms, her concept of the word *cancer,* and her experiences with cancer in other family members are potential major factors. In addition, her spiritual beliefs about the cause of the problem, her ethnic identity and newly arrived refugee status, her acceptance or rejection of a "sick role," and her social network's assessment of her condition and recommendations for treatment may also be influencing her to choose traditional healing treatments over surgery, radiation, and chemotherapy.

147. D. *parent*. Arthur Kleinman's three sectors of healers are popular or lay, folk, and professional. The popular sector includes everyday people whose authority is acquired through experience, such as parents, neighbors, and community members. The folk sector includes sacred or secular healers, whose authority derives from inheritance, apprenticeship, religious position, or divine choice. The category includes pastors, rabbis, imams, priests, astrologers, psychics, and lay midwives. The professional sector includes people whose authority is achieved by schooling and by licensure, evaluated by the profession's organizations and sanctioned by the government. Professional healers include physicians; nurses, nurse practitioners, and nurse midwives; physician assistants; clinical psychologists; social workers; chiropractors; and dentists. This designation extends to other health professionals such as physical therapists and pharmacists, who have become subject to increasingly rigorous standards for licensure and certification since Kleinman proposed his categories.

148. B. *displacement*. The student experiences his anger as directed at a person other than the professor who just made him wait. The student is still angry, but the object of the anger has shifted or been displaced. Conversion connotes having physical symptoms generated by disavowed psychological conflict. Projection describes the mechanism of a person perceiving their own thoughts and feeling as coming from the outside world. Reaction formation refers to overt action that is the opposite of what a person unconsciously thinks or feels. Repression involves pushing experience out of consciousness so that it is nonrecoverable.

149. D. *apraxia* is the loss of ability to do simple, specific coordinated movements, such as tying shoelaces or drinking from a straw. Agnosia is the loss of the ability to recognize the import of sensory stimuli (e.g., tactile agnosia is the inability to recognize objects by touch). Anosognosia is unawareness or denial of a neurological deficit despite the presence of a clear disability. Aphasias are difficulties with the comprehension or production of language. Aprosody is the loss of the normal variations in stress, pitch, and rhythm of speech that convey emotional expression.

150. E. *recommend nicotine replacement or bupropion to reduce potential weight gain*. Weight gain from smoking cessation is real, but not a valid reason to continue smoking. Increased exercise or the use of bupropion or nicotine replacement may reduce the amount of weight gain. No matter what the patient's genetic risk, smoking is the most serious, modifiable cardiovascular risk factor that he has. Although the patient is rationalizing an addiction, smoking cessation is generally not built around 12-step programs. These target the social, interpersonal, and spiritual consequences of addictions that have adverse effects on relationships. Nicotine addiction is more prosocial, and group support, for which there is limited evidence of efficacy, primarily involves education, behavioral techniques, and encouragement. The counselor's psychodynamic speculation may be valid, but addressing the issues in formal mental health treatment is not likely to be necessary or sufficient to induce habit change. Obesity by itself is not clearly a risk factor. If the patient's father was obese and had heart disease, the problem may have been related to hyperlipidemia, which can be modified by diet and drugs.

151. D. *Thiamine*. Clinically manifested as Korsakoff's syndrome, the memory gaps associated with thiamine (vitamin B1) deficiency are generally filled in by confabulation. Korsakoff's syndrome results from long-term alcohol abuse and is only treatable if detected early, prior to neuronal damage. Wilson's disease is an autosomal recessive disorder, characterized by defective copper metabolism; its clinical presentation may resemble schizophrenia. Niacin deficiency causes pellagra, which causes dermatitis, inflammation of mucous membranes, and diarrhea, as well as psychic disturbances. Deficiencies in potassium, seen mainly in people taking diuretics or who are hospitalized and maintained on IV fluids with insufficient potassium replacement, lead to muscle cramping and cardiac conduction abnormalities. Zinc deficiency early in life produces anemia, short stature, hypogonadism, impaired wound healing, and geophagia (eating dirt). Zinc deficiency in an adult may cause hair loss and immune dysfunction.

152. B. *fixed interval*. The medication is taken on a preset, unchanging time schedule. Note that if the patient feels more pain, he cannot obtain more medication. A continuous schedule would be one where the patient takes medication whenever he feels in pain. Fixed

and variable ratio schedules provide relief depending on how many times a behavior is done (e.g., pain is reported). Noncontingent suggests that reinforcement is not in any way linked to a stimulus (e.g., feeling of pain).

153. E. *USDA subsidies to cattle farmers, quality of produce in local grocery stores, frequency of fast food consumption by coworkers, personal food preferences.* USDA farm subsidies are an example of a factor at the outermost level of the social ecological model (society) that could affect dietary intake. Crops that are subsidized by the government may be cheaper and represent a larger portion of the US food supply than do crops that do not receive subsidies. The abundance of such foods and their relatively low cost, in turn, can make them more likely to be consumed by any given individual and by the population as a whole. The quality of produce in local grocery stores (which may be influenced by the aforementioned society-level factor of subsidies) is a community-level variable that can affect dietary intake. At the interpersonal level, the behaviors (including fast-food consumption) of one's coworkers and other acquaintances may influence an individual's dietary choices. A personal taste or distaste for certain foods is an individual-level variable affecting dietary intake.

154. D. *stopping smoking.* After 2 years of abstinence, risk for heart attack returns to the level of people who have never smoked. Stopping smoking is difficult. The success rate of a single attempt to quit is below 10% without formal help and about 20% with help. Losing weight and modifying diet are almost always good ideas, but the impact of stopping smoking will be more dramatic. Weight lifting may improve muscle tone, but will not provide the benefits of a cardiovascular workout. Cholesterol-lowering medication is useful but must be combined with diet to be effective.

155. B. *disease, but not illness.* H. Y. has an objective physical health problem without the subjective self-label of illness. Sickness refers to the social role assumed by patients who are then relieved of duties and responsibilities. She is performing all her tasks and so is not disabled.

156. A. *classical conditioning.* The child first cried when given the shot by the nurse. Now he cries when he sees the nurse, without any shot being involved. Thus, he has the same distress response, but it has become generalized to a new stimulus. Fading, negative reinforcement, positive reinforcement, and shaping all refer to operant conditioning.

157. E. *token economy.* This is an example of secondary reinforcement. The boy receives stickers that have no intrinsic value, but are reinforcing because of what they signify. Biofeedback requires trial-and-error practice to modify an internal physiological state by learning to change some proxy external stimulus (e.g., using a heart monitor to learn to control heart rate). Desensitization and flooding are treatments for phobias. Shaping involves reinforcing successively better approximations of desired behaviors (e.g., a child putting away some toys, then most toys, then all toys).

158. B. *limbic system:* hippocampus, hypothalamus, anterior thalamus, cingulate gyrus, and amygdala. The limbic system constitutes the circuit through which emotional responses reverberate. The cerebellum is important for learning skills and for some memory functions. The neocortex is a control mechanism and handles most higher-level thought processes. The pineal body is the site of melatonin synthesis, and is also involved in regulating sleep. The reticular activating system helps control sleeping and waking.

159. B. *fidelity.* Fidelity refers to the ethical principle of faithfulness to one's duties and obligations as a professional. Beneficence is acting in the best interests of patients. Although the principle of beneficence might apply to the clinician's behavior in this example, it does not apply as well as the principle of fidelity. The principle of medical honesty refers to truthfulness in dealings with patients. Justice in medicine is the fair administration of medical services. Trust is not an ethical principle.

160. B. *patient passivity during encounters with clinicians.* Characteristics of paternalism in provider–patient relationships include professional dominance, patients serving as passive recipients of medical information and services, and the provider's assumption that patients adhere to the provider's decisions about medical management. In contrast, the other choices offered are characteristics of a contractual, patient-centered relationship between professionals and patients.

161. E. *Traditional healing practice.* Traditional healing may take forms unfamiliar to Eurowestern practitioners. Linear bruises on the back, chest, or extremities may result from the Southeast Asian practice of "coining." For illnesses caused by bad wind, or built-up pressure, rubbing the body with a mentholated cream followed by rubbing a silver coin vigorously over the area is believed to release the pressure, thus relieving the illness. Coining has been confused with child abuse. Families have been reported to child protective services by practitioners ignorant of the practice. Mongolian spots are congenital hyperpigmented areas, most often seen on the lower back or buttocks. The hyperpigmentation fades with age but may never disappear completely. Sepsis can present as petechiae that progress to purpura, ecchymoses, and frank hemorrhage. Petechiae are usually distributed widely over the entire body.

162. A. *acknowledging differences in understanding of health-related issues.* The preferred clinician–patient relationship includes respect for the roles of the professional as the provider of medical expertise and the patient as the autonomous recipient of services, respectively. This relationship values mutual exchange of information, active involvement of patients in all aspects of their care, collaborative decision making, and respect for differences in background and understanding of health-related issues. The other options provided are concepts and beliefs consistent with traditional (but increasingly outdated) paternalistic clinician–patient relationships.

163. E. *lead to fewer conflicts when shared between patient and provider.* An explanatory model (EM), Kleinman's term for describing people's ideas about a sickness event, has five components: etiology of the condition, timing and mode of onset of symptoms, pathophysiological processes, natural history, and appropriate treatments. Ethnic identity is not one of the five components. EMs change over time as more information is gathered and as the disease unfolds. Different people hold different EMs about the same sickness event, but Kleinman's theory predicts that greater agreement between the patient and the provider about the explanatory model for an illness episode, leads to fewer conflicts about diagnosis and management.

164. B. *depression.* The typical signs and symptoms of grief resemble those of a major depressive episode. While some of these symptoms exist in the other options provided, they are most characteristic of depression. Over time, simple grief differs from depression in that it tends to evolve into wistful sadness and may be assuaged by rituals of mourning and comfort from others.

165. C. *disturbed source identification.* Studies of memory and false memory have shown that the ability to correctly identify the source of a perception or belief may be manipulated separately from the belief itself. For example, if a person watches an event and then hears a description with different details, the person may think they witnessed something that never happened, not recognizing that the false memory came from the description. Schizophrenic hallucinations often seem to the person to be coming from outside, rather than from within the brain, another example of source misidentification. Not knowing whether one dreamed an experience or actually lived it also exemplifies this phenomenon. Short-term memory is measured by giving the person unrelated objects to remember and asking them to list the objects after a period of distraction or delay. Dissociation is a state of trance in which some perceptions are not registered or are registered in a distorted fashion, and often not remembered accurately. Impaired concentration is measured by history and performance on serial sevens and digit span tests. Poor judgment is inferred from history and from the person's responses to conventional hypothetical situations.

166. A. *less likely to communicate their intentions.* Because they are less likely to give warning, preventive intervention is more difficult. Older persons, like the rest of the population, find firearms the method of choice for completed suicide. Being older does not connote more practical experience with suicide. Older people have a lower incidence of clinical depression than other age groups in the population. Over the last 3 decades of the 20th century, government programs for older persons and general prosperity in the country meant that they were no more likely to live in poverty than people in other age groups.

167. D. *the formation of a subsystem with relatively closed boundaries around it* is most common

during the first months of a marriage. Most young married couples do not completely cut off or disengage from their parents unless there has been a major rift, such as around the choice of spouse. Enmeshment with parents would intrude on the couple's time together and their identity as a unit, and is developmentally inappropriate in young adulthood. An open boundary around the couple's relationship would make it difficult to establish their own identity as a couple.

168. B. *sexual activity for both genders is most frequent in the 20s and declines with age.* However, this does not mean that sexual activity is confined to these ages. Many older people experience sexual desire and arousal. The best predictor of whether an older person is having sexual relations is the availability of a partner, making marital status a good predictor for both genders. The University of Chicago study found that married people have more sex than single people. Although peak sexual activity differs among women, it rarely peaks in their 50s. The relationship between sexual activity and socioeconomic status is not linear. More sexual activity seems to occur in lower and very high socioeconomic groups.

169. D. *divorce is most common between the ages of 30 and 45.* Couples who marry young are at higher risk for divorce. More than 50% of adults remarry within 5 years after becoming divorced. Divorced people of any age tend to remarry, practicing so-called serial monogamy. Someone who is divorced once is more likely to get divorced again.

170. B. *Conduct disorder.* Antisocial personality disorder is characterized by a pervasive pattern of disregard for, and violation of, the rights of others. Although the diagnosis of a personality disorder, in this case, antisocial personality disorder, is not made in individuals younger than 18, to prevent applying a permanent label to problems that may remit with maturity, symptoms do appear before the diagnostic threshold is reached. The diagnosis of antisocial personality disorder thus requires evidence of conduct disorder (i.e., similar symptoms appearing before the age of 15). Alcohol use disorder, gambling disorder, major depressive disorder, and oppositional defiant disorder are frequently comorbid with antisocial personality disorder, but are not required to make the diagnosis.

171. E. *Vascular dementia.* The patient's age, history of hypertension and diabetes, relatively rapid onset, and lateralizing neurological signs all suggest vascular dementia. Alzheimer's dementia has a more insidious onset, and lateralizing signs are not an associated feature. Creutzfeldt-Jacob disease is a rapidly progressive dementia that is fatal within 2 years. Huntington's disease is an autosomal dominant disorder that develops insidiously prior to age 40. Pick's disease is a rare dementia; clinical findings are similar to those of Alzheimer's dementia.

172. D. *Speaking in language that is similar to the patient's* facilitates relationship building. Asking questions and conveying responses at the patient's language level increases understanding and also allows the patient to discuss the illness without being overwhelmed with jargon or other confusing medical terminology. *Empathy* is best defined as understanding another person's thoughts and feelings. Using words that both parties understand facilitates this process. The other answers illustrate courtesy and attentiveness more than empathy per se.

173. E. *transference by the patient.* Transference is bringing into current life the experiences, beliefs, and perceptions of previous relationships. If the patient had experienced previous relationships marked by criticism, subsequent relationships (including the clinical encounter) may be perceived in a similar fashion. While the behavior of people with personality disorders may be hard to understand, it is most appropriate to consider situational explanations before labeling a patient with a diagnosis that implies long-term pathology. This provider is understandably surprised by the patient's irate response to what was intended as straightforward education and, as such, is not demonstrating the inappropriate reaction expected in a countertransference response. In this case, the patient is not denying that he has a knee pain or weight problem, but is inappropriately upset with the provider's efforts to assist him with those problems. There is nothing in the vignette to suggest that the provider is not being empathetic.

174. E. *problems or complications brought on by medical treatment.* The term *iatrogenic effect* is frequently applied to the negative consequences of drug therapy (e.g., superinfection

following antibiotic therapy), but the broader concept applies to any adverse condition resulting from receiving medical care (e.g., wound dehiscence following surgery).

175. B. *Enmeshed.* Enmeshed families are most likely to have difficulty with an individual separating and establishing their own identity. Disengaged families usually have less difficulty with independence. Multigenerational and overprotective families may have some difficulty with separation, but not to the extent of an enmeshed family. Extended family refers to membership in a group, rather than to how people in that group rely on each other.

176. B. *"Patients come first when care is really needed."* This physician's family has supported traditional principles of physician obligation in patients for 20 years. Inherent in that obligation is recognition that patients' needs come first in situations where medical services are necessary. While a spouse is an adult partner who can choose such a lifestyle and make a commitment to such principled behavior, a practitioner's children may feel hostage to disappointment, such as lack of contact with the physician parent or feeling unable to rely on parental support or presence. Obligations as a physician and obligations as a parent may conflict rather than overlap, making it essential that the physician be explicit about the motivation behind what may otherwise be felt as confusing and rejecting behavior.

177. A. *has a history of maltreatment or abuse by an intimate partner.* Epidemiological investigation has shown that a history of victimization is associated with both chronic pelvic pain and irritable bowel syndrome. Her headaches are classic migraines. Although the association of migraines with victimization is less clear, the fact that she does not have regular medical care despite having a recurrent, chronic illness is also a clue that she has been recently victimized in a relationship. Controlling abusive partners often prevent their victims from accessing routine supports such as preventive health care. The common thread among her various conditions is the effect of severe stress on monoamine neurotransmitter systems that control pain thresholds and autonomic nervous system activity. ER providers often dismiss such patients as drug seeking, since their pain does not correlate with clear tissue injury. Conversion disorder describes patients with

symptoms that do not have recognized pathophysiology and are associated with an identifiable psychological conflict, again possible but not likely here. Although panic disorder patients are intensely concerned about somatic symptoms, this patient's symptoms are not those of panic attacks, which by definition have acute onset and subside quickly. Pain is generally not a panic symptom. The diagnosis of malingering implies that she is only feigning symptoms, although in this case she has symptoms with a known pathophysiology, in a classic pattern, and with typical comorbidities. Malingering and drug seeking should not be the first hypothesis the clinician adopts. Illness anxiety disorder (formerly hypochondriasis) describes a conviction of severe illness in the face of contradictory evidence. The vignette does not describe the patient as magnifying her symptoms or being overly concerned about their implications.

178. E. *respect for autonomy.* The principles of beneficence (improving patients' welfare), justice (assuring fair distribution of health care services), and nonmaleficence (not intentionally harming patients) do not directly apply to the behavior described. Moral virtue refers to behaviors that conform to generally accepted moral standards.

179. D. *Nonmaleficence* refers to not intentionally harming one's patients. Adherence to the other principles and behaviors requires specific action by the clinician: Beneficence involves improving patients' welfare, justice requires assuring fair distribution of health care services, moral virtue means behaving according to moral standards, and respect for autonomy is encouraging patient involvement and self-rule in medical management decisions.

180. B. *her relationship with her care providers.* The patient's relationship with her care providers will allow thoughtful discussion of all treatment options and decisions regarding her end-of-life care. Her caregivers will know her as a patient and person, aware not only of her medical history but also her philosophy of life and death. Given her capacity (ability to make appropriate decisions regarding her medical management) and terminal medical condition, decisions regarding her care should not be unduly influenced by input from her sister, her insurance company, regulatory bodies, or the nursing home administration.

181. C. *Obsessive-compulsive disorder.* People with obsessive-compulsive disorder have prominent obsessions (ideas, thoughts, or impulses that create significant anxiety) and compulsions (repetitive or ritualistic activities that reduce the anxiety generated by the obsessions). In the vignette, the girl has obsessions about germs that are tied to compulsive activities, including taking long showers and cleaning the steering wheel of her car. People with obsessive-compulsive personality disorder show pervasive patterns of perfectionism and inflexibility; often, they have trouble making decisions because the perfectionism interferes. However, stereotypic obsessions and ritualistic responses are not part of the diagnosis. Obsessive-compulsive personality traits are similar to the qualities of the personality disorder but do not impair social and occupational functioning. Generalized anxiety disorder is defined as anxiety and worry about a variety of events and activities for the majority of the day over a 6-month period. Illness anxiety disorder (formerly, hypochondriasis) is characterized by fears that minor bodily or mental symptoms may indicate a serious illness, leading to self-diagnosis and preoccupation with one's body.

182. E. *show greater confidence in their interpersonal skills.* However, gender continues to increase certain stresses for female physicians. Lower pay or salaries, less confidence in the business aspects of practice, and the demands of balancing family and child-rearing duties are examples often cited as increasing the stress of women physicians, relative to men. The old misconception that female surgeons would be likely to perform fewer operations has been repeatedly disproved.

183. C. *because a family member has a history of substance abuse.* Transference refers to responses based on a person's own emotional needs originating in familial or developmental relationship experiences. While choices A, B, and D may reflect important childhood issues, the emotional transference of familial substance abuse is likely unconscious and thus more accurately reflects this process. Wanting to be like a character on television is a conscious choice (i.e., an imitation), not the unconscious attachment that transference implies.

184. D. *80%.* Compulsivity, which has positive and negative aspects, is a common trait in many physicians. Anecdotally, it is certainly common in other health care providers and professionals in other domains as well.

185. C. *enmeshed.* Enmeshed families are characterized by unusually strong emotional connectedness. Family members have difficulty making autonomous choices and acting independently when necessary and appropriate. Exiting from the family, even briefly to attend kindergarten, can produce exaggerated separation anxiety.

186. C. *Fine hair on the back and arms,* or lanugo. The girl presented in the vignette illustrates anorexia nervosa, binge purge pattern. She is 20% below normal body weight for her height and within the usual age range for onset of the condition. Another classic sign is amenorrhea. Note that binge and purge behavior, a well-recognized sign of bulimia, also occurs in about 50% of all anorexics. Sadness suggests the possibility of depression, a common accompaniment to anorexia nervosa. Anorexia is not consistently linked to rashes, loss of tendon reflexes, high heart rate, or light sensitivity. However, in the severest forms of the illness, idiosyncratic medical complications, such as bradycardia, may appear.

187. E. *validity* means that the test assesses what it is supposed to assess; in this case, that the screening test actually assesses suicidality. To have validity (accuracy), a test must first have reliability (precision or consistency), but having reliability tells us nothing about validity. Administration refers to how the test will be given. Bias reflects a tendency of the test or tester to produce skewed results.

188. E. *validity.* Does the test assess qualities that are important to being a bank teller? Does it separate success from failure or help to predict who will be successful in this particular job? Bias is a deviation from truth and suggests a flaw in the test itself, or in its administration. Convergence is a type of validity, but not the type of interest here. For convergence, different tests that purport to assess the same thing would give the same result. Precision and reliability refer to consistency – that is, does the test give the same result every time it is taken (test-retest reliability)?

189. E. *predictive validity* means that the validating criterion (success in school) will exist in the future. Construct validity requires that the test's assessment be consistent with some

underlying theoretical perspective. Content validity means that the items on the test relate to the subject matter being assessed. Criterion-related validity means that the test matches some existing criterion, as when a person diagnosed as depressed endorses the necessary symptoms on a depression inventory. Face validity means that, on first impression, the items on the test seem to be about the subject being assessed.

190. D. *Subway: 12-inch sub – hearty Italian bread with Black Forest ham, Swiss cheese, and ranch dressing – and a bowl of vegetable beef soup.* Despite the traditionally fattier meats (ham and beef) and the sandwich being topped with cheese and creamy dressing, this fast-food meal is actually the healthiest dinner selection of the five choices listed, totaling 755 kcal, 18 g of total fat, and 5 g of saturated fat. This meal provides only slightly more than a third of the calories of a standard 2,000-kcal adult diet, only about one quarter of the recommended total fat intake of no more than 30% of total calories from fat, and less than one quarter of the saturated fat recommendation of less than 10% of total daily calories. The other selections weigh in as follows: (A) Chili's Cobb Salad and sweet corn soup: 1,500 kcal, 76 g of fat, 36 g of saturated fat (75% of an adult's daily calories in one meal!); (B) Outback Steakhouse ribs and fries: 1,190 kcal, 76 g of fat, 33 g of saturated fat (more than half of a day's calories and about 1.5 times the saturated fat recommendation for an adult!); (C) Red Lobster shrimp and Caesar salad: 820 kcal, 51 g of fat, 7 g of saturated fat (the total calories in this dish are better than most, and the saturated fat is OK, but the total fat is more than three quarters of the daily adult recommendation); (E) Wendy's Chicken Fillet Sandwich and small fries: 790 kcal, 33 g of fat, 6.5 g of saturated fat (although not nearly as hefty in calories, this single meal contains about half of the maximum recommended daily calories from fat for an adult). The take-home messages here are that fast food is not always bad, salads are not always good, and some of our favorite restaurant meals are loaded with much more than the flavor that makes them so enticing.

191. C. *has not menstruated in the past year.* Current research separates the perimenopause from menopause, the latter term being appropriate for a woman who has not menstruated for the past year. Hot flashes, disturbed sleep, and irregular menses are common symptoms of perimenopause, a period of declining ovarian function that may last for years before cessation of menses, and extend beyond it. Perimenopausal women are less able to conceive than younger women, but women who do not wish to become pregnant should use contraception until they are fully menopausal, as pregnancy is still possible up to that point.

192. C. *Muscarinic.* The question presents a patient with symptoms of anticholinergic intoxication, a result of antagonism of the muscarinic receptors. Antagonism of brain dopamine receptors produces antipsychotic effects. Antagonism of histamine receptors is linked to other central nervous system (CNS) effects, including drowsiness. The effect of blocking CNS norepinephrine receptors is not simple; stimulating them may increase anxiety but relieve symptoms of depression. Many of the drugs prescribed to people with schizophrenia increase prolactin, producing breast growth, lactation, and, in women, inhibiting normal menstrual cycling.

193. E. *Whatever activity she thinks she is likely to do consistently.* The question, What is the best exercise or activity for weight loss? has no right answer. Just about any physical activity can aid in weight loss, provided that an individual burns more calories than they consume. The amount of calories burned by a particular regimen is a product of not only the particular mode of activity but also the intensity and duration of that activity. The four activities and intensities listed actually all burn the same number of calories (about 210 kcal for a 150-lb [68-kg] woman). When it comes to providing physical activity guidance for weight loss, the best activity is the one (or more) that an individual is willing and able to do.

194. C. *85–115.* The IQ has a mean of 100 and standard deviation of 15. In a normal distribution, 68% of the scores will be within 1 standard deviation of the mean (plus and minus), 50% of the scores will be over 100, and 50% will be under 100. About 2.5% of the population will have scores under 70 or over 130. A score of 70 is the IQ criterion cutoff for intellectual disability. However, adaptive functioning deficits (in conceptual, social, and practical domains), as well as IQ, are used for a diagnosis of intellectual disability.

195. E. *Schizotypal personality disorder,* by DSM-5 criteria. J. G. evidences a pervasive pattern of acute discomfort with, and a reduced capacity for, close relationships (lack of close friends and extreme social anxiety) as well as cognitive or perceptual distortions and eccentricities of behavior including odd thinking and speech, odd beliefs (in telepathy), suspiciousness, inappropriate affect, and eccentric appearance and behavior. Antisocial personality disorder is the diagnosis applied to people who exploit others, cannot confirm to rules, and express no remorse for their actions. A person who has a borderline personality disorder is in constant chaos, with unstable mood, self-image, and relationships. A narcissist sees the world and self in grand terms. The schizoid person has no friends, but likes it that way and just wants to be left alone.

196. D. *night terrors.* Night terrors are a sleep disorder that occurs during the transition from Stage 3 to Stage 4 (deep) sleep, usually about 90 min after the child has fallen asleep. Night terrors have the classical presentation described here and are associated with difficulty arousing the child. Night terrors tend to run in families and can be a precursor of temporal lobe epilepsy. Acute adjustment reaction is a time-limited stress-induced disorder. Bruxism is teeth grinding that occurs in Stage 2 sleep. Hypnogogic hallucinations occur while falling asleep and are one of the symptoms of narcolepsy. Nightmares are essentially bad dreams that occur in REM sleep.

197. A. *has complete information about the surgical procedure and recovery.* Knowing what is going to happen reduces stress and allows for faster recovery with less reported pain. Good relationships with hospital medical personnel are the best predictor of satisfaction with hospital stay, but have not been shown to shorten recovery time. Giving pain medication on demand tends to lessen the patient's fear of pain, but does little to reduce the need for the medication.

198. B. *create plans.* The child's ability to plan how to gratify impulses is what makes the twos so terrible. Not only are children this age impulsive, but they also can negotiate around simple impediments meant to protect and contain them. Because the ability to imagine alternatives does not become manifest until the child is 5 or 6 years old, the 2-year-old's plan is *the*

plan and no amount of logic will induce him or her to du something different. Children can distinguish facial features from early infancy. Although 2-year-olds have some idea of the standards of good and bad conduct, these standards are not internalized; instead, a child of this age seeks simply to not get caught. Rule-based play is characteristic of middle childhood.

199. E. *Thematic Apperception Test* (TAT). For the TAT, a projective personality test, patients are presented with a number of ambiguous pictures and asked to create a story about what they see. Stories are scored for unconscious themes such as the need for power, need for intimacy, or need for achievement. The MMPI, an objective personality test that is multidimensional and norm referenced, provides a profile of the person's personality. The other choices are tests that seek to characterize neurological or developmental impairment.

200. E. *the tendency for the body to maintain a particular state.* Homeostasis is an optimal state where demands on the body are balanced by appropriate responses. Note that homeostasis is a dynamic state that changes over time with development and maturation. The central issue is a biological balance between the organism and the environment, not psychology vs. physiology. Balancing sexual and aggressive drives is a core dynamic in classic psychoanalytic (Freudian) psychology.

201. D. *have strong psychological need for control over situations.* Type A or cardiovascular disease–prone behavior pattern connotes greater anger, sense of time urgency, and need for control. The response to stress, not the exposure to stress, defines Type A. There is no relationship between Type A and problem solving or social withdrawal.

202. A. *Bender Visual-Motor Gestalt Test* looks at cortical functioning related to mental representation, retention, and reproduction of presented figures. The Draw-A-Person and Rorschach tests are projective tests intended to assess a patient's unconscious content and preoccupations. The Luria-Nebraska Neuropsychological Battery includes a wide-ranging group of standardized instruments seeking to generate a complete picture of the patient's neurological functioning. The Wechsler Memory Scale examines short-term

memory and might be used to assess a patient with suspected Alzheimer's dementia.

203. E. *the projective hypothesis* assumes that responses to ambiguous stimuli reveal information about the person responding. Reaction formation is a psychological defense mechanism postulated by Freud in which real but unconscious feelings are hidden by acting in an opposite manner (e.g., love is manifested as hate). Subjective press is the perceived field of stimuli-directing behavior. The Gestalt laws of perception focus on the role of context and mental set in governing what is perceived.

204. E. *Fatigue, hyperpigmentation of the skin, hyperkalemia*. Although fatigue is common in restrictive anorexia nervosa as weight loss occurs and metabolism decreases, the skin does not become hyperpigmented. Hyperkalemia is associated with starvation in developing countries with significant protein-calorie malnutrition, but the diet of most patients with eating disorders has enough high-quality protein to preclude kwashiorkor, which also takes at least several months to develop and generally is associated with chronic malnutrition. The triad of fatigue, hyperpigmentation, and hyperkalemia suggests adrenal insufficiency (Addison's disease). Insufficiency of adrenal mineralocorticoids leads to hyperkalemia. In consequence, the body secretes additional ACTH to try to stimulate adrenal function. ACTH also stimulates melanin production, leading to darkening of the skin, often most noticeable in skin creases that do not tan. Early satiety is associated with gastric atony; bradycardia is a sign of hypometabolism; and hypoglycemia is associated with low caloric intake. All these are seen in anorexia nervosa. Similarly, constipation and hypothermia are characteristic consequences of low caloric intake. Although not often measured as part of routine screening, mild elevations of liver enzymes can be seen with low weight due to poor caloric intake. True loss of appetite occurs later in the course of the illness, but orange/yellowish discoloration of the skin may be seen. A high intake of carotene-containing vegetables and the relatively low thyroid activity (*sick euthyroid syndrome*) associated with malnutrition and weight loss accounts for this, as thyroid hormone is needed to metabolize carotene. Neutropenia is also associated with weight loss. Hypogonadotropic amenorrhea is a clas-

sic element of anorexia nervosa. Alopecia also occurs with starvation, but may be worse after weight restoration, when new hairs enter the growing phase, and resting hairs fall out.

205. B. *be able to use symbols to represent reality*. The preoperational stage lasts from about 2 to 7 years of age. During this stage, children leave behind preoccupation with sensations and motion and represent the world to themselves as composed of constant objects. Putting together simple picture puzzles (e.g., putting a single piece into a large cut out space of the same shape on a board), exploring the environment by physically manipulating objects, and needing to have an object present to trigger thought are more closely linked to the sensorimotor stage (ages birth to 2). Sophisticated, but inflexible, thought processes are the hallmarks of concrete operations (ages 7 to 12).

206. A. *Emotionally cutoff*. Emotional cutoff is more likely to create pseudoindependence than true independence. The need to completely abandon a relationship in order to exert autonomy suggests that the patient has learned an "all or none" approach (i.e., complete absorption vs. no contact) to interacting with others.

207. A. *construct validity*. Does the test match the abstract theoretical notion represented by the trait of obsessiveness? Content validity means that the items on the test seem related to the subject matter being assessed. Criterion-related validity means that the test matches some existing criterion, as when a person diagnosed as depressed endorses the necessary items on a depression inventory. Face validity means that, on first impression, the items on the test seem to be about the subject being assessed. Predictive validity refers to a match between the test results and validating criteria that will exist in the future

208. B. *consider this test, since its reliability is very strong*. A number close to 1.00 indicates very good reliability. A number over 1.00 is not mathematically possible.

209. D. *Action*. The patient is actively working on behavior change but has done so for < 6 months, placing her in the action stage. With precontemplation, the patient is not thinking about changing a behavior and has no intention of changing within the next 6 months. In

contemplation, the patient is thinking about changing within the next 6 months, but is not committed to it. In the preparation stage, the pros and cons have been weighed, and the patient decides to start working on change by developing a plan and intending to change within the next 30 days. In the maintenance stage, the patient is trying to not relapse and has changed for > 6 months.

210. B. *accountable.* Accountability of care is the disclosure of standards of care to the public and an acceptance of responsibility by providers for the judgment of the public.

211. A. *Changing to a drug covered by his insurance plan.* Barriers to nonadherence include cost, side effects, and a complicated medical regimen. Exploring whether cost is an issue and changing to a drug covered by insurance would decrease the burden on the patient and would make the treatment more attractive to anyone, regardless of financial status. Explaining the health hazards of elevated blood pressure and the side effects of the medication would be a good idea but will not, in themselves, change the patient's behavior. Increasing the number of pills he has to take each day will make him even less likely to take his medication. Attending a hypertension support group is useful for many people, but will not address the financial issue that is probably the source of his nonadherence.

212. E. *Valproic acid* is teratogenic in the first trimester, for which it has a "black box" warning. It can cause major congenital malformations including neural tube defects in up to 5% of pregnancies and decreased IQ scores in individuals exposed in utero. Carbamazepine is also associated with neural tube defects in the first trimester but the incidence appears to be < 1%. Lamotrigine and risperidone have a FDA pregnancy Category C rating (animal reproduction studies have shown an adverse effect on the fetus with no adequate and well-controlled studies in humans, but potential benefits may warrant use of the drug in pregnant women despite potential risks). Lithium is considered a weak teratogen in the first trimester (although it is associated with Ebstein's anomaly).

213. A. *Bipolar I disorder.* Lithium, the anticonvulsants, and the antipsychotics used as monotherapy or in combination, are mainstays of treatment for mood stabilization and for mania with bipolar I disorder. Lamotrigine is FDA approved for depression prophylaxis in bipolar disorder.

214. C. *Lithium* alone has been found to reduce the risk of suicide attempts and death by suicide in patients with bipolar disorder.

215. D. *Performance of well-practiced material is less likely to decline under high stress conditions.* Well-practiced material does not have to be pulled out of memory, a person just performs it "rote." An example of this is the overpracticing done in preparation for a "code" so that everything goes smoothly in that high stress situation. Moderate stress environments are the most conducive to learning new material and actually more conducive than low stress environments. Stress plays a significant role in learning and performance. Performance of all tasks except overlearned tasks declines in high stress situations.

216. E. *Word salad.* Thought process is the way thoughts are connected or associated. Word salad is an incoherent mixture of words and phrases. Circumstantiality is overly and unnecessarily detailed speech that is indirect and delayed in reaching the point, although thought does eventually get to the original point. Clang association is a manner of speaking in which groups of words are chosen for their similarity in sound rather than logical meanings. Neologisms are new words that are created by the user, often by combining syllables. Neologisms have idiosyncratic meaning for the user but are meaningless to others. Tangentiality is a pattern of speech full of oblique and irrelevant references such that the speaker is unable to get to the original point of the issue.

217. C. *Ideas of reference.* Thought content consists of the topics that occupy a person's thoughts. Ideas of reference refers to an individual interpreting wrongly that incidental events relate to themselves (e.g., thinking people on TV are talking to or about oneself). Depersonalization is a perceptual state in which one's thoughts and feelings are detached from oneself and seem unreal. Hallucinations are perceptions occurring in the absence of external stimuli. Obsessions are thoughts that are preoccupying, intrusive, and often disturbing and unreasonable. Ruminations are mood-congruent

Practice Exam Answers

concerns about which one thinks deeply and carefully.

218. C. *70.* The mode is the most frequently occurring score. There are two 70s and only one of every other number.

219. C. *70.* The median is the middle number. Note that you must first rank order (highest to lowest or lowest to highest) the scores to identify the middle number. For an even number of subjects, add the two middle numbers together and divide by two.

220. B. *his limited activity.* In general, athletes are able to tolerate short-term dependency, social isolation, and pain better than inactivity. He is old enough to understand the cause-and-effect relationship between his accident and his injury.

221. D. *major depression.* When depressed, children and adolescents are often more irritable than sad. Very brief upswings of mood are common, even when the child or adolescent is predominantly depressed. This vignette describes sleep disorder, changes in appetite, self-loathing, and lack of usual interests, along with suicidal ideation. Her social isolation and falling grades are signs that her problems are affecting general functioning, making depression the most appropriate diagnosis. Attention-deficit/hyperactivity disorder (ADHD) typically shows up earlier in life, although the diagnosis may be missed if the child is able to compensate in school. In any case, ADHD is not associated with changes in sleep, appetite, and energy. Dissatisfaction with body image is common in both normal and ill adolescents, but body dysmorphic disorder implies that the person is completely preoccupied with some physical characteristic. In addition, concern specifically about weight is excluded from the criteria for this disorder. Borderline personality disorder is characterized by *a pervasive pattern* of instability of interpersonal relationships, self-image, and affect along with marked impulsivity. Fears of abandonment (real or imagined) and frantic efforts to avoid it are prominent. Borderline personality disorder is typically not diagnosed until after age 18 because some instability in these areas is expected in normal adolescents during this stage of development, when identity is being forged. Puberty can contribute to mood lability and intensification of moods, but normal

puberty is not associated with deteriorating general adjustment and suicidal ideation. In girls, the risk of major depression rises with puberty, and the hormonal changes of adolescence may be part of the pathophysiology of depression. However, it is a mistake to dismiss mood symptoms as "just hormones" when they have potentially serious consequences.

222. E. *Tests of intelligence generally attempt to measure ability, not achievement.* IQ tests measure capacity (how much the child is able to learn), not achievement (how much the child actually learned). A number of different definitions of intelligence exist, and a number of different types of intelligence have been proposed (e.g., emotional intelligence). IQ is a derived measurement; intelligence is the inference from that measurement. A number of researchers have demonstrated some racial bias in IQ tests, leading to the development of "culture-free" tests. A good test administrator should take these biases into account.

223. A. *HMO.* Only prepaid health care systems, such as HMOs, benefit from keeping patients healthy. Prepay means the provider already has the money and benefits if the patient does not become sick and require health care services. If patients stay healthy, the provider makes more money. Under fee-for-service systems, as in the other choices offered in this question, the provider only makes money when the patient accesses care.

224. C. *an increase in AIDS prevalence.* The conceptual formula is (prevalence = incidence × duration). Therefore, if mortality decreases, duration increases, which leads, in turn, to an increase in prevalence. In the question, no data are presented for infection rates among family members, changes in medical care, the number of people practicing safe sex, or the survival rate after diagnosis.

225. C. *Halstead-Reitan Neuropsychological Test Battery.* This battery is a wide-ranging set of standardized instruments seeking to generate a complete picture of the patient's neurological functioning. The Bender Visual-Motor Gestalt Test looks at cortical functioning related to mental representation, retention, and reproduction of presented figures. The California Personality Inventory provides a profile of the patient in a manner similar to the MMPI. The Luria-Nebraska Neuropsychological

Battery provides an assessment similar to the Halstead-Reitan based on different standardized tests. The Thematic Apperception Test is a way of assessing the patient's unconscious needs and preoccupations.

226. B. *generalized anxiety disorder.* The diagnosis requires that symptoms such as those described be present for at least 6 months. Anxiety is a normal, transient emotional response. The diagnosis of generalized anxiety disorder is made when the emotional state endures and impairs the person's general functioning. Agoraphobia is fear of situations from which escape is difficult or help unavailable in the event of panic-like symptoms. The diagnosis of panic disorder requires *recurrent* (> 1) *unexpected* (with no obvious cue or trigger) panic attacks. At least one of the panic attacks needs to have been followed by 1 month or more of recurrent worry about having more panic attacks or their consequences and/or a significant maladaptive change in behavior due to this fear. No panic attacks are described by the patient in the vignette. Obsessive-compulsive disorder features obsessions (ideas that will not go away) or compulsions (actions a person feels compelled to perform, usually to control obsessions). Social phobia is a fear of appearing inept or shameful in public, either in general, or limited to certain situations.

227. C. *progressive relaxation.* The student is practicing a behavioral strategy to reduce physiological arousal and allow for better concentration on the exam. Biofeedback is the technique of using an external monitoring devices to obtain information about an involuntary function of the central or autonomic nervous system, in order to gain some voluntary control over that function. For example, a person reducing their heart rate by observing their heart rhythm on a cardiac monitor. Meditation is a systematic method of focusing attention on a neutral stimulus, a practice that increases control of physiological responses. Self-hypnosis is a technique for altering mental state and can include making suggestions to oneself about what to think, feel, or do in a given situation. A stress response would entail the manifestation of reactions to stress.

228. B. *Dieting to get in shape for the cross-country team.* Dieting for any reason is the greatest risk factor for this girl. In susceptible individuals, dieting often leads to increasingly more restrictive intake. Moreover, cross-country running is dominated by very thin athletes, providing constant reminders of a thin ideal. A competitive individual may focus on being the thinnest runner. Although teasing about weight is now considered a form of bullying, even when done in jest, it is only important in the context of an individual who is already highly vulnerable to developing an eating disorder (i.e., the "last straw"). Early pubertal development can lead to a girl feeling as if she "does not fit in" or "stands out." However, there is no consistent pattern of pubertal development associated with developing an eating disorder. Although dieting in the family can be a trigger, maternal influence is generally stronger; her father being on a diet to treat hypercholesterolemia is less likely to precipitate an eating disorder. Parental separation and conflict can have both positive and negative effects; patients often note that the decrease in parental fighting actually reduces their stress level.

229. C. *mania.* Mania in this case is illustrated by poor judgment, unrealistic self-appraisal, irritability, and pressured speech. The patient's recent job loss is a soft clue that he is having a mood episode, since mania may be triggered by events that could just as well induce depression. His personalized and idiosyncratic interpretation of proverbs and judgment questions is also typical of mania. Delusional disorder is also associated with unrealistic thinking, but connotes a long-standing pattern of false belief, without disorganization of thought or impaired concentration. The patient's scanty clothing and labile mood could be considered histrionic (seductive and emotionally exaggerated), but these traits can also be seen in the context of acute mania. Masked depression is not a well-accepted term. When used, it connotes someone who denies feeling depressed and who may primarily complain of somatic symptoms. On systematic questioning, however, the person with masked depression will have depressive ideation (hopelessness, worthlessness, helplessness, suicidal thoughts) and neurovegetative signs (anhedonia, sleep problems, apathy, changes in energy and appetite, bodily anxiety). Manic patients often seem narcissistic (self-absorbed, manipulative, and grandiose), but narcissistic personality disorder does not imply an acute change in mental status, signs of cognitive impairment, or

grossly poor judgment. In any case, personality disorders cannot be diagnosed based on a person's immediate state; by definition, they begin early in life and are evident across many situations.

230. A. *concept formation.* The clinician in this description is developing a classification scheme. This type of thinking is also called inductive reasoning. Convergent thinking focuses on determining the *single* best answer by manipulating existing knowledge. Hypothesis testing involves seeking evidence that is consistent with, or that contradicts, a given proposition. Insight suggests some sudden realization about a situation or relationship. Stimulus discrimination entails noting the difference between two or more experiences.

231. B. *defining how experiences are described and what is remembered.* Reality is created as linguistic labels are assigned. The words we use to describe a situation help to give context, and therefore meaning, to events. Recent research suggests that humans are hardwired for language and that children can discriminate linguistic from nonlinguistic patterns from an early age. Sound can have an associational meaning that precedes language. Sensation and perception are not limited by language, although recollection of them may be. The meaning of words is altered by the way they are pronounced or the intonation that accompanies them (prosody), but reality is linked to the linguistic labels, not to the particular form of their expression.

232. A. *a delusional episode.* Delusion refers to a false belief that is not shared by others in the same culture. If we all believe that walking under a ladder will bring bad luck, that is a shared belief and, therefore, an aspect of culture. If I think this by myself with no support from others, we call it a delusion. An hallucination is a perception of a stimulus (e.g., seeing or hearing something) when such a stimulus does not exist. An illusion is a misperception of an existing stimulus. Gaps in memory can be filled in with fictitious content called confabulation. Sensory distortions, like illusions, involve misperceiving something.

233. B. *intelligence is generally defined in terms of verbal ability and problem-solving skills.* Most IQ tests assess intelligence by assessing these capacities. Although as much as 70% of intelligence may be derived from heredity, the role of environment is critical to determining a person's ultimate functional capacity. Most measures of intelligence require convergent thinking (i.e., looking for preset solutions to the problems presented). In some cultures, a slower, more reflective approach is seen as a sign of higher intelligence. Cross-cultural testing finds few to no differences in intelligence among races, if the tests are unbiased. Racial differences that appear within the US disappear when people are tested in their countries of origin.

234. B. *Circumstantiality, tangentiality, flight of ideas, loose associations.* Circumstantiality may be nonpathological, especially in people who are anxious or trying to communicate by giving extra details. Tangentiality implies that the person is having trouble following a train of thought or suppressing associations, and unaware that they are not logical and goal directed. Flight of ideas is a more severe form of tangentiality, when the connections between ideas may be discernible, but off the point, pressured, and idiosyncratic. As thought disorder becomes more severe, the logical connections between ideas are lost, and the person connects things by superficial rather than semantic qualities (e.g., by the sound of a word rather than the sense, termed *clanging*). With loose associations, the connections are random or arbitrary.

235. A. *accurate empathy* is the ability to understand the patient in the patient's terms and to have the patient confirm that understanding with the clinician. Clinical judgment refers to decisions about diagnostic procedures and recommendations for treatment. Concept formation refers to gathering information to identify the common elements of a class of disorders. Divergent thinking is looking for creative, new, "out of the box" solutions to problems. Paralinguistic communication refers to the nonverbal cues that punctuate and give context to verbal communications.

236. D. *self-control contracting.* The patient contracts with herself, so that when a goal is reached, she gets a reward. Cognitive rehearsal is the process of visualizing action before actually attempting it. Cognitive restructuring refers to relabeling or reframing the situation. Problem solving refers to any cognitive routine to

arrive at an acceptable solution to a presented dilemma. Skills training involves working with persons as individuals or in a group to help them learn and practice particular behaviors such as basic social skills (greeting and conversing with others).

237. B.   *cognitive restructuring.* The student is being urged to change the assumptions they have made about the outcome of future behaviors. Positive cognitions are more likely than negative cognitions to lead to productive behaviors. The mechanism behind this observation is unknown but may relate to positive cognitions making the person feel more relaxed, under control, and optimistic – three emotional states that enhance performance. Cognitive rehearsal is the process of visualizing action before actually attempting it. Problem solving refers to executing a cognitive routine to arrive at an acceptable solution to a presented dilemma. In self-control contracting, a person contracts with themselves that, when a goal is reached, a reward will be received. Skills-training involves working as an individual or in a group to learn and practice particular behaviors. The target skill may be technical (learning how to do a certain job) or social (learning how to share).

238. B.   *are working at being part of the adult culture.* Most young adults want to be a part of the adult world. Their dreams and aspirations flow from their life experience and the culture outside the immediate family. Seeking independence can make stable intergenerational relationships difficult. Young adulthood is a time for making commitments to intimate relationships and to career. Advice from older persons is sought and valued.

239. A.   *They connect various cortical storage sites to form combined memories.* Memories are encoded all over the cortex. The hippocampus serves as an index or locator permitting them to be retrieved. The cerebellum serves as a trainer and guide for learning motor skills. The thalamus forwards incoming sensory input to the cortex.

240. C.   *Determining if the attacks were associated with a stressor.* Diagnosis of panic disorder requires that the patient have recurrent *unexpected* attacks (not associated with a situational trigger – that is, they are "out of the blue"), with at least one of the attacks being followed by 1 month or more of persistent concern about having more attacks or having the consequences of an attack (losing control, "going crazy") or a significant maladaptive behavior change as a result of the attacks. Determining if Mr. I. has anxiety at other times is helpful in assuring that no other anxiety disorder diagnoses are missed, but does not differentiate panic disorder from another anxiety disorder with panic attacks. Determining if the attacks have led to actual fainting is not relevant to differentiating among diagnosis. Determining if the attacks are associated with low blood sugar could help identify a potential medical illness (as opposed to a psychiatric illness) as the etiology or as a contributing factor of the panic attack. Determining the duration of the attacks is not helpful as most panic attacks less than 10 min.

241. A.   *Becoming a parent.* All of the options listed may prompt individuals to reflect on their identity and place in life, but nothing conveys the enduring meaning of becoming an adult as much as the advent of a child. Parenthood represents a psychological, social, and financial break from the past.

242. E.   *the consequences of behavior.* In this operant conditioning paradigm, what happens after the behavior is the key event. Anything that makes the behavior more likely to be repeated is called a positive reinforcer. Any stimulus event that makes the behavior less likely is called punishment. If stimuli occur spontaneously and are unconnected to behavior, they will have no effect, or can result in the unintentional conditioning of "superstitious" behavior. Genetics provides the substrate for behavior, but it is the appearance of stimuli in the environment that conditions the response. The level of drive can determine the intensity of responses, but not the learning of the actual response set.

243. A.   *administer a Mini–Mental State Examination,* which will give specific information about deficit areas. The Wechsler Adult Intelligence Scale is a test for assessing intelligence, not dementia. Family members' recollections and a 2-day observation lack structure and systematic data gathering. Computed tomography is likely to be normal at this stage.

244. C.   *eating, bathing, and going to the toilet.* The other activities are frequently performed on a

daily basis, and may be important to a patient's safety at home, but are not included in formal ADL listings and assessment. Ambulating and stair climbing are key components of the Medical Outcomes Study 36-item Short Form Health Survey (SF-36), a frequently used survey to assess the overall health status of people in the general population.

245. D. *response extinction.* When reinforcement stops entirely, a behavior tends to stop, although it may unexpectedly reappear in the future as spontaneous recovery. Note that if the reinforcer is not stopped completely, an intermittent reinforcement schedule is initiated, which will make the behavior even harder to stop in the future. Free operant behaviors are not associated with any clear conditioning regimen. Negative reinforcement is anything that, when removed, makes a given behavior more likely in the future. Positive reinforcement is anything that, when applied, increases the chance of the behavior happening again. Stimulus generalization occurs when a similar, but not identical, stimulus elicits the same response.

246. E. *Response extinction.* This is an example of systematic desensitization. Note that the fear is not attacked directly. Instead, the feared object is gradually introduced while another response (relaxation) is in place. While the new response (feeling relaxed) is in place, the old response (becoming fearful) cannot occur and extinction results. Aversive conditioning is the use of noxious stimuli to inhibit an already learned response. A critical period (e.g., imprinting) is a time in a developmental sequence when specific (e.g., environmental) stimuli have especially great impact on subsequent learning and development. Negative reinforcement is anything that, when removed, makes a given behavior more likely to occur in the future. Positive reinforcement is anything that, when used, increases the chance that the behavior will happen again.

247. D. *information about the consequences of behavior is reinforcing.* The vignette describes an example of biofeedback in which an internal physiological state is altered by using externally provided cues. In this instance, it is the information provided by the gauge, not the actual physiological change, high-frequency behavior, or motor performance, that is reinforcing.

248. D. *structured games and sports.* Between 6 and 12 years of age, play becomes truly interactive. Children need structures and rules to govern their increasingly elaborate play. Developing a sense of competency is a key task of development at this age. Children want to participate and show what they can do. To be relegated to the sidelines as one just watching is often taken as a sign of social shame. Same-gender play is generally preferred by both sexes. This is not a time for fantasy, but a time for doing in reality, a time for demonstrating that the child can make things happen. Children at this age also have preferred playmates and develop semi-exclusive play groups. Children do not seek to play with just anyone, but crave the company of their "friends."

249. A. *encouraged to continue with school activities such as team sports and physical education.* The child has a medical condition, but one that, with proper attention, need not limit his quality of life. To encourage the child's withdrawal from normal activities risks stigmatizing him and reducing his chances of developing and maintaining supportive peer friendships. There is absolutely no reason for the child to take on the sick role and seek exemption from regular activities. To label the child as "unfit" risks harming him more than the disease itself will. With proper management, the child can live a full, happy life without an increase in school absences or exemption from family chores.

250. A. *dependent on the reinforcement value of relationships.* Social learning involves our sense of, and the value we place on, other people and our relationships with them. The principles of classical and operant conditioning still apply. Social learning is a key part of individual survival and depends on the feedback of environmental cues, like any other type of learning. In this case, however, how we regard, and are regarded by, other people is the primary reward or motivation for behaviors.

251. B. *Endocrine.* Neurological responses to stress are electrochemical and instantaneous, and typically transient. By contrast, endocrine responses involve the release of hormones into the blood stream. This produces a slower but more prolonged response, due to reliance on the circulatory system for transportation of the active agents to the target organ.

252. C. *the context in which arousal occurs.* The context, and the individual's past experience with that context, will define the meaning and the labeling of the emotion. Whether arousal is felt as joy or anger depends on the cues available to us in the behaviors of others and our own cognitive attributions.

253. E. *90%.* Some of the most dramatic advances in medicine at the end of the 20th century were in the area of neonatal intensive care. Low birthweight infants, who would have faced certain death in the 1960s and 1970s, now routinely survive.

254. B. *25%.* Although survival rates for premature infants have improved dramatically over the past few decades, the child who survives is at higher risk for disabilities than a full-term infant. Long-term respiratory difficulties are common, as are a host of impairments due to hypoxia.

255. A. C*onflict theory – adaptation.* The hallmark of this situation is conflict about change. The question is whether or not the system will adapt to the new request, or will seek to maintain its current routine. Resolution will likely depend on the power of external influences and the perception of possible gains within the hospital organization.

256. D. *Parentified.* When a child is parentified, they are placed in the position of assuming parental authority over household decisions, especially those that include supervising and disciplining siblings. Typically, the oldest child, especially the oldest daughter, is given this role. Resentment from the other children in the family can lead to emotional isolation. Inability to spend time with peers because of home responsibilities can lead to social isolation. Depression is a common outcome.

257. B. A*pproach-avoidance.* The taste of the food reinforces approach behavior, while the probability of unwanted weight gain serves as a negative reinforcer for avoidance behavior. In the conflict presented, the approach reinforcer (good taste) is more immediate and so may influence behavior more strongly. The long-term negative reinforcer (that it will make a person fat in the unspecified future) is not only deferred to some later time but is also less certain to occur than the pleasure of the taste right now. The notion of an oedipal conflict comes from psychoanalytic, not behavioral, psychology.

258. A. *Disengaged.* The strength of disengaged families lies in fostering independence and autonomy. This process may occur at the expense of not teaching members how to work together, and nurture and support one another.

259. E. *injury,* as confirmed annually by epidemiological data. After age 1, injuries of all types are the leading cause of death among children. Automobile accidents account for a substantial proportion of these deaths, although fire-related accidents and environmental poisoning are also prominent causes of injury leading to significant morbidity and mortality.

260. A. *cognitive styles.* Cognitive style denotes individual differences in taking in and coping with life experiences, by the way the individual assigns meaning to them (e.g., seeing an event as frightening, or reassuring, as unique or generalized, as severe or trivial). Cognitive styles, like computer programs, process incoming information in idiosyncratic ways depending on each person's past experience. Defense mechanisms are psychoanalytic concepts in which people cope with uncomfortable emotional states by means of unconscious (nonrational) mental processes. Delusions are false beliefs not shared by others of the same culture. Schemas are the mental patterns or templates against which a person compares experiences and then categorizes them and assigns meaning to them. Sensations are the result of physiological perception.

261. B. *intellectualization* cloaks an experience in abstract terms and removes it from the immediacy of emotional experience – that is, thoughts replace emotions. Denial is the refusal to accept some clear feature of external reality. Projection entails seeing one's own thoughts or feelings as part of the external world. In repression, an event and any reactions to it are forgotten and generally not retrievable. Sublimation provides satisfaction by channeling unacceptable impulses into socially acceptable outlets.

262. C. *habituation* occurs when a stimulus loses its novelty and no longer evokes the same level of initial response. Threshold detection is the lowest level at which a stimulus can be perceived. Just noticeable difference is the smallest difference between two stimuli that allows them to be distinguished. Accumulated fatigue is the result of sleep deprivation over time and

is a common problem among new parents. Not enough information is presented about the parents' general activity level, however, to make this diagnosis. Adjustment reaction suggests difficulty coping with a new or stressful situation. The wife may be less likely to habituate, because, for her, the child's cry is a cue for action. She is likely to become more, not less, attuned to it over time.

263. B. *higher for Hispanics who immigrated to the US than those remaining in their country of origin.* Suicide rates shift over time. Currently, the suicide rate for people in their teens and 20s is similar to that of the population average, about 12 per 100,000. Suicide is one of the leading causes of death among teenagers, because their overall death rate is low. Suicide rates are highest among white males. In fact, two of every three successful suicides are committed by white males. Suicide rates tend to be higher in industrialized countries as a result of the *anomie* (a sense of normlessness or being unsure what rules govern behavior) referred to by Durkheim.

264. C. *psychiatric hospitalization with one-to-one monitoring.* Because 50% of all patients with schizophrenia attempt suicide and 10% are successful, precautions should be taken. Concomitant substance abuse raises the risk. Danger of suicide is the clearest reason to hospitalize a person for psychiatric reasons. Discharge, even with referral to a self-help program or outpatient therapy, gives the patient the opportunity to carry out the commands of the voices he hears. The immediate threat to life should be addressed before initiating any treatment of the substance abuse problem.

265. D. *show concern and ask what assistance she would like to help her manage the diabetes.* The patient has a long history of diabetes mellitus and poor adherence to treatment recommendations. Although the patient may benefit from additional dietary counseling and information about the health consequences of poorly controlled diabetes, she has likely received this information during previous visits. Rather than confront the patient about her reasons for not adhering to the treatment plan or ensuring that she understands that the diabetes is her problem, the best first step is to demonstrate concern about her and to communicate that her opinions regarding her

treatment are valued. An authoritarian provider–patient relationship has not produced the desired results in the care of this patient. Her future medical management should be more patient centered.

266. B. *Enrollment in an experimental drug protocol with poor results.* Anything that might increase a sense of hopelessness increases the risk for suicide. If anything, her level of schooling and her lifetime job suggest that she is at less risk for suicide. Suicide rates are higher among individuals with higher socioeconomic status (defined as a combination of education plus occupation). Having a family member as a caregiver means reduced isolation and, so, reduced suicide risk.

267. C. *Have her breathe into an airsickness bag* is the most readily available way to control her hyperventilation and reduce the "air hunger" that is causing her to gasp for breath. A panic attack is an overwhelming event that cannot be controlled by simply trying to calm a person down or telling a story. Her acute symptoms must be addressed before trying to gather information about the frequency of attacks. Giving the woman a hard candy is unlikely to have an effect on the panic attack and might actually put her at risk for choking.

268. C. *delays in learning to crawl.* Infants who sleep on their stomachs have a risk of SIDS 2 to 3 times that of infants who sleep on their back. Educating parents to place their infants to sleep on their back has been key to reducing the incidence of SIDS. However, children who spend more time on their back have less practice lifting and balancing themselves and, therefore, show delays in learning to crawl, which normally occurs at about 7 to 9 months of age. Speech and social smile are not delayed by placing infants on their back, because this position allows for a broader visual field and may even facilitate these developmental tasks. Auditory discrimination has no known relationship to sleeping position. Thumb-sucking behavior occurs with relatively equal frequency whether the child is placed on the stomach or on the back.

269. B. *E for Energy.* In the mnemonic, *E* stands for energy, which is typically decreased in major depressive disorder. *A* is for appetite. *I* is actually for loss of Interest. Involutional melancholia is a term formerly used for depres-

sive bouts occurring during menopause in women. This condition is now treated as a major depressive episode. *P* is for psychomotor retardation. Leaden paralysis is a term used by patients with atypical depression to describe their extreme sense of fatigue. They report that symptoms they feel include a heaviness in their arms and legs similar to having lead weights attached to them, slowing down their movements. The full mnemonic *SIG E CAPS* stands for Sleep (problems), Interest (reduced), Guilt, Energy (fatigue), Concentration (reduced), Appetite (lack of), Pleasure and/or Psychomotor change (anhedonia and/or leaden paralysis), and Suicidal ideation or behavior.

270. C. *Drive.* Drive theory concerns the motivational influence of survival instincts such as the need for food, water, air, and sex. Arousal theory focuses on the need of the organism to maintain an optimal, but idiosyncratic, level of activation. Cognitive theory focuses on the labeling of behavior and the mapping of activity within a perceived environment. Expectancy theory frames motivation in terms of conditioned, expected associations. Sociocultural theory points out that the impetus for many behaviors can be linked to the specific social and cultural milieu in which they occur.

271. E. *peer victimization for being lesbian.* Multiple studies have found that peer victimization due to homophobic bias increases the risk for suicide in LGBT youth. LGBT youth who come from highly rejecting families are at increased risk for suicide attempts. Having parental support is protective. The majority of LGBT youth who attempt suicide have some form of mental disorder at the time of the attempt; not having one is protective. Although there have been a few published studies linking homosexuality in male adolescents with suicide attempts, no such association has been found for girls. Having a handgun in the house offers a lethal means that increases risk, but making it inaccessible by keeping it locked in a gun safe significantly reduces that risk.

272. B. *immature behavior and lower self-esteem.* Boys who develop later are treated as if they are younger, and may feel deficient when they compare themselves with their peers. Athletic ability is more likely in those who experience early puberty, due to the boost in muscle development provided by testosterone.

No relationship has been found between the timing of puberty and academic ability, delinquency, or musical ability.

273. E. *Selective serotonin reuptake inhibitor.* The only selective serotonin reuptake inhibitor (SSRI) approved by the FDA for the treatment of bulimia nervosa is the antidepressant fluoxetine. Other studies suggest that all SSRIs reduce binge eating and purging even in patients with bulimia who are not depressed. Patients may respond to normal doses initially, but often require doses that are 2 to 4 times higher to reduce binge/purge behavior. Antiemetics reduce nausea and vomiting but do not prevent self-induced vomiting or other forms of purging. Although some antipsychotic medications have demonstrated effectiveness, and some reduce nausea and vomiting in other conditions, they are not typically prescribed for simple bulimia nervosa. Appetite suppressants are not effective in the treatment of this disorder and, depending on the category of drug, may be addictive. Likewise, although benzodiazepines and other anxiolytics may help reduce anxiety, they do not help with the underlying behaviors and also are potentially addictive.

274. B. *In early treatment, the focus is on behavior change and not underlying psychiatric pathology.* The Maudsley method and other family-based approaches focus on empowering the parents first to take control of the affected patient's eating, and then gradually to relinquish it back to the patient as their weight and state of starvation return to normal. These approaches are intentionally "agnostic" about the causes of the pathological food-related behavior. The method teaches parents to exert their existing authority and to provide a structured, nurturing, limit-setting meal time experience (which may or may not involve conflict) so that healthy weight is reestablished. They cannot make the child eat, although they can withhold rewards, such as phone time or games, if the child refuses to eat or resorts to binge/purge behavior. These rewards may be gradually restored when the child reaches milestones of recovery (e.g., eats a normal meal, gains weight, returns to a normal heart rate or blood pressure). Searches for the cause(s) of the eating disorder are not helpful, as they, tend to focus on blame, fault, and guilt, which are all disempowering. At one time, treatment focused on the underlying psy-

chopathology in the individual and the family, with the assumption that once these were resolved, weight restoration would occur on its own. This has proved to be incorrect. The poor nutritional and metabolic state resulting from an eating disorder also impedes effective mental health treatment. As the affected child demonstrates the ability to maintain normal weight (although often with continuing disordered thought patterns about food), parents take a less active role. Parents do not need to monitor their child's caloric intake, but they do need to remain aware of the possibility of relapse and pay attention to any return of disordered eating behaviors.

275. E. *the human body is in its peak physical condition from 20 to 30 years of age.* Patients may rely on medical professionals to tell them what is "normal" at every phase of life. "Feeling old" may be a sign of daily stress or perhaps the beginning of mild depression. The patient should be encouraged to elaborate on what she means by "feeling old." Athletic activity should be encouraged to foster cardiovascular fitness, maintain bone density, and promote better mental health. Brain cell development peaks in utero, while complexity is highest during the teenage years. Peak intellectual achievement may occur very late in life, but is most common in the 40s.

276. C. *aphasia.* The most common type of aphasia (nominative, dysfluent or Broca's aphasia), results from lesions in Broca's area in the left hemisphere and compromises the ability to produce speech, although comprehension is intact. Receptive, fluent, or Wernicke's aphasia indicates lesions of Wernicke's area. These impair comprehension, with speech that may be fluent but syntactically and semantically imprecise. Conduction aphasia results from lesions of the tract connecting the two brain areas. Such lesions damage the ability to repeat what one has heard, despite intact comprehension and speech production. Thus, these three aspects of the Mini–Mental State Examination test different aspects of aphasia. Agnosia is the inability to recognize objects or parts of one's own body. Amnesia is loss of memory. Apraxia is the inability to perform learned actions such as tying one's shoes, putting on a shirt, drawing, or copying a drawing. Disturbance of executive function encompasses problems doing things in sequence, suppressing impulses, or directing attention

at will. The MMSE is a well-standardized, bedside test that systematically assesses each domain, to aid recognition of both focal and diffuse brain pathology. The copyrighted MMSE is especially helpful in dementia, a global brain state that may affect most or all of these abilities. The freely available Montreal Cognitive Assessment Test (MoCA) measures naming, comprehension, praxis, executive function, and memory, but not repetition. It has replaced the MMSE in many settings.

277. A. *a desire to enhance cognitive development.* The need refers to the desire or impulse for cognitive growth and activity. Type A behavior patterns are hard driving and competitive, but distinct from the desire for cognitive engagement and development. Ability offers the potential for cognitive activity, but not the drive. The desire to have children does not spring from cognitive need. The desire for dominance and control over others is separate from internal cognitive enhancement.

278. C. *increased capacity for interpersonal relationships.* Task-oriented behaviors continue as career goals are identified, and are supported by increased experience with complex decision making. With experience, perspective increases and with it the capacity to manage and control impulsive behavior. The focus on the creation of an independent identity fades with maturation into young adulthood. Sense of self emerges more from the reality of relationships and less from the idealization of self.

279. E. *the proportions of sexually active single men and women are nearly equal.* The common belief that single women vastly outnumber single men is untrue. Fewer than 20% of young adults choose long-term singlehood. Most periods of singlehood relationships last less than 3 years. Singlehood has career advantages in terms of the hours that can be spent working, and it can foster an increased sense of psychological autonomy. Overall, only 6% of males and 3% of females are homosexual. Many of these individuals are married, and half of homosexuals who are married have children. It is no more true to say that most single people are homosexual than it is to say that married people cannot be homosexual.

280. B. *pseudodementia.* The Mini–Mental State Examination (MMSE) is particularly helpful

for differentiating dementia of the Alzheimer's type from depression with reversible cognitive impairment or "pseudodementia," a condition that is quite common in older, depressed people. The cognitive problems of depression are mostly those of processing speed, effortful concentration, and motivation to perform. Depressive ideation makes people overestimate their impairments. Demented patients, by contrast, may be unaware of their deficits. They tend to have problems that stem from different areas of brain cortex (marked by deterioration of short-term memory, aphasias, apraxia, disorientation, and disturbance of executive functioning). Scores below 24 on the MMSE are a reliable indicator of dementia, if the patient has made a good effort. The maximum MMSE score is 30 and scores > 27 typically indicate normal cognition. Scores between 24 and 27 require careful assessment to distinguish early dementia from other forms of cognitive impairment. In this case, subacute onset, past personal history of depression, and depressive ideation support the depression diagnosis. Delirium connotes an acute change in mental status due to some metabolic, toxic, or circulatory condition that does not permanently damage brain tissue but disrupts the function of the reticular activating system. Delirious patients may score very low on any form of mental status evaluation due to their fluctuating level of consciousness and global brain dysfunction, but a 3-month course of illness is not consistent with delirium. Generalized anxiety disorder is associated with agitation, worry, bodily anxiety, and dread. By definition, it lasts at least 6 months. It tends to develop earlier in life, or after significant trauma. Subcortical dementia differs pathologically and clinically from Alzheimer's dementia. In later stages, both seem similar, but early in the course of illness, parietal lobe and hippocampal functions are more disturbed in Alzheimer's dementia, leading to amnesia, psychosis, aphasia, and apraxia. In contrast, subcortical pathology preferentially disrupts the basal ganglia and frontal lobes, affecting motor activity, mood, executive functioning, social behavior, and judgment. Although patients with any form of dementia may seem apathetic, self-doubt and feelings of futility are associated more specifically with depression.

281. A. *establishing a collegial relationship with parents typically begins during young adulthood.* Only as a young adult can the child begin to see the parent as a mutual participant in the adult world. Many young adults describe their sense of self by contrasting it with their parents. Financial assistance from parents to help pay for adult children's education, a first home, or having children is usually accepted with gratitude. The process of questioning family origins and making commitments often begins in adolescence. Adult relationships are different from those between parents and their young children. Although old patterns can linger, the young adult's capacity for independence and self-determination alters the balance of power in the relationship.

282. E. *natural, supernatural, and social worlds.* An ethnic group's shared ideas about the natural, supernatural, and social worlds influence its system of maintaining health and treating disease. The natural realm includes the connections between people and the earth's elements of soil, water, air, plants, and animals. The social realm encompasses individual qualities and the appropriate interaction between people of different ages, genders, lineages, and ethnic groups. The supernatural realm connotes beliefs about birth, death, afterlife, reincarnation, spirits, and interactions between the spiritual world and the human world. To fully understand any ethnic group's perspective about health and disease, we must put it into context with other aspects of that culture, such as beliefs about natural hazards, what a person is or should be, the kinship system, and the meaning of suffering, life, and death.

283. A. *cognitive rehearsal is the process of visualizing action before actually attempting it.* Like an actor, the player visualizes the task to be accomplished before attempting it. Cognitive restructuring involves changing the assumptions that are behind future behaviors. Problem solving refers to a cognitive routine to arrive at an acceptable solution to a presented dilemma. In self-control contracting, a person contracts with themselves that, when a goal is reached, a reward will be received. Skills training involves learning and practicing particular behaviors with the aid of an instructor or model.

284. D. *Convergence of NMDA and non-NMDA receptor activation slows, prolongs, and increases the efficiency of the synapse, facilitating complex sensory learning.* This conver-

gence signals that the stimuli are important and provides inducement for the structural changes required for long-term memory. Stimulation of the non-NMDA receptors triggers the depolarization that releases magnesium blockade of NMDA receptors. This results in combined NMDA and non-NMDA receptor activation and produces a prolonged synaptic response.

285. B. *25% increase in height and 50% increase in weight.* Weight increases more than height as physical development progresses. The period just before puberty is when the greatest growth in height ("growth spurt") occurs.

286. D. *Earlier height gain in girls reflects the body's adaptation to reproductive functioning.* There is no evidence that the eating habits or nutrition of boys and girls differ appreciably. Most growth occurs during delta sleep and is unaffected by waking time or activity level, nor is growth related to the attention that is paid to the child. Although boys and girls show slight differences on standardized tests (boys do better on mathematics and visual-spatial problems, while girls do better on verbal tasks), this is more likely related to cultural mores and social roles than to intrinsic developmental differences.

287. D. *improved health and nutrition.* Childhood diseases, in general, have little impact on the timing of puberty. Although many things have been cited as consequences of global warming, change in the timing of puberty is not one of them. Given higher infant survival rates, later age at first marriage, and longer life expectancy, the social demand would be for later puberty, not earlier.

288. B. *Duration.* Chronic pain is generally defined as lasting beyond reasonable expectancy for a particular injury. Pain that lasts longer than 6 months is commonly considered chronic. Intensity refers to the patient's level of discomfort. Family history will reveal any predisposing factors. The site and cause of the pain are useful in planning management and in estimating the probable level of residual disability.

289. B. *Hypothalamus and the pituitary gland.* The hypothalamus regulates the endocrine balance that is central for pubescent development. It also regulates eating, body temperature, and

the sleep/wake cycle. Efferent pathways from the hypothalamus control the pituitary gland by both neural projections and communicating blood supply. The adrenal gland is made up of two parts. The adrenal medulla produces the epinephrine responsible for the fight-or-flight response. The adrenal cortex produces both cortisol and aldosterone, hormones that mobilize nutrients, regulate the response to inflammation, and regulate the balance of salts and body fluids. Thyroid hormone regulates metabolism and helps maintain the functioning of neuronal structures. Although abnormal functioning of the thyroid or adrenal glands may influence growth, theses glands are end organs for the regulatory processes originating in the hypothalamus and pituitary gland.

290. A. *are at the stage of concrete operations,* according to Piaget's theory of cognitive development. During this stage, children can abstract from their experiences, but have trouble understanding general abstractions such as hypothetical situations. The capacity for abstraction is gained as the child transitions to the stage of formal operations. Capacity for understanding in the situation presented is linked to development, not educational level. Measured IQ is remarkably stable from about age 5 onward. Although an infant may be distractible, a boy of this age should be able to pay attention long enough to absorb an age-appropriate explanation of diabetes. In general, children and even adolescents do trust those who care for them. When rebellion does occur, it is manifested as symbolic struggles for identity, not rejection of everything related to the parents or other adults.

291. D. *developmental struggles are relatively minor.* Progression to adulthood follows a reasonably continuous pattern. The stresses and strains of adolescence make for good drama, but do not reflect the experience of most teenagers. Most adolescents derive their core values from those of their parents. Boys and girls experience roughly similar adjustment difficulties to adolescence per se, although girls have some increased biological and social risks during this period. Actually, girls' increased vulnerability to the onset of mood, anxiety, and eating disorders begins with puberty and extends through the reproductive years (i.e., 14 to 45 years). Girls may lose self-confidence and become more internalizing during adoles-

cence. They are also more liable to experience sexual abuse or exploitation.

292. E. *intense concern about social and peer relationships.* In girls, adjustment to the physical changes of puberty typically occurs at 11 to 13 years. Although intimate relationships become increasingly important during middle adolescence (14–17 years), peer relationships still predominate. This is the first age at which career preference may be carried into action, but career preference is unlikely to be a middle adolescent's main preoccupation. The desire for conformity is likely to be stronger than the desire for recognition.

293. D. *Placebo effect.* The placebo effect is a change in the patient's illness attributable to the symbolic import of a treatment. Patients in studies designed as described in the question do not know if they are receiving the drug being studied or an inert pill. Assuming all other treatments are identical, the placebo effect should be the same (contribute equally to the findings in both groups) and, therefore, be eliminated as a differentiating factor. Specific treatment effect refers to the therapeutic mechanism (e.g., antimicrobial action) of the new drug being studied and is usually what the study is intended to measure. Nonspecific treatment effects are those unrelated to the drug being studied, such as how clinic staff treat the patients. Natural course of the disease refers to fluctuations in disease severity that occur irrespective of treatment. Investigator bias refers to how investigators' preconceived ideas of research outcomes affect study results. Though double-blind studies, in which neither the investigator nor the subject know whether the subject is receiving active drug or placebo, partly control for investigator bias, bias may affect other elements such as the duration of the trial, choice of study population, or outcome measures.

294. B. *accidents, suicide, and homicide.* These data are collected and reported by the Centers for Disease Control and Prevention (CDC). These three top causes of death have been unchanged for decades, reflecting the increase in risk-taking behavior associated with adolescence and young adulthood (15 to 24 years). Taking risks reflects the inadequate consideration of long-term consequences, feelings of invulnerability, impulsivity, and poor judgment seen in this age group, especially among males.

295. D. *appropriate.* Care is appropriate when the "right thing is done in the right way by the right person for the right reason." These are criteria for professional competency and comprehensiveness. Appropriateness is therefore defined by professional standards of care.

296. C. *meaning of the pain.* A classic study done during World War II showed that soldiers with similar degrees of injury expressed different levels of pain, as measured objectively by how much narcotic they required for relief, depending on the meaning of their injuries. Those for whom the injury meant they would be sent home were in measurably less pain than those who expected to return to combat. Like any other subjective, conscious experience, pain is influenced by how much attention is paid to it, which, in turn, is a factor of what the pain means. The person's general state of morale (hopeful, cheerful, empowered vs. depressed, hopeless, helpless) also influences subjective pain, as shown by the efficacy of treatment for depression in reducing pain. Every other option presented (availability of narcotics, degree of tissue injury, general fitness, and time of day) may influence pain but was matched between soldier groups. In research terms, these are controlled conditions that highlight the effect of the variable of interest.

297. A. *gender identity* refers to the psychological sense of self. Gender identity is more strongly determined by culture and parental assignment than by the physical genitalia with which the child was born. People with a mismatch between physical sex and psychological identity are termed transsexual. Parental identification refers to the child's focus on and attachment to parental figures, and is one of the major contributors to gender identity. Sex role schemas are mental templates or categories that help provide an understanding of the differences in male and female behaviors. Sex role stereotypes reflect inflexible notions of what constitutes appropriate behaviors for males and females. Sexual orientation refers to the gender of a person's preferred sexual partner, either homosexual or heterosexual.

298. E. *reductions in infant mortality rates.* Life expectancy at birth is defined as median survival time. Therefore, anything that results in loss of life at a young age has a disproportionate impact on life expectancy. All of the other options are associated with better health and

reduced mortality, but occur too late in life to have the same impact on life expectancy as infant mortality

299. B. *bias.* A tester who knows the hypothesized outcome may unwittingly act to confirm it. A placebo effect is found when the patient shows improvement even though the intervention lacks any known therapeutic benefit. Construct validity refers to the degree to which the test matches a given theoretical concept. This is not the issue here. Reliability is the extent to which the test results are reproducible or consistent. Stigma is a problem with most psychiatric diagnoses. Patients feel and can be treated with a level of shame not associated with illnesses considered strictly "physical."

300. E. *moderate levels of arousal are best for optimal performance.* The Yerkes-Dodson law states that excessively high arousal (high anxiety) impedes performance, while low arousal (apathy) fails to provide the necessary motivation to do well.

301. C. *egocentrism* – that is, the inability to see the world from another's point of view. In this classic demonstration, children are presented with a diorama of mountains and asked to describe what a person standing on the other side of the mountains would see. In early developmental stages, children can only respond in terms of what they see and cannot imagine the perspective of the other person. Centration is the tendency for young children to focus attention on one aspect of the situation while neglecting other possibly relevant aspects. Conservation is knowing the amount of substance stays the same despite a change in shape or form. Magical thinking (preoperational stage) is the belief that thinking about something will actually cause it to occur. Piaget's object permanence is the capacity to realize that objects exist even if they cannot be directly sensed, and is demonstrated by asking the child to find an object that has been covered. Attaining object permanence is an indication that the child has reached Piaget's preoperational stage.

302. A. *animism.* The child's tendency to attribute the qualities of living things to inanimate objects may be reinforced by fairy tales and other stories. Artificialism is the belief that all things are created, and symbolization is the process

by which one thing stands for other things. Autism is a psychiatric condition manifested as an inability to relate to other people, a preference for sameness in the environment, and lack of language development. Magical thinking is believing that thought equals action; the child believes their desires actually cause events to occur.

303. C. *10,000.* Most of these words are descriptive of things in the child's environment or are used to denote events in the child's life. Children at this age are, however, still mastering some of the finer points of grammar, such as tenses.

304. D. *initiative vs. guilt.* Autonomy vs. shame becomes important at the time of toilet training, generally between ages 2 and 4. Adolescence, ages 12 to 18, is the time when issues of identity predominate. Industry vs. inferiority corresponds with the Freudian latency period, ages 6 to 12. During that period, children strive to display their competencies to themselves and others. Trust vs. mistrust is paramount during the first 2 years of life, as children learn whether or not they can depend on their caretakers. Basic trust is considered the foundation of all future relationships.

305. E. *society's moratorium on growing up.* Pressure to grow into adult roles quickly would leave little social space for the subculture. MTV reflects the subculture, but did not create it. Drug use can be a part of adolescent exploration, but is not the force that created the subculture. The existence of the teenage subculture predates the age of computers.

306. E. *slower rate of metabolism.* All of the other options presented may affect sensitivity to medication in any given individual, at any age. However, lower metabolic rate and decreased clearance due to age-related declines in liver and kidney function relate particularly to older persons.

307. A. *Alzheimer's disease* accounts for 50% to 70% of all dementias in older people. The patient's age and presentation argue against "normal senility." The gradual onset tends to rule out tumor or stroke. The patient is not reported to be taking other medications, nor is the pattern of cognitive change described consistent with any particular medicine regimen. Loss of memory, decreased ability to dress oneself,

repeatedly leaving the stove on, and failing to recognize family members is not a normal part of the aging process.

308. A. *a high-frequency behavior or reward can be used as a reinforcer for a low-frequency target behavior.* A behavior that occurs frequently has high value and can, therefore, be used to reinforce other behaviors that are less common. The valance of low-frequency behaviors is variable (i.e., they can be aversive or merely neglected), and so they do not predictably influence behavior. Moderate levels of arousal are associated with optimum performance, but moderate-frequency behaviors do not optimize learning. Individuals do seem to engage in behavior that they find desirable, but this statement is unrelated to the Premack principle.

309. B. *balancing life's accomplishments and failures.* Maintaining ego integrity requires that one make reasonable decisions based on a fair appraisal of external life circumstances. A person aged 64 has quite a bit of life to look back on, but if she does not have a serious disease, she is not close to death. The issue now is, does she feel a sense of accomplishment and purpose that bring her satisfaction and peace as she grows older? Or does it seem to her that she has wasted her life, and has more regrets than successes? Note that in the face of despair at this stage, Erikson's recommended therapeutic intervention is "regression in the service of the ego." This means mentally returning to a previous developmental stage and revisiting, understanding, and accepting previous life-defining decisions. Once these earlier decisions are reviewed, the person can move forward with a firmer foundation of "ego strength" (i.e., a sense of still being oneself and an active agent in one's life, in the face of the gradual loss of capacities that comes with aging).

310. E. *successful negotiation of transitions.* This implies anticipating the need for change and making adjustments in activities and expectations to accommodate these changes. Accepting change means accepting new roles in both work and personal life, and learning to fulfill the demands of these roles. It is impossible to move through life without experiencing some loss. Coping with losses and arranging a new life pattern in the face of them is key to "successful" development across the lifespan.

311. D. *illustrations of how people interpret bodily signs and symptoms in culturally specific ways.* Entities that are recognized by certain groups but not others have been studied as folk illnesses or culture-bound syndromes. These entities are physical ailments. Within a particular interpretive framework, each has a specified etiology and pathophysiology, although not necessarily ones that can be tested by the tools of Western medical science. Models of causation also determine methods of treatment. Some culturally specific conditions may also be understood as expressions of mental or social distress, with specific symbolic meanings. Eating disorders, which embody a cultural ideal of body shape and a nutritional environment that distorts healthy eating, are products of Eurowestern culture, understood and classified within the culturally valued framework of biomedical sciences. Folk illnesses and culture-bound syndromes are not separate categories of diseases, just other examples of how all signs and symptoms are culturally interpreted. The use of culturally derived categories is not a sign of ignorance or lack of education.

312. C. *include increases in adrenal steroids, beginning as early as age 7.* Older psychological developmental theories described middle childhood as a time of "latency" when sexual concerns are mostly irrelevant. While this is a reasonable claim at the psychological level, physical sexual development is a continuous process that begins in middle childhood with an increase in adrenal steroids. External markers of puberty follow from subsequent changes in estrogen, testosterone, and progesterone in both girls and boys.

313. B. *complexity of synaptic connections.* More complex connections provide the neural substrate for increasingly sophisticated behavior and thought patterns. It is not the size of the brain as measured by head circumference that matters most, but the evolving connections between brain areas and cells. The absolute number of neurons declines throughout development. The mechanisms of neuronal processing do not change, nor do new neurotransmitters appear.

314. C. *expression of adult sleep architecture.* Sleep patterns, such as length of sleep cycle and differentiation among sleep stages, mature to adult-like patterns between 10 and 13 years

of age. Function-specific activity increases as certain areas of the brain become more adept at specialized tasks. Hemispheric differentiation is established during infancy and is a central organizing principle for brain functioning. Delta wave activity occurs in the deepest stages of sleep and is never primary in waking brain function. The amount of delta activity actually declines with age; as a result, the deepest stages of sleep do not occur in older people. Alpha wave activity suggests a disengagement from external stimuli and is most easily fostered by closing the eyes. As children explore and become more involved in the outside world, alpha wave activity is likely to decrease.

315. A. *Deficits in executive functions* such as reasoning and decision making. Persons with ADHD show no essential differences on visual discrimination tasks, although they may have difficulty adhering to the instructions of the testing situation. They may show deficits in visual-spatial tracking tasks. Deficits in attention make processing verbal directions more difficult, not easier. ADHD does not make children more susceptible to childhood infectious diseases. Social difficulties in children with ADHD are extremely common. The Multimodal Treatment Study of Children with ADHD (MTA) found that 52% fell in the socially rejected category, and less than 1% were of popular status. When children who did not fit in any category were excluded from the study, 80% of the children with ADHD fell into the rejected group. Prior studies have shown that children with ADHD have peer rejection scores 1 standard deviation above the mean, and 60% are 2 standard deviations or more above the mean.

316. C. *evaluate and characterize the psychological attributes of other people.* Children become less egocentric and are able to see the world from others' point of view as they mature. They are also able to classify these perceived differences and characterize people as having different "personalities." Manipulation of abstract concepts such as anticipating the future, predicting in hypothetical situations, and having a personal philosophy are all characteristic of Piaget's stage of formal operations, which generally occurs after age 12. However, the ability to think abstractly develops over time, and some children in later middle childhood are beginning to have this capability.

317. D. *be seen as good.* At this boy's stage of development, being good means following the rules. Knowing and following the rules is likely to garner approval of supervising adults and allows the child to generate self-approval by internalizing these standards. The issue here is not avoiding either embarrassment or punishment from others, but achieving a positively valued sense of self. The directions given by the child are the result of trying to adhere to the rules and not the result of a desire to dominate others. The child seeks rules, not to replace the parents, but to be like them and to please them by being a "good boy."

318. D. *Reflex, imprinting, one-trial, classical, operant, social.* The sequence moves from lower-level central nervous system to higher-level cortical functioning.

319. C. *physical changes can be predicted from social and interpersonal factors.* People who have and enjoy social relationships early in life show less physical decline later in life. The exact reasons for this finding are unclear. It may be that generally healthy people have more interpersonal relationships, that these relationships benefit physiological functioning over time, or that the presence of social relationships serves to buffer stressful life events, and so reduce physiological strain. Most individuals report signs of aging beginning in their 40s. However, different people manifest signs of aging at different times. Wrinkles and physical decline occur across a wide variety of ages. Women do not age earlier than men, though social norms valuing young women may make them more sensitive to external signs of aging. In fact, women's life expectancy is, on average, 15 years longer than that for men.

320. B. *the female menstrual cycle begins to change during the 30s and 40s,* the beginning of the process that culminates in menopause. Recent research has found no differences in the age of onset of menopause in different ethnic or racial groups. The number of children a couple has is not related to sexual activity at older ages. Sexual desire in males is neither the cause nor consequence of sperm production. Men continue to produce sperm, although in declining quantity, throughout life.

321. A. *body dysmorphic disorder* connotes undue preoccupation with some trivial or imagined

physical defect. Everyone evaluates personal appearance differently from how others perceive it. In body dysmorphic disorder, the person's distorted image of a body part must cause distress and impair function. Delusional disorder typically involves more complex and pervasive false beliefs than preoccupation with a single physical trait. Factitious disorder describes someone who induces illness to obtain the benefits of the sick role to gratify unconscious needs for attention, sympathy, and relief from responsibility. Malingering involves feigning illness for conscious secondary gain, such as receiving opiates, escaping military duty, receiving compensation, or avoiding prison. Civilian malingerers may have antisocial personality traits. Social phobia may be associated with similar avoidance of social situations, but the root is fear of ridicule, humiliation, or rejection.

322. B. *establish that the e-mail link is secure.* The Health Insurance Portability and Accountability Act (HIPAA) requires that all protected health information (PHI) sent via e-mail be secure. Home systems may not be secure. While timeliness, keeping e-mails brief, and transmitting the minimum information necessary are important components of provider–patient correspondence, they are not as important as the provider's responsibility to first ensure that PHI is protected. At the conclusion of the exchange, all correspondence should be placed in the patient's medical record.

323. C. *the clinician controls medical decision making.* Behaviors that decrease patients' involvement in their medical care and the decision-making process also decrease adherence to treatment. The other options provided are associated with *increased* patient adherence to treatment regimens.

324. D. *most adult children and their parents have positive feelings about each other.* Older parents continue to be sources of help and advice for their adult children, and children of older people constitute their major support system during times of illness or other personal crises. Once they have their own children, adults tend to look at their parents differently, with a new understanding of the problems and dilemmas of parenthood. Feelings of dependency on parents continue throughout the lifespan, although the behaviors that express this dependency change over time. Child–parent, not

sibling, relationships tend to hold the extended family together and provide a shared identity among family members even into middle age.

325. C. *10%.* One in 10 children in the US is born prematurely. The risk for prematurity is higher in African American mothers, teenage mothers, mothers from lower socioeconomic groups, and mothers who smoke.

326. D. *show more anger when challenged.* Although emotional expressions differ across cultures, cross-cultural studies show that greater anger when challenged seems to be almost universal for males. The other options are more culture specific.

327. A. *Alcohol.* Fetal alcohol syndrome is the leading prenatal cause of mental retardation, and the most preventable. Convincing women who are pregnant, or are likely to become pregnant, to avoid alcohol consumption is the simplest known method for reducing the risk for retardation. Babies and children whose mothers took anticonvulsants (especially sodium valproate or valproic acid) during pregnancy are at increased risk for various complications, including impaired intellectual development. These impairments do not generally reach the level of global mental retardation, and anticonvulsant use is far less common than alcohol use among women of reproductive age. Children of mothers who use cocaine may evidence withdrawal reactions following birth, but they develop normally if the postnatal environment is sufficiently stable and nurturing. Opiate (e.g., heroin, methadone) use is associated with neonatal withdrawal symptoms and diffuse neurodevelopmental deficits, but not with mental retardation in particular. Women who smoke have a harder time becoming pregnant in the first place, and if they continue smoking after the child is born, their child is at increased risk for asthma and sudden infant death syndrome (SIDS).

328. D. *Prolactin.* Parkinson's disease is characterized by reduced levels of dopamine in the substantia nigra. A number of treatments, including L-dopa, are available. Dopamine is a prolactin-inhibiting factor. Thus, prolactin levels can serve as a rough indicator of overall dopamine levels in the brain. Acetylcholine is more closely associated with Alzheimer's dementia. Norepinephrine is linked to mood disorders. Lower levels of GABA are associated with

anxiety disorders. Serotonin is implicated in a wide variety of disorders including mood disorders, anxiety, and schizophrenia.

329. B.   *5-HT2* activity works to modify appetite by means of phosphoinositide, a secondary messenger. Stimulation of the 5-HT1 receptors causes contraction of the gastrointestinal system and inhibits central nervous system activity. The action of the 5-HT3 receptors is not clear at this time. Stimulation of the 5-HT4 receptors increases adenylate cyclase activity. The answer "all of the above" is incorrect because the action of appetite is specific to the 5-HT2 receptor.

330. D.   *Symbolic interaction – latent pattern maintenance.* Communication is possible when actions have a common meaning within a shared frame of reference. In this case, the assumptions about the meaning of the action (rolling the patient over) were different. The nurses rolled the patient over to prevent bedsores, but the action prevented the patient from sleeping and communicated to the patient that sleeping would be fatal. Conflict theory examines the social structures and processes that emerge as the result of competition for dominance and other scarce resources. Implicit theory refers to the subjective theory of action that organizes and gives meaning to the world in which a person moves. Structural functional analysis examines how organizational and situational components work to allow the attainment of specific ends. Integration maps the process by which the diverse components of a system are able to function together as a whole.

331. E.   *reliability.* The reliability of a test provides information about how likely it is that a particular test will give the same results on a consistent basis, so that any change represents real change and not just random fluctuation. Adaptive capacity has nothing to do with evaluating how useful a test may be. Bias is deviation from truth and reflects an inability of the test to accurately represent reality. Concurrent validity means that other, external criteria confirm the results of the test. Content validity means that the items on the test relate to the subject matter being assessed.

332. A.   *Altruistic.* The soldier sacrificed himself to save a friend. The term *anomic suicide* stems from the term *anomie*, which connotes the

condition of normlessness and lack of social rules. Anomic suicides occur in situations of social upheaval and chaos, when normative rules are unclear. Egoistic suicide is associated with a personal agenda, such as revenge on a loved one. Fatalistic and heroic suicide are not part of Durkheim's typology.

333. B.   *Compulsive gambling that only occurs on weekends.* Compulsive gambling represents an unaddressed addiction that often becomes progressive. Clinicians can practice in limited roles with HIV. Impairment after stroke depends on the location of the stroke, not the stroke per se. Medical professionals have high levels of successful drug rehabilitation. Problems with keeping records is more likely to reflect poor skills rather than impairment.

334. E.   *somatic symptom disorder.* Somatization is a term that generally connotes the expression of distress in physical rather than psychological terms. Somatic symptom disorder describes a long-standing pattern of having one or more somatic symptoms that are excessively distressing or result in significant disruption of daily life for more than 6 months. How we experience our bodies is highly influenced by the balance between central norepinephrine, histamine, interleukins, acetylcholine, dopamine, and endogenous opiates, which are, in turn, regulated by serotonin, and other neurological factors. The thresholds and stability of these neurological processes are, in turn, affected (sensitized or desensitized) by prior experience and elements of the current environment. Attributing somatic distress entirely to psychological processes is especially easy to do when a patient is convinced of an unproven cause for the distress. Patients are "accused" of somaticizing when, in fact, they and their physicians lack a common language and a common framework for understanding the way in which they experience bodily sensations. There are many reasons people avoid social situations and cannot fill normal social expectations. Avoidant personality is only diagnosed if the patient expresses a desire for relationships but avoids them for fear of consequences such as rejection, humiliation, or exploitation. Malingering is often invoked to explain why a distressed person with no objective signs of disease seeks attention, but it cannot be diagnosed without evidence that the person is not actually in distress (or has purposefully inflicted distress) and is seeking

secondary gain. Obsessive-compulsive disorder involves intrusive thoughts about contamination, danger, being harmed or doing harm to others associated with compulsions to try to control these thoughts. Panic disorder does present with multiple somatic complaints, but these come in acute bursts and follow a typical pattern related to peripheral autonomic arousal (pounding heart, air hunger, dizziness, restlessness) and are associated with overestimation of how dangerous the symptoms are.

335. E. *Licensing* is required in order to be granted legal permission to deliver medical care. Certification recognizes achievement of a higher standard of competency by a professional organization, but is not required for practice. Practitioners can choose to participate in whichever insurance plans they like, or none at all. This choice includes both Medicaid and Medicare. Health care practitioners can also charge fees as they see fit and may, for example, set up a payment system for patients paying out-of-pocket that recognizes ability to pay as a factor in determining charges (e.g., a "sliding scale").

Contributors

Forrest C. Bennett, MD
(Selected Theories of Development; The Fetus, Newborn, and Infant; Toddlerhood and the Preschool Years)
Professor of Pediatrics (retired)
University of Washington School of Medicine
Seattle, WA
fbennett@u.washington.edu

Martha A. Bird, MD
(Practice Exam)
Professor
Department of Psychiatry and Behavioral Sciences
James H. Quillen College of Medicine
East Tennessee State University
Johnson City, TN
birdma@etsu.edu

Richard J. Botelho, BMedSci, BMBS, MRCGP (UK)
(Motivating Healthy Behaviors)
Professor of Family Medicine (retired)
University of Rochester
Rochester, NY
rbotelho@me.com

José L. Calderón, MD
(Understanding and Improving Health Literacy)
Associate Professor
Charles R. Drew University of Medicine & Science
Los Angeles, CA
doxstox@g.ucla.edu

Marlene Camacho-Rivera, ScD, MPH
(Culture and Cultural Competence in Health Care)
Assistant Medical Professor
CUNY School of Medicine
The City College of New York
New York, NY
mcamacho-rivera@med.cuny.edu

John E. Carr, PhD – Editor
(Cognition, Communication, and Social Interaction; Emotion and Learning; Evolving Models of Health Care; Predisposition; Principles of Psychotherapy; Stress, Adaptation, and Stress Disorders)
Professor Emeritus
Departments of Psychiatry & Behavioral Sciences and Psychology
University of Washington
Seattle, WA
jcarr@u.washington.edu

Marissa E. Carraway, PhD
(The Provider–Patient Relationship)
Licensed Psychologist
Clinical Assistant Professor
Department of Family Medicine
Brody School of Medicine
Associate Graduate Faculty
Department of Psychology
East Carolina University
Greenville, NC
carrawaym15@ecu.edu

Jillian S. Catalanotti, MD, MPH, FACP
(The US Health Care System)
Associate Professor of Medicine and of Health Policy Management
The George Washington University
Washington, DC
jcatalanotti@mfa.gwu.edu

Alexander L. Chapman, PhD, RPsych
(Suicide)
Professor & Coordinator, Clinical Science
Department of Psychology
Simon Fraser University
Burnaby, BC
Canada
alchapma@sfu.ca

Tingyin T. Chee, MD, MPA
(The US Health Care System)
Resident Physician
The George Washington University
Washington, DC
tychee3@gmail.com

Stephanie H. Cho, MD
(Somatic Symptom and Related Disorders)
Psychosomatic Medicine Fellow
LAC + USC Medical Center
Los Angeles, CA
stephanie.cho.md@gmail.com

Stephen R. Cook, MD, MPH, FAAP, FTOS
(Obesity)
Associate Professor of Pediatrics
Golisano Children's Hospital
University of Rochester Medical Center
Rochester, NY
stephen_cook@urmc.rochester.edu

Jayanth Dasika, MD
(Pain)
Assistant Professor
Department of Anesthesiology
University of Florida
Jacksonville, FL
jayanth.dasika@jax.ufl.edu

Erin M. Denney-Koelsch, MD
(Palliative Care)
Palliative Care Program
Department of Medicine
University of Rochester Medical Center
Rochester, NY
erin_denney-koelsch@urmc.rochester.edu

Kristin A. Evans, PhD
(Obesity)
Senior Research Analyst
IBM Watson Health
Armonk, NY
kaevans@us.ibm.com

James A. H. Farrow, MD
(The Adult Years)
Professor of Pediatrics & Medicine
Tulane University School of Medicine
New Orleans, LA
jfarrow@tulane.edu

Jessica F. Ferreira, BA
(Suicide)
Clinical Psychology Graduate Student
Simon Fraser University
Burnaby, BC
Canada
jferreir@sfu.ca

Jonathon M. Firnhaber, MD
*(The Medical Encounter and Clinical
Decision Making)*
Associate Professor
Vice Chair of Academic Affairs
Residency Program Director
Department of Family Medicine
Brody School of Medicine at East Carolina
University
Greenville, NC
firnhaberj@ecu.edu

Julia B. Frank, MD – Editor
*(Anxiety Disorders; Disruptive, Impulse-Control,
and Conduct Disorders; Evolving Models of
Health Care; Introduction to Psychopathology;
Neurocognitive Disorders: Delirium and
Secondary Symptoms; Neurocognitive
Disorders: Dementia; Obsessive-Compulsive
and Related Disorders; Personality Disorders;
Pharmacological Interventions for Psychiatric
Disorders; Practice Exam; Principles of
Psychotherapy; Somatic Symptom and Related
Disorders; Stress Disorders; Bereavement, and
Dissociative Disorders; The Nervous System; The
Psychiatric Evaluation)*
Clinical Professor of Psychiatry
Former Director of Medical Student Education in
Psychiatry
George Washington University School of
Medicine and Health Sciences
Washington, DC
jfrank@mfa.gwu.edu

Maria F. Gómez, MD
(Substance-Related and Addictive Disorders)
Associate Professor of Clinical Psychiatry and
Behavioral Sciences
Albert Einstein College of Medicine
Associate Director, Psychosomatic Medicine
Montefiore Medical Center
Bronx, NY
mfgomez@montefiore.org

Frederic W. Hafferty, PhD
*(Theories of Social Relations and
Interprofessional Collaboration)*
Professor of Medical Education
Division of General Internal Medicine and
Program in Professionalism and Values
Mayo Clinic
Rochester, MN
fredhafferty@mac.com

Douglas C. Haldeman, PhD
*(Health Care Issues Facing Lesbian, Gay,
Bisexual, and Transgender Individuals)*
Professor and Chair
Doctoral Program in Clinical Psychology
College of Graduate and Professional Studies
John F. Kennedy University
Pleasant Hill, CA
doughaldeman@aol.com

Mariel R. Herbert, MD
*(Disruptive, Impulse-Control, and Conduct
Disorders; Personality Disorders;
Pharmacological Interventions for Psychiatric
Disorders)*
University of Maryland School of Medicine
Baltimore, MD
mherbertmd@gmail.com

Lisa D. Herzig, MD
*(Selected Theories of Development; The Fetus,
Newborn, and Infant; Toddlerhood and the
Preschool Years)*
Assistant Professor
Developmental Behavioral Pediatrics
Seattle Children's Hospital
University of Washington School of Medicine
Seattle, WA
lisa.herzig@seattlechildrens.org

Michael C. Hosokawa, EdD
*(Health Care in Minority and Majority
Populations)*
Professor
Department of Family and Community Medicine
University of Missouri School of Medicine
Columbia, MO
hosokawam@health.missouri.edu

Rory P. Houghtalen, MD
*(Anxiety Disorders; Depressive and Bipolar
Disorders; Appendix: Psychological Testing)*
Clinical Professor of Psychiatry
University of Rochester School of Medicine and
Dentistry
Adjunct Clinical Faculty
Rochester Institute of Technology Physician
Assistant Program
Rochester, NY
roryh@rochester.rr.com

Ryan F. Houghtalen, BS, RN
(Depressive and Bipolar Disorders)
University of Rochester School of Nursing
Rochester, NY
ryan_houghtalen@urmc.rochester.edu

Girardin Jean-Louis, PhD
(Chronobiology and Sleep Disorders)
Associate Professor
Department of Medicine
SUNY Downstate Medical Center
Brooklyn, NY
girardin.jean-louis@nyumc.org

Joel L. Kent, MD
(Pain)
Associate Professor of Anesthesiology
Director, Division of Pain Medicine
University of Rochester
School of Medicine and Dentistry
Rochester, NY
joel_kent@urmc.rochester.edu

Ian M. Kodish, MD, PhD
*(Cognition, Communication, and Social
Interaction; Emotion and Learning;
Predisposition; Stress, Adaptation, and Stress
Disorders; The Nervous System)*
Assistant Professor
Department of Psychiatry and Behavioral
Sciences
University of Washington
Seattle, WA
ian.kodish@seattlechildrens.org

Richard E. Kreipe, MD
(Eating Disorders)
Professor of Pediatrics
University of Rochester
Rochester, NY
richard_kreipe@urmc.rochester.edu

Eric D. LaMotte, MD
(Energy Homeostasis)
Clinical Instructor, Division of General Internal
Medicine
University of Washington Medical Center
Seattle, WA
lamotte@uw.edu

Lars C. Larsen, MD
*(The Medical Encounter and Clinical Decision
Making; The Provider–Patient Relationship)*
Professor Emeritus
Department of Family Medicine
Brody School of Medicine
East Carolina University
Greenville, NC
larsenl@ecu.edu

Keyne C. Law, MA
(Suicide)
Psychology Intern at the Medical University of
South Carolina
Doctoral Candidate in Clinical Psychology
Department of Psychology
The University of Southern Mississippi
Hattiesburg, MS
keyne.law@eagles.usm.edu

Patricia M. Lenahan, LCSW, LMFT, BCETS
(Geriatric Health and Successful Aging)
Adjunct Faculty
University of Southern California
Dworak Peck School of Social Work
Los Angeles, CA
plenahan@usc.edu

Sonja M. Lillrank, MD, PhD
(Schizophrenia and Other Psychotic Disorders)
Assistant Director for Psychiatry
Counseling and Psychiatric Services
Assistant Professor for Psychiatry
Georgetown University
Washington, DC
sml87@georgetown.edu

Nguyen Mai, PhD
(Pain)
Department of Neuroscience
University of Rochester
Rochester, NY
nguyen_mai@urmc.rochester.edu

Roland D. Maiuro, PhD
(Interpersonal Violence and Abuse)
Associate Professor of Psychiatry & Behavioral
Sciences (retired)
University of Washington School of Medicine
Seattle, WA
rmaiuro@prodigy.net

Christopher R. Martell, PhD, ABPP
*(Health Care Issues Facing Lesbian, Gay,
Bisexual, and Transgender Individuals)*
Lecturer
Clinic Director Psychological Services Center
University of Massachusetts – Amherst
Amherst, MA
cmartell@umass.edu

J. LeBron McBride, PhD, MPH
(The Family)
Director of Behavioral Medicine
Director of Clerkship
Floyd Medical Center
Family Medicine Residency Program
Rome, GA
lmcbride@floyd.org

Elizabeth A. McCauley, PHD, ABPP
(The School Years)
Professor
Department of Psychiatry and Behavioral Sciences
Department of Child and Adolescent Psychiatry
and Behavioral Health
Seattle Children's Hospital
University of Washington School of Medicine
Seattle, WA
eliz@uw.edu

Hilary H. McClafferty, MD, FAAP
(Complementary and Integrative Medicine)
Associate Professor
Department of Medicine
University of Arizona College of Medicine
Tucson, AZ
hmcclafferty@email.arizona.edu

K. Ramsey McGowen, PhD
(Poverty and Homelessness)
Associate Dean for Curriculum, Office of
Academic Affairs
Professor Emeritus of Psychiatry and Behavioral
Sciences

James H. Quillen College of Medicine
East Tennessee State University
Johnson City, TN
mcgowen@mail.etsu.edu

Barret Michalec, PhD
*(Theories of Social Relations and
Interprofessional Collaboration)*
Associate Dean of Interprofessional Education
Associate Professor of Sociology
University of Delaware
Newark, DE
bmichal@udel.edu

Emily F. Myers, MD
*(Selected Theories of Development; The Fetus,
Newborn, and Infant; Toddlerhood and the
Preschool Years)*
Assistant Professor of Pediatrics
Seattle Children's Hospital
University of Washington School of Medicine
Seattle, WA
emily.myers@seattlechildrens.org

João V. Nunes, MD – Editor
*(Chronobiology and Sleep Disorders; Disorders
of Infancy, Childhood, and Adolescence;
Evolving Models of Health Care; Predisposition;
Substance-Related and Addictive Disorders; The
Nervous System)*
Associate Medial Professor, Physiology and
Pharmacology
Chairman, Department of Behavioral Medicine
Sophie Davis School of Biomedical Education
The City College of New York
New York, NY
nunes@med.cuny.edu

David W. Pantalone, PhD
*(Health Care Issues Facing Lesbian, Gay,
Bisexual, and Transgender Individuals)*
Associate Professor of Psychology
Department of Psychology
University of Massachusetts – Boston
Boston, MA
david.pantalone@umb.edu

Michael Peroski, DO
*(Neurocognitive Disorders: Delirium and
Secondary Syndromes; Neurocognitive Disorders:
Dementia)*

University of Maryland
Sheppard Pratt Psychiatry Residency
Baltimore, MD
mperoski@som.umaryland.edu

Richard R. Pleak, MD
*(Disorders of Infancy, Childhood, and
Adolescence)*
Associate Professor of Psychiatry
Hofstra Northwell School of Medicine
Hempstead, NY
rpleak@northwell.edu

Michael I. Posner, PhD
(Brain Networks in Health and Illness)
Professor Emeritus of Psychology
University of Oregon
Eugene, OR
mposner@uoregon.edu

Timothy E. Quill, MD, FACP, FAAHPM
(Palliative Care)
Professof of Medicine, Psychiatry, and Medical
Humanities
Palliative Care Division
Department of Medicine
University of Rochester Medical Center
Rochester, NY
timothy_quill@urmc.rochester.edu

Mary K. Rothbart, PhD
(Brain Networks in Health and Illness)
Adjunct Professor of Psychology in Psychiatry
Weill Medical College of Cornell University
New York, NY
Professor Emerita of Psychology
University of Oregon
Eugene, OR
maryrothbart@yahoo.com

Dennis C. Russo, PhD, ABPP
*(The Medical Encounter and Clinical Decision
Making; The Provider–Patient Relationship)*
Clinical Professor of Family Medicine and
Psychology
Head of Behavioral Medicine
Department of Family Medicine
Brody School of Medicine
East Carolina University
Greenville, NC
russod@ecu.edu

Olle Jane Z. Sahler, MD – Editor
*(Evolving Models of Health Care;
Complementary and Integrative Medicine;
Practice Exam)*
Professor of Pediatrics, Psychiatry, Medical
Humanities and Bioethics, and Oncology
University of Rochester School of Medicine &
Dentistry
Golisano Children's Hospital
Rochester, NY
oj_sahler@urmc.rochester.edu

Kaliris Y. Salas-Ramirez, PhD
(Sexuality and Sexual Disorders)
Assistant Medical Professor
Department of Physiology, Pharmacology and
Neuroscience
The Sophie Davis School of Biomedical Education
CUNY School of Medicine
New York, NY
ksalasram@ccny.cuny.edu

Charles P. Samenow, MD, MPH
*(Sexuality and Sexual Disorders; Physician
Health, Impairment, and Misconduct)*
Associate Professor
Department of Psychiatry and Behavioral Sciences
George Washington University School of
Medicine
Washington DC
csamenow@mfa.gwu.edu

Ellen A. Schur, MD, MS
(Energy Homeostasis)
Associate Professor of Medicine
Co-Director, UW Medicine Weight Loss
Management Center
Director, Metabolic Imaging Subcore, UW
Nutrition and Obesity Research Center
Division of General Internal Medicine
Department of Medicine
University of Washington
Seattle, WA
ellschur@u.washington.edu

Azizi Seixas, PhD
(Chronobiology and Sleep Disorders)
Assistant Professor
Department of Population Health
NYU School of Medicine
New York, NY
azizi.seixas@nyumc.org

Margie H. Shaw, JD, PhD
(Moral, Ethical, and Legal Issues in Patient Care)
Division of Medical Humanities & Bioethics
University of Rochester School of Medicine and
Dentistry
Rochester, NY
margie_shaw@urmc.rochester.edu

Taylor B. Starr, DO, MPH
(Eating Disorders)
Instructor and Fellow in Adolescent Medicine
University of Rochester School of Medicine
Rochester, NY
taylor_starr@urmc.rochester.edu

Nancy K. Sugg, MD, MPH
(Interpersonal Violence and Abuse)
Associate Professor
Department of Medicine
University of Washington School of Medicine
Seattle, WA
sugg@u.washington.edu

Christine E. Tran-Boynes, DO
(Practice Exam)
Clinical Associate
Department of Psychiatry and Behavioral
Sciences
Johns Hopkins University School of Medicine
Baltimore, MD
ctranboynes@gmail.com

Peter P. Vitaliano, PhD
(Stress, Adaptation, and Stress Disorders)
Professor of Psychiatry and Behavioral Sciences
School of Medicine
University of Washington
Seattle, WA
pvital@uw.edu

Ferdinand Zizi, MBA
(Chronobiology and Sleep Disorders)
Clinical Instructor
Department of Health Sciences
SUNY Downstate Medical Center
Brooklyn, NY
ferdinand.zizi@nyumc.org

Subject Index

Praise for This Edition

"The fourth edition of this text book continues the wonderful tradition of providing for medical students or other health professions, in a single source, information usually found in textbooks from various disciplines, including psychology, biology, health psychology, public health, and clinical medicine. It is a true primer introducing vocabulary, concepts, theories, and the integration of the behavioral and biological sciences in a clear, understandable manner. Information obtained from this book will provide an outstanding foundation to add more advanced and expert knowledge for the health care clinician and researcher."

Barry A. Hong, PhD, ABPP, Professor of Psychiatry and Medicine at Washington University, St. Louis, MO

"This excellent textbook emphasizes the importance of an integrated science approach, combining behavioral, social, and biological sciences, to understanding health, illness, and health care. It draws on up-to-date research evidence to explore the mechanisms by which bio-behavioral interactions occur. In the context of an increasingly wide recognition of the significance of behavioral and social sciences in medical and health education and practice, this excellent text book should be required reading for all students involved in health care – and indeed for practitioners."

Jeni Harden, PhD, MPh, MA, Director of Education, Usher Institute of Population Health Sciences and Informatics, University of Edinburgh, UK

"This latest edition continues the editors' outstanding success in bridging the exciting worlds of the physiological and behavioral-social contributions to quality health care. Today's providers are undergoing an unprecedented transformation into integrated systems of care, increasingly bringing the best of interdisciplinary science to the clinical bedside. The text's clinical vignettes provide vivid, real-life applicability for both aspiring and seasoned colleagues."

Patrick DeLeon, PhD, MPH, JD, former President of the American Psychological Association

"This is an amazing text! It integrates biological, psychological, and social aspects of health, wellness, and illness states. It integrates current concepts of ethics and interprofessional teamwork with integrative medicine and culture. It addresses, in one book, such issues as sexuality, gender and sexual orientation, the patient–physician relationship, palliative care and end-of-life issues, clinical decision-making, psychotherapy and psychoeducation, the organization of the medical system and current payment mechanisms, and the public health system. It even addresses the concerns of impaired physicians. This book is wonderful for fourth-year medical students no matter what field they are going into, generalists in pediatrics, internal medicine and family medicine, as well as all health professionals who are interested in a holistic and scientific approach to the healing process."

Benjamin Siegel, MD, Professor of Pediatrics and Psychiatry, Boston University School of Medicine and Boston Medical Center, MA

"Extending beyond the biopsychosocial approach to an integrated sciences model, The Behavioral Sciences and Health Care is an exceptionally thoughtful guide to understanding the exciting new findings in behavioral neuroscience and genetics, social biology, and behavioral medicine and, even more importantly, how to apply this understanding to improve health and health care delivery."

Robert M. Rohrbaugh, MD, Professor and Deputy Chair for Education and Career Development, Residency Program Director, Department of Psychiatry, Yale University School of Medicine, New Haven, CT